A BIOGRAPHICAL DICTIONARY OF CORK

A BIOGRAPHICAL
DICTIONARY OF
CORK

Tim Cadogan
&
Jeremiah Falvey

FOUR COURTS PRESS

Typeset in 9 pt on 11.5 pt AGaramond by
Carrigboy Typesetting Services, County Cork for
FOUR COURTS PRESS LTD
7 Malpas Street, Dublin 8, Ireland
e-mail: info@four-courts-press.ie
and in North America for
FOUR COURTS PRESS
c/o ISBS, 920 NE 58th Avenue, Suite 300, Portland, OR 97213.

A catalogue record for this title is available
from the British Library.

ISBN (10–digit) 1–84682–030–8
ISBN (13–digit) 978–1–84682–030–4

Printed in England
by MPG Books, Bodmin, Cornwall.

CONTENTS

ABBREVIATIONS

ADC	aide-de-camp
BA	Bachelor of Arts
BCL	Bachelor of Civil Law
B.Comm.	Bachelor of Commerce
BD	Bachelor of Divinity
BE	Bachelor of Engineering
B.Sc.	Bachelor of Science
CBC	Christian Brothers' College
CBE	Commander of the British Empire
CBS	Christian Brothers' School
CHAS	Cork Historical & Archaeological Society
CIE	Córas Iompair Éireann (Irish Transport Company)
Connradh na Gaeilge	The Gaelic [language] League
CYMS	Catholic Young Men's Society
Dáil Éireann	The lower house of the Irish parliament
DD	Doctor of Divinity
DED	District Electoral Division
D.Litt.	Doctor of Literature
D.Sc.	Doctor of Science
DSO	Distinguished Service Order
FAI	Football Association of Ireland
fl.	*floruit* (period of the most successful part of subject's career)
FRS	Fellow of the Royal Society
GAA	Gaelic Athletic Association
H.Dip.	Higher Diploma of Education
IRA	Irish Republican Army
IRB	Irish Republican Brotherhood
IRFU	Irish Rugby Football Union
ITGWU	Irish Transport & General Workers' Union
JCHAS	*Journal of the Cork Historical & Archaeological Society*
JHC	Junior Hurling Championship
JP	Justice of the Peace
KC	King's Counsel
LDF	Local Defence Force

LL.D	Doctor of Laws
LSS	Licentiate in Sacred Scripture
MA	Master of Arts
MB	Bachelor of Medicine
MCC	Member of the County Council
MD	Doctor of Medicine
MHC	Minor Hurling Championship
MP	Member of Parliament
M.Sc.	Master of Science
NFL	National Football League
NHL	National Hurling League
NS	National School
NUI	National University of Ireland
PBC	Presentation Brothers' College
PLG	Poor Law Guardian
QC	Queen's Counsel
QUB	Queen's University, Belfast
RAF	Royal Air Force
RDC	Rural District Council
RDS	Royal Dublin Society
RHA	Royal Hibernian Academy
RIC	Royal Irish Constabulary
RNLI	Royal National Lifeboat Institution
RTÉ	Irish Radio and Television
Seanad Éireann	The upper house of the Irish parliament
SFC	Senior Football Championship
SHC	Senior Hurling Championship
s.p.	*sine prole* (without issue)
TCD	Trinity College, Dublin
TD	Teachta Dála (member of Dáil Éireann)
UCC	University College, Cork
UCD	University College, Dublin
UCG	University College, Galway
UDC	Urban District Council
VC	Victoria Cross
VS	Vocational School

INTRODUCTION

It was in no spirit of chauvinism that we embarked on the compilation of a dictionary of Cork biography. In recent decades, there has been an unprecedented growth of interest and participation in local history throughout County Cork. While both the local history activist and the armchair devotee now have an increasing range of published reference sources, both at national and local level, to draw upon, there is a dearth of reference material in the biographical sphere. This is not to ignore the excellent, but focused *Beathaisnéis* series of volumes, which have been a welcome addition to history shelves, or the work of Henry Boylan and other biographical compilers. Fashions in local history research change and many persons worthy of further study are forgotten because their careers are only encountered by accident. We would like to think that our compilation would stimulate interest in further research into the lives and careers of some of our subjects.

Our range of coverage is not limited by fields of endeavour, but sought to include all those whom we considered had achieved a degree of noteworthiness and who had died before the start of 2006. There are however some areas that we targeted for inclusion. We have endeavoured to include the Members of Parliament who represented Cork constituencies from the Act of Union and the members of Dáil Eireann who represented Cork constituencies since the foundation of the Irish Free State. We have also, insofar as they could be identified, included Cork-born persons who represented other constituencies in those parliaments. Inclusiveness has been easier in the parliamentary area than in others and we are conscious that in some of these, our trawling of sources has been less effective. Where possible, we have included a date of death for an entry and these have been gleaned from newspapers and other published sources. We have rarely resorted to civil or church records to establish such data, mainly because of time constraints.

We would like to acknowledge the kindness of Kieran Wyse, Niamh Cronin, Bill Power, Colman O Mahony, Jim Herlihy, Richard Henchion, Liam O'Regan, Philip O'Regan, Audrey O'Sullivan, Hilary O'Sullivan and all others who assisted in our researches over several years.

TIM CADOGAN

JEREMIAH FALVEY

A

ABELL, Abraham (1782–1851) Born Cork, the son of **Richard Abell**, a Quaker of Pope's Quay, and brother of **John Abell**, **Richard Abell**, and **Joshua Abell**. He was employed as a clerk in the Murphy firm of merchants and brewers at Morrison's Island. He was a founder member of the Cork Literary and Scientific Society and of the Cuvierian Society. He was also a treasurer of the Cork Library and a manager of the Cork Institution. In a wider field, he was a member of the Royal Irish Academy, the Irish Archaeological Society, the Camden Society, and the South Munster Antiquarian Society. An avid collector of miscellanea, he left a library of over 4,500 books at his death. He died on 12 February 1851. [Life by R.S. Harrison (1999)]

ABELL, James (1751–1818) Born Cork, the son of Joseph Abell. He operated as a businessman at Morrison's Island and later lived on the Old Blackrock Road. During his retirement, he was heavily involved as a Quaker activist in the temperance movement. He died on 10 September 1818.

ABELL, John (1791–1861) Born Cork, the son of **Richard Abell**, and brother of **Abraham** and **Joshua Abell**. On his marriage, he set up as a hardware merchant in Limerick and helped with other Quakers in relief works there during the Famine. He had a great interest in astronomy and, on his retirement, he built an octagonal towerhouse at Corbally for his observations. He published *The Turkish Bath as an Antidote for the Cravings of the Drunkard* (1859).

ABELL, Joshua (1793–1846) Born Cork, the son of **Richard Abell**, and brother of **Richard Abell**, **John Abell**, **Abraham Abell**, and **Mary Knott**. He was educated at the Quaker school at Ballitore, Co. Kildare. He opened an educational academy in Dublin in 1818, and six years later, founded the Hibernian Peace Society. His interests lay in geology, electricity, and in publishing (founding and editing the *Dublin Literary Gazette*). He was also a member of the Royal Dublin Society.

ABELL, Richard (1750–1801) Born Cork, the father of **Abraham Abell**, **Joshua Abell**, **Richard Abell**, **John Abell**, and **Mary Knott**. He operated as a merchant from his residence at Pope's Quay. As a member of the Cork Committee of Merchants, he was involved in upholding Cork's premium reputation in the beef and butter sectors at the end of the eighteenth century. He was one of the leaders of the city's Quaker community.

ABELL, Richard (1789–1840) Born Cork, the son of **Richard Abell** of Pope's Quay, merchant, and brother of **Abraham Abell**, **Joshua Abell**, **John Abell**, and **Mary Knott**. He studied at Edinburgh University where he qualified as a doctor with a special interest in phrenology. In 1828, he drew a crowd of 2,000 people in Dublin's Rotunda to hear him lecture on the subject.

ABRAHAM, William (1840–1915) Born Limerick, of a family in the nursery trade. He worked for some years in the employment of his brother-in-law, Peter Tait, a Limerick merchant. He then opened his own nursery business at South Hill, Limerick. Having been active in the land agitation, he was elected as nationalist MP for Limerick West in 1885, but did not seek re-election in 1892. In June 1893, he was returned unopposed as MP for Cork North East on the resignation of **Michael Davitt** and retained that seat until his defeat by **William O'Brien** in the general election of 1910. In June of that year, he succeeded to the Dublin Harbour seat of **T.C. Harrington** until his death in London on 2 August 1915. A Congregationalist, he was buried in the Nonconformist section of St Pancras Cemetery, East Finchley, London. He was a notable public speaker and a former treasurer of the Irish Parliamentary Party.

ADAMS, Andrew L. (d. 1882) Born Scotland, the son of a physician and classical scholar. On retiring as an army surgeon, he was appointed as professor of Zoology at the Royal College of Science, Dublin, in 1873. A year previously, he was elected a fellow of the Royal Society. In 1878, he was appointed as professor of Natural History at the Queen's College, Cork (now UCC). While at Cork, he published *A Monograph of the British Fossil Elephants* (1877, 1881). He also published *The Wanderings of a Naturalist in India* (1867), *The Western Himalayas and Cashmir* (1867), *Notes of a Naturalist in the Nile Valley and Malta* (1870) and *Field and Forest Rambles, with Notes and Observations on the Natural History of Eastern Canada* (1873).

ADAMS, James W. [VC] (1839–1903) Born Cork, the son of a local magistrate. He was educated at TCD where he graduated BA (1861). Having been ordained in 1863, he ministered in England and three years later left for Bengal to work as an army chaplain. In 1874, he was posted to Kashmir where he built a church of pine logs with his own hands. During the Afghan campaign of 1879, he risked his life in saving some soldiers who were in danger of drowning with the enemy close at hand. For this he was awarded the VC, which he received in London in 1881. On his return to India, he ministered to the soldiers in various campaigns. In 1886, 'Padre Adams' returned to England and held several rectories before his death at Oakham, Leicestershire, on 20 October 1903. In the previous June, he had been conferred with an honorary degree of MA by TCD.

ADAMS, Richard (1846–1908) Born Castle-townbere, Co. Cork, the son of Bryan Adams,

customs official. He was educated at Queen's College, Cork (now UCC), where he graduated in law. He was called to the Bar in 1873 and to the Inner Bar in 1889. He began his journalistic career on the *Cork Examiner* and later worked for the *Morning Star* under the editorship of **Justin McCarthy**, before being appointed as editor of the *Southern Reporter* in 1868. During his tenure, the *Reporter* was subjected to a few noteworthy libel cases. He practised on the Munster Circuit from 1873 and was one of the most outstanding wits of his day. He was appointed a county court judge for Limerick in 1894. He died on 14 April 1908.

ADDERLEY, Thomas (d. 1792) He was the eldest son and heir of Edward Adderley of Gloucestershire. He was MP for Charlemont (1752–60), Bandon (1761–76) and Clonakilty (1776–92) – a total of forty continuous years in parliament. He was also a freeman of Kinsale (1755). He built and owned the town of Innishannon and, in 1749, he established a linen industry there – largely made up of sixty Huguenot émigré families. The enterprise lasted until his death in 1792.

AGAR, Charles (1736–1809) Born Gowran Castle, Co. Kilkenny. He was educated at Christ Church, Oxford, where he graduated MA (1762) and DTL (1765). He was consecrated as Church of Ireland bishop of Cloyne on 20 March 1768. He later became Archbishop of Cashel (1779) and of Dublin (1801). In the secular sphere (where he possessed great wealth and influence), he was created Baron Somerton (1795), Viscount Somerton (1800) and earl of Normanton (1806). He died on 14 July 1809. [Portrait by Gilbert C. Stuart; Life by A. Malcomson (2002)]

AHERN, James (1868–1949) Born Ballingeary, Co. Cork, the son of John Ahern, builder, and Mary Lucey, teacher. He worked for a while at Inchigeela NS, and having graduated BA by 1896, was appointed as a professor of mathematics and the teaching of Irish at De la Salle

Training College, Waterford. He was intimately connected with the founding and expansion of various Connradh na Gaeilge branches in Counties Waterford and Cork. His two-part Irish-English phrasebook, *Leabhar Mion-chainte* (1901 and 1902) was a notable success. In 1902, he also published an annotated edition of *Tadhg Gabha* (by 'Beirt Fhear'). His adaptation and condensed version of **Gerald Griffin**'s *Collegians* (under the title, *The Colleen Bawn*) appeared in the *Knapsack Library* in 1945 and ran to several printings. He also published a booklet on **Thomas Davis** in 1945. However, his enthusiasm for the Gaelic revival movement declined following the War of Independence and the subsequent civil war. He died on 18 October 1949 and was buried in Ballygunner, Co. Waterford.

AHERN, Liam (1916–1974) Born Castle-quarter, Dungourney, Co. Cork, the son of Eamonn Ahern, MCC (1921–53), and a nephew of **John Dineen**. He was educated locally and at Pallaskenry Agricultural College, Co. Limerick. On the death of his father in 1953, he was co-opted to Cork County Council and remained a member until his death. He was a member of Seanad Éireann from 1957 to 1973. Having unsuccessfully contested Cork North East as a Fianna Fáil candidate in the 1965 general election, he won the seat in February 1973. He died on 13 July 1974, and was buried in Mogeely Cemetery. His son, Michael Ahern, is a current junior government minister.

AHERN, John (1911–1997) Born Leamlara, Lisgoold, Co. Cork, the son of a schoolteacher. He was educated at St Colman's College, Fermoy; St Patrick's College, Maynooth and at the Lateran University, Rome. He was ordained for the diocese of Cloyne in 1936. He was subsequently appointed to the staffs of St Colman's, Fermoy (1940–4) and Maynooth College (1946–57), where he was professor of Canon Law. He was consecrated as bishop of Cloyne on 9 June 1957. He resigned (on age grounds) on 17 February 1987 and retired to Nazareth House, Mallow. He died on 25 September 1997 and was buried in the grounds of St Colman's Cathedral, Cobh.

AHERN, Thomas (1884–1970) Born Ballymacoda, Co. Cork, the son of Patrick Ahern, farmer. He worked as a draper's assistant in Midleton and emigrated to Fremantle, Western Australia, in 1910. He went into the drapery business and moved to Perth in 1912 where he worked as a store manager until 1922. In that year, he acquired a controlling interest in a drapery and furniture concern and, as Ahern's Ltd, expanded into a large chain of department stores. He took an interest in local Roman Catholic affairs and served as president of Perth Chamber of Commerce. He died on 22 May 1970 and was buried at Karrakatta Cemetery, Perth, of which he was a trustee.

AHERNE, Michael ['Gah'] (d. 1946) Born Blackrock, Cork, the brother of **Paddy ('Balty') Aherne**, and brother-in-law of **Eudie Coughlan**. He was a forward with Blackrock Hurling Club and won four All-Ireland SHC medals with Cork (1926, 1928–9 and 1931). In the 1928 final against Galway, he notched up a record score of 5–4. He also won two NHL medals (1926 and 1930), a Railway Cup medal in 1929, and an All-Ireland JHC medal in 1925. He died at Glenvera Hospital, Cork, on 30 December 1946 and was buried in the family plot at Ballintemple.

AHERNE, Paddy ['Balty'] (d. 1971) Born Blackrock, Cork, the brother of **Michael ('Gah') Aherne** and brother-in-law of **Eudie Coughlan**. He was a forward with Blackrock Hurling Club and won five All-Ireland SHC medals (1919, 1926, 1928–9 and 1931). He also won two NHL medals (1926 and 1930) and a Railway Cup medal in 1931. He died at his Ballintemple residence on 2 October 1971 – the eve of a Blackrock victory in the County hurling championship final. He was buried in Ballintemple Cemetery.

AIKENHEAD, Mary (1787–1858) Born Eason's Hill, Cork, the daughter of Dr David

Aikenhead. She was raised in the Protestant faith, but converted to Roman Catholicism in 1803 following the death of her father who had converted on his deathbed in 1801. At the request of the archbishop of Dublin, she founded the first Irish congregation of the Sisters of Charity on 22 August 1815. Prior to her death at Our Lady's Mount, Harold's Cross, Dublin, on 22 July 1858, she had founded ten houses in Ireland as well as St Vincent's Hospital, Dublin – the first hospital in Ireland to be administered by nuns. She was buried in the cemetery of St Mary Magdalen Convent, Donnybrook. [Lives by S. Atkinson (1879) and anon. (1925); Letters (Dublin, 1914); Commemorative plaque at Eason's Hill]

ALDWORTH, Elizabeth (1693–1772) Born Doneraile Court, the only daughter of Arthur St Leger, 1st Viscount Doneraile (1st creation). Having secretly watched the proceedings of a masonic lodge at Doneraile Court *c.*1710, she was initiated into the lodge and was subsequently known as 'The Lady Freemason'. On 7 April 1713, she married Richard Aldworth of Newmarket Court, Co. Cork. She had two sons, Boyle and St Leger, with the latter eventually becoming Viscount Doneraile of the second creation. She died on 11 May 1772 and was buried in St FinBarre's Cathedral, Cork. [Memoir by J. Day (Cork, 1914, 1926, 1941)]

ALDWORTH, Lady Mary (1840–1920) She was the eldest daughter of Francis Bernard, 3rd earl of Bandon. In 1863, she married Colonel Richard W. Aldworth (1825–1899), landowner, of Newmarket, Co. Cork. As well as running her household, she became involved in local politics and served as a Poor Law Guardian. She played a leading part in the activities of the unionist/imperialist Primrose League in the last two decades of the 19th century. The Primrose League, which had been founded in memory of British Premier Benjamin Disraeli (1804–81) by Lord Randolph Churchill (1849–95) to propagate the principles of Tory democracy, was, in Ireland, the unionist counterpart to the growing nationalist Home Rule movement and had over 4,000 members in County Cork by 1891. Lady Aldworth was the 'ruling councillor' of the Mitchelstown 'Habitation' (branch). She died on 10 January 1920.

ALEXANDER, Conel H. O'D. (1909–1974) Born Cork, the son of **Conel W. L. Alexander**, professor of Civil Engineering at UCC. On his father's death, the family moved to Birmingham, where he developed as a chess player, winning the British Boys' Championship in 1926 and the senior title in 1938 and 1956. By 1950, he had become an international grandmaster. He twice won the Hastings International Tournament (1947 and 1953) – an amazing feat for a part-timer. He represented Great Britain in five Chess Olympiads (1933, 1935, 1937, 1954 and 1958). He was educated at King's College, Cambridge, where he graduated with a First in Mathematics (1931), and then went on to teach mathematics at Winchester School. On the outbreak of World War II, he joined the staff of the Government Code and Cipher School where he worked on the problem of breaking the German naval codes. After the war, he was in charge of research and development at the Government Communication Headquarters (GCHQ) at Cheltenham. He later became the chess correspondent of the *Sunday Times* and *The Spectator*, and was also the author of several books on chess. He died in Cheltenham on 15 February 1974.

ALEXANDER, Conel W.L. (1879–1920) Born Imlick, Co. Donegal, the son of Joseph Alexander and father of **Conel Hugh O'Donel Alexander**. He was educated at schools in Derry and Bangor. He attended the Queen's University, Belfast where he graduated BE (1901) and Birmingham University where he graduated M.Sc. (1905). He worked as the Assistant Engineer of Birmingham (1902–6) before his appointment as professor of Civil Engineering at UCC in 1906 (to 1920). Having a keen interest in rugby, he played for Ulster (1899–1901) and served as president of the IRFU

(1909–10). In 1912, he was a member of the Munster Senior Cup-winning UCC team and in the same year, was instrumental in acquiring the Mardyke grounds for UCC from the IRFU. He was also dean of the Faculty of Engineering of the NUI from 1909. He died on 17 December 1920.

ALEXANDER, William T. (1818–1872) Born Cork. He became a surgeon in the British Navy and developed an interest in botany. His 'Fungi of Cloyne' was published in the *Phytologist*.

ALLEN, Richard (1786–1873) Born Cork. He was educated at the Quaker-run Newtown School, Waterford, where he was one of the first pupils. In 1810, he returned to the school as a qualified teacher and superintendent. He published *A Catechism of Religious Faith and Practice* (1834).

ALLEN, William P. (1848–1867) Born Bandon, Co. Cork, the son of a bridewell keeper. He became a Fenian, who, along with two colleagues, Michael Larkin and **Michael O'Brien**, attacked a police van on its way to Manchester Gaol on 18 September 1867. A policeman was killed in the attack. On the strength of flimsy evidence, the 'Manchester Martyrs' were hanged in Manchester Gaol on 23 November 1867.

ALLIN, Thomas (c.1837–1909) Born Midleton, Co. Cork, the son of Thomas Allin, a prominent flour miller. He was educated at Midleton College and TCD where he graduated BA (1859). He was ordained in the Church of Ireland and held many curacies in various Irish dioceses before retiring to Weston-super-Mare, England. He was a keen botanist and published *The Flowering Plants and Ferns of the County Cork* (1883). He was also the author of *Universalism Asserted, on the Authority of Reason, the Fathers and Holy Scripture* – a doctrine which asserted that, ultimately, everybody will be saved. He died at Chelston, Torquay, on 4 March 1909.

ALLMAN, George J. (1812–1898) Born Cork, the eldest son of James C. Allman of Bandon, brewer and distiller, and brother of **Richard**

Lane **Allman**. He was educated at TCD where he graduated BA (1839), MB (1843), and MD (1847), but abandoned medicine to study marine zoology of which he was an early pioneer in England. In 1844, he succeeded his namesake, William Allman (1776–1846), as professor of Botany at TCD. He was elected as a fellow of the Royal Society in 1854. In 1855, he was appointed as Regius Professor of Natural History at Edinburgh – a position he held until his retirement in 1870. For his work, he received the Brisbane Medal of the Royal Society of Edinburgh, the Cunningham Medal of the Royal Irish Academy, and the Gold Medal of the Linnaen Society (1896). He died near Poole, Dorset, on 24 November 1898.

ALLMAN, Richard L. (c.1812–1904) Born Bandon, Co. Cork, the son of James C. Allman, brewer and distiller, and brother of **George James Allman**. He became the senior partner in the family business when George opted for an academic career. The Allmans, who were Presbyterians, had long been to the fore in Liberal politics in Bandon and on the late withdrawal of **Alexander Swanston** from the April 1880 election, Richard was brought in as a candidate. Defeated by **Percy Brodrick Bernard**, he was successful in the June by-election which was caused by Bernard's resignation. He was Bandon's last MP as the constituency was disenfranchised in 1885. He died at his Bandon residence, 'Woodlands', on 23 December 1904 and was buried in Ballymodan Graveyard, Bandon.

AMBROSE, Edward (1814–1890) Born Cork. He studied sculpture at the Royal Academy, London, and later in Paris, Rome, and Louvain. On his return to London around 1851, he exhibited at the Royal Academy, the Royal Irish Academy, and at the Cork Exhibition of 1852. He returned to Cork for his final years where he lived at Lough Road. He took a great interest in the swans on The Lough and received a small annual grant from Cork Corporation to feed them. He died on 29 April 1890.

AMBROSE, James (1813–1856) Born Bandon, Co. Cork. He emigrated to England where he was convicted of robbery and deported to Botany Bay. Finding his way to the United States and adopting the name 'Yankee Sullivan', he became a successful bare-knuckle boxer, opened a saloon, and challenged Tom Hyer for the championship of America. A bout was arranged between them at Rock Point, Maryland, in February 1849 when Sullivan retired in the 16th Round. Subsequently, on Hyer's retirement from the ring, Sullivan claimed the title. He was then challenged for the title by John Morressey, a Tipperaryman. Their contest in New York ended in uproar, with Sullivan walking away from the ring after a dispute, thereby conceding the title by default. Leaving New York, where he had been involved in the Tammany Hall political organisation, Sullivan moved to San Francisco where he made progress in city politics. However, he was arrested by a vigilante committee pledged to clean up local politics and lodged in jail. He was found dead in his cell on 31 May 1856. The cause of death was never established, leading to speculation of suicide or assassination.

ANDERSON, John (1747–1820) Born Portling, near Dumfries, Scotland. He arrived in Cork in 1780 and, as a 'Protestant Stranger', was made a freeman of the city. He quickly gained a reputation in the commercial life of the city and county and, in 1789, he established the first Irish mail coach service. With borrowings of £40,000, he purchased a large estate (including the town of Fermoy) which he developed into a commercial centre. In 1800, he ventured into banking when he established the Fermoy Bank. The turning point in his fortunes came in 1807 when he purchased a large part of the nearby Barrymore estate – a move which ultimately led to the failure of his bank in 1816. He died in London on 13 July 1820. [Life by **N. Brunicardi** (1987); Commemorative plaque at Anderson's Quay (which he firstly developed), Cork]

ANGLIN, Arthur H. (1850–1934) Born Cork. He graduated at Queen's College, Cork (now UCC) with a First and Gold Medal in 1868. He obtained further honours at St Peter's College, Cambridge, where he graduated in 1874. For the next three years he engaged in research work at Cambridge and at other universities before returning to Cork as professor of Mathematics in 1887. He held this post until his retirement in 1913. He died at his residence, 4 Fernhurst Villas, College Road, on 25 January 1934 and was buried in St Finbarr's Cemetery.

ANGLIN, Timothy W. (1822–1896) Born Clonakilty, Co. Cork, the son of Francis Anglin, an East India Company employee. He was educated locally and worked as a teacher before emigrating in 1849 to Saint John, New Brunswick, Canada. He was shortly (through his newspaper, the *Saint John Weekly Freeman*) to become an advocate of the reform of the Irish Roman Catholic community. In 1861, he was elected to the New Brunswick House of Assembly as an independent. An opponent of the Canadian confederation, he was appointed an executive councillor in the New Brunswick anti-confederate government of 1865. However, in the following November, he resigned his position as a result of the abuse which he was receiving as a supposedly Fenian supporter. He was elected to a seat in the first general election for the Canadian House of Commons in 1867, firstly as an independent and then as a Liberal. His great moment came when he was elected as Speaker of the Canadian House of Commons in March 1874 and held this position until the defeat of the Liberals in 1878. Thereafter his career went into decline although he sat on various government commissions. He died of a blood clot to the brain in Toronto on 3 May 1896. His son, Francis, became the Chief Justice of the Canadian Supreme Court, while his daughter, Margaret, became an internationally renowned actress. [Life by W.M. Baker (1977)]

ANSTER, John (1795–1867) Born Charleville, Co. Cork, the son of John Anster, distiller. He was educated at TCD where he graduated BA (1816) and LL.D (1825). He was called to the

Irish Bar in 1824 and was appointed as registrar of the High Court of Admiralty in Ireland in 1837. He was awarded a pension on the Civil List in 1841. From 1850 until his death, he was professor of Civil Law at TCD. As well as publishing poems and articles in periodicals, he was the first translator of Goethe's *Faust* into English (1835 and 1864). He died in Dublin on 9 June 1867.

ANSTEY, Thomas C. (1816–1873) Born London, the son of Thomas Anstey, an early settler in Tasmania. Thomas Junior was reared in Tasmania and later studied at the University of London. He was called to the English Bar in 1839. A convert to Roman Catholicism, he returned to Tasmania with his Irish-born wife, Harriet Strickland, in 1840 and campaigned for Roman Catholic rights there before returning to England. A natural interest in the Irish Question and friendship with William Smith O'Brien (1803–64) earned him the nomination as an Irish confederate for Youghal Borough in the 1847 election. He was elected with a comfortable majority. In 1852, having abandoned Youghal, he contested a seat at Bedford where defeat ended his parliamentary career. Having been appointed as Attorney General of Hong Kong in 1854, he clashed with the authorities and was suspended. He then settled in India and practised at the Bombay Bar. He died in Bombay on 12 August 1873, mourned by the native population of all creeds, whose legal cases he had espoused.

ANTHONY, Richard S. (1875–1962) Born Cork. He worked in the printing department of the *Cork Examiner*. He first entered national politics as an unsuccessful Labour candidate for Cork City in the 1923 general election. He was elected to the Dáil in 1927, but was expelled from the Labour Party in 1931 for having voted in favour of the Public Safety Act. He was re-elected in 1932, 1933, and 1937 as an independent Labour deputy but lost his seat in 1938. He was once again re-elected in 1943 and 1944, but lost again in 1948 – this time as an official Labour candidate. He was a member of Seanad Éireann

(1948–51 and 1954–7). A linotype operator by profession, he was president of the Cork Typographical Society from 1920, and was also chairman of Cork Workers' Council (1923–6). He also served on Cork Corporation and was Lord Mayor for one term (1942/43). He died at the South Infirmary Hospital on 3 January 1962 and was buried in St Finbarr's Cemetery.

ARCHDEACON, Nicholas (d. 1823) Born Monkstown, Co. Cork, of a dispossessed Jacobite family. He was educated at Redington Academy, Great Island, and later studied for the priesthood at the Irish College, Douai, and at Louvain. During the Reign of Terror in 1793, he was arrested as a foreigner in Paris. Following his return to Ireland, he was appointed as bishop of Kilfenora and Kilmacduagh on 12 October 1800. He died on 27 November 1823.

ARMSTRONG, George F. (1845–1906) Born Co. Dublin, the son of Edmond John Armstrong. He was educated at TCD and was professor of English and History at Queen's College, Cork (now UCC) from 1870 until 1905. In 1890, he assumed by deed poll the additional surname of Savage, i.e. Savage-Armstrong, as senior male representative of the Savages of the Ards, Co. Down, his mother's family. A noted poet, he was nominated for the English Poet Laureatship in 1896, but was not selected. His works include *Ugone* (1870), *The Tragedy of Israel* (1872), *Victoria Regina* (1887), *Mephistopheles in Broadcloth* (1888), and *Poems Lyrical and Dramatic* (1892). He also wrote a family history entitled, *The Savages of the Ards Peninsula* (1891). He died in Co. Down on 24 July 1906. [Selection of works by S.S. Mills (1917)]

ARNOTT, Sir John (1814–1898) Born Auchtermuchty, Fifeshire, Scotland, and educated locally. With a partner, he opened a small drapery business in Patrick's Street, Cork, in 1837. The enterprise failed and Arnott left for Belfast where he became successful. He returned to Cork in the late 1840s and became well established in the drapery/clothes manufacture area. He served three times as mayor of Cork (1859–61) and was knighted by the lord lieutenant in November 1859 on the occasion of the laying of the foundation stone of the new St Patrick's Bridge. He was also elected as a Liberal MP for Kinsale in 1859 and served until 1863 when he resigned his seat. His business interests were legion. He was the founder of the Arnott's chain of stores, the owner of Arnott's Brewery and a chain of bakeries. In 1873, he purchased the *Irish Times* and from 1872 until 1897 was the owner of the Passage and Rushbrooke Docks. He established both Cork Park and Baldoyle racecourses. He also had interests in railway and shipping companies and purchased the duke of Devonshire's Bandon estates for £250,000 in 1896. He survived major losses in the 1870s only to recover his position and go on to new heights. In 1859, he published an important pamphlet on the conditions of children in the Cork Workhouse. He was a noted philanthropist, at one time using the sobriquet 'Timothy Tightboots' to mask his charitable donations. He exerted great influence in ensuring the passing of the Irish Poor Law Relief Bill. Though of Presbyterian persuasion, he gave generously to both Protestant and Roman Catholic causes; his will included charitable bequests totalling £45,000. He was created a baronet in 1896. He resided at Fir Hill, Monkstown, Co. Cork, and later at 'Woodlands', Montenotte, where he died on 28 March 1898. He was buried in St Luke's Graveyard, Douglas. [Commemorative plaque at his former drapery store, 51/54 Patrick's Street, Cork]

ASHE, St George (1657–1718) Born Castle Strange, Co. Roscommon, the son of a Co. Meath landlord. He was educated at TCD where he graduated BA (1676), MA (1679), BD (1687) and DD (1692). He was appointed as Provost of TCD in 1692 and three years later he became a member of the Irish Privy Council. He was consecrated as Church of Ireland bishop of Cloyne on 18 July 1695. He was subsequently translated to the dioceses of Clogher (1697) and Derry (1717). He died on 27 February 1718 and was buried in Christ Church Cathedral. His daughter, Catherine, married **Charles Crow**, bishop of Cloyne.

ASHLIN, George Coppinger (1837–1922) Born Carrigrenane House, Little Island, Co. Cork, the third son of John Mason Ashlin and his wife Dorinda Coppinger (of Midleton). The father died while George was an infant. He was educated in Liege (Belgium), at Oscott College and at the Royal Academy, London. From 1856 to 1860, he studied architecture under Edward Welby Pugin, the son of the celebrated architect, Augustus Welby Pugin (1812–1852). He practised in Ireland in partnership with E.W. Pugin and married his partner's sister, Mary, in 1867. His principal architectural works include SS. Peter and Paul's Church, Cork, and St Colman's Cathedral, Cobh, but he was responsible for about fifty other churches as well as public and private contracts (including Portrane Asylum, Co. Dublin, and Clery's Department Store, Dublin) in Ireland. In his later years, Thomas A. Coleman joined him as partner. He died at his residence, St George's, Killiney, Co. Dublin, on 10 December 1921. He was elected a member of the Royal Hibernian Academy in 1885 and president of the Royal Institute of Architects of Ireland in 1901.

ATKIN, Robert T. (1841–1872) Born Clonakilty, Co. Cork, the fourth and youngest son of William Francis Atkin of Fernhill. Following the father's death, the family moved to France where Robert was educated. He was married in London in 1863 and in the following year he emigrated to Queensland, Australia, and became editor of the *Brisbane Guardian*. On being taken over by its rival, the *Brisbane Courier* in 1868, he and a partner established the *Queensland Express* and when this failed in 1871, he and two other journalists founded the *Brisbane Colonist*. By this time, his health was failing and he died at Sandgate, Brisbane, on 25 May 1872. He had won a seat on the State Legislative Assembly in 1868 but a petition was lodged against him and he resigned before the investigation was completed. However, he was returned in 1870 but again resigned through ill-health two months before his death. He was a prominent member of the Brisbane Hibernian Society.

ATKINS, Henry St J. (1896–1987) Born St Claire's Avenue, Cork, the son of Patrick Atkins. He was educated at North Monastery CBS and at UCC where he graduated B.Sc. (1915) and M.Sc. (1923). He taught at North Monastery (1915–20), at PBC, Cork (1921–6) and was professor of Mathematics at St Patrick's College of Education, Dublin (1928–36). He was appointed as professor of Pure Mathematics at UCC in 1936 (to 1954) and as college registrar in 1943 (to 1954). He was elected as president of UCC in 1954 and served until his retirement in 1963. He was the recipient of an honorary D.Sc. from the National University of Ireland in 1955. He died at the Bon Secours Hospital, Cork, on 12 October 1987 and was buried in St Finbarr's Cemetery.

ATKINS, William (1812–1887) Born Cork, the son of Ringrose Atkins, MD. He came under the influence of his architect uncle by marriage, **George R. Pain,** and his first commission was for the Chapel of Mount Jerome Cemetery, Dublin (1845), which he won by competition. His first major commission (and also his most prominent) was for the Cork Lunatic Asylum (1847–52). Other commissions include St Marie's of the Isle Convent (1850), Cork Dominican Priory (1850) and Lindville Asylum, Cork (1855). His commissions for the Church of Ireland include those at East Ferry, Midleton (1865), Leighmoney, Kinsale (1865); Rooska, Bantry (1868); Ardfert (1868), Killarney (1869) and

Corkbeg, Whitegate (1881, completed posthumously). His architectural reputation rests on 'Oakpark', Tralee, a country house which was commissioned by Maurice Fitzgerald Soudes (1857–61) and now considered one of the finest Gothic Revival houses in Ireland. He died on 5 January 1887. [Essay by J. Williams in A. Bernelle (ed.), *Decantations* (1992)]

ATKINSON, George M.W. (c.1806–1884) Born Queenstown (Cobh), Co. Cork. He went to sea as a ship's carpenter and developed an interest in marine painting. He exhibited marine subjects at the Royal Irish Academy. His 'Visit of the Queen and Prince Albert to Queenstown in 1849' was lithographed and published. He died at Cobh on 7 January 1884. His sons, George Mounsey (d. 1908), Richard Peterson (*fl.* 1856–82), and Robert, as well as his daughter, Sarah (*fl.* 1880–1915), were painters and art enthusiasts.

AUSTIN, Michael (1855–1916) Born Cork, the son of John Austin. He was educated at the Christian Brothers Schools, Cork, and was apprenticed to the printing trade in 1869. As a member of the Typographical Society, he became prominent in trade unionism. In 1891, he was elected vice-president of a national conference to establish the nucleus of an annual trade union congress. In the 1892 general election, he was elected as MP for Limerick West which he represented until his retirement in 1900. He was one of the first Labour/Nationalists elected to the House of Commons. He also served as a member of the Royal Commission on Labour. He died at his London residence, 54, Doddington Grove, on 18 February 1916.

B

BADHAM, Bettridge (d. 1744) Born Cork, the son of Alderman Thomas Badham. He was MP for Charleville (1713–14) and Rathcormick (1743–4). He presented the address of the 'Sovereign, Bailiffs and Freemen' of Charleville to King George I when he succeeded to the throne in 1714. He died at Ballyheen in July 1744.

BAKER, [A.A.] William (1925–1991) Born Dunedin, Connaught Avenue, Cork, the son of Arthur Baker, commercial traveller. Following his secondary schooling, he left Cork in 1944 to enlist in the British Army. He was demobbed at the end of the war and took up journalism, mainly writing short stories for magazines. In the early 1950s, he became editor of Panther Books where he devised the 'house name' scheme – a syndicate of writers producing mass-market fiction, the copyright of which was owned by the publishers. Later, in 1956, he took over the management of the Sexton Blake Library for Amalgamated Press using the same system, contributing to the series of novelettes himself as well as editing other contributions. When the series was discontinued in 1963, he bought the rights to the Sexton Blake character and leased it to Mayflower Books. By now, he was turning out a diverse range of *genre* novels himself (beginning in 1955 with *Without Warning*) and in 1968, opened his own publishing house, W. Howard Baker. He wrote under various pseudonyms including W. Howard Baker, W.A. Ballinger, Nicola Devon, and Peter Saxon. As Ballinger, he wrote *Rebellion* (1966), and as Saxon, *The Disoriented Man* (1966) which was made into a film, *Scream and Scream Again* (1969). However, most of his books were entertainments for the mass-market paperback trade. He died in London on 13 February 1991.

BAKER, George (1816–1886) Born Cahir, Co. Tipperary, or Cork, the son of a Quaker, Richard Harris Baker (1785–1859). At the time of his marriage in 1848, he had established a baking business in Cork and was a pioneer in the craft of biscuit manufacture. Around 1860 he set up, with his partner, George Simpson, the biscuit company of Baker, Simpson & Co. which operated in the area between Patrick Street and Paul Street. There was also a confectionery and refreshment saloon in French Church Street. As well as supplying the home market, biscuits were exported as far away as China and the West Indies.

BALDWIN, Augustus W. (1776–1866) Born Russell Hill, Lisnegatt, Bandon, Co. Cork, the sixth of sixteen children of Robert Baldwin, gentleman, and brother of **William Warren Baldwin**. The family emigrated to Canada and he joined the Royal Navy in 1794. He saw service against the French both off Canada and in the English Channel and eventually rose to the rank of captain in January 1817. In that year, he retired from active service and settled on a small estate near Toronto, Ontario (then in Upper Canada). He was appointed as a local magistrate and as a commissioner of claims. He also went into banking and shipbuilding, and in 1831, he became a Conservative member of the Legislative Council of Upper Canada. Following the Canadian constitutional crisis of 1836, he was appointed to the new legislative Council of the United Province of Canada in June 1841. However, he resigned from that body shortly afterwards. He held directorships in the Bank of Upper Canada and in the British America Assurance Company. He died at his estate, Russell Hill, Toronto, on 5 January 1866.

BALDWIN, Connell J. (1777–1861) Born Cloheena, Kilnamartra, Co. Cork, the son of Dr James Baldwin, MP, and brother of **Herbert Baldwin**. He was a cousin of Daniel O'Connell (1775–1847), the Liberator. He was educated by the Jesuits in France and joined the Royal Navy at the age of 14 years. Two years later, he was invalided out of the navy and then fought in many of the major battles of the Peninsular War where he reached the rank of captain. He saw further service in Britain and the West Indies and, in 1826, he raised a regiment to serve under the Emperor of Brazil. Two years later, he emigrated to Canada and settled on a small estate in the Gore Township near Toronto, Ontario, and built both a school and a church there. Representing the Roman Catholic interest, he was nominated as a Reform candidate in the 1841 state election. However, as his rival was an Orangeman, he withdrew in order to avoid bloodshed. He served as a local magistrate and as a militia commander from 1835 to 1851. During the cholera epidemic of 1847, he turned his home into a private hospital and cared for many destitute immigrants. He died on a visit to Toronto on 14 December 1861.

BALDWIN, Herbert (1782–1861) Born Cloheena, Kilnamartyra, Co. Cork, the third son of Dr James Baldwin and brother of **Connell J. Baldwin**. His mother was the paternal aunt of 'The Liberator', Daniel O'Connell (1775–1847). The Baldwins were substantial landowners and Herbert, whose family were Roman Catholics, inherited over 2,000 acres in Co. Cork. Having studied medicine, he opened a practice in Cork City in 1805 and four years later, he entered local politics. In the general election of 1830, he unsuccessfully contested Cork City as a Liberal radical, but two years later he was returned as a Repeal MP for the same constituency. Though again defeated at the polls in 1835, he regained his seat on petition. He retired in 1837 and died at his Cloheena residence, on 17 January 1861.

BALDWIN, William W. (1775–1844) Born Knockmore, Carrigaline, Co. Cork, the fifth of the sixteen children of Robert Baldwin, gentleman. He was the uncle of **Robert Baldwin Sullivan**. In 1797, he graduated with a medical degree from the University of Edinburgh and in the following year most of the family, including William, emigrated to Toronto, Ontario. As there was not much of a demand for his medical skills, he studied law and was called to the Bar in 1803. In 1808, he became a registrar of the Court of Probate and a year later was appointed as a district court judge. By the 1820s he had become a large landowner and a wealthy man with a large country residence. A Whig, Baldwin was elected to the Upper Canadian House of Assembly in the general election of 1820, but lost the seat in 1824. With another parliamentary defeat in 1830, he decided to retire from politics. In 1836, largely through the influence of his neighbour, **Sir Francis Hincks**, he was elected as president of the Constitutional Reform Society of Upper Canada and also chairman of the Toronto Political Union. On account of this, he was dismissed from his judgeship by his bitter enemies in the Tory administration. A staunch Anglican, he was an opponent of the extreme Canadian Orangeism of the time and was tolerant of both Dissent and Roman Catholicism. His liberal opinions were later to exert a huge influence on federal Canadian politics. He died in Toronto on 8 January 1844.

BALL, Anne E. (1808–1872) She lived in Youghal, Co. Cork, where she undertook the study of seaweeds. She assisted W.H. Harvey in his *Phycologia Britannica*. Her brother was **Robert Ball**.

BALL, Robert (1802–1857) Born Queenstown (Cobh), Co. Cork, of an old Youghal family. He was the brother of **Anne Elizabeth Ball**. While working in the Irish Under-Secretary's office in Dublin, he took an interest in natural history. However, in a reorganisation of the office in 1852, he was placed on the retired list as he 'devoted much attention to scientific pursuits, and it was not expected that public servants should be thus occupied.' In 1844, he had been appointed as director of the TCD Museum and became secretary of the Queen's University in Ireland in 1851. He received an honorary degree of LL.D from TCD in 1850 in recognition of the donation of his large collection of natural history and of his other services to that college. He was also elected as a fellow of the Royal Society. He died on 3 March 1857. His son, Sir Robert Ball, FRS (1840–1913), became the Astronomer Royal for Ireland (1874–92). Another son, Valentine, became professor of Geology and Mineralogy at TCD.

BARRETT, Eaton S. (1786–1820) Born Cork. He was educated in London and at TCD where he graduated BA (1805) and was later called to the Middle Temple. He wrote both prose and poetry, including his satirical poem *All the Talents* (1807) which ran to nearly 20 editions in less than a year. His *All the Talents in Ireland* was also written in 1807. He later published *Women* (1810), *My Wife, What Wife?* (1815) and *The Heroine* (1822). He also was the founder of the London satirical newspaper, *The Comet*. He died of tuberculosis in Glamorgan, Wales, on 20 March 1820.

BARRETT, Frederick W. (1875–1949) Born Tivoli, Cork, the youngest son of William Barrett of Silver Springs. He joined the 15th Hussars in 1897 and became interested in polo when his regiment was in India. He was a skilful polo player and captained the British team which won the Westchester Cup in 1914. He served in France during World War I and when he resigned in 1919, he had risen to the rank of major. He later won a gold medal with the British team at the Antwerp Olympics (1920) and a bronze four years later at the Paris Olympics. He went on to become a successful horse trainer, especially with the 1931 Scottish Grand National winner, *Annadale*. He died in Wiltshire in 1949 and was buried in St Bride's, Pembrokeshire.

BARRETT, Jack (1911–1979) Born Kinsale, Co. Cork. He came to prominence as a hurler with his native town before starring for Cork and winning an All-Ireland SHC medal in 1941. He also won two NHL medals in the Cork colours and six Railway Cup medals for Munster. On retirement from the playing field, he became a prominent GAA administrator. He was vice-chairman of Cork County Board (1954–9) and chairman (1966–72, 1973–4). He was also chairman of the Munster Council of the GAA (1959–62). He was narrowly defeated in the election for the presidency of the GAA in 1961. A cattle dealer, he died suddenly while inspecting stock near Midleton on 16 February 1979. He was buried in St Eltin's Cemetery, Kinsale.

BARRETT, John (d. 1693) Born Castlemore, Mallow, Co. Cork. He sat as a member for Mallow in the 'Patriot Parliament' of James II in 1689. On the confiscation of his estate in 1691, he left for France and rose to the rank of colonel in Dorrington's Irish regiment. He was killed following the battle of Landen in 1693.

BARRETT, Stephen D. (1913–1976) Born Cork, the second child of George Barrett of York Terrace, Summerhill, and grandson of Joseph Barrett, lord mayor of Cork (1905–7). He was educated at Christian Brothers College, Cork, and at UCC where he graduated BCL. In 1931, he joined the staff of the *Cork Examiner*. He was called to the Bar in 1946 and resigned from the *Examiner* in the following year as chief sub-editor and assistant leader-writer. He unsuccessfully contested Dáil elections in Cork City (1948 and 1951), before winning a by-election in 1954 as a Fine Gael candidate. He retired from national politics in 1969, having also been a member of Cork Corporation (1950–69) and having been elected Lord Mayor in 1960. He was appointed a judge of the Circuit Court in November 1973 and was on the Galway Circuit at the time of his death. He was taken ill on a journey to County Tipperary and died at the North Infirmary Hospital, Cork, on 8 September 1976. He was buried in St Joseph's Cemetery. He was the author of *The Almost People* (1973) – a collection of essays.

BARRY, Anthony (1901–1983) Born Cork, the son of James J. Barry, a grocer who specialised in teas and wines. He was educated at North Monastery CBS and left school at the age of fourteen to enter the family business. He joined the National army on its foundation and resigned at the end of the civil war with the rank of captain. He developed the tea-blending side of the business and established 'Barry's' as a premier tea firm. A founding member of Cumann na nGaedheal, he was **W.T. Cosgrave**'s 'man' (election agent) in Cork. He sat on Cork Corporation for many years and also served as Lord Mayor (1961/62). He represented Cork City in the Dáil (1954–7 and 1961–5) and was also a member of Seanad Éireann (1957–61). He was a member of Cork City library committee for an unprecedented fifty years (1929–79). A keen photographer, his studies of Cork in the 1950s and 1960s were published as *No Lovelier City: a Portrait of Cork* (1995). He died at the Bon Secours Hospital, Cork, on 24 October 1983 and was buried in St Finbarr's Cemetery. His son, Peter, served as a Fine Gael TD, Tánaiste, and Minister of Foreign Affairs, and also served as lord mayor of Cork (1970/71). His daughter, Terry (Kelly), served as mayor of Limerick (1983) while his granddaughter, Deirdre (Clune), was returned as lord mayor of Cork (2005).

BARRY, David (d. 1947) Born Glanworth, Co. Cork. He took an active part in the War of Independence, serving with the Limerick Flying Column. He was later adjutant of the Cork No. 2 Brigade and registrar of the Dáil Éireann court in North East Cork. He represented Fermoy RDC as an *ex officio* member of Cork County Council (1922–4). In 1924, he founded the Irish Tourism Association in Cork, which, by the late 30s had become a nationwide organisation. He oversaw the opening of the Irish Tourist Office in Regent Street, London. He died at his home at Mount Merrion, Dublin, on 15 March 1947 and was buried in Kilcrumper Cemetery, Fermoy.

BARRY, David FitzDavid (1605–1642) Born Co. Cork, the grandson of **David FitzJames de**

Barry, Viscount Buttevant. He succeeded to the title at the age of 16 and married 13-year old Alice Boyle, the daughter of **Richard Boyle**, 1st earl of Cork. In 1627, he was created 1st earl of Barrymore by King Charles I. He took the royalist side during the Confederate War and took part in the battle of Liscarroll on 3 September 1642. He died three weeks later at Castlelyons and was buried in the earl of Cork's tomb at St Mary's Collegiate Church, Youghal, Co. Cork.

BARRY, David FitzJames de (1550–1617) Born Co. Cork, the son of James FitzRichard Barry Roe, Viscount Buttevant. He succeeded to the title in 1581 as his elder brother, Richard, being deaf and dumb, was disbarred. He was a supporter of the Desmond Rebellion, but changed allegiance when he was attacked by the English under Governor Zouch in May 1582 and suffered heavy losses. He remained loyal to the English Crown and an opponent of Hugh O'Neill during the Nine Years War. He died at Barryscourt Castle, Carrigtohill, on 10 April 1617.

BARRY, Denis (1885/6–1923) Born Cullen, Riverstick, Co. Cork. In his early 20s, he was a prominent hurler with Blackrock, winning four-in-a-row County Championships (1910–13), Croke Cup medals (1910 and 1913), a Munster Senior medal (1912), and a County Junior football medal with Lees (1910). In 1915, he left Cork for Kilkenny city where he worked as a draper's assistant. Prominent in the Republican movement, he was arrested following the 1916 Rising and was lodged in Wakefield Detention Barracks. Following the Treaty, he took the Republican side and was Chief of the Republican Police in Cork City during its occupation by the anti-Treaty forces. During this period, he masterminded a famous escape by Republican prisoners from Spike Island. He was arrested in 1923 and was interned in Newbridge Camp. He went on hunger strike and died at the Curragh Military Hospital on 20 November 1923. He was buried in St Finbarr's Hospital, Cork. [Commemorative plaque and monument at Riverstick]

BARRY, Edmond (1837–1900) Born Midleton, Co. Cork, the son of Edmond Barry, publican. He was educated locally and entered St Patrick's College, Maynooth, where he was ordained for the Cloyne diocese in 1858. He subsequently served as curate at Aghada, Mitchelstown and Youghal until his appointment as parish priest of Rathcormac in 1885. He was an authority on Ogham inscriptions and published several articles on the subject. His most enduring work, *Barrymore: Records of the Barrys of Co. Cork*, was published in 1902, having appeared in serial form in *JCHAS* from 1899 to 1902. He was a member of the Royal Irish Academy and a vice-president of the Royal Society of Antiquaries of Ireland. He died at Rathcormac on 23 May 23 1900 and was buried in Bartlemy Graveyard.

BARRY, Sir Edward (1698–1776) Born Cork, the son of Nathaniel Barry, apothecary. He was educated at TCD where he graduated BA (1717) and at Leyden University where he graduated MD. He was later awarded the MD of TCD (1740) and Oxford University (1761). He was also a fellow of the College of Physicians, Dublin (1740) and a fellow of the Royal College of Physicians, London (1762). He was elected a fellow of the Royal Society in 1733. In 1720, he commenced his practice on 'Orrery Quay', Cork, and lived there for twenty years. He was made a freeman of Cork in July 1733. In 1739, he moved to Dublin where he established his practice on College Green and in 1751, he built Mespil House as a country seat. He was MP for Charleville from 1743 to 1760. He was also vice-president of the Physico-Historical Society of Ireland – the body which supported the publication of the histories of **Charles Smith**. He was appointed as Physician General of the Army in 1745 and was professor of Physic at TCD from 1754 to 1761. In the latter year, he moved to England where he was awarded the MD of Oxford University and licensed to practise in London. He was made a baronet in 1773. He died in 1776. His publications include, *A Treatise on the Consumption of the Lungs* (1726), *A Treatise of the Three different Digestions*

and Discharges of the Human Body, and the Diseases of their Principal Organs (1759), *Observations, Historical, Critical, and Medical, on the Wines of the Ancients, and the Analogy between them and the Modern Wines* (1775), and five papers to the *Edinburgh Medical Essays and Observations* [Some correspondence in Countess of Cork and Orrery (ed.), *The Orrery Papers* (2 vols, 1903)]

BARRY, Edward (1852–1927) Born Rosscarbery, Co. Cork, the son of Garrett Barry, a tenant farmer and land agent to the Carbery estate. He was educated at Castleknock College, Co. Dublin. Having been for a number of years chairman of the Clonakilty Board of Guardians, he was elected to the House of Commons in 1892 as an anti-Parnellite MP for South Cork. He retained his seat uncontested until the December 1910 election when he was defeated by the O'Brienite candidate, **John Walsh**. A cousin of **O'Donovan Rossa**, he was one of a minority group in the Irish Parliamentary Party which recommended a temporary withdrawal from parliament in 1907. He was also the first tenant farmer to represent a Cork constituency in parliament. He died at his residence, 'Newmill', Rosscarbery, on 7 December 1927.

BARRY, Garrett S. (1789–1864) Born Leamlara House, Lisgoold, Co. Cork, the son of Standish Barry, a representative of one of the few old Roman Catholic gentry families in County Cork. He was educated at TCD where he graduated BA (1809) and was called to the Irish Bar in 1811. He was one of two Roman Catholics who were among the 79 founders of the Cork and County Club in 1828. He was elected as high sheriff of Cork in 1830 and two years later he was elected as a Liberal MP for Cork County. He retained his seat until his retirement in 1841. Though opposed to the payment of tithes, he did not favour the Repeal movement. He died at Leamlara House on 26 December 1864.

BARRY, George R. (1825–1867) Born Cork, the son of John Richard Barry. He spent part of his youth in Mauritius, but by 1850, he operated as a merchant in Bengal and owned tea plantations in the East Indies. Returning to Ireland, he took up residence at Lota Lodge, purchased part of Lord Fermoy's estate for £9,600 in 1865 and part of The O'Donoghue's estate for £3,610 in 1866. Having been adopted as the Liberal candidate for Cork County in 1865, he was returned at the head of the poll. In 1866, his Indian investments began to unravel and he became embroiled in financial difficulties. These helped in no small way to hasten his premature death at St Leonard's, near Hastings, East Sussex, on 31 January 1867.

BARRY, Gerald (*fl.* **1624–1642**) Born Co. Cork, a member of the Barrymore family. He saw service with the Spanish army in Germany and the Low Countries, and wrote an account of the 1625 Siege of Breda (1628). He was promoted to the rank of colonel and was employed by the King of Spain to raise troops in Ireland. He returned to Ireland and took part in the Rising of 1641 as a commander of the Munster forces. He returned to Spain in the following year when he was declared an outlaw by the English Government. He published *A Discourse of Military Discipline* (1634).

BARRY, James (**1741–1806**) Born Blackpool, Cork, the son of a builder, publican, and sea captain. He developed a strong interest in painting. He went to Dublin in 1763 where he exhibited at the Royal Dublin Society. While there, he met with Edmund Burke who brought him to London and introduced him to Sir Joshua Reynolds (1723–92). The latter advised him to work in Italy and, with the help of an allowance from Burke, he arrived in Rome in September 1766. He returned to London in 1771 and exhibited at the Royal Academy. For over six years (1777–83) he worked on the decoration of the Great Room of the Society of Arts at the Adelphi and exhibited there in 1783 and 1784. In 1782 he was appointed as professor of Painting at the Royal Academy, but owing to his hostility to his fellow-members, was eventually expelled

from the institution. For the remainder of his life, he lived aloof from society and in extreme poverty. He died on 6 February 1806 and following his lying in state at the Adelphi, he was buried in the crypt of St Paul's at the expense of Sir Robert Peel (1788–1850). [Self-portraits at the National Portrait Gallery, London, and at the Victoria and Albert Museum, London; Exhibition booklet, Cork Municipal Art Gallery (2005)]

BARRY, John (**1792–1838**) Born Bandon, Co. Cork. He converted to Methodism in 1809 and was admitted into the reserve itinerant ministry. Having attended a Bandon meeting in 1823 which was addressed by the 'St Paul of Methodism', Adam Clarke (*c.*1762–1832), he became interested in missionary work. He and his family left for Jamaica in February 1825 and were there when an uprising by the slaves against the planters took place in December 1832. He was then posted to, in turn, Toronto, Montreal and Bermuda (arriving there a fortnight after slavery had been abolished on the island). However, he became seriously ill in 1836 and returned briefly to England. He died in Montreal on 21 June 1838. Barry was a fine preacher who, at all times, spoke out against slavery and social injustice. He was also very interested in the education of the poorer classes and in the Sunday Schools system.

BARRY, John (**1875–1938**) Born Freemount, Co. Cork, the eldest son of Simon Barry, farmer. He was educated at St Colman's College, Fermoy, and at St Patrick's College, Maynooth, where he was ordained in June 1899. In that year, he left for Melbourne, Australia, where, in March 1917, he was appointed as administrator of Melbourne Cathedral and as chancellor of the archdiocese. These appointments were confirmed two months later by the new archbishop of Melbourne, his fellow-Corkman, **Daniel Mannix**. In 1924, he was appointed as bishop of Goulburn, New South Wales, and immediately embarked on a building programme which included a new cathedral in Australia's capital, Canberra. He died of a heart disease on 22 March

1938 at Sydney and was buried at Kenmore, Goulburn.

BARRY, John G. (1926–1989) Born Conna, Co. Cork, the eldest son of Joseph Barry. He was educated at Mount Melleray School and at UCC where he graduated BA (1947) and MA (1949). He later completed a doctoral thesis (1952) on the function of coarb and erenagh in the Irish Church. From 1950 to 1962, he worked as an assistant librarian at the National Library of Ireland, serving mainly in the Genealogical Office. During this period, he undertook for the Irish Manuscripts Commission a report on the duke of Devonshire's Irish estates (*Analecta Hibernica*, 22, 1960) and 'A Guide to the Records of the Genealogical Office' (*Analecta Hibernica*, 26, 1970). His O'Donnell Lecture, 'The study of family history in Ireland', was published in 1957. In 1962, he was appointed a statutory lecturer in History at UCG and three years later he was appointed to the newly-created professorship of Medieval History at UCC. He was in poor health for some time before his death, which occurred on 6 August 1989.

BARRY, John Milner (1768–1822) Born Bandon, Co. Cork. He was educated at Edinburgh University where he graduated MD (1792). He held the Lectureship in Agriculture at the Cork Institution for many years prior to his resignation in 1815. The author of several medical treatises, he founded the Cork Fever Hospital and introduced vaccination into Ireland when he vaccinated in Cork in 1800. He contributed many articles on vaccination, fevers and related topics to various books and journals. He was also a strong advocate of the education of women. He died in Cork on 16 May 1822.

BARRY, Kathy (1909–1982) Born Dalton's Avenue, Cork, the daughter of John Barry. A renowned beauty, she ran a small provisions shop (now demolished) in Dalton's Avenue, off the Coal Quay. She was famous for her crubeens which were always in great demand once the pubs had closed. There was also a chance of a few glasses of cider for special customers. Her name lives on in a verse of 'The Boys of Fair Hill' and also in the rugby chant, 'We'll Crown Kathy Barry Queen of Ireland'. It is still said of badly defeated teams that, 'They wouldn't "bate" Kathy Barry'. She spent her final days living across the road at No. 6, Corporation Buildings. She died at the Mercy Hospital on 27 December 1982 and was buried in St Joseph's Cemetery.

BARRY, Kevin (1930–1999) Born Cork. He was educated at UCD where he graduated BE. In 1952, he joined the Wimpey Construction Company and worked on various projects in the Middle East, Africa, West Indies and South America. In 1971, he was involved in the construction and siting of Europe's largest oil drilling and production platforms in the North Sea. For his work in North Sea oil development, he was awarded the Queen's Silver Jubilee Medal in 1977. He served as deputy chairman and chief executive of Brown and Root Wimpey Highlands Fabricators from 1979 until 1983. He was awarded the OBE in 1989. He died as a result of a car accident on 3 September 1999.

BARRY, Lodwick (1591–1616) Born Co. Cork. He was educated at Oxford and his real name was probably James Barry, the second son of Lord Barrymore. A dramatist, he wrote *Ram Alley or Merry Tricks*, which was produced in London in 1610. This would probably have made him Ireland's first dramatist.

BARRY, Margaret (1917–1989) Born Peter Street, Cork, the daughter of a banjo player. At the age of sixteen and following the death of her mother, she became a street singer and banjo player, operating largely in the Ulster counties. Displaying a unique voice and style, she collected a large repertoire of popular songs. In the mid-1940s, she was brought to London by Alan Lomax where she sang with Michael Gorman, fiddler, of Tubbercurry, Co. Sligo. Recordings followed and the duo performed in many of the main concert halls in Britain and America. She spent her last years in Banbridge, Co. Down and died in 1989.

BARRY, Michael J. (1817–1889) Born Cork, the son of Michael Joseph Barry, and nephew of Bishop **John England**. Being a follower of the Young Ireland movement, he was a frequent contributor of poems to its organ, *The Nation*. However, following the unsuccessful rising of 1848, he abandoned the nationalist movement and became editor of the *Cork Southern Reporter* (*c.*1850) as well as a contributor to *Punch*. He later became a leader-writer for *The Times* and served as a police magistrate in Dublin. He died at his George's Street (now Oliver Plunkett Street), Cork, residence on 23 January 1889 and was buried in an unmarked grave in St Joseph's Cemetery. His publications included *Songs of Ireland* (1845), *Echoes from Parnassus* (1849), *A Waterloo Commemoration* (1854), *Lays of the War* (1855), *Irish Emigration Considered* (1863), *The Kishogue Papers* (1872) and *Heinrich and Leonora – an Alpine Story* (1886).

BARRY, P. (*c.*1825–1907) Born Cork. He trained as a journalist and later moved to London where he wrote on social issues, including, *Wealth and Poverty Considered* (1869) and *The Workman's Wrongs and the Workman's Rights* (1870). He died in London in 1907.

BARRY, Pat (1928–2000) Born Glanmire, Co. Cork. He was educated locally and at UCC, winning a Fitzgibbon Cup hurling medal with the latter. Along with seven brothers, he was the mainstay of many Sarsfields hurling and football teams from the mid-1940s until the late 1960s. As a half-forward, he was a member of the Cork teams which won the All-Ireland Senior Hurling Championship treble (1952–54), captaining the side in 1952. He also won four Railway Cup and two National League hurling medals with Cork. He died at the Mercy Hospital, Cork, on 18 December 2000 and was buried in Kilcrumper New Cemetery, Fermoy.

BARRY, Sir Redmond (1813–1880) Born Ballyclough, Glanworth, Co. Cork, the third son of Major-General Henry G. Barry. He was educated Bexley School, Kent, and at TCD where he graduated BA (1837). A year later, he was called to the Bar and then emigrated to Australia in 1839. In 1850, he was appointed as solicitor-general of Victoria and a year later he was appointed to the bench of the Supreme Court of Victoria. He was knighted in 1860. He became first chancellor of Melbourne University in 1853 and held this position until his death. He was the founder of Melbourne Public Library (now the State Library of Victoria). He took a great interest in public libraries and before the foundation of the Melbourne one, he would open his own house at night to interested readers. He also had a high regard for the Aborigine people and defended many of them for no fee. He pronounced the death sentence on the celebrated outlaw, Ned Kelly (1855–80), and died twelve days after Kelly's execution, on 23 November 1880. He was buried in Melbourne General Cemetery. [Portraits at La Trobe Library and at Melbourne University; Biographical article by A. Sutherland in *Melbourne Review*, 7 (1882).]

BARRY, Richard G.G. (1914–2000) Born 'Greenville', Carrigtohill, Co. Cork, the son of Thomas G. Barry, gentleman. He was educated at Presentation Brothers College, Cork, and Douai Abbey School, Berkshire, before graduating MB at UCC in 1937. He took up junior medical posts in Bristol and London before joining the Army Medical Corps in 1940. During World War II, he saw service in Norway, India, Iraq, Iran, Egypt and Italy. He then studied paediatrics in London and Derbyshire before he graduated MD in 1948. In the following year, he returned to practise in Cork and was appointed as paediatrician to the Erinville, Mercy and Bon Secours hospitals. His specialist interest in gastroenterology was mainly responsible for the huge drop in Cork's infant mortality in the 1950s. He was appointed as lecturer in Paediatrics at UCC in 1951 and as professor in 1970. He was voluntary paediatrician to St Anne's Adoption Society from 1954 and was awarded the Papal Benemerenti Medal in 1989 for his work for the society. He was a fellow of both the Royal College of Physicians of London (1971) and of the Royal College of Physicians of Ireland (1978). He died at Cork University Hospital on 19 October 2000 and was buried in Carrigtohill Cemetery.

BARRY, Robert (1588–1662) Born Britway, Castlelyons, Co. Cork, the son of David Barry. He was educated at the Jesuit College, Nantes, and on his return to Ireland, he became chaplain to Ellen Barry, countess of Ormond. He was consecrated as bishop of Cork on 25 March 1648. During the Confederation of Kilkenny period, he supported the papal nuncio, Archbishop Rinuccini (d. 1665). Following the Confederate War, he fled to Nantes where he became assistant to the bishop there. He died on 26 June or 6 July 1662 and was buried in Nantes Cathedral.

BARRY, Tadhg (d. 1921) Born Blarney Street, Cork. He was educated at Blarney Street and North Monastery schools. He became a member of the Irish Republican Brotherhood (IRB) in 1910 and joined the Irish Volunteers in 1913. Two years later, he was imprisoned for a seditious speech. He became a full-time official of the ITGWU in 1917 and contributed many articles to its organ, *The Voice of Labour*. Having become an alderman of Cork Corporation, he was arrested at Cork Courthouse in January 1921 and was imprisoned on Spike Island. He was subsequently transferred to Ballykinlar Internment Camp, Co. Down, where, unarmed, he was shot dead by a sentry on 15 November 1921. He was buried in the Republican plot in St Finbarr's Cemetery, Cork, on 21 November. He was prominent in Cork GAA circles where he served as chairman of the City Division and as delegate to Cork County Board. He was the author of *Hurling and How to Play It*. He contributed poetry to the various Cork periodicals under such nom-de-plumes as 'Méirleach', 'Ciotóg' and 'Tadhg'. He was also the author of *Songs and Other [C]rhymes of a Gaol-Bird: written in Cork Military and Civil Prisons … 1916–17*.

BARRY, Tom (1898–1980) Born Killorglin, Co. Kerry, the son of Thomas Barry, a police constable. The family subsequently moved to Rosscarbery and Bandon. He joined the British army and served in Mesopotamia during World War I. On his return home after the war, he joined the Republican movement and commanded the West Cork Flying Column of the IRA in many engagements during the War of Independence. He married Leslie Price of Dublin (see **Leslie de Barra**) in 1921. He took the anti-Treaty side during the Civil War and continued in the IRA following the cease-fire of 1923 until the late Thirties. In June 1946, he stood as an Independent in a Cork Borough by-election but finished at the bottom of the poll. He worked at the Cork Harbour Commissioners from 1927 until 1965 and served for a while in the Southern Command during the Emergency. He died on 2 July 1980 and was buried in St Finbarr's Cemetery. [Autobiography (1949); Life by M. Ryan (2003); His 'Flying Column' by E. Butler (1971); Life-size bronze by **Seamus Murphy;** Commemorative plaque at 64 Patrick's Street, Cork]

BARRY, Vincent C. (1908–1975) Born Sunday's Well, Cork, the youngest of eleven children of a postal official. He was educated at North Monastery CBS, Cork, and at UCD where he graduated B.Sc. (1928), M.Sc. (1929), and D.Sc. (1939). He worked in the department of Chemistry, UCG, as a researcher of marine algae. In 1944, he was awarded a fellowship by the Medical Research Council of Ireland to study tuberculosis. He contributed scientific terminological data to T. de Bhaildraithe (ed.), *English-Irish Dictionary* (1959). He was elected president of the Royal Irish Academy in 1970 and served until 1973. He died in Dublin on 4 September 1975.

BARRY, William (d. 1706) Born Cork. He was educated at the Dominican Convent at Toulouse where he became professor of Philosophy. He returned to Ireland as a Dominican friar but left again for France following the Jacobite defeat.

He later became prior of the Dominican Convent at Louvain. He died in the Royal Hospital at Chateau-Thierry, France, in 1706.

BARRY, William (1841–1875) Born Co. Cork. He worked as a journalist on several local papers before settling in London where he became the editor of a major newspaper. He was cast as the hero in William Black's novel, *Shandon Bells*. He published two volumes of essays. He died in London in 1875.

BARRY, William (1872–1929) Born Midleton, Co. Cork, the son of Edmond Barry, baker and grocer. He was educated at Midleton CBS, St Colman's College, Fermoy, and at All Hallows College, Dublin. He was ordained in 1898 and ministered in Australia where he was a member of the staff of St Mary's Cathedral, Sydney. He was appointed as parish priest of Chatswood and was consecrated as coadjutor archbishop of Hobart, Tasmania, in 1919. He succeeded to the archbishopric in the following year. He died at St Benedict's Hospital, Melbourne, on 18 June 1929.

BARRY, William Gerard (d. 1940) Born Carrigtohill, Co. Cork, the son of Patrick Barry, JP. He studied at the Cork School of Art where his teacher was **Henry Jones Thaddeus**. He worked in Paris and Etaples before returning home in 1888. In the previous year he had won the Taylor Prize of the Royal Dublin Society for his best known work, 'Times Flies', which was then exhibited at the Royal Academy, London. He subsequently travelled widely and worked in Canada, the United States and the South Pacific. He finally settled in France, firstly in the Riviera and then at St Jean de Luz. He died on 19 March 1940 when a bookcase fell on him.

BARRY, Zachary (1827–1898) Born Fermoy, the son of David Barry, doctor. He was educated at TCD where he graduated BA (1849) and LL.D (1868). He was ordained in 1851 and ministered in Liverpool before emigrating two years later to Freemantle, Western Australia, to work as a government chaplain for the Society for the Promotion of the Gospel. With growing deafness posing a problem for his ministry, he returned to Ireland in 1862 as secretary of the Irish Church Home Missions. He returned to Sydney in 1865 where he ministered until his retirement in 1893. His reputation rests with his career as a controversialist, a militant Protestant, and a supporter of Orangeism. His bias also extended to the Anglo-Catholic element of his own denomination, the Church of England. With a Presbyterian clergyman, he founded and edited the *Protestant Standard* – a publication not noted for its tolerance! In 1874, he was one of the founders of the Public Schools League, which was closely based on the Irish National School system. He died at Paddington, Sydney, on 4 October 1898 and was buried in Randwick Cemetery there. His publications include *Do Catholic Bishops Swear to Persecute Protestants?* (1867), *An Erring Sister's Shame* (1867) and *The Danger Controlled* (1868).

BARTER, Richard (1802–1870) Born Cooldaniel, Kilmichael, Co. Cork, the father of **Sir Richard Barter**. Having qualified as a doctor at the Royal College of Physicians, London, he returned to Ireland and practised as a dispensary doctor at Inniscarra. In 1842, he opened the Hydropathic Institute at St Anne's, Blarney. He later developed hot air and vapourless (Turkish) baths and travelled widely to explain his methods. He died at Blarney on 3 October 1870. He published *The Turkish Bath, with a View to its Introduction into the British Dominions* (1856).

BARTER, Richard (c.1824–1896) Born Macroom, Co. Cork. Having an interest in sculpture, he entered the Royal Dublin Society's school in 1844. He went to live in London for a short period, where he became a friend of the Irish sculptor, **John Foley**. In 1853, he settled in Blarney near the Hydropathic Institute of his namesake, Dr **Richard Barter**, where he spent the rest of his life with the exception of occasional visits to London. As a sculptor, he underachieved, but was very popular with his artistic friends. He died at St Anne's Hospital, Cork, on 5 January 1896.

BARTER, Sir Richard (1837–1916) Born Mallow, Co. Cork, the son of Dr **Richard Barter**. He was educated at Flyn's College, Dublin. He inherited St Anne's Hill Farm and developed it as a centre of excellence in dairy farming. He contributed pamphlets on aspects of dairying and was an enthusiastic promoter of the Munster Dairy School (estab. 1881) of which he was hon. secretary from its foundation. He was an outstanding stockbreeder of Kerry cattle and Large York pigs. He was knighted in 1911 for his services to agriculture and dairying. He was also chairman of the Cork and Muskerry Railway Company and a president of the Munster Agricultural Society. He died at St Anne's Hill on 16 August 1916 and was buried in Inniscarra Graveyard.

BASTABLE, Charles F. (1855–1945) Born Charleville, Co. Cork, the only son of R. Bastable, clergyman. He was educated at Fermoy College and at TCD where he graduated BA (1878), MA (1882), and LL.D (1890). He was called to the Bar in 1881. A year later, he was elected to the Whately Chair of Political Economy at TCD and retained this until his retirement in 1932. He simultaneously held the professorship of Jurisprudence and Political Economy at Queen's College, Galway (now UCG) from 1883 to 1903 – a position which he resigned on his appointment as professor of Jurisprudence and International Law. He was also Regius Professor of Laws at TCD from 1908 until 1932. His research interests were in economics rather than in law and he gained an international reputation in the fields of public finance and international trade theory. His publications included *The Theory of International Trade* (1887, 1903 [4th ed.]), *The Commerce of Nations* (1892), and *Public Finance* (1892, 1903 [3rd ed.]. He contributed articles to the 9th, 10th, and 11th editions of *Encyclopaedia Brittanica*. He died at his Rathgar, Dublin, residence on 3 January 1945. [Life by G.A. Duncan (1946)]

BEALE, Abraham (1793–1847) Born Cork, the son of Thomas Beale, and brother of **George Beale**. On his ironmongery business lapsing into bankruptcy in 1819, he was disowned by his fellow-Quakers, but was later re-admitted when all outstanding debts were cleared. He then went into partnership for a while with his relative, **James Beale,** and they operated their ironmongery business on Patrick's Quay. He took a great interest in the Cork Mechanics' Institution and during the Famine, he was one of the secretaries of the Cork Friends Auxiliary Relief Committee. He died in 1847.

BEALE, George (1791–1834) Born Cork, the son of Thomas Beale and brother of **Abraham Beale**. He practised as an architect and was responsible for the design and plans of the Quaker Meeting House at Grattan Street, Cork, which was built in the year of his death.

BEALE, James (1798–1879) Born Cork. He set up in business on Penrose Quay as a ship-builder, whose company (the St George Steam Packet Company) commissioned the *Sirius*, the first steamship to make the trans-Atlantic crossing (31 March to 22 April 1838). He worked for a while as partner with his brother-in-law, **Robert John Lecky**, running a ship-repair yard at Penrose Quay. He was also an enthusiastic watercolour painter and travelled extensively in Italy, Norway, and Morocco. His 'A Storm off the Bay of Tangiers' and 'Skelligs Night on the South Mall' hang in the Crawford Gallery, Cork. [Commemorative plaque at Penrose House, Penrose Quay, Cork]

BEALE, Joshua (1720–1789) Born Cork, the son of Joshua Beale and grandson of **Joseph Pike**. He ran a timber business and resided in Sunday's Well. He was one of the leaders of Cork's Quaker community and took a prominent part in quelling the labour unrest in Cork during and after the American War of Independence. He died at the home of his nephew, **Joshua Beale** at Myrtle Hill, Cork.

BEALE, Joshua (1763–1833) Born Cork, the nephew of **Joshua Beale**. He was educated at the Quaker School, Ballitore, Co. Kildare. He was a co-founder of the Cork Dispensary and Humane Society in 1787 and was a member of the original committee. This society helped nearly 12,500 patients in the first four years of its existence. He was also a supporter of the Cork Anti-Slavery Society. Even though he had been finally disowned by the Cork Quakers in 1823, he continued to live by Quaker principles for the remainder of his life.

BEALE, William G. (1871–1923) Born Cork, of the seed-merchant firm of Harris & Beale (1791) of Grand Parade. He was shot on 16 March 1923 by two gunmen as he returned to his house at St Luke's. A pacifist, he was apparently shot as a reprisal for an execution. He died at the South Infirmary Hospital on 20 March and was buried at the Friends' Burial Ground, Capwell.

BEAMISH, Charles E. St J. (1908–1984) Born Dunmanway, Co. Cork, the third son of Francis George Beamish of Larne, Co. Antrim and younger brother of **Sir George Robert Beamish**. He served as a Group Captain in the RAF in England, America and the Far East during World War II and was awarded the DFC, the American Legion of Merit and the American Silver Star. He was an international rugby player and was capped 12 times for Ireland (1933–8). He also represented Ulster and the Barbarians. He died in Templemore, Co. Tipperary in 1984.

BEAMISH, Francis B. (1802–1868) Born Beaumont House, Ballintemple, Cork, the eighth son of **William Beamish**, merchant, landowner, and brewer. He was the brother of **North Ludlow Beamish**. He was educated at Rugby School, England. He represented Cork City as a Liberal MP for two periods (1837–41 and 1853–65). He was elected as mayor of Cork in 1843 and served as high sheriff of the city in 1852. He was one of the few Cork Protestants who supported the Emancipation and Repeal movements of Daniel O'Connell. He died at his English residence, Beaumont Lodge, Totnes, Devon, on 1 February 1868.

BEAMISH, Sir George R. (1905–1967) Born Dunmanway, Co. Cork, the second son of Francis George Beamish of Larne, Co. Antrim, schools inspector. He was the elder brother of **Charles E. St J. Beamish**. He rose to the rank of Air Vice-Marshal and served in six different war theatres during World War II. He was subsequently appointed as commandant of the RAF College at Cranwell and was knighted in 1955. He also excelled at rugby and represented Ireland 25 times (1925–33). He toured Australia and New Zealand with the British and Irish Lions in 1930 and played a total of 21 games in that tour. He also represented Midland Counties and played his club rugby for the RAF and Leicester. He died at Castlerock, Co. Derry, on 13 November 1967.

BEAMISH, North Ludlow (1796–1872) Born Beaumont House, Ballintemple, Cork, the fifth son of **William Beamish**, merchant, landowner and brewer. He was the brother of **Francis B. Beamish**. He joined the 4th Royal Irish Dragoons in 1816 and was promoted to the rank of major in 1826. He was also an author of note and his best-known work is his *History of the King's German Legion* (2 vols, 1834). He also published *Antiquitates Americana* (1841) and *The Uses and Application of Cavalry at War* (1855). He was a fellow of the Royal Society. He died at Annemount, Glounthaune, Co. Cork, on 27 April 1872 and was buried at St Michael's Graveyard, Blackrock.

BEAMISH, North L.A. (1842–1923) Born Annemount, Glounthaune, Co. Cork, the eldest son of **North Ludlow Beamish**. He was educated at TCD where he graduated BA. He became a director of Beamish and Crawford Brewery Ltd and was a keen cattle breeder and exhibitor. He acted as treasurer for the Munster Agricultural Society for many years and worked on the committee which organised the Cork International Exhibition of 1902. He died suddenly on 16 May 1923 while staying at the Shelbourne Hotel, Dublin. He was buried in the Old Church Cemetery, Cobh.

BEAMISH, Richard H. (1861–1938) Born Ashbourne House, Glounthaune, Co. Cork, the elder son of Richard Piggott Beamish, merchant and brewer. He was educated at Hailebury College and lived in Sweden for a number of years (his mother was Swedish). He was both mayor and high sheriff of Cork (1906 and 1911) and was chairman and managing director of Beamish and Crawford Brewery Ltd (1901–30). In the 1922 general election, he was an unsuccessful independent candidate, but was elected as a TD for the Progressive Association in 1923. He sat until 1927 when he did not seek re-election. At the first annual election to Cork Corporation in June 1930, he was returned as an alderman, but attended no meetings after December 1931 when he took up residence in England. He was responsible for laying out the gardens at Ashbourne House. He died at Weybridge, Surrey, on 23 February 1938.

BEAMISH, William (1760–1828) Born Willsgrove House (later Beaumont House), Cork, the third son of William Beamish, Esq. He entered the Royal Navy but quickly transferred to the army where he served with the 19th Regiment during the American War of Independence. On retiring from the army, he established himself as a Cork merchant and was made a freeman in 1790. In 1791, the Cork Porter Company was acquired by Beamish, **William Crawford** and two others, trading under the title of 'Beamish & Crawford'. Five of his eleven sons became partners in the firm on his death. He died on 17 April 1828 and was buried at Desert Serges, Enniskeane. [Bust by **John Hogan** at St Michael's Church, Blackrock]

BECHER, John R.H. (d. 1929) Born Ardralla, Skibbereen, Co. Cork, the son of Michael Becher. He was educated at TCD where he graduated BA (1886) and MA (1890). In 1890, he was ordained for the Church of Ireland ministry and held curacies in Kerry and Waterford before serving as rector of Tallow (1897–1901). He held further rectories in Youghal (1901–6), Baltimore (1906–18), Killaconenagh (1918–21), and Kilmocomoge (1921–6). He also served as archdeacon of Ross (1917–26). During his residence in Baltimore, he took an active interest in maritime affairs and was greatly responsible for the lifeboat station being located there in 1919. For his exploits in the rescue of twenty-three men from the S.S. *Alondra* on the Kedge Rocks in December 1916, Archdeacon Becher was awarded the RNLI Silver Medal for conspicuous bravery. He retired in 1926 owing to ill health and went to live in Kenya. He died, following an operation, at Nakuru Hospital, Kenya, on 8 May 1929.

BECHER, Thomas (d. 1709) He served as a militia officer under **Roger Boyle**, earl of Orrery, in the 1660s. During the Williamite War, he served as a colonel at the battle of the Boyne and was reputed to have been presented with a watch by King William. He was a beneficiary of the Williamite Plantation and was MP for Baltimore (1692, 1695–9 and 1703–9). He was ancestor of the Wrixon-Becher line through the mother of **Sir William Wrixon Becher**. He died in 1709.

BECHER, Sir William Wrixon (1780–1850) Born Cecilstown, Co. Cork, the eldest son of William Wrixon, by his wife Mary, a Becher heiress. William thus assumed the additional surname of Becher. In 1819, he married the celebrated actress, **Eliza O'Neill**, who promptly terminated her stage career. In 1818, he was elected MP for Mallow and having retained the seat in 1820, he retired from politics in 1826. An extensive landowner, he was created a baronet in 1831. He died in October 1850. In a survey of 1876, his son, Sir Henry Wrixon Becher, owned a total of 19,291 acres in counties Tipperary and Cork.

BEDDY, James P. (1900–1976) Born Cobh, Co. Cork. He was educated at O'Connell Schools, Dublin, and at UCD where he obtained doctorates in Law and Economic Science. He joined the Revenue Commissioners and then worked with the Industrial Credit Company (1933–69). He served on many State authorities including the Industrial Development Authority, An Foras Tionscail, and the Educational and Social Research Institute. He also lectured in Commerce at UCD. He wrote *Profits: Theoretical and Practical Aspects* (1940). He died at St Michael's Nursing Home, Dún Laoghaire, on 28 September 1976 and was buried in Dean's Grange Cemetery.

BEECHER, Seán (1936–1997) Born Middle Parish, Cork. He was educated locally and at UCC where he graduated B.Comm. During his time at UCC, he represented the Irish Universities in soccer on three occasions at international level. Most of his working life was spent as a clerical officer with Cork County Council, but he was also a Labour Party activist and a devotee of St Finbarr's Hurling and Football Club, whom he served for a time as club secretary. Having published a well-received popular history of Cork, *The Story of Cork* (1971), he took early retirement from Cork County Council around 1990 to concentrate on writing. His *Dictionary of Cork Slang* was published in 1983. Other books followed, combining careful research with a popular touch: *The Blues: a history of St Finbarr's club* (1984), *Day by Day: a miscellany of Cork history* (1992), *An Gaeilge in Cork City* (1993) and a novel, *The Fastnet File* (1997). He died suddenly in Cork on 29 December 1997 and was buried on Inishmore in the Aran Islands.

BELCHER, Thomas W. (1831–1910) Born Bandon, Co. Cork. He was educated at TCD where he graduated MA (1854) and MD (1862). He later became a senior fellow and librarian at the Royal College of Physicians, Dublin. However, he decided on a career in the church and was ordained in 1869. He served in England where he wrote many diverse works in history, music, and theology as well as his memoirs. He died in Bristol on 27 March 1910.

BELFORD, Charles (1837–1880) Born Cork. He emigrated with his two younger brothers, Alexander and Robert, to Toronto in 1857 and worked on the staff of *The Leader* newspaper which was owned by his great-uncle. With the demise of that newspaper in 1871, he was appointed as editor of the newly founded Conservative *Toronto Mail* in April 1872. While working for this paper, he founded with his two brothers the publishing firm of Bedford Brothers, which was the first Canadian company to publish cheap pirated reprints of popular authors, including Mark Twain (1835–1910) and Anthony Trollope (1815–82). Many other Canadian publishers followed suit. They also published *Bedford's Monthly Magazine* which was devoted to literature and the arts. In 1878, Charles, through ill health, was forced to withdraw from the company and from the *Mail*. He moved to Ottawa where he died on 19 December 1880.

BELL, Robert (1800–1867) Born Cork, the son of a magistrate. He was educated at TCD but did not graduate. He moved to London in 1828, having previously commenced his journalistic career in Dublin. As well as editing a 24-volume collection on the English poets, he also wrote plays, biographical works, and two novels – *Hearts and Altars* (1852) and *Ladder of Gold* (1856). He died in London on 12 April 1867 and was buried in Kensal Green Cemetery near the grave of his friend, the English author, W.M. Thackeray (1811–63).

BENN, Sir Arthur S. (1858–1937) Born Eglantine, Douglas, Cork, the eldest son of Rev. J.N. Benn, rector of Carrigaline and Douglas (1855–72, when he retired and moved to England where he died in 1874), and elder brother of **Ion H. Benn**. He was also the grandson of the 2nd Lord Castlemaine. He was educated at Clifton College and at the Inner Temple, and lived in Canada for some years before returning to England in 1902. He contested parliamentary seats in 1905 and 1910 before his election as Conservative MP for Plymouth in 1910 (to 1918). He later served for the Drake Division of Plymouth (1918–29) and for Sheffield Park (1931–35). He was a director of the international Chambers of Commerce from its foundation to 1927 and president of the British Chambers of Commerce (1921–3). He was knighted in 1918 and was created 1st Baron Glenravel of Kensington in 1936. He died (*s.p.*) on 13 June 1937 and the title became extinct.

BENN, Sir Ion H. (1863–1961) Born Eglantine, Douglas, Cork, the third son of Rev. J.N. Benn, rector of Carrigaline and Douglas (1855–72, when he retired and moved to England where he died in 1874), and younger brother of **Arthur S. Benn**. He was also the grandson of the 2nd Lord Castlemaine. A company director and businessman, he was mayor of Greenwich (1901/2) and contested the Greenwich constituency in the 1906 general election as a unionist and tariff reformer. He was Unionist MP for Greenwich (1910–22). He served in World War I and was awarded the DSO and the Croix de Guerre. He was knighted in 1920. He died on 12 August 1961.

BENNET, William (1746–1820) Born in the Tower of London. He was educated at Emmanuel College, Cambridge, where he graduated BA (1767), MA (1770), BD (1777) and DD (1790). He was consecrated as Church of Ireland bishop of Cork and Ross on 13 June 1790. He was subsequently translated to the diocese of Cloyne (1794). An expert on Roman Britain, he was elected as a fellow of the Royal Society (1790). He died in London on 16 July 1820 and was buried in Plumstead, Kent. [Monument (1823) by J. Heffernan (1788–1847) at Cloyne Cathedral]

BENNETT, Bill (1877–1967) Born Killeady, Ballinhassig, Co. Cork. He was an Irish champion road bowler at various times up to the age of 50 years. He was also a noted athlete, winning Irish titles in the shot putt (for 'distance' and 'over the bar') and high jump. While stationed in South Africa during the Boer War, he won four Cape Championships on the same day. He died in 1967.

BENNETT, Edward Hallaran (1837–1907) Born Charlotte Quay, Cork, the youngest son of Robert Bennett, Recorder of Cork, and grandson of **William S. Hallaran**. He was educated at TCD where he graduated BA, MB, M.Ch (1859) and MD (1864). In 1863, he became a fellow of the Royal College of Surgeons of Ireland, and a year later he took up the position of University anatomist and surgeon at Sir Patrick Dun's Hospital, Dublin. He was appointed as professor of Surgery at TCD in 1873. He was president of the Royal College of Surgeons from 1884 to 1886. A fracture of the thumb which he identified in 1880, is named after him ('Bennett's Fracture'). He died in Dublin on 23 June 1907. [Bronze portrait medallions by O. Sheppard at TCD and Sir Patrick Dun's Hospital]

BENNETT, George (1824–1900) Born Bandon, Co. Cork, the son of Joseph Bennett, pawnbroker and merchant. He was educated at Bandon Grammar School and at TCD where he graduated BA (1847). He published *The History of Bandon* in 1862 and a further enlarged version in 1869. Through the influence of his fellow townsman, Henry Baldwin, he sold most of his Bandon holdings in 1873 and emigrated to Oregon, USA, with two of his sons, leaving his wife and another son behind. He died of a heart attack at Bandon, Oregon, on 18 October 1900, and was buried in the local graveyard.

BENNETT, Henry (1766–1828) Born Haremount, Macroom, Co. Cork, the son of Philip Bennett, sheriff (1774) and mayor (1748) of Cork. He worked as an apprentice solicitor on the Grand Parade, and, on marrying the daughter of one of the partners, he himself became a partner in the firm of Heard and Colburn. He wrote poetry for *Bolster's Quarterly*

Magazine and other periodicals. With **John Toleken**, he composed the well-known song, 'St Patrick was a Gentleman', which was sung by them while posing as ballad mongers at a Cork masquerade ball in 1814 or 1815. He was the author of a comic opera, entitled, 'The Election', which was published in *The Freeholder*.

BENNETT, John (d. 1536) A priest of the diocese of Cloyne, he was appointed as bishop of Cork and Cloyne on 28 January 1523. He was probably a descendent of Richard and Alice Bennett, the founders of St Mary's, Youghal, following the creation of the collegiate church there by Thomas Fitzjames Fitzgerald, 8th earl of Desmond. On his appointment, he established his episcopal residence in Youghal and expanded the fine library at St Mary's – the catalogue of which still exists. He died in May or early June 1536.

BERESFORD, Lord John George (1773–1862) Born at Tyrone House, Dublin, the son of the 1st Marquess of Waterford. He was educated at Eton and at Christ Church, Oxford. He was consecrated as Church of Ireland bishop of Cork on 24 March 1805. He was translated to the diocese of Raphoe in 1807 and to Clogher in 1819. He became archbishop of Dublin in 1820 and of Armagh in 1822. He died at Donaghadee, Co. Down, on 18 July 1862 and was buried in Armagh. [Portrait by S. Catterton Smith, snr. (1854)]

BERGIN, Osborn J. (1873–1950) Born Sunday's Well, Cork, the son of Osborn R. Bergin, insurance agent. He was educated at Cork Grammar School and at Queen's College, Cork (now UCC), where he studied classics. While at college, he became interested in Irish and, failing to find tuition in Cork, travelled to Eyeries in Beara where he was taught by Pádraig Ó Laoghaire, a local teacher. Having become a lecturer in Celtic Studies at Queen's College, he engaged in further studies in Irish at Berlin and at Freiburg where he took his doctorate in 1906. He returned to Ireland where he was appointed

as professor of Early and Medieval Irish at UCD in 1909 – a position which he held until 1940 when he became the first director of the School of Celtic Studies at the Dublin Institute for Advanced Studies. However, he resigned from this position in the following year and devoted the rest of his life to Irish philology. As well as his many important articles to journals such as *Eiriú* and *Studies*, he was the general director of the *Dictionary of the Irish Language* which was published by the Royal Irish Academy. He died in Dublin on 6 October 1950 and was buried in St Finbarr's Cemetery, Cork. [Assessments by G. Ó Murchadha in *Studies* (December, 1950), and by **D.A. Binchy** *The Osborn Bergin Memorial Lecture* (1970)]

BERGIN, William (1864–1942) Born Co. Kildare, the son of Charles Bergin. He was educated at Tullabeg College, Co. Offaly, and at TCD where he graduated MA. In 1895, he was appointed as professor of Natural Philosophy at Queen's College, Cork (now UCC), a position he occupied until his retirement in 1931 when he was appointed as emeritus professor of Physics. He married Aileen Grace Lane, the daughter of **Denny Lane**. He died at the Mercy Home, Cork, on 29 December 1942.

BERKELEY, George (1685–1753) Born Thomastown, Co. Kilkenny. He was educated at Kilkenny College and at TCD where he graduated BA (1704) and MA (1707). He was consecrated as Church of Ireland bishop of Cloyne on 19 May 1734. He died in Oxford on 14 January 1753 and was buried in Christ Church Cathedral there. The publications associated with his Cloyne episcopate include *The Analyst* (1735), *The Querist* (1735), *A Discourse addressed to Magistrates* (1736), *Siris* (1744 and 1747), *Further Thoughts on Tar Water* (1752), *A Miscellany* (1752), and *A Word to the Wise* (1752). [Life by A.A. Luce (1949); Works edited by A.A. Luce and T.E. Jessop (9 vols, 1941–57); Life and Letters by A.C. Fraser (1871); Memorials at Christ Church, Oxford, and at St Colman's Cathedral, Cloyne]

BERMINGHAM, John (1921–2000) Born Spring Lane, Blackpool, Cork. At the age of fourteen, he went to work at D. and A. O'Leary, printers, of Washington Street. He was elected as a Fine Gael member to both Cork County Council and Cork Corporation in 1955, and in the following year, he became a member of the National Organisation for Rehabilitation (later the National Rehabilitation Board). He was a founder member of the Cork Polio and General Aftercare Association (later Cope Foundation) and became its chief executive and chairman. He retired in 1989 after 35 years of service. He served as lord mayor of Cork (1969/70) and was also made a freeman of Cork. He stood as a Fine Gael Dáil candidate for Cork Borough in 1954 but was unsuccessful. He died at Cork University Hospital on 1 November 2000 and was buried in St Finbarr's Cemetery.

BERNARD, Charles B. (1811–1890) Born Grosvenor Street, London, the second son of **James Bernard**, 2nd earl of Bandon and his wife, Mary, the daughter of Archbishop **Charles Brodrick**. He was the brother of **Henry Boyle Bernard** and of **Francis Bernard**. He was consecrated as bishop of Tuam on 30 January 1867. He died at the see house, Tuam, on 31 January 1890.

BERNARD, Francis (1663–1731) He was the son of Francis Bernard and Elizabeth Freke. He worked as a barrister and was attainted by the 'Patriot Parliament' of King James II. On the conclusion of the Williamite War, he was restored to parliament and made a rapid rise in the judiciary culminating in his appointment as Judge of the Common Pleas in 1715, the year in which he re-built Castle Bernard, Bandon. He was MP for Clonakilty (1692–5) and Bandon (1695–1727). The ancestor of the earls of Bandon, he died on 29 June 1731 and was buried at Ballymodan Church.

BERNARD, Francis (1810–1877) Born Grosvenor Street, London, the eldest son of **James Bernard**, 2nd earl of Bandon and his wife, Mary, the daughter of Archbishop **Charles Brodrick**. He was the brother of **Charles Brodrick Bernard**, bishop of Tuam, and of **Henry Boyle Bernard**. He was educated at Eton and at Oxford University where he graduated MA. He succeeded his father as MP for Bandon on 6 January 1831. He was returned in the general election of the following May but resigned his seat in July. On the resignation of **J.D. Jackson**, he was returned as Conservative MP for Bandon in February 1842. He sat for Bandon until 1857 when he succeeded his father as 3rd earl of Bandon. He died on 17 February 1877.

BERNARD, Henry B. (1812–1895) Born Grosvenor Street, London, the third son of **James Bernard**, 2nd earl of Bandon and his wife, Mary, the daughter of Archbishop **Charles Brodrick**. He was the brother of **Charles Brodrick Bernard**, bishop of Tuam, and of **Francis Bernard**. He was educated at Eton and at Oxford. On the death of his uncle, **William Smyth Bernard**, in 1863 he was elected MP for Bandon and retained the seat in the Conservative interest until his defeat by **William Shaw** in the 1868 general election. He then retired from public life. An honorary colonel of the South Cork Militia, he died at his residence, Coolmain Castle, Kilbrittain, on 14 March 1895 and was buried in Ballymodan Churchyard, Bandon.

BERNARD James (1785–1856) He was the eldest son of Francis Bernard, 1st earl of Bandon and his wife, Henrietta Boyle, the only daughter of Richard Boyle, 2nd earl of Shannon. He was the brother of **Richard Boyle Bernard** and **William Smyth Bernard**. He married Mary Brodrick, the daughter of Archbishop **Charles Brodrick** and their children included **Francis Bernard**, 3rd earl of Bandon; Bishop **Charles Brodrick Bernard**, and **Henry Boyle Bernard**. James sat as MP for Youghal (1806–7; 1818–20), Cork County (1807–18), and Bandon (1820–6 and 1830–1). He succeeded as 2nd earl of Bandon in November 1830. He died on 31 October 1856.

BERNARD, Percy B. (1844–1912) He was the eldest son of Bishop **Charles Brodrick Bernard** of Tuam. He was educated at Oxford and served as private secretary to the lord lieutenant, the duke of Marlborough, from 1876 until 1880. In the general election of 1880, he was returned as Conservative MP for Bandon, but resigned his seat some few months later. Through his second marriage, the Bernard family inherited the Kirwan seat of Castle Hacket, Co. Galway. He died at his Blackrock, Co. Dublin, residence on 18 July 1912 and was buried in Tuam.

BERNARD, Percy R.G. (1904–1979) Born Gillingham, Kent, the son of Lt. Col. R.P.H. Bernard. He joined the RAF and became one of the first officers to win a DSO (1940). He was transferred to the Far East theatre and was in command of a group of Beaufighters whose main task was to attack Japanese convoys. In one twenty-eight-day period, a total of 700 Japanese craft were destroyed. He was subsequently decorated by the American Air Force, being awarded the DFC and Bronze Star. After World War II, he was appointed in 1955 as commander-in-chief of the NATO Second Tactical Air Force with the acting rank of air marshal. He retired in 1963 and returned to Bandon where he built a house near the ruins of his ancestral home, Castle Bernard. He donated part of his lands to Bandon Golf Club – a gesture which enabled the course to be expanded from 9 to 18 holes. He was also an active member of the Bandon Game Protection Association and of the Bandon Anglers' Association. He died at the Bon Secours Hospital, Cork, on 8 February 1979. He was 5th and last earl of Bandon, having succeeded in 1924.

BERNARD, Richard B. (1787–1850) He was the second son of Francis Bernard, 1st earl of Bandon, and brother of **James Bernard** and **William Smyth Bernard**. In the general election of 1812, he was returned as MP for Bandon. He resigned his seat in 1815. He subsequently entered the ministry of the Church of Ireland and became dean of Leighlin. He died in 1850.

BERNARD, William S. (1792–1863) He was the fourth son of Francis Bernard, 1st earl of Bandon, and brother of **James Bernard** and **Richard Boyle Bernard**. He was educated at a military academy in Kent and, having entered the army in 1809, saw service in the Peninsular War. In 1857, he retired from the army with the rank of lieutenant colonel in the 17th Lancers. He was high sheriff of Cork in 1820 and Conservative MP for Bandon (1832–5). In 1857, when his nephew, **Francis Bernard**, the sitting MP, succeeded to the earldom, he was re-elected to the Bandon seat which he continued to represent until his death on 6 February 1863.

BERRY, Henry F. (1847–1932) Born Mallow, the son of Parsons Berry, MD. He was educated at Wright's School, Mallow, and at TCD where he graduated BA, MA, and D.Litt. He entered the Public Record Office, Dublin, in 1868 as an assistant deputy keeper, and having risen to the rank of deputy keeper in 1899, he retired in 1912. He had also qualified as a barrister. He was the editor of *Early Statutes and Ordinances of Ireland* (1907) and of *Register of Wills and Inventories, Diocese of Dublin 1457–83* (1898). He also published many articles in the *Journal of the Royal Society of Antiquaries of Ireland* and in the *Proceedings of the Royal Irish Academy*. A founder member of the Cork Historical and Archaeological Society, he contributed many articles to the *JCHAS*, including some on the Mallow area. His 'Mallow and some Mallow Men' which appeared in the *JCHAS* (1924–8) was published as a collection in 1928. In 1918, on inheriting the Co. Tipperary estates of his wife's family, he took the name, Twiss. His Tipperary residence, Bird Hill House, was burned during the War of Independence and as a result, he and his wife moved to England and permanently resided there. He died at his residence on Beacon Road, Bournemouth, on 27 August 1932.

BINCHY, Daniel A. (1899–1989) Born Charleville, Co. Cork. He was educated at Clongowes Wood College and at UCD where he graduated BA and MA. He later took a

D.Phil. at the University of Munich and was called to the Bar in 1921. In 1924, he was appointed as professor of Jurisprudence and Roman Law at UCD and undertook further studies at the Ecole des Chartes, Paris. He entered the Irish diplomatic service as Minister Plenipotentiary to Germany (1929–32). An active opponent of Fascism, he published *Church and State in Fascist Italy* (1941) under the aegis of the Royal Institute of International Affairs. After World War II, he spent a period at Corpus Christi, Oxford, before being appointed to the Dublin Institute of Advanced Studies as professor at the School of Celtic Studies in 1948. He became a Senior Professor there in 1950. He wrote many articles on all aspects of early Celtic society and published his monumental *Corpus Iuris Hibernici* (6 vols, 1978) in which the major texts dealing with early Irish law are examined. He died on 4 May 1989 and his body was donated for medical research.

BOLSTER, Evelyn [Sr M. Angela] (1925–2005) Born Mallow, Co. Cork, the daughter of Michael Bolster. She joined the Mercy Community at St Maries of the Isle, Cork, where she took the religious name of Angela. She studied history at UCC where she graduated PhD in 1963. Her thesis was published in 1965 as *The Sisters of Mercy in the Crimean War*. In 1972, she commenced her major undertaking, *A History of the Diocese of Cork* (4 vols, 1972–93) – thus bringing the history of the diocese up to the episcopate of **William Delany**. In 1984, she became diocesan archivist of the diocese of Cork and Ross. She was also vice-postulator for the cause of beatification and canonisation of the Mercy foundress, Catherine McAuley (1778–1841), on whose life and work she published five books, including, *The Correspondence of Catherine McAuley, 1827–1841* (1989). She was also author of *The Knights of Columbanus* (1979) and of *A History of Mallow* (1971). She died on 2 February 2005 and was buried in the community cemetery at St Maries of the Isle.

BOOLE, George (1815–1864) Born Lincoln, the son of a minor tradesman. He was the father of **Ethel Lilian Voynich**. He studied both the classics and modern languages and opened a school in the locality in 1835. He then turned to the study of mathematics and his progress was so quick that he was appointed as professor of Mathematics at the Queen's College, Cork (now UCC), in 1849. He was later conferred with the degree of LL.D by TCD and the degree of DCL by the University of Oxford. He was also a fellow of both the British Academy and Irish Royal Academy. His world-wide reputation rests with his *An Investigation of the Laws of Thought* (1854) which had previously been published in pamphlet form under the title *The Mathematical Analysis of Logic* (1847). He died at his Ballintemple home on 8 December 1864, from a fever as a result of a wetting on his way to college. He was buried in St Michael's Churchyard, Blackrock. [Life by D. McHale (1985); Miscellany by P.D. Barry (1969); Memorial window at the Aula Maxima, UCC; Commemorative plaque at his former residence, 5 Grenville Place, Cork]

BOSANQUET, J.E. (*fl.* 1854–1861) He was a landscape painter and photographer who carried on his business at Patrick Street. He occasionally exhibited at the Royal Hibernian Academy. His son, J. Claude Bosanquet, was also a landscape artist.

BOURNE, William Sturges (1769–1845) Born London, the only son of John Sturges, the chancellor of the diocese of Westminster. He assumed the additional surname of Bourne in 1803. He sat in the English Commons from 1798 until 1831 when he retired from politics. From 1815 to 1818, he was MP for Bandon – the only Irish constituency which he represented. During his career he held several minor cabinet posts. He died at his residence, Fleetwood House, Southampton, on 1 February 1845.

BOWEN, Edward (1780–1866) Born Kinsale, Co. Cork. He was educated at Drogheda Academy and was brought to Quebec City, Quebec (then in Lower Canada) in 1797. He qualified as a lawyer in 1803 and was appointed as Attorney General of Lower Canada in 1808. However, he was forced to withdraw as a prior appointment to the post had been made in London. He was compensated for this in the following year when he was appointed as a King's Counsel (KC). In turn, he became a judge at Quebec (1812), president of the Court of Appeal (1839–43), and chief justice of the Superior Court (1849). His knowledge of French and of French law was a great asset to his career as his English-speaking brothers on the Bench were totally limited in that area. Despite the large income from his legal work and the large tracts of land he had been given or bought, he was not always in a sound financial state, as the support of his sixteen children took a heavy toll. He died in Quebec on 11 April 1866.

BOWEN, Elizabeth D. Cole (1899–1973) Born Dublin, the only child of Henry Cole Bowen (1862–1930) of Bowen's Court, Faraghy, near Kildorrery, Co. Cork. Her ancestor, Henry Bowen of Gower, Wales, had come to Ireland as a soldier in Cromwell's army. Following on her education in Kent, she settled in London after World War I and became well known in literary circles. On her father's death in 1930, she inherited Bowen's Court (completed 1775) and continued to spend most of her summers there. She was awarded a CBE in 1948 and the D.Litt. of TCD in the following year. On her husband's death in 1952, she returned to Co. Cork to live. However, she sold the estate in 1959 and the house was then demolished by the new owner. She died in London on 22 February 1973. Her novels include *The Hotel* (1927), *The Last September* (1929), *To the North* (1932), *The House in Paris* (1935), *The Death of the Heart* (1939), *The Heat of the Day* (1949), *A World of Love* (1955), and *Eva Trout* (1969). An account of her family, *Bowen's Court*, and of her childhood, *Seven Winters*, were both published in 1942. Her first collection of short stories, *Encounters*, was published in 1923. [Critical biography by V. Glendinning (1977)]

BOWLES, William (1705–1780) Born Cork. He gave up his profession as a lawyer and then took up the study of science in Paris. Through a meeting with Don Antonio de Ulloa (a future admiral of the Spanish fleet) in 1752, he was appointed as a superintendent of state mines in Spain and was commissioned to establish a natural history collection. His *Introduction a la Historia natural, y a la Geographia fisica de Espagne* (1775) was translated into several languages. He died in Madrid on 25 August 1780.

BOYD-BARRETT, Chevalier James R. (c.1904–1976) Born Loughborough, Leicestershire. He was educated at Belvedere College, Clongowes Wood, Dublin School of Art, and at the University of London. In June 1928, he began a private practice as a architect in Cork. Among the buildings designed by him were four of Cork's 'Rosary of Churches', Bon Secours Hospital and Convent, North Monastery Primary Schools, the monastery and chapel at Deerpark, the engineering and recreational buildings at UCC, ten new churches in the diocese of Kerry, the chapel and seminary at Killarney, and the Bon Secours Hospital, Tralee. His major national design was for the Department of Industry and Commerce in Kildare Street, Dublin. For his services to ecclesiastical architecture, he was conferred with the Knighthood of the Order of St Sylvester (1963) which bestowed the title of 'Chevalier' on him. He died at the Bon Secours Home, Cork, on 1 November 1976 and was buried in St Finbarr's Cemetery.

BOYLE, Charles (1674–1731) Born Chelsea, London, the son of Roger Boyle, 2nd earl of Orrery and grandson of **Roger Boyle**, the 1st earl. He was MP for Charleville (1695–99) and also sat in the English Parliament for Huntingdon (1700–3). He succeeded as 4th earl of Orrery in 1703. His claim to fame is his association with the 'Orrery' (a mechanical model of the solar system) which was made for him and to which he gave his name. He died on 28 August 1731.

BOYLE, Courtenay (1770–1844) He was the third son of the 7th earl of Cork and Orrery. A naval officer, he was elected as MP for Bandon at the November 1806 general election, but did not seek re-election at the following one six months later. He eventually reached the rank of vice-admiral in the British Navy. He died on 21 May 1844.

BOYLE, Henry (1682–1764) Born Castle-martyr, Co. Cork, the second son of the Hon. Henry Boyle, and grandson of **Roger Boyle**, 1st earl of Orrery. He was a member of the Irish House of Commons from 1707 (Midleton, 1707–13 and Cork County, 1715–56) until 1756 when he was created earl of Shannon and sat in the House of Lords. From 1733 until 1753 he was Speaker of the Commons and as an 'undertaker' who organised blocs of parliamentary votes, was probably the most powerful politician in the country (he was nicknamed 'The Colossus of Castlemartyr'). His resignation from the speakership cost the Irish administration an unprecedented pension of £2,000 a year for thirty-one years in addition to the earldom. **Charles Smith's** *History of Cork* was dedicated to him. He died in Dublin on 27 September 1764. [Portraits by Stephen Slaughter (1744, 1745); Bust in bas-relief by John Dixon; Bust by John van Nost (1754)]

BOYLE, Henry (1771–1842) He was the eldest son of Richard Boyle (1727–1807), 2nd earl of Shannon. He was MP for Clonakilty (1793–7) and for Cork County (1797–1800), having also been elected for Rathcormack. He sat for Cork County in the English Commons (1801–7). In the general election of 1807 he was returned for both Bandon and Youghal but took neither seat as he succeeded to the earldom on the death of his father a few days after the election. In 1817, he changed his political allegiance from the Tories to the Whigs. He served as lord lieutenant for County Cork from 1831 until his death on 22 April 1842.

BOYLE, John (1563–1620) Born Kent, an elder brother of **Richard Boyle**, 1st earl of Cork. He was educated at the University of Oxford where he was awarded the degree of DD. He was appointed as Church of Ireland bishop of Cork, Cloyne, and Ross on 25 August 1618. He died at Bishopscourt, Cork, on 10 July 1620, and was buried in the Boyle Chapel at St Mary's Collegiate Church, Youghal.

BOYLE, John (1803–1874) He was the third son of the 8th earl of Cork and Orrery. In 1827, he was elected MP for Cork County in a by-election caused by the death of Viscount Ennismore. He was elected for Cork City in 1830, was re-elected in the following year, but was defeated in 1832. He died on 6 December 1874. His son, Robert Boyle, was an unsuccessful Liberal candidate for Cork County in 1868.

BOYLE, Michael (1609–1702) He was the eldest son of Archbishop **Richard Boyle**. He was educated at TCD where he graduated BA (1637) and DD (1661). He was consecrated as Church of Ireland bishop of Cork, Cloyne, and Ross on 27 January 1661. He later became arch-bishop of Dublin (1663) and archbishop of Armagh (1678). He was the last bishop to have been appointed as Lord Chancellor of Ireland (1665–85). In 1669, he founded the town of Blessington, Co. Wicklow, near which he built a 'magnificent seat' and which was plundered by Jacobite forces during the Williamite War. He died on 10 December, 1702, and was buried in St Patrick's Cathedral, Dublin. [Monument (1702) by W. Kidwell (d. 1736) at Blessington]

BOYLE, Richard (d. 1645) He succeeded his cousin, **John Boyle**, as Church of Ireland bishop of Cork, Cloyne, and Ross in 1620 (the date of the patent was October 24). His brother was Michael Boyle (c.1580–1635), the Church of Ireland bishop of Waterford and Lismore. He was translated to the archbishopric of Tuam on 30 May 1638. On the outbreak of the 1641 Rebellion, he took refuge in Galway. He died in Cork on 19 March 1645 and was buried in St FinBarre's Cathedral.

BOYLE, Richard (1566–1643) Born Canterbury, Kent. He came to Ireland as an Elizabethan adventurer and, as deputy escheator of Crown lands, he built up a substantial estate which was augmented through his marriage in 1603 to Catherine, the daughter of Sir William Fenton, the secretary of the Irish Privy Council. He later purchased Sir Walter Raleigh's (c.1552–1618) seigniory of over 80,000 acres – an area which stretched from Lismore to Bandon. He also got hold of the lands of St Mary's College, Youghal, for which he had later to pay a substantial fine. However, by then his total income from his various estates came to a massive £20,000 a year. He was created 1st earl of Cork in 1620 and later served as one of the Lords Justices of Ireland. He died on 15 September 1643 and was buried in the south transept of St Mary's Collegiate Church, Youghal, which he had purchased as a private chapel. [Life by N. Canny (1982); Remembrances edited by A.B. Grosart (5 vols, 1886)]

BOYLE, Richard (d. 1665) He was the son of Richard Boyle (1612–1698), 2nd earl of Cork and 1st earl of Burlington. During the war with the Dutch, he served as a volunteer on board the 'Royal Charles' under the command of the future King James II (the then duke of York). On 3 June 1665, he, along with Viscount Muskerry and the earl of Falmouth, were killed by the same cannon shot from one of the Dutch ships. The diarist, Samuel Pepys (1633–1703), described the scene – 'They were killed… with one shot, their blood and brains flying in the duke's face and the head of Mr Boyle striking down the duke, as some say.'

BOYLE, Richard (1612–1698) Born Youghal, Co. Cork, the second son of **Richard Boyle**, 1st earl of Cork. At the age of 12, he was knighted by the lord deputy, Viscount Falkland, when on a visit to Youghal. Through his marriage in 1635 to Elizabeth Clifford, the heiress of the future earl of Cumberland, he acquired an influential position at the court of King Charles I. When the Irish Rebellion broke out in 1641, he returned to assist his father and fought with three of his brothers at the battle of Liscarroll in September, 1642. He succeeded as 2nd earl of

Cork on his father's death in 1643 and remained a royalist supporter during the period of the English civil war. During the Cromwellian period, he lived quietly at Lismore in relatively poor circumstances. However, things gradually improved and he benefited from the restoration of Charles II in 1660 when he was created earl of Burlington by a grateful king. He held the position of lord treasurer of Ireland from 1660 until 1695. He had a great interest in architecture and art and sold substantial parts of his Irish estates to finance his extravagant building schemes, including Burlington House, in Piccadilly, London. He died on 13 January 1698. [Life edited by T.C. Barnard and J. Clark (1995)]

BOYLE, Richard (1809–1868) He was the eldest son of **Henry Boyle**, 3rd earl of Shannon. Having come of age in 1830, he was returned as MP for Cork County in the general election of that year. Though he was re-elected in 1831, he withdrew from the general election of 1832. He succeeded to the earldom in April 1842 on the death of his father. He died on 1 August 1868.

BOYLE, Roger (1621–1679) Born Lismore, Co. Waterford, the eleventh child and fifth son of **Richard Boyle**, 1st earl of Cork. He attended TCD (1630–4) and later toured Europe with his brother, Lewis (1636–9). In 1641, the year in which the Irish Rebellion (which led to the Confederate War) broke out, he married Margaret Howard, the daughter of the earl of Suffolk. Initially, he supported the royalists in the Confederate Wars (1641–1649) but later switched his allegiance to the Irish forces of the English Parliament. He met with Cromwell when the latter overwintered in Youghal in 1649/50. He was a prominent figure in the restoration of Charles II to the English throne in 1660 and in September of that year, he was created 1st earl of Orrery and appointed as president of Munster for life. To fit his new positions, he built a huge residence in the barony of Orrery which he named 'Charleville' in honour of the restored king (the mansion was burned by the duke of Berwick during the

Williamite War). However, due to the rivalry of the 1st Duke of Ormonde, he was removed from office and spent his remaining years at Castlemartyr which he had inherited and rebuilt. He died on 16 October 1679 and was buried in the Boyle Chapel in St Mary's Collegiate Church, Youghal. He was also a man of letters. His *Treatise on the Art of War* (1677) was dedicated to Charles II. His plays *Henry V* and *Mustapha* were performed at the royal court. [Life by K.M. Lynch (1965)]

BRADLEY, Michael (d. 1922) Born Dunmanway, Co. Cork, where he carried on a harnessmaking business in Main Street. In the general election of June 1922, he was a Labour candidate in the Cork combined constituency of Mid-, North, South, South-East, and West Cork. He won the second seat behind General **Michael Collins**, but never took his place in the Dáil owing to poor health. He died at the South Infirmary, Cork, on 6 December, 1922, and was buried in Dunmanway Cemetery.

BRADY, Nicholas (1659–1726) Born Bandon, Co. Cork, the son of Major Nicholas Brady. He was educated at Christ Church, Oxford, where he graduated BA (1682) and at TCD where he graduated BA (1685) and MA (1686). He entered the church and held various livings in the diocese of Cork as well as being chaplain to Bishop **Edward Wetenhall**. He supported the Williamites in the ensuing war and later gained valuable preferments in England, being, as well, chaplain to King William III and to Queens Mary and Anne. With the English Poet Laureate, Nahum Tate (1652–1715), he published in 1696 a metrical version of the Psalms. He also published a translation of the *Aeneid* and a tragedy, *The Rape, or the Innocent Impostors*, which was performed at the Theatre Royal, London, in 1692. He died at Richmond, London, on 20 May 1726.

BRADY, William Maziere (1825–1894) Born Dublin, the youngest son of Sir Nicholas W. Brady, lord mayor of Dublin. He was educated

in England, at Portora Royal School, Co. Fermanagh, and at TCD where he graduated BA (1848), BD (1858) and DD (1863). He was ordained in the ministry of the Church of Ireland in 1849. In 1851, he was appointed perpetual curate of St Dolough's, Dublin, and rector of Farahy, Co. Cork. He became vicar of Clonfert, Co. Cork, in 1859, but resigned this position in 1864. In 1863, his *Clerical and Parochial Records of Cork, Cloyne, and Ross* was published in three volumes. He published several pamphlets in favour of the disestablishment of the Church of Ireland. After disestablishment, he resigned his benefices and went to live in Rome and was subsequently received into the Roman Catholic Church. As a result of his researches in the Vatican archives, he published, in three volumes, *The Episcopal Succession in England, Scotland, and Ireland 1400–1875* (1876/77). He died at the Vatican on 19 March 1894 and was buried in the Campo Santo of St Lorenzo Fuori le Mure, Rome. He acted as private chamberlain to Popes Pius IX and Leo XIII.

BRANSFIELD, Edward (1783–1852) Born Ballinacurra, Midleton, Co. Cork, the son of a sea captain. Having served on various ships of the Royal Navy, he obtained his master's certificate and was assigned to the *Andromanche* to investigate a sighting of land off Cape Horn. Having transferred to the *Williams*, he hoisted the Union Jack and buried some English coins in a metal container on 22 January 1820 to claim the subsequently-named King George Island for Britain. He died in Brighton in 1852. Today, his name is perpetuated in the South Shetlands area of Antarctica by such placenames as Bransfield Island, Bransfield Rock, Bransfield Straits, and Mount Bransfield.

BRASH, Richard R. (1817–1876) Born Cork, the son of William Brash, builder. He also became a builder but added to it the profession of architect. A member, with **John Windele**, of the South Munster Antiquarian Society, he was a keen student of early architecture and contributed articles on Irish round towers to the journals of several learned societies. His *Ecclesiastical Architecture of Ireland to the Close of the Twelfth Century* was published in 1875, and his *The Ogham-Inscribed Monuments of the Gaedhil*, edited by G.M. Atkinson, was published posthumously in 1879. He died at his residence at Sunday's Well on 18 January 1876 and was buried in St Finbarr's Cemetery.

BRASIER, Brooke W. (1879–1940) Born Carrigaline, Co. Cork, the eldest child of Brooke Brasier, gentleman. In 1898, he married Lady Charlotte Moore, youngest daughter and co-heiress of the 5th Earl Mount Cashell. An expert in land rental and leasing, he settled in East Cork at Shanagarry House and soon ventured into both local and national politics. He was elected to Cork County Council and, in 1932, he was returned as an independent TD for East Cork. However, he failed to be re-elected in the following year. He joined Fine Gael and, in 1935, spent a period in jail at the Curragh Camp during the Land Annuities campaign. He was re-elected to the Dáil for the revised constituency of South East Cork in 1937 and 1938, heading the poll on both occasions. He died at his residence on 30 August 1940 and was buried in Ballyvinny Graveyard, Watergrasshill.

BREEN, Dermot (1924–1978) Born Waterford, the sixth child of James Breen. When he was five years old, the family moved to Cork. He was educated at Farranferris College and at PBC, Cork. He was appointed as organiser of the first Tóstal Chorcaí in 1953 and as director of Cork International Choral Festival in 1954 (to 1959). He established and directed the Cork International Film Festival from its inception in 1956. In 1965, he established his own consultancy firm in Cork. He was appointed as Irish Film Censor in June 1972. He died unexpectedly in Dublin on 5 October 1978.

BRENAN, James (1837–1907) Born Dublin. He studied art at the School of Art, Leinster House, and at the Royal Hibernian Academy. Having studied decorative art in London, he obtained various teaching positions there, and in Dublin and Birmingham. In 1860, he was appointed as headmaster of the Cork School of Art and held the post until 1889. He was involved in the Cork Exhibition of 1883 and had a keen interest in the promotion of the lace industry. In the following year, the first lace class was established at the Convent of Mercy, Kinsale, and soon Brenan was visiting ten lace-making classes in various convents throughout the county. He exhibited at and was a member of the Royal Hibernian Academy (elected in 1878). In 1889, he took up the position of headmaster of the Metropolitan School of Art in Dublin. He died on 7 August 1907.

BRENAN, James B. (1825–1889) Born Cork, the son of **John Brenan**. He never left Cork and established himself as a fine local portrait painter. He exhibited at the Royal Hibernian Academy, of which he was a member, from 1843 until 1886. He died on 22 April 1889.

BRENAN, John (c.1796–1865) Born Fethard, Co. Tipperary, the father of **James B. Brenan**. Following studies at the Royal Dublin Society's School, he settled in Cork and gained a reputation as a landscape painter. He exhibited at the Royal Hibernian Academy between 1826 and 1864.

BRENAN, Joseph (1828–1875) Born Cork. He worked as a journalist and was a frequent contributor to *The Nation*, the organ of the Young Ireland movement. Following the abortive Young Ireland uprising of 1848, he founded another newspaper, *The Irishman*, in 1849. With its suppression in the same year, he fled to America and settled in New Orleans. Despite his blindness, he continued to write poetry for several Irish journals and papers. He died in 1875.

BRENNAN, Joseph (1887–1976) Born Bandon, Co. Cork, the son of Joseph Brennan, merchant. He was educated at Clongowes College, UCD, and Christ's College, Cambridge. He joined the Civil Service in 1911 and worked in the Chief Secretary's Office, Dublin Castle, where, as first division clerk, he specialised in financial matters (1912–20). Following Independence, he became Comptroller and Auditor-General of the Provisional Government in 1922 and Secretary of the Department of Finance in 1923. He served until 1927 when he was appointed as chairman of the Currency Commission. This body was replaced by the Central Bank in 1942 and Brennan became its first governor (his signature appeared on Irish banknotes from 1928 to 1953). He also served on many other government commissions until his retirement in 1953. In 1938, he was conferred with the honorary degree of LL.D by the National University of Ireland. He died on 3 March 3, 1963. [Life by L. Ó Broin (1982)]

BRIDE, Thomas F. (1849–1927) Born Cork, the son of Henry Nelson Bride. He was brought to Melbourne, Australia, as a child. He was educated at the University of Melbourne where he graduated in law with first class honours in 1873 and subsequently took his doctorate in 1879. He worked as assistant librarian at the university from 1873 until 1881 when he was appointed as librarian of the Melbourne Public Library. Having made great improvements in the library, he resigned in 1895 to take up a position as curator of the estates of deceased persons. Outside of his official duties, Bride was a man of many parts. He was elected a fellow of the Royal Geographical Society in 1885 and in the following year he was a member of the Australian Antarctic Exploration Committee. He was also the founder of the Melbourne Technical Schools Association and served on the councils of both the University of Melbourne and the Working Men's College. His great disappointment was being an unsuccessful candidate in the Victoria general election of 1880. He died in Melbourne on 7 April 1927.

BRINKLEY, John (1766–1835) Born Woodbridge, Suffolk. He was educated at Caius College, Cambridge, where he graduated MA (1791) and DD (1806). In 1792, he was appointed as professor of Astronomy at TCD and as Director of Dunsink Observatory. He was consecrated as Church of Ireland bishop of Cloyne on 8 October 1826, and thereafter devoted most of his time to his episcopal duties. He was president of the Royal Irish Academy from 1822 until his death. He was also president of the British Astronomical Society (1831–3). He died in Leeson Street, Dublin, on 14 September 1835, and, following a Latin eulogy by the professor of Oratory at TCD, was buried in the crypt of the college chapel. [Statue by **John Hogan** at TCD; Monument by **John Hogan** at St Colman's Cathedral, Cloyne]

BRODERICK, Timothy S. (1893–1962) Born Cork. He was raised in Youghal where he attended the local CBS. He then studied at UCC where he graduated BA, B.Sc. in 1913. He undertook postgraduate studies at TCD before taking up a teaching post at Exeter University. He was elected a fellow of TCD in 1930 and was appointed Donegal Lecturer in Mathematics. In 1944, he was appointed Erasmus Smith professor of Mathematics there. He was elected a senior fellow in 1958 and in the following year was appointed as temporary provost for six months – then an unprecedented position for a Roman Catholic. He collapsed and died at Dalkey Railway Station on 4 April 1962 and was buried in Dean's Grange Cemetery, Dublin.

BRODERICK, William J. (1877–1957) Born Youghal, Co. Cork, the son of William Broderick, JP, MCC, farmer and butcher. He entered local politics in 1914 when he was elected to Youghal UDC, and, in 1917, he represented the Urban District Councils of Munster at the Irish Convention. In June 1925, he was elected to Cork County Council as a Cumann na nGaedheal (later Fine Gael) candidate and two years later, he was elected as chairman of that body – a position which he held until his death. During his 32-year membership of the Council, he contested a total of seven elections and was returned on the first count on six occasions. He served as a Fine Gael TD for East Cork (1932–7), County Waterford (1938–43), and for South East Cork (1943–8). He died at his Youghal residence on the North Main Street on 16 June 1957 and was buried in Youghal Cemetery.

BRODRICK, Alan (c.1654–1728) The second son of **Sir St John Brodrick**, the founder of the borough of Midleton. A lawyer by profession, he practised on the Munster Circuit and following the Williamite War, he was appointed as solicitor general for Ireland in 1695. He was returned to the 1702 Parliament as MP for Cork City and was immediately chosen as Speaker of the House of Commons. He was the leader of the main Whig opposition to the ruling Tories during the later reign of Queen Anne and on her death in 1714, the Whigs came into power under King George I. He was appointed as Lord Chancellor (1714–25) on becoming a peer and became 1st Viscount Midleton in 1717. As well as his personal acquisitions, he inherited the Midleton estates as his elder brother, Thomas, had no issue. He died at Ballyannan Castle, Midleton, in 1728.

BRODRICK, Charles (1761–1822) Born Peper Harrow, Surrey, the fourth son of George Brodrick, 3rd Viscount Midleton. He moved to Midleton in 1784 to look after his brother's (the 4th Viscount) estates. Having married the daughter of **Richard Woodward**, bishop of Cloyne in 1786, he entered the church in the following year and immediately gained preferment in his father-in-law's diocese. He was consecrated as Church of Ireland bishop of Clonfert on 22 March 1795. Having been translated to the diocese of Kilmore in 1796, he was advanced to the archbishopric of Cashel in 1801 and was appointed in addition, as coadjutor to the archbishop of Dublin during the latter's illness (1811–19). He died on 6 May 1822 and was buried in Midleton Graveyard. His two sons succeeded as 6th and 7th Viscounts Midleton, while his daughter, Mary, married **James Bernard**, the 2nd earl of Bandon.

BRODRICK, Sir St John (1627–1711) Born Wandsworth, Surrey, the son of Sir Thomas Brodrick. He came to Ireland in the aftermath of the 1641 and, through skilful alliances, he acquired substantial estates, especially in Midleton which was incorporated as a parliamentary borough in 1670. He was MP for Kinsale (1661) and for Cork County (1692–99). His second son, **Alan Brodrick**, 1st Viscount Midleton, succeeded to his estates. He died in January 1711 and was buried in Wandsworth.

BRODRICK, William St John F. (1856–1942) Born London, the son of William Brodrick, 8th Viscount Midleton. He was educated at Eton and at Balliol College, Oxford, where he graduated BA. Turning to politics, he was elected as Liberal MP for West Surrey (1880) and later for Guildford (1885–1906). He was appointed as Secretary of State for War (1900) and as Secretary of State for India (1903–6). However, he was defeated in the general election of 1906. He succeeded as 9th Viscount Midleton in the following year and was created 1st earl of Midleton in 1920. At this time, he was the leader of the Southern Unionists and played a prominent part in the Irish Convention and later, in 1921, he participated in the Truce negotiations with Eamon de Valera (1882–1975). Having refused the offer of the Irish lord lieutenancy from the British Prime Minister, David Lloyd George (1863–1945), he withdrew from Irish politics. He died at his residence, Peper Harow, Surrey, on 13 February 1942. He published *Ireland – Dupe or Heroine?* (1932), and *Records and Reactions, 1856–1939* (1939).

BROPHY, Robert J. (c.1865–c.1958) Born Cork. A journalist by profession, he began his career c.1890 with the *Kilkenny People*, but returned to Bandon where he worked as a news correspondent before moving to Cork c.1900 when he joined the staff of the *Cork Constitution*. When the paper's offices were wrecked during the civil war and the paper closed, he moved to Dublin c.1926 and took up a sub-editorial post on the *Irish Independent*.

Between 1909 and 1922, under the pseudonym of 'R.J. Ray', he wrote five plays all of which were produced at the Abbey Theatre. One of the 'Cork Realists', along with **T.C. Murray** and **Lennox Robinson**, his plays deal with prejudice and brutality in Irish life, both in town and country. The plays, none of which have been published, were 'The White Feather' (1909), 'The Casting-out of Martin Whelan' (1910), 'The Gombeen Man' (1913), 'The Strong Hand' (1917) and 'The Moral Law' (1922). Though his fellow-realists prospered after 1922, Ray's career halted despite the fact that the work of no other playwright of his stature in the early twentieth century remains unpublished. He lived in Clontarf, Dublin, until *c.*1958 when he died suddenly following a collapse on a Dublin street.

BROSNAN, Seán (1916–1979) Born Dingle, Co. Kerry. He was educated at De la Salle Training College, Waterford, from where he graduated as a primary teacher. He later studied at UCD, TCD, and at the King's Inns where he qualified as a barrister. As a Kerry footballer, he won four All-Ireland SFC medals (1937, 1939–41) and a Railway Cup medal with Munster (1941). He settled in Youghal and was elected as a Fianna Fáil member for Cork North East in 1969. He lost his seat in 1973 but regained it a year later in a by-election following the death of Deputy **Liam Ahern**. He died at his Youghal residence on 18 April 1979 and was buried in North Abbey Cemetery there.

BROUNKER, William (1620–1684) Born Castlelyons, Co. Cork. He was educated at Oxford where he graduated MD. Having published several scientific works, he became the first president of the Royal Society and held this position for fifteen years. Holding the title of 2nd Viscount Castlelyons, he died at Westminster in 1684.

BROWNE, Francis (1880–1960) Born Buxton Hill, Sunday's Well, Cork, the son of James Browne, miller and tanner. He was the nephew of Bishop **Robert Browne** of Cloyne. He was

educated at CBC, Cork; Belvedere College, Castleknock College and at UCD. In 1915, he was ordained as a member of the Jesuit Order and served in World War I as a military chaplain. He was awarded the Military Cross, and the Belgian Croix de Guerre. He took a great interest in photography from an early age and photographed many subjects on the ill-fated *Titanic* before it left Cork Harbour on its maiden voyage. For the remainder of his life, he provided a remarkable photographic insight into Irish life – both political and social. Luckily, his glass negatives have been saved for posterity. He died in Dublin on 7 July 1960. [Life by E.E. O'Donnell (1994)]

BROWNE, Jemmett (1703–1782) Born Cork, the son of Edward Browne, merchant and 'Senatoris Corcagiensis'. He was educated at TCD where he graduated BA (1724). He was consecrated as Church of Ireland bishop of Killaloe on 9 October 1743 and was subsequently translated to Dromore (1745), Cork (1745), and Elphin (1772). He was raised to the archbishopric of Tuam in 1775. He was a firm opponent of John Wesley when the latter preached in Cork. The builder of Riverstown House, he died there on 15 June 1782. He was buried in the episcopal chapel at Ballineaspaig (Bishopstown) and later re-interred in the foundations of the present St FinBarre's Cathedral.

BROWNE, Peter (*c.*1670–1735) Born Co. Dublin. He was educated at TCD where he graduated BA (1686), MA (1691) and DD (1699). He was elected as provost of TCD in 1699 and became Church of Ireland bishop of Cork and Ross in 1710. He built his country episcopal residence at Ballinaspig (Bishopstown), of which part of the chapel remains. A High Tory, he fell foul of the Cork Whigs and Williamites in the 'Drinking to the Memory of the Dead' controversy of 1713 (it is he who is the 'bishop of Cork' referred to at the conclusion of the Orange oath). His famous *Analogy* of 1733 deals with the problem of human understanding.

He died on 25 August 1735 and was buried at Bishopstown. His remains were later re-interred in the foundations of the present St FinBarre's Cathedral. [Life by A.R. Winnett (1974)].

BROWNE, Robert (1844–1935) Born Charleville, Co. Cork, the uncle of **Francis Browne**. He was educated at St Colman's College, Fermoy (a member of the first class in 1859) and at St Patrick's College, Maynooth, where he was ordained in 1869 for the diocese of Cloyne. He taught at Fermoy from 1870 to 1874 when he was moved to Maynooth. He became president of Maynooth in 1885 and was responsible for the completion of the college chapel and the building of the exhibition hall there. He was consecrated as bishop of Cloyne on 19 August 1894 and was given the formidable task of finishing St Colman's Cathedral at Queenstown (now Cobh) which was consecrated, free of debt, in 1919. He came to national and international notice in 1912 when he and six of his priests successfully sued the *Dundee Courier* concerning an allegation of indiscriminate dismissals of Protestant shop assistants by Queenstown Roman Catholic traders. His conduct during the proceedings was praised by many Church of Ireland ministers. He died on 23 March 1935 after an episcopate in Cloyne of forty-one years duration and was buried in the crypt of St Colman's Cathedral.

BROWNE, William H. (1800–1877) Born Ballinvonear, Mallow, Co. Cork, the son of Henry Browne, barrister. He was educated at Charleville School and at TCD where he graduated BA (1822) and LL.D (1828). Following his ordination in 1824, he served as curate of Whitechurch until February 1828 when he was appointed as colonial chaplain at Launceston, Tasmania, Australia. His main duties had to do with the jail, the prisoners' barracks and the house of correction. In 1834, he published the *Jail Manual*, a selection of prayers to be used in places of confinement. His Protestant militancy lost him some clerical and lay friends – especially so when he signed 'The

Solemn Declaration of the Association of Members of the Church of England for maintaining in Van Diemen's Land (i.e. Tasmania) the Principles of the Protestant Reformation'. His main reputation rests, however, with the savings movement. He was one of the chief movers in the foundation of the Launceston Bank of Savings in 1835 and he also advocated the provision of savings facilities through post offices. He retired from the active ministry in 1868 through ill health, and was appointed as archdeacon of Launceston in 1870. He died there on 18 June 1877. He had published *Sunday Services adapted to the Use of Country Congregations* in 1876.

BRUEN, Jimmy (1920–1972) Born Belfast, the son of James Bruen of Wilton, Cork, bank official. He was a member of the Cork Golf Club team which twice won the Barton Shield (1937–8) and the Irish Senior Cup (1939). He took the British Boys' title in 1936 with a massive 11 and 9 victory and followed this by winning the Irish Close Championship in 1937 and 1938. He won three Irish Amateur Open Championships (1937–9) and played in the Walker Cup in 1938 which was won by the British and Irish team for the first time. After World War II, in 1946, he took the British Amateur title and played in two further Walker Cups (1949 and 1951). He represented his country twenty-four times in home internationals and became an international selector (1959–62). On a more local note, he won the Cork Scratch Cup on four successive occasions (1938–41) at his home club, Cork GC, where he served both as captain and president. He died of a heart attack at the Bon Secours Home, Cork, on 3 May 1972 and was buried privately. [Life by G. Crosbie (1998); Plaster by **Seamus Murphy**]

BRUNICARDI, Niall (1913–1997) Born Dublin, the son of Major Dominic Brunicardi who was awarded the Military Cross for his service in World War I. He was educated at Belvedere College where he excelled at languages. He graduated BA (1935) and LL.B (1837)

at UCD before joining the Irish army after the outbreak of World War II. He was stationed at the Curragh Camp (1940–7) where he served in a teaching role. He saw further service at Army Headquarters, Dublin (1947–58), where he was involved in the translation service. He then left the army in 1958 and joined the Irish navy as an education officer until his retirement from service in 1969 with the rank of lieutenant-commander. Earlier, in 1961, he spent six months as an interpreter during the beginning of the Congo crisis. He then worked as a language teacher at Mitchelstown VS (1969–73) and at Fermoy VS (1973–80). In his retirement, he graduated MA at UCC (1989), having become a partner in the Fermoy publishing company, Éigse Books, some years previously. His own publications included *John Anderson of Fermoy: The Forgotten Benefactor* (1980), *Haulbowline, Spike and Rocky Islands in Cork Harbour* (1982), *Christ Church, Fermoy* (1984), *The Bridge at Fermoy* (1985), *St Patrick's Church, Fermoy* (1986) and *John Anderson – Entrepreneur* (1987). He also wrote many articles in journals and local newspapers. He died at his Fermoy residence on 1 January 1997 and was buried in Kilcrumper Cemetery. [Beathaisnéis le R. Ó Glaisne (1997)]

BUCK, Adam (1759–1833) Born Cork, the son of a silversmith and elder brother of **Frederick Buck**. He gained an early local reputation as a painter of miniatures. In 1795, he went to London and exhibited over 171 contributions at the Royal Academy over the following thirty-eight years. He also exhibited at the British Institution and at the Society of British Artists. He died in London in 1833.

BUCK, Frederick (1771–c.1840) Born Cork, the son of a silversmith and the younger brother of **Adam Buck**. He also practised for a long period as a painter of miniatures in his native city and especially during the Peninsular War as many embarking army officers gave him orders to draw their portraits. Trade was so brisk that he used light prints on which he would paint the face and relevant regimental colours.

BUCKLEY, Daniel (1890–1918) Born Boherbue, Co. Cork, the son of Daniel Buckley, baker. While he was a young man, the family moved to nearby Kingwilliamstown (now Ballydesmond). He decided to emigrate to the US and boarded the ill-fated *Titanic* at Cobh. On the night of 15 April 1912, as the liner was sinking, he boarded one of the lifeboats with some other men. However, as the men were being ordered off the boat by armed ship's officers, a woman (believed to have been Madeline Astor, the wife of American billionaire, John Jacob Astor) threw a shawl over him, thereby ensuring his survival. He then worked in a Manhattan hotel before joining the Irish-manned 69th Regiment of the US Army in June 1917. The regiment was subsequently re-formed as K Company of the 165th US Infantry and Buckley was posted to the front in France. He was shot by a German sniper in October 1918, less than a month before the end of World War I. His remains were later brought home and re-interred in Ballydesmond Cemetery early in 1919. He composed the popular ballad, 'Sweet Kingwilliamstown'.

BUCKLEY, G.H. (d. 1836) He was a Cork architect and sculptor who died of consumption while still young. In 1828, he exhibited at the Mechanics' Institute in Cork. Many of his monuments are in St Joseph's Cemetery where he himself is buried. He died in Cove (now Cobh) on 6 June 1836.

BUCKLEY, John (*fl. c.*1835) He painted portraits, miniatures, and landscapes in Cork. His silhouette, which was done by **A.A.C. Edouart** in 1835, is in the National Gallery of Ireland.

BUCKLEY, Mars (*c.*1825–1905) Born Mallow, Co. Cork. He emigrated with his wife and child to Melbourne, Australia, in 1851, and went into the drapery business with a partner, C.J. Nunn. He was so successful that, by the 1860s, his commercial operations were grossing some £40,000 a year. In 1866, he was one of the founders of the Commercial Bank of Australia. Following Nunn's suicide in 1891, he sold the concern and later, having survived a run on the Australian banks, opened his own operation which he described as 'The Oldest-Established Drapery House in Victoria, and the Most fashionable resort for Shopping in Australia'. He died at his mansion, 'Beaulieu', Melbourne, on 9 October 1905. [Life by G. Meudell (1935)].

BUCKLEY, Michael B. (1831–1872) Born Cork, whose parents occupied 'a humble station in life'. He was educated at Hartnett's Classical School and at the Mansion House School before entering St Patrick's College, Maynooth, in 1849. While at Maynooth, some of his poems were published. He was ordained at Ovens, Co. Cork, in 1855 and commenced his ministry in several country parishes before returning to Cork City where he acquired a reputation as a preacher and lecturer. In 1868, his *Life and Writings of Rev. Arthur O'Leary* was published and he was transferred to the curacy of SS. Peter & Paul's. In 1870, he was one of two priests appointed to visit North America to fundraise for the new cathedral. He lectured throughout Canada, in Boston, and in New York. The project was deemed an outstanding success, but his health was impaired by the regime and his strenuous itinerary. He arrived back in Ireland in October 1871 and recuperated for a while at Sunday's Well. He died at his sister's home on 17 May 1872 and was buried in St Joseph's Cemetery. His *Sermons, Lectures, etc.* (1874) was published posthumously with a memoir of his life by Rev. Charles Davis.

BUCKLEY, Sir Patrick A. (1841–1896) Born Inane, Castlehaven, Co. Cork, the son of Cornelius Buckley, farmer and merchant. He was educated at Sedward's School, Skibbereen, at St Colman's College, Fermoy and at the Irish Colleges of Paris and Louvain. While at Louvain, he was selected to lead the Irish recruits for the Papal Brigade from Ostend to Vienna. He served with them in defence of Pope Pius IX for a while, before returning to his studies and subsequently to Ireland. He emigrated to Queensland, Australia, where he completed his legal studies and was admitted to the Victorian Bar. He settled in New Zealand where he became head of a legal practice in Wellington. Shortly after his arrival, he entered the Provincial Council and held the post of provincial solicitor in the last administration under that system. In 1878, he entered the New Zealand Legislative Council, and in 1884 he became colonial secretary and leader in the Upper House (until October 1887). In 1891, he joined a Liberal government as attorney general and in the following year, he was once again appointed as colonial secretary. He resigned both offices in December 1895 when he was made a judge of the New Zealand Supreme Court. He had been knighted in 1892. He died at Lower Hutt, near Wellington, on 18 May 1896. His only sister, Ellen, was the second wife of **Jeremiah O'Donovan Rossa** but died at the age of 20. His brother, Dr Cornelius Buckley, was a noted physician in San Francisco.

BUCKLEY, Seán (1873–1963) Born Bandon, Co. Cork, the second son of John Buckley, builder. He was educated locally. He took an active part in organising Sinn Féin and the Irish Volunteers, serving a prison term in 1918. He acted as intelligence officer on the formation of the 3rd Cork Brigade, IRA, and was in active service in that area until the Truce. Taking the republican side during the Civil War, he was appointed director of civic administration under General Liam Lynch (1890–1923). Having been captured by Free State troops following the republican evacuation of Cork City, he was imprisoned but was released after a forty-three-day hunger strike. While in prison, he was elected as a Republican TD for West Cork, but failed to retain his seat in 1927. In 1938, standing as a Fianna Fáil candidate, he was again returned for West Cork and retained his seat until 1948 when he was returned for the South Cork constituency. He was re-elected in 1951 but did not seek re-election in 1954. He represented the Bandon area on Cork County Council from

1921 to 1928 and from 1945 until his death. A building contractor by profession, he resided at Coolfadda, Bandon. He was a director of the *Southern Star* newspaper (1918–29), and was also chairman of that company (1926–7). He died at the Bon Secours Hospital, Cork, on 1 December 1963 and was buried in Bandon Cemetery.

BUCKLEY, Tim – see under **Ó BUACHALLA, Tadhg (1863–1945)**.

BUCKLEY, William (*fl.* 1905) Born Cork. A short-story writer and novelist, he wrote for numerous newspapers including *The United Irishman*. His novel *Croppies, Lie Down* (1903) dealt with the Rising of 1798. In 1907, he published a short-story collection, *Cambia Carty*, which is set in Youghal.

BUCKTON, William (d. 1793) In a death notice of the *Cork Gazette* of 4 September 1793, he is described as 'the celebrated Statuary'. He was especially noted for his chimneypieces.

BULLEN, George (1816–1894) Born Clonakilty, Co. Cork. He moved to London when a young man and initially worked as a teacher at Southwark. In 1838, he became an assistant in the printed books section of the British Museum. Following several promotions, he was appointed in 1875 as the keeper of printed books – the top position in the department which he had entered thirty-seven years previously. Under his supervision, the museum catalogue was begun in 1881. He retired in 1890, having received an honorary degree of LL.D from the University of Glasgow in the previous year. He was also a vice-president of the British Library Association and a fellow of the Society of Antiquaries. He died at Kensington, London, on 10 October 1894 and was buried at Highgate Cemetery.

BUNBURY, Thomas (1829–1907) Born Shandrum, Co. Cork, the son of William Bunbury, the local rector. He was privately educated and studied at TCD where he graduated BA (1852), MA (1863), and DD. He held incumbencies in the dioceses of both Cloyne and Limerick before being appointed as dean of Limerick in 1872. He was consecrated as Church of Ireland bishop of Limerick on 1 November 1899. He died on 19 January 1907.

BUNWORTH, Charles (1704–1772) Born Newmarket, Co. Cork, the second son of Richard Bunworth, gentleman farmer. He was educated locally and at TCD where he graduated BA (1727) and MA (1730). He was ordained deacon (1730) and priest (1731) – both in St Colman's Cathedral, Cloyne. He held various preferments in the diocese of Cloyne and was rector of Buttevant at his death. He was a patron of **Barry Yelverton** and **John Philpot Curran** (to whom he was most probably related by marriage) in their pre-TCD days and was also the great-grandfather of **Thomas Crofton Croker**. His reputation rests with his patronage of, and interest in, Irish traditional music. A fine harper himself, his rectory was the meeting place of scores of travelling bards where songs, stories, and poems were exchanged. His harp ('The Bunworth Harp', made 1734) ultimately came into the possession of Crofton Croker who sold it on. It is now in the possession of the Museum of Fine Arts, Boston. He died on 14 September 1772 and was buried in Buttevant Graveyard.

BUNWORTH, Richard (1918–1992) Born Cork. He was educated at Rockwell College and joined the army in 1937. He was commissioned as second lieutenant in 1939. He was appointed as officer commanding the Irish contingent during the Congo crisis in 1960 and also served as a UN military observer during the Middle East wars of 1967 and 1973. He was the assistant Army Chief of Staff when he retired in 1978. He died in 1992.

BURCHILL, George (1820–1907) Born Bandon, Co. Cork, the son of Thomas Burchill. The family emigrated to Canada in 1826 and settled in Miramihi, New Brunswick. He started as a clerk in a shipyard and eventually rose to the position of business manager. In 1850, he went into partnership with master builder **John Harley** to purchase the yard. On bad business advice, the partnership was dissolved in 1859 and Burchill went into the timber business, organising the purchase of logs, having them sawn and then exported (by ship to Great Britain and by rail to the US). He was particularly successful following the end of the American civil war and in 1881 he founded the firm of Geo. Burchill and Sons. He later went into the logging business and was years ahead of his time in the facilities he provided at the logging camps (thus making the cost of his own logs higher that the ones he purchased from others). He retired in 1904 and died on 18 June 1907 at Nelson, New Brunswick. [Company profile by B. Glendenning, MA thesis, Univ. of Montreal (1978)]

BURGES, William (1827–1881) Born London, the son of a civil engineer. He entered the University of London to study engineering but left soon after, in 1844, to work in an architect's office. Following several visits to the Continent, he won an international competition in 1856 for a design of Lille Cathedral. He later designed Brisbane Cathedral, decorated the Chapter House at Salisbury Cathedral, rebuilt the eastern end of the chapel of Waltham Abbey, and decorated the interior of the chapel of Worcester College, Oxford. In 1862, he prepared his design for the new St FinBarre's Cathedral, Cork – his *magnum opus*. He presented 'the golden angel' at the eastern end as a consecration gift. He died in London on 20 April 1881.

BURKE, James D. (1833–1904) Born Limerick, the son of John Burke, cabinetmaker. He received his early education at Sexton Street CBS. He entered the novitiate of the Christian Brothers at Mount Sion, Waterford, in June 1852, and three months later was transferred to North Monastery CBS where he continued his training and began his teaching career. With the exception of the years 1890–6 (when he was in Dublin as assistant to the superior-general of his Order), he spent the remainder of his life in

Cork. His interests and innovative ideas soon made him a pioneer in Irish scientific and technical education. Among his colleagues at North Monastery were the architect, Brother **Austin Riordan** and (Brother) John Holland (1840–1914), the inventor of the submarine. In 1869, with the financial help of **Denny Lane**, **Martin F. Mahony**, **Joseph P. Ronayne** and **Richard Caulfield**, he opened a science hall at North Monastery which, by 1875, included an experimental department in physics and chemistry operated by the pupils. In 1876, he began work on his Industrial and Art Museum, which, in time, grew into a huge selection of curios. Two years later, he became Superior of the school – a position which he held until his retirement in 1899. In 1897, he began the building of the **Gerald Griffin** Memorial Technical School where hundreds of Cork's craftsmen and tradesmen were trained. On 16 March 1904, as he was crossing Patrick Street, he was hit by a horse-drawn carriage and died at the North Infirmary Hospital on the 25th. Following a funeral of huge proportions, he was buried in the community plot at North Monastery. [Life by D.V. Kelleher (1988)]

BURKE, James M. (1873–1936) Born Skibbereen, Co. Cork, the eighth son of Patrick Burke, shopkeeper. He was educated at Hogan's University School, Skibbereen, and at UCC where he graduated BA. He was admitted to the Bar in 1900 and practised on the Munster Circuit. He worked as editor of the *Cork Sun* (1903–5) and of the *Southern Star* for several periods after 1915. He was chairman of Skibbereen UDC (1906–21) and of Skibbereen RDC (1906–20, in succession to his brother, Daniel) by virtue of which he was an *ex-officio* member of Cork County Council. A reluctant candidate at the 1933 general election, he topped the poll in West Cork for Fine Gael. He sat until 1936. He died in a Clonakilty nursing home on 10 September 1936 and was buried in Abbey Cemetery, Skibbereen. He was the author of a 'History of the Carberies' in serial form, and of many other historical articles.

BURKE, John (1842–1919) Born Kinsale, Co. Cork, the son of Denis O'Hara Burke, fisherman. He went to sea and was in America at the outbreak of the civil war. He returned to Ireland and then signed on a ship taking Irish emigrants to Brisbane, Australia, where he arrived in August 1862. He jumped ship and worked locally as a seaman until he secured a master's certificate to command in sheltered waters only. He later became a shipowner, operating a full coastal service. He retired in 1915 when the management of the company was taken over by one of his sons, John Edward Burke (1871–1947), and continued to prosper under the latter's son, John Augustine Burke (1896–1972), before being taken over in 1968.

BURKE, Liam (1928–2005) Born Glanmire, Co. Cork, the son of Bill Burke, farmer, and a nephew of **Tadhg Manley**. He worked as a car sales manager before entering local politics in Cork Corporation in 1967 and took a Dáil seat for Cork North Central two years later. He lost his seat in 1977 and was elected to the Seanad. However, in a by-election in Novemebr 1979, he was again returned to the Dáil but lost narrowly in 1989 and again returned to the Seanad. Three years later, he regained his Dáil seat by the narrow majority of 14 votes. The 'great survivor' retired from the political arena in 2002 when he did not contest the general election. He served as lord mayor of Cork in 1984, and during the *Cork 800* celebrations in 1985, he was conferred with an honorary doctorate by UCC. An avid 'follower of the dogs', his greyhound, Henrietta, won the famed Waterloo Cup in 2003. He died at the Bon Secours Hospital, Cork, on 21 August 2005 and was buried in St Finbarr's Cemetery.

BURKE, Rickard O'S. (1838–1922) Born Kinneigh, Dunmanway, Co. Cork. In 1853, he joined the Cork Militia but went to sea when the militia was disbanded in 1856. He was in New York when the American civil war broke out and joined the 15th New York Light Infantry and fought in the battle of the Bull Run. He became an army engineer and rose to the rank of colonel by the time the war ended. He had joined the Fenians early in the civil war and was sent from Dublin to Liverpool to procure arms for the movement. He was to take charge of the Waterford area during the planned Fenian Rising of 1867, but with its failure, he became involved in the re-organisation of the movement and was subsequently arrested and lodged in Clerkenwell Prison. In an attempt to free Burke, an explosion demolished part of the prison wall, killed eight people and maimed a further 120. Burke was sentenced to 15 years' penal servitude, was released in 1872 and returned to the US two years later where he was employed as a clerk in the War Department. He later worked as a railway engineer for the Mexican National Construction Company and served as assistant city engineer and assistant harbour engineer in Chicago. He died in Chicago on 11 May 1922. [Life by M.C. Lynch and S. O'Donoghue (1999)]

BURTON, Philip (1910–1995) Born Curragh, Kanturk, Co. Cork, the fifth child of Francis John Burton. Two of his uncles, **John Guiney** and **Patrick Guiney**, were nationalist MPs for Cork North. He was also a first cousin of **Dave Guiney**, the athlete and sports journalist. He joined the Cumann na nGaedheal Party (later Fine Gael) in 1932 and later became the District Staff Officer (North Cork) for the Blueshirt organisation. During the 'economic war' of the Thirties, he was imprisoned for a year at Arbour Hill detention prison. During World War II, he was appointed as a Battalion Commander of the Local Defence Force (LDF) and he retained this position until 1966. He was elected to Cork County Council as a Fine Gael member in 1942 and subsequently served as chairman (1957, 1959–61, and 1976). He was TD for Cork North East (1961–69) and for Mid-Cork (1969–73). Following his 1973 defeat at the polls, he served as a member of the Seanad (1973–7). He died on 3 January 1995 and was buried in Kanturk Cemetery.

BUSTEED, John (1895–1964) Born Cork. He was educated at North Monastery CBS and won the first Honan Scholarship to UCC in 1913. However, his academic career was interrupted during World War I when he left college and joined the Irish Guards. On his return, he completed his B.Comm. degree and, having obtained a NUI travelling studentship, graduated M.Comm. For a time, he was assistant editor of *The Statist*, a weekly magazine. In 1924, he was appointed as professor of Economics at UCC – a position he held until his death. He served on several government commissions, including the Banking Commission, on which he produced a personal minority report. However, his major influence was in the fields of trade union relations and adult education. In 1959, he chaired the discussions that led to the amalgamation of the Irish Trades Union Congress and the Congress of Irish Unions. He died at the Bon Secours Hospital, Cork, on 9 August 1964 and was buried privately.

BUTLER, John (1716–1800) Born at Grange, Fethard, Co. Tipperary, the third son of Edmund Butler, 8th Baron Dunboyne. He was Roman Catholic bishop of Cork from June 1763 until 1786. In that year, he unexpectedly succeeded his nephew as 12th Baron Dunboyne. In pursuit of an heir, he resigned his bishopric on 13 December and requested permission from Pope Pius VI to marry. When this was refused, he converted to Protestantism and married his cousin. However, the marriage proved to be childless. He was received back into the Roman

Catholic Church on his deathbed. He died at Dunboyne Castle on 7 May 1800. [Life by C. Costello (1978)]

BUTT, Isaac (1813–1879) Born Co. Donegal, the only son of a clergyman. He was educated at the Royal School, Raphoe; at Midleton College, and at TCD where he graduated BA (1835). He was called to the Irish Bar in 1838 and soon acquired a firm reputation before being called to the Inner Bar in 1844. He established a Dublin weekly called the *Protestant Guardian*, but, under the influence of effects of the Famine, he turned to nationalism. He defended both the Young Irelanders and the Fenians following their failed revolts. He was called to the English Bar in 1859. He sat in the English Commons as MP for Youghal (1852–65) and for Limerick (1871–79). He founded the Home Rule movement in 1870, but, even though retaining the leadership, eventually lost control of the party to **C.S. Parnell** and his supporters. He died at Dundrum, Dublin, on 5 May 1879. [Life and career by D. Thornley (1964)]

BUTTS, John (c.1727–1765) Born Cork. He established a local reputation as a landscape painter. He moved to Dublin around 1757 and engaged in all kinds of artistic work to provide for his large family. However, his intemperance eventually won out and he died in poverty in May 1765. He was acknowledged by his friend, the painter **James Barry**, as the latter's 'first guide'.

C

CAHILL, Bernie (1930–2001) Born Bere Island, Co. Cork, the son of Daniel Cahill, local businessman and shopkeeper. He was educated at Rockwell College, Blackrock College, and at UCC where he graduated B.Sc. in dairy science (1951). He held various positions in the British dairy sector before returning to Ireland in 1967 to set up Express Dairies (his British employer) new dairy processing centre at Ballineen, Co. Cork. This new venture, trading as Carbery Milk Products and Carbery Distillers, was a huge success especially in the production of alcohol from whey, which was sold to the producers of Bailey's Irish Cream liqueur. He served on various boards including An Bord Bainne (1977–88) and Heineken Brewery Ireland. He also spent periods as chairman of Feltrim Mining and Irish Sugar before its privatisation as Greencore plc in 1991. In that year, he was appointed as chairman of Aer Lingus and as executive chairman two years later when the company faced major financial difficulties. With State aid, voluntary retirements, and the sale of Team Aer Lingus (a maintenance subsidiary company) to a Danish concern, he was able to turn the company back into a profit situation. He died on 17 August 2001 following a boating accident near his home in Schull, Co. Cork, and was buried on his native island.

CALLAGHAN, Daniel (1760–1824) Born Cork, the son of a local merchant, and father of **Daniel Callaghan** and **Gerard Callaghan**. He became, according to **Daniel Owen Madden**, 'the greatest merchant that Ireland (has) produced'. A daring speculator and businessman, his success was copperfastened by winning major government contracts which made him a fortune during the French wars and enabled him to invest £130,000 in land in Cork and Limerick. His enterprises were diverse and included the principal distillery in Cork around 1800. He died at his residence, Lotabeg, Cork, on 29 March 1824 and was buried in Shandon Graveyard.

CALLAGHAN, Daniel (1786–1849) Born Cork, the son of **Daniel Callaghan** and brother of **Gerard Callaghan**. Engaging in the enterprises founded by his father, he succeeded him as head of the business in 1824. In March 1830, he was elected as MP for Cork City in a by-election arising from Gerard's election in 1829 being declared void. Elected with Tory support, he later became a Repealer and a Liberal Repealer. He retained his seat until his death, though in 1835, he held the seat only on the elected Conservatives being unseated on petition. In poor health in his latter years, he died at his residence, Lotabeg, Cork, on 29 September 1849 and was buried in Shandon Graveyard.

CALLAGHAN, Gerard (d. 1833) Born Cork, the third son of **Daniel Callaghan** (1760–1824) and brother of **Daniel Callaghan** (1786–1849). He was educated in England where he became a zealous convert to the Church of England. His apostasy, however, only became known when he was elected as MP for Dundalk as a Tory in 1818. In 1820, 1826, and 1829, he contested Cork City and though successful in 1829, was unseated on petition being deemed ineligible because he was a government contractor. His brother, Daniel, won the vacant seat, but did not vacate it for Gerard at the 1830 general election. Though leader of Cork City Toryism during the 1820s, he spent vast amounts of money (in vain) to win parliamentary representation. He died suddenly at his residence, Sidney House, Cork, on 24 February 1833 and was buried in the family vault in Shandon Graveyard. [Sketch by **Daniel O. Madden** in *Revelations of Ireland in the Past Generation* (1848)]

CALLAGHAN, John (1605–1654) Born Killone, Macroom, Co. Cork, the son of Dermot MacCallaghan. He left for France in 1627 where he studied at Nantes, Rennes, La Flece and at the Sorbonne. During the period of the Confederation of Kilkenny, he opposed the papal nuncio, G.B. Rinuccini (d. 1665). On his return to France, he published a number of pamphlets which advocated Jansenist principles. He also wrote his *Vindiciae Catholicorum Hiberniae* (Paris, 1650) which was highly critical of Rinuccini's tactics at the Confederation. He died in 1654 in Paris and was buried at the Jansenist stronghold of Port Royal.

CALLANAN, Jeremiah J. (1795–1829) Born Cork. He enrolled at Maynooth College in 1818 to study for the priesthood but left and studied for two years at TCD before his money ran out. Following a spell with the 18th Royal Irish Regiment, he returned to Cork and worked in the school of **William Maginn** who introduced some of Callanan's poems to *Blackwood's Magazine*. His collection, over six years, of ballads, poems and stories throughout Munster is unfortunately lost. In a state of failing health, he left Ireland for Lisbon in 1827 where he died of tuberculosis on 19 September 1829. His *Collected Poems* appeared posthumously in London (1833) and were reprinted in Cork (1847 and 1861). [Life by J. Higgins (1981)]

CALVERT, Frederick (1780–1834) He was a landscape painter who worked in Cork in the early nineteenth century. In 1807, he published an aquatint entitled 'Parliament Bridge, Cork'. He eventually left Cork to live in England where he published many lithographs and drawings and also a book entitled, *Lessons on Landscape Colouring, Shadowing, and Pencilling*. Some of his works were exhibited at the Royal Hibernian Academy in 1834. He died at Lambeth, London on 4 May 1834 leaving a widow and twelve children.

CANTWELL, Noel (1932–2005) Born Mardyke Walk, Cork. He developed an early interest in cricket and soccer, playing junior soccer with his local side, Western Rovers. He made his League of Ireland debut with Cork Athletic before being transferred to West Ham United in 1952. He made 248 appearances for West Ham (including a Second Division title in 1958) before being transferred to Manchester United in 1960, then in the process of team rebuilding following the Munich airport disaster. He captained United to a famous FA Cup victory in 1963. He became chairman of the Professional Players' Association in 1966, but left that post in the following year when he was appointed as manager of Coventry City. He left the club in 1972 to manage Peterborough United but left in 1977 for a managership spell in the North American Soccer League. He returned to manage Peterborough in 1986 before his retirement in 1988. He made his international debut in 1953 and eventually earned thirty-six caps with twenty-two of those as captain. An avid cricketer, he represented his country in five internationals, including one against the West Indies. He died in Peterborough on 7 September 2005. [Autobiography (1965)]

CARBERY, Mary Lady (1867–1949) Born St Alban's, Herts., England, the second daughter of Henry Toulmin. She studied at the Royal Academy of Music, London. In 1890, she met and married Algernon Freke, 9th Lord Carbery, and went to live at his ancestral home, Castlefreke, Rosscarbery, where her son, **John E. Carbery**, was born. Lord Carbery died of consumption in England in 1898. She then married **Arthur W. Sandford** and divided her time between his Cork home and Castlefreke, until the latter residence was destroyed by fire in 1910. She edited *Mrs Elizabeth Freke: Her Diary 1671–1714* (1913) and was also the author of *The Germans in Cork* (1917) – a satirical pamphlet on the political situation in 1917. This was published anonymously. From around 1920 onwards, the Sandfords lived in England and on the Continent. Her *Children of the Dawn* was published in 1923. As 'Mary Carbery', she published *The Farm by Lough Gur* (1937, 1973) –

the reminiscences of Mary Fogarty of Lough Gur, Co. Limerick. She also published *Happy World* (1941), a memoir of her early life to the age of seventeen. She died at Eye Manor, the residence of her son, Christopher, on the Welsh border, on 6 February 1949 and was buried in Eye Churchyard. [Her grandson, Jeremy Sandford, edited *Mary Carbery's West Cork Journal 1898–1901* (1998).]

CARBERY, John E. (1892–1970) Born John Freke, and succeeding in 1898 as 10th Lord Carbery, he changed his name by deed poll in 1920. He was the son of Algernon Freke, 9th Lord Carbery, and **Mary Lady Carbery**. He is mainly remembered as a peerless aviator at various Cork airshows in the early 1920s. He also featured as a member of the Rhodesian 'Happy Valley' group in James Fox's *White Mischief* (1982), which was subsequently made into a major film. He died on 25 December 1970.

CAREW-SMYTH, Ponsonby M. (1860–1939) Born Cork, the son of Emmanuel Uniacke Smyth, gentleman, and Catherine Giles (née Carew). Having an interest in art, he studied in Belfast and later at South Kensington where he was also employed as a teacher. Following a period of further study in Paris, he married in 1890 and in the following year emigrated to Melbourne where he was appointed as inspector of drawing at the department of Education. He took a great interest in the link between primary and technical education and also in the provision of adequate teacher training. His *Austral Drawing Books* provided the basis for the teaching of drawing in the state of Victoria until 1927. He was the main organiser of various drawing and craft exhibitions and also served as acting director of the National Gallery of Victoria from 1936. He died at his residence at South Yarra, Victoria, on 9 October 1939.

CAREY, Edmund (1883–1943) Born Midleton, Co. Cork, the son of John P. Carey, publican. His premises were destroyed by the British military on New Year's Day 1921 as an official reprisal. He served on Cork County Council (1925–43) and was elected as a Cumann na nGaedheal TD for Cork East in 1927. He lost his seat in the general election of 1932 and unsuccessfully contested the general elections of 1938 and 1943 as a Fine Gael candidate. He died at Midleton Cottage Hospital on 26 August 1943 and was buried in the local cemetery.

CAREY, John R. (1834–1923) Born Cork, the son of John Westropp Carey, soldier. He was educated at Dr Hamblin's College, Cork, and emigrated to Australia in 1853 to join in the gold rush. However, he soon set up as a general agent, supplier and auctioneer at Castlemaine, Victoria. He moved to New Zealand in 1862 and became a partner in a similar business in Auckland. From 1869 until 1873, he was captain of the Auckland Troop of the Royal Cavalry Volunteers and probably saw action in the Maori wars. Following his marriage in 1873, he and his business partner returned to Australia and set up in Sydney where he was the major partner in a steamboat company. He later established the Sydney Tramway & Omnibus Company which eventually failed in 1899. However, he had better luck with his foray into the newspaper business when he established the successful Sydney *Daily Telegraph* in 1879. He was a major contributor to local charities and was a trustee of the Savings Bank of New South Wales. He died on 9 June 1923 and was buried in the Anglican section of South Head Cemetery, Sydney.

CAREY, Tadhg (1919–1995) Born Kinsale, Co. Cork. He grew up in Dillon's Cross, Cork, where he attended the local St Patrick's NS. He later attended North Monastery CBS and entered UCC on a City University Scholarship in 1936. He became a member of the teaching staff at UCC in 1939 and graduated MA in Mathematical Science (1942). He later became registrar of the college (1954–78) and was also appointed as professor of Mathematical Statistics. He was elected as president of UCC in 1978 and served until his retirement in 1989.

He died at Cork University Hospital on 8 February 1995 and was cremated at Glasnevin Crematorium, Dublin.

CARLETON, Hugh (1739–1826) Born Cork. He was educated at TCD and was called to the Irish Bar in 1764. He eventually rose to become Lord Chief Justice and 1st Viscount Carleton. Though he was the guardian of **Henry Sheares** and **John Sheares**, the Cork United Irishmen, it was he who condemned them to death. In the Emmet Rising of 1803, the Dublin mob killed Lord Kilwarden in mistake for Carleton. He died in Dublin in 1826.

CARPENTER, George T. (1908–2005) Born Maymount, Cork, the son of William Carpenter, insurance agent. An all-round sportsman, he represented Ireland in fencing at the Helsinki (1952) and Rome Olympiads (1960). Among his other sporting interests were rowing, rugby, sailing, water-skiing, and badminton. He was the owner of the popular Club Hotel, Glenbrook, which he purchased in 1947. He died at his Kinsale home in August 2005. [Autobiography (2003)]

CARROLL, Isaac (1745–1816) Born Cork, the son of Edward Carroll (of an Ulster Jacobite family) who had married a Quaker woman, Sarah Bell. With his brother, John Carroll (1740–1819), he operated an extensive timber and general supply business at Devonshire's Marsh. The firm was also extensively involved in the hogshead- and barrel-staves trade which was one of Cork's main exports in the early nineteenth century. The firm gave its name to Cork's 'Carroll's Quay'.

CARROLL, Isaac (1828–1880) Born Aghada, Co. Cork, the son of James Carroll (1795–1874). He developed a strong interest in botany and collaborated with **Thomas Allin** in his study of lichens. He contributed extensively to Moore and Moore's *Cybele Hibernica* of 1866. A total of 400 specimens of his lichen collection were later sold to the Natural History Museum, London.

He also studied Lapp, Norwegian, and Icelandic flora. He arranged the herbarium at the newly-founded Queen's College, Cork (now UCC).

CASEY, John (1820–1891) Born Kilbehenny, Mitchelstown, Co. Cork. A native Irish speaker, he qualified as a national teacher and worked in Cappoquin, Tipperary Town and Kilkenny. Through his conversations with a graduate who was dying of tuberculosis, he developed an interest in mathematics. Following correspondence with the mathematicians, **George Salmon** and **Richard Townsend**, he entered TCD where he graduated BA (1862). He worked as a teacher at Kingstown (now Dún Laoghaire) School from 1862 until 1873. He became a member of the Royal Irish Academy in 1866 before serving as professor of Mathematics in Cardinal Newman's Catholic University (1873–81). He reluctantly refused (at the request of Archbishop Paul Cullen of Dublin) a similar and more lucrative offer from TCD. In 1875, he became a fellow of the Royal Society. He lectured at University College, Stephen's Green (later UCD) from 1881 until his death in Dublin on 3 January 1891.

CASEY, John S. (1846–1896) Born Baldwin Street, Mitchelstown, Co. Cork, the son of Jeremiah Casey. He was educated locally and, in his early years, worked in Geary's public house in North Main Street, Cork. Being active in the Fenian movement, he wrote letters in the Fenian *Irish People* under the pseudonym, 'Galtee Boy'. He was arrested in 1865, convicted of Fenian membership and sentenced to five years penal servitude. The first two years were served in Portland Gaol, before he was transported to Freemantle penal colony on the *Hougoumont* in 1867 along with sixty-one other Fenians. He was granted a free pardon in May 1869 and returned to Ireland in the following year. In a series of letters to various newspapers in 1876, he highlighted the plight of tenants of the Buckley Estate on the Galtee Mountains. Arising from these articles, he was sued for criminal libel by Buckley's agent, Patten Smith Bridge. Defended by the noted advocate, **Isaac Butt**, the verdict was a split decision which amounted to an acquittal. For a time in the 1880s, he acted as secretary of the Mitchelstown branch of the National Land League. He later became coroner for Co. Limerick, a position which he held until the time of his death which occurred at his Baldwin Street residence on 23 April 1896. He was buried in Mitchelstown Cemetery. His *Journal of a Voyage from Portland to Freemantle on board the Convict Ship 'Hougoumont'*, was published as a limited edition in 1988.

CASEY, Patrick (1873–1940) Born Ballynoe, Co. Cork. He was educated at St Colman's College, Fermoy, and at St Patrick's College, Maynooth, where he was ordained in 1896. Following postgraduate studies at the Dunboyne Institute, Maynooth, he worked on the staffs of St Kieran's College, Kilkenny, and St Colman's College, Fermoy. He then ministered in Bally-macoda, Fermoy, Mallow, and Newmarket, before being consecrated as bishop of Ross at St Patrick's Pro-cathedral, Skibbereen, on 15 September 1935. He died in Skibbereen on 15 September 1940 and was buried in the grounds of his cathedral. His uncle, a noted Land League cleric, was the parish priest of Abbeyfeale, Co. Limerick.

CASEY, Seán (1922–1967) Born Cork. He was educated at PBC, Cork, and worked in the clerical department of CIE from 1941 to 1954. His entry into public life came in 1950 when he was elected to Cork Corporation as a member of the Labour Party. He unsuccessfully stood for Cork Borough in the general elections of 1948 and 1951, and in a by-election in 1954. Later that year, he won a Dáil seat and retained it until his death. He served as lord mayor of Cork in 1956, 1962 (when he played host to President J.F. Kennedy) and in 1966. He was nearing completion of his third term when his death occurred on 29 April 1967 at the South Infirmary Hospital. He was buried in St Finbarr's Cemetery.

CASEY, William (*fl.* 1780–1828) He worked as an engraver from an address in Henry Street, Cork. His bookplates of 'Timothy Mahony'

(1780), 'O'Callaghan' (1800), and 'John Wrixon' are recorded.

CASEY, William L. (1835–1870) Born Cork. Having studied at the Cork School of Design, he was appointed as second master at the Limerick School of Art in 1854. He eventually settled in London and spent a period as master of St Martin's Lane Academy. He is especially noted for his portraits and subjects in water-colour. He died in London on 30 September 1870.

CASHMAN, Joseph (1881–1969) Born Black-pool, Cork. From childhood, he was fascinated by cameras and photography. He first worked for the Cork printing firm, Guy and Co., and from 1902 to 1910 he worked in the photo-engraving department of the *Cork Examiner*. He spent the following two years with the *Cambria Daily Leader* of Swansea. From 1912 to 1923, he was head of the photo-engraving department of *The Freeman's Journal* and on its cessation, he set up his own studio in Dublin and specialised in bloodstock photography. In 1929, he was recruited to head the photographic department of the *Irish Press* where he spent the rest of his career. He was the leading photographic annalist of the turbulent years (1910–30) in Ireland. Selections from his photographic archive were published under the title, *Ireland: the Revolutionary Years*. He died at his residence, 13 Manon Place, Dublin, on 1 January 1969.

CAULFIELD, Richard (1823–1887) Born Cork. He was educated at TCD where he graduated BA (1845), LL.B (1864) and LL.D (1866). Having been elected as fellow of the Royal Society of Antiquaries (1862), he was appointed as librarian at the Cork Institution (1864) and later at Queen's College, Cork (now UCC) in 1876. He edited the Council books of Cork, Youghal and Kinsale and other primary historical collections including the Pipe Roll of Cloyne (1859) [re-edited with commentary by P. MacCotter and K.W. Nicholls (1996)]. He died at the Royal Cork Institution on 3 February

1887 and was buried in Douglas Churchyard. Among his many publications were *The Life of St Fin Barre* (1864) and *Sigilla Ecclesiae Hibernicae Illustrata* (1853). [Biographical article by J.P. McCarthy in *JCHAS* (1987)]

CAVENDISH, Charles C. (1793–1863) He was the fourth and youngest son of George A.H. Cavendish, 1st earl of Burlington (new creation) and grandson of William Cavendish, 4th Duke of Devonshire. He was a Liberal MP from 1820 until 1857 and was created 1st Baron Chesham in January 1858. He represented the constituency of Youghal (1841–7) and died on 10 November 1863.

CHALMERS, J. (*fl.* 1801–1820) He worked in Dublin as a landscape and scene painter until he was employed in the Cork Theatre. In 1819, he was appointed as drawing-master at the Cork Institution. He exhibited landscapes at the Cork Society for the Promotion of the Fine Arts.

CHAPPELL, William (1582–1644) Born Nottinghamshire, the son of Robert Chappell. He was educated at Corpus Christi College, Cambridge, where he became a Fellow in 1607. He stayed for twenty-seven years and had the poet, John Milton (1608–74), as a pupil. He was appointed as dean of Cashel and provost of TCD in 1634. However, he was appointed as Church of Ireland bishop of Cork and Ross on 11 November 1638 and resigned the provostship two years later. He criticised **Richard Boyle**, 1st earl of Cork, on the dilapidated state of St Mary's Collegiate Church, Youghal (for which Boyle was responsible). Boyle was brought before the Irish Parliament about the matter and severely cautioned. On the outbreak of the 1641 rebellion, he left Cork for Dublin en route for England. Despite being refused a pass, he eventually escaped and returned to his native county. He died at Derby on Whit Sunday, 14 May 1649, and was buried in Bilsthorpe. His works included *Methodus Concionandi* [trans. 'A Mode of Assembly'] (1648) and *The Use of Holy Scripture* (1653).

CHARLES, John J. (1845–1912) Born Cookstown, Co. Tyrone, the son of David H. Charles, doctor. He was educated at Queen's College, Belfast; University College, London; and Edinburgh University. He pursued further studies in Paris, Bonn and Berlin. He was appointed as professor of Anatomy at Queen's College, Cork (now UCC), in 1875 (to 1907). He was the author of numerous anatomical papers in various medical journals in England, France and Germany. He died in Dublin in August 1912.

CHATTERTON, Lady Henrietta (1806–1876) Born England. In 1824, Henrietta (née Iremonger) married Sir William Chatterton of Castle Mahon, Co. Cork. She illustrated and wrote *Rambles in the South of Ireland during the year 1838* and *Home Sketches and Foreign Recollections* (1841).

CHATTERTON, Hedges E. (1819–1910) Born Cork, the eldest son of Abraham Chatterton, and first cousin of **James C. Chatterton**. He was called to the Bar in 1843 and subsequently attended TCD where he graduated LL.D in 1849. He was called to the Inner Bar in 1858. He was appointed as solicitor general for Ireland in 1866, as attorney general in 1867 and as vice-chancellor in the same year – a position which he was to hold until 1904. In 1867, he also represented Dublin University (TCD) as a Conservative MP. He died in August 1910.

CHATTERTON, Sir James C. (1796–1872) Born Cork, the second son of Sir James Chatterton, Baronet, of Castle Mahon, Blackrock, and first cousin of **Hedges E. Chatterton**. He had a successful military career, serving throughout the Peninsular War and attaining the rank of general. He was high sheriff of Cork in 1851 and on his brother's death in 1855, succeeded to the baronetcy as the 3rd and last baronet. He contested the parliamentary constituency of Cork City as a Conservative candidate on six occasions (returned as MP in February 1835, unseated on petition in May 1835, unsuccessful in 1837 and 1841, elected in a by-election in November 1849, defeated in 1852, and again in a by-election in 1853). During his tenure as MP, he opposed the extension of the Public Libraries Act to Ireland. He was Master of the Provincial Grand Lodge of Munster Freemasons for many years. He died on 5 January 1872.

CHESTER, William B. (1820–1893) Born Mallow, Co. Cork, the son of John Chester, vicar of Ballyclough. He was educated at TCD where he graduated BA (1846), MA (1856) and BD/DD (1883). He was consecrated as Church of Ireland bishop of Killaloe on 24 February 1884. He died in Dublin on 27 August 1893 and was buried in Parsonstown (now Birr) Graveyard.

CHINNERY, Sir Brodrick (d. 1808) Born Midleton, Co. Cork, the fourth son of George Chinnery, clergyman and headmaster, and brother of Bishop **George Chinnery.** In the Irish Parliament, he sat for Castlemartyr (1783–90) and for Bandon (1790–1800). He was created a baronet in August 1799. After the Union, he represented Bandon in the British House of Commons. He died in May 1808 and was buried in Midleton Graveyard.

CHINNERY, George (1719–1780) Born near Mallow, Co. Cork, the son of George Chinnery, clergyman and headmaster, and brother of **Sir Brodrick Chinnery**. He was educated at TCD where he graduated BA (1740), MA (1743) and LL.D (1751). He succeeded his father as headmaster of Midleton College in 1750 and served until his resignation in 1775. He was consecrated as Church of Ireland bishop of Killaloe on 7 March 1779 and was translated to Cloyne on 15 February 1780. He died on 13 August of that year and was buried in Midleton Graveyard.

CHURCH, Sir Richard (1784–1873) Born Cork, the son of a Quaker merchant. He joined the British army at an early age and following service in Egypt and Italy, he took up the cause of Greek independence from Turkey as a result of an expedition to the Greek islands. In 1815, he attended the Congress of Vienna to lobby for the Greeks. He was knighted in 1822 and immediately left for Greece where he commanded the Greek forces in the west of the country during the Greek War of Independence (1821–30). He eventually took Greek citizenship, and became a member of the Council of State and inspector-general of the army. He died in Athens on 30 March 1873. [Life by E.M. Church (1895)]

CLANCY, William (1802–1847) Born Cork, the son of Daniel Clancy. He studied at St Patrick's College, Carlow, and at St Patrick's College, Maynooth, where he was ordained in 1823. He served in the Cork diocese until 1830 when he was appointed as professor of Moral Philosophy and Hebrew at Carlow. In 1834, he was appointed as coadjutor bishop of Charleston, South Carolina, and three years later was transferred to the vicarate of British Guiana. He retired from this position in 1843 and returned to his native city. He died at his town residence in Clarence Street, Cork, on 19 June 1847 and was buried in the precincts of the North Cathedral. He also had a residence at Orienville, Little Island.

CLAYTON, Robert (1695–1758) Born England, the son of Dr John Clayton, clergyman. He was educated at Westminster School and at TCD where he graduated BA (1714), MA (1717), LL.B (1718), LL.D (1722) and DD (1730). He was consecrated as Church of Ireland bishop of Killala on 23 January 1730. He was translated to the diocese of Cork and Ross on 19 December 1735 and to Clogher on 26 August 1745. In 1751, he published *An Essay on Spirit* – an anti-Trinitarian work which sparked off a huge controversy and denied him promotion to the archbishopric of Tuam. As he was about to be deprived of his bishopric, he took ill and died in Dublin on 26 February 1758. He was buried in Donnybrook Churchyard, Dublin. [Life by A.R. Winnett in *Studies in Church History*, vol. 9, D. Baker, ed. (1972); Plaster bust by John van Nost]

CLEAVER, Euseby (1746–1819) Born Buckinghamshire, England, the son of a schoolmaster and brother of William Cleaver, bishop of St Asaph, Wales. He was educated at Westminster School and at Christ Church, Oxford, where he graduated BA (1767), MA (1770), and DD (1783). He was consecrated as Church of Ireland bishop of Cork and Ross on 28 March 1789. He was translated to the diocese of Ferns on 13 June of that year. His residence and property at Ferns were plundered in the 1798 Rising, but he escaped personal injury. In 1809, he was promoted to the archbishopric of Dublin. Two years later, when he was found to be of unsound mind, Archbishop **Charles Brodrick** of Cashel was appointed as coadjutor. Cleaver died at Tunbridge Wells, Kent, in December 1819. (His grandson, Rev. Euseby Digby Cleaver (1826–94), was a noted Gaelic scholar and was vice-president of Connradh na Gaeilge in 1893. A sod from Gugán Barra was placed in the coffin at his funeral in Wales.) [Portrait by Gilbert C. Stuart]

CLEBURNE, Patrick Ronayne (1828–1864) Born Bridepark Cottage, Ovens, Co. Cork, the son of Joseph Cleburne, physician. He attended TCD for a period and subsequently enlisted in the British Army. He emigrated to the United States and settled in Helena, Arkansas. Joining the Confederate army when the civil war broke out in 1861, he quickly rose to the rank of brigadier-general. He took part in many campaigns and was so successful that he was nicknamed 'The Stonewall Jackson of the West'. He was killed at the battle of Franklin, Tennessee, on 30 November 1864. His remains were reinterred in Evergreen Cemetery, Helena, in 1870. [Lives by H. and E. Purdue (1973); and M.P. Joslyn (1997]

CLERKE, Agnes M. (1842–1907) Born Skibbereen, Co. Cork, the sister of **Ellen M. Clerke**. An astronomer of note, she published *The History of Astronomy* (1885), *The System of the Stars* (1890) and contributed more than fifty articles to the *Edinburgh Review*. In 1903, she

was elected as an honorary member of the Royal Astronomical Society. She died at South Kensington, London, on 20 January 1907. [Life by Lady Huggins (1907); M. Bruck (2002)]

CLERKE, Ellen M. (1840–1906) Born Skibbereen, Co. Cork, the sister of **Agnes M. Clerke**. As well as being a scientist, she was also an accomplished linguist and contributed to many German and Italian publications. She published *The Flying Dutchman* (1881), *Fable and Song in Italy* (1899), *Flowers of Fire* (1902) and monographs on Jupiter (1892) and Venus (1893). She was also a leader writer and occasional editor of *The Tablet*. She died at South Kensington, London, on 3 March 1906. [Life by Lady Huggins (1907)]

CLERKE, Sir Thomas H. S. (1792–1849) Born Bandon, Co. Cork. He joined the British army and having lost a leg in 1811 during the Peninsular War, was assigned to depot duties on the recommendation of the duke of Wellington. A noted linguist, he was the first editor of *Colborn's United Service Magazine* (1842). In 1833, he was elected as a Fellow of the Royal Society and also held the fellowships of the Royal Astronomical and Geological Societies. He died at Brompton Grove, London, on 19 April 1849.

CLERY, Sir Cornelius F. (1838–1926) Born Cork, the son of a wine merchant. He was educated in Dublin and at the Royal Military College, Sandhurst. He developed an interest in military education and was promoted to the position of professor of Tactics at Sandhurst. On leaving the college in 1875, he published *Minor Tactics*, the most influential of British military handbooks of the period. He later saw service in Cape Province, South Africa, and in Egypt where he was made chief-of-staff of the army of occupation. He returned to England and took up positions at the staff college and at the War Office. In 1899, he returned to South Africa on the outbreak of the Boer War where he commanded the Second Infantry Division at the relief of Ladysmith. However, his actions did not seem to go down well with the War Office and he was recalled to England in October 1900. He retired from the army five months later. He died in London on 25 June 1926.

CLIFFORD, Sir Augustus W.J. (1788–1877) Born England. He joined the navy in 1800 and served until 1831 before his retirement with the rank of admiral. He sat as MP for Bandon (1818–20) and for Dungarvan (1820–2). He resigned his seat in February 1822 but was returned for Bandon again in a by-election of July 1831. He sat until December 1832 when he was appointed as Gentleman Usher of the Black Rod, a post which he held until his death. He was knighted in 1830 and created a baronet in 1838. He died at his residence in the House of Lords on 8 February 1877.

CLIFFORD, Sigerson (1913–1985) Born Cork, the son of Michael Clifford. The family moved to Co. Kerry in 1915 and he was educated at Cahirciveen CBS. He joined the civil service in 1932 and served until his retirement in 1973. His plays include 'The Devil's Dust', 'The Great Pacificator', 'Nano', 'The Glassy Man' and 'The Wild Colonial Boy'. He also published some poetry collections – *Travelling Tinkers* (1951), *Lascar Rock* (1953) and *Ballads of a Bogman* (1955). He was also the co-author of *The Tragic Story of the Coleen Bawn* (1966), which was adapted from **Gerald Griffin**'s *The Collegians*. He died at Glenageary, Co. Dublin, on 1 January 1985 and was buried in Cahirciveen.

COATES, William P. (1883–1963) Born Kinsale, Co. Cork. He became a British Socialist Party activist in London and in 1913 he married Zelda Kahan, a Russian émigré and fellow-socialist. In May 1918, he returned to Ireland to avoid conscription and was appointed Irish Transport & General Workers Union (ITGWU) organiser in Waterford. Here he extended unionisation into the surrounding countryside. In April 1919, he returned to London and became an organiser for the British Socialist

Party. He later became secretary of the 'Hands Off Russia' campaign and of the Anglo-Russian Parliamentary Committee (1924–63). With his wife, he wrote and published many books about life in Soviet Russia, their best known being a two-volume publication, *A History of Anglo-Soviet Relations* (1944, 1958). He died in Manor House Hospital, London, on 8 August 1963.

COGAN, Philip (1748–1833) Born Cork. He became a chorister and later a lay vicar at St FinBarre's Cathedral. He moved to Dublin and was appointed to a similar post at Christ Church Cathedral in 1772. He was later appointed, in 1780, as organist at St Patrick's Cathedral in that city and held the post until 1802. He also established himself as a music teacher and among his pupils was Thomas Moore (1779–1852), the poet. He was a founder member and vice-president of the Irish Music Fund Society and directed many performances of Handel's *Messiah* which were organised by the society for the support of poverty-stricken musicians. He wrote two comic operas, *The Ruling Passion* (1778) and *The Contract* (1782), for Dublin audiences. A master harpsichordist and pianist, he also wrote many sonatas and concerti for those instruments as well as three violin sonatas. He died at the residence of his son-in-law in Old Dominick Street, Dublin, on 3 February 1833 and was buried in Glasnevin Cemetery.

COGHILL, Nevill H.K.A. (1899–1980) Born Castletownshend, Co. Cork, the second son of Sir Egerton B. Coghill, Bart., a noted amateur landscape painter. His mother was Hildegarde Somerville, sister of **Edith O. Somerville**, the novelist. Educated at English public schools, he served in the Balkans in the last months of World War I, before studying at Exeter College, Oxford, where he read History and English. In 1924, he was elected a research fellow of Exeter and a year later became a fellow and librarian there. He specialised in medieval literature and among his published works are, *The Poet Chaucer* (1949, 2nd ed., 1967), the Penguin edition of *The Canterbury Tales* (1951) ['creating for the first time since the Middle Ages a nation-wide audience for Chaucer'], and *Shakespeare's Professional Skills* (1964). In 1957, he was elected to the Merton Chair of English Literature at Oxford. He was also a noted dramatic producer, especially for the spectacular outdoor perform-ances of the Oxford University dramatic society in the 1940s. In the year of his retirement (1966), he directed Richard Burton (an ex-pupil) and Elizabeth Taylor in 'Doctor Faustus' at the Oxford Playhouse and was co-director with Burton of the film version (with almost the same cast) which was filmed in Rome in the following year. This was followed in 1968 by his highly successful musical stage version (with Martin Starkie) of *The Canterbury Tales*, which ran for five years at the Phoenix Theatre, London. He died in a Cheltenham (Gloucester) nursing home on 6 November 1980.

COHALAN, Daniel (1858–1952) Born Kilmichael, Co. Cork, the uncle of Bishop **Daniel Coholan** of Waterford. He was edu-cated at St Vincent's College, Sunday's Well, and at St Patrick's College, Maynooth, where he was ordained in 1883. He was professor of Dogmatic and Moral Theology at Maynooth from 1886 until 7 June 1914 when he was consecrated as coadjutor bishop of Cork. He succeeded as bishop of Cork on 29 August 1916. He is noted for his decree of excommunication of 12 December 1920 on members of the Republican movement and also for his sincere though banal attempt at a rapprochement with Cork Anglicans in 1937. He died on 24 August 1952 and was buried at the cathedral of St Mary and St Anne. Among his publications were *Trinity College and the Commissions* (1908), *De Deo Creatore* (1909), *De Incarnatione* (1910), *Trinity College: its Income and its Value to the Nation* (1911) and *De Sanctissima Eucharistica* (1913).

COHALAN, Daniel (1884–1965) Born Kilmichael, Co. Cork, the nephew of Bishop **Daniel Coholan** of Cork. He was educated at PBC, Cork, and at the Irish College, Rome,

where he was ordained in 1906. Following postgraduate studies in Rome, he acted as Dean of Residence at UCD (1910–22). He then ministered in Cork at St Patrick's Church, the North Cathedral and St Finbarr's West before his consecration by his uncle as bishop of Waterford on 4 April 1943. He died on 27 January 1965 and was buried in the grounds of Holy Trinity Cathedral, Waterford.

COLBERT, James (c.1898–1955) Born Douglas Road, Cork, the son of Patrick Colbert. He was educated at North Monastery CBS and at Mount Melleray School, Co. Waterford, before entering All Hallows College, Dublin, where he was ordained on 19 June 1921. He subsequently ministered in the vicariate of the Cape of Good Hope, South Africa, until his retirement in 1948. He was made vicar apostolic of Port Elizabeth in June 1939 and, in the same year, was consecrated bishop of Port Elizabeth in Rome. Though one of the youngest bishops in the world at the time, ill health forced him to retire in 1948. His latter years were spent as director of a boarding school for native coloured children at Izeli in the Eastern Province. He died at Port Elizabeth on 8 January 1955.

COLE, John H. (1830–1909) Born Woodview, Innishannon, Co. Cork, the son of Thomas C. Cole, JP. He was educated at TCD where he graduated BA (1858). For the previous three years, he had been a lieutenant in the South Cork Infantry. Having been ordained deacon (1858) and priest (1860), he held various curacies in the diocese of Cork, Cloyne, and Ross until appointed as rector of Leighmoney parish in 1869. In 1897, he began work on a supplementary volume to **William M. Brady**'s succession lists for the Church of Ireland united diocese of Cork, Cloyne, and Ross. Six years later, his *Church and Parish Records of the United Diocese of Cork, Cloyne, and Ross* was published (1903). He also contributed a series of articles, 'Innishannon and its Neighbourhood' to the *JCHAS* (1907). He died at Woodview, Innishannon, on 15 May 1909 and was buried in Innishannon Graveyard.

COLEMAN, John C. (1914–1971) Born Cork, and educated at North Monastery CBS. He worked in the Ford car assembly plant and in the Irish Assurance Company before entering the service, in 1941, of the Irish Tourist Association and later the publicity department of Bord Fáilte. An Irish pioneer in speleology, he published a number of articles (as well as an MA thesis at UCC [1965]) on the subject. He was president of the Irish Speleological Society, a fellow of the Royal Geographical Society, and president of the Irish Mountaineering Club. His *Caves of Ireland* (1965) became the definitive work on the subject. His masterpiece, however, was his *Journeys into Muskerry* (1950) which was illustrated by his own drawings. It became one of the first modern Irish walking guides, and, with his *The Mountains of Killarney* (1948), was reprinted several times. He lived in Dublin from *c*.1945 and died of a heart attack while motoring on 20 April 1971. He was buried in Dean's Grange Cemetery, Dublin.

COLLINS, Denis B. (1861–1894) Born Lough Ine, Skibbereen, Co. Cork. He was educated locally, in Limerick, and in Cork. He emigrated to the US in 1882, and having studied for the priesthood, was ordained in New York in 1888. He wrote poetry for many newspapers and periodicals, including the Dublin *Irish Monthly*, the *Boston Pilot*, and *Donahoe's Magazine*. He died at West Winfield, New York, on 16 October 1894.

COLLINS, Dominic (1553–1602) Born Youghal, and also known by his Irish name, Dominic Ó Coileáin. Following service in the Spanish army, he joined the Society of Jesus (Jesuits) in 1598 as a lay brother. He returned to Ireland immediately after the battle of Kinsale (4 December 1601) and assisted in the defence of Dunboy Castle. He was arrested shortly afterwards and executed in Youghal. He was beatified in 1992.

COLLINS, Eugene (1822–1895) Born Kinsale, Co. Cork, the eldest son of Daniel Collins. With his brother, he was a partner in the Kinsale firm of Collins & Co. In 1854, he married Marianne Taunton of Grandpont House, nr. Oxford, whose uncle, Sir William Elias Taunton, was a judge of the Court of Queen's Bench. He stood as a Liberal candidate for his native Kinsale in 1865, but lost narrowly to the sitting MP, **Sir George Conway Colthurst**. He returned to the fray in 1874 when he stood as a Home Ruler and comfortably defeated a Conservative opponent. He retained the seat in 1880 but retired in 1885 when the Kinsale borough was disenfranchised. He died at Bayswater, London, on 10 March 1895.

COLLINS, James P. (*c*.1824–1847) Born Co. Cork, the only son of Patrick Collins. In 1837, his family emigrated to Saint John, New Brunswick, Canada, where he was apprenticed to a local physician. Following further studies in Paris and London, he began to practise at Saint John in August 1846. In May of the following year, a typhus epidemic broke out in North America, largely as a result of Irish immigration in the wake of the Famine. Partridge Island near Saint John was a quarantine area for the immigrants and Collins was appointed as one of two assistant medical officers there, having been promised that his efforts would be of great benefit to his future employment prospects. Within two months Collins was dead, having contracted the disease. He died on 2 July 1847 and, following a huge funeral, was buried in the Roman Catholic cemetery in Indianstown. His remains were twice dis-interred before being finally buried near Fort Howe in 1949. A Celtic cross was erected to his memory on Partridge Island.

COLLINS, Jerome J. (1841–1881) Born Arbutus Lodge, Cork, the son of Mark Collins, salt and lime manufacturer of South Main Street. He was educated at the Cork Lancasterian School and at St Vincent's Seminary. He joined a local engineering firm and was clerk-of-works on the construction of the North Gate Bridge in 1863. He emigrated to the United States two years later, probably because of his Fenian involvement, and in June 1867 he founded the Clan na nGael movement in New York. He joined the staff of the *New York Herald* in 1870 and established himself as a pioneer of press weather-forecasting. In 1877, he inaugurated a system of cabled storm-warnings to Europe. Two years later, he was a crew member of the *Jeanette* polar expedition under the command of G.W. De Long and financed by the *Herald*. The expedition turned into a disaster and resulted in the deaths of nineteen of the thirty-five participants, including Collins who died *c*.30 October 1881 at the Lena Delta in Siberia. A relief expedition recovered the bodies in March 1882, and having been transported to the United States via Hamburg, were given a public funeral in New York. However, Collins' body was exhumed and was returned to Ireland in early 1884. He was finally laid to rest at Curraghkippane Cemetery, near Cork, where his grave is marked by a Celtic cross. [Commemorative plaque at South Gate Bridge, Cork]

COLLINS, John (1889–1961) Born Drimoleague, Co. Cork. He joined the African Missions Society in Cork, and following studies at its Wilton College, was ordained in 1913. He then worked on the Liberian mission where he spent almost the next fifty years. In 1934, he was appointed as vicar apostolic of Liberia and bishop of Tula, being consecrated at the North Cathedral, Cork, in September. Owing to ill health, he resigned his vicariate in 1960 and died in Monrovia, Liberia, on 3 March 1961.

COLLINS, John T. (1887–1971) Born Cloncorban, Kilmeen, Co. Cork, the eldest of seven children of Timothy Collins, farmer. He was related to the poet **Seán Ó Coileáin** and to **Jeremiah O'Donovan Rossa**. He was educated at Rossmore NS and joined the staff of Cork Mental Hospital in 1909. He worked there until his retirement as Head Mental Nurse in 1952. He was one of the outstanding local historians of his time, contributing historical articles (under the pseudonym of 'Heber') to the *Cork Examiner*, *Evening Echo* and other newspapers, as well as over forty articles (commencing in 1934) to the *JCHAS*. His field of expertise was in the study of the native Irish families of County Cork and their vicissitudes from the 16th century onwards – a topic on which he wrote and spoke with authority. He also made several broadcasts on local history and was a member of the Cork County library committee for many years. He died at his Western Road residence on 4 June 1971 and was buried in St Finbarr's Cemetery.

COLLINS, Michael (1781–1832) Born Clonakilty, Co. Cork, the son of a harness-maker. He entered St Patrick's College, Maynooth, in 1798, but was one of the several students who were expelled in 1803 on account of their nationalist sympathies. He was then admitted to Carlow College where he was ordained and afterwards became professor of Belles-Lettres. He was appointed as parish priest of Castletownroche in 1811 and two years later he was transferred to the parish of Creagh and Tullagh, which included the town of Skibbereen. In 1822, he obtained the site on which the present Pro-Cathedral was built under his supervision. In 1824, he gave evidence before the select committee into the disturbed state of Ireland. In 1827, he was appointed coadjutor bishop with right of succession to Bishop **William Coppinger** whom he succeeded as bishop of Cloyne and Ross in August 1831. However, his episcopate was very brief as he died of an apoplectic seizure in Skibbereen on 8 December 1832. He was buried in his cathedral. [Monument by **John Hogan** at St Patrick's Cathedral, Skibbereen]

COLLINS, Michael (1890–1922) Born Clonakilty, Co. Cork, the son of a small farmer. He was the brother of **Margaret Collins-O'Driscoll** and uncle of **Seán Collins**. In 1906, he went to London to take up a clerkship in the Post Office savings bank. While there, he joined the Irish Republican Brotherhood and returned to Dublin to fight at the GPO in the Easter rising of 1916. Following a term of imprisonment in Britain, he returned to Dublin where he took a leading part in the organisation of

Sinn Féin and the Irish Volunteers. With the sweeping success of Sinn Féin in the general election of 1918, he was made, in turn, minister of Home Affairs and of Finance of the first Dáil Éireann. He played a pivotal part in the Anglo-Irish War of Independence (1919–21) as the director of intelligence of the IRA. He was a member of the Irish delegation which negotiated the Anglo-Irish Treaty (6 December 1921) and was appointed as chairman and minister for Finance of the Provisional Government to implement it. With the outbreak of the Irish civil war on 28 June 1922, he was appointed as commander-in-chief of the Irish Free State army. He was killed by rifle fire during an engagement with anti-Treaty forces at Béal na Bláth, near Bandon on 22 August 1922. His remains were taken to Dublin, and following a state funeral, were buried at Glasnevin Cemetery. [Lives by **F. O'Connor** (1937), L. Ó Broin (1980), T.P. Coogan (1990) and J.A. Mackay (1996); Biopic directed by N. Jordan (1996); Bronze cast bust at Fitzgerald Park, Cork / heroic-size marble at the Municipal Gallery, Dublin / circular bronze plaque at Sam's Cross, Clonakilty / and plaster cast of bronze plaque at Collins Barracks, Cork – all by **Seamus Murphy**]

COLLINS, Paddy (1903–1995) Born Cork. He was educated at North Monastery CBS. He played at corner back for Glen Rovers in the 1920s during the club's rise through junior and intermediate ranks, and later won seven Cork County SHC medals with the club. He won two All-Ireland SHC medals (1929 and 1931) and a NHL medal (1930). In the famous All-Ireland decider of 1931, 'Fox' (as he was known) played in all three games against Kilkenny before the title went to Cork, thus becoming the first Glen Rovers player to win an All-Ireland senior hurling medal. In that year also, he was a member of the Munster hurling team which won the Railway Cup. When his playing days were over, he devoted much of his time in an administrative capacity to Glen Rovers and also served as a Cork hurling selector for many years. He died in Wales (at his daughter's residence) on

17 February 1995 and was buried in St Finbarr's Cemetery.

COLLINS, Patrick A. (1844–1905) Born Ballinafana, Fermoy, Co. Cork, the son of Bartholomew Collins, farmer. When the father died in 1847 Mrs Collins disposed of his large lease and emigrated to the United States where she settled in Chelsea, Massachusetts. Ten years later, the family moved to Ohio, but Patrick returned to Boston in 1859. He joined the Fenian movement in 1864 and later the Democratic Party. While attending Harvard Law School (which he had entered in 1871), he was elected to the Massachusetts Lower House (1868–69) and to the Senate (1870–71). He graduated LL.B in 1871 and went into service that same year. In 1880, he supported the Irish leader, **Charles S. Parnell,** on his American visit and was elected as president of the American Land League. He was elected to the US Congress in 1882 and reluctantly served three terms until 1888. Having helped President Grover Cleveland (1837–1908) regain the White House in 1893, he was appointed as US consul-general to London. He was later elected as the second Irish-born mayor of Boston in 1901 and 1903. In failing health, he died suddenly at Hot Springs, Virginia, on 14 September 1905 and, was buried in Holyhood [*sic*] Cemetery, Brookline, Mass. An estimated 100,000 people attended the obsequies. [Life by M.P. Curran (1906)]

COLLINS, Seán (1918–1975) Born Clonakilty, Co. Cork, the son of Seán Collins and nephew of General **Michael Collins** and **Margaret Collins-O'Driscoll**. He was educated at Dominican College, Newbridge, at UCD and at the King's Inns. He was called to the Bar in 1940. He served as Fine Gael TD for West Cork for two periods (1948–57, 1961–9), and was defeated in the elections of 1947 and 1969. He died at St Finbarr's Hospital, Cork, on 11 April 1975 and was buried in St Finbarr's Cemetery.

COLLINS-O'DRISCOLL, Margaret (1878–1945) Born Woodfield, Clonakilty, Co. Cork, the eldest daughter of Michael Collins, farmer, and sister of General **Michael Collins**. She was the aunt of **Seán Collins**. She was educated locally and at Baggot Street Training College, Dublin and was Principal of Lisavaird Girls Schools (1896–1922). In 1901, she married **Patrick O'Driscoll**, a journalist, who was briefly the editor of the *Southern Star* newspaper. He later worked on the staff of the *Cork Free Press* and as a member of the Dáil reporting staff. In 1923, Margaret was elected as a Cumann na nGaedheal TD for Dublin North and represented that constituency until defeated in 1933. She was vice-president of Cumann na nGaedheal in 1926/27. She died on 17 June 1945 and was buried in Glasnevin Cemetery.

COLTHURST, David La Touche (1828–1907) Born Lucan, Co. Dublin, the third son of **Sir Nicholas C. Colthurst**, Bart., and brother of **Sir George C. Colthurst**. Following his education at Eton College, he joined the army in 1847 and served with distinction in the Crimean War. He retired with the rank of lieutenant colonel in 1872. Being both a Roman Catholic (he converted in the early 1860s) and a supporter of Home Rule, he was a surprise nominee for the 1879 by-election for Cork County. Adopted by the Farmers' Club and approved by the Cork Branch of the National Land League, he comprehensively defeated his Conservative opponent, namely, his nephew, Sir George Colthurst. In the 1880 general election, he narrowly won the second Cork County seat from A.J. Kettle, the Parnellite Home Rule candidate. He did not seek re-election in 1885. He died at his residence, Ardrum Lodge, Bournemouth, on 19 January 1907.

COLTHURST, Sir George C. (1824–1878) He was the eldest son of **Sir Nicholas C. Colthurst**, and brother of **David La Touche Colthurst**. He succeeded to the baronetcy on the death of his father in 1829. He was educated at Harrow School. In 1846, he married the only daughter and heiress of St John Jefferyes and thus acquired the estate and castle of Blarney. A

substantial landowner, he was recorded as the owner of 31,260 acres in Co. Cork in 1876. In 1863, he was elected as a Liberal MP for Kinsale and retained the seat until his retirement in 1874. It was he who built the modern Colthurst residence at Blarney and who fostered cricket among his employees and tenants at Ballyvourney. He died of gout at Buxton, Derbyshire, on 24 September 1878.

COLTHURST, Sir Nicholas C. (1789–1829) He was the only son of Sir Nicholas Colthurst, and father of **David La Touche Colthurst** and **Sir George C. Colthurst**. He succeeded to the baronetcy on the death of his father in 1795. From 1812 to his death, he sat as a Conservative MP for Cork City. He died at Brighton, East Sussex, on 22 June 1829.

COMMINS, Andrew (1832–1916) Born Ballybeg, Co. Carlow, the son of John Commins. He was educated at Carlow College, Queen's College, Cork (now UCC), where he graduated MA in 1854 and at London University where he graduated LL.D in 1858. He was called to the English Bar in 1860 and practised on the Northern Circuit. He sat as a Home Rule MP for Roscommon (1880–92) but was defeated on the anti-Parnellite ticket in 1892. In the following year, he was returned in a by-election for Cork South East and retained the seat until his retirement in 1900. He contributed verse to the Young Ireland paper, *The Nation*, under the pseudonym 'John Dawe, Jr.' He died in Liverpool (where he had lived for many years) on 7 January 1916.

CONDON, Edward O'Meagher (1835–1915) Born Brigown Hill, Mitchelstown, Co. Cork. The family emigrated to the US when he was two years of age. He later fought in the American civil war. He joined the Fenian movement and returned to Ireland as an organiser. He was involved with **William P. Allen**, Michael Larkin, **Michael O'Brien** and others in an attack on a police van in Manchester on 18 September 1867 in which a police sergeant was shot. Having been condemned to death, his sentence was commuted to 10 years' penal servitude on account of his American citizenship. He returned to live in the US but later revisited Ireland. He wrote *The Irish Race in America* (1889). He died in New York on 17 December 1915.

CONDON, Seán (1923–2001) Born Cork. A stylish hurler, he played at half-forward with St Finbarr's and eventually became an icon of that club. He won four All-Ireland SHC medals (1942–4 and 1946). In 1944, he captained the Munster hurling team to victory in the final of the Railway Cup. Previously, in 1941, he had captained Cork to an All-Ireland minor hurling title. He was also a footballer of note and won an All-Ireland junior medal in 1951. He died at Cork University Hospital on 27 October 2001 and was buried in St Finbarr's Cemetery.

CONDON, Thomas (1822–1907) Born Ballinafana, Fermoy, Co. Cork, the son of John Condon, stonecutter. The family emigrated to the United States in 1833 and settled in Michigan. In 1849, he entered Auburn Theological Seminary, New York, and in 1852 was accepted by the Mission Board of the Congregational Church for the Oregon mission. He married in October of that year and the couple set out by ship from New York, round Cape Horn, to San Francisco, and finally to Portland, Oregon. Following his ordination, he served various congregations throughout the eastern part of the state. While at high school, he had developed a keen interest in geology and later, in addition to his pastoral work, he made a geological survey of most of Eastern Oregon publishing his researches in numerous journals. He was appointed as professor of Geology and Natural History at the University of Forest Grove, Oregon in 1873 and three years later was appointed to a similar chair at the University of Eugene, Oregon. As state geologist, he published *A Preliminary Report to the Legislative Assembly* (1874) and *Oregon Geology* (1910). He also published *The Two Islands and What Came*

of Them (1902). He died at his daughter's residence near Eugene, on 11 February 1907. The town of Condon, Oregon, is named in his honour. [Lives by E.C. McCornack (1928); and R.D. Clark (1989)]

CONDON, Thomas (1835–1864) Born Kilfinane, Co. Limerick. His family moved to Cork in 1843 where he was educated and eventually qualified as an engineer. He moved to London in 1862 to pursue his career but was forced to return to Cork through ill health. He showed great promise as a poet and was involved in a translation of Dante shortly before his death. He died at Sunday's Well on 9 April 1864 and was buried in St Joseph's Cemetery. [Critical review by T. Burke in *Hibernian Magazine* (1884)]

CONNELL, George M. (*fl.* 1830–1882) Born Cork. He operated as a painter of miniatures from his studio in Fitton Street, Cork. He exhibited at the Royal Hibernian Academy and at the Cork Exhibition of 1852. In 1879, he moved to Dublin and was appointed as a painter of miniatures to the lord lieutenant, the duke of Marlborough. He died in Dublin in 1882 – the last of the Irish painters in his field.

CONNELL, Vivian (1905–1981) Born Carrigaline, Co. Cork. He was largely self-educated and earned a subsequent reputation as a playwright and novelist. His plays 'Throng o' Scarlet' (1941) and 'The Nineteenth Hole of Europe' (1943) were followed by the novels *The Chinese Room* (1943), *The Golden Sleep* (1948) and *The Hounds of Cloneen* (1951). He settled in France but died in Bray, Co. Wicklow, in August 1981.

CONNER, Henry D. (1859–1925) Born Manch, Ballineen, Co. Cork, the son of Daniel Conner. He was educated at Stratford-on-Avon and at TCD where he graduated MA. He was called to the Bar in 1882 and to the Inner Bar in 1899. In the general election of 1910, he contested the Dublin constituency of St Stephen's

Green and was returned as a Unionist candidate. He was appointed as the first circuit court judge for County Cork in 1922 and for Dublin City and County in 1924. He died on 24 July 1925. He was the author of *The Fishery Laws of Ireland* (1892) and other legal commentaries.

CONNER, Rearden (1907–1991) Born Cork, the son of an RIC constable. He emigrated to London and worked as a landscape gardener before turning to broadcasting and writing. His novels included *Shake Hands with the Devil* (1933), *The Sword of Love* (1938), *The Singing Stone* (1951), *Men Must Live* (1937), *A Plain Tale from the Bogs* (1937) and *Epitaph (*posthumously, 1994). He died in Dublin in August 1991. His entire estate was willed to the Leonard Cheshire Foundation.

CONNOLLY, Cornelius (d. 1974) A native of Coolnagrane, Skibbereen, he was active in the War of Independence, having joined the Volunteers in 1913 and later the IRB. He was commandant of the Skibbereen battalion. Imprisoned in 1919, he was one of a party of prisoners who staged a daring and spectacular escape from Strangeways Prison near Manchester. He joined **Tom Barry**'s Flying Column in March 1921 and took part in the attack on Rosscarbery Barracks later that month. Connolly took the pro-Treaty side during the Civil War. In 1923 he was elected to Dáil Éireann as a Cumann na nGaedhal TD for West Cork. He did not contest the 1927 election. He died at his residence, Lisanuhig, Skibbereen at an advanced age on 5 April 1974 and was buried in the New Cemetery, Skibbereen.

CONNOLLY, Thomas L. (1815–1876) Born Cork, the son of Christopher Connolly, dealer and soldier. He was baptised in South Parish Church and his father died when he was three years old. He came under the influence of Father **Theobald Mathew** and studied at the Capuchin Frascati School in Rome. Following his ordination in Lyons in 1838, he returned to Dublin where he worked as a prison chaplain for a few years. In 1842, he emigrated to Nova Scotia, Canada, as secretary to the bishop of Halifax. Ten years later, he was consecrated as bishop of Fredericton, New Brunswick and two years later he founded the Sisters of Charity at St John, New Brunswick. He was elevated to the archbishopric of Halifax in 1859 and built Saint Mary's Cathedral there. Mindful of the delicate denominational balance which existed in Canada, he was a firm supporter of the idea of a confederation. Consequently, he was strongly anti-Fenian ('that pitiable knot of knaves and fools') and opposed the idea of a Fenian monument in Nova Scotia. He took a prominent part in the First Vatican Council and died in Halifax on 27 July 1876.

CONNOR, Charles (1788–1826) Born Co. Cork. He was educated at TCD but did not graduate on account of his being a Roman Catholic. He went to London where he commenced on a successful stage career in 1816.

CONWAY, Kate J. 'Birdie' (d. 1936) Born Carrigaline, Co. Cork. She studied at Cork School of Music under its principal, A. Teur, and took elocution lessons from J.W. Flynn. Her soprano voice first earned her recognition in the Cork Operatic Society before she embarked on a professional operatic career under the stage name, Mlle. del Rita. One of her early professional leading roles was in Sir Charles V. Stanford's (1852–1924) 'Shamus O'Brien' (1896) where she co-starred with Joseph O'Mara. She appeared at venues in Europe and the United States before retiring prematurely from the professional circuit around 1900. Her last public appearance was at the old Cork City Hall in a 1914 charity concert. She was involved with Connradh na Gaeilge in Cork from its foundation and was one of the pioneers of the Cumann na mBan movement in Cork, being president of the Shandon branch at the time of the Treaty. She took the pro-Treaty side in the civil war and devoted much time to the welfare of the Free State army in the early

1920s. She also devoted much of her time to the Magdalen Asylum, Sunday's Well. She died at Golden Grove, Douglas Road, Cork, on 21 February 1936 and was buried in Carrigaline. [Account in L. Condon, *Cumann na mBan and the Women of Ireland* (1969)]

COOK, Charles H. (*c.*1830–*c.*1906) Born Bandon, Co. Cork. He worked as a portrait painter in Cork and twice exhibited at the Royal Hibernian Academy. He eventually moved to England and died at Scarborough.

COOKE, William (*c.*1740–1824) Born Cork. He left Cork in 1766 and established a reputation as an author in London following introductions to Oliver Goldsmith and Edmund Burke. His didactic poem *Conversation*, which was published in 1807 (and had reached four editions by 1815), describes the celebrated Literary Club which was founded by Samuel Johnson (1709–84) and Sir Joshua Reynolds (1723–92) in 1764. He died in London on 3 April 1824.

COOMBES, James (1924–2000) Born Strand Road, Clonakilty, Co. Cork. He was educated at Farranferris College and at St Patrick's College, Maynooth. Following his ordination in 1949, he spent the rest of his clerical life in the diocese of Ross in his native West Cork. He was appointed as administrator in Castlehaven (1976) and Skibbereen before becoming parish priest of Timoleague (1986). A trenchant defender of 'family values' and outspoken critic of the 'permissive age', he was an outstanding local historian. His published work includes *A History of Timoleague and Barryroe* (1969), *Utopia in Glandore* (1970) and *A bishop of Penal Times* (1981). He co-founded and edited *Seanchas Chairbre* of which three issues appeared (1982–93). He retired on the occasion of his golden jubilee in 1999 and took on the role of curate in Clogagh where he died on 11 June 2000. He was buried in Timoleague churchyard.

COPPINGER, John (b. 1723) Born Lisapoole, Co. Cork, the son of James Coppinger. On leaving Ireland, he purchased an estate at Roscoff, Brittany, which was later confiscated during the French Revolution (it was returned to his son, James, on the restoration of the Bourbons). He crossed over to Cornwall, where he settled on a farm at St Austell. He features in Cornish folklore as 'Cruel Coppinger'.

COPPINGER, William (d. 1696) Born Ballyvolane, Cork, the son of Stephen Coppinger, gentleman. He acted as high sheriff of Cork during the Jacobite period. He was attainted by the Williamite government and later settled in France. He died there in 1696 and his widow was granted a state pension by King Louis XIV.

COPPINGER, William (1753–1831) Born St Finbarr's Parish, Cork, into one of the oldest merchant families of the city. He was educated in Paris and considered a military career, but entered the Irish College there and was ordained to the priesthood in 1780. Returning to his native city, he was briefly a curate in St Finbarr's before being appointed as parish priest of Passage West and vicar general of Cork diocese in 1784. In December 1787, he was appointed coadjutor with right of succession to **Matthew McKenna**, bishop of Cloyne and Ross and succeeded him in June 1791. On his appointment as coadjutor, he became parish priest of Youghal where he resided and where he built the parish church, largely from his own resources. However, he came into conflict with the Orange faction of the town and moved to Cove (now Cobh) where he resided at Mount Crozier. During his episcopacy, the pre-cathedral chapel and Ballymore church were built. A prolific pamphleteer and letter-writer (especially during the Veto Controversy of the early 1800s), he published translations of the *Imitatio Christi* (1795), of Scheffmaker's *Catechism* and J.B. Bossuet's (1627–1704) *Exposition of the Doctrines of the Catholic Church* (1789). His *Life of Nano Nagle* (a funeral sermon) was published in 1794. He died at Cove of 6 August 1831 and was buried in the grounds of the old chapel. His remains were later transferred to the crypt of St

Colman's Cathedral, Cobh. [Chalk drawing by J. Comerford at the National Gallery, Dublin; Engraved in stipple by C. Rolls]

CORBET, William (1779–1842) Born Ballymacthomas, off Blarney Street, Cork, the son of Frederick Corbet, gentleman farmer. He was educated at TCD where he graduated BA (1797) but was expelled on account of his membership of the United Irishmen. He went to France and was a member of Napper Tandy's (c.1737–1803) small French expeditionary force which landed in Co. Donegal in 1798, but which, on hearing of General Humbert's defeat at Ballinamuck, headed for Norway. He was subsequently arrested in Hamburg and was returned to Dublin where he was lodged in Kilmainham Gaol. He escaped, rejoined the French army, and eventually rose to the rank of general. In 1831, he was appointed as Commander-in-Chief of the French forces in Greece. He died at St Denis on 12 August 1842.

CORBETT, Daniel (fl. c.1750) He worked in Cork as an engraver in the middle of the 18th century. He was the father of **John Corbett**, artist, and of **Joseph Corbett**, sculptor. Nine of his engravings appeared in **Charles Smith's** *History of Cork*. [Marble bust by **John Hogan** at the Royal Hibernian Academy]

CORBETT, John (1779/80–1815) Born Cork, the son of **Daniel Corbett,** engraver, and a brother of **Joseph Corbett**, sculptor. Showing talent at an early age, he was sent to London to study portraiture under his fellow-Corkonian, **James Barry**. He returned to Cork and pursued a successful but short-lived career. He died of a brain fever in February 1815. [Portrait by himself at the age of nineteen]

CORBETT, Joseph (fl. c.1792) Born Cork, the son of **Daniel Corbett**, engraver, and a brother of **John Corbett,** artist. He showed great promise as a sculptor and was awarded a £30 premium by the Royal Dublin Society for a piece in marble. He later worked with the

sculptor, Edward Smyth, on the Dublin Custom House.

CORBY, Henry (d. 1917) He was educated at Queen's College, Cork (now UCC) and was later appointed as professor of Obstetrics and Gynaecology there in 1883 (to 1924). He was a consultant physician at Cork Maternity Hospital and a surgeon at the South Infirmary Hospital. Among his publications were papers entitled 'Industry and Ability', 'Bacteria, the Foes and Friends of Man' and 'Some Medical Aspects of School Life'. He was high sheriff of Cork in 1904 and was president of the Incorporated Medical Practitioners' Association. He died in Cork in April 1917.

CORKERY, Daniel (1878–1961) Born Mullinroe, Clondrohid, Co. Cork. The family later moved to Macroom where they had a meal and general grocery business. During the War of Independence, he was officer commanding 7th Battalion, Cork No.1 Brigade. In the 1921 election to the Second Dáil, he was elected as a Sinn Féin TD for the County Cork constituency and was re-elected in 1922 as an anti-Treaty candidate. He represented North Cork as Republican TD (1923–7) and for Fianna Fáil (1927–32; 1933–7). In 1937, he was defeated as a candidate for West Cork and was subsequently chosen to sit in Seanad Éireann (1938–48). A shopkeeper by occupation, he was president of Macroom GAA Club for many years and his death occurred on 23 April 1961 while watching his club play a senior football championship match at Glantane. He was buried in St Colman's Cemetery, Macroom.

CORKERY, Daniel (1878–1964) Born Gardiner's Hill, Cork, the son of William Corkery, carpenter. He was educated at PBC, Cork and at St Patrick's College of Education, Dublin, where he qualified as a primary teacher in 1908. He was employed at St Patrick's NS, Gardiner's Hill, Cork, where his pupils included **Frank O'Connor** and **Seamus Murphy**. He joined Connradh na Gaeilge and founded the

Cork Dramatic Society with **Terence McSwiney**. He resigned from primary school teaching in 1921 and worked as an art teacher and inspector of Irish with the Cork County technical education committee until his appointment as professor of English at UCC in 1931. On his retirement in 1947, he was awarded an honorary D.Litt. of the National University of Ireland. In 1950, he was appointed as a member of the Arts Council and he also served as a member of Seanad Éireann (1951–4). He is best known for his authorship of *The Hidden Ireland* (1924) – a work which deals with the position of Gaelic poetry in the eighteenth century and which aroused and still arouses controversy in its interpretation. He also wrote *The Threshold of Quiet* (1916), *Synge and Anglo-Irish Literature* (1931) and *The Fortunes of the Irish Language* (1954). His short story collections include, *A Munster Twilight* (1916), *The Hounds of Banba* (1920), *The Stormy Hills* (1929), *Earth out of Earth* (1939) and *An Doras Dúnta* (1953). His plays consisted of 'The Labour Leader' (1919), 'The Yellow Bittern' (1920), 'Resurrection' (1924) and 'Fohnam the Sculptor' (1939). With **Séamus Ó hAodha**, he wrote the miracle play, 'Clochar' (1919). He died at Passage West on 31 December 1964 and was buried in St Joseph's Cemetery, Cork. [Lives by G.B. Saul (1973) and P. Maume (1993); Headstone at St Joseph's Cemetery, Cork, and life-size bronze at Cork Municipal Gallery – both by **Seamus Murphy**]

CORRY, Martin J. (1889–1979) Born Cork, the son of Martin G. Corry, an RIC head constable. He was educated at PBC, Cork, but went into farming when his father purchased a farm in Mourneabbey on his retirement in 1904. The family moved in 1916 to another farm at 'Sunville', Glounthaune. Here he became involved in the activities of the Cork No. 1 Brigade of the IRA and spent periods of imprisonment in Cork, Belfast and Wormwood Scrubs. He took the anti-Treaty side during the civil war and was interned in Newbridge detention camp until January 1924. He was elected as the first Fianna Fáil TD for East Cork

in the 1927 general election and continued in that capacity until the general election of 1969. With the exception of a two-month period in 1974, he sat on Cork County Council from August 1924 until his death – a total of over 54 years. He also sat on Cobh UDC (1950–67). He held many positions in the various farming organisations in which he was active until his death at 'Sunville' on 14 February 1979. He was buried in Midleton Cemetery.

COSGRAVE, William T. (1880–1965) Born Dublin. In 1909, as a member of Sinn Féin, he was elected to Dublin Corporation. He took part in the Easter Rising of 1916 and was sentenced to death which was later commuted to penal servitude for life. However, in early 1917, he was released under an amnesty. He was returned as a Sinn Féin MP for Kilkenny in the 1918 General Election and was elected as minister for Local Government in the first Dáil. In 1922, he supported the Treaty and following the deaths of Arthur Griffith and **Michael Collins**, he was appointed as president of the Executive Council of the Irish Free State. In April 1923, he became leader of the newly-launched Cumann na nGaedheal Party, the precursor of modern Fine Gael. He represented Cork City in the Dáil (1927–44). He died in Dublin on 16 November 1965. [Life by S. Collins (1996)]

COSGROVE, William [VC] (1888–1936) Born Upper Aghada, Co. Cork. He worked locally as a farm labourer before enlisting in the Royal Munster Fusiliers in 1910. Having served in Burma for five years, he was posted to the Dardannelles with the First Battalion of the regiment. On 26 April 1915, 'Corporal Cosgrove pulled down the posts of the enemy's high wire entanglements single–handed, notwithstanding a terrific fire from front and flanks' (reads the citation) – an action for which he was awarded the Victoria Cross. He was also promoted to the rank of sergeant. Because of his wounds (fifty-three in all), he was invalided home and was used in recruiting drives. Following the disbandment of the regiment in 1922, he served with the Northumberland Fusiliers in India and Burma, retiring with the rank of staff-sergeant. Cosgrove, who was 1.98m (6ft. 6in.) tall, died at the Queen Alexandra Military Hospital, London, on 14 July 1936 following a long illness. He was buried in Upper Aghada Cemetery.

COTTER, Edward (1902–1972) Born Bantry, Co. Cork. During the War of Independence, he was an active member of the Bantry Company, IRA, of which he was a section commander at the Truce. He took the Republican side in the civil war and was interned in Cork and Newbridge for a year. He was elected as a member of Bantry Town Commissioners (1941) and of Cork County Council (1942–72). He was unsuccessful in a 1949 by-election but was elected as a Fianna Fáil TD for West Cork in 1954 and sat until his retirement in 1969. A licensed vintner in Bantry, he died at Bantry Hospital on 11 December 1972, having been in poor health for some years. He was buried in Abbey Cemetery, Bantry.

COTTER, Sir James (c.1630–1705) Born Ballinsperrig, Carrigtohill, Co. Cork, the son of Edmond Cotter, gentleman. He was the father of **James Cotter**. A noted soldier, he fought on the Royalist side during the English civil war. Having had his estates handed back at the Restoration, he created a sensation in 1664 when he arranged the assassination in Switzerland of John Liste, one of the party who had signed the death warrant of King Charles I. He again played a leading part when he was a commander of the Munster Jacobite forces during the Williamite War. Under the Treaty of Limerick, he was once again restored to his estates.

COTTER, James (1689–1720) Born Ballinsperrig, Carrigtohill, Co. Cork, the son of **Sir James Cotter**. A Jacobite and a Tory, he was named in the Irish Parliament as being involved in a Dublin riot during the general election of 1713. When the Whigs came into power in the following year through the death of Queen Anne, he became a prime target of the Cork leaders of that party. Following a farcical trial, 'Seamus Óg' was executed on 7 May 1720 having being convicted of raping a Quaker woman, Elizabeth Squibb. He was buried in Carrigtohill Graveyard on the following night. [Profile by B. Ó Buachalla in O'Flanagan and Buttimer (eds), *Cork: History and Society* (1993)]

COTTER, Sir James L. (c.1787–1834) Born Rockforest, Mallow, Co. Cork, the son of Sir James Laurence Cotter, Bart. He was educated at TCD where he graduated BA (1808) and LL.B/LL.D (1820). He sat as MP for Mallow (1812–20). He succeeded to the baronetcy on the death of his father in February 1829. He died on 31 December 1834.

COTTER, Patrick (1760–1806) Born Kinsale, Co. Cork. He developed into a giant by the age of 18 and was contracted to exhibit all over Britain – his parents being paid at the rate of £50 a year for three years. He exhibited widely in England from the age of eighteen as 'Patrick Cotter O'Brien, the Kinsale Giant'. He left £2,000 when he died at Clifton, Bristol, on 8 September 1806. He was buried in the Roman Catholic Chapel at Trenchard Street, Bristol. His remains were discovered during excavations in the 1970s and his height was computed at 2.46m (8' 1") by the department of Anatomy of Bristol University before being re-interred. [Life by G. Frankom and J.H. Musgrave (1976); Plaster casts of hands at the museum of the Royal College of Surgeons, London]

COTTER, Thomas Y. (1805–1882) Born Bantry, Co. Cork, the son of a naval purser. Following a period as a naval cadet, he studied medicine in London. In December 1835, he was appointed as first colonial surgeon of South Australia and took up duties in January 1837. However, the task of providing medical services for both newcomers and prisoners proved too difficult for him and he was suspended in August 1839. Having served in various medical positions, he finally settled as medical officer in

Port Augusta, South Australia, in 1870. He died there on 9 January 1882. He was also interested in literary matters and spent periods as editor of the *South Australian Magazine* and the *South Australian Almanack*. [Life by J.B. Cleland (1941)]

COTTER, William (1866–1940) Born Cloyne, Co. Cork. He entered St Patrick's College, Maynooth, in 1885 and was ordained in 1892. He left for the English Mission and served at Ryde, Isle of Wight, in the new diocese of Portsmouth (1882). He was appointed to the cathedral chapter in 1900, and five years later, he was consecrated as auxiliary bishop of Portsmouth. He succeeded to the bishopric in 1910. He died at Portsmouth on 24 October 1940. At the time of his death, part of his diocese (the Channel Islands) was under German occupation.

COTTRELL, Con (1917–1982) Born Bally-hooleen, Ballinhassig, Co. Cork, and was educated at Goggin's Hill NS. He first played competitive hurling in 1940, but by 1946 had won five All-Ireland SHC medals (1941–4 and 1946). His most regular position was at centre-field, where he played in 1947 when Cork went down by a single point to Kilkenny. He played his club hurling with Ballinhassig, but won a County Louth SFC medal with Cooley Kickhams when he was a clerical student in the Rosminian Order. He retired from the game in 1947 on his ordination to the priesthood. He worked at St Patrick's, Upton, for many years and was also superior of St Joseph's School for the Blind, Dublin, for a long period. He spent his last years, in declining health, at Upton and died at Cork Regional Hospital on 3 March 1982. He was buried in the Community Cemetery, Upton.

COUGHLAN, Eugene ['Eudie'] (b. 1900) Born Blackrock, Cork, the son of Patrick Coughlan, fisherman, who won All-Ireland SHC medals in 1893 and 1894. He was the brother-in-law of **Michael ('Gah') Aherne** and **Paddy ('Balty') Aherne**. He won five All-Ireland SHC medals (1919, 1926, 1928–9 and 1931); two NHL medals (1926 and 1930); and two Railway Cup medals (1928–9).

COURTNEY, T.C. (1895–1961) Born Cork. He was educated at North Monastery CBS, at PBC, Cork; and at UCC where he graduated BE. He worked as an engineer with the Cork, Bandon, and South Coast Railway Company, on the assembly of the Ford plant at The Marina, and on new installations at the Harland and Wolff Shipyard, Belfast. He joined the National Army Corps of Engineers in 1922 and rose to the rank of major before resigning in 1925. He then worked as an engineering inspector at the department of Local Government and Health, and after a spell as County Surveyor of Tipperary, he became the chief engineering advisor to his former department in 1934. During World War II, he was appointed as chairman of the Turf Development Board and a month after taking up this position in 1941, he was responsible for organising 25,000 bog workers in 946 bogs. In February 1949, he was appointed as manager of CIE (Córas Iompair Éireann) until his retirement through ill health in August 1958. While at CIE, he played a key role in the introduction of diesel-powered loco-motives, in improved rolling stock, and in the development of the Great Southern Hotels. He died in Waterville, Co. Kerry, on 15 August 1961.

COUSSMAKER, George (c.1792–1821) He was the only son of Colonel K.H.G. Coussmaker and Catherine Southwell, the eldest daughter of the 20th Baron de Clifford. The Southwell/de Clifford family controlled the Kinsale borough for which Coussmaker was MP (1813–21). He died, unmarried, in 1821, and the de Clifford baronetcy subsequently descended through his only sister, Sophia, Baroness de Clifford.

COVENEY, Hugh (1935–1998) Born Cork, the son of Patrick F. Coveney, quantity surveyor. He was educated at CBC, Cork; and at Clongowes Wood College. He entered the family business, of which he became the principal partner. One of Cork's leading businessmen, he entered politics in 1979 when he was elected as a Fine Gael member of Cork Corporation and later served as lord mayor (1982/83). He was elected to the Dáil in 1981 as a TD for Cork South but lost his seat in February of the following year. However, he regained the seat in the following November and held it until November 1987. He was persuaded to contest a by-election in November 1994, which he won, and was appointed as minister for Defence and the Marine in the following month. Controversially, he was forced to resign his ministry in May 1995 and was appointed as minister of state in the department of Finance and Office of Public Works – a position which he held until 1997. He died on 14 March 1998 as a result of a cliff-top accident at Robert's Cove, near his Minane Bridge residence. He was buried in St Michael's Cemetery, Blackrock. Coveney was a prominent yachtsman and captained the Irish team in the 1979 Admiral's Cup.

COVENY, Robert (1809–1878) Born Springfield, Tracton, Co. Cork, the son of Robert Coveny, landowner. With his brother, Thomas, he emigrated to Sydney, Australia, in 1835 where the brothers opened a supply business. Following bankruptcy in 1843 (with the debts being cleared a year later), the brothers parted company in 1845. Robert went into the wholesale and retail business of imported goods such as tea, wine, tobacco, soaps, sugar etc. He took a keen interest in public affairs, and, in 1856, was one of the organisers of the reception for the ex-Young Irelander, Charles Gavan Duffy (1816–1903), the future Prime Minister of Victoria. He was also one of the main movers in the establishment and administration of St Vincent's Hospital, Sydney. He died on 16 November 1878.

COX, Sir Richard (1650–1733) Born Bandon, the son of Captain Richard Cox. His family having lost heavily during the Confederate War (1641–49), he studied law at Gray's Inn and was called to the Bar in 1673. He built up a successful law practice and was appointed as

recorder of Kinsale. He also founded the town of Dunmanway where he had his estate. An ardent advocate of the Protestant interest, he left Ireland for Bristol during the pro-Catholic lord lieutenantcy of Richard Talbot, earl of Tyreconnell (1686–90). He returned to Ireland with the forces of William of Orange and took part in the battle of the Boyne. In 1691, he was appointed as military governor of Cork and was knighted by the lord lieutenant, Lord Sydney, in the following year. An ardent Tory, he was appointed as Irish Lord Chancellor in 1703 but fell foul of the Whigs in 1707 and was removed from office. He served as chief justice of the Queen's Bench from 1711 to the Hanoverian succession of 1714 when he was again forced to leave office. He died in Dunmanway on 3 May 1733. His *Hibernia Anglicana, or The history of Ireland from the conquest thereof by the English to this present time* (1689 and 1690) treats of Irish history from a colonial perspective. [Portrait at the Royal Hospital, Kilmainham, Dublin.]

CRANITCH, Micheál (1912–1999) Born Rathcormac, Co. Cork, the son of Matthew Cranitch. He was educated locally, at Fermoy CBS and at De la Salle Training College, Waterford, where he qualified as a primary school teacher. He spent most of his career as principal teacher at Rathduff National School, Co. Cork. He later attended UCC where he graduated MA. An accomplished Irish traditional musician and Gaelic revivalist, he was a lifelong member of the Grenagh GAA Club. He also served as chairman of the Cork County library committee and as a member of many Cork cultural societies. In 1969, he was appointed to Seanad Éireann as a nominee of Taoiseach **Jack Lynch**. He lost the seat in 1973 having served as Cathaoirleach from January to June of that year. He regained the seat in 1977 as a member of the agricultural panel and served until 1982. He died at his Rathduff residence on 23 November 1999 and was buried in Grenagh Cemetery.

CRAWFORD, Arthur F. SHARMAN (1862– 1943) Born Crawfordsburn, Co. Down, the fourth son of Arthur Johnston Sharman-Crawford, barrister and company director. A director of Beamish and Crawford Ltd, he was a generous benefactor to Cork. He provided the site and building of the Sharman-Crawford Technical School and provided scholarships and financial support to the Cork School of Art. He was also a governor of the Cork Dairy Institute and a founder member of Cork Golf Club. He died at his residence, Lota Lodge, on 14 July 1943 and was buried in St Lappan's Cemetery, Little Island. [Commemorative plaque at entrance to the Crawford College of Art and Design, Sharman Crawford Street, Cork]

CRAWFORD, William (*fl.* 1790–1800) Born Crawfordsburn, Co. Down, the fourth son of James Crawford, landowner. In 1792, he founded the brewing firm of 'Beamish and Crawford' with **William Beamish** and two others. He built a new residence, 'Lakelands', at Blackrock. His son, William (d. 1840), was a founder of the first School of Art in Cork. [Memorial statue by **John Hogan** at the Crawford Art Gallery]

CRAWFORD, William H. (1812–1888) Born 'Lakelands', Blackrock, Cork, the son of William Crawford (d. 1840) and grandson of **William Crawford**. With Richard Pigott Beamish, he took over the Beamish and Crawford Brewery in 1850. An ascetic, he was a noted local benefactor and philanthropist. In 1885, he provided £20,000 for the building of the Crawford Science and Art Schools, and also endowed the new St FinBarre's Cathedral and Queen's College, Cork (now UCC). He died on 16 October 1888. [Commemorative plaque at the Crawford Art Gallery, Emmet Place, Cork]

CREAGH, James (1701–*c.*1790) Born Co. Cork. He emigrated to France while a young man and subsequently became an officer in Lord Clare's regiment. He was seriously wounded at the battle of Fontenoy in 1745 and lost an eye at the battle of Rosbach in 1767. He retired on pension in 1771 and saw the outbreak of the French Revolution.

CREAGH, Peter (d. 1705) Born Limerick, the grand-nephew of Richard Creagh (*c.*1525–1585), archbishop of Armagh. Having been educated on the Continent, he entered the church and was consecrated as bishop of Cork and Cloyne by Pope Clement X in 1676. During the fallout from the Popish Plot (1678), he was obliged to go into hiding in his diocese. However, he was discovered and imprisoned in Dublin. Following the accession of James II in 1685, he was appointed as archbishop of Tuam and later as archbishop of Dublin. With the defeat of James, he followed the Jacobite court to France and was appointed by James as archbishop of Dublin on 9 March 1693 – a position which he was unable to take up. He died in Strasbourg on 20 July 1705.

CREAN, Eugene (1854–1939) Born Douglas Street, Cork, the son of Charles Crean, publican. A carpenter by trade, he was involved in the trade union movement in Cork city and as a representative of the Carpenters' Society, was elected president of the Cork United Trades Workers Association. In 1892, he was chosen as an anti-Parnellite nationalist candidate to contest Queen's County in the general election and was duly elected, retaining his seat in 1895. Five years later, he was selected to contest the South East Cork constituency as a nationalist candidate. He defeated the Healyite candidate, Matthew Hickey. He retained his seat to 1918, having stood as an O'Brienite candidate in the two elections of 1910. He was also a member of Cork Corporation and was elected mayor of Cork in 1899. He was the last bearer of the title 'Mayor' (changed to 'Lord Mayor' in 1900). He was a patron of the GAA in its early years and was president of Cork County Board (1890/1891). He died at his Douglas Street residence on 12 January 1939.

CREEDON, Mary A. (1811–1855) Born Co. Cork, the daughter of John Creedon. In July 1839, she entered the Sisters of Mercy Order in Dublin and took the name of Sister Mary Francis on her profession in 1841. In that year she renewed her acquaintance with Bishop M.A. Fleming of Saint John's, Newfoundland, whom she had previously met in Newfoundland while visiting her married sister. Fleming saw the need for separate schools for 'the children of the wealthy classes, who were both able and anxious to pay for their education' and where they would be taught 'the elegant and fashionable accomplishments of the day'. Sister Mary Francis and two other volunteers began their work in Newfoundland in June 1842 and opened their first school with forty-two pupils in the following year. However, by 1847, she was left alone and the school closed. Yet she resisted all attempts to recall her to Dublin and began ministering to the elderly and the poor. Her luck changed in December 1850 when her niece was professed and a young novice arrived from Ireland. This ensured the ultimate success of the Order in Newfoundland. She died on 15 July 1855 in Saint John's and was buried at Belvedere Orphanage. [Sketch by P. O'Neill in *Remarkable Women of Newfoundland and Labrador* (1976)]

CROFTS, Ambrose (1894–1963) Born Cork. He was educated at North Monastery CBS, Cork, and studied for the priesthood in Rome. He was ordained as a member of the Dominican Order in 1919. On his return to Ireland, he ministered in Dublin where he became deeply involved in the activities of the Catholic Young Men's Society, becoming its national organiser for a time. From 1938 until 1946 he was appointed as vicar provincial of the Dominican Order in Australia and New Zealand. On his return to Ireland in 1949, he was put in charge of Dominican Publications. In 1962, he was appointed as prior at Holy Cross, Sligo. He died at Garden Hill Nursing Home, Sligo, on 28 September 1963 and was buried in Sligo Cemetery.

CROKE, Thomas W. (1824–1902) Born Ballyclough, Co. Cork, the son of William Croke, estate agent. He was educated at Charleville Endowed School, at Menin in Belgium, and at the Irish College in Rome

where he graduated DD on 1847. He returned to Ireland and served as a curate in Charleville and Midleton before taking up the position of professor of Ecclesiastical History at Newman's Catholic University, Dublin. He then served as president of St Colman's College, Fermoy (1858–66), where he supervised the building of the new college. He was appointed as parish priest of Doneraile in 1866 and attended the First Vatican Council in 1870 as a theological advisor to the bishop of Cork, **William Delany**. While attending the council, he became friendly with the future Cardinal Manning of Westminster, and mainly through Manning's influence, was appointed as bishop of Auckland, New Zealand, in that year. Despite a successful episcopate in New Zealand, his health failed and in 1875, he was raised to the archbishopric of Cashel. He was a strong supporter of the various nationalist movements (especially the Land League), and of athletics and Gaelic games. He became the first patron of the Gaelic Athletic Association and Croke Park is named in his honour. He died at his residence at Cashel on 22 July 1902 and was buried at his cathedral in Thurles. [Life by M. Tierney (1976)]

CROKER, Richard (1841–1922) Born Ballyva, near Clonakilty, Co. Cork, but the family emigrated to New York in 1844. He began work as a machinist but soon entered local politics as a Tammany (a group of New York Democrats) member and became an alderman in 1868. 'Boss' Croker was appointed city coroner in 1873 with a salary of $25,000. He succeeded as Tammany leader in 1886 and remained in that position until his retirement to England in 1903, having amassed a vast fortune. He set up as a horse trainer in Berkshire. When he was refused permission to train at Newmarket, he returned to his native land in 1907 and bought the Glencairn Estate near Leopardstown. In that same year, his horse, Orby, won both the English and Irish Derbies. On his wife's death in 1914, he married a young Cherokee Indian princess – a move which was opposed by his family and which resulted in subsequent litigation over his property. He died on 29 April 1922 and was buried at Glencairn. He is remembered for his definition of an honest politician as, 'A man who, when he's bought, stays bought'.

CROKER, Temple H. (1729–c.1790) Born Sarsfield's Court, Glanmire, Co. Cork. He was educated at Westminster School and at Christ Church, Oxford, where he graduated BA (1750), and MA (1760). From his position as chaplain to the earl of Hillsborough, he was given a living in Kent. However, due to financial circumstances, he was declared bankrupt in 1773. He was then 'exiled' to a rectory at St Christopher's in the West Indies where he published four sermons under the title *Where am I? How came I here? What are my wants? What are my duties?* He also published numerous articles on literature and science including *Orlando Furioso* (1755) and *The Satires of Ludovico Aristo* (1759). He was the editor of *The Complete Dictionary of Arts and Sciences* (3 vols, 1764–6).

CROKER, Thomas Crofton (1798–1854) Born Cork, the son of an army major. As an amateur draughtsman, he exhibited in Cork in 1817. In the following year, he departed for London but frequently returned home. In 1830, he married Marianne, the daughter of the artist, Francis Nicholson. For his *Researches in the South of Ireland* (1824), Nicholson and Marianne drew the views, while he provided the antiquarian details during their tour of 1821. He also published *Fairy Legends and Traditions in the South of Ireland* (1825). This publication of folk traditions received wide acclaim and was translated into German by the Brothers Grimm. He also published *Legends of Killarney* (1831), *The Adventures of Barney Mahoney* (1832) and *My Village Versus Our Village* (1832). His folk song collections included *Popular Songs of Ireland* (1839), *Historical Songs of Ireland* (1841), *The Keen in the South of Ireland* (1844) and *Popular Songs Illustrative of the French Invasion of Ireland* (1845/1847). He died at Old Brompton on 8 August 1854. [Portrait by Daniel Maclise in *Maclise's Portrait Gallery* (1898)]

CROLY, David G. (1829–1889) Born Clonakilty, Co. Cork, but grew up in New York. Having enrolled at the University of the City of New York for a year, he took a job as reporter for the New York *Evening Post* and subsequently for the New York *Herald*. In 1858, he married Jane Cunningham, who is regarded as America's first lady journalist. Following periods of management with the New York *World* and *Daily Graphic*, he resigned from newspaper journalism in 1878. Previously, in 1873, he had founded a magazine, the *Modern Thinker*, which ran to only three issues. He developed a great interest in the new philosophical theory of Positivism and published in 1871 his *Primer of Positivism*. However, he is mainly remembered for a still earlier publication entitled, *Miscegenation* (1864), which advocated breeding between black and white people 'to attain the fullest results of civilisation'. Thus a new word, 'miscegenation', entered the English language. He died on 29 April 1889. His son, H.D. Croly (1869–1930), was also a noted journalist and author.

CRONIN, Edmund J. (c.1897–1946) Born Liscullane, Charleville, Co. Cork, the son of John Cronin, farmer and JP. He joined the IRA in December 1920 and was attached to 'C' company, 4th batt., Cork No. 2 brigade. Following the Treaty, he joined the Free State Army and had risen to the rank of commandant on his resignation in 1927. In February 1932, he founded the Army Comrades Association (ACA) which became known from April 1933 as the Blueshirts and of which General Eoin O'Duffy (1892–1944) assumed the presidency in July 1933. Cronin split with O'Duffy and for some time led a rival Blueshirt organisation. In December 1936, he unsuccessfully attempted to obtain permission from General Franco (1892–1975) to form a rival Irish Brigade to fight in the Spanish Civil War. He farmed in the Charleville area until 1939 when he moved to Worcester, England, as a commercial representative. Widowed in

1942, he returned to Dublin for health reasons in the following January and died in a Leeson Street nursing home on 12 March 1946. He was buried at Shandrum Graveyard, Co. Cork.

CRONIN, Elizabeth (1879–1956) Born Ballyvourney, Co. Cork, the daughter of Seán Ó hIarlaithe, schoolteacher. 'Bess' Cronin was educated locally and spent her teenage years on an uncle's farm nearby. She imbibed the songs and stories of the locality where her family had a strong tradition in poetry and music. She married Seán Ó Cróinín and lived at Carraig an Adhmaid, Ballymakeera. In the 1940s and '50s, she became the focus of attention of international folksong collectors and was regularly featured on BBC radio programmes. The piper, Seamus Ennis, called her 'The Muskerry Queen of Song'. She died at Macroom Hospital (she lived at her son's residence in Cork Street) on 2 June 1956 and was buried in Reilig Ghobnatan, Ballyvourney. *The Songs of Elizabeth Cronin, Irish Traditional Singer* (2000), was compiled and edited by her grandson, Daibhí Ó Cróinín, and was accompanied by two CDs. She was the mother of Donncha Ó Cróinín (d. 1990), the Irish scholar, and of **Seán Ó Cróinín**, folklore collector.

CRONIN, Jerry (1925–1990) Born Coolagown, Fermoy, Co. Cork. He was educated at Conna NS and at Fermoy CBS. He was secretary of the Mallow Board of the Beet Growers' Association before his election in 1965 as Fianna Fáil TD for Cork North East. He was also a founder member of the Mallow Industrial Development Association and first secretary of Mallow Show Society. He was parliamentary secretary at the department of Agriculture and Fisheries (1969–70) and minister for Defence (1970–3). He also served on Cork County Council from 1967 to 1970. Having been elected as an MEP in 1979 (to 1984), he did not seek re-election to the Dáil in the general election of 1981. While serving as an MEP, he was a member of the EC Parliamentary Committee of Regional Policy and Planning. Following a long illness, he died at Cork Regional Hospital on 19 October 1990 and was buried in St Joseph's Cemetery, Mallow.

CROOKE, Sir Thomas (d. *c*.1624/5) A 'New English' adventurer, he was one of the principal financiers (largely from the assets of piracy) of the huge pilchard industry which prospered in the Baltimore district in the first half of the seventeenth century. At its most prosperous, this industry had a turnover of £30,000 a year and was the main cause of the 'Sack of Baltimore' in 1631. He procured a charter for Baltimore from King James I and the incorporation took place on Lady Day (25 March) 1613 with Crooke as its first member. He was made knight and baronet in March 1624. He died 'shortly afterwards' and has given his name to Crookstown.

CROSBIE, George (1864–1934) Born Cork, the son of **Thomas Crosbie**, proprietor of the *Cork Examiner*, and father of **George Crosbie (1899–1972)**. He was educated at St Vincent's Seminary, Cork, and at Tullabeg College, Co. Offaly. Though called to the Irish Bar, he never practised. He joined the *Cork Examiner* in the 1880s and became chairman of Thomas Crosbie and Co. on his father's death in 1899. He was one of the founders (and for seventeen years the chairman) of the Cork Industrial Development Association. He was also the intermediary in the purchase of Cork Park by Henry Ford and of Rushbrooke Docks by Furness Withy. He was an unsuccessful UIP (United Ireland Party) candidate in the keenly fought Cork City by-election of 1909 and was also unsuccessful in his attempt to gain a Seanad seat in 1924. However, he was elected to the Seanad as a Government nominee in 1932. He died at his residence, Knockrea Park, Cork, on 26 November 1934. He was the author of the play, 'The Casting Vote, or, Paddy Flaherty's Vision' which was published in Dublin (1920).

CROSBIE, George (1899–1972) Born Cork, the second son of **George Crosbie (1864– 1934)**, newspaper proprietor. He was educated at CBC, Cork, and at Clongowes Wood College. He served in the British Royal Navy in World War I. He joined the Maritime Inscription on its foundation in 1940 and became its first commanding officer in Cork. In February 1941, he was commissioned as lieutenant-commander in the Irish Marine Service and throughout the Emergency he served as commanding officer of the Marine Depot at Haulbowline and as marine executive officer, Southern Command. He later retired with the rank of Commander. He was a director of Thomas Crosbie & Co. Ltd and also held directorships in several other companies. As chairman of the Cork Opera House Company (1958–69), he played a leading role in the rebuilding of the present Cork Opera House following the destruction by fire of the old building. In 1959, he was a member of the commission of inquiry to advise on the setting up of a new television service and was one of the first appointees to the RTÉ Authority. He was also a prominent sportsman, being president of the Golfing Union of Ireland (1938–42) and admiral of the Royal Cork Yacht Club (1958–64). He died at the Mercy Home, Cork, on 6 February 1972 and was buried in St Finbarr's Cemetery.

CROSBIE, James (1902–1984) Born Cork, the son of James Crosbie of the *Cork Examiner* publishing family. He was educated at PBC, Cork; Clongowes Wood College and at the King's Inns, Dublin. He was called to the Bar in 1925 and practised on the Munster Circuit for some years before joining the family business as a director on his father's death in 1931. He was a member of Seanad Éireann (1938–51; 1954–7) and was an unsuccessful Fine Gael candidate for Cork Borough in the 1944 general election. He was a member of the Irish delegation to the Council of Europe (1949–56) and was elected vice-president of that body in 1956 – the first Irishman to be so honoured. From 1954 to 1961, he was the Irish representative on the European Commission for Human Rights. He was chairman of Thomas Crosbie & Co. Ltd from 1970 until ill health forced him to resign in 1975. He died at the Bon Secours Hospital, Cork, on

16 February 1984 and was buried in St Finbarr's Cemetery.

CROSBIE, Thomas (1827–1899) Born Ardfert, Co. Kerry, the father of **George Crosbie (1864–1934)**. He was educated locally and at the age of fifteen, he joined the reporting staff of the *Cork Examiner* which had been founded in the previous year by **J.F. Maguire**. One of his contemporaries at the newspaper was the future parliamentarian, **Justin McCarthy**, who was to remain a lifelong friend. He later became Maguire's partner and the effective managing director of the newspaper. On Maguire's death in 1872, he bought out the proprietorship. Under his management, the *Cork Examiner*, previously published three times weekly, became a daily. The *Evening Echo* was launched in 1892, and a weekly edition, the *Cork Weekly Examiner* appeared in 1895. He served as president of both the Irish Association of Journalists and of the Institute of Journalists. In October 1897, he was forced to retire from active business through ill health and died at his Aghada, Co. Cork, residence on 30 June 1899. He was buried in St Finbarr's Cemetery.

CROSS, Eric (1903–1980) Born Newry, Co. Down, the son of a British official in the diplomatic service. He was educated in England and had a reputation as a chemist and as an inventor. His publication of *The Tailor and Ansty* (1942) caused a sensation when it was banned under the Censorship of Publications Act. The book dealt with the conversations of **Tadhg Ó Buachalla** (Tim Buckley), a story-teller of Gougane Barra, Co. Cork, and his wife, Anastatia (Anstey). Cross died a recluse at Cloona Lodge, Westport, Co. Mayo, on 5 September 1980. He was buried in Knappagh Cemetery. [Analysis by J. Cahalan in *Éire-Ireland* (1979); Life-size bronze by **Seamus Murphy**]

CROSS, Philip (1824–1888) Born Shandy Hall, Coachford, Co. Cork, the son of Philip Cross, landowner. Having obtained a medical qualification, he joined the British Army and rose to the rank of surgeon-major in the 53rd Regiment, serving in the Far East, Africa and Canada. In 1869, he married Mary Laura Marriott, sixteen years his junior, in Picadilly, London. They lived for some years in Canada, where they had four children, before he retired to Shandy Hall. Cross was, as his father had been, irascible and litigious, and his unpopularity caused his wife, in 1886/87, to become depressed. In 1887, he began an adulterous affair with the governess, Effie Skinner. Laura Cross was severely ill in May 1887 and died on 2 June, according to Dr Cross, of typhoid fever. She was buried on 4 June 4 and less than a fortnight later, Cross married Ms Skinner. Following exhumation of Laura's remains, he was arrested and charged with murdering his wife by arsenic poisoning. His trial, which began on 13 December 1887, was a *cause célebre*. His behaviour and reputation doomed him, despite flaws in the prosecution case. He was convicted and sentenced to death. He was executed in Cork Prison on 10 January 1888.

CROTTY, Bartholomew (1769–1846) Born Clonakilty, Co. Cork, the son of a prosperous weaver. He was educated locally and at Lisbon (under the patronage of Bishop **Matthew McKenna**) where he became professor of Philosophy in 1791 and rector in 1801. He returned to Ireland in 1811 and was chosen as president of St Patrick's College, Maynooth. He was consecrated as bishop of Cloyne and Ross on 11 June 1833. He died on 3 October 1846 and was buried in the chapel of Presentation Convent, Midleton. Following the dismantling of the chapel, his remains were re-interred at St Colman's Cathedral, Cobh, in October 1998.

CROW, Charles (1655–1726) Born Hawkeshead, Lancashire, England. He was educated at Queen's College, Oxford and at TCD where he graduated BA (1676), MA (1679) and DD (1693). He was consecrated as Church of Ireland bishop of Cloyne on 15 September 1702. He died on 26 June 1726 and was buried in his cathedral. His library was subsequently purchased for £1,100 by the Cork Diocesan Chapter and later formed the nucleus for the St FinBarre's Cathedral Library – a collection which is now housed at UCC. By his will, he established a grammar school at Cloyne.

CROWLEY, Denis O. (b. 1852) Born Castletownbere, Co. Cork. He was educated locally and emigrated to the United States *c*.1862. He settled in Boston where he was employed in a printing house. In 1875, he moved to San Francisco and studied for the priesthood, being ordained in December 1883. While in Boston, he had written poetry for the *Boston Leader*, the *American Gael*, the *Irish World* and the *Irish American*. He also wrote for the *San Francisco Monitor* and for *Donahoe's Magazine*. He published *Irish Poets and Novelists* and some of his poems were included in *Poets of America*.

CROWLEY, Flor (1910–1980) Born Behagullane, Dunmanway, Co. Cork, the son of Lawrence Crowley, farmer. He was educated locally and at St Patrick's College of Education, Dublin. He worked as a primary school teacher at Behagh (1931–67) and Bandon (1967–75). He was a prominent athlete in the weight-throwing and shot events, winning over forty championship events at county and provincial level. He also won a national championship in the hammer event. A Munster road-bowling champion in 1950, he was one of the prime movers in the formation, in 1954, of Ból Chumann na hÉireann, of which he was chairman until his death. He also oversaw the development of the European dimension of bowling from 1969. Under the penname 'Raymond', he wrote a bowling column for the *Southern Star* for many years. He also published a reminiscence of rural life, *In West Cork Long Ago* (1979). He died on 25 July 1980 and was buried in Bandon Cemetery.

CROWLEY, Flor (1934–1997) Born Cork, the son of Jerome Crowley. He was educated at PBC, Cork, but worked in Dublin for eight years before he established a successful auctioneering firm in Bandon. He played senior rugby at PBC and later played with both Dolphin and Wanderers. Having unsuccessfully contested a Mid-Cork by-election as a Fianna Fáil candidate in March 1965, he was returned to the Dáil in the following month. He represented South West Cork as a TD (1969–77 and 1981–2) and was also a member of Seanad Éireann (1977–81 and 1982–3). He was a member of Cork County Council (1967–79) and of Cork Corporation (1967–71). He died at his residence, 'Craigie', Bandon, on 16 May 1997 and was buried in Bandon Cemetery. His son, Brian Crowley, was elected to the European Parliament in 1994 and is currently a member.

CROWLEY, Frederick H. (1891–1945) Born Dromtariffe, Banteer, Co. Cork, the son of Michael N. Crowley, a woollen manufacturer and a member of Cork County Council (1899–1908). He took a prominent part in the War of Independence, including the attack on Rathmore RIC barracks. He was a member of Kerry County Council from 1917 and sat as a Fianna Fáil TD for County Kerry (1927–37) and Kerry South (1937–45). He married Honor Boland, the daughter of J.P. Boland (MP for South Kerry, 1900–18, and the first Irish-born winner of an Olympic gold medal) in 1939. Following his death at his residence, Danesfort, Killarney, on 5 May 1945 and his burial in Muckross Cemetery, Mrs Crowley succeeded him as a TD and was returned for South Kerry in every general election up to and including 1965. She died in the following year.

CROWLEY, John (1870–1934) Born Waterfall, Cork. He was educated at Queen's College, Cork (now UCC), and at Edinburgh where he qualified as a doctor in 1897. Following a year working in London, he was Medical Officer for a County Mayo district for the rest of his life. A member of Sinn Féin from its foundation, he was a battalion commander in the IRA and his house was regularly raided by the British military. In the 1918 general election, he was elected as the Sinn Féin member for North Mayo, but, following an attempt on his life in

the following year, he went 'on the run' in County Cork. He took the Republican side in the civil war and in 1922 was arrested by Free State troops and imprisoned in Ballina until his release by republican forces when they captured the town. He represented the constituencies of Mayo North West (1921–3) and Mayo North (1923–27). He died at his residence at Bally-castle, Co. Mayo, on 16 February 1934 and was buried in the nearby Doonferry Cemetery.

CROWLEY, Peter O'Neill (1832–1867) Born Ballymacoda, Co. Cork, the son of a prosperous farmer. He was the grand-nephew of Rev. **Peter O'Neill** who was flogged in Youghal on suspicion of being a member of the Society of United Irishmen. He joined the Fenian movement and was a leader in East Cork during the rising of 1867. On 5 March, he led the raid on the nearby coast-guard station at Knockadoon where a quantity of arms was taken. However, when it became clear that the East Cork operation was a fiasco, most of the Fenians dispersed while O'Neill Crowley and a few others headed for North Cork to make contact with other units. He was shot dead in an engagement with police and soldiers at Kilclooney Wood, near Kildorrery on 31 March. He was buried in the grounds of Ballymacoda Church alongside his grand-uncle.

CUMMINS, Geraldine (1890–1969) Born Cork, the daughter of **W.E. Ashley Cummins** and sister of **Robert C. Cummins**. She was privately educated and was later an Irish hockey international. A feminist, she founded the Munster Women's Franchise League with **Suzanne Day** and **Edith O. Somerville**. With Day, she wrote two plays, 'Broken Faith' (1913) and 'Fox and Geese' (1917) which were pro-duced by the Abbey Theatre. In 1920, she married the major Irish poet, Austin Clarke (1896–1974) but the marriage broke up after ten days for reasons of non-consummation. Her two novels, *The Land They Loved* (1919) and *Fires of Bealtaine* (1936) were both feminist in character. She also published a collection of short stories, *Variety Show* (1959). Her two religious novels, *The Childhood of Christ* (1937) and *After Pentecost* (1944) were claimed by her to have been written by a member of the primitive Christian Church using her as a medium. She died in Cork on 24 August 1969 and was buried in St Lappan's Graveyard, Little Island.

CUMMINS, Robert C. (*c.*1887–1975) Born Cork, the third child of **W.E. Ashley Cummins** and brother of **Geraldine Cummins**. He was educated at Cheltenham College and at UCC where he qualified MD. During World War I, he served with the Royal Army Medical Corps at Salonika, Greece. He was consultant physician to Cork's Erinville Hospital for fifty years and was also a member of the staff of both the Victoria and Eye, Ear, and Throat hospitals. He was author of *Unusual Medical Cases: a Cork Physician's Memories* (1962) and co-author with his sister, Geraldine, of *Healing the Mind* (1957). He died at St Luke's Home, Cork, on 19 February 1975 and was buried in St Lappan's Graveyard, Little Island.

CUMMINS, W.E. Ashley (1858–1923) Born Blackrock, Cork, the son of Dr W.J. Cummins, and father of **Robert C. Cummins** and **Geraldine Cummins**. He was educated at Queen's College, Cork (now UCC), where he graduated MD with first class honours and was awarded the Gold Medal. As a Queen's College rugby player, he represented Ireland in 1879 and 1881–2. He was professor of the Practice of Medicine at UCC (1897–1923). He was also consulting physician to the Lying-In Hospital, Cork, and to the Eye, Ear, and Throat Hospital, Cork. He was president of the Cork Medical and Surgical Society for many years. He died at his residence, 'Woodville', Glanmire, on 18 October 1923 and was buried in St Lappan's Graveyard, Little Island.

CUMMINS, William (1872–1943) Born Kilbrittain, Co. Cork. He was educated locally and at St Patrick's Training College, Dublin, where he qualified as a primary teacher. He took up a teaching position in Co. Kildare, and later became principal of Newbridge NS. A promi-

nent member of the Irish Labour Party, he was chairman of Newbridge Town Commissioners for over a decade and was also very prominent in Co. Kildare Irish language circles. In February 1923, he was elected to fill a vacancy in Seanad Éireann and remained a member until his death. He died at the Drogheda Memorial Hospital, The Curragh, on 27 July 1943 and was buried in Kilbrittain Cemetery.

CÚNDÚN, Pádraig P. (1777–1857) Born Ballymacoda, Co. Cork. At about the age of 49 years, he gave up farming and emigrated to America with his wife and young family. He resumed the agricultural life at Utica, New York State. His political sympathies had been formed through the influence of Rev. **Peter O'Neill**, the parish priest of Ballymacoda who had suffered as a suspected United Irishman during the Rebellion of 1798. Cúndún had written many Irish songs and poems prior to his emigration, but resumed around 1833 when his debts were paid in America. His favourite poetic form was that of the 'aisling' – a tradition he had continued from his fellow-Ballymacoda parishioner, the poet **Piaras Mac Gearailt**. He died in 1857.

CUNNINGHAM, Marney (1933–2000) Born Cork, the son of Jack Cunningham. He was educated at PBC, Cork, and at UCC where he graduated BE. Carrying on the family tradition, he excelled in rugby and represented Munster both at schoolboy and senior level. He was a member of the UCC team which won the Munster Senior Cup in 1955 and played his first international against France in January of that year. Having gained seven international caps, his playing career came to a premature end when, at the age of 22 years, he decided to study for the priesthood at Upholland College, Lancashire. He later became parish priest at St Charles Church, Swinton, Lancashire, and ministered there until his retirement several months before his death on 31 May 2000.

CURRAN, John Philpot (1750–1817) Born Newmarket, Co. Cork, the father of **Sarah**

Curran, the betrothed of the patriot, Robert Emmet (1778–1803). He was educated at Midleton College, at TCD and at the Middle Temple. He was called to the Irish Bar in 1775 and became a King's Counsel in 1782. A Whig, he sat for Rathcormac in the Irish Commons from 1783 until 1797. He defended many of the leaders of the United Irishmen following the rebellion of 1798. Even though he opposed the Act of Union, he became master of the Irish Rolls and a member of the Privy Council in 1806. He received a pension of £2,700 a year on his retirement in 1814 when he moved to London. There he associated with Thomas Moore (1779–1852), Lord Byron (1788–1824) and Richard Brinsley Sheridan (1751–1816). He was described by the novelist, Jane Austen (1775–1817), as 'the ugliest man imaginable but completely irresistible'. He died in Middlesex on 14 October 1817 and was buried privately. His remains were re-interred in Glasnevin Cemetery, Dublin, in 1834. [Life by L. Hale (1958); Portrait by Robert Lucius West (1827)]

CURRAN, Sarah (1782–1808) Born New-market, Co. Cork, the youngest daughter of **John Philpot Curran**, the advocate. Following her secret engagement to the patriot, Robert Emmet (1778–1803), and the latter's execution in September, 1803, she was disowned by her father and was looked after by a Quaker family at Glanmire. Two years later, she married a Captain Sturgeon in Cork. She died in Hythe, Kent, on 5 May 1808 and was buried in Newmarket Cemetery. She is remembered in Thomas Moore's air, 'She is far from the Land'. [Life by M. Barry (1985)]

CUTHBERT, John (1815–1874) Born Cork, the son of Gilbert Cuthbert, excise officer. Following his apprenticeship as a shipwright, he emigrated to Sydney, Australia, in 1834. He bought some land at Darling Harbour and established a shipyard which concentrated on the building of steamships. It soon became one of the largest shipbuilding concerns in Australia employing over 300 mechanics of all descriptions. Despite a serious strike in 1871, he quickly recovered his market and, in 1872/73, built six battle cruisers for the British Admiralty for use in the suppression of the Polynesian slave trade. Noted for his charitable and generous donations, he died in Sydney on 8 December 1874.

D

DACEY, John R. (1854–1912) Born Cork, the son of Thomas Dacey, barrister. On his father's death, the family moved to Victoria, Australia, in 1858. He worked as an agricultural blacksmith, was married in 1878, and moved to Sydney in 1883 where he set up as a coachmaker. He became interested in local politics, and having been successful in local elections, was returned to the state Legislative Council as a Labour member in 1895. He served as the Parliamentary Party's treasurer from 1901 until 1910, when he was a surprise ministerial omission from Labour's first cabinet. However, following the resignations of two cabinet members, he was chosen as Colonial Treasurer but unfortunately had not the opportunity to show his true talents as he died on 11 April 1912. He was accorded a state funeral to Botany Cemetery, Sydney. The Sydney suburb of Daceyville is named after him.

DALY, Francis J. (1886–1950) Born Cork, the son of Maurice Daly, businessman. He was educated at Monkstown NS, at PBC, Cork; and at Clongowes Wood College. He was active in the Sinn Féin movement and was chairman of the O'Growney Branch of Connradh na Gaeilge. He was appointed as a member of Cork Harbour Commissioners in 1920 and served as chairman on two occasions (1920–3, 1925–7). In 1922 and 1927, he unsuccessfully contested a Dáil seat in Cork Borough as a Farmers' candidate. He was elected to Cork Corporation in 1930 and served as lord mayor in 1930 and 1931. In 1943, he was elected to Dáil Éireann for Cork Borough as a Fianna Fáil TD (having been previously associated with Cumann na nGaedheal). He did not seek re-election in 1948. His principal business interest was as a director of Messrs. Suttons Ltd, with which he had a long association. He was also a director of

National Flour Mills Ltd and other Cork businesses. He died at his residence, 'Northcliffe', Blackrock, on 18 February 1950 and was buried in St Finbarr's Cemetery.

DALY, Jack (1867–1932) Born Kilworth, Co. Cork, the son of James Daly, innkeeper. He was the father of **Patrick Daly**. He was elected to Fermoy Rural District Council about 1900 and was later co-opted as a member of Cork County Council (1911–14). In the 1923 general election, he took the East Cork seat as an Independent Labour candidate. He held this seat until his death but changed his allegiance to the Cumann na nGaedhal Party in later years. He also sat on the County Council for a second period (1925–32). He died at his residence, Ballinglanna House, Kilworth, on 23 February 1932 and was buried in Kilcrumper Cemetery.

DALY, John (c.1829–1905) Born Cork, the son of John Daly, butter merchant. Following his education at Clongowes Wood College, he became a prominent Cork merchant and sat as a member and alderman of Cork Corporation for many years. He was also elected mayor of Cork on three occasions (1871–3). He unsuccessfully contested the Tralee constituency as a Home Rule candidate in the 1874 general election and narrowly lost a by-election contest for Cork City in 1876. In the notable general election of 1880, he headed the poll for Cork City. However, he resigned his seat in February 1884 owing to financial difficulties which culminated in bankruptcy. He then emigrated to Australia and settled near Sydney. In 1895, he was seriously injured in a railway accident while on his way to a Michael Davitt reception committee meeting. He recovered from his injuries (having lost four fingers and a foot) and returned to Cork where he resumed his commercial interests. He died at his home, 'Sunnyside', Monkstown, on 13 October 1905.

DALY, John C. (1912–1987) Born Cobh, the son of Eugene Daly, policeman. An Irish international rugby prop-forward, 'Christy' played for Cobh Pirates, Cork Constitution, London Irish and also represented the Barbarians. He gained seven international caps (1947–8) and his greatest moment came in March 1948, when he scored the winning try against Wales which won the Triple Crown for Ireland for the first time since 1899. Following this success, he switched over to Rugby League and represented Huddersfield for many years, winning a League Championship with them. He later played for Featherstone Rovers. He died in Huddersfield in 1987. [Sketch by **Dave Guiney** in J.M. Kidney, *Skull and Cross-Bones* (1990)]

DALY, Patrick (1901–1948) Born Kilworth, Co. Cork, the son of **Jack Daly**. He was educated locally and at Mount Melleray School, Co. Waterford. On his father's death in 1932, he was co-opted to Cork County Council and served until 1945. He was elected to the Dáil as a Fine Gael deputy for East Cork in the general election of 1933. He lost his seat in 1943 and was unsuccessful again in 1944. He died in 1948.

DANCKERT, Hugh (b. 1826) Born 9 Prince's Street, Cork, the son of John Dankert, wine merchant. He practised in Cork as a painter of miniatures (including one of **John Francis Maguire**) and also painted portraits in oils.

DAUNT, Achilles (1832–1878) Born Rincurran, Kinsale, Co. Cork, the eldest son of Achilles Daunt of Tracton Abbey. He was educated at TCD where he graduated BA (1854), MA (1866) and DD (1877). He was awarded the Gold Medal for Classics in 1853. Following his ordination, he was appointed to numerous preferments in the dioceses of Cork, Meath, and Dublin. In 1875, he became dean of Cork on the promotion of **Robert S. Gregg** to the bishopric of Ossory. He died at **Richard Barter's**

Hydropathic Institute, Blarney, on 17 June 1878 and was buried at Mount Jerome Cemetery, Dublin. He was a noted evangelical preacher in Dublin, drawing huge congregations to his sermons and building the new Church of St Matthias there. [Memoir by F.R. Wynne (1879)]

DAUNT, William O'Neill (1807–1894) Born Tullamore, Co. Offaly. He joined the Repeal Association and sat in the British House of Commons as a Repeal MP for Mallow in 1832, but was unseated on petition. He had previously converted to Roman Catholicism in 1827. He was afterwards a supporter of the Young Ireland movement and was a frequent contributor to its organ, *The Nation*. His historical works included *A Catechism of the History of Ireland* (1844), *Personal Memoirs of the Late Daniel O'Connell* (1848) and *Ireland since the Union* (1888). His novels included *Innisfoyle Abbey* (1840), *Saints and Sinners* (1843), *Hugh Talbot* (1846) and *The Gentleman in Debt* (1851). He died at Kilcascan, Ballineen, Co. Cork, on 29 June 1894. [Diaries, under the title, *A Life Spent in Ireland*, edited by A. Daunt (1896)]

DAVIES, Rowland (1649–1721) Born Gilabbey, Cork, the son of Rowland Davies of Bandon. He was educated at TCD where he graduated BA (1671), MA (1681) and LL.D (1706). He was ordained in 1671 and became dean of Ross on 26 December 1678. He wrote a manuscript account of the diocese of Ross (1682) but withdrew to England during the Jacobite period. He returned to Ireland with the forces of William of Orange and wrote an account of his part in the campaign which was subsequently edited and published by **Richard Caulfield** in 1857. He became dean of Cork in 1710 and also wrote several pamphlets on religious disputational themes. He died at Dawstown, Matehy, Co. Cork, on 11 December 1721 and was buried in St FinBarre's Cathedral. [Portrait at Ross Deanery, Rosscarbery]

DAVIS, Francis (1810–1885) Born Ballincollig, Co. Cork. He moved to Belfast where he worked as a muslin weaver. As 'The Belfast Man', he wrote poetry for the Young Ireland newspaper, *The Nation*. He was also the editor of the short-lived, *Belfast Man's Journal*. He died in 1885. [Works edited by C. O'Grady (1878)]

DAVIS, Thomas Osborne (1814–1845) Born Mallow, Co. Cork, the son of an army surgeon. He was educated at TCD where he graduated BA (1836). He was called to the Irish Bar in 1838. A year later, he joined the Repeal Association but growing impatient with Daniel O'Connell's strategies, he founded, in 1842, the Young Ireland movement (and its organ, *The Nation*) with Charles Gavan Duffy (1816–1903) and John Blake Dillon (1814–66). He clashed with Daniel O'Connell on the issue of the Queen's colleges shortly before his death in Dublin on 16 September 1845. His ballad, 'A Nation Once Again', became practically an Irish national anthem until the demise of the Irish Parliamentary Party in 1918. He also wrote some other enduring ballads including 'Clare's Dragoons', 'The West's Asleep' and 'The Lament for Eoghan Rua O'Neill'. He published *Speeches by the Rt. Hon. **John Philpot Curran**, with a Memoir* (1844). [Lives by Charles Gavan Duffy (1892), and J.M. Hone (1934); Statue by **John Hogan** at the mortuary chapel of Mount Jerome Cemetery, Dublin; Portrait by H. McManus; Life-size bronze at Mallow Castle, and bronze tablet at 72, Main Street, Mallow, by **Seamus Murphy**]

DAVITT, Michael (1846–1906) Born Straide, Co. Mayo, but raised in Lancashire. Having joined the Fenians in 1865, he became secretary of the Irish Republican Brotherhood three years later but was jailed in 1870. He spent seven years in Dartmoor Gaol and returned to Ireland, having spent a short time in America. With **C.S. Parnell**, he founded the National Land League in late 1879 and became a pivotal figure in the land struggle. He opposed Parnell after the 'Parnell Split' of 1890. He was elected as MP for Cork North East in a by-election of February 1893 but resigned his seat in the

following June. He retired from politics in 1899 and died on 31 May 1908. He was buried in his native village. His publications include, *Leaves from a Prison Diary* (1884), *The Defence of the Land League* (1891), *The Boer Fight for Freedom* (1902), *Within the Pale* (1903) and *The Fall of Feudalism in Ireland* (1904). [Lives by D.B. Cashman (1908), F. Sheehy-Skeffington (1908), and T.W. Moody (1982)]

DAY, Robert (1836–1914) Born Cork. He was one of the most notable antiquarians of his day and a collector of archaeological artefacts, coins, medals etc. He contributed dozens of articles to the learned journals both locally, nationally and in Britain. He was the joint editor of the Cork Historical and Archaeological Society's annotated reprint (1893) of **Charles Smith's** *History of Cork*. He was also president of the CHAS from 1894 until his death. He was a fellow of the Society of Antiquaries and was a member of the Huguenot Society, the Royal Numismatic Society, and the Bibliographic Society. He became an alderman of Cork Corporation in 1880 and served as high sheriff in 1893. His public service was also marked by officerships in the Cork Literary and Scientific Society, Cork Savings Bank, and South Infirmary Hospital. He was also the Governor of the Commercial Buildings. He died at his residence, Myrtle Hill House, Cork, on 10 July 1914. The sale of his famous collection ('the greatest dispersal of its kind which ever took place in Ireland') commenced on 7 September 1915 and the 1,500 lots (exclusive of other portions which had previously been sold in London) were sold off over the following five days.

DAY, Robert (c.1879–1949) Born Kilgarvan, Co. Kerry. He came to live at 269 Old Youghal Road, Cork, at an early age. He worked in the Metropole Laundry and, following the death of **Tadhg Barry**, he became branch secretary of the Irish Transport and General Workers' Union in 1921. In the same year, as an alderman of Cork Corporation, he led the 'take-over' of the Cork Harbour Board – an episode which secured a minimum wage for dock workers. He stood as a Labour candidate in the general election of 1922 and topped the poll for Cork City. However, he lost his seat in the election of the following year. Crippled by arthritis, he was a complete invalid before the age of forty. He died at his residence, 9 Nicholas Street, Cork, on 1 May 1949 and was buried in Rathcooney Graveyard.

DAY, Suzanne Rouvier (1890–1964) Born Cork, the daughter of **Robert Day (1836–1914)**. A feminist, she founded the Munster Women's Franchise League with **Geraldine Cummins** and **Edith O. Somerville**. She was elected as a Cork Poor Law Guardian in 1912 and caused some controversy in local government circles when, in 1916, she published *The Amazing Philanthropists* ('being extracts from the letters of Lester Martin, PLG') – a work which was highly critical of the Poor Law system. She collaborated with Cummins in the production of 'Broken Faith' (1913) and 'Fox and Geese' (1917) which were both produced by the Abbey Theatre. She also wrote plays independently such as, 'Out of a deep Shadow' (1912) and 'Toilers' (1913). These were socially-committed dramas on the lot of female sweatshop workers. She served as a nurse on the Western Front during World War I and in 1918 wrote a book entitled, *Round About Bar-le-Duc*, which dealt with her experiences there. Her *Where the Mistral Blows* (1933) is a travel book on Provence. She was a member of the London Fire Service during World War II. She died there in 1964.

DEADY, John C. (1849–1884) Born Kanturk, Co. Cork. He was educated at Mount Melleray School, Co. Waterford, and studied for the priesthood for a time. He contributed poetry to a large number of newspapers including *The Nation*, the *Cork Examiner* and the *Cork Herald*. The 'Poet of Duhallow' died at Banteer on 19 August 1884.

DEAN, Kennedy (*fl.* 1795) Born Cork, the son of Hugh Primrose Dean, a landscape painter of Scottish descent who had settled in Cork. Following a spell in the British Navy, he returned to Cork and worked as a painter and drawing master.

DEANE, Sir Thomas (1792–1871) Born Dundanion, Blackrock, Cork, the son of Alexander Deane, a prominent Cork builder. He was the father of **Sir Thomas N. Deane** and grandfather of **Sir Thomas M. Deane**. He also became a successful building contractor and quickly became prosperous. He then turned to the study of architecture and later designed such Cork buildings as Queen's College (now UCC), the Bank of Ireland, the Commercial Buildings (now part of the Imperial Hotel), the portico of Cork Courthouse etc. With his junior partner in the firm of Deane & Woodward, Benjamin Woodward (1816–61), he was responsible for the design of the Oxford University Museum (1855) in which the carver brothers from Ballyhooly, John and James O'Shea, executed some of their celebrated ornamentation. In 1830, he was elected as mayor of Cork and was knighted in the same year. He was elected as a member of the Royal Hibernian Academy in 1860 and also served as president (1866–8). He was also president of the Institute of Irish Architects. He died at Monkstown, Dublin, on 2 October 1871 and was buried in Blackrock Graveyard, Cork. [Family sketches by J. Coleman, *JCHAS*, xxi (1915); and F. O'Dwyer (1997); Commemorative plaque at the Imperial Hotel, Cork]

DEANE, Sir Thomas M. (1851–1933) Born Ferney, Blackrock, Cork, the eldest son of **Sir Thomas N. Deane** and grandson of **Sir Thomas Deane**. He was educated privately and at TCD where he graduated BA (1872). He was also an architect and was a pupil of **William Burges**, but his pencil sketchbooks, which are in the National Gallery of Ireland, show his diverse talents as an artist. He studied architecture in France and Italy (1875–8). Carrying on the family tradition, he went into partnership with his father and was responsible for such buildings as the Church of Ireland College of

Education, Dublin; the Royal College of Science (now Government Buildings), Dublin; and the Anthropological Museum and Physiological Laboratory, Oxford. He was elected as a member of the Royal Hibernian Academy in 1910. In 1911, he was knighted by King George V while on a visit to Dublin. He died at his residence in Penmacnmawr, Wales, on 3 February 1933. [Family sketches by J. Coleman, *JCHAS*, xxi (1915); and F. O'Dwyer (1997)]

DEANE, Sir Thomas N. (1828–1899) Born Dundanion, Blackrock, Cork, the son of **Sir Thomas Deane** and father of **Sir Thomas M. Deane**. He was educated at Rugby School and at TCD where he graduated BA (1849). In 1850, he joined the firm of Deane & Woodward, and on his father's death in 1871, took over the firm. In Dublin, he was responsible for the design of the National Library and National Museum at Kildare Street (1885–90) – for which he was knighted at the official opening in 1890. He also designed St Ann's Church, Dawson Street; the Natural History Museum, the National Gallery, and the RDS Lecture Theatre at Leinster House (now the Dáil Chamber). At Oxford, he was responsible for the design of the Meadow Building (1863), the Clarendon Laboratory (1867), and the Pitt-Rivers Museum (1885). He subsequently became inspector of National Monuments. He also painted landscape and watercolours and was a frequent exhibitor at the Royal Hibernian Academy from 1863 until 1898 (he was elected as a member in 1864). He died in Dublin on 8 November 1899. [Family sketches by J. Coleman, *JCHAS*, xxi (1915); and F. O'Dwyer (1997)]

DEASY, Denis (1853–1884) Born Bandon, Co. Cork, the son of a master cooper. He was employed in Dowden's store and later as a goods clerk on the Cork & Bandon Railway. Attracted to the Fenian movement, he was sworn into the Irish Republican Brotherhood and was one of a group of 'Dynamiter' conspirators based in Cork and Liverpool. He was arrested in Liverpool on 28 March 1882, having arrived from Cork in possession of bomb-making equipment. He (and others) were put on trial in Liverpool, found guilty of treason and sentenced to life imprisonment. He died in Chatham Prison on 17 May 1884. His remains were returned to Bandon and were buried in Kilbrogan Cemetery. An imposing Celtic Cross was erected over his grave in March 1907.

DEASY, Liam (1896–1974) Born Kilmacsimon Quay, Innishannon, Co. Cork. He left school at the age of thirteen to work in Bandon. He joined the Irish Volunteers in 1917 and formed a company in Innishannon, of which he was elected captain. On the formation of the West Cork Brigade, he was appointed adjutant and on the death of **Charlie Hurley**, he was appointed brigade commander – a position which he held until the Truce. He was one of the founders of Ideal Weatherproofs Ltd and later became the managing director of Trimproof Ltd, an associated company. In June 1940, he enlisted in the Irish Army for the duration of the Emergency. In the following year, he was promoted to the rank of commandant and appointed a command staff officer with responsibility for organising the Local Defence Force (LDF). In 1942, he was promoted to the staff of GHQ, Dublin, in the directorate of the LDF. In 1973, his *Towards Ireland Free*, an account of the War of Independence in West Cork, was published. It earned a rejoinder from General **Tom Barry** in the form of a pamphlet, entitled, *The Reality of the Anglo-Irish War in West Cork*. He died at St Ann's Hospital, Dublin, on 20 August 1974 and was buried at Bohernabreena Cemetery. His account of the Civil War, *Brother against Brother* was published posthumously in 1982.

DEASY, John (1856–1896) Born Cork, the son of M. Deasy, civil engineer. He was educated at the Model Schools, Anglesey Street. He farmed extensively at Bishopstown and came to political prominence as a member of the Cork Board of Guardians. In February 1884, he was chosen as the Home Rule candidate to contest the seat vacated by **John Daly** and was returned in the by-election after his defeat of **William Goulding**. He represented Mayo West as a Nationalist and latterly as an anti-Parnellite MP (1885–93). Owing to ill health, he resigned his seat in July 1893. He was called to the Bar in 1888 and practised on the Munster Circuit. In 1891, he married a Miss Tynan from Carlow and he died of consumption in Carlow on 24 February 1896.

DEASY, Rickard (1812–1883) Born Clonakilty, Co. Cork, the son of a brewer. He was educated at TCD where he graduated BA (1835), MA (1847) and LL.D (1860). He was called to the Bar in 1835 and to the Inner Bar in 1849. He served as MP for Co. Cork from 1855 until 1861. In that year, he was appointed as a judge at the Court of Exchequer. He became Lord Justice of the Court of Appeal in 1878. He died in Dublin on 6 May 1883 and was buried at Dean's Grange Cemetery.

DEAVES, Ebenezer (1765–1809) Born Cork, the son of Ebenezer Deaves (1731–1777), a Quaker textile manufacturer, and of Elizabeth Harvey. He invested in marshy 'development land' at Penrose Quay but died at the early age of 44 years. The business was administered in trust for his two sons, **Reuben Harvey Deaves** and Thomas Harvey Deaves, while his widow was left with £30,000 of stock.

DEAVES, Reuben Harvey (1794–1854) Born Cork, the son of **Ebenezer Deaves**. In 1822, he and his brother, Thomas Harvey Deaves (1797–1849), paid off their late father's trustees and established a timber import business on Lavitt's Island. They were also involved in the purchase and sale of ships and both of them sat as Cork harbour commissioners. However, their company went bankrupt in 1848 but they eventually paid their creditors.

DEAVES, Thomas (b. 1738) Born North Abbey, Cork, the son of Anthony Deaves (1702–1779) whose Quaker family originally came from Gloucestershire. He had two bleach-greens at Blarney and in 1787 he built a five-storey cotton-spinning mill in the village. Unfortunately, owing to the large investment in new technology, he went bankrupt in the following year. He was also expelled from the Cork Quaker Meeting for issuing false credit bills.

De BARRA, Leslie M. (1893–1984) Born Dublin (née Price). She qualified as a teacher and worked in Belfast. She took part in the Easter Rising and was director of Cumann na mBan until 1923. On marrying General **Tom Barry** in 1921, she moved to Cork. She was a founder member of the Irish Red Cross Society in 1939 and served as its chairperson from 1950 until the early '70s. In recognition for her work on behalf of the Red Cross, she was awarded the Dunant Medal of the International Red Cross Committee in 1978. She was also chairperson of the Irish National Committee for Refugees (1955–60) and national president of the relief agency, Gorta (1960–5). She was awarded an honorary LL.D degree from the National University of Ireland. She died at St Finbarr's Hospital, Cork, on 9 April 1984 and was buried in St Finbarr's Cemetery.

DEEBLE, Richard (1675–1718) Born Cork, the son of George Deeble. A clockmaker, he was commissioned by Cork Corporation to provide clocks both for the Council Chamber (1706) and for the Exchange at Castle Street (1709). After his early death, his Quaker co-religionists took care of his nine children.

DEERING, Michael (d. 1901) Born Limerick, but spent the prime of his life in Cork where he was employed for a number of years by Messrs. Arnott and Co., and latterly filled an important position in Murphy's Brewery at Lady's Well. He was a member of the GAA from its inception in 1884 and was instrumental in bringing four Tipperary clubs to Cork in 1886 for the first official hurling tournament in the city. In 1890, he was elected president of the Cork County GAA Board and steered the association through the political crisis of the early 1890s. He was elected president of the GAA in 1898 – a position which he held until his death at Quaker Road, Cork, on 25 March 1901. He was buried in St Joseph's Cemetery, where an imposing Celtic Cross was erected over his grave by the GAA and unveiled on 26 October 1902.

DELACOUR, James (1709–1781) Born Killowen, Blarney, Co. Cork, the eldest son of John Delacour of Cork. He was educated at TCD where he graduated BA (1732) and MA (1735). Following his ordination, he served as a Church of Ireland curate at Ballinaboy from 1744 until 1755. Fancying himself as a prophet, he was known locally 'the mad parson' but the high standard of his poetry does not reflect this. He wrote many collections which were locally published (1770, 1778, and 1807). His *Abelard to Eloisa* (1730) is a reply to Alexander Pope's (1688–1744) *Eloisa to Abelard*. He was buried in Shandon Churchyard, Cork. [Poetry selection in *JCHAS* (1894)]

DELANY, William (1804–1886) Born Bandon, Co. Cork. He was educated locally and at St Patrick's College, Maynooth, where he was ordained in 1827. He served in several chaplaincies and curacies before being appointed as parish priest of Bandon in 1845. Two years later, he became bishop of Cork on 15 August 1847. He died on 14 November 1886 and was buried in the grounds of the Cathedral of St Mary and St Anne. Shortly before his death, he had laid the foundation stone of St Finbarr's College, Farranferris. [Statue, *in sede*, by J. Lawlor (1889) in cathedral grounds]

DELAUNE, Thomas (*c.*1635–1685) Born Brinny, Co. Cork. A Roman Catholic, he converted to the Baptist faith and moved to England where he kept a school. When he published his *Plea for the Nonconformists* in 1683 (with seven subsequent reprints), he was imprisoned at Newgate with his wife and two children. A year later, he wrote *A Narrative of the Sufferings of T.D.* By that time, his wife and children had perished from starvation and he himself was to follow in 1685. The writer and Nonconformist, Daniel Defoe (1660–1731), reprinted Delaune's *Plea* and criticised the London Baptists for not raising the £67 fine which would have freed the unfortunate Delaune.

DEMPSEY, Martin J. (1922–1998) Born Grange, Fermoy, Co. Cork, the twelfth and last child of Patrick Joseph Dempsey. He was educated at Grange NS, at St Colman's College, Fermoy, and at UCD where he studied as a night student. In 1941, he entered the civil service as a higher executive officer and remained there until 1964. From 1948, he was a well-known and popular singer and actor in various media. He had some poems published in *The Bell* and wrote five plays (1950–5) which were never published. He died at his Dublin home on 23 November 1998 and was buried in Fingal Cemetery, Balgriffin.

DENNEHY, Henry E. (1823–1902) Born Fermoy, Co. Cork, the fifth son of John Dennehy, wine merchant. He was educated at St Patrick's College, Maynooth, where he was ordained in 1851. He ministered in Queenstown (Cobh) from 1852 to 1874 – for the last two years as Administrator. In 1874, he was appointed as parish priest of Kanturk and subsequently became archdeacon of Cloyne. He administered the diocese between the death of Bishop **John McCarthy** and his successor's consecration. He was the author of several published works on subjects as diverse as the Early Church, disestablishment, and land reform. His two-volume 'religious romance', *Alethea* (1895) was critically acclaimed though published under the pseudonym of 'Cyril'. His last work, *The Flower of Asia* (1901), was also a novel. A lecture by him in 1872 is the genesis of the *History of Great Island*, edited and expanded by James Coleman. He died at Kanturk on 19 September 1902 and was buried in Fermoy.

DENNEHY, Sir Thomas (1829–1915) Born Brooklodge, Fermoy, Co. Cork. He was educated at the Irish College in Paris where he was a classmate of Archbishop **Thomas Croke** of Cashel. Following the outbreak of the Paris Uprising of 1848, he joined the British army. He was posted to India where he took part in many campaigns including the suppression of the Indian Mutiny of 1855. He was governor of Dholepore in Ragapootna (1878–85) during the minority of the future Maharajah. On his return from India, he was appointed to the household of Queen Victoria (1819–1901) and subsequently to that of King Edward VII (1841–1910). He retired in 1910. He had been knighted in 1896 and had attained the rank of major general. He died in Youghal on 14 July 1915 and was buried in Midleton Cemetery.

DE NORAIDH, Liam (1888–1972) Born Kilworth, Co. Cork, the son of David Norris, commercial traveller. He spent some time as a teacher but returned to Kilworth where he opened a hardware shop. Having a great interest in Irish traditional music, he was employed (1940–3) by the Irish Folklore Commission to gather songs in various Munster Gaeltacht areas and counties. As recording equipment was unavailable owing to World War II, he was forced to write down the songs (300 in all) as he heard them. He died on 21 January 1972 and was buried in Kilworth Cemetery. [Part of his collection in *Ceol ón Mhumhain* (1965)]

DE RÓISTE, Liam (1882–1959) Born Tracton, Co. Cork, the son of Edward Roche, primary teacher. At the age of 17, he began work in a Cork drapery store before taking a post at Skerry's College, which led to a teaching position there. He joined Connradh na Gaeilge in 1899 and was a founder-member (and for many years, secretary) of Coláiste na Mumhan, Ballingeary. He was also a founder member of the Cork Celtic Literary Society which led to his involvement with the Cork Industrial Development Association of which he was secretary. He was vice-chairman of the Cork branch of Sinn Féin from its foundation in 1906 and was prominent in the Volunteer movement in its early days. He

was elected as a Sinn Féin TD to the First Dáil in 1918 and to the Second Dáil in 1921. He was elected to the Third Dáil in 1922 as a pro-Treaty candidate. However, he retired from national politics in 1923. In 1921, a force of Black and Tans raided his Sunday's Well home (which he had left some time previously) and murdered Rev. Seamus O'Callaghan who was visiting. He later helped found the Irish International Trading Company and worked there until 1956. From 1945, he represented the Civic Party on Cork Corporation for two periods. He died at the Bon Secours Home, Cork, on 15 May 1959 and was buried in St Joseph's Cemetery. He was the author of a pamphlet, *A message to the man: thoughts for the thinker, work for the worker* (1908) and a drama, 'The Road to Hell' (1908). [Life by D. Ó Murchadha (1976)]

DESMOND, Anna M. (1839–1921) Born Bantry, Co. Cork, the daughter of Patrick Desmond, lawyer. Having been educated at home, she joined the Convent of Mercy community in Cappoquin, Co. Waterford, in 1862 and took her final vows in November 1865. In 1871, she volunteered for the Australian mission and arrived in Brisbane, Queensland, in 1872. As Sister Benigna, she taught music and did much charitable work. She eventually became head of the community, and, in 1902 she was appointed as mother superior of the Order's motherhouse at Townsville, Queensland. She visited Ireland in the following year where she persuaded other nuns to work in Australia and also helped the Christian Brothers to establish a school at Townsville. She died on 24 November 1912 and was buried in Townsville Cemetery.

DESMOND, Cornelius (1896–1993) Born Kilmeedy, Milstreet, Co. Cork, the son of Bartholomew Desmond, farmer. He was educated locally and served in the 1st Batt., 4th Cork Brigade of the IRA during the War of Independence. He later moved to Cork where he helped found the Irish Transport and General Workers' Union (now SIPTU). He was a founder member of Fianna Fáil but later left that party in the late 1930s and joined the Labour Party, becoming its vice-chairman. He unsuccessfully contested a Cork City by-election in 1956, but served in Seanad Éireann (1961–5) and as lord mayor of Cork (1965/66). His son, Barry Desmond, was a Labour TD, Minister for Foreign Affairs, and a member of the European Court of Auditors. He died on 16 November 1993.

DESMOND, Daniel (c.1913–1964) Born Crosshaven, Co. Cork. He was educated locally and at the School of Commerce, Cork. A builder's clerk, he became the secretary of the Federation of Irish Rural Workers in 1947. He unsuccessfully contested County Council (in 1942) and Dáil (in 1944) elections. However, he was elected to the County Council in 1947 and to the Dáil for Cork South in 1948 as a Labour Deputy. He was parliamentary leader of the Labour Party during the second Inter-Party Government and was later deputy leader of the party. He was almost entirely responsible for the passing of the Local Government Superannuation Servants Act of 1956 which ensured a pension scheme for road workers. He died at St Stephen's Hospital, Glanmire, on 9 December 1964 and was buried in St Patrick's Cemetery, Crosshaven. His wife, **Eileen Desmond**, succeeded him as TD for Mid-Cork (1965–9, and 1973–87). [Headstone by **Seamus Murphy** at Crosshaven Cemetery]

DESMOND, Eileen (1932–2005) Born Eileen Harrington at the Old Head of Kinsale and educated at the local Convent of Mercy from where she entered the civil service in the department of Posts and Telegraphs. She succeeded her late husband, **Daniel Desmond**, TD, in a by-election for the Mid-Cork constituency in March 1965 – an event which led Taoiseach Seán Lemass to call a general election. On being re-elected to the Dáil, she was appointed as Labour spokesperson on education. She lost her seat in the general election of 1969 and was further unsuccessful in a by-election in 1972. In the meantime, she worked as a senator from 1969 until her re-election for Mid-Cork in 1973. She subsequently served as minister for Health and

Social Welfare, but because of illness, this only lasted for nine months to March 1982. Again, owing to illness, she did not contest the general election of 1987. Previously, she had won a seat in the Munster constituency of the European Parliament in 1979 and served until 1981. She died in Cork University Hospital on 6 January 2005 and was buried in St Patrick's Cemetery, Crosshaven.

DESMOND, Peter (1926–1990) Born Cork. He was capped four times on the Irish soccer XI, and was a member of the team which defeated England (1–0) at Goodison Park, Liverpool, in September 1949 – the first foreign international side to gain an away victory over England. In a long playing-career, he lined out for Waterford, Shelbourne, Middlesborough, Southport, York City and Hartlepool. He died while on holiday in Devon in mid-September 1990 and was buried in Middlesborough.

DESMOND, William (1874–1941) Born Cork. He partook in the family firm of T. Desmond & Sons of Conway's Yard, and was also the owner of Desmond's Hotel. He sat as a Fine Gael TD for Cork City (1932–7) and also served a term as lord mayor of Cork (1940/41), having been a member of Cork Corporation for over thirty years. He died at his residence on 5 September 1941 and was buried in St Joseph's Cemetery. He was well known in hunting and rugby circles and was a successful amateur jockey in his younger days, winning his first race at Cork Park on his father's horse. His son, T.N. Desmond, BL, was a circuit court judge and president of the Munster Agricultural Show Society.

DICKINSON, Charles (1792–1842) Born Cork. He was educated at TCD where he graduated BA (1815), MA (1820) and DD (1834). He was consecrated as Church of Ireland bishop of Meath on 27 December 1840. He was a strong advocate of the national schools system. He died of typhus on 12 July 1842 and was buried in St Ann's Church, Dawson Street, Dublin. [Sketch by J. West (1845)]

DILLON, Brian (1830–1872) Born Banduff, Rathcooney Road, Cork, the son of Edward Dillon. As a child, he suffered a bad fall which resulted in curvature of the spine, lifelong ill-health, and stunted growth. The family opened a public house at the crossroads now known as Dillon's Cross, and Brian received his education at city schools including the Cork School of Art. He then went to work as a clerk in the South Mall law office of W.P. Coppinger, solr., and soon became involved in nationalist organisations, including the Fenian movement of which he became a local leader. In 1865, he was arrested in the Fenian 'clampdown', charged with conspiracy and was sentenced to ten years penal servitude. He served five years in Pentonville Gaol and later at Woking Gaol where his health deteriorated and where he was released on compassionate grounds. His return to his native city was marked by a huge demonstration of support. His health continued to decline and he died at his home on 17 August 1872. Following temporary interment at St Joseph's, he was later re-buried in Rathcooney Graveyard. [Life by W. McGrath (1952); Commemorative plaque at Dillon's Cross, Cork]

DINAN, Ellen (*c.*1829–1901) Born Macroom, Co. Cork, the daughter of Thomas Dinan. The family emigrated to Philadelphia, USA, when she was a child. In 1849, she entered the Sisters of St Joseph and took the religious name of Mary Bernard. She made her final profession in Toronto in March 1852, having been a member of the first group of her Order which arrived in that city in October 1851. The group lived in great poverty at an orphanage and supplemented their earnings from menial tasks by begging on the streets. She was put in charge of the novices until her term expired in 1856. By that time, the number of sisters in the house had risen to forty. For the next four years, Sister Bernard spent periods in different houses but returned to Toronto in 1860 where she was appointed as assistant to the superior general. She succeeded to that post in 1869 and served until 1874 when she was deposed by Archbishop J.J. Lynch of Toronto for 'imprudence in governing' as a result of a bogus press report of a convent affair between a priest and a nun. After a five-year 'limbo period', she ministered near Toronto (1880–7) when she returned to the city just before Lynch's death. In that year, she became superior at the Sacred Heart Orphanage at Sunnyside on the banks of Lake Ontario. She died on 20 September 1901, just a few weeks before the fiftieth anniversary of the arrival of the original four to Toronto. [Life by M.B. Young (1986)]

DINEEN, John (1866–1942) Born Garrylaurence, Clonmult, Co. Cork, the son of Maurice Dineen, farmer. He became involved in public life as a member of Midleton Board of Guardians and Rural District Council. In 1911, he was elected to Cork County Council and was identified with the Redmondite faction (to 1914). He became a Sinn Féin supporter and, on account of this, he was removed from his position as a JP. He then acted as a County Judge of the Republican Courts. He was the subject of two kidnapping attempts during the period 1920–2 and his house was burned down during the civil war. In 1922, he was elected to Dáil Éireann as a Farmer's Party representative in Cork East. He was re-elected in the following year, but lost his seat in the general election of 1927. He had remained a member of Cork County Council until 1925 when he did not seek re-election. He died at his Clonmult residence on 16 October 1942 and was buried in the local cemetery. He was a brother-in-law of Bishop **Patrick Casey** of Ross and an uncle of **Liam Ahern**, TD.

DIXON, Richard (*fl.* 1570) Born London (?), the son of William Dixon who, in 1544, obtained the grant of the Carmelite Friary of Cloncurry, Co. Kildare. He held various livings in the Church of Ireland and was a canon of St Patrick's Cathedral, Dublin. The Lord Deputy, Sir Henry Sidney (1529–86), recommended him to Queen Elizabeth I (1533–1603) for the dioceses of Cork and Cloyne. She replied on 17

May 1570 that 'We are pleased that Richard Dyxon, being by you very well commended for his learning and other qualities, shall have the bishoprics of Cork and Cloyne'. The royal patent for the appointment was issued on 6 June. However, he was deprived of his temporalities almost a year later on the charge that, 'Richard Dyxon, bishop of Cork less that twelve months, who has a married wife, has, under colour of matrimony, retained a woman of suspected life as his wife'. He had been compelled by the Royal Commissioners to do public penance at Christ Church Cathedral, Dublin, but 'did it in hypocrisy and pretence of amendment'. He was deprived of the temporalities of his diocese on 8 November 1571. He returned to England and probably settled at Wakefield, Yorkshire.

DOBBIN, Katherine Lady (1868–1955) Katherine Wise was born in Bristol, the daughter of a solicitor. She came to Cork on her marriage in 1887 to Sir Alfred Graham Dobbin, a Cork merchant and tobacco manufacturer. They lived in Montenotte, but in 1939, they took up residence at the Imperial Hotel. She exhibited watercolour subjects at the Royal Hibernian Academy from 1894–1947. Some of her Cork views are at the Crawford Gallery. She died in 1955.

DONEGAN, Bartholomew (c.1910–1978) Born Milford, Co. Cork. During the 'Emergency', he served as an LDF officer. He was elected as a Fianna Fáil member of Cork County Council for the Kanturk area in 1945 and was returned at each subsequent election until his death. Having unsuccessfully contested a Dáil seat in North Cork in 1954, he became a TD for the same constituency in 1957. With a constituency revision, he sought re-election for North East Cork in 1961, but was unsuccessful as he also was in 1969 for Mid-Cork. In November 1963, he was elected to Seanad Éireann in a by-election caused by the death of a sitting member. He served as chairman of Cork County Council in 1971. A farmer and horse-breeder of Blossomville, Newtown, Charleville, he died on 26 August 1978 and was buried in Deliga Cemetery.

DONELAN, Anthony J.C. (1846–1924) Born Co. Armagh, the son of Lt.-Col. Anthony Donelan of the 48th Regiment. He attended Sandhurst Military College and served in the British army where he rose to the rank of captain. He served as MP for East Cork (1892–1911), East Wicklow (1911–18) and was chief whip of the Irish Parliamentary Party under John Redmond (1856–1918). He was closely involved with the establishment of the naval dockyards at Haulbowline. He died at his residence, Ballynona Lodge, Midleton, on 12 September 1924 and was buried in Dungourney Churchyard.

DONOVAN, Charles (1863–1951) Born Calcutta, the son of an Irish civil servant in the Bengal Civil Service. Following his attendance at Queen's College, Cork (now UCC), and at TCD, he graduated MD from the Royal University of Ireland. He returned to India and entered the Medical Service in 1891. He was appointed as professor of Biology at Madras University and superintendent of Royapettah Hospital. In 1903, along with William Leishman (who was working independently in England), he discovered the parasite, later named *Leishmania donovani*, which was responsible for kala-azar, a major infectious Indian disease. He retired from the Indian Medical Service in 1920 and settled in Gloucestershire. He was a frequent visitor to Timoleague where his sisters lived at Ummera House. In 1936, he published a *Catalogue of the Macrolepidoptera of Ireland*. He died in 1951.

DONOVAN, Daniel F. (1763–1821) Born Cork. He was educated in France and was ordained as a member of the Capuchin Order. Following the outbreak of the French Revolution, he was expelled from the Irish convent at Bar-sur-Aube on 27 May 1790 ('and is supposed to have become chaplain to the family of a French nobleman in Paris'). His escape from the guillotine, as told by Hayes in his *Biographical Dictionary of the Irish in France*, is described as 'legend' by Capuchin historians. He returned to Cork and one of his appointments was to the chaplaincy of Cork Gaol where he ministered specially to the condemned. It was he who welcomed Father **Theobald Mathew** into the Cork Capuchin community and acted as his mentor. He also served as provincial of the Irish Capuchins (1816–19). He died in Cork on 14 February 1821.

DONOVAN, Finbarr (d. 2001) Born South Parish, Cork. He was educated at UCC where he graduated in mathematics and physics and undertook postgraduate studies there, at Cambridge and at Leeds University. One of the pioneers of Irish computer studies, he worked in this area at Aer Lingus, AIB, ITT, and USIT World. He was also associated with the establishment of the computer department at the University of Limerick. He was conferred with a doctorate from TCD only three weeks before his death. Though a scientist, he had a deep interest in ecclesiastical history. He edited C. Ó Conbhuidhe's *Studies in Irish Cistercian History* (1998) and was the author of *The Cistercian Abbeys of Tipperary* (1999). He died on 27 July 2001 and was buried in St Finbarr's Cemetery, Cork.

DONOVAN, Jeremiah (d. 1862) Born Macroom, Co. Cork. He entered St Patrick's College, Maynooth, in September 1811 and was subsequently ordained a priest of the diocese of Cloyne. He was professor of Classics at Carlow College (1816–20) and in February 1820 was appointed as professor of Rhetoric at Maynooth. In 1829, Dr Donovan published his *Translation of the Catechism of the Council of Trent*, described by his mentor, Bishop James W. Doyle of Kildare and Leighlin ['JKL'] (1786–1834), as 'the best translation into English of a Latin work that I have ever read'. Owing to poor health, he resigned his Maynooth post in September 1834, went to live in Rome and travelled extensively in Italy. The result of his researches, *Rome, Ancient and Modern, and its Environs*, was subsequently published in four volumes. Following a period of convalescence in England, he retired to St Joseph's Seminary, Clondalkin, Co. Dublin. He subsequently went to Paris to seek medical advice and died there while undergoing an operation on 11 December 1862.

DONOVAN, Patrick J. [Patsy] (1865–1953) Born Queenstown (now Cobh), Co. Cork, the son of Jeremiah Donovan who emigrated to the United States and was followed by his family when Patsy was three years old. As a teenager, he worked in a mill in Lawrence, Maine, and earned a reputation in local leagues as a baseball player. He turned professional and made his debut in 1890. He spent seventeen years in the major professional leagues and, by 1903, was the highest-paid player, earning $8,000 a year from the St Louis Cardinals. On retiring in 1907, he managed teams for a period, including five major ones. As a scout for Boston Red Sox, he discovered and recommended the legendary Babe Ruth (1895–1948) in 1914. In later life, he worked as a high school coach. He died in Lawrence on 23 December 1953.

DOOLEY, Tom (1846–1935) Born Cork. He was a member of the GAA from its foundation and was reputed to have attended the initial meeting at Hayes' Hotel, Thurles. A member of St Finbarr's hurling club, he was its hon. secretary from the club's foundation before being elected as secretary of the Cork County Board (1894–1900). He was also chairman of that Board from 1900 to 1904. In 1901, he was elected as the first secretary of the Munster Council and was later a member of the Central Council of the GAA (1904–8). During this time, he advocated the adoption of the provincial government system in the GAA. He was elected as the first vice-president of Cork County Board in 1916, and held this position until his death. He died at his Pouladuff Road residence on 16 November 1935 and was buried at Waterfall Cemetery where a Celtic cross was unveiled at his grave by **J.J. Walsh** in January 1939.

DORAN, Charles Guilfoyle (1835–1909) Born Knocknaskea, Co. Wicklow, the son of a builder. He studied architecture and engineering in his father's office, but simultaneously began a journalistic career, contributing to several newspapers and journals. In 1863, he was associated with the foundation of the *Galway American* (later the *United Irishman and Galway American*). A year later, he became national secretary of the National Brotherhood of St Patrick, a Fenian political front. He fled to Paris after the '67 when he became a member and secretary of the Supreme Council of the IRB. In 1868, he became clerk of works on the St Colman's Cathedral building project and spent most of the rest of his life in Queenstown (now Cobh). He was active in local politics and served as chairman of the Town Commissioners and initiated the Tibbotstown waterworks scheme. He later moved to Cork and resided at Union Quay. He died on 19 March 1909 and was buried in St Joseph's Cemetery. In the following year, his substantial private library was sold by auction.

DORGAN, Val (1934–2001) Born Cork, the son of Patrick Dorgan, ex-soldier who had fought in World War I. He was educated at North Monastery CBS and studied medicine for a time at UCC before pursuing a career in journalism with the *Cork Examiner*. His forty-three years as a journalist were spent with this newspaper and covered sport, European and Northern Ireland affairs. He eventually attained the position of chief editorial writer and retired from the newspaper in 1996. In 1987, he won the European Journalist of the Year Award. He joined the Glen Rovers club at an early age and later won several county championship hurling medals in the company of his hurling hero, **Christy Ring**, whose career he described in his book, *Christy Ring* (1980). His play, 'The Hurler', which investigated the relationship between republicanism and the GAA, was produced at UCC's Granary Theatre. He took up golf in his retirement and wrote a golfing column entitled, 'View from the Bunker'. He died at the Bon Secours Hospital, Cork, on 2 June 2001 and was buried in St Joseph's Cemetery.

DOWDALL, James C. (1873–1939) Born Cork, the brother of **Thomas P. Dowdall**. He was educated at PBC, Cork, and in Denmark. He joined the family business and was one of the founders in 1905 of Dowdall, O'Mahony Ltd. He took a prominent role in industrial development, was president of the Cork Industrial Development Association, and held directorates in numerous leading companies. He was a member of the governing body of UCC, where, in 1926, he was conferred with an honorary degree of LL.D. He was also a member of the senate of the National University of Ireland. Like his brother, **Thomas Dowdall**, he changed allegiance and joined the Fianna Fáil Party in 1927. He was a member of the first Seanad Éireann in 1921. He died at Holyhead on his way back to Ireland on 28 June 1939 and was buried in St Finbarr's Cemetery.

DOWDALL, Jenny (1899–1974) Born Dublin as Jane Doggett, the daughter of an employee of a Smithfield ostling company. A nurse by occupation, she married Senator **James C. Dowdall** (as his second wife) in 1929 and moved to Cork. She entered local politics in the mid-1940s as a Fianna Fáil representative and was nominated to Seanad Éireann in 1951 where she served until her defeat in the 1961 election. She also served as Cork's first woman Lord Mayor (1959/60). In 1964, she became one of the first two women to be appointed to the Council of State. She died in the Mercy Hospital, Cork, on 10 December 1974 and was buried in St Finbarr's Cemetery.

DOWDALL, Thomas P. (c.1871–1942) Born Cork, the brother of **James C. Dowdall**. He was educated at PBC, Cork, and in Denmark. He joined his uncle's firm, Dowdall Brothers Ltd, and in 1905, he was one of the founders of Dowdall, O'Mahony Ltd, a firm which engaged in the manufacture of butter and margarine. After the Treaty, he joined the Cumann na nGaedhal Party but, around 1927, he changed his allegiance to Fianna Fáil and represented Cork City in the Dáil (1932–42). A founding member of the Industrial Development Authority (IDA), he was chairman of Dowdall, O'Mahony and of Cash and Co. at the time of his death. He died at the Bon Secours Home on 7 April 1942 and was buried in St Finbarr's Cemetery.

DOWDEN, Edward (1843–1913) Born Cork, the son of John Wheeler Dowden, linen merchant. He was the brother of **John Dowden** and nephew of **Richard Dowden (Richard)**. He was educated at Queen's College, Cork (now UCC), and at TCD where he graduated BA (1863). He was appointed to the new chair of English Literature at TCD in 1867 – a position which he held until his death. He was subsequently awarded the LL.D of Edinburgh University and the DCL of the University of Oxford. His works include *Shakespeare, His Mind and Art* (1875), *A Shakespeare Primer* (1877) and *A Life of Shelley* (1886). Shortly before his death he wrote a little book of poems, *A Woman's Reliquary* for his second wife, Elizabeth. He died in Dublin on 4 April 1913. [Life by H.O. White (1943)]

DOWDEN, John (1840–1910) Born Cork, the son of John Wheeler Dowden, linen merchant. He was the brother of **Edward Dowden** and nephew of **Richard Dowden (Richard).** He was educated at TCD where he graduated BA (1861) and DD (1876). In 1874, he was appointed as professor of Theology at Edinburgh Theological College. He became the Scottish Episcopal bishop of Edinburgh in 1886. A founder of the Scottish Historical Society, he wrote many historical and theological works including *The Celtic Church in Scotland* (1894) and *The Medieval Church in Scotland* (1910). He died on 30 January 1910. [Portrait by J. Bowie]

DOWDEN (Richard), Richard (1794–1861) Born Bandon, Co. Cork, the son of Richard Dowden (*c.*1769–1823) and uncle of **Edward Dowden** and **John Dowden**. He is referred to as 'Richard Dowden Richard' to distinguish him

from his father. The family moved to Cork where he operated as a merchant and was manager of Jennings Soda Water Company of Paul Street. He was elected as mayor of Cork in 1845. He had a keen interest in botany and published *Walks after Wild Flowers, or the Botany of the Bohereens* (1852). He was also president of the Cork Cuvierian Society. He was a staunch Unitarian and collaborated with Father **Theobald Mathew** to promote the temperance movement. He died on 4 August 1861. [Commemorative plaque at Paul Street Shopping Centre]

DOWNES, Dive (1653–1709) Born Northamptonshire, England, the son of Lewis Downes, clergyman. He was educated at TCD where he graduated BA (1671), MA (1675), BD (1686) and DD (1692). He was consecrated as Church of Ireland bishop of Cork and Ross on 4 June 4 1699. Having married four times, he died in Dublin on 13 November 1709 – the same day as the birth of his daughter, Anne. His important 'Journal of a Tour through the Diocese of Cork and Ross' (in 1699) was later published in **W.M. Brady**, *Clerical and Parochial Records of Cork, Cloyne, and Ross* (1863–4) and in *JCHAS*, xv (1909), T.A. Lunham (ed.).

DOWNING, Denis J. (1844–1871) Born Skibbereen, Co. Cork, the second son of Mortimer Downing, hardware merchant. **Jeremiah O'Donovan Rossa**, a relative, lodged with the family from 1848 to 1853 and Downing and his brothers were original members of the Phoenix Society and joined the Fenians. He was one of those arrested for membership of the Phoenix Society in 1858. He went to the United States where, on the outbreak of the American Civil War in 1861, he enlisted in a New York regiment and was commissioned as first lieutenant in December of that year. He fought in the Shenandoah campaign and on the advance on Gordonsville. However, he was captured in the second battle of the Bull Run and taken prisoner to Richmond, Virginia. He was exchanged in December 1862 and rejoined his regiment at Fredricksberg where he was promoted to first lieutenant and to captain shortly afterwards. He was seriously wounded at the battle of Gettysberg and lost a leg as a result. On the night after the battle of Fredericksburg, Downing sang **T.D. Sullivan**'s ballad 'Ireland Boys Hurrah', a Phoenix Society marching song. The chorus was taken up by the Irish Brigade of the Union army, then by the whole army for six miles along the river, and finally by the Confederate lines across the river. In February 1864, Downing was appointed a captain in the Invalid Corps and a major and lieutenant-colonel a year later. In 1866, he was appointed a first lieutenant in the regular army. In a state of ill-health, he returned to Ireland in 1871 and died at Castletownshend shortly afterwards on 14 May 1871. He was buried in Skibbereen.

DOWNING, Ellen M.P. (1828–1869) Born Cork. She wrote poetry for the Young Ireland newspaper, *The Nation*. She eventually entered a convent and contributed poems to the *Cork Magazine* and the *Irish People*. She died on 27 January 1869. Her *Poems for Children* (1881), was published posthumously. [Collections edited by J.P. Leahy (1868, 1879 and 1880)]

DOWNING, Timothy McCarthy (1814–1879) Born Kenmare, Co. Kerry, the second son of Eugene Downing, merchant, and Helena McCarthy (of the McCarthys of Killfaddamore). He was educated locally and around 1830 was apprenticed to his elder brother, F.H. Downing, solicitor, of Kenmare. Having qualified as a solicitor, he set up practice in Skibbereen in 1836, taking from the outset a prominent role in the public affairs of the town. He was prominent in famine-relief bodies and defended the members of the Phoenix Society at their trial in 1857. During the 1850s and 60s, he purchased several estates in the Encumbered Estates Court and was returned in 1875 as the owner of over 3,400 acres in Co. Cork and 600 acres in County Kerry. In 1868, he was returned as Liberal MP for Cork County and as a Home Ruler in 1874. He retained his parliamentary seat until his death. He died at his residence, Prospect House, Skibbereen, on 10 January 1879 and was buried in Caheragh Old Cemetery. Only one of his seven sons (Eugene) survived him and he just by a few months, with the property passing to the McCarthys of Glencurragh. He left his residence to the bishop of Ross. It later served as the diocese of Ross episcopal residence and currently as the Parochial House.

DOWSE, Charles B. (1862–1934) He was the son of John R. Dowse, Dean of Ferns. He was educated at TCD where he graduated BA (1855), MA (1893) and BD/DD (1912). He held numerous clerical posts in the diocese of Ferns and Dublin. He was consecrated as Church of Ireland bishop of Killaloe on 11 June 1912 but was soon translated to the united diocese of Cork, Cloyne, and Ross following the death of Bishop **William Meade** on December 23 of the same year. In failing health, he resigned from his position on 15 September 1933 and died at Kensington Court, London, on 13 January 1934.

DOYLE, Joseph ['Jack'] (1913–1978) Born Queenstown (now Cobh), Co. Cork, the second child of Michael Doyle, merchant seaman. In 1930, he joined the Irish Guards and took an interest in boxing. Two years later, he was the heavyweight champion of the brigade of Guards. He left the army to pursue a professional boxing career as a heavyweight, which lasted ten years (1932–42). In 1933, he boxed Jack Peterson for the British heavyweight title and Lonsdale Belt but was disqualified in the second round. He combined his boxing career with those of singer, film actor and vaudeville artist. His best-known film was as the eponymous hero in *McGlusky the Sea Rover* (1935). Following his marriage to the film star, Movita (who later married actor, Marlon Brando), the couple drew huge crowds all over Ireland while on various tours during World War II. Following a divorce in 1945, he settled in London and performed as a wrestler. His later years were marked by heavy drinking and relative poverty. He died at Paddington Hospital, London, on 13 December 1978 and was buried in Old Church (Clonmel) Graveyard, near Cobh. [Life by M. Taub (1990)]

DOYLE, Jeremiah J. (1849–1909) Born Kilmurry, Co. Cork, the son of Daniel Doyle, farmer. He was educated at Mount Melleray School, Co. Waterford, and at All Hallows College, Dublin, where he was ordained in 1874 for the diocese of Armidale, New South Wales. Following a successful ministry, he was consecrated as the first bishop of Grafton, New South Wales, in August 1887. However, he chose to reside at Lismore (100km north of Grafton) and, in 1900, succeeded in changing the diocese's name to that of Lismore with the cathedral named after St Carthage. His episcopate was entirely successful with great increases in the number of churches and schools and in the number of religious communities which settled in the diocese. He died at Lismore on 4 June 1909 and was buried in his cathedral.

DREW, Oliver (1883–1938) Born Drew's Ville, Evergreen, Cork. In 1900, while still a schoolboy at PBC, Cork, he won the Fermoy doubles handball tournament. Still in his teens, he travelled to America in 1902 to contest the World Handball Championship against Mike Egan. Drew won the first leg of the fifteen-game rubber on 22 May 1903, but an argument over expenses left the match unfinished. He later won the Championship of America in 1906. He died in Chicago in May 1938.

DRISCOLL, Denis (1762–1811) Born West Cork to a Roman Catholic family of sufficient means to afford him an education for the priesthood on the Continent (possibly in Spain). Having been ordained, he served in Cork for some time, but in August 1789, he became a minister of the Church of Ireland and was appointed as curate assistant of the French Reformed Church until the termination of his licence in 1791. Having experienced two forms of authority, he now embraced a third, namely radicalism. As editor, and later as proprietor of the *Cork Gazette* newspaper, he published

extreme views on economics and religion and espoused the views of Thomas Paine (1737–1809). In 1794, he was prosecuted for one of his diatribes, found guilty of libel, and sentenced to two years' imprisonment. On his release, undaunted, he continued his writings in the *Gazette* but faced with another prosecution in 1797, he was forced to abandon the newspaper in return for the dropping of the case. Facing poverty, he obtained a passport to emigrate to America in 1799. He resumed his career as a radical propagandist in New York and became an adherent of Deism. He became editor of the Deists' new magazine, the *Temple of Reason* (1800–2), before establishing the *American Patriot*, an anti-Federalist journal, in Baltimore in September 1802. In January 1804, he became owner/editor of the well-established *Augusta Chronicle* in Georgia and mellowed his politics to a moderate republicanism. In declining health, he retired from journalism in December 1810 and died at Augusta on 10 March 1811.

DRUMMOND, James (c.1784–1863) Born Scotland. He settled in Cork in 1809 on being appointed as curator of Cork Botanical Garden (now St Joseph's Cemetery). In the following year he became an associate of the Linnean Society. He left Ireland for Australia in 1829 where he worked as a professional plant collector, specialising in orchids. His brother, Thomas, was also a noted botanist and collected in North America for the Glasgow Botanical Garden.

DRUMMOND, John J. (d. 1896) He studied at the Cork School of Art and later practised as a subject painter in the city. He eventually moved to London where he worked for a while as a drawing master to the royal family. He was subsequently headmaster of the Llanelli and Bath Schools of Art. He died in 1896.

DUGGAN, George (1812–1876) Born Mallow, Co. Cork, the son of John Duggan. When George was an infant the family emigrated to Canada to join John's brother in Hamilton, Ontario. George moved to Toronto in 1828 to study law and was called to the Bar in 1838. When his brother, John, was called to the Bar in 1840 they formed the law firm of Duggan and Duggan. An Orange district master, George was elected to the Legislative Assembly in 1841 and sat until his defeat in 1847. However, in an effort to neutralise the Orange faction, he was appointed by his Reformer opponents as recorder of Toronto in 1851. He was promoted as judge of the Toronto County Court in 1868 and held this appointment until his death. He died in Toronto on 14 June 1876 and his funeral cortege numbered seventy carriages.

DUGGAN, Lucy (c.1898–1978) Born Ballyheeda, Ballinhassig, the daughter of Thomas Duggan (d. 1909), school teacher, whose wife also was a teacher at Ballyheeda National School. She was the granddaughter of the transported Fenian, Thomas Duggan, and the sister of Archdeacon Tom Duggan. She qualified as a primary teacher and later studied at UCC where she was appointed as professor of Education in 1949. She held this position until her retirement in 1962. She died at the Bon Secours Hospital, Cork, in 1978 and was buried in Ballyheeda Graveyard.

DUNBAR, John (1827–1878) Born Cork, the third son of Joseph Dunbar, grocer and merchant. He was educated at Clongowes Wood College and at TCD where he graduated BA (1849) and MA (1865). He was called to the Irish Bar in 1849 and to the Middle Temple in 1854. He practised on the English Home Circuit and was on the parliamentary staff of the *Daily News* before practising for some years at the Bombay Bar. On his retirement from the Bombay Bar, he was elected MP for New Ross as a Liberal Home Ruler. He represented New Ross until his death. He died, following a long illness, at his chambers in the Middle Temple, London, on 3 December 1878.

DUNLEA, John [VC] (1831–1890) Born Douglas, Cork. He joined the British army and was posted to India with the 93rd Regiment where he rose to the rank of lance-corporal. On 16 November 1857 during the Indian Mutiny, he

was the first regimental soldier to break through the breaches at Secundra Bagh, Lucknow – an action which earned him the Victoria Cross. He died in Cork on 17 October 1890.

DUNNE, John (1845–1919) Born Mitchelstown, Co. Cork, the son of Michael Dunne, farmer. He was educated at Mitchelstown CBS, Mount Melleray School, Co. Waterford, and at All Hallows, Dublin, where he was ordained in 1870. He was posted to the Australian diocese of Bathurst, New South Wales, where, following a successful ministry, he was appointed as vicar-general of the diocese in 1900. In the following year, he succeeded as bishop. He was noted as a great promoter of new schools and churches and was nicknamed 'The Builder Bishop'. He died of cancer at his see house on 22 August 1919 and was buried in Bathurst Cemetery.

DUNNE, Seán (1956–1995) Born Waterford. He was educated at Mount Sion CBS and at UCC. As well as being the literary editor of the *Cork Examiner*, he also wrote poetry and reviews, contributed to literary broadcasts and edited several publications. He published *The Poets of Munster: an Anthology* (1985), *In My Father's House* (1991), *An Introduction to Irish Poetry* (1992), *The Cork Anthology* (1993), *The Road to Silence* (1994), *Something Understood* (1995) and *The College: a Photographic History of University College, Cork* (1995). His poetry collections include *Against the Storm* (1985), *The Sheltered Nest* (1992) and *Time and the Island* (posthumously, 1996). He died at his residence in Magazine Road on 3 August 1995 and was buried in St Oliver's Cemetery, Co. Cork.

DUNSTON, John (1853–1927) Born Moneyvollahane, Castlehaven, the son of a farmer. He emigrated to Canada as a young man and subsequently moved to New York, where he worked as a waiter before opening his own restaurant, the 'Manhattan Oyster Bar', in 1891. In 1915, he purchased the property on Sixth Avenue, between 44th and 45th Streets, where he established 'Jack's Restaurant', one of New York's most popular bar/restaurants of its day. 'A tall, distinguished-looking man, wearing long white moustaches of late years and always clad in immaculate tuxedo', he was reputed to have thrown away the key when he first opened in 1891 and his establishments never closed. He fell foul of Prohibition and was forced to close 'Jack's' in May 1925. He died in New York on 28 December 1927 and was buried in Calvary Cemetery. His estate, principally consisting of real estate in Manhattan, was valued at $1,575,000 net, at probate.

DWYER, James (1795–1889) Born Co. Tipperary. James Dwyer became familiar with Cork through his dealing in the cattle trade. In 1820 he established a store in Great George's Street (now Washington Street), which grew over the years to become the largest wholesale company in southern Ireland and supplied the retail trade countrywide. He also took an active role in public life, was prominent in the Young Ireland movement in Cork and was a member of Cork Corporation and an alderman. A new warehouse headquarters for the Dwyer enterprise was built in Washington Street in 1874. James Dwyer died at his Sunday's Well residence on 15 September 1889 and was buried at St Finbarr's Cemetery.

DWYER, William (1887–1951) Born Cork, into a prominent business family and was educated at Downside Abbey, England. In 1928, he established the Sunbeam Knitwear Company in Blackpool, Cork. This firm became known as Sumbeam Wolsey Ltd in 1933 when the Irish business of Wolsey, an English textile firm, was acquired. In the late 1940s, further factories were built at Youghal (Seafield Fabrics) and Midleton (Worsteds and Woolcombers). By 1950, the combined workforce of the Dwyer firms numbered 2,000 people. He unsuccessfully contested a Cork City seat for Fine Gael in the 1943 general election, but, standing as an independent candidate in 1944, he topped the poll. However, he resigned his seat in 1946. He again contested a seat as an independent candidate in 1948, but this time for the East Cork constituency. He failed to win a seat. Following a brief illness, he died at the Bon Secours Home on 10 May 1951, and was buried privately. Throughout his life, he was a significant contributor to many charities. In 1945, he commissioned **Seamus Murphy** to design the Church of the Annunciation, Blackpool, which he had built in memory of his daughter, Maeve, and which he presented to Cathedral Parish.

E

EAMES, Sir William (1821–1910) Born Cork. He joined the Royal Navy as an assistant engineer in 1844 and served in the Crimean War (1854–1855). He was appointed as Chief Inspector of Machinery in 1870 and Chief Engineer of Chatham Dockyard (1869–1881). He was knighted in 1902 and died in London on 28 February 1910.

EDWARDS, Fred J. [VC] (1894–1964) Born Queenstown (now Cobh), Co. Cork. In World War I, he served as a Private in the 12th Battalion of the Middlesex Regiment. In an action at Thiepval (France) on 26 September 1916, the line of advance was held up by machine gun fire with all the officers either killed or wounded. Edwards, on his own initiative, dashed out to the gun emplacement and disabled it with grenades, thus enabling the advance and saving a dangerous situation. For his action, he was awarded the Victoria Cross on 25 November 1916. He died at Richmond, Surrey, on 9 March 1964, and was buried there.

EGAN, Barry M. (1879–1954) Born Cork, grandson of William Egan the founder of the noted Cork jewellery firm (1820). He went to Paris as a young man and studied the art of ecclesiastical furnishings and silversmithing. On his return to Cork, he established 'Egans' as a centre of excellence in those areas. He was both chairman and manager of the firm. He was a founder member of the Irish Tourist Association and served a term as its president. In 1920, when he was both president of Cork Chamber of Commerce and acting lord mayor following the death of **Terence McSwiney**, the family business was destroyed during the burning of Cork and he was forced to spend some time in Paris for his own safety. In June 1927, he was elected to the Dáil as a Cumann na nGaedhal member and served until 1932. He did not seek re-election in 1932 but was an unsuccessful candidate in the following year. He died at his residence, Charlotte House, Queen Street, on 3 March 1954, and was buried in St Joseph's Cemetery.

EGAN, Michael (1866–1947) Born Cork. He became active at an early age in the trade union movement in Cork and was vice-president of the Cork United Trades (1904 and 1905) and president (1906, 1907, and 1913). He was the Labour representative on the Irish Anti-Conscription Committee which met in Dublin during World War I. He was elected to Cork Corporation for the North West Ward in 1917 and was a member of the Corporation up to its dissolution in 1924. In November of that year, he was elected to Dáil Éireann as a Cumann na nGaedheal TD in a by-election which arose from the resignation of Professor **Alfred O'Rahilly**. He was unsuccessful in seeking re-election in 1927 and also in seeking re-election to the restored Corporation. He was a member of the Cork Harbour Board from 1925 to 1946. A resident of Commons Road, he died at the North Infirmary Hospital on 3 March 1947, and was buried in St Finbarr's Cemetery.

ELLIOTT, Alfred G. (1828–1915) Born Cork, the son of William Elliott, shopkeeper. He was educated at Foley's School, Cork, and at TCD where he graduated BA (1858) and MA (1879). He was ordained in 1858 and served various parishes in the Irish northern dioceses. He was consecrated as bishop of Kilmore on 17 October 1897. A strong anti-home ruler, he was also a noted collector of books and *objets d'art*. He died at the See House, Kilmore, Co. Cavan, on 28 September 1915, and was buried privately. He left his books to the Kilmore see house library.

ELMORE, Alfred (1815–1881) Born Clonakilty, Co. Cork, the son of a retired army surgeon. He went to London c.1827 to follow an art career and exhibited at the Royal Academy in 1834. Following further studies on the Continent, he returned to London in 1844 and exhibited at both the Royal Academy and at the British Institution in successive years. He became a member of the Royal Academy in 1857, and was elected as an honorary member of the Royal Hibernian Academy in 1878. He died at Kensington on 24 January 1881.

EMMET, Christopher Temple (1761–1788)
Born Hammond's Marsh, Cork, the eldest son of Robert Emmet, MD, and brother of the patriot, Robert Emmet (1778–1803), and **Thomas Addis Emmet**. He was educated at TCD where he graduated BA (1780). A very successful barrister, he was called to the Bar in 1781 and to the Inner Bar in 1787. He died in York Street, Dublin on 4 March 1788.

EMMET, Thomas Addis (1764–1827) Born Hammond's Marsh, Cork, the son of Robert Emmet, MD, and brother of the patriot, Robert Emmet (1778–1803), and **Christopher Temple Emmet**. He was educated at TCD where he graduated BA (1783). He then graduated MD at the University of Edinburgh. Because of the death of his brother, Christopher, in 1788, he abandoned medicine and took an LL.B degree at TCD in that year. He was called to the Bar in 1790. Having joined the Society of United Irishmen, he was arrested after the 1798 rebellion and went into exile with his family to Port George, Scotland. On his release in 1802, he went to France and had interviews with both Napoleon (1769–1821) and his Foreign Minister, Talleyrand (1754–1838), on the prospects of an invasion of Ireland. However, subsequent to his brother Robert's failed rebellion in 1803, he settled in the United States where he was very successful at the New York Bar. He died in New York on 14 November 1827, and was buried in St Mark's Churchyard there.

ENGLAND, John (1786–1842) Born Cork, the brother of Rev. **Thomas Richard England** and uncle of **Michael J. Barry** and **Thomas England**. He studied at Carlow College from 1803 until his ordination to the priesthood in 1808. He was president of St Mary's College (the short-lived Cork diocesan seminary) from 1814 until 1817. Of strong nationalist views, he published his *School Primer of Irish History* in 1815 and in the following year, as a trustee of the *Cork Merchantile Chronicle*, was fined £100 arising out of an article in that paper. This, along with his anti-Vetoist principles, led to tensions with Bishop **John Murphy** of Cork and other members of the Irish hierarchy. He was appointed as parish priest of Bandon in 1817. In September 1819, Murphy, in a reply to *Propaganda Fide*, referred to him as 'capable of ministering to Catholics in North America where he will not find the same vexatious politico-religious problems which obtain in this country.' Three years later, he was appointed by papal bull as bishop of Charleston, South Carolina, and was consecrated in Cork on 21 September of that year. His American episcopate was a very successful one. His establishment of the *United States Catholic Miscellany* (1822–1861), the first Roman Catholic newspaper published in America, was a significant achievement. He was noted for his friendship towards the Negroes but nevertheless, he defended slavery, holding that the Negroes were much better treated than Irish peasants. On 8 January 1826, he addressed the American House of Representatives in the presence of President John Quincy Adams (1767–1848). He died in Charleston on 11 April 1842 and was buried there. [Life by P. Guilday (2 vols, 1927); Works by A. Reynolds (5 vols, 1849), and by S.G. Messmer (7 vols, 1908); Engravings by J. Peterkin (1843) and J. Sartain]

ENGLAND, Thomas (d. 1869) Born Bandon, Co. Cork, the son of Michael England. He was the nephew of Bishop **John England** and Rev. **Thomas R. England**. He had commenced art studies in Cork when he became involved in the Young Ireland agitation in 1848. On its collapse, he emigrated to the US, settling in California in 1851. He quickly made his mark as an ecclesiastical architect. His obituary states that, 'To him are due almost all of Catholic art we possess in California. St Mary's Cathedral (the fine college now occupied by the Christian Brothers), Grass Valley Cathedral, Stockton Church, and St Francis Church, San Francisco – the latter the most beautiful edifice on the coast – are a few of the buildings designed and executed by him.' He died in San Francisco on 23 October 1869.

ENGLAND, Thomas Richard (1790–1847) Born Cork, the brother of Bishop **John England** and uncle of **Thomas England**. A noted biographer, he was, in turn, parish priest of Glanmire and Passage West. His publications included *Letters and Memoirs of Abbe Edgeworth* (1810), *A Short Memoir of an Antique Medal, bearing on one Side the Representation of the Head of Christ, and on the other, a curious Hebrew Inscription, lately found at Friar's Walk, near the City of Cork* (1819), and *The Life of Rev. Arthur O'Leary* (1822). He died on 18 March 1847.

ENGLEDOW, Charles J. (1860–1932) Born County Dublin, the son of Rev. W.H. Engledow, formerly archdeacon of Barbados. He was educated at Cambridge University and entered the Colonial Office in 1879. He was ADC to the governor of Grenada and subsequently to the governor-in-chief of the Windward Islands. He was high sheriff of County Carlow in 1893 and resided at Burton Hall there. In 1895, he was elected MP for Kildare North as an anti-Parnellite nationalist, but lost his seat in 1900 when standing as a Healyite. He then purchased Rostellan Castle, became a Poor Law Guardian of the Midleton Union, and was elected to Cork County Council in 1908. However, standing as an O'Brienite, he failed to retain his seat in 1911 and 1914, though he served as a co-opted member for a few months in 1914. He died at his residence, 'Glenmervyn', Glanmire, on 18 December 1932.

ENGLISH, William J. [VC] (1882–1941) Born Cork. He joined the British army and rose to the rank of lieutenant in the 2nd Scottish Horse. During the Boer War, he held a gun position on his own during a Boer attack at Bloemfontein on 3 July 1901. With his ammunition exhausted, he ran through cross-fire on open ground and back again to his own position. He later served in both World Wars and rose to the rank of lieutenant colonel. He was drowned near Egypt on 4 July 1941.

EVANS, Thomas E. (1813–1896) Born Cashel, Co. Tipperary, the son of Thomas M. Evans, doctor. He was educated at Armstrong's School, Cork, and at TCD where he graduated BA (1838). Following his ordination in 1839, he held various positions in the dioceses of Ferns, Cloyne, and Cork. He was a poet of note and also published *The Pyramids of Egypt* (1837). He died on 11 July 1896.

F

FAGAN, Robert (1745–1816) Born Cork. He studied art and in 1768 left for Rome where he resided for many years. He specialised in painting portraits of the many Irish and British aristocrats on the 'Grand Tour'. He was also a keen antiquarian and worked on the archaeological excavations at the ancient Roman port of Ostia. In 1799, during the French occupation of the city, he sent an important collection of pictures, the Altieri Claudes, to England. He also exhibited at the Royal Academy. He was appointed as British Consul General for Sicily and Palermo and committed suicide in Rome on 26 August 1816.

FAGAN, William Addis (1832–1890) Born Cork, the second son of **William Trant Fagan**. Having been educated at Stonyhurst, he entered the 12th Royal Lancers as a cornet in 1855 and retired in 1867 with the rank of captain. He was elected as a Liberal MP for Carlow Borough in 1868, but did not seek re-election in 1874. He died on 14 March 1890.

FAGAN, William Trant (1801–1859) Born Cork, the eldest son of James Fagan, merchant, and father of **William Addis Fagan**. He was educated at Southall Park, Middlesex. Having become mayor of Cork in 1844, he was elected as a Repeal MP for Cork city in 1847 but resigned his seat in 1851. He regained the seat in 1852 as an independent Liberal and retained it in 1857 and 1859. He published *The Life and Times of Daniel O'Connell* (1847). He died in London on 16 May 1859 and was buried in St Joseph's Cemetery, Cork.

FALKINER, Riggs (d. 1797) Born Cork, the son of Caleb Falkiner, merchant, and nephew of Daniel Falkiner, lord mayor of Dublin (1739). He established a bank in Cork in the early 1760s – trading as 'Falkiner and Mills' until 1770. Other partners were involved in the business in later years. He was MP for Clonakilty (1768–76) and for Castlemartyr (1776–83). He was created a baronet in 1778 (the title is still extant). He lived at Garryhesta, near Ovens, before building the original mansion at Annemount, Glounthaune, which is named after his second wife. His will was proven on 3 August 1797.

FALVEY, Thomas (*fl. c.*1815–1832) Born Cork. Having taken up painting in his native city, he set out for the Continent when one of his pictures was rejected as 'unfit' by a local committee. On his return, he failed to win adequate patronage with the exception of his 'The Institution of the Order of St Francis' which was commissioned by Father **Theobald Mathew**. He then headed for a new life in America, but died in 1832 shortly after his arrival there.

FARREN, Elizabeth (countess of Derby) (1759–1829) Born Cork, the daughter of an apothecary. Her career as an actress started as a child when her widowed mother moved to England and she went on to appear in major London productions at the Haymarket Theatre and Drury Lane. She retired from the stage in 1797 when she married Edward Stanley, 12th earl of Derby, as his second wife and by whom she had three children. She died in Lancashire on 29 April 1829.

FARRINGTON, Anthony (1893–1973) Born Cork, the son of Thomas Farrington, analytical chemist and treasurer of the Cork Historical & Archaeological Society from its foundation to his death in May 1924. Anthony was the younger brother of **Benjamin Farrington** and nephew of **Stephen Foreman**. He was educated at Cork Grammar School and at UCC where he graduated BE (1921). In that year and having a strong interest in geology, he joined the staff of the Geological Survey of Ireland. He had held a demonstratorship in engineering for a few months at UCC. In 1928, he was appointed as resident secretary of the Royal Irish Academy (1928–1961) and as librarian of the same institution (1934–61). He was also editor of the Academy's *Proceedings* (1945–65). He was a founder member of the Geographical Society of Ireland in 1934 and later served as its president (1943–6, 1951–60) and as editor of its journal, *Irish Geography* (1944–5 and 1951–60). In recognition of his work on glacial geology and geomorphology, he was awarded the degree of D.Sc. by TCD in 1936. He was a founder member of An Taisce (The Irish National Trust) and served on its council for many years. He died at a Bray, Co. Wicklow, nursing home on 23 February 1973, and was buried in Calary Churchyard, Co. Wicklow. He was the father of the playwright and RTÉ actor, Conor Farrington.

FARRINGTON, Benjamin (1891–1974) Born Cork, the son of Thomas Farrington, analytical chemist and treasurer of the Cork Historical & Archaeological Society from its foundation to his death in May 1924. Benjamin was the elder brother of **Anthony Farrington** and nephew of **Stephen Foreman**. He was educated at TCD where he graduated BA (1915) and at UCC where he graduated MA. He worked as an assistant in the Classics Department of QUB (1916–20) before moving to Cape Town where he was appointed, in turn, as lecturer in Greek (1920–22), senior lecturer in Classics (1922–30), and professor of Latin (1930–35). He returned to Europe in 1935 on his appointment as lecturer in Classics at Bristol University. In the following year, he was appointed as professor of Classics at University College, Swansea, where he stayed until his retirement in 1956. He was the author of more than a dozen published works, the best-known of which were *Science in Antiquity* (1936, 2nd ed., 1969), *Science and Politics in the Ancient World* (1939), *Greek Science: its meaning for us* (2 vols, 1944–8; rev. ed. in one volume, 1953),

Francis Bacon: philosopher of industrial science (1949, rev. ed., 1973), *Aristotle: the founder of scientific philosophy* (1965), and *What Darwin really said* (1965). He died on 17 November 1974.

FAWSITT, Diarmaid (1884–1967) Born Bandon, Co. Cork, the son of Boyle T.H. Fawsitt. He was educated at Blarney Street CBS, Cork. He became secretary of the Irish Industrial Development Association in 1911 (to 1919) in succession to E.J. Riordan, and was one of those who negotiated the establishment of Henry Ford and Son in Cork. He was a founder member of the Volunteer movement in Cork and attended the first meeting in the City Hall in December 1913. He served as Consul General for Ireland in the United States (1919–21) and as assistant secretary at the Department of Industry and Commerce (1922–23). He was called to the Bar in 1928 and to the Inner Bar in 1938. He served as an acting Circuit Court judge (1941–43) and then as a Circuit Court judge on the Eastern Circuit (1943–56). He died at St Joseph's Nursing Home, Dublin, on 27 April 1967, and was buried in St Fintan's Cemetery, Sutton.

FEEHAN, John M. (1916–1991) Born Cashel, Co. Tipperary. He was educated at Thurles CBS, Rockwell College, and UCG. He was commissioned as an officer of the Irish army in 1939 and rose to the rank of captain. He co-founded the Mercier Press, Cork, in March 1944, and subsequently opened the Mercier Bookshop. His publications included *An Irish Publisher and His World* (1969), *Tomorrow to be Brave* (1972), *The Wind that round the Fastnet Sweeps* (1978), *The Shooting of Michael Collins* (1981), *Bobby Sands and the Tragedy of Northern Ireland* (1983), *Operation Brogue* (1984), *The Irish Bedside Book* (1980), and *The Statesman* (1985). He was the co-author of *The Comic History of Ireland* (1951, 1964). He resigned his army commission in 1950 and died on 21 May 1991.

FENTON, Sir Maurice (d. 1664) Born Mitchelstown, Co. Cork, the son of Sir William Fenton and grandson of Sir Geoffrey Fenton who obtained large estates in the wake of the Desmond Rebellion. Maurice sat as MP for Cork County in Cromwellian Parliament of 1659. A year previously, he had been made a baronet by Cromwell. However, the title became extinct when his son, Sir William Fenton, died unmarried. The Mitchelstown estates then passed to the King family of Co. Roscommon, who later became earls of Kingston. Maurice died in 1664.

FIHELLY, John Arthur (1882–1945) Born Timoleague, Co. Cork, the son of Cornelius Fihelly, customs officer. A year after his birth, the family emigrated to Brisbane, Queensland. At the age of 13, he was employed as a telegraph messenger boy and later worked in the department of Trade and Customs as a clerk. He played rugby for both Queensland and Australia and was one of the founders of Rugby League football in Australia. He was a member of the first Australian league side to tour England in 1908/9. He later became president of the Queensland Amateur Rugby League Board. In 1912, he was elected to the Queensland Legislative Assembly and served as Minister Without Portfolio from 1915 until 1918. His pro-Irish position made him many enemies and following his denunciation of the British Government in 1916, the state governor, Sir **Hamilton Goold-Adams**, refused to speak to him. He became secretary for railways in 1918 and a year later the ministry of justice was added to his responsibilities. However, due to his personal behaviour, he lost his seat in 1921 and was appointed as agent-general of the government. He finally resigned from state politics in 1924. He became a successful local politician, but following an accident in 1926 in which his skull was fractured, his health deteriorated. He died in Brisbane on 2 March 1945, and was accorded a state funeral.

FINN, Edward (1767–1810) Born Cork. He was a member of the Society of United Irishmen. Following the failure of the 1798 rebellion, he escaped to Bordeaux and entered the French army. He rose to the rank of colonel in the Lanciers de Bergh regiment. In 1802, he settled as a merchant in Bordeaux, but rejoined his old regiment at the commencement of the Peninsular War. He was killed in October 1810 while defending the bridge at Azava, Spain. He was buried by a Corkman, Colonel O'Donovan of the British army, whom he had known since his childhood.

FINNY, John Magee (1841–1922) Born Cork, the son of T.H.C. Finny, Rector of Clondulane, Fermoy. His mother was Frances Magee, the daughter of Archbishop **William C. Magee**. He was privately educated and was a senior exhibitioner at TCD in 1864. He became King's Professor of the Practice of Medicine at TCD (1882–1910) and president of the Royal College of Physicians (1890–92). He died on 7 December 1922, and was buried in Mount Jerome Cemetery, Dublin.

FISHER, William (1817–1895) Born Cork. He studied art in Italy as a young man and became a member of the Florentine Academy. Having taken up residence in London by 1840, he exhibited at both the Royal Academy and at the British Institution. He also exhibited at the Royal Hibernian Academy and at the Cork Exhibition of 1852. He died in London on 23 March 1895.

FITZGERALD, Barbara (1911–1982) Born Cork, the daughter of John A.F. Gregg (1878–1961), archbishop of Armagh. She was educated in England and at TCD. Following her marriage to Michael Fitzgerald Somerville, she spent much of her time in West Africa. She worked with the intelligence services in England during World War II and subsequently lived in Armagh. Her novels *We Are Besieged* (1946) and *Footprints upon Water* (posthumously, 1983), deal with the fortunes of Anglo-Irish families in a changing Ireland. She died in Co. Dublin on 21 May 1982.

FITZGERALD, Charles C. Penrose (1841–1921) Born Corkbeg, Whitegate, Co. Cork. He joined the British navy in 1854 at the age of thirteen and rose to the rank of admiral. He retired in 1905 and died at Folkestone on 11 August 1921. He published *The Life of Admiral Tryon* (1897) and two autobiographies, *Memories of the Sea* (1913) and *From Sail to Steam* (1916).

FITZGERALD, Denis P. (1871–1948) Born Cork. He was educated at PBC, Cork, and at Queen's College, Cork (now UCC) where he graduated BA (1890) and MB (1896). He was lecturer in Anatomy at UCC (1897–1908) and House Surgeon at the Eye, Ear, and Throat Hospital, Western Road. In 1909, he succeeded Professor **John J. Charles** as professor of Anatomy, a post he held until his retirement in 1942. He had been dean of the faculty of Medicine from 1940. He published numerous papers on anatomy and his pastime of historical research made him a recognised authority on Cork local history. He died at the Mercy Home, Cork, on 2 January 1948, and was buried in St Joseph's Cemetery.

FITZGERALD, John (1825–1910) Born Hanover Street, Cork. He was educated at Blackmoor Lane NS, Sullivan's Quay CBS, and North Monastery CBS. At the age of 15, he was apprenticed to his brother-in-law, Michael Murphy, a successful London cabinet-maker. However, he returned to Cork and worked as a chemist's assistant at Queen's College (now UCC) before resuming work in cabinet making with Cornelius O'Keefe of Grattan Street. In his 20s, he turned his attention to wood-carving, the occupation to which he subsequently devoted himself both as teacher and craftsman. He was also a talented artist. However, he is best remembered as a poet and antiquary. His verse was published in collected form in *Gems of the Cork Poets* (1883), and after his death in *Legends, Ballads, and Songs of the Lee* (1913). Under the pseudonyms 'Cock o'Sinbarry's' and 'The Bard of the Lee', his best known verses are 'The Green Hills of Cork' (or 'Beautiful City') and 'Cork is the Eden'. His antiquarian writings were published in Cork newspapers, in the *JCHAS*, and in a small volume, *Echoes of '98*

(1898). He recorded old Cork in sketches and drawings also. He died on 14 May 1910, and was buried in St Joseph's Cemetery.

FITZGERALD, Sir John Fitzedmund (1528–1612) He was the son of Edmund Fitzjames Fitzgerald and cousin of John Fitzedmund Fitzgerald whom he succeeded as seneschal of Imokilly. Unlike his cousin, he opposed the Kildare rebellion of 1569 and was made sheriff of County Cork. He remained loyal to the English Crown through the two Desmond rebellions and was knighted at Cloyne in 1602 by Sir George Carew (1555–1629), President of Munster. He also received a pension. Previously, in 1591, he had succeeded in having himself appointed dean of Cloyne (though a layman!); a move which enabled him, through the Diocesan Chapter, to alienate the episcopal demesne at Cloyne in fee simple to one of his dependants. He died on 15 July 1612 and was buried in Cloyne Cathedral. [Tomb in north transept, St Colman's Cathedral, Cloyne.]

FITZGERALD, Mick (1881–1920) Born Ballyoran, Castlelyons, Co. Cork. He was educated in Fermoy and joined the Irish Volunteers there in February 1914. When the Fermoy battalion of the IRA was formed in 1918, he was appointed quartermaster under **Liam Lynch**. He was arrested and sentenced to three months' imprisonment in Cork Jail in June 1919. He was a participant in the daylight attack on a military party in Fermoy on 7 September 1919. He was arrested on the following morning and remanded in custody until he was charged on 20 April 1920 with the murder of Private Jones. After serving eleven months in jail, he went on hunger strike on 11 August 1920. He died on 17 October, the 67th day of his hunger strike. He was buried in Kilcrumper Cemetery on 20 October 1920.

FITZGERALD, Richard [VC] (1831–1884) Born Cork. He became a gunner in the Bengal horse artillery. During the Indian War, he and sergeant Diamond remained at their gun post at

Bolandshahr on 28 September 1857, when the other members of their unit had either been killed or wounded. Under sustained heavy fire, they cleared the road of the attackers. He died in India in 1884.

FITZGERALD, Richard (1881–1956) Born Midleton, Co. Cork, the son of a draper and local politician. He studied for the priesthood and was ordained in 1902. He served as a curate in Macroom before being appointed as vice-president of Salamanca theological college, Spain. He was consecrated as bishop of Gibraltar in 1927. He played a prominent part in the reconstruction of Gibraltar after World War II. He died on 15 February 1956 and was buried in Gibraltar.

FITZGERALD, Robert Uniacke (1751–1814) Born Corkbeg, Whitegate, Co. Cork, the son of Robert Uniacke who, in 1718, had been granted the Corkbeg estate by a grand-uncle, Robert Fitzgerald, on condition that the surname would be changed to Fitzgerald. He was the elder brother of **Sir Thomas Judkin Fitzgerald**. He succeeded to the estate on his father's death in 1778, was a Colonel in the North Cork militia and was elected for Cork county in the Irish parliament in 1798. Pro-Union, he continued to sit for Cork county in the imperial parliament until 1806. He died at his seat, Corkbeg, on 20 December 1814 and was buried in Corkbeg Graveyard.

FITZGERALD, Sir Robert Uniacke Penrose (1839–1919) Born Corkbeg, Whitegate, Co. Cork, the eldest son of Robert Penrose Fitzgerald, landlord. He was educated in England and graduated from Cambridge in 1863. In the 1860s, he travelled widely in Tibet and India. He unsuccessfully contested the Youghal parliamentary seat as a Conservative in the 1874 general election. However, he sat as Conservative MP for Cambridge from 1885 until 1906. As owner of 6,000 acres (of which he farmed 1,000 acres), he took a prominent role in the Cork Defence Union and the Property Defence Association during the Land League period. He

was knighted in 1896. He died at his London residence on 10 July 1919, his 80th birthday.

FITZGERALD, Seamus (1896–1972) Born Cobh, Co. Cork. He was educated at PBC, Cobh, and became an apprentice at the naval dockyard, Haulbowline. He joined the Irish Volunteers in 1916 and was interned at Frongoch following the rising of that year. He was subsequently interned several times during the War of Independence. In 1920, he was president of the East Cork Republican District Court and chairman of Queenstown (Cobh) UDC (a position which he filled on ten occasions up to 1950). He was also a member of Cork County Council (1920–2 and 1932–6). He was the youngest member of the 2nd Dáil and voted against the Treaty. A founder member of Fianna Fáil, he was a member of Seanad Éireann (1934–6) and sat as a TD for Cork city (1943–4). However, he was unsuccessful in the Dáil elections of 1922, 1923, 1927, and 1944. He was a member of Cork Harbour Commissioners for fifty-two years (1920–72) and also served as chairman (1936–42), was the founder and chairman of Fitzgerald and Co. (Grand Parade) and of CRETCO, a founder director of Aer Rianta, Irish Steel, and Cork Dockyard Ltd (of which he was chairman from 1941 to 1958), and a director and first chairman of Verolme (Cork) Dockyard. He as awarded an honorary degree of LL.D by UCC. He died at his residence, 'Carrigbeg', Summerhill, on 23 April 1972 and was buried in St Colman's Cemetery, Cobh. [Life-size bronze by **Seamus Murphy**; Papers in Cork Archives Institute, who published *A descriptive list of the papers of Seamus Fitzgerald LLD* (1999).]

FITZGERALD, Sir Thomas JUDKIN (1755–1810) Born Corkbeg, Whitegate, Co. Cork, the son of Robert Uniacke who, in 1718, had been granted the Corkbeg estate by a grand-uncle, Robert Fitzgerald, on condition that the surname would be changed to Fitzgerald. He was a younger brother of **Robert Uniacke Fitzgerald**. Judkin was the surname of his mother. Thomas was educated at TCD where he graduated BA

(1773). On the outbreak of the Rebellion of 1798, he was requested to act as highsheriff of Tipperary. His ruthless tactics led to an award of £500 damages to a Mr Wright of Clonmel who had been flogged. He petitioned the Irish Parliament against the award. He failed in this, but an Indemnity Act was amended to include him and he received a large pension from the English Government. He was knighted in 1801. He died on 24 September 1810.

FITZGERALD, William (1814–1883) Born Lifford, Co. Donegal. He was educated at Midleton College and TCD where he graduated BD and DD (1853), having been previously professor of Moral Philosophy (1847) and professor of Ecclesiastical History (1852). He was consecrated as bishop of Cork, Cloyne, and Ross on 8 March 1857. He was translated to the diocese of Killaloe in 1862. He died on 24 November 1883. His publications during his Cork episcopate include *The Duties of Parochial Clergy* (1857), *The Duty of Catechising the Young* (1858), *A Letter to the Laity of Cork*, 'Lord Wodehouse's Bill for Legalizing Marriages with a deceased Wife's Sister' [Speech in the House of Lords, March 20, 1859] (1860), *Thoughts on Present Circumstances of the Church of Ireland* (1860), *The Revival of Synods* (1861) and *An Essay on the Study of the Evidences of Christianity* (1861).

FITZGERALD, William (1832–1896) Born Mogeely, Co. Cork, the nephew of Bishop **William Keane** of Cloyne. He was educated locally and at the Irish College, Paris, where he was ordained in 1857. For the next twenty years, he worked on the staff of St Colman's College, Fermoy, becoming its president in 1874. He was consecrated as bishop of Ross on 11 November 1877 at the Pro-Cathedral, Skibbereen. He died on 24 November 1896, and was buried alongside his uncle in St Colman's Cathedral, Cobh.

FITZGERALD, William O'Brien (1906–1974) Born Cork, the son of William Fitzgerald, clerk of the crown and peace. He was educated at Belvedere College and the King's Inns. He was called to the Bar in 1927 and to the Inner Bar in 1944. Following a highly successful career at the Bar, he was appointed in 1966 by Taoiseach Jack Lynch as a judge of the Supreme Court. He was promoted to the post of Chief Justice in 1972. He died on 17 October 1974.

FITZGIBBON, Denis (1921–1998) Born Cork, the son of Edwin Fitzgibbon. He was educated at PBC, Cork, and excelled in rugby, playing for Dolphin and Munster. He studied accountancy and moved to Dublin where he worked for Smithfield Motors. He had a successful business career in the motor trade, becoming sales director of Volkswagen Ireland in 1960 and managing director of Toyota in 1975. He also served as chairman of the Marketing Institute of Ireland. In the 1950s, he became a nationally known entertainer using the name, 'Din Joe'. From 1953 to the early 1970s, he presented the popular radio programme, 'Take the Floor', which became essential light entertainment listening and was recorded live at venues around the country. He published *Laughter Unlimited* – a collection of his jokes and stories. He died in Dublin on 23 November 1998 and was cremated.

FITZGIBBON, Edmund Fitzjohn (*c.*1552–1608) He was the son of John Óg Fitzgerald (*alias* Fitzgibbon) and was known as 'The White Knight'. His father had been attainted and his lands seized in 1546, but Edmund was able to lease them back from the crown in 1576. A further lease was made in 1579 which also included those lands which had reverted to the crown on the death of his mother, Ellen (née Condon). He narrowly escaped the implication of being a supporter of the Desmond rebellion and was appointed as sheriff of Cork in 1596. He was again under suspicion after the battle of Kinsale, but his capture of James Fitzthomas Fitzgerald ('The Súgán Earl') in the Mitchelstown caves in 1601 saved his reputation from the point of view of the English authorities. In 1604, he was created Baron Clangibbon by King James I (1556–1625) with restoration of his ancient title in tail male, but he and his son died before the patent was issued by the Irish parliament. He died at Castletown on 23 April 1608, the day after the death of his son, Maurice. They were buried firstly at Kilbehenny but a week later, were re-interred at Kilmallock, Co. Limerick.

FITZGIBBON, Edmund Gerald (1825–1905) Born Cork, the son of Gibbon Carew Fitzgibbon. He worked as a clerk in London and emigrated to Victoria, Australia, in 1852. In 1854, he was employed as a clerical assistant in the office of Melbourne city council, and through the deaths of two of his immediate superiors, he was appointed as town clerk of Melbourne in 1856. He was responsible for numerous advances in the provision of items such as tramways, public lighting, asphalt pathways, effluent control etc., for the city. In 1891, he was appointed as full-time chairman of the Melbourne and metropolitan board of works and supervised the provision of the city's massive sewage system. He was admitted to the New South Wales Bar in 1860 but was an unsuccessful candidate for the state election in 1861. He was prominent in the movement to abolish the system of transportation of convicts, and he also advocated the abolition of state assistance to denominational schools. He died at his residence on 12 December 1905. [Portraits at Melbourne city council and board of works; Statue near Prince's bridge, Melbourne]

FITZGIBBON, Edwin (d. 1938) Born Dungourney, Co. Cork. He served on the staff of Rochestown College before taking up a lectureship in philosophy at UCC and eventually being appointed to the professorship. He promoted hurling among the students and organised inter-varsity competitions for which he donated a trophy (the Fitzgibbon cup) in 1912. He retired from his professorship in 1937 when he was succeeded by a fellow-Capuchin, Father **James Edward O'Mahony**. He died in 1938.

FITZPATRICK, Joseph J. (1877–1910) Born Cork, probably the son of Patrick Fitzpatrick of Anglesea Terrace, machinist. He was educated at North Monastery CBS and later joined the Irish Christian Brothers in 1894. He taught, in turn, at Synge Street CBS, Dublin, Sexton Street CBS, Limerick and at Wexford CBS before returning to Synge Street in 1907. He had a great interest in the teaching of Irish and his publications include *Aids to the Pronunciation of Irish* (1905), *Aids to Irish Composition* (1907) and *Sequel to Aids in Irish Composition* (1907). He died of tuberculosis at Jervis Street private hospital, Dublin, on 5 October 1910, and was buried in Glasnevin Cemetery.

FITZPATRICK, Thomas (1860–1912) Born Cork, the son of a buyer in Grant's drapery establishment. Having begun his artistic career with the Cork company of Guy's, he moved to Dublin as a lithographic artist where he made his reputation as political cartoonist, magazine illustrator, illuminator (helped by his daughter, Mary) and photo-engraver. He became chief cartoonist for the *National Press* and later the *Weekly Freeman* as well as other pictorial publications. In 1905, he founded *The Leprechaun,* a humorous monthly review of topical comment and satire. His political cartoons, like those of his mentor, **John Fergus O'Hea**, presented a rival image to those of *Punch* and illustrated wittily a key period in Irish history. He also painted in oil and watercolours. He fell ill in 1911 and his daughter, Mary, took over the editorship of the magazine, which survived to 1915. He died in Dublin on 16 July 1912 and was buried in Glasnevin Cemetery.

FLAVIN, Martin (1841–1916) Born Cork, the eldest son of Timothy Flavin. He was a butter merchant and a prominent businessman, was chairman of the Cork-Macroom Railway Co. and was a director of the Cork Imperial Hotel Co. Being an Alderman on Cork Corporation in 1891, he was selected to stand as the anti-Parnellite candidate in the by-election arising from **C.S. Parnell**'s death. He was elected MP, defeating both the future Irish nationalist leader, John Redmond (1856–1918), and a Unionist candidate. However, due to ill health, he did not contest the 1892 general election and, in later years, took no active part in politics. He died at his Summerhill, Cork, residence on 30 December 1916.

FLEISCHMANN, Aloys G. (1880–1964) Born Dachau, Bavaria, the son of Alois Fleischmann, and father of **Aloys G. Fleischmann** (1910–92). He was educated locally and at the Royal Conservatoire of Music, Munich, where he graduated with a master's degree and studied with the famous German composer and organist, Josef Rheinberger (1839–1901). In 1906, he succeeded his father-in-law, Hans Swertz, as organist at St Mary's Cathedral, Cork – a position which he held for nearly forty years. He was also appointed to the staff of the Cork School of Music and was conductor of the choir there. As a German national, he was interned in the Isle of Man during World War I and was conductor of the camp orchestra. With his wife, Tilly (a gifted concert pianist and teacher), the couple were a major influence in the development of music in the city and beyond. In 1954, he was presented with the Papal medal, 'pro ecclesia et pontifice', for his services to church music. He died at St Patrick's Hospital, Cork, on 3 January 1964 and was buried in St Finbarr's Cemetery. [Family archive at UCC]

FLEISCHMANN, Aloys G. (1910–1992) Born Munich, the son of **Aloys G. Fleischmann** (1880–1964) and his wife, Tilly (née Swertz). He was reared in Cork, educated at Farranferris College and graduated MA from UCC (1932). Following a period of postgraduate study at the Academy of Music, Munich, he was appointed as professor of Music at UCC in 1936 where he served until his retirement in 1980. His contribution to the musical life of Cork, through his teaching and through the many societies and agencies which he founded or supported, was unique. He was the founder of and conducted the Cork Symphony Orchestra for fifty-six years, an entry which appears in the *Guinness Book of Records*. He was also the founder and director of the Cork International Choral and Folk Dance Festival for a period of thirty-three years. With **Joan Denise Moriarty**, he founded the Cork ballet company and conducted at many of its performances. He was made a freeman of Cork in 1978 and was also a member of Aosdána. His many compositions encompass the entire musical spectrum. His publications include *Music in Ireland* (1952) and *Sources of Traditional Irish Music, 1583–1855* (2 vols, posth., 1998). He died at his Ballyvolane residence, 'Glen House', on 21 July 1992 and was buried in St Finbarr's Cemetery. [Remembrances by contemporaries and annotated catalogue of his music by S. de Barra in R. Fleischmann (ed.), *Aloys Fleischmann (2000)*; Family archive at UCC]

FLEWETT, William Edward (1861–1938) Born Dublin, the son of a prison governor. He was educated at Erasmus Smith high school and TCD where he graduated BA (1885). Following his ordination in that year, he was appointed as a curate at St FinBarre's cathedral and as dean of residence at Queen's College, Cork (now UCC). He later held rectories in Midleton, Mallow and St Luke's (where he ministered for twenty years). On the resignation of Bishop **Charles Dowse** in 1933, he was elected as bishop of Cork, Cloyne, and Ross and was consecrated on 30 November of that year. He died while on holiday at Glandore on 5 August 1938 and was buried at Frankfield graveyard, Douglas.

FLINN, Hugo (1879–1943) Born Cork, the son of Hugh Flinn, a leading fish merchant whose headquarters were in Liverpool. He was educated at Dungarvan, Kinsale, Mungret College and Clongowes Wood College. He qualified as an engineer at the Royal University of Ireland and took up a position as electrical engineer with Liverpool corporation. He returned to Ireland in 1914 and, for some years, superintended his father's fish interests. On the latter's death in 1920, he disposed of the business and set up as an electrical engineer in Cork, opening one of the city's first wireless establishments in Mac Curtain Street. In 1927, he launched a 'No Income Tax' campaign and was elected to the Dáil as a Fianna Fáil TD for the borough of Cork in September 1927. A TD from 1927 to his death, he served as parliamentary secretary to the minister for Finance from 1932. He was appointed as the Turf Controller around 1940. He died at his residence, 'Cooleen', Rushbrooke, on 28 January 1943 and was buried in St Finbarr's Cemetery.

FLYN, William (c.1740–1811) He was the nephew of Lawrence Flyn, a prominent Dublin bookseller and publisher. He was also the grand-uncle of the Jesuit, **Robert Haly**. By 1768, he was established as a bookseller, printer, and publisher 'at the Sign of Shakespear, near the Exchange' in Cork. From 1768 to 1802, he was publisher and printer of the *Hibernian Chronicle* newspaper, originally published in quarto and subsequently in folio size. In 1771, he published *The Modern Monitor, or Flyn's Speculations*, a selection of essays from the *Hibernian Chronicle*. By 1801, the *Hibernian Chronicle* was printed by his son-in-law, **James Haly**, under whom it was continued as the *Cork Merchantile Chronicle*. He died at George's Quay, Cork, on 4 December 1811.

FLYNN, James Christopher (1852–1922) Born London, the son of Daniel Flynn of White-church, Co. Cork. He was educated at CBC, Cork. He came to prominence in the Land League period and was imprisoned during the Plan of Campaign (1886–90). He was elected as MP for Cork North at the 1885 general election and was returned unopposed at each of the five subsequent elections until his retirement in January 1910. He took the anti-Parnellite side in the 1890s and also served as secretary to the Cork Evicted Tenants' Association. He died at his residence, 4 York Terrace, Cork, on 15 November 1922 and was buried in St Finbarr's Cemetery.

FLYNN, Patrick (b. 1894) Born Ballinadee, Co. Cork, the son of Patrick Flynn. While still a teenager, he won the Irish Four-Mile championship in May 1913. He emigrated to the United States in September 1913 and continued his exploits as a top long-distance runner. In 1917, he went to France with the American Expeditionary Force and was wounded in the shoulder in 1918. Despite this, he returned to athletics in 1920 and was selected on the US team for the Antwerp Olympiad, having won the 3,000m steeplechase in the US championships. At Antwerp, a fall at the water jump dashed his hopes of gold, but he finished in second place to take the silver medal. Though he is commemorated by a 1998 memorial in Ballinadee, his later life and career in the US is not known.

FOGARTY, Francis J. (1899–1973) Born Cork, the son of Michael Fogarty. He was educated at Farranferris College, Cork. He joined the RAF at the age of eighteen and on the outbreak of World War II, he commanded the 37th Bomber Squadron. He was promoted as senior staff officer to No. 4 Group Bomber Command and played a pivotal role in the bombing of Germany towards the end of that war. After the war, he commanded the Mediterranean Allied air forces and served as an aide-de-camp to Queen Elizabeth II (b. 1926) before his retirement in 1957. He died on 12 January 1973.

FOLEY, Allen J. (1835–1899) Born Cahir, Co. Tipperary, the son of an RIC constable. When he was ten years old, the family moved to Dungourney, Co. Cork, where his father had obtained the position of parish clerk. He was educated at Midleton College until the age of eighteen when he left for America. In the meantime, he had taken singing lessons from the rector of Dungourney, Rev. William Wilson. His great 'basso profundo' voice (with a range of two octaves) was quickly recognised and soon he was earning extra money through singing in a church choir. He left America for Europe in 1861 and made his debut, as 'Signor Foli', in the following year. For the remainder of his life, he was in constant demand in the fields of opera, oratorio and concert. He died of double pneumonia at Southport, Merseyside, on 20 October 1899. [Life by D. Reynolds (1994)]

FOLEY, James 'Fox' (c.1910–1952) Born Geraldine Place, Cork, the son of Patrick J. Foley (d. 1936), an employee of Cork telephone exchange. His early sporting success was as a hurler, winning County juvenile and minor medals with the Geraldines in 1920 and 1925 respectively. His career as an outstanding soccer goalkeeper began in junior football with Blackrock Rovers, before joining Cork FC with whom he won his first FAI Cup medal in 1934. In that same year, he made his international debut, winning the first of seven caps in a World Cup qualifier against Belgium. He was transferred to Glasgow Celtic (also in 1934) where he gained the remainder of his caps. He played briefly for Plymouth Argyle in 1938 before signing for Cork City in 1938. He played for Cork United in the 1940s and won a further two FAI Cup medals (1941, 1947). The 1947 cup final replay was his last senior match, but he was subsequently coach to Evergreen United, the Cork League of Ireland side. He died at the Bon Secours Hospital, Cork, on 14 October 1952 after a short illness. He was buried in St Joseph's Cemetery.

FORDE, James (b. 1824) Born Cork. A talented artist who lived in George's Street and who flourished in the middle of the nineteenth century.

FORDE, Patrick (d. 1972) Born Kayser's Hill, Barrack Street, Cork, the son of John Forde. He was educated at Sullivan's Quay CBS. He unsuccessfully contested the Mid Cork constituency as a Fianna Fáil candidate in the 1965 general election. He was elected to Cork County Council in 1967 and was returned to the Dáil for the Mid Cork constituency in 1969. He died unexpectedly at his residence in Fivemilebridge, Ballygarvan (where he was a successful publican) on 13 May 1972 and was buried in Killingley Cemetery.

FORDE, Samuel (1805–1828) Born Cork, the son of a tradesman who had apparently deserted his family. In 1818, he commenced his artistic career under J. Chalmers (*fl.* 1801–20), the master of the newly founded Cork School of Art. He acquired great skill in the art of distemper painting but was not quite as successful at portraiture. He was master of the Cork Mechanics' Institute and was an intimate friend of **Daniel Maclise**. His 'Fall of the Rebel Angels' (1828) was exhibited at the Royal Hibernian Academy and now hangs at the Cork School of Art. He also painted the 'Crucifixion' at St Patrick's cathedral, Skibbereen. He died of consumption on 29 June 1828 and was buried in St FinBarre's Churchyard. [Self-portrait at the Crawford Gallery, Cork]

FOREMAN, Stephen (1868–1936) Born Cork, the son of William Foreman, provisions merchant and uncle of **Anthony Farrington** and **Benjamin Farrington**. He was a contributor to the *New Ireland Review* from 1895 and was the author of three collections of poems, *City of the Crimson Walls* (1895), *The Abhorred Shears* (1905) and *The Sanctuary and the Wilderness* (n.d.). He also wrote four novels, *Errors of the Comedy* (1911), *Overflowing Scourge* (1911), *The Fen Dogs* (1912) and *The Terrible Choice* (1913). For many years, he was a prominent member of the Cork Operatic Society. He died at his residence, 3 Redcliffe, Western Road, Cork, on 24 February 1936.

FORREST, John (1820–1883) Born Buttevant, Co. Cork, the son of Benjamin Forrest. He was educated at Bandon High School, St Patrick's College, Maynooth; and at the Gregorian University, Rome, where he graduated DD in 1847. In that year, he was ordained and returned to Ireland to take up parish duties and in 1850 he began his career as a teacher in Dublin. Having failed to secure lectureships in Maynooth and at the Catholic University of Ireland, he resigned from his teaching post and went back to parish work. However, he was recommended by Cardinal Paul Cullen (1803–78), archbishop of Dublin, as rector of the new St John's College, Sydney – a post which he took up in September 1860. The college was a complete failure, largely because of the attitude of the local archbishop.

In 1873, Forrest was offered £400 a year by the new coadjutor archbishop to resign from the college which at the time boasted of one resident student! In 1875, he was appointed as parish priest of Balmain, Sydney. He died there on 3 August 1883.

FOSTER, William (c.1744–1797) The son of Anthony Foster, Chief Baron of the Irish Exchequer, he was educated at TCD where he graduated BA (1765), MA (1767), and DD (1789). He was consecrated as Church of Ireland bishop of Cork and Ross on 14 June 1789. He was subsequently translated to Kilmore (1790) and Clogher (1796). His brother, John Foster (1740–1828), was the last Speaker of the Irish House of Commons. He died on 4 November 1797.

FOX, Joseph F. (b. 1853) Born Harbour Row, Queenstown (now Cobh), the son of Thomas Fox, grocer. He was educated at St Colman's College, Fermoy, and at Queen's College, Cork (now UCC). He emigrated to New York and became a professor at St Francis Xavier's College, where he graduated MA, before taking a medical degree at the University of Cincinnati. He practised medicine and surgery at Troy, New York State, and was active in nationalist circles. He was a member of the New York executive of the National League of America and was founder of the Irish National Federation of America. He returned to Ireland in 1885 and was selected as nationalist candidate for the Tullamore division of Queen's County (Offaly). He was duly returned and sat as the MP from 1885 until 1900, latterly as an anti-Parnellite. He resided at Wilmount Castle, Cobh, for a time in the 1890s, but later returned to the United States

FRANKS, Sir John (1770–1852) Born Bally-magoold, Mallow, Co. Cork. He was educated at TCD where he graduated BA (1788) and LL.B (1791). A friend of **John Philpot Curran**, he was called to the Bar in 1792 and to the Inner Bar in 1823. In 1825, he was appointed as a judge of the Calcutta Supreme Court and was knighted before his departure. He resigned from

this position through ill health in 1834. He died in Dublin on 11 January 1852.

FRANKS, Sir Thomas Harte (1808–1862) Born Carrig Castle, Mallow, Co. Cork. He joined the British army in 1825 as an ensign in the 10th Regiment. In 1842, his regiment was posted to India where, with the rank of lieutenant colonel, he served with distinction in the two Sikh Wars (1845–6 and 1848–9) and in the Indian revolt of 1857. Following a disagreement with Field Marshal Sir Colin Campbell (1792–1863), he returned to England where he was promoted to the rank of major general and was knighted. With his health ruined, he died at Tetsworth, Oxfordshire, on 5 February 1862.

FREEMAN-JACKSON, Harry (1911–1993) Born Pakistan. He served in the British army in World War II and spent four years in a German POW camp. Retiring with the rank of captain, he and his wife settled near Mallow immediately after the war and he became master of the Duhallow Hounds. He became an internationally known horseman and represented Ireland in the Three-Day Event in four consecutive Olympiads (1952, 1956, 1960 and 1964), the first Irish Olympian to do so. He acted as *chef d'équipe* on a fifth occasion. He won the prestigious Burghley horse trial event in 1963, and in 1966, was *chef d'équipe* of the Irish team which won the Three-Day Event World Championship (his daughter, Virginia, was a member of the team). In the same year, he was awarded the Texaco Equestrian Sportstar of the Year. He was also a leading amateur steeplechase jockey, and won a Foxhunter's Chase at Cheltenham, a Galway Plate and finished in second place in the Irish Grand National. He died at his home, Cool-na-Grena, Mallow, on 21 July 1993 and was buried in St Gobnait's Cemetery.

FRENCH, Seán (d. 1937) He was educated at CBC, Cork, where he excelled at rugby, being on the senior team during his final years. He studied chemistry and for a number of years was partner in a well-known Cork firm of pharmaceutical chemists. He was active in the Republican movement and was interned on several occasions during the War of Independence. In 1920, he was elected to Cork Corporation of which he was to remain a member until his death. He served as lord mayor from 1924 until his death, with the exception of the years 1930 and 1931. He was elected to Dáil Éireann as a Fianna Fáil TD for Cork Borough in 1927, having unsuccessfully contested a 1924 by-election as a Republican candidate. He did not seek re-election in 1932 and unsuccessfully contested the seat again in 1933. He died unexpectedly on 12 September 1937 of pneumonia at the North Infirmary Hospital and was buried in St Finbarr's Cemetery.

FREWEN, Moreton (1853–1924) He was the son of Thomas Frewen, MP for South Leicestershire. He was educated at Cambridge University and later travelled in the United States where he operated a ranch for some years. He had a reputation for reckless financial and political schemes. Having inherited an estate at Innishannon, Co. Cork, he was elected as an O'Brienite MP for Cork North East in the general election of December 1910. He resigned in July 1911 in order to provide a seat for **T.M. Healy**. He was a brother-in-law of Randolph Churchill (1849–95) and his niece was Sir Edward Carson's (1854–1935) second wife. He died on 2 September 1924. [Lives by A. Leslie (1966) and by A. Andrews (1968)]

FURLONG, Walter (1893–1973) Born Wolfe Tone Street, Cork, the son of James Furlong, policeman. He was educated at North Monastery CBS and inherited a tailoring business in South Main Street from his grandfather, Tim O'Callaghan, a Fenian. He joined the Irish Volunteers in 1916 and was a member of 'G. company', 1st battalion, 1st Cork brigade of the IRA. He was arrested and was interned for nearly a year in Bere Island. He took part in the discussions which led to the formation of the Fianna Fáil party in 1926 and represented that party on Cork Corporation for many years, though it was as an Independent that he was elected as lord mayor in 1951. He was elected as a Fianna Fáil TD for Cork Borough in 1944. He lost his seat in 1948 and unsuccessfully sought to regain it in 1951. He died at St Finbarr's Hospital, Cork, on 11 December 1973 and was buried in St Joseph's Cemetery.

G

GAGGIN, John Boles (c.1830–1867) Born Co. Cork, of an Anglo-Irish Protestant family. He served as a lieutenant in the Royal City of Cork Regiment of Militia of Artillery but emigrated to Vancouver Island, Canada, in April 1859. In the following October, he was appointed by the governor as a magistrate and as an assistant gold commissioner along with other minor public duties at Port Douglas. The 'regular jolly Irishman from Cork' was very popular despite his being 'a whale for drink'. In January 1866, the magistracy at Port Douglas was abolished but Gaggin was appointed magistrate for the Kootenay district. His superior reported that he was doing a good job and had 'knocked off the drink *in toto*, excepting lager beer'. In failing health, he died at Wild Horse Creek, Kootenay, on 27 May 1867 – the day after one of his police constables had been murdered.

GALLAGHER, Frank (1898–1962) Born Cork, the son of James J. Gallagher, secretary to Dwyer & Co. Ltd. He was educated at PBC, Cork, and, for a short period, at UCC. He was employed as a young journalist by the *Cork Free Press* and sent to London to cover the parliamentary debates on Irish home rule. Following the Easter rising of 1916, he joined the IRA and collaborated with Robert Erskine Childers (1870–1922) to publish the *Irish Bulletin*. He took the anti-Treaty side during the civil war and was interned. In 1931, he became the first editor of the *Irish Press* through his appointment by Eamon de Valera (1882–1975). On leaving this newspaper in 1936, de Valera appointed him as deputy director of Radio Éireann. He was also director of the Government Information Bureau for two terms (1938–48 and 1951–4). He worked at the National Library from 1954 until his death. He died in Dublin on 16 July 1962. He published *Days of Fear* (1928) and, under the

pseudonym 'David Hogan', *The Four Glorious Years* (1953).

GALLAGHER, Rory (1949–1995) Born Ballyshannon, Co. Donegal. He was reared in Cork where he attended North Monastery CBS. While a member of the group, 'Taste' (which he had joined in 1965), their album, *On the Boards*, reached the British Top Ten in 1970. He decided to go solo in 1971 and made the Top Ten with his *Live in Europe* album. By then he was regarded as the world's top blues guitarist. He died on 14 June 1995, and was buried in St Oliver's cemetery, Cork. His now rare *Rory Gallagher Boxed* (4 CDs) was produced in 1992. [Memorial at Rory Gallagher Square, Cork]

GALLWEY, Sir Michael Henry (1826–1912) Born Greenfield, Clonakilty, Co. Cork. He was educated at TCD where he graduated BA (1849). He was called to both the Bar and Inner Bar in 1889. Having settled in South Africa, he became attorney general for Natal Province (1859–90) and went on to become chief justice there (1890–1). In the meantime, he was appointed as president of the Transvaal and Zululand boundary commission. He died on 25 July 1912.

GALVIN, Edward (1882–1956) Born Newcestown, Co. Cork. He was educated at Bandon, Farranferris College, and St Patrick's College, Maynooth. He was ordained in 1909 and was appointed to a parish in Brooklyn, New York. In 1912, he left for missionary work in China but returned to Ireland in 1916 to recruit. With Rev. John Blowick (1888–1982) of Maynooth, he founded St Columba's Foreign Missionary Society, which was later established at Dalgan Park, Co. Meath. In 1920, he left for China with the first group of the new society. He was consecrated bishop in 1927, and, with the capture of Hupeh

Province by the Japanese in 1939, his work was severely curtailed. When the Communists came to power in 1949 following a civil war, he was arrested and placed under house arrest until his expulsion in 1952. He died on 23 February 1956 and was buried at Dalgan Park. [Lives by W.E. Barrett (1965) and P. Mac Caomhánaigh (1967)]

GALVIN, John (1907–1963) Born Bandon Road, Cork. He was elected to Cork Corporation in 1952 and was a member of Cork Health Authority and of the South Cork Board of Public Assistance. In 1956, he won a Dáil seat in a by-election as a Fianna Fáil TD for Cork City. He was also a prominent member of St Finbarr's and president of Lough Rovers Hurling and Football Club. He died at his Bandon Road residence on 11 October 1963 and was buried in St Finbarr's Cemetery. His widow, **Sheila Galvin**, held his seat in the subsequent by-election.

GALVIN, Sheila (1914–1983) Born Cork. As Sheila Murphy, she married **John Galvin**, licensed vintner, of Bandon Road, an alderman of Cork Corporation and a Fianna Fáil TD for Cork Borough (1956–63). Following the premature death of her husband, she contested and won the resultant by-election and sat as a Fianna Fáil deputy for Cork City. She was the second woman to represent a Cork constituency in Dáil Éireann and the first since 1927. She did not seek re-election in the subsequent general election of April 1965. She died on 20 March 1983.

GARDINER, Sir Thomas Robert (1883–1964) Born Cork, the son of a Post Office surveyor. He was educated at Edinburgh University where he graduated MA (1905). In the following year, he entered the Post Office. Having held many positions in that service, he rose to the position of director-general in 1936. At the outbreak of World War II, he became Permanent Secretary of the Ministry of Home Security. In late 1940, he returned to his position in the Post Office and directed the service until his retirement in 1945. He was appointed KBE (1936), KCB (1937), GBE (1941), and GCB (1954). In 1949,

he was awarded an honorary degree of LL.D by Edinburgh University. He died in London on 1 January 1964.

GEBRUERS, Staf (1902–1970) Born Antwerp, Belgium. He received his early education in local Jesuit schools and later studied at the Antwerp Conservatoire and at the Lemens Institute for Church Music, Mechelen (Malines). He came to Ireland in 1924 to take up the position of organist and carilloneur at St Colman's cathedral, Cobh. He remained there for the rest of his life and was an important contributor to the musical life of both county and country. For many years, he was professor of Music at the Cistercian seminary at Mount Melleray, Co. Waterford. He arranged many popular songs and published a popular hymn-book, the *Cantuarium*. He also wrote a comic opera, 'The Adamless Eden', and translated a life of Joseph Damien the Leper (1840–89) from the Flemish. In 1958, he organised the Carillon Festival of Ireland, an event which featured many recitals by prominent international carilloneurs. He died at the Mercy Hospital, Cork, on 24 April 1970 and was buried in St Colmans's Cemetery, Cobh.

GIBBINGS, Robert John (1889–1958) Born Cork, the son of Rev. Edward Gibbings, a canon of St FinBarre's Cathedral. Having studied medicine for two years at UCC, he went to the Slade School of Art, London, in 1911 to study art and wood engraving. In 1915, he was shot through the neck while serving with the Royal Munster Fusiliers at the Gallipoli landings. He was invalided out of the army and became a founder member of the Society of Wood Engravers, of which he was the first secretary. In 1923, he purchased the Golden Cockerel Press, and during the next decade the company produced 72 books with Gibbings as director and book designer until he sold the business in 1933. By this time, he was gaining a reputation as a travel writer who used his own illustrations. In 1938, he was conferred with an honorary degree of MA by the NUI. He died at Headington,

Oxford, on 19 January 1958 and was buried at Long Wittenham. His publications included *Twelve Wood Engravings* (1921), *The Seventh Man* (1930), *John Graham, Convict* (1937, repr. 1956), *Blue Angels and Whales* (1938), *Sweet Thames Run Softly* (1940), *Coming down the Wye* (1942), *Lovely is the Lee* (1945), *Over the Reefs* (1948), *Sweet Cork of Thee* (1951), *Coming down the Seine* (1953), *Trumpets from Montparnasse* (1955) and *Till I End My Song* (1957). [Life by M. Andrews (2003); Bibliography by A.M. Kirkus, P. Empson, and J. Harris, eds) (1962); Studies by Balston (1949) and by Empson (1959)]

GIBBONS, Geraldine (1817–1901) Born Kinsale, Co. Cork, the daughter of Gerald Gibbons. She was educated in Cork, but the family emigrated to Sydney, Australia, in 1834. With her sister, she joined the newly arrived Sisters of Charity and was professed in July 1847. She was one of the founders of St Vincent's hospital, Sydney, and succeeded her sister as superior of the Sisters of Charity. She was subsequently requested by her archbishop to be the superior of his newly founded Good Samaritan Order – an order following a modified Benedictine Rule. She was now superior of two flourishing congregations. However, due to local pressures, she relinquished both positions in 1859 (Charity) and 1876 (Samaritan). She then ministered to the poor in Hobart, Tasmania, until 1885 when she returned to Sydney. She died at Marrickville, New South Wales, on 15 October 1901.

GIBSON, Joseph Stafford (1837–1919) Born Kilmurry, Co. Cork. He lived for most of his life in Spain and travelled widely on the Continent where he produced a huge collection of watercolours which were presented to the Crawford Gallery in 1919 along with his coin collection. He also willed the sum of £14,790 'for the furthering of Art in the City of his boyhood'. He had been a friend of **James Brenan**, headmaster of the Cork School of Art.

GILBERT, John (1846–1915) Born Newcastle, England. He exhibited watercolours at the Royal Hibernian Academy from 1885 to his death. He was also involved in the organisation of exhibitions in Cork in the 1880s. He died on 8 August 1915.

GILHOOLY, James (1847–1916) Born Bantry, Co. Cork, the son of Peter Gilhooly, coastguard officer. Educated privately, he established an extensive grocery business in Bantry and was involved in local politics, serving as Chairman of Bantry town commissioners and Bantry rural district council at various times. In 1867, the authorities believed him to be a Fenian 'Head Centre' in the Bantry area. He entered Parliament in 1885 as Nationalist MP for West Cork and retained the seat in eight elections (four of them contested) up to his death. After the 'Parnell Split', he joined the anti-Parnellite faction and from 1910, was an O'Brienite and chairman of the All-for-Ireland League. He was a member of Cork County Council as an *ex officio* member of Bantry RDC from its foundation in 1899. During the Land League period, he was imprisoned on a few occasions – serving a three-month term for his role in the 'No Rent Manifesto' of 1881. He died at Goulding's nursing home, Cork, on 16 October 1916 and was buried in Abbey Cemetery, Bantry.

GILLMAN, Henry (1833–1915) Born Kinsale, Co. Cork, the son of Edward Gillman. He was educated at the Hamilton Academy, Bandon. The family later emigrated to the United States in 1850 and settled in Detroit, Michigan. He worked on the US Geodetic Survey of the Great Lakes and on other topographic and hydrographic surveys. He was elected as a fellow of the American Association for the Advancement of Science in 1875. He served as librarian of the Detroit public library from 1880 to 1885 and in the following year he was appointed as American consul in Jerusalem. He returned to Detroit in 1891 where he wrote extensively before his death on 30 July 1915. His publications include *Wild Flowers and Gardens of Palestine* (1894), *Hassan, a Fellah* (1896) and *Vericourt Westhrop and Issue* (1903). He also wrote a volume of poems, *Marked for Life* (1863).

GILLMAN, Sir Webb (1870–1933) Born Clonteadmore, Coachford, Co. Cork, the youngest son of Herbert Gillman. He was educated locally and at Dulwich military college. He served in the Boer War and in World War I where he rose to the rank of major general (1916). He rose to the rank of lieutenant general in 1926 while serving as inspector of artillery at the War Office. He was master general of the Ordnance and member of the Army council from 1927 to 1931, and was made a general in the latter year. He died at King Edward VII Hospital for Officers, London, on 20 April 1933.

GLOVER, Edward A. (1815–1862) Born Mount Glover (now Mount Corbett), Churchtown, Mallow, Co. Cork, the eldest son of James Glover, gentleman. He was educated at TCD where he graduated BA (1837). He was called to both the Irish (1840) and English Bars but did not practise for very long. A Liberal in politics, he unsuccessfully contested parliamentary seats at Beverley (1852), Canterbury (1854), and Abingdon (1854, but did not go to the polls), before being elected for Beverley in March 1857. He was unseated in the following August and in April 1858, was sentenced to three months imprisonment for having made a false declaration as to his property. This was, in fact, the last prosecution under that particular heading as the qualification was abolished in 1858. He died on 17 March 1862.

GOLDEN, Eddie (1915–1983) Born Cork. He was reared in Australia but returned to Cork at the age of 11 years. He was educated at North Monastery CBS and at UCC where he was the first person to take a history degree entirely through Irish. His life-long interest in acting was developed during his teens under Rev. **James C. O'Flynn** and he played many Shakespearean roles in the Cork Opera House in his early 20s. Minor film roles in England in 1945 and 1947 coincided with his professional stage career, commencing in London productions of O'Casey and P.V. Carroll. He toured the United States with the Gate Theatre Company

and appeared on Broadway before joining the Abbey Theatre in 1949. As an actor and director, he had many successes and was acknowledged as one of the leading Irish stage actors of his generation. In 1970, he was appointed as artistic director of the Irish Theatre company and, in 1976, took a year's leave-of-absence to work with the Lyric Theatre in Belfast. He died in the Royal Victoria Eye and Ear Hospital, Dublin, on 29 March 1983 and was buried in Bohernabreena cemetery, Dublin.

GOLDEN, Peter (1877–1926) Born Masseytown, Macroom, Co. Cork, the youngest child of Terence Golden, schoolteacher, and second cousin of **Terence MacSwiney**. He was educated at Knocknagoun NS, Rylane, but, with the death of his father in 1886, he went to work on a relation's farm at Rylane. He emigrated to the United States in 1901 and joined his brother and sisters at St Louis, Missouri. Having studied at the St Louis School of Elocution and Dramatic Art, he began a stage career and had moved to New York by 1913. He had an abiding interest in Irish politics and established the first Sinn Féin branch in the US in St Louis. He was later employed as a journalist by the *Gaelic American* whose editor was the Fenian, John Devoy (1842–1928). In 1919, he was appointed as secretary of the Irish Progressive League and was to the forefront in organising campaigns in support of Irish political and economic freedom. While the War of Independence was in progress, Golden, as national secretary of the American Association for the Recognition of the Irish Republic, toured the US to elicit support through speeches, lectures, readings, and concerts. As a supporter of Eamon de Valera (1882–1975), he opposed the Irish Treaty, but returned to Ireland during the height of the civil war in an unsuccessful attempt to broker a settlement. He returned to the US where he continued to campaign and raise funds for the Republican cause. In failing health, he died at Denver, Colorado, on 19 March 1926, while on his way to Pasadena, California. He was buried in Denver but was re-interred in St Finbarr's

Cemetery, Cork, on 14 July 1926. He published *A Voice Crying in the Wilderness* (1904) and *Impressions of Ireland* (1923). His poetry collections include *The Voice of Ireland* (1913), *To Arms and Other Poems* (1913), *Ballads of Rebellion* (1914) and *Songs of the Irish Republic* (1923). [Life by J. Herlihy (1994)]

GOOKIN, Robert (d. 1667) Born Courtmacsherry, Co. Cork, the younger son of **Sir Vincent Gookin** by his first wife, and brother of **Vincent Gookin**. He fought as a captain in the Confederate Wars, initially on the Royalist side, but changed allegiance to the forces of the English parliament in 1648. He received large grants of land under the Cromwellian Plantation. However, in 1660, with the restoration of King Charles II (1630–85) pending and the possibility of his land grants being declared null and void, he conveyed his lands to **Roger Boyle**, 1st earl of Orrery (one of the chief Irish movers of the Restoration), and leased them back for 100 years. He died in February 1667.

GOOKIN, Sir Vincent (c.1590–1638) Born (probably) in Kent, the son of John Gookin, gentleman. He was the father of **Robert Gookin** and **Vincent Gookin**. He came to Ireland early in the seventeenth century to take up the position of Surveyor-General and settled at Castle Mahon, Bandon. He eventually became one of the wealthiest men in Munster, largely through the income from his fishery at Courtmacsherry. Even though knighted in 1631, he fell foul of both the Irish parliament and Lord Deputy Wentworth in 1634 through his publication of a violent anti-Irish pamphlet addressed to the latter. With a large fine and severe parliamentary censure pending, he fled to England and died at his residence at Highfield, Gloucestershire, on 5 February 1638.

GOOKIN, Vincent (c.1616–1660) Born (probably) Courtmacsherry, Co. Cork, the elder son of **Sir Vincent Gookin** by his first wife, and brother of **Robert Gookin**. Having disposed of his father's Gloucestershire property, he settled in Ireland. During the Cromwellian period, he represented the boroughs of Kinsale and Bandon. He was firmly against the policy of transferring the dispossessed native Irish landowners to Connacht and, in 1655, he published a pamphlet in London, *The Great Case of Transplantation Discussed*, in support of his opinions. This, in turn, was severely criticised by one of the transplantation commissioners, Colonel Richard Lawrence, who accused Gookin of being a 'degenerate Englishman corrupted by the Irish.' Gookin replied in the same year with another London pamphlet, *The Author and Case of Transplanting the Irish into Connaught vindicated from the unjust Aspirations of Col. R. Lawrence.* The controversy led to the appointment of Henry Cromwell as chief governor of Ireland in September to replace the ruling military clique. As Surveyor-General of Ireland, he was appointed in 1656, along with Sir William Petty (1623–87) and Myles Symner (c.1610–86), to carry out the Down Survey which mapped out the sequestrated lands. He died intestate probably in early 1660, as his will was proven on 17 January of that year.

GOOLD, Thomas (c.1766–1846) Born Co. Cork, the son of Sir John Goold. He was educated at TCD where he graduated BA (1786) and MA (1791). He witnessed the initial stage of the French Revolution of 1789 and wrote a pamphlet in defence of the views of the orator, Edmund Burke (1729–97), on the French situation. Between this time and 1791, it seems that he whittled away some £10,000 of his inheritance on various entertainments in Dublin. He was called to the Bar in 1791 and soon established a large practice. He was a strong opponent of the Act of Union. He was appointed a King's sergeant-at-law in 1830 and master-in-chancery two years later. He died at Lisadell, Co. Sligo, on 16 July 1846.

GOOLD-ADAMS, Sir Hamilton John (1858–1920) Born Jamesbrook, Midleton, Co. Cork, the fourth son of Richard Wallis Goold-Adams, high sheriff of Cork. Having served an apprenticeship on a training vessel, he changed careers and, in 1878, was commissioned in the Royal Scots Regiment. He served in South Africa from 1884 until 1901 and rose to the rank of major. He was lieutenant governor of the Orange River Colony from 1901 until 1907. He was knighted in 1902 and returned to England in 1911. In that year, he was appointed as high commissioner to Cyprus and three years later he became governor of Queensland, Australia. In a turbulent term of office, which included World War I, he left Brisbane in January 1920 to retire in England. However, he took ill on the journey and died in Capetown, South Africa, on 12 April.

GOSNELL, Samuel (d. *p*.1818) Born Cork, the son of Henry Gosnell, apothecary. Under the pseudonym, 'Fogarty O'Fogarty', he wrote many witty poems in *Blackwood's Magazine* and in the *London Gazette*. He was the editor of the witty Cork paper, *Something New* which he founded c.1818. He worked as a surgeon.

GOULD, James A. (1812–1886) Born Cork. He entered the Augustinian Order and was educated in Rome. He was ordained in Perugia in 1835. Having returned to Cork for three years, he set out for the Australian mission in 1838. He was consecrated as the first Roman Catholic bishop of Melbourne in August 1848. This was a time of rapid population growth in Melbourne and in the goldfields, which resulted in a great need for both educational and ecclesiastical facilities. He visited Ireland in 1851 in an effort to recruit more priests and other religious for his diocese. In March 1874, he was raised to the dignity of archbishop when Melbourne was designated as a metropolitan see. On 21 August 1882, he was fired on at Brighton, Victoria (where he resided) by Patrick O'Farrell, a brother of the man who had wounded the duke of Edinburgh in Sydney in 1868. He died in Brighton on 11 June 1886 and was buried in St Patrick's Cathedral, Melbourne – which he had built.

GOULD, Abbé Thomas (1657–1734) Born Cork. He went to France in 1678 and studied at Poitiers prior to his ordination. He was sent to Thouars to work at the conversion of the Huguenots – a task which he accomplished so successfully that he was given the abbacy of St Laon and a pension by King Louis XIV. He published (in French) *A Letter to a Gentleman of Bas Poitou* (1705), *A Treatise on the Sacrifice of the Mass* (1724), *A Conversation to explain the Doctrine of the Catholic Church on the Holy Scriptures* (1727) and *A Collection of the various Objections which Protestants make against the Catholics ... and the Responses of the Catholics* (1735). He died at Thouars in September, 1734.

GOULDING, William (1817–1884) Born Birr, Co. Offaly, the son of Joshua Goulding. He was educated at Mountmellick grammar school. Following his marriage, he settled in Cork where he became a prominent businessman, and, in time, the founder of the Goulding chemical manures firm. Having failed to win a parliamentary seat in the general election of 1874, he went on to become a Conservative MP for Cork City (1876–80). However, he was again unsuccessful in the 1880 and 1884 elections, and was the last Conservative MP to sit for that constituency. He died on 8 December 1884. His elder son, William Joshua, was created a baronet in 1904, while his younger son, Edward Alfred, sat as an MP for English constituencies (1895–1906, 1908–22). He was created a baronet in 1915 and raised to the peerage as Baron Wargrave in 1922.

GRACE, William R. (1832–1904) Born Glanmire, Co. Cork, the son of James Grace, who had taken part in the struggle for Venezuelan independence. He ran away to sea, but, with his father's support, he moved to Peru where he was joined by his brother, Michael, and founded the chandler firm of Grace Brothers & Co. Through ill health, he was forced to leave Peru with Michael remaining to manage the company. He settled in New York in 1865 and founded W.R. Grace & Co. which engaged in huge business deals with the Peruvian Government. However, as a result of the War of the Pacific between Chile, Bolivia, and Peru in 1879, the latter country became practically bankrupt with a huge national debt. This debt was taken over by Grace who, with Lord Donoughmore and other British financiers, established the Peruvian Corporation Ltd which received enormous concessions in silver mining, oil, railways, sugar, nitrates etc. He also became a shipping magnate with the founding of the Grace Steamship Company. In 1895, Grace further broadened his horizons with other huge developments all over South America when he established William R. Grace & Co. – an amalgamation of all his companies. Having an interest in local politics, he was elected as the first Roman Catholic mayor of New York in 1880 and was re-elected for a further term in 1884. He died in March 1904 and was buried at Holy Cross Cemetery, Brooklyn. [Life by P. Hevner (1888); Sketch by J. Thompson in *World's Work* (May 1904)]

GRAVES, Clotilde I.M. (1864–1932) Born Buttevant Barracks, Co. Cork, the daughter of Major W.H. Graves. She was educated at a convent in Lourdes, France, and converted to Roman Catholicism. She was a noted novelist and dramatist and wrote under the pseudonym 'Richard Dehen'. Many of her plays, including *Nitocris* (1887) and *The Lover's Battle* (1902), were performed in London and New York. Her successful novels included *A Well-Meaning Woman* (1894), *The Dop Doctor* (1910) and *Between Two Thieves* (1914). She died in Middlesex, England on 3 December 1932.

GRAVES, Philip P. (1876–1953) Born Cheshire, England, the son of Alfred Percival Graves. On his retirement in 1946, he purchased Ballylickey House, Bantry, and opened it as a private hotel. An Oxford graduate, he served in World War I and was foreign correspondent for the London *Times* (1906–46). He published numerous papers on butterflies, moths, and dragonflies. He died at Ballylickey on 3 June 1953.

GREEN, George C. (1863–1940) Born Airhill, Glanworth, Co. Cork, the son of James S. Green, QC, and brother of **Max S. Green**. He

was educated at TCD where he graduated BA. He was called to the Bar in 1886 and to the Inner Bar in 1906. He was professor of English Law at UCC (1902–8) and was appointed a circuit court judge for Armagh and Louth in 1909 (to 1921) and afterwards for Fermanagh. He died at his Blackrock, Co. Dublin, residence on 7 February 1940 and was buried privately.

GREEN, Max S. (1864–1922) Born Airhill, Glanworth, Co. Cork, the son of James S. Green QC, and brother of **George C. Green**. He was educated at TCD and at the Royal College of Sciences where he qualified as a civil engineer. From 1885 to 1897, he was engaged in various public and private engineering projects and then served as Engineer to the Prison Service (1897–1906). He was appointed as private secretary to the Irish viceroy in 1907 and served until 1912. The son-in-law of the Irish Parliamentary Party leader, John Redmond (1856–1918), he was shot dead while attempting to apprehend robbers at St Stephen's Green, Dublin, on 3 March 1922.

GREEN, William S. (1847–1919) Born Youghal, Co. Cork, the only son of Charles Green, merchant. He was educated at Midleton College and at TCD where he graduated BA (1871) and MA (1874). Having been ordained as a Church of Ireland minister in 1873, he was for many years the rector of Carrigaline. However, on being appointed a government commissioner on fisheries, he resigned from the church ministry in 1889. Being both an adventurer and a naturalist, he travelled widely. In 1881, he was the first to climb Mount Cook in the New Zealand Alps. He then worked in tropical forests and surveyed glaciers in the Canadian Selkirks for the Canadian government. From 1885–89 (under the auspices of the Royal Irish Academy) he studied, with A.C. Haddon, the zoologist and anthropologist, the marine fauna of the south west of Ireland. He became chief inspector of fisheries in 1900 and retired in 1914. He was also a commissioner of the Congested Districts Board (1892–1909). He published *The*

High Alps of New Zealand (1883) and *Among the Selkirk Glaciers* (1890). He was also the reputed author of the novel *Grania Waile* (1895) under the pseudonym of 'Fulmar Petrel'. He died at West Cove, Co. Kerry, on 22 April 1919. [Short biography in R.L. Praeger, *The Way that I Went* (1935)]

GREER, Thomas (1837–1905) Born Sydney Place, Cork, the eldest son of Alfred Greer, a Quaker merchant of Dungannon, Co. Tyrone, and Helena, the eldest daughter of **Joshua Carroll**. His father established a successful paper factory near Cork and, following the death of Helena, married Peggy Bowen-Colthurst in 1853 and resided in Dripsey House. Soon afterwards, the family converted to the Church of Ireland. Thomas was educated at a private school at Clifton, Bristol. He was high sheriff of Carrickfergus (1870) and of County Tyrone (1876). He was Conservative MP for Carrickfergus from 1880 to its disenfranchisement in 1885. He died on 20 September 1905.

GREGG, John (1798–1878) Born Cappa, Kilrush, Co. Clare, the son of a small landowner. He was educated at TCD where he graduated BA (1825), DD (1860) and was ordained in 1826. He was consecrated as Church of Ireland bishop of Cork, Cloyne and Ross on 16 February 1862. He is the first recorded Church of Ireland bishop to have preached a sermon in Irish. The present St FinBarre's Cathedral was built (1865–70) during his episcopate. He was succeeded at Cork by his son, **Robert S. Gregg**, who eventually became Primate of Ireland. He died at his Cork see house on 26 May 1878, and was buried in Mount Jerome Cemetery, Dublin.

GREGG, Robert S. (1834–96) Born Kilsallaghan, Co. Dublin, the son of Bishop **John Gregg**. He was educated at TCD where he graduated BA (1857), MA (1860) and DD (1873). He was ordained in 1857 and became dean of Cork in 1874. In the following year he was consecrated as Church of Ireland bishop of Ossory. He succeeded his father as bishop of Cork, Cloyne

and Ross on the latter's death on 26 May 1878. He provided, at his own cost, the reredos and much of the marble panelling of the new St FinBarre's cathedral. He was elected as archbishop of Armagh in 1893. He died at his Armagh see house on 10 January 1896 and was buried at Douglas Cemetery, Frankfield, Cork.

GRIERSON, Charles McIver (1864–1939) Born Queenstown (now Cobh). His family moved to Plymouth where he was educated. He later moved to London and, in 1900, he returned to Ireland and settled in Sligo. Here he produced many watercolours which he frequently exhibited at the Royal Hibernian Academy. He died on 25 September 1939.

GRIFFIN, Gerald (1803–1840) Born Limerick, the son of Patrick Griffin, brewery manager. His writing career began in his native city, but in 1823 he set out for London to advance his literary career. However, he returned to Limerick in 1827 due to ill health and continued to write there and in Dublin during the following decade. Becoming disillusioned with writing, he burned his manuscripts and entered the Christian Brothers in 1838. He was transferred to North Monastery CBS, Cork, in the following year where he worked as a teacher. He died of typhus on 12 June 1840 and was buried in the community plot at North Monastery. His novels include *Tales by the O'Hara Family* (1825), *Holland-Tide* (1827), *The Collegians* (1829), *The Rivals* (1829), *Tracy's Ambition* (1829) and *the duke of Monmouth* (1836). His story-collections include *Tales of the Munster Festivals* (1827), *Tales of My Neighbourhood* (1835) and *Talis Qualis, or Tales of the Jury Room* (posthumously, 1842). His first play, *The Tragedy of Aguire* (c.1820) was destroyed with his manuscripts, while *Gisippus* (1842) was produced in London after his death. [Life by J. Cronin (1978)]

GRIFFITHS, Thomas (d. 1746) Born Shandon, Cork, the son of George Griffiths. With the blessing of the Cork Quaker Meeting, he emigrated to Philadelphia in 1716. In 1723, he became secretary of the Free Society of Traders and served as mayor of the city in 1729, 1730, and 1733. He also sat on the Provincial Council (1733) and was a judge of the Philadelphia Supreme Court (1739–43). He died in 1746.

GROGAN, Nathaniel (1740–1807) Born Cork, the son of a turner. His early interest in art was opposed by his father. Having enlisted in the army, he served both in America and the West Indies. On his return to Cork, he painted landscapes and also decorated the Vernon Mount residence. In 1782, he exhibited at the Free Society of Artists in London and subsequently enjoyed a considerable reputation in Cork. He died at his residence at The Mardyke in 1807 and was buried in St FinBarre's Churchyard. A collection of his pictures was exhibited at the Cork Exhibition of 1852. His two sons, Nathaniel and Joseph, were also painters.

GROVE-WHITE, James (1852–1938) Born Melbourne, Australia, the eldest son of Major H.T.F. White of the 40th Regiment and a native of Kilbyrne, Doneraile, Co. Cork. He was educated at Elizabeth College, Guernsey, and at the Lycée Imperial, Caen. He joined the 57th Regiment in 1873, and following a distinguished army career, he retired in 1903 with the rank of colonel. At the outbreak of World War I, he returned to the service and served in France (1916–17) as a staff officer. He returned to his family estates in Cork and Waterford, residing at the family home at Kilbyrne. He was a keen agriculturalist and actively engaged in improved methods of husbandry. He was chosen as high sheriff for Co. Waterford in 1910 and later represented the Farmers' Party in Cork County Council from 1925 to 1928 when he did not seek re-election. He was a passionate local historian who became a member of Cork Historical & Archaeological Society on its foundation in 1892 and was a frequent contributor to the society's journal (*JCHAS*) from 1893. He was vice-president of the society in 1913 and acted as its president until his death. His *magnum opus* is his 'Historical and Topographical Notes on Buttevant, Castletownroche, Doneraile, and Mallow, and Places in their Vicinity' which appeared as a separately paginated appendix to the *JCHAS* (1911–24) and was published on its completion in four volumes. Copiously illustrated and with comprehensive indices, 'Grove-White', as it is known, is an invaluable compendium of the history and antiquities of North East Cork. He died at Kilbyrne on 2 November 1938.

GUBBINS, Beatrice (1878–1944) Born Bottomstown, Co. Limerick, the daughter of Thomas Wise Gubbins who moved to Cork to run Wise's distillery on the North Mall. In 1897, she held her first exhibition at the Royal Hibernian Academy and her last one in 1937. She resided at Dunkathel House where many of her watercolours are now exhibited. She travelled extensively in Europe and North Africa and was also a keen aviator. From 1900 to 1939, she was the secretary of the Queenstown Sketching Club. She died at Dunkathel House on 12 August 1944, and was buried in St Lappan's graveyard, Little Island.

GUEST, Montague J. (1839–1909) Born London, the third son of Sir Josiah J. Guest, MP. The Guest Ironworks at Dowlais, Glamorgan, was the largest of its kind in Wales. In 1869, Guest, as a Liberal opposed to home rule, was elected MP for Youghal and represented the borough until 1874. He subsequently was MP for Wareham, Dorset (1880–5). He died on 9 November 1909.

GUINEY, Dave (1921–2000) Born Kanturk, Co. Cork, the son of **John Guiney**, nephew of **Patrick Guiney** and first cousin of **Phil Burton**. One of Ireland's most versatile athletes, he took five Irish Youth titles in the discus, shot putt, javelin, long jump, and high jump – all in one afternoon in 1941. An Irish record holder in the shot putt, he represented his country in that event on twelve occasions between 1944 and 1956. He won the British AAA shot putt title in 1948 and represented Ireland at the London Olympics later in that year. He left the Civil

Service in 1946 when he was refused leave to compete in the European Championships in Oslo and then went into sports journalism. He worked as sports editor for Independent Newspapers, the *Irish Press,* the *Sunday Mirror* and as a sports correspondent for many newspapers, including the *Cork Evening Echo.* He acted as *chef de mission* for the Irish team at the Barcelona Olympics of 1992. His books included *Gold, Silver, Bronze, The Days of the Little Green Apples, A Little Wine and a Few Friends, Ireland's Olympic Heroes, The New York Irish* and *Ireland's Olympians.* He died at the Mater Hospital, Dublin, on 14 October 2000 and was cremated at Glasnevin Crematorium.

GUINEY, John (1868–1926) Born Kanturk, Co. Cork, the son of Timothy Guiney, clerk of Kanturk Union, brother of **Patrick Guiney**, father of **Dave Guiney** and uncle of **Phil Burton**. He was educated at St Colman's College, Fermoy, at Castleknock College, and at the National University, Dublin. He qualified as a solicitor in 1892 and opened a practice in Kanturk. In 1913, he was elected, unopposed, as an independent nationalist (O'Brienite) MP for Cork North in succession to his late brother, Patrick. He died in 1926.

GUINEY, Patrick (1862–1913) Born Kanturk, Co. Cork, the eldest son of Timothy Guiney, clerk of Kanturk Union, brother of **John Guiney**, uncle of **Dave Guiney** and **Phil Burton**. He was educated at St Patrick's Monastery, Mountrath, Co. Laois. He became a farmer and served on Cork County Council (1908–11). He was elected as an independent nationalist (O'Brienite) MP for Cork North in January 1910. He was re-elected in December of that year when he also contested (unsuccessfully) Kerry East. He died on 12 October 1913 and was buried in Clonfert Cemetery, Newmarket.

GUINNESS, Richard S. (1797–1857) Born Dublin, the second son of Richard Guinness, barrister and nephew of the brewer, Arthur Guinness (1725–1803). He was elected as Conservative MP for Kinsale in the 1847 general election, but was unseated on petition in the following year. He later represented Barnstaple, Devon (1854–7). He was father-in-law of the 1st earl of Iveagh. He died on 28 August 1857.

GUMBLETON, William E. (1840–1911) He was the son of George Gumbleton, clergyman, by his second marriage. He attended Brasenose College, Oxford, but did not graduate. He toured Europe with his mother and eventually settled on the family estate, Belgrove, Great Island, *c.*1870, where he became interested in horticulture. He specialised in the propagation of rare plants and wrote many articles in garden and botanical magazines. The African daisy, *arctotis gumbletonii,* was named in his honour by the famous English botanist, Sir Joseph Hooker (1817–1911). He died at his residence on 4 April 1911. His botanical library was subsequently transferred to the National Botanical Gardens, Glasnevin, Dublin.

GWYNN, Denis R. (1893–1973) Born Dublin, the third son of Stephen Gwynn, writer and scholar. He was educated at Clongowes Wood College, St Enda's, Rathfarnham, and UCD where he graduated BA (1914), MA (1915) and D.Litt (1932). He served (as did his father) in France during World War I (1916–7), but was invalided home. He began work as a journalist in London and in Dublin where he was editor of *The Dublin Review.* During World War II, he farmed in Hampshire. He returned to Ireland and was appointed as research professor of Modern Irish History at UCC in 1948, a position he held until his retirement in 1962. He acted as editor of Cork University Press (1954–62) and wrote a regular column called 'Now and Then' in the *Cork Examiner.* As well as being a writer of biography, he also published *Young Ireland and 1848* (1949). He died at his home at Malahide, Dublin, on 10 January 1973 and was buried at Stamullan, Co. Meath.

H

HALES, Seán (1880–1922) Born Ballinadee, Co. Cork, the son of Robert Hales, farmer, and brother of **Thomas Hales**. He was active in the Volunteer movement, was arrested in 1916 and imprisoned for nine months. On his release, he took part in the military campaign. In 1919, he became O/C of the Bandon battalion in succession to Thomas, who became brigade O/C. He took a leading part in the engagements at Brinny, Newcestown and Crossbarry. In June 1920, he was elected to Cork County Council for the Bandon area and in May of the following year, he was elected to the Second Dáil as a Sinn Féin TD for West Cork. Unlike Thomas, he took the pro-Treaty side and was elected to the Third Dáil in June 1922. On 7 December 1922, he and Pádraig Ó Máille were shot at as they emerged from the Ormond Hotel, near the Four Courts, Dublin. Ó Máille escaped death, but Hales was fatally wounded and died shortly afterwards. In reprisal, the Government executed Liam Mellows and three other prisoners the following day – an action which was publicly condemned by the Hales family. He was buried in Innishannon Cemetery. [Memorial statue at Bandon]

HALES, Thomas (d. 1966) Born Ballinadee, Co. Cork, the son of Robert Hales, farmer, and brother of **Seán Hales**. He was a member of the Irish Volunteer movement from its foundation and attended the Volunteer National Convention in Dublin in 1915 as a delegate. Following the Easter Rising of 1916, he helped to re-organise the Volunteers in Cork and in January 1919 he was elected the first brigade commander of the Cork 3rd Brigade of the IRA with which he saw active service. He was arrested in June 1920, sentenced to two years imprisonment, but was released at Christmas 1921. He resumed his rank during the Civil War (taking the opposite side

to Seán, who was pro-Treaty), was arrested in November 1922 and was detained in prison until Christmas of 1924. Even though he was co-opted as a member of Cork County Council in January 1923, he did not seek election in 1925 but later served from 1934 until 1942. In 1933, he was elected to Dáil Éireann as a Fianna Fáil TD for West Cork but lost his seat four years later when he stood as an independent Republican. He later stood unsuccessfully as an independent candidate for West Cork (1944) and as a Clann na Poblachta candidate for Cork South East (1948). He died at St Finbarr's Hospital, Cork, on 29 April 1966 and was buried in St Patrick's Cemetery, Bandon.

HALES, William (1747–1831) Born Cork, the son of Rev. Samuel Hales, a Cork clergyman. He was educated at TCD where he graduated BA (1769) and was appointed as professor of Oriental Languages. He entered the church and was appointed as rector of Killeshandra, Co. Cavan, in 1788. He wrote over twenty works on history, chronology, mathematics and theology. He died on 30 January 1831.

HALL, J. Compton (1863–1937) Born Cork. He was educated at King William's College, Isle of Man, and later qualified as an architect, being elected as a fellow of the Royal Institution of British Architects. He specialised in church and private house restorations and designed Dunham Hall for William Grey, 9th earl of Stamford. He was also a noted landscape artist and was a member of the Society of British Artists. He died on 6 April 1937.

HALLARAN, William Saunders (c.1765– 1825) Born Castlemartyr, Co. Cork, the son of William Hallaran. He graduated MD from Edinburgh University and, on the establishment of the Cork Lunatic Asylum in 1791, was appointed as its first medical superintendent. He was a pioneer in the humane treatment of the insane, which treatment he enunciated in his *Enquiry into the Causes producing … the Number of Insane … With Observations on the Cure of Insanity* (1810, 2nd ed., 1818). In 1799, he opened his own private asylum at 'Cittadella', off Blackrock Road. He was also senior physician to the South Infirmary Hospital. He died at his South Mall residence on 17 December, 1825. His grandson, **Edward Hallaran Bennett**, was an eminent surgeon, whose name is recalled in 'Bennett's Fracture'. [Commemorative plaque at 43, South Mall, Cork]

HALLIDEN, Patrick J. (1880–1960) Born Lyre, Banteer, Co. Cork, the eighth child of William Halliden. He was educated at Lyre NS where he became a monitor under the direction of his mother, Margaret. He subsequently entered St Patrick's College of Education, Dublin, where he qualified as a primary teacher in 1902. He was later appointed as principal of Lyre Boys' NS, a post which he held until his retirement in 1945. He was the founder of the Irish Dairy Shorthorn Breeders' Society in 1920. He served as a member of Cork County Council (1945–50) and was a prominent member of its various committees. He was also a life vice-president of the National Athletic and Cycling Association of Ireland (NACAI) and a founder member of Lyre GAA club in 1933. As a candidate for the County Cork Farmers' Association, he was elected as TD for the North Cork constituency in 1943. He later joined Clann na Talmhan (Farmers' Party) and became its chairman. While supporting the Inter-party government as an independent, he resigned from Clann na Talmhan on 29 April 1951, in protest against the administration's policy on milk. He did not contest the 1952 general election. He died at his daughter's residence, 'Tencourt', Blackrock, Cork, on 9 June 1960 and was buried in Lyre Cemetery.

HALLINAN, Sir Eric (1900–1985) Born Midleton, Co. Cork, the son of Edward Hallinan, flour miller. He was educated at Downside School, UCC and TCD. He was called to the Irish Bar in 1924 and to the English Bar in 1927. He entered the British colonial service and eventually rose to the position of chief justice of Cyprus (1951). He died on 13 April 1985 and was buried in Midleton Cemetery.

HALLISSY, Timothy (1869–1958) Born Blarney, Co. Cork. He was educated at Queen's College, Cork (now UCC), at the Royal College of Science, Dublin, and at the Royal University, Dublin. He held degrees in chemistry, physiology, and agricultural science. He taught agricultural science at Mount Bellew, Co. Galway, before joining the Geological Survey of Ireland in 1906 as a temporary professorial assistant. He became senior geologist to the Survey in 1921 and succeeded Professor Grenville A.J. Cole (b. 1859) as director in 1928. He collaborated with Cole in the publication of *The Handbook of the Geology of Ireland* (1924) which became a primer for geology students. In the previous year, he had published *Barytes in Ireland*. He retired from the GSI in November 1939 and died at his Terenure, Dublin, residence on 13 July 1958.

HALY, James (1763–1850) Born Cork, the third son of Simon O'Grady Haly of Ballyhaly, Co. Cork. He was the father of **Robert Haly** and brother of **Sir John Haly**. Through his mother, Anne Barry of Leamlara, Co. Cork, he was related to the leading Roman Catholic families of the county. In 1788, he married Ellen Flynn, eldest daughter of the printer, William Flynn, whom he succeeded in the business. Haly was the first printer and publisher of the *Cork Mercantile Chronicle* which, in 1802, succeeded Flynn's long-established *Hibernian Chronicle*. In addition to printing and publishing, Haly was one of the leading city booksellers. He died at his Coburg Street residence on 4 or 5 January 1850.

HALY, Sir John (d. 1799) Born Cork, the son of Simon O'Grady Haly of Ballyhaly, Co. Cork. He was the brother of **James Haly** and the uncle of **Robert Haly**. He qualified as a doctor and had a successful practice in Cork. He was knighted in 1785 and admitted a freeman of Cork in 1793. (His third wife, Lady Haly [née Fuller] was among the dancing partners of the future King William IV (1765–1837), when, as prince, he visited Cork in 1787.) His obituary credited him as being 'one of the first physicians to introduce in Cork a safe method of vaccination'. He died at his residence, White Street, Cork, on 20 March 1799.

HALY, Richard (1730–1816) Born Ballyhaly, Co. Cork, the son of John Haly, landowner. He entered the French service as a soldier in Rothe's regiment of the Irish Brigade and fought in the battles of Fontenoy and Lauffelt. He married into a French aristocratic family and settled at Abscon in Flanders. He died in 1816 at his chateau near Amboise. His sister, Elizabeth, married Charles Lucas (1713–1771), the Dublin radical opposition MP.

HALY, Robert (1796–1882) Born Cork, the son of **James Haly**, the nephew of **Sir John Haly** and the grand-nephew of **William Flyn**. He was educated at Stonyhurst College and commenced his training at Hodder, near Stonyhurst, in 1814. He was ordained at Fribourg in 1828 and returned to Dublin in 1829. A noted preacher, he was twice rector of Clongowes Wood College (1836–40, 1842–50). He also served periods as superior of St Francis Xavier's Church in Dublin (1851–6) and of the Jesuit community in Galway (1859–65). He directed Jesuit parish missions throughout Ireland during his career, until he suffered a stroke in 1877. His latter years were spent in Dublin, where he died on 1 September 1882. He was buried in the Jesuit plot in Glasnevin.

HAMILTON, Liam (1928–2000) Born Mitchelstown, Co. Cork, the eldest of five children of Richard Hamilton, former Garda and chemist's assistant. He was educated at Mitchelstown CBS. He entered the civil service by competition, and having been assigned to the department of Justice, worked in the High Court Office, Dublin. Having undertaken further studies at UCD and at the King's Inns, he was called to the Bar in 1956. In the preceding year, he had won the John Brooks Exhibition at the Inns. He joined the Labour Party in 1958 and was an unsuccessful local election candidate for the Rathmines Ward of Dublin Corporation. He was called to the Inner Bar in 1968 and was appointed a judge of the High Court in 1974. He presided over the Special Criminal Court for many years. He was appointed president of the High Court in 1985 and chief justice of Ireland in 1994. Previously, in 1991, he conducted the Beef Tribunal which investigated alleged malpractice in the beef industry. The tribunal lasted for thirty months and, at the time, was the most expensive in the history of the state. In March 1999, he was appointed by the Government to inquire into what became known as 'The Sheehy Affair' and which led to the resignations of two judges. He retired in January 2000 but accepted the invitation to direct the inquiry into the Monaghan and Dublin bombings of 1971. However, he was forced, through illness, to resign his commission. He died at St Vincent's Hospital, Dublin, on 29 November 2000 and was buried in Shanganagh Cemetery.

HAMMOND, Thomas Chatterton (1877–1961) Born Cork, the youngest son of Colman M. Hammond, farmer. He was educated at Cork Model Schools and following a religious conversion in Dublin, he entered TCD in 1899 and graduated BA in 1903. He became a minister of the Church of Ireland in 1905 and married a Corkwoman, Margaret McNay, a year later. In 1910, he became rector of St Kevin's, Dublin, and became well known for his anti-Roman Catholic polemic. In 1919, he was appointed to the important position of superintendent of the Irish Church Missions and later toured Canada and Australia. In 1936, he took up the position of principal of Moore Theological College in Sydney and built up its reputation as a centre for Anglican evangelicalism. From 1939, he was also a canon of St Andrew's Cathedral,

Sydney. He served as grand chaplain of the Federated Loyal Orange Grand Council of Australasia from 1936 until his death in Sydney Hospital on 16 November 1961. He was buried in North Suburbs Cemetery. Among his works were *Authority in the Church* (1921), *In Understanding Be Men* (1936), *Perfect Freedom* (1938), Reasoning Faith (1943) and *The New Creation* (1953). He also wrote many pamphlets and gave many radio broadcasts in defence of Protestantism. [Life by W. Nelson (1994)]

HANLEY, Gerald (1916–1992) Born Cork, the brother of the novelist and playwright, James Hanley (1901–85). He worked in East Africa during the late Thirties and joined the British army on the outbreak of World War II. His novels are based on his experiences and observations in Africa and the Far East. These include *Monsoon Victory* (1946), *The Consul at Sunset* (1951), *The Year of the Lion* (1953), *Drinkers of Darkness* (1955), *The Journey Homeward* (1961), *Without Love* (1957) and *Noble Descents* (1982). He died in 1992.

HARDING, Edward J. (1804–1870) Born Cork. He worked in watercolours, oils, and miniatures and featured at the Cork Exhibition of 1852.

HARLEY, John (1800–1875) Born Court-macsherry, Co. Cork, the second son of a schoolmaster. In 1823, he joined his brother William in Miramichi, New Brunswick, Canada, and worked in a shipyard. He soon rose to the position of master builder and in 1850, he became, with **George Burchill**, a partner in the purchase of a shipyard. When the partnership ended in 1857, he carried on alone until 1866, by which time he had been responsible for the construction of some sixty-two ships of the highest quality. In 1864, his bark, the *Sea Mew*, took only sixteen days to travel from Miramachi to Liverpool. He spent his last years as an inspector of lights and as a harbour master. He died in Miramichi on 16 September 1875 and was buried in Newcastle, New Brunswick.

HARMAN, George R.A. (1874–1975) Born Crosshaven, Co. Cork, the son of Samuel Harman, clergyman. He was educated at TCD where he graduated as a medical doctor. He played his club rugby with TCD and represented Ireland twice during the 1899 season when the side took the Triple Crown. He represented both Munster and Leinster at interprovincial level. He was also prominent on the TCD cricket XI. He died at his residence in Downderry, Cornwall, on 14 December 1975 at the age of 101 years.

HARRINGTON, Edward (1852–1902) Born Castletownbere, Co. Cork, the son of Denis Harrington and younger brother of **Timothy C. Harrington**. He was educated locally and became an assistant teacher in Bantry, transferring to Castletownbere in 1877. Soon afterwards, he moved to Tralee where he joined the staff of the *Kerry Sentinel* newspaper which had been founded by his brother, Tim. On the departure in 1882 of Tim to become secretary of the National Land League, Edward took over the proprietorship and editorship of the *Sentinel*. In 1885, he was elected MP for West Kerry and retained his seat until 1892, when, standing as a Parnellite candidate, he was defeated. In the late 1880s, he was twice imprisoned for publishing 'seditious articles' in the *Sentinel* and was fined £500 for comments on the *Times* Commission judges. After 1892, he devoted himself to the running of his newspaper. He died at his residence in Nelson Street, Tralee, on 29 May 1902 and was buried in the New Cemetery, Tralee.

HARRINGTON, Michael (d. 1810) Born Carrigtohill, Co. Cork. He studied at the Irish College, Paris, and was ordained priest for the diocese of Cloyne *c.*1775. He returned to Ireland and leased a holding at Ballybrassil, Great Island, where he established the Redington Academy to cater for the education of Roman Catholic boys. Among his pupils were Daniel O'Connell (1775–1847), the Liberator, and his brother, Maurice. However, the school did not survive for long after his death which took place on 22 February 1810. He was buried in Templerobin Graveyard, Ballymore, Cobh. [Sketch by T. Cadogan in *Harbour Lights* (1988)]

HARRINGTON, Sir Stanley (1856–1949)
Born 'Leeview', Cork, the son of William Harrington, retail and wholesale chemist/druggist. He was educated at Beaumont College and Queen's College, Cork (now UCC) where he graduated BA. With his brothers William B. and Ignatius, he established the Shandon Chemical Works at Commons Road in 1885. Later offshoots of the firm were Harrington Brothers Ltd, London, and from 1922, Harrington & Goodlass Wall. In 1896, they formed another company, The Cork Chemical & Drug Company. Originally the managing director, Stanley succeeded to the chairmanship on the death of William B. He was president of Cork Chamber of Commerce (1892/3) and some-time chairman of Thomas Lyons & Company, having married in 1883 Catherine Lyons, the daughter of the founder. He was knighted in 1907 on the occasion of the visit of the Prince of Wales and was made a privy councillor in 1918. He died at his residence, 'Araglin', Rushbrooke, Co. Cork, on 31 July 1949.

HARRINGTON, Timothy C. (1851–1910)
Born Castletownbere, Co. Cork, the son of Denis Harrington and elder brother of **Edward Harrington**. He entered TCD in 1884 but did not graduate. He worked as a teacher at the Dominican School, Tralee, and while there he founded and edited the *Kerry Sentinel* in 1877. He became secretary of the Irish National Land League in 1882, and, following periods of imprisonment, he and **William O'Brien** of Mallow were the main strategists of the League's 'Plan of Campaign' of 1886. Previously, in 1883, he had entered parliament as MP for Westmeath. He continued to sit for the Harbour Division of Dublin from 1885 until his death. He was called to the Bar in 1887 and often appeared for his leader, **C.S. Parnell**. Following the 'Parnell Split' of 1890, he took the side of

Parnell. He acted as leader of the rump on Parnell's death until John Redmond (1856–1918) took over in January 1892. He played a pivotal role in uniting the Irish Parliamentary Party under Redmond in 1900. He served as lord mayor of Dublin from 1901 until 1904. He died in Dublin on 12 March 1910 and was buried in Glasnevin Cemetery.

HARRINGTON, Timothy R. (d. 1937) Born Castletownbere, Co. Cork. He commenced his journalistic career on the staff of the *Cork Herald* around 1890. He then moved to Dublin as chief reporter of the *Daily Nation* and subsequently filled the same role in the *Irish Daily Independent*. When the latter paper was converted into a halfpenny morning newspaper under the title of the *Irish Independent* by **William Martin Murphy** in 1904, he selected Harrington as editor-in-chief in July of that year. Harrington remained in that post until 1931, though severe nervous breakdowns in 1924 and 1925 curtailed his energy latterly and forced his retirement in August 1931. He remained a director of Independent Newspapers Ltd until his death which occurred at his residence, 'St Finbarr's', Ailesbury Road, Dublin, on 24 September 1937. He was buried in Glasnevin Cemetery.

HARRIS, Joseph (1789–1800) Born Cork, the son of Joseph and Jane Harris, Quakers. Having been predeceased by his father, Joseph died of measles at the age of 11 years. His sufferings and related attitudes are recorded in *Some Account of Joseph Harris, a Child of Eleven Years old* which was published in Cork in 1814.

HARRIS, W. Richard (1846–1923) Born Cork, the son of Richard Harris, labourer, and brother of **Mary Jones**, better known as 'Mother Jones'. The father emigrated to America in 1835. The family later joined him in Toronto to where he had temporarily moved. Richard (jnr.) was educated in Toronto and Quebec where he came under the patronage of Bishop Lynch of Toronto. In 1869, he was sent to Rome to complete his studies and was ordained priest in June 1870. Returning to Toronto, he ministered in various parishes, becoming dean of St Catherine's parish in 1884. Two years later, he became president of the Canadian Institute, a pioneering organisation in the study of archaeology. From the early 1890s onwards, Harris was the most prolific Roman Catholic author of his generation in English-speaking Canada. His early books all dealt with the history of Roman Catholic missions in Canada, most notably his *The Catholic Church in the Niagara Peninsula, 1623–1895* (1895). In 1896, he attended the Irish Race Convention in Dublin as a delegate from the Toronto archdiocese. He resigned from his Toronto deanery in 1901 and, over the next decade, travelled widely and continued to publish. He spent a seven-year period in Utah (1905–12), publishing *The Catholic Church in Utah* (1909). He returned to Toronto in 1913 and became chaplain to an industrial school. In the last decade of his life, he published a further six books, including two travel books on Mexico and contributed many scholarly papers to archaeological journals. He died in Toronto on 5 March 1923.

HARTLAND, Henry A. (1840–1893) Born Mallow, Co. Cork, the son of William Baylor Hartland, nurseryman, whose family had been gardeners and nurserymen in County Cork since the 1770s. He was the brother of **William Baylor Hartland**. He was educated at CBC, Cork, and at the Cork School of Art. Following some work in Cork and Dublin, he settled in Liverpool and acquired an instant reputation. He exhibited at the Royal Hibernian Academy and at the Society of Artists in London. He was also a member of the Liverpool Academy and of the Society of Painters in watercolours. Following a fall from a cliff, he died in Liverpool on 28 November 1893.

HARTLAND, William B. (1836–1912) Born Mallow, Co. Cork, the son of William Baylor Hartland, nurseryman, whose family had been gardeners and nurserymen in County Cork

since the 1770s. He was the brother of **Henry A. Hartland**. His father died in 1848 and five years later, William was apprenticed to his cousin, Joseph Bullen Hartland in Cork. He established his own nursery business in 1878 on a 10-acre site at Árd Cairn, Ballintemple. He achieved notability for his promotion of daffodils as a popular flower and his *Little Book of Daffodils* catalogue first appeared in 1884. He collected daffodil bulbs from old castle and monastic grounds around Ireland for his breeding stock and used the same methods to promote tulips. His *Original Little Book of Irish-grown Tulips* appeared in 1896. He also collected old varieties of apple trees and built up stocks of Irish varieties. A flamboyant self-promoter, he was, nevertheless, an important figure in Irish horticultural history. In 1884, he published *Wayside Ireland* – an account of a trip which he made to Achill Island and a commentary on the areas through which he passed (2nd ed., 1895). He died at the Protestant Incurables Home, St Luke's, Cork, on 15 September 1912 and was buried in Douglas Graveyard.

HARTOG, Marcus M. (1851–1924) Born London, the second son of Professor Alphonse Hartog. He was educated at Trinity College, Cambridge, where he graduated MA (1874) and at London University where he graduated D.Sc. Having worked at the Botanical Gardens, Ceylon, and at Owen College, Manchester, he was appointed as professor of Natural History at Queen's College, Cork (now UCC) in 1882. He subsequently became professor of Zoology there (1909–21). He published articles in the leading botany and zoology journals and also published a book, *Problems of Life and Reproduction*, in 1913. With Professor Mary Hayden, he also published *A Study of the Irish Dialect of English*. On his retirement, he went to live in Paris where he died on 21 January 1924.

HARTY, Abraham (*fl. c.*1830) He was the son of a Quaker, Thomas Harty of London. With his brother, Joseph, he ran three bakeries in Cork and resided at 71 Patrick Street. On the night of 3 September 1836, a phial of vitriol was thrown into his face by a member of a group of disgruntled bakers. The culprits were sentenced to death, but a Quaker campaign against the death sentence which was led by **Abraham Abell**, succeeded in a commutation of the sentence to that of transportation.

HARVEY, Joshua (1790–1871) Born Youghal, Co. Cork, the son of Thomas Harvey. Having qualified as a doctor, he took a great interest, like most Quakers, in the temperance movement. He was a founder member of the Dublin (later Hibernian) Temperance Society. He published *Some Observations and Advice addressed to the mechanic and industrious Classes on the Use of ardent Spirits* (1830).

HARVEY, Reuben (1734–1808) Born Youghal, Co. Cork, the father of **Reuben Harvey (1770–1830)**. He later resided at Pleasant Field, Blackrock (the site of the Ursuline Convent). He took an interest in the American War of Independence and corresponded with George Washington (1732–99) as an intermediary with the British government. When a group of American sailors were imprisoned in Kinsale, Harvey and other Quakers assisted them in their plight – an action which was commended by the American Congress.

HARVEY, Reuben (1770–1830) Born Cork, the son of **Reuben Harvey (1734–1808)**. Following in his father's footsteps, he was appointed as American Consul in Cork. He also served on the committees of the Cork School for the Deaf and the Cork Lancasterian School.

HARVEY, Joshua Reuben (1804–1878) Born Cork, the son of **Reuben Harvey (1770–1830)**. Having studied medicine at Cork, Edinburgh and Dublin, he was appointed in 1839 to the Lying-In Hospital at Mardyke Street and was the first physician at the South Infirmary hospital. He was a frequent contributor to the *Dublin Quarterly Journal of Medicine*.

HASTIE, James (1786–1826) Born Cork, of a Quaker family. He joined the British army and was posted to India with the 56th Regiment of Foot. As a result of his conduct during a fire, he was recommended for a commission, but in the meantime, he was appointed as assistant government agent to the court of King Radama I of Madagascar. He became a close friend of the king and accompanied him on his many campaigns before he finally established his royal authority over the other tribes on the island. The manuscript journals of Hastie's geographical and anthropological observations of the island were deposited among the Colonial State Papers at the Public Record Office, London. He died at Antananarivo, Madagascar, on 18 October 1826 and was buried in a special vault which had been prepared for his remains by the king.

HAUGHTON, Benjamin (1855–1932) He lived in Montenotte, Cork, and served on the bench as a magistrate and later as a member of Seanad Éireann (1922–28). During the War of Independence, he played a major part in the activities of the Irish White Cross, a relief organisation. He served on the board of the North Infirmary hospital and was connected with the Cork Improved Buildings Company, which promoted affordable and better housing to those who needed it. He died on 5 October 1932, and was buried in the Cork Quaker Cemetery.

HAUGHTON, John B. (1750–1833) He was the son of a Quaker, Benjamin Haughton (1705–77) of Edenderry, Co. Offaly, who settled in Cork on his marriage to Sarah Cambridge. He had been educated at the Quaker school at Ballitore, Co. Kildare. He opened a hardware business on the North Main Street in 1785 and later lived at Cleve Court, Blackrock. He eventually went bankrupt in the difficult times of the second decade of the nineteenth century, but this was remedied when some of his extensive properties were sold and the business put into the trusteeship of his sons-in-law. This firm survives to the present day as 'Brooks Haughton' on South Terrace.

HAWES, Benjamin (1797–1862) Born Lambeth, London, the son of Benjamin Hawes, soap manufacturer. He entered the family business and held office as a magistrate and as deputy lord lieutenant for Surrey. In 1832, he was elected as a Liberal MP for Lambeth and sat for that constituency until 1847. In March 1848, he was elected MP for Kinsale in a by-election. He sat for the constituency until his resignation in February 1852 in order to devote his full attention to the post of deputy Secretary for War. Following the Crimean War, he was appointed as permanent under-secretary to the War Office – a post which he held until his death at Queen Anne's Gate, Westminster, on 15 May 1862.

HAYES, Seamus (1924–1989) Born Cork but the family later moved to Dublin. He became interested in showjumping and had a distinguished career. He won the BSTA National Jumping Competition (1948–50); best rider at the Horse of the Year Show at Wembley (1949–50 and 1952); the *Daily Mail* Cup (1961 and 1963) and the British Showjumping Derby (1961 and 1964). On three occasions, he was a member of the Irish team which won the Aga Khan Cup at the Dublin Horse Show (1961, 1963 and 1967). However, he is best remembered for the great victories he gained on his mount, *Goodbye*. He died in 1989.

HAYES, Seán (1886–1928) Born Cregg, Rosscarbery, Co. Cork, the son of Denis Hayes. He was educated at Glandore NS and entered the Civil Service in London in 1904, transferring to Dublin in 1912. He joined the Irish Volunteers and took part in the Easter Rising of 1916. He was interned at Frongoch until the general amnesty of December 1916, and then returned to West Cork. In late 1917, he became editor of the *Southern Star* newspaper, a position he continued to hold intermittently until 1919. In the general election of 1918, he was returned unopposed for Sinn Féin in West Cork. He was also returned in the elections of 1921 and 1922 as a pro-Treaty TD. He did not seek re-election in

1923. During the civil war, he was military governor of Newbridge Prison and afterwards was appointed to a position in the GPO stores, Dublin. He died at his Clontarf, Dublin, residence on 24 June 1928 and was buried in Glasnevin Cemetery.

HAYES, Tim (1936–2005) Born Cobh, the son of Timothy Hayes. He spent some years as a seaman before returning to Cobh where he worked in the local dockyard. Certainly not a claustrophobe, he determined to beat the world record for the underground endurance test by being buried in a coffin. Following a pseudo-funeral, which attracted huge publicity and clerical criticism, he was buried at Ballymore, Cobh, on Christmas Day, 1965. He emerged 101 hours later for his Christmas dinner, having beaten the existing world record of a hundred hours. During his subterranean adventure, the burial site was visited by many thousands of people. He was subsequently buried on many occasions all over Ireland. He died at his Cobh home on 10 July 2005 and was finally buried at the Old Church Cemetery, Cobh.

HAYES, William E. (1915–1987) Born Cork, but raised in Sheffield where he played for the English Schoolboys soccer XI. He was signed by Huddersfield Town as an amateur (1932) and then as a professional (1934). He played with the Huddersfield club until 1941 when he returned to Cork. He helped Cork United to win four League of Ireland titles and two FAI Cup runners-up medals before returning to Huddersfield in September 1946. He subsequently made 181 First Division appearances for Huddersfield before his transfer to Burnley in February 1950. He retired in 1952, having also made four international appearances for Northern Ireland (1937–9) and two for Éire (1946–7). He opened a garage at Accrington, Lancashire, and died on 22 April 1987.

HAYMAN, Samuel (1818–1886) Born South Abbey, Youghal, Co. Cork, the eldest son of Matthew Hayman, Esq. The Haymans had been established in Youghal since the 17th century. He was educated at Youghal, Clonmel and TCD where he graduated BA (1839). He entered the Church of Ireland as a minister in 1842 and served as a curate in various parishes until his appointment as rector of Ardnageehy (1863–7). He then held rectorships at Templeroan (1867–72) and at Carrigaline with Douglas (1872–5). In 1874, he was made a canon of the diocesan chapter and in the following year, when his parishes were divided, he resigned Carrigaline and became rector of Douglas. He established a reputation as an historian and antiquarian through his publications on the history of Youghal [*The Annals of Youghal* (1848, 1851, 1852 and 1858) and *The Guide to Youghal, Ardmore, and the Blackwater* (1860, 1861)]. He also published the *Unpublished Geraldine Documents* (1870–81), and wrote articles in the *Gentleman's Magazine* and other journals. He was a member of the Royal Society of Antiquaries of Ireland. He died on 15 December 1886 and was buried in Douglas Graveyard.

HEALY, Augustine A. (1904–1987) Born Castle Road, Blackrock, Cork. 'Gus' was educated at North Monastery CBS and later worked as a dental mechanic. He suffered a fall during his childhood which resulted in a spinal deformity. Having taken up swimming as a therapeutic exercise, he became interested in the sport and later served as president of the Irish Amateur Swimming Association (1943/44). He was also a keen follower of rugby and was president of the Munster Branch of the IRFU (1945). He had a long association with the Cork Shakespearean Company and with its founder, Rev. **James C. O'Flynn**. He was also associated with Cork Film Festival and with the building of the new Cork Opera House. He became a member of Cork Corporation in 1943 and twice served as lord mayor of Cork (1964/65 and 1975/76). He was also a member of Cork County Council (1960–74). He made his debut in national politics in 1957 when he won a seat for Fianna Fáil in Cork Borough and was elected as chairman of the Fianna Fáil

Parliamentary Party two years later. Defeated in 1961, he was nominated to Seanad Éireann and served until 1965 when he regained his Dáil seat. He was a TD until 1977 when he did not seek re-election. He died at Cork University Hospital on 10 July 1987 and was buried in St Finbarr's Cemetery.

HEALY, Francis J.B. (1872–1931) Born Queenstown (Cobh), the son of J. Healy, JP, and cousin of **Tim Healy** and **Maurice Healy**. He was educated at Tullabeg College, Tullamore, at Clongowes Wood College and at TCD. He was called to the Bar in 1893 and practised on the Munster Circuit. He became an activist in the separatist Irish-American Alliance faction of the Ancient Order of Hibernians, in which he served as Grand Master (c.1909–15). He was prominent in defending separatist prisoners charged under the Defence of the Realm Act. He was co-opted to Cork County Council in 1913. Having been deported following the Easter Rising of 1916, he was put forward by **William O'Brien**'s All-for-Ireland League as a candidate in the West Cork by-election of 1916 and was narrowly defeated. He subsequently supported Sinn Féin and took the Republican side in the Civil War. He was a keen local historian and contributed many articles to newspapers and to journals such as the *JCHAS* and the *Journal of the Ivernian Society*. He died at his residence, Wilmount Castle, Cobh, on 7 August 1931 and was buried in Ballymore Graveyard.

HEALY, James N. (1916–1993) Born Turner's Cross, Cork. Following the death of his mother, the family moved to Lincoln Place, Grattan Hill, when he was six months old. He was educated at St Angela's School, at CBC and at UCC where he graduated B.Comm. However, he opted for a career on the stage and, as well as appearing both in drama and variety, also produced many Gilbert and Sullivan comic operas. He also founded the Group Theatre and a professional theatre group, the Theatre of the South. He had a lively interest in local history and published *The Castles of County Cork* in

1988. He died at the Bon Secours Hospital, Cork, on 27 May 1993 and was buried privately.

HEALY, Maurice (1859–1923) Born Bantry, Co. Cork, the third son of Maurice Healy, Poor Law Union clerk, and brother of **Tim Healy** and **Thomas J. Healy**. He was also the nephew of **A.M. Sullivan** and **T.D. Sullivan**. His mother died shortly after his birth and the family moved to Lismore where he was educated at the local CBS. He was admitted a solicitor in 1882. He was MP for Cork City from 1885 to 1900, in which year, standing as a Healyite nationalist, he was defeated. He was returned again for Cork City from May 1909 to January 1910 and for Cork North East from March to December 1910, now as an O'Brienite. From December 1910 until the General Election of 1918, he again represented Cork City. His forte in parliament was land law and he was a close confidant of his brother, Tim. He died at his residence, Temple Hill, Ballintemple, Cork, on 9 November 1923 and was buried in St Joseph's Cemetery. He was the father of Maurice Healy (1887–1943), the author and barrister.

HEALY, Tim (1855–1931) Born Bantry, Co. Cork, the second son of Maurice Healy, Poor Law Union clerk, and brother of **Maurice Healy** and **Thomas J. Healy**. He was also the nephew of **A.M. Sullivan** and **T.D. Sullivan**. He was educated at Fermoy CBS but left for England at the age of 13 where he took up a job as a railway clerk in Newcastle-on-Tyne. On moving to London in 1878, he became immersed in nationalist parliamentary politics through his job as a correspondent at Westminster and soon came under the influence of **C.S. Parnell**. He was returned unopposed as MP for Wexford in 1880 and a year later he was instrumental in the adoption of the 'Healy Clause' in the Land Act. He subsequently represented Monaghan (1883) and South Londonderry (1885) before the 'Parnell Split' of 1890 in which he played a leading anti-Parnellite role. In the meantime, he had been called to the Irish Bar in 1884 (Inner Bar 1910) and had built up a large practice.

When the Irish Parliamentary Party was reunited under John Redmond in 1900, his talent for disruption was recognised when he was expelled two years later. However, through the influence of Cardinal Michael Logue (1840–1924) and **William Martin Murphy**, he was able to retain his parliamentary seat for North Louth (1891) until 1910 when he joined **William O'Brien's** All-for-Ireland League and was returned for Cork North East. A supporter of Sinn Féin, he (reluctantly) resigned his seat in favour of that party's candidate before the General Election of 1918. On the foundation of the Irish Free State, he was appointed as Governor-General – a position which he held until the end of his term on 31 January 1928. He died on 26 March 1931 and was buried at Glasnevin Cemetery. His works include *Why is there an Irish Land Question and an Irish Land League?* (1881), *Why Ireland Is Not Free, a Study of Twenty Years in Politics* (1898), *Stolen Waters* (1913), *The Great Fraud of Ulster* (1917), *The Planter's Progress* (1921) and *Letters and Leaders of My Day* (2 vols, 1928). [Lives by L. O'Flaherty (1927), M. Sullivan (1943) and F. Callanan (1996)]

HEALY, Thomas J. (1854–1925) Born Bantry, Co. Cork, the eldest son of Maurice Healy, Poor Law Union clerk, and brother of **Maurice Healy** and **Tim Healy**. He was also the nephew of **A.M. Sullivan** and **T.D. Sullivan**. He was educated at Lismore CBS and was admitted a solicitor in 1888. He was elected as an anti-Parnellite MP for Wexford North in a March 1892 by-election. He retained his seat until his defeat in the General Election of 1900. He died in 1925.

HEARD, John I. (1787–1862) Born Kinsale, Co. Cork, the son of John Heard whose ancestors had settled near Bandon in the late 16th century. He was educated at Peterhouse, Cambridge, where he graduated BA (1808). Following the death of Lord de Clifford in 1832, he purchased the urban portion of the de Clifford estates, thereby becoming the proprietor of half of the town. In 1839, he was high sheriff of Cork. He was elected as Liberal MP for the borough of Kinsale in 1852 and sat until 1859 when he declined to contest the seat. He died in Kinsale on 1 September 1862 and was buried in St Multose's Church. [Mural commemorative tablet in St Multose's]

HEARN, Thomas (1875–1952) Born Collinstown, Co. Westmeath, the eldest son of Daniel J. Hearn, clergyman. He was educated at TCD where he graduated BA (1898) and LL.B (1902). Following his ordination in 1898, he ministered in Cork and Youghal and held canonries at the cathedrals of Cork and of Ross. He was later chancellor of St FinBarre's Cathedral (1926–34) and archdeacon of Cork (1933–38). He was consecrated as bishop of Cork, Cloyne and Ross on 13 November 1938. He died at his residence in Bishop Street, Cork, on 14 July 1952 and was buried in St Lappan's Graveyard, Little Island.

HEAZLE, William (d. 1872) Born Cork, the son of an organist at Shandon. He studied art at the Cork School of Art (1850) and at Kensington, London. Having refused a teaching position in London, he returned to Cork and exhibited at the Royal Hibernian Academy in 1861. Shortly afterwards he decided to give up art altogether and to study medicine. Unfortunately, before qualifying as a doctor, he died at his father's house in Queen Street in 1872.

HEDGES, Sir William (1632–1701) Born Coole, Macroom, Co. Cork, the eldest son of Robert Hedges of Youghal. He was sent to Constantinople (Istanbul) as head of the Levant Company but returned to England c.1671. In 1681, he was elected as a director of the East India Company and acted as governor of Bengal Province from 1682 until 1687. When he returned to England in that year, he was knighted by King James II (1633–1701). He became sheriff of London in 1693 and a year later was appointed as a director of the Bank of England. He died in London on 5 August 1701 and was buried at Stratton, Wiltshire. [Diary edited by H. Yule]

HEGARTY, Sir Daniel (1849–1914) Born Summerhill, Cork, the son of Daniel Hegarty, merchant. An alderman of Cork Corporation, he was elected as mayor of Cork in late January 1900, narrowly defeating, by a single vote, the future Lord Mayor, Sir Edward Fitzgerald (1846–1927), after whom Fitzgerald Park is named. With the Boer War in full swing, tensions were high between the nationalist and unionist members of the corporation. Fuel was added to fire when Queen Victoria (1819–1901) paid her last visit to Ireland in the following April. Following an address of welcome at the Viceregal Lodge (now Áras an Uachtaráin) by Mayor Hegarty, the queen, on her return to England, confirmed by royal charter the new title of 'Lord Mayor' and a knighthood on Cork's First Citizen. On his return, the corporation refused to pay the enrolment fee for the charter and, eventually, Hegarty paid the fee out of his own pocket. He died on 20 November 1914.

HELY-HUTCHINSON, Christopher (1767–1826) He was the son of **John Hely-Hutchinson (1724–1794)** and brother of **John Hely-Hutchinson (1757–1832)** and **Richard Hely-Hutchinson**. He was called to the Bar in 1792 and sat as MP for Taghmon (Wexford) in 1795. He fought against the forces of General Humbert (b. 1767) at the battle of Ballinamuck in 1798. He represented Cork in the British Commons (1801–12) and then Longford (1812–19). During some of that period, he served in the Russian army.

HELY-HUTCHINSON, John (1724–1794) Born John Hely at Gortroe, Mallow, Co. Cork. He was the father of **John Hely-Hutchinson (1757–1832)**, **Richard Hely-Hutchinson** and **Christopher Hely-Hutchinson**. He was educated at TCD where he graduated BA (1744) and was called to the Bar in 1748. In 1751, he married Christina Nixon, the heiress of Richard Hutchinson, and assumed the new name. In the Irish Parliament, he sat for Lanesborough (1759–61), Cork City (1761–90) and for Taghmon (1790–4). His election as provost of TCD in

1774 led to much controversy, as he was unqualified for the position. Furthermore, the circumstances of his appointment were seen to compromise the independence of the university. A liberal Protestant, he supported the various Catholic Relief Acts (1774–93). He died at Buxton, Derbyshire, on 4 September 1794. His *Commercial Restraints of Ireland*, which was published anonymously in 1779, was ordered to be burnt by the public hangman but was well received by the advocates of free trade.

HELY-HUTCHINSON, John (1757–1832) He was the son of **John Hely-Hutchinson (1724–1794)** and brother of **Richard Hely-Hutchinson** and **Christopher Hely-Hutchinson**. He was educated at Eton and at TCD where he failed to graduate. He became MP for Cork City (1790–1800) while, at the same time, he pursued a successful army career. He took part in the suppression of the 1798 Rebellion and later saw service in Egypt against the forces of Napoleon (1769–1821), rising to the rank of general in 1813. In 1825, he succeeded his brother, Richard, as the 2nd earl of Donoughmore. He died on 29 June 1832.

HELY-HUTCHINSON, Richard (1756–1825) He was the eldest son of **John Hely-Hutchinson (1724–1794)** and brother of **John Hely-Hutchinson (1757–1832)** and **Christopher Hely-Hutchinson**. He was educated at TCD where he graduated BA (1775) and LL.D (1783). He sat in the Irish parliament for both Sligo and Taghmon (Wexford). He commanded the Cork Legion during the 1798 Rebellion and as a supporter of the Act of Union, he was created 1st earl of Donoughmore in 1800. He served as postmaster general of Ireland from 1805 to 1809. A firm supporter of Catholic Emancipation, he represented that lobby at the British House of Lords until the Veto Controversy of 1813. He died on 22 August 1825 and was succeeded as 2nd earl by his brother, John.

HENEGAN, David (c.1705–p.1774) Born Cork. He was educated at the Irish College,

Paris, and at the Sorbonne where he graduated DD. In 1762, he was appointed as the provisor at the Irish College for the Munster ecclesiastical province. He was a contributor of many Irish biographies and articles to the *Dictionnaire de Moreri* of 1759. He was also vicar general to the exiled Bishop **John O'Brien** of Cloyne and certified the latter's dictionary, *Focalóir Gaoidhilge-Sax-Bhéarla* (1768). In May 1774, he established a bursary at the Irish College for the education of one student from the diocese of Cork.

HENNESSY, Henry (1826–1901) Born Cork, the second son of John Hennessy of Ballyhennessy, Listowel, Co. Kerry, and elder brother of **Sir John Pope Hennessy**. He worked as a civil engineer and had an interest in physics and mathematics. In 1849, he was appointed as Librarian at Queen's College, Cork (now UCC). He was invited in 1855 by Cardinal J.H. Newman to take the chair of Physics at the newly founded Catholic University. He subsequently became professor of Applied Mathematics at the Royal College of Science (1874–91). He was elected as a fellow of the Royal Society (1858) and served as vice-president of the Royal Irish Academy (1870–73). He died in Bray on 8 March 1901. His publications included *On the Study of Science in its Relation to Individuals and Society* (1858 and 1859), *On the Freedom of Education* (1859) and *The Relation of Science to modern Civilisation* (1862).

HENNESSY, John J. (1847–1920) Born Cloyne, Co. Cork, the son of Michael Hennessy. He was brought to the United States when a child and was educated at CBC (St Louis) and at seminaries in Missouri and Wisconsin. He was ordained at St Louis in November 1869 and engaged in missionary work in the St Louis diocese to 1888. He was consecrated as bishop of the newly-created see of Wichita in November 1888. He died at Wichita, Kansas, on 13 July 1920 and was buried there.

HENNESSY, Sir John POPE- (1834–1891) Born Cork, the son of John Hennessy of

Ballyhennessy, Listowel, Co. Kerry and younger brother of **Henry Hennessy**. He was educated at Queen's College, Cork (now UCC), and was called to the Bar in 1861. In 1859, he was elected as the first Irish Roman Catholic Conservative to the British parliament as a member for King's Co. He lost this seat in 1865 and then took on the role of colonial governor of the Windward Islands, Hong Kong and Mauritius. He was knighted in 1880 but was suspended from office six years later through a quarrel with a government official. He was returned to Parliament as an anti-Parnellite member for Kilkenny in 1890 but died at his residence, Rostellan Castle, Co. Cork, on 7 October 1891 (the day after Parnell's death). He was buried in St Joseph's Cemetery, Cork. [Life by James Pope-Hennessy (1964)]

HENNESSY, Michael J. (*fl.* 1923–32) A native of Cobh and an accountant by profession, he was active in Connradh na Gaeilge as a young man. He was elected to the Third Dáil as an Independent TD for the Cork East/North East constituency. In the election of 1923 to the 4th Dáil, he was returned as a Cumann na nGaedheal TD for the East Cork constituency and was re-elected in both of the 1927 general elections. He failed to retain his seat at the 1932 general election. He resided at 11 O'Rahilly Street Cobh. He left Cobh in the 1950's and moved to Portsmouth, where he was still living in the early 1970s.

HENNESSY, Patrick (1915–1980) Born Cork, the son of an army officer. When the Troubles began, he was taken to Arbroath, Scotland. He developed an early interest in art and studied at Dundee College of Art, Scotland. He returned to Ireland on the outbreak of World War II in 1939 and worked both in Dublin and Cork. He was elected as a member of the Royal Hibernian Academy in 1949 and exhibited there in 1952. In his later years, he lived and worked both on the Continent and in Morocco. He died at the Royal Free Hospital, London, on 30 December 1980 and was cremated at Golders Green Crematorium.

HENNESSY, Richard (1720–1800) Born Ballymacmoy, Kilavullen, Co. Cork, the son of James Hennessy, a minor North Cork landowner. Contrary to popular belief, he had not been an officer in the French Army at the battles of Fontenoy, Dettingen etc., though he did enter Clare's regiment where his service was short and undistinguished. In 1765, the year in which he established his distilling business at Cognac on the River Charente, he married Ellen Barrett, his cousin's widow, who, in turn, was a first cousin of the orator and statesman, Edmund Burke (1729–97). While conditions in the brandy business were difficult for most of his life, his house eventually prospered and has continued to the present day. He died at his estate, La Billarderie, Cognac on 8 October 1800.

HERLIHY, Donal (1908–1983) Born Knocknagree, Co. Cork. He was educated at St Brendan's College, Killarney, and at the Irish College, Rome, where he was ordained in 1931 and subsequently graduated DD and LSS. He worked on the staff of Jeffer's Institute, Tralee (1933–9) and at All Hallows College, Dublin (1939–47) where he was appointed as professor of Sacred Scripture. He was appointed as vice-rector of the Irish College, Rome, in 1947 and as rector from 1951 to 1964. He was consecrated as bishop of Ferns on 15 November 1964. He died on 2 April 1983 and was buried at St Aidan's Cathedral, Enniscorthy. His reputation was posthumously besmirched by the revelations of his failure to deal adequately with accusations of sexual abuse by some of his priests during his episcopacy.

HERLIHY, Nora (1910–1988) Born Ballydesmond, Co. Cork, the daughter of Denis J. Herlihy, teacher. She was educated locally, at Mercy Convent, Newcastlewest and at Carysfort College of Education, Dublin, where she qualified as a primary teacher. She initially worked in Waterford but later in various Dublin schools. She became interested in the Irish Co-operative Movement and, while studying for an evening degree at UCD, she and two other students founded the Dublin Central Co-operative Society of which she acted as secretary. She then made a study of the US and Canadian credit union systems and this led to the establishment of the Credit Union Extension Service in 1957. In the following year, the first credit union branch was formed in Dublin, and soon the movement spread to her native county when Ballyphehane Credit Union came into existence in 1960. In the same year, the Credit Union League of Ireland was founded with Nora acting as secretary. She later became part-time manager of the League whose member-branches were regularised by the passing of the Credit Union Act of 1966. She was later honoured with the distinction of a life director of the movement. She died in Dalkey, Co. Dublin, on 7 February 1988 and was buried in Ballydesmond Cemetery. [Life by A.G. Culloty (1990); Memorial museum, Ballydesmond, Co. Cork]

HERON, John (d. 1913) Born Bandon, Co. Cork. He was educated locally and at Queen's College, Cork (now UCC), where he graduated BE (1871). However, he abandoned an engineering career, took up chemistry and studied at the Royal College of Chemistry. In 1877, he was assistant chemist at Worthington's Brewery, Burton-on-Trent, and six years later was chemist at the Anglo-Bavarian Brewery. In 1885, he was chemist at Gorton Hill sugar factory, Battersea, London. Ten years later, he established himself in London as a brewer's analyst and consultant, having previously been elected as the first president of the Institute of Brewing. Following his death in 1913, his laboratory was carried on by his son.

HERON, William (1742–1819) Born Cork. He emigrated to America and settled in Redding Ridge, Connecticut, before the American Revolution. In this conflict, he took the side of the colonists and represented Redding Ridge at four sessions of the Connecticut Assembly (1778–82). However, he turned to espionage and operated as a British agent. He was so successful that he was never under the suspicion of the colonists who indeed regarded him as 'one of theirs'. Following the War of Independence, he again sat in the Connecticut Assembly (1784–96). He died on 8 January 1819.

HERVEY, Frederick Augustus (1730–1803) Born London, the grandson of the 1st earl of Bristol. He was educated at Corpus Christi College, Cambridge, where he graduated MA (without examination) in 1754. Through the influence of his brother, George William Hervey, the Irish Lord Lieutenant, he was consecrated as Church of Ireland bishop of Cloyne on 31 May 1767. He became a member of the Irish Privy Council (1767) and was awarded a DD by TCD in the following year. He was translated to the lucrative diocese of Derry in 1768. In 1770, he was awarded another DD degree from Oxford. He succeeded as the 4th earl of Bristol in 1779 and was elected a Fellow of the Royal Society in 1782. An eccentric (Horace Walpole once quipped 'There are men, women and Herveys'), he lived mostly on the Continent and bought huge quantities of paintings, statues, and other works of art to adorn his two Irish residences. He also undertook the task of building a colossal family seat at Ickworth, Suffolk. Through his involvement with the Irish Volunteers, he lost all political power and was shunned by the Irish establishment. He died at Albano, Italy, on 18 July 1803 and was buried at Ickworth. [Lives by W.S. Childe-Pemberton (2 vols, 1924), and B. Fothergill (1974); Bust (n.d.) by J. Wilton (1722–1803); Wax portrait by I. Gosset (1713–99) at Ickworth; Family portrait at the National Gallery, Dublin.]

HICKEY, James (1886–1966) Born Ballinagar, Mallow, Co. Cork, the eleventh of twelve children of John Hickey. He was educated at Rahan NS and came to Cork in 1913 where he worked in various capacities before becoming a trades union official in 1917. He was elected as a Labour Party member of Cork Corporation in 1934 and served as lord mayor (1938–9) and 1943. He also completed the term of **Seán French** who died in office in September 1937.

Having failed to win a Cork City Dáil seat for Labour in 1937 (by the narrow margin of 35 votes), he subsequently represented this constituency (1938–43 and 1948–54). Defeated by his running mate, **Seán Casey** in 1954, he became a member of Seanad Éireann (1954–7). He was the first chairman of the Cork City branch of the Irish Red Cross and was also an active member of Cork CYMS. He died at his St Luke's residence on 7 June 1966 and was buried at Rahan Cemetery.

HICKEY, Maurice (1915–2005) Born Cork, the son of Maurice Hickey. He was educated at PBC (Cork), Rochestown College and UCC where he graduated with distinction in medicine in 1941. He worked in Nottingham and London before his appointment as consultant thoracic surgeon to London County Council. He returned to Ireland in 1948 and worked under the aegis of Dr Noel Browne (1915–97), the minister for Health, performing operations in Dublin, Cork and Castlerea on a weekly round. Having been transferred to Cork, he worked at St Finbarr's Hospital, at Sarsfield's Court (Riverstown) and finally at Cork University Hospital. By this time, his pioneering techniques in heart surgery had gained for him an international reputation. He was conferred with the freedom of Cork in 1992. He died on 16 May 2005 and was buried in St Columba's Cemetery, Douglas.

HICKEY, William (1787–1875) Born Murragh, Bandon, Co. Cork, the eldest son of Dr Ambrose Hickey, the local rector. He was educated at St John's College, Cambridge, where he graduated BA (1809) and at TCD where he graduated BA (1832). He was ordained as deacon in the Church of Ireland at Cork in 1811. In 1820, he was incumbent at Bannow, Co. Wexford (in the diocese of Ferns) where he was co-founder of the South Wexford Agricultural Society. He moved to Kilcormick in 1826 and made many improvements in his parish. He studied farming and, writing as 'Martin Doyle', he published *Hints to Small Farmers* (1830)

which ran to numerous editions up to 1867. He followed this by tens of other publications on practical farming and husbandry. For his efforts, he was elected as a member of the Royal Dublin Society. He died at Mulrankin, Co. Wexford, on 24 October 1875. [Sketch by T. Cadogan in *Bandon Historical Journal* (1989)]

HIGGINS, Joseph (1885–1925) Born Ballincollig, Co. Cork, the son of William Higgins, teacher and local historian who, following a jail term for his part in the Fenian Rising of 1867, worked at the Royal Gunpowder Mills, Ballincollig. Joseph worked in Cork as a clerk in the tea firm of Newsom & Sons of French Church Street and studied sculpture by night at the Crawford School of Art. He eventually took up teaching positions in Youghal, Fermoy and Midleton, and later lived permanently in Youghal. Among his clay models were studies of **Michael Collins**, **Daniel Corkery** and **W.F. Stockley**. He died of tuberculosis on 25 November 1925. [Life by O. Murphy (2005); Commemorative plaque at 13/14 French Church Street, Cork]

HILL, Arthur (1846–1921) Born Cork, the son of **Henry Hill (1807–1887)** and father of **Henry Haughton Hill (1882–1951)**. He was educated at Queen's College, Cork (now UCC), where he graduated BE (1869) and at the University of London. He travelled through Europe studying buildings and all types of architecture. He was the co-editor of the book, *The Domed Churches of Charente*. He joined his father's firm in 1869 and took over its running on the latter's death in 1887. Among his local works were the Munster and Leinster Bank head office (now AIB), South Mall; Cork Technical Schools; the chemical laboratories at UCC, and the Imperial Hotel. For many years, he was also lecturer in Architecture at UCC. He died on 25 February 1921, and was buried in the graveyard of St Colman's Cathedral, Cloyne. [Commemorative plaque at the Metropole Hotel, Cork]

HILL, Henry (1807–1887) A Cork architect, the son of **William Hill (c.1766–1844)**, and father of **Arthur Hill**. He was the brother of **William Henry Hill** (*c.*1800–1860). He was also an able watercolourist. He joined the family firm in Georges Street (now Oliver Plunkett Street), Cork. Among his works are the Saints Joachim and Anne's Home (Anglesey Street), Christ Church (Rushbrooke) and Park House (Youghal). He provided the illustrations for Mr and Mrs Hall's *Ireland* (3 vols, 1841–3). He died at his residence on Blackrock Road on 27 May 1887 and was buried in the graveyard of St Colman's Cathedral, Cloyne.

HILL, Henry Haughton (1882–1951) Born Cork, the son of **Arthur Hill**, architect. He studied at the Liverpool University School of Architecture where he graduated BA. He then joined his father's firm and collaborated with him in such Cork landmarks as the College of Commerce (Morrison's Island), the Dairy Science (now Geography) Building (UCC) and the premises of Cash and Co. (now Brown Thomas plc), Patrick Street. Like his father, he worked as lecturer in Architecture at UCC. He also had a great interest in painting. He died at St Aubyn's, Monkstown, Co. Cork, in 1951.

HILL, Sir Hugh (1802–1871) Born Graig, Doneraile, Co. Cork, the son of James Hill, Esq. He was educated at TCD where he graduated BA (1821). He studied at King's Inns and at the Middle Temple, London. He was called to the English Bar in 1841 and to the Inner Bar in 1851. In 1858, he was appointed as a judge at the Queen's Bench and was also knighted. However, in 1861, he was forced to retire through ill health and died at the Royal Crescent Hotel, Brighton, on 12 October 1871.

HILL, Martin (1905–1976) Born Cork, the son of **William H. Hill**. He was educated at Malvern College and at Oriel College, Oxford, where he graduated MA. Following further studies at the London School of Economics and at the University of Vienna, he took up a position in the economic and financial sections of the League of Nations. In 1946, he took up a permanent staff position at the United Nations as special adviser to the Secretary-General. Following his retirement in 1970, he acted as special consultant to the Secretary-General for a further two years before becoming a special fellow of the United Nations Institute for Training and Research. Among his publications were *The Economic and Financial Organisation of the League of Nations* (1945), *Immunities and privileges of International Officials* (1947) and 'The Administrative Committee on Co-ordination' in *The Evolution of International Organizations* (1966). He died at Princeton, New Jersey, on 18 May 1976.

HILL, Thomas (1775–1859) he was the son of **William Hill (1739–1779)** and brother of **William Hill** (*c.*1766–1844). He was an architect and died at Passage West in 1859, leaving an estate of £2,000.

HILL, William (1739–1779) A Protestant gentleman who lived in Cloyne. He was the father of **William Hill** (*c.*1766–1844) and **Thomas Hill (1775–1859)**.

HILL, William (*c.*1776–1844) The architect of the Church of Ireland diocese of Cloyne, he was the son of **William Hill (1739–1779),** brother of **Thomas Hill (1775–1859)** and father of **William Henry Hill** (*c.*1800–1860).

HILL, William Henry (*c.*1800–1860) An architect of George's Street, Cork (the present Oliver Plunkett Street). He was the son of **William Hill** (*c.*1766–1844). His younger brother, Henry, was also an architect.

HILL, William Henry (1837–1911) Born Cork, the son of **William Henry Hill** (*c.*1800–1844) and father of **William Henry Hill (1865–1941)**. He was educated locally and graduated from Queen's College, Cork (now UCC), and the Royal University with a BE degree. He worked as an apprentice architect with his uncle, Henry, and was subsequently appointed architect to the Church of Ireland diocese of Cloyne and held that post until Disestablishment in 1869. He worked on the architectural aspects of the restoration of Cork Courthouse after the disastrous fire of 1891. He died at his residence, Audley House, Patrick's Hill, Cork in 1911.

HILL, William Henry (1865–1941) Born St Patrick's Hill, Cork, the son of **William Henry Hill (1837–1911)**, architect, to whose practice he succeeded. He was the father of **Martin Hill**. He represented the seventh architect of the Hill family through four generations. Following family tradition, he was architect to the Munster dioceses of the Church of Ireland. Among his many commissions were the restoration of Cork Courthouse following the fire of 1891, Cork and Youghal mental hospitals, St Luke's Church, the 1888 extension to the Crawford Art Gallery and the planning of the Cork and Muskerry Railway. He was one of the first motorists in Cork, a long-time member of the CHAS and a council member of the Royal Society of Antiquaries of Ireland. He died on 31 October 1941 at Currabinny, Crosshaven, and was buried in Douglas graveyard.

HINCKS, Edward (1792–1866) Born Cork, the eldest son of **Thomas Dix Hincks**, a Presbyterian minister. He was also the brother of **William Hincks** and **Sir Francis Hincks**. He was educated at Midleton College and at TCD where he graduated BA (1811). In 1825, he was preferred to the rectorship of Killyleagh, Co. Down, where he remained for the rest of his life. He was an expert on the deciphering of Egyptian, Assyrian, Babylonian, Median and Persian cuneiform inscriptions and contributed many articles to the Royal Irish Academy. He died at Killyleagh on 3 December 1866. [Commemorative plaque at entrance to the Unitarian Church, Prince's Street, Cork]

HINCKS, Sir Francis (1807–1885) Born Cork, the youngest son of **Thomas Dix Hincks**, a Presbyterian minister. He was the brother of **Edward Hincks** and **William Hincks**. He emigrated to Canada in 1831 where his interest

in journalism led to the establishment of *The Examiner* newspaper in 1838. He entered the Canadian parliament in 1841 and three years later founded the *Montreal Pilot* newspaper. A Liberal in politics, he became Prime Minister of Canada in 1851. He resigned in 1854, having been accused by Orangemen of favouring Roman Catholics during the Gavazzi Riots [the anti-papal campaign of Allesandro Gavazzi (1809–89)] of June 1853. He returned to England and was later appointed as governor of Barbados (1855–62) and of British Guiana (1862–69). In 1869, he returned to Canada and served as finance minister in the Canadian Government from which he resigned in 1883. He died in Montreal on 8 August 1885. [Reminiscences (1884); Life by R.S. Longley (1943)]

HINCKS, Thomas (1818–1899) Born Exeter, the son of **William Hincks**. He succeeded his father in the Unitarian ministry and served in Cork, Dublin, and in England. He graduated BA at London University and was elected a fellow of the Royal Society in 1872. He published the zoological treatises *Zoophytes* (1868) and *Polyzoa* (1880). He died at Clifton, Bristol, on 25 January 1899.

HINCKS, Thomas Dix (1767–1857) Born Dublin, the son of a customs official. He was the father of **Edward Hincks**, **William Hincks**, and **Sir Francis Hincks**. He entered TCD in 1784 but did not graduate. In 1788, he attended Hackney New College where he was a pupil of the chemist and discoverer of oxygen, Joseph Priestley (1733–1804). He ministered at the Unitarian Church, Princes Street, Cork, in 1790 and was ordained in 1792. He opened a school which operated from 1791 until 1803, and in that year he was elected as a member of the Royal Irish Academy. He also wished to found an institution in Cork on similar lines to the Royal Dublin Society. With the support of Sir Thomas Newport, the chancellor of the Irish Exchequer, a charter to establish the Cork Institute was issued on 31 January 1808. The old Custom House was acquired as a premises for the new institute. In 1815, he served as a tutor at the Fermoy Academy. While in Cork, he was the editor of the quarterly *Munster Agricultural Magazine*. He was appointed as professor of Hebrew and headmaster of the Belfast Academical Institution in 1821 and served there until 1836. He was awarded the LL.D of Glasgow University (1834). His daughter, Hannah, was an expert on algae. He died in Belfast on 24 February 1857 and was buried at Killyleagh, Co. Down. He published *Letters ... in Answer to Paine's Age of Reason* (1795 and 1796) [Commemorative plaque at entrance to Prince's Street Unitarian Church, Cork].

HINCKS, William (1794–1871) Born Cork, the son of **Thomas Dix Hincks**. He was also the brother of **Sir Francis Hincks** and **Edward Hincks**. He served as a Presbyterian minister at Cork (1815), Exeter (1816–22) and Liverpool (1822–7). He became professor of Natural History at Manchester College, York (1842–9) and professor of Natural History at Queen's College, Cork (now UCC) (1849–53). His appointment as professor of Natural History at University College, Toronto, in 1853 was made at the expense of the famous English scientist and humanist, T.H. Huxley (1825–95). He was elected as president of the Canadian Institute from 1869 until his death and was for several years the editor of its *Canadian Journal*. He died in Toronto on 10 September 1871. [Biographical article by C.R.W. Biggar in *University of Toronto Monthly*, 2 (1901–2)]

HOARE, Edward W. (1779–1870) Born Ballycrenane, Kilcredan, Co. Cork, the younger son of Sir Edward Hoare, MP and landowner. In 1790, he joined the Royal Navy and was promoted to the rank of lieutenant five years later. Having seen action against the French in Malta and Egypt, he was advanced to the rank of commander in 1805 and to captain in 1810. With two companies of soldiers on board, he took part in the attack on Java on 5 June 1811. He was on half-pay from 13 August 1812. He was later promoted to the rank of admiral and died at Ryde, Isle of Wight, on 6 January 1870, and was buried at Castle Haven there.

HOARE, Edward W. (1863–1920) Born Carrigrohane Castle, Co. Cork, the son of Captain William Jesse Hoare. He was privately educated and later attended New Veterinary College, Edinburgh. He subsequently became a member (1886) and a fellow (1892) of the Royal College of Veterinary Surgeons. In addition to his private Cork practice, he was appointed as lecturer in Veterinary Science at UCC. He acted as extern examiner to many universities and institutions, as well as being a member of the board of examiners at the Royal College of Veterinary Surgeons and editor of the *Veterinary News*. His publications included, *A System of Veterinary Medicine* (2 vols, 1916) and *Veterinary Therapeutics* (3rd ed., 1916). He died at his residence at Clover Hill, Blackrock, Cork, and was buried privately. [Comments in M. Jesse Hoare, *The Road to Glenanore* (1975)]

HOBBS, Dan (1883–1962) Born near The Lough, Cork. During his lifetime, he was Cork's best-loved comedian and concert compere. A founder-member of 'The Warblers' (a noted concert group in Cork [1916–29]), he was a regular on the old Opera House stage and also performed in Dublin's Theatre Royal and on Radio Éireann. He was managing director of the well-known Patrick Street drapery business which bore his name. A keen sportsman, he was a successful racing cyclist in his youth, hunted his own pack of beagles (The Lough Foot Beagles), and was closely associated with St Finbarr's GAA club and with boxing in Cork. He died at his residence, Mount Kieran, The Lough, on 6 July 1962 and was buried in St Finbarr's Cemetery.

HOGAN, Edmund (1831–1917) Born Belvelly, Cobh, Co. Cork, the son of William Hogan, stonemason. A member of the Society of Jesus, he studied for the priesthood in Rome. He was appointed as Todd Professor of Celtic at the Royal Irish Academy, and, on the foundation of

UCD, he became professor of Irish Language and History (1887). He published *Cath Ruis na Ríg for Bóinn* (1892), *Distinguished Irishmen of the 16th Century* (1894), *History of the Irish Wolf Dog* (1897), and *Onomasticon Goedelicum, an Index to Gaelic Names of Places and Tribes* (1910, repr. 1993). He was co-editor of Charles O'Kelly's (1621–95) *Macariae Excidium* (1894). He also compiled a phrase book for Connradh na Gaeilge in 1899. He died in Dublin on 26 November 1917. [Obituary by Dr Douglas Hyde in *Studies* (Dec., 1917)]

HOGAN, James (1898–1963) Born Kilrickle, Loughrea, Co. Galway, the son of Michael Hogan. He was educated at Clongowes Wood College and at UCD (1915–19) where he gained a brilliant reputation. He was active in UCD's Cumann Gaedhealach and was enrolled as a member of the 3rd Dublin battalion of the Irish Volunteers. He did not participate in the Easter Rising of 1916 as he was at home on holidays. During the War of Independence, he was a member of the East Clare Flying Column. He was appointed as professor of History at UCC in 1920, the youngest-ever professorial appointment at that college. He served in the Free State Army until his resignation in 1923 when he returned to academic life in Cork. He held the professorship until his retirement in 1960. During the Blueshirt period, he belonged to the intellectual wing of that movement, but soon disillusionment set in. In 1936, he unsuccessfully contested the Galway constituency as a Fine Gael candidate in a by-election which was caused by the death of his brother, Patrick Hogan, who had been minister for Agriculture (1922–32) in the Cumann na nGaedheal government. For many years, he was a member of the governing body of UCC and of the Senate of the NUI. In 1928, he was a founder member of the Irish Manuscripts Commission and was joint editor (with Professor Eoin Mac Neill) of the commission's organ, *Analecta Hibernica*. He died on 23 October 1963 and was buried privately. His publications include *Ireland in the European System* (1920), *Could Ireland become Communist?* (1935) and *Election and Representation* (1943). [Volume of essays by D. Ó Corráin (ed.) (2001)]

HOGAN, John (1800–1858) Born Tallow, Co. Waterford, the son of a Cork builder. Following an apprenticeship as a carver in Cork to the architect, **Sir Thomas Deane**, he attended anatomy lectures and copied casts at the gallery of the Cork Society of Arts. Having come to public notice, he received a commission from Bishop **John Murphy** to carve twenty-seven statues in wood and a bas-relief of Leonardo da Vinci's 'Last Supper' for the North Cathedral. With the help of private subscriptions, he arrived in Rome in early 1824 to undertake further studies and eventually to set up a studio there. He visited Ireland in 1829 where he exhibited at the Royal Irish Art Union and received further commissions. He was also awarded the gold medal of the Royal Dublin Society. In 1837, he was elected as a member of the Society of the Virtuosi del Pantheon – the first member from the British Isles. With the rise of the Young Italy revolutionary movement in 1848, he left Rome and settled in Dublin. He died on 27 March 1858 and was buried at Glasnevin Cemetery. [Portrait by B. Mulrenin at the National Gallery of Ireland, Dublin; Commemorative plaque at his former residence, 7 Cove Street, Cork]

HOGAN, John (1805–1892) Born Mallow, Co. Cork, the son of Thomas Hogan. Following the death of his mother, his father and himself emigrated to Baltimore, Maryland, in 1816. However, Thomas died in the following year and John was taken into an apprenticeship with a boot manufacturer. In 1821, he converted to Methodism and served as a peripatetic minister on the Baltimore and St Louis Circuits. However, in 1830, he was forced to abandon the ministry through ill health and he went into business as a general merchant at Edwardsville, Illinois. In 1836, he was elected to the Illinois legislature, but failed to be elected to Congress two years later. A series of his articles was published in 1854 under the title of *Thoughts about the City of St Louis* and this was the cause of bringing large numbers of Irish immigrants to the city. In 1857, he was appointed as postmaster of St Louis and when the American civil war broke out, he paid the salaries of the postal officials out of his own pocket (and earning the nickname of 'Honest John Hogan'). Happily, he was elected to Congress in 1864. He died on 5 February 1892. [Recollections by S.H. Boogher (1927)]

HOLLAND, Michael (1855–1950) Born Clonakilty, Co. Cork. The family moved to Cork shortly after his birth. He was employed at the Cork drapery firm of Dwyer & Co. for many years. He studied at the Cork School of Art and afterwards produced many illuminated addresses. He also started a successful hand-made lace industry. He was a member of the Cork Historical and Archaeological Society for a total of fifty-eight years. He was secretary and editor of the *JCHAS* (1934–6) and president of the Society (1942–6). For many years in the Thirties, he contributed a pictorial strip in the *Cork Examiner* and *Cork Weekly Examiner*, entitled, 'This Quaint Old Cork of Ours'. He also contributed many articles to the *JCHAS* and to other local journals. He died at the South Infirmary Hospital on 6 November 1950 and was buried in St Finbarr's Cemetery.

HOLMES, Sir John (c.1640–1683) Born Mallow, Co. Cork, the son of Henry Holmes, Esq., and younger brother of **Sir Robert Holmes**. At the English Restoration in 1660, he joined his brother as a captain in the Royal Navy and served from 1664 until 1679. He was knighted in 1672. He sat as MP for Newtown, Isle of Wight, from 1677 until his death. In June 1679, he fought a duel with his fellow-MP, John Churchill, the future 1st duke of Marlborough (1650–1722), who laid siege to Cork in 1690. He was buried at Yarmouth on 23 June 1683.

HOLMES, Sir Robert (1622–1692) Born Mallow, Co. Cork, the son of Henry Holmes,

Esq., and elder brother of **Sir John Holmes**. He served in the Royalist army during the English civil war and during the Commonwealth he campaigned in France with the Duke of York (the future King James II). At the Restoration in 1660, he was appointed by York (now Lord High Admiral) as a sea captain. From 1663 until 1667, he was involved in the great sea-battles with the Dutch fleets and was knighted in 1665. He was returned to the English parliament as MP for Winchester in 1668 and was also appointed as captain-general and governor of the Isle of Wight where he built a large mansion. He again saw action against the Dutch off the Isle of Wight in 1672 but afterwards returned to his governing and parliamentary duties. He died on 18 November 1692 and was buried in Yarmouth. [Life by R. Ollard (1969)]

HOOPER, John (1846–1897) Born Cork, the son of Patrick Hooper and father of **Patrick J. Hooper**. He joined the staff of the *Cork Herald* in 1861 and was the newspaper's editor. In November 1883, he was elected as alderman for the North West Ward of Cork Corporation. In the general election of December 1885, he was selected as nationalist candidate for Cork South and elected with a massive majority. At the end of 1887, he was imprisoned under the Coercion Acts for publishing reports of suppressed branches of the National Land League and spent two months in Tullamore Gaol. He resigned his parliamentary seat in May 1889. He was parliamentary correspondent of the *Freeman's Journal* for some time, before becoming editor of the *Evening Telegraph* in 1892 – a position he held at his death which occurred in Dublin on 20 November 1897. He was buried in Glasnevin Cemetery. His health had been precarious ever since his incarceration in Tullamore a decade earlier.

HOOPER, Patrick J. (1873–1931) Born Cork, the son of **John Hooper**. He joined the staff of the *Freeman's Journal* in 1892 and served as London editor (1912–16) before returning to Dublin as chief editor (1916–24). He had previously qualified as a barrister at Gray's Inn in 1915. In 1927, he was elected to fill a vacancy in Seanad Éireann and in the following year was re-appointed for the third triennial period during which he was elected Leas-Chathaoirleach on the death of Senator P.W. Kenny in April 1931. He died at his Morehampton, Dublin, residence on 6 September 1931 and was buried privately at Glasnevin Cemetery.

HORAN, Thomas P. (1854–1916) Born Midleton, Co. Cork, the son of a policeman. He emigrated to Australia and became a top-class cricketer. He represented Australia on fifteen occasions and toured England in 1878 and 1882. A right-hander, he scored 4,027 runs in a career which included 106 matches. He died on 16 April 1916.

HORGAN, Denis (1871–1922) Born Fermoyle, Banteer, Co. Cork, the son of Jeremiah Horgan, farmer. He was educated at Banteer NS. A gifted shot-putter and all-rounder, he won a total of thirteen British AAA shot titles (1893–99, 1904, 1905, 1908–10, and 1912) and broke the world record many times. In 1901, he was suspended for a year for competing in the Highland Games, but did not resume until late 1903. Unaccountably, he was not selected for the Paris Olympiad of 1900, or for New Orleans Olympiad of 1904. He left for America in late 1905 and joined the auxiliary section of the New York police department. Representing Britain, he took the silver medal at the London Olympics of 1908 at the age of thirty-seven years, despite having been brutally attacked by an Italian gang while on street patrol in the previous November. He was retired on pension and returned home for a while. He took the American AAU title in 1909. He was never defeated in the shot by a European athlete – only by Americans. Having won the AAA shot title in 1912, he retired from competition, having won forty-two major national titles and innumerable prizes. He died on 30 May 1922 and was buried in Lyre Cemetery, Co. Cork.

HORGAN, John (1834–1907) Born Macroom, Co. Cork, the son of John Horgan, shopkeeper. He practised as a solicitor in Cork city from 1861 and was secretary of the Cork Law Society. He was also local agent for the Cork politician, **Joseph Philip Ronayne**. With his wife and family, he emigrated to Sydney, New South Wales, in 1875 and practised as a solicitor there. However, with the loss of a libel suit (with subsequent bankruptcy) and the death of his son, he moved to Perth, Western Australia, in 1881. He again went into legal practice and was soon landed in trouble on many fronts. His luck temporarily changed for the better when, through his activities in the Kimberley gold rush and new railroad construction, he won the Perth seat on the Western Australian Legislative Council in 1888. However, he lost his seat in the following year and the conservative elements in Perth made sure that he was 'out for good'. He went through several legal partnerships but ultimately practised alone. He died, in debt, on 8 July 1907 and was buried in East Perth Cemetery.

HORGAN, John (1876–1955) Born Limerick, the son of an ironworker who was a native of Aherla, Co. Cork. The family later returned to Cork city where he qualified as a plumber. He served on Cork Corporation from 1911 until 1950. He was elected to the Dáil in 1927 as a Centre Party TD, but was unsuccessful in the following general election. He later joined the Fine Gael Party and served as lord mayor of Cork (1941/42). He died at his Glasheen Road residence on 27 June 1955 and was buried in St Finbarr's Cemetery. His grandson, Judge Seán O'Leary, served as lord mayor of Cork (1972/73).

HORGAN, John J. (1881–1967) Born Cork. He was educated at PBC and at Clongowes Wood College, Co. Kildare. Having become a solicitor in 1902, he supported the Irish Parliamentary Party and took a keen interest in the affairs of Connradh na Gaeilge. He sat on the board of the Cork Harbour Commissioners for an unprecedented forty-nine years. He also took a great interest in Cork arts and was chairman of Cork Opera House for many years. He sat as coroner at the Kinsale inquest for the victims of the *Lusitania* disaster in 1915. His publications included *Great Catholic Laymen* (1908), *Home Rule, a Critical Consideration* (1911) and *The Complete Grammar of Anarchy* (1918). He died in Cork on 21 July 1967. [Autobiography (1948); Headstone at St Finbarr's Cemetery, Cork, and life-size bronze by **Seamus Murphy**]

HORNE, Jonathan T. (1894–1978) Born College Road, Cork, the son of Jonathan Horne, drapery store supervisor. 'Jock' was educated at the Cathedral School (Dean Street), Cork Grammar School and at TCD where he graduated B.Mus. He was appointed as organist and choirmaster at St Canice's Cathedral, Kilkenny. In 1922, he succeeded his mentor, Dr Eveling, to the same position at St FinBarre's Cathedral. In that year, he was admitted as an associate of the Royal College of Organists. From then, until his retirement in 1977, he was one of the great influences in the musical life of Cork. He was a founder member of the Cork Oratorio Society, the Cork Gilbert & Sullivan Society, and was for thirty years on the staff of the Cork School of Music where he taught piano, organ and the theory of music. He was also the conductor of the school's choir for which he composed the song, 'The Lake Lark'. He died at Thame, Oxfordshire, on 24 November 1978 and was cremated. His ashes were buried in the family plot at St Finbarr's Cemetery.

HOVENDEN, Thomas (1840–1895) Born Dunmanway, Co. Cork, the son of Robert Hovenden, gaolkeeper. With the death of both his parents, he was placed in a Cork orphanage at the age of six years. He served as an apprentice to a Cork carver and gilder and studied at the Cork School of Design. He emigrated to the United States where he continued his artistic studies in New York. In 1874, he moved to Paris

where he studied for a further six years. On his return to America, he took up a teaching post at the Pennsylvania Academy. In 1882, he was elected to the National American Academy. He was especially noted for his paintings of American Negro life. He died tragically while attempting to save a little girl from an oncoming train at Norristown, Pennsylvania, on 14 August 1895.

HOWARD, Frederick John (1814–1897) He was the only son of Colonel Frederick Howard (killed at Waterloo), the third son of the 5th earl of Carlisle. He was connected to the dukes of Devonshire by his mother's second marriage and, in 1837, he married the sister of the 7th duke. He represented Youghal in parliament (1837–1841), but unsuccessfully contested Bridgnorth in 1841. He served as private secretary to his cousin, the 7th earl of Carlisle during the latter's term as Irish viceroy (1855–8, 1859–64). He died on 28 February 1897.

HOWARD, James Scott (1798–1866) Born Bandon, Co. Cork, the son of John Howard. He emigrated to Canada in 1819 and was appointed to the staff of the Toronto post office. He eventually rose to the rank of postmaster in 1828. However, he fell under suspicion as a rebel supporter in the Upper Canada rebellion of 1837 and was dismissed from his post. For the next four years he tried in vain to clear his name and even though the state's Executive Council granted that he had been politically neutral, he failed to recover his post. However, through the efforts of **Sir Francis Hincks**, he was given the post of treasurer of the Home District. He died in Toronto, on 1 March 1866. He published *A statement of facts relative to the dismissal of James S. Howard, esq., late Postmaster of the City of Toronto, U.C.* (1839).

HOWARD, Jeremiah J. (1849–1922) Born Brookpark, Kilcorney, Co. Cork, the son of John Howard, tenant and middleman. He was educated in Macroom and at St Colman's College, Fermoy. He went into agriculture, became involved in the National Land League, and supported **C.S. Parnell**. His marriage to Elizabeth Casey of Blackpool brought with it a substantial farm at Lehenagh – where Cork Airport stands today. He soon became involved in public life and served both as secretary of the Cork Agricultural and Industrial Association and as a member of the Cork Board of Guardians. He was returned unopposed for the Ballincollig electoral division in the first county council election in 1899 and was elected as chairman of that body at the inaugural meeting of 22 April of that year. He was re-elected annually until 1906 when he did not stand. (Following the death of his wife, he had re-married in 1902 and his brother-in-law, John Horgan of Castlewhite, was co-opted in his stead.) He was appointed as a member of the Land Commission in 1905 and continued to serve until ill health forced him to resign. He died in a private hospital in London in late November 1922, and was buried in St Joseph's Cemetery, Cork.

HUDSON, Edward (1743–1821) Born Castle-martyr, Co. Cork. He was an eminent Dublin dentist and lived in Grafton Street. He wrote poetry and had a reputation as an artist. He privately published his *Ode on St Cecilia's Day* (1788) under the pseudonym, 'A Patrician'. He died on 8 October 1821. His son, William E. Hudson (d. 1853), was a well-known music antiquary, while his nephew, Edward Howard, was a close friend of the poet and bard, Thomas Moore (1779–1852).

HUMPHREYS, John (1776–1864) Born Cork, the son of a Quaker, Joshua Humphreys, and brother of **Joseph Humphreys**. He ran a school on the North Main Street on the principles of the great Swiss educationalist, J.H. Pestalozzi (1746–1827). He served as assistant secretary of the Cuvierian Society and as librarian of the Royal Cork Institution where his extensive collection of shells was eventually deposited. He died in July 1864.

HUMPHREYS, Joseph (1787–1859) Born Cork, the son of a Quaker, Joshua Humphreys, and brother of **John Humphreys**. He moved to Dublin where he worked as superintendent of the National Institute for the Education of Deaf and Dumb Children of the Poor in Ireland at Glasnevin. He died in 1859.

HUNGERFORD, Margaret Wolfe (1855–1897) Born Mileen, Rosscarbery, Co. Cork, the daughter of Canon Fitzjohn Stannus Hamilton of Ross Cathedral. She was educated at Portarlington College, Co. Laois. At the age of 17 years, she married Edward Argles, a Dublin solicitor and, following his death, she married Henry Hungerford of Bandon in 1892. Among her thirty light novels are *Molly Bawn* (1878), *A Little Irish Girl* (1891), *Nor Life Nor Maid* (1892), *The Red House Mystery* (1893), *The Hoyden* (1894) and *Lady Verner's Flight* (1893). She died in Bandon of typhus on 24 January 1897.

HUNGERFORD, Thomas (1823–1904) Born Cork, the son of Emanuel Hungerford, a captain in the South Cork Militia. When Thomas was five years old, the family emigrated to Australia, where Captain Hungerford took up cattle ranching at Baerami Creek, New South Wales. Thomas was educated at Maitland, New South Wales, and took over his father's ranch in 1852. From then on he expanded on a huge scale so that by 1881, his company of Hungerford & Sons was renting millions of acres in Queensland, South Australia and New South Wales. He took a great interest in the affairs of the Aborigines, learnt their language, and compiled a dictionary for his own use. In 1875, he was elected to the state Legislative Assembly, but was unseated on petition. However, he was returned in 1877 and sat until his retirement in 1880 to attend to his business. Misfortune struck in the early 1890s when depression and drought ruined the viability of his holdings and his herd of 50,000 cattle. He died at Ashfield, near Sydney, on 4 April 1904. The town of Hungerford, Queensland, near the border with New South Wales, is named after him.

HUNTER, John H. (1839–1910) Born Bandon, Co. Cork, the son of William Hunter. He was educated locally and at Queen's College, Cork (now UCC). In 1859 he emigrated to Canada to continue his studies at the University of Toronto where he graduated BA (1861) and MA (1862). He married in 1862 and shortly after was appointed headmaster of Beamsville Grammar School. He was appointed to a similar position at Dundas in 1865. In 1868, he organised the Ontario Grammar School Masters' Association and at a public meeting of the association in the following year, roundly criticised Upper Canada College in Toronto for glaring abuses. In the same year he also criticised the province's chief superintendent of education over his attitude to local authorities. In 1871, he was appointed as principal of St Catharine's Grammar School and in that year he took on the Senate of Toronto University over its practice of having closed sessions. He moved to his last school, the Ontario Institute for the Education and Instruction of the Blind, at Brandford in 1874. Here he was responsible for many innovative ideas including telegraphy, raised-dot printing systems and an American method of music teaching for the blind. Things came to a head in 1879 when, following a dispute with his bursar, he was subjected to a government enquiry and was relieved of his duties. However, one of the provisions of the enquiry was that Hunter would be appointed to another government job, and, within a short time, he was made Ontario's first inspector of insurance. As the insurance industry was unregulated at the time, he was given the task to examine existing legislation and to inaugurate a system of control. This was realised in 1892 with the passing of the Insurance Corporations Act and in that year he was appointed as both the province's registrar and inspector of Friendly Societies. Now he became interested in actuarial science and in January 1897 he published an actuarial table based on the experience of the Canada Life Insurance Company from 1847 to 1893. This table was the first of its kind to have been based on Western social classes and was adopted by the National Fraternal Congress in the United States. Through his annual inspectorial reports, Hunter, 'the father of fraternalism in Ontario', laid the foundations for subsequent legislation in the 20th century. Originally trained as a teacher of English, Hunter also pursued a minor literary career. He wrote poetry for many local journals and, in 1882, the government of Ontario selected him to compile and edit the *Royal Readers* for widespread use. He died of pneumonia at his Toronto residence on 6 October 1910. Despite his many investments in debentures and land-development, he had never taken out a life-insurance policy!

HUNTER, Thomas (d. 1932) Born Castletownroche, Co. Cork, the eldest son of Con Hunter. A member of Connradh na Gaeilge, he joined the Irish Volunteer movement on its foundation. He worked as a draper's assistant in Dublin and later, in partnership with fellow-Republican, Peadar Clancy, conducted a drapery business ('The Republican Outfitters') in Talbot Street. During the Easter Rising of 1916, he was a commandant at Jacob's biscuit factory. After the rising, he was sentenced to death but this was later commuted to penal servitude for life. During his term at Lewes Jail, he was vice-commandant under Eamon de Valera (1882–1975). Released under the general amnesty of 1917, he was returned unopposed as the Sinn Féin MP for Cork North East in 1918. He was arrested again in March 1920 and was imprisoned in Mountjoy Jail where he and Clancy organised a prisoners' protest that secured the release of the republican prisoners. In the 1921 general election, he was elected as TD for Cork East/North East, but, standing as an anti-Treaty candidate in 1922, he lost his seat. In poor health for his latter years, he died at Glanworth on 11 March 1932 and was buried in Castletownroche Cemetery.

HURLEY, Charlie (1892–1921) Born Baurleigh, Kilbrittain, Co. Cork. At an early age, he went to work in Bandon, but studied in his spare time. He successfully sat a civil service examination for the post of 'boy clerk' and was appointed to Haulbowline (1911–15). He was promoted to Liverpool, but declined the offer as acceptance would entail conscription in the British Army. He was already involved in the Irish Volunteer movement when he returned to West Cork where he operated as an organiser for the movement. Arrested for the possession of arms, he was later sentenced to five years' penal servitude. He was released in late 1918 and returned to West Cork where he was chosen brigade commander of the Cork 3rd brigade of the IRA following the arrest of **Tom Hales**. He took part in many engagements and led the West Cork Flying Column during the illness of General **Tom Barry**. On 15 February 1921, he was wounded in an attack on the military at Upton, but was killed a month later in a gunfight at Ballymurphy on 19 March 1921. He was buried at Clogagh graveyard.

HURLEY, Jeremiah (1891–1943) Born Rea, Terelton, Co. Cork. While he was still a child, his family moved to Clogheen, near Cork. He was educated at Sunday's Well NS, at UCC and at St Patrick's College of Education, Dublin. He qualified as a national teacher and worked in Blackpool NS until he became a full-time public representative in 1937. A member of the Labour Party, he was elected to Cork Corporation in 1931, and having unsuccessfully contested Cork Borough in 1932 and 1933, was elected to Dáil Éireann for Cork South East, which he represented until his death. He served as president of the Irish National Teachers' Organisation (1934/35) and was also a member of Cork County Council (1942/43). He died unexpectedly at his residence at Mount Pleasant Road, Cork, on 2 February 1943 and was buried in St Finbarr's Cemetery, Cork.

HURLEY, Jim (1902–1965) Born Clonakilty, Co. Cork. He joined the local battalion of the IRA in 1918 and two years later, at the age of 18, became the battalion commander. During the civil war, he was interned in Cork Gaol and at the Curragh. He worked as town clerk of Clonakilty (1924–32) and in other local government posts in Counties Meath (1933–5), and Longford (1935–7). He was appointed as secretary of the Cork Board of Health (1937–42), as county manager of Meath (1942–3) and as Cork assistant county manager (1943–4). In November 1944, he was appointed as secretary and bursar of UCC of which he was a B.Comm (1932) and BA (1940) graduate. He later graduated MA (1955) and remained in the college post until his death. In his 20s, he was an outstanding GAA player. At club level, he turned out for Clonakilty, UCC and Blackrock. He won four All-Ireland SHC medals with Cork (1926, 1928–9 and 1931), an All-Ireland JHC medal (1925), and a Munster SFC medal (1928). He also won three Railway Cup hurling medals with Munster (1928, 1930–1). He died at the Bon Secours Hospital, Cork, on 10 February 1965 and was buried in St Mary's Cemetery, Clonakilty.

HURLEY, John J. (d. 1961) Born Durrus, Co. Cork. He travelled widely in his youth and went to China in the early years of the 20th century. During the Chinese Revolution (1911), he acted as a military adviser to the nationalist forces and was personally decorated for his service by Sun Yat Sen (1867–1925), the provisional president of the Republic of China. He returned to Ireland during World War I and served as an intelligence officer in the IRA during the War of Independence when he was a confidante of some of the leading figures. In 1925, he was the producer of *Land of her Fathers*, one of the first films made in Ireland and the first to feature the Abbey Players. Michael Mac Liammoir (1899–1978) played the lead and Barry Fitzgerald (1888–1961) made his screen debut. The film was screened in the Grafton Cinema, Dublin, on 1 October 1925. However, the only copy was either lost or stolen in New York some time later. He died at his residence at Sandymount Avenue, Dublin, on 24 March 1961 and was buried in Dean's Grange Cemetery.

HURLEY, Seán (1887–1916) Born Maulagow, Drinagh, Co. Cork. He was educated at the local NS and in Clonakilty. Having passed the civil service examination, he was called to the post office in London in 1906, but later obtained a position in Harrod's Stores. He joined Connradh na Gaeilge League and the GAA in London and was also sworn into the IRB. He was one of the Irish Volunteers who, in 1916, arrived in Dublin from Britain to take part in the planned uprising. On Saturday, 29 April, he was seriously wounded while defending a barricade near the Fr. Mathew Hall. Following the surrender, he was taken to the Richmond Hospital where he died. The only County Cork Volunteer to die in the Dublin Easter Rising, he was buried in Glasnevin Cemetery.

HUSSEY, Philip (1713–1783) Born Cloyne, Co. Cork, the son of a local clothier. Following a spell in the navy as a boy, he practised as a portrait painter under the patronage of the Irish Lord Chancellor, John Bowes. With further reputations as a botanist and a musician, he twice visited London where he was quite popular. He died in Dublin in June 1783.

HUTCH, William (1844–1917) Born Buttevant, Co. Cork. He was educated at St Colman's College, Fermoy, and at the Irish College, Rome. He was president of St Colman's College from 1881 to 1892, prior to his appointment as parish priest of Midleton in 1892. In September 1903, he was made archdeacon of the diocese of Cloyne. He was the author of two substantial biographies, *Nano Nagle, her Life, her Labours and their Fruits* (1875) and *Mrs Ball, Foundress of the Institute of the Virgin Mary … a biography* (1879). He also translated *The Spiritual Exercises of St Ignatius* from the Italian. He died at the Mercy Hospital, Cork, on 31 May 1917 and was buried in Rosary Cemetery, Midleton, adjoining the new parish church – the construction of which he had inspired and directed.

HUTCHINS, Ellen (1785–1815) Born Ballylickey, Bantry, Co. Cork, the daughter of Thomas Hutchins, gentleman. She suffered from lifelong ill health and around 1802 was

encouraged by the specialist, Professor Whitley Stokes (1763–1845), to take up the study of botany as an open-air activity. Under his tutelage and that of James Mackey to whom he introduced her, she became an authority on the botany of Bantry Bay and a prominent figure in the field of cryptogamic botany in which she specialised and corresponded with leading English botanists in that field. She was also a talented botanical artist. Her *Early Observations on the Flora of Southwest Ireland* was published posthumously and records her correspondence with the botanist, Dawson Turner [ed. M.E. Mitchell (1999)]. She died at the family residence, 'Ardnagashel', Ballylickey, on 9 February 1815, and was buried in an unmarked grave at Bantry Graveyard.

HUTCHINS, Patricia (1911–1985) Born Ardnagashel, Bantry in 1911, she was educated privately and at schools in the Isle of Wight and Worthing. She married the Derry-born poet and critic Robert Greacen in 1946 and settled in London; they divorced in 1966 and she subsequently moved back to Bantry. She worked in Fleet Street and wrote on documentary film. Her first book (a children's story), *Ivan and his Wonderful Coat,* was published in 1945. Her subsequent books, for which she is best known, were *James Joyce's Dublin* (1950), *James Joyce's World* (1957) and *Ezra Pound's Kensington* (1965). She died at Ardnagashel in 1985.

HUTCHINSON, Clive D. (1949–1998) Born Cork, the son of Ven. Archdeacon Hutchinson, rector of Blackrock. He was educated at Midleton College and at TCD where he read history and political science. He received his moderatorship at TCD in 1971, but changed career and graduated as a chartered accountant in 1974, having established a successful accountancy partnership in Cork. A life-long ornithologist, his first recording appeared on the *Irish Bird Report* of 1960, when he was eleven years of age. In addition to numerous contributions to journals and reports, he published six books, *The Birds of Dublin and Wicklow* (1975),

Ireland's Wetlands and their Birds (1979), *Watching Birds in Ireland* (1985), *Birds in Ireland* (1989), (with Margaret Ridgway) *The Natural History of Kilcolman* (1990) and *Where to watch Birds in Ireland* (1994). He was the founding editor (1977) of the journal, *Irish Birds* and remained in that position until 1984. He was closely associated with Cape Clear bird observatory from 1967 to his death from an incurable illness in early 1998.

HUTSON, Marshall C. (1903–2001) Born Nottingham, England. He studied at the Nottingham School of Art and afterwards in London. He moved to Ireland in his twenties and began teaching at the Crawford School of Art, Cork, where he was vice-principal from 1930 to 1962. He had wide artistic interests and taught a wide range of subjects, but was primarily a painter and sculptor. He regularly exhibited at the Royal Hibernian Academy from 1931 and became a member in 1982. Among his sculpture commissions are works at UCC, Cork School of Commerce and Cork City Library. His bust of Rev. **James C. O'Flynn** is in Passage West Town Park. He died at the Beaumont Nursing Home, Cork, on 31 October 2001 and was buried in St Michael's Cemetery, Blackrock.

HYDE, John (d. 1832) Born Castlehyde, Fermoy, Co. Cork, the son of John Hyde, MP for Co. Cork in the Irish parliament (1769–76). He was high sheriff of Co. Cork in 1808. The brother-in-law of Henry Boyle, 3rd earl of Shannon, he married Elizabeth O'Callaghan, the daughter of Viscount Lismore. He was MP for Youghal (1820–26). He died at Castlehyde on 13 February 1832.

HYDE, Tom (1899–1937) Born Ballinacurra, Midleton, Co. Cork, the son of Cornelius Hyde, merchant. He was educated at Midleton CBS and Rochestown College and then went into the family business. During the War of Independence, he was a member of the 4th battalion of the 1st Cork brigade of the IRA and subsequently joined the Free State army in 1922,

with the rank of captain. In October 1934, he chaired a Dublin meeting which attempted to heal the Blueshirt split and to reconcile the differences between General Eoin O'Duffy (1892–1944) and Commandant **Edmund Cronin**. He subsequently joined the Irish Brigade which was organised by O'Duffy and fought on the nationalist side in the Spanish Civil War. His unit left for the front in November 1936, and three months later, on 19 February 1937, he was killed in the brigade's first engagement on the Madrid Front – mistakenly shot by a unit of General Franco's forces from the Canary Islands.

HYNES, John T. (1799–1869) Born North Cathedral Parish, Cork, the son of John Hynes. Following his early education in Cork, he joined the Irish Franciscans in Rome in February 1819. However, he left in the following September to join to join the Irish Dominicans and was professed in June 1820. He went to the United States in the following year and was ordained in Kentucky in June 1822. He ministered for a short time in Ohio before returning to Cork to work in the Dominican community there. In 1825, he was sent to work in the West Indies where he spent ten years. He again returned to Cork before being appointed as coadjutor to the suffragan bishop of Corfu, Greece, in 1838. He lived in Corfu for a short while before he was forced to leave owing to the political situation. He moved to Rome and was appointed as administrator apostolic of Demerara, British Guiana, in 1843 to succeed Bishop **William Clancy**. On his appointment as Vicar Apostolic in 1946, he took six Irish Ursuline nuns to establish schools etc. in the region. He resigned his post in 1857 and took up residence in Monkstown, Co. Dublin, where he devoted much of his time to the Irish business affairs of his nephew, Bishop **James A. Gould** of Melbourne. He spent his winters in France where he died on 30 March 1869, at the Hotel Maurice, Paris. His remains were brought back to Cork and were buried in St Finbarr's Cemetery. An imposing monument marking his grave was later erected by the Dominican bishop of Cork, **Thomas A. O'Callaghan**. [Calendar of correspondence in *Archivium Hibernicum*, 28 (1966)]

HYNES, Samuel F. (1854–1931) Born Cork. He was registered as a student at the Cork School of Art in 1869. By the 1880s, he had established a successful architectural practice at South Mall which specialised in ecclesiastical and educational projects. His designs (mainly Gothic Revival) include churches at Glounthaune (1880s) and Castletownroche (1896); Gougane Barra Oratory (*c.*1900), Farranferris College (1885), Bishop's House, Redemption Road (1885); and **Gerald Griffin** and Bro. (**Dominic) Burke** Schools, North Monastery. He died at his Blackrock residence on 28 June 1931 and was buried in St Finbarr's Cemetery.

I

IRWIN, Clarke H. (1858–1934) Born Bandon, Co. Cork, the son of William Irwin, clergyman. He was educated at Bandon Grammar School, Queen's College, Cork (now UCC); Magee College, Derry; and the University of Bonn. He also graduated MA (1879) from the Royal University of Ireland, and DD (1915) from the Presbyterian Theological Faculty of Ireland. He ministered in Bray, Co. Wicklow, and in Melbourne, Australia. He was editor of Presbyterian newspapers such as the *Presbyterian Churchman* (Dublin) and the *Australian Weekly* (Melbourne). He was an accomplished linguist, editing the Gospels in nine languages and specialising in some African dialects. For thirty-five years, he was the editor of the Religious Tract Society. He died in London on 2 March 1934.

IRWIN, Mary Jane (1846–1916) Born Strand Street, Clonakilty, Co. Cork, the daughter of Maxwell Irwin and wife of **Jeremiah O'Donovan Rossa**. Her father and brothers were nationalist in sentiment and probably at least Fenian sympathisers. She was educated at Sacred Heart Convent, Roscrea, Co. Tipperary, and was still in her teens when she married the twice-widowed Fenian, Rossa, in November 1864. He was imprisoned from 1865 to 1871, but his wife was a tower of strength to him during that period and for the rest of his life. On his release and subsequent exile, she followed him to the US. Thirteen children were born to the marriage, six of whom died in infancy. Over the signatures 'MJI' and 'Cliodhna', she contributed poetry to the *Irish People* and subsequently did so for the *Irish People* of New York. Her poetry collection, *Irish Lyrical Poems* was published in New York in 1868. In 1906, she returned with Rossa to reside briefly in Cork. She died at her New York residence (on West 135th Street) on 17 August 1916 and was buried in St Peter's Cemetery, New Brighton.

IVORY, Thomas (1732–1786) Born Cork, where he initially worked as a carpenter. He moved to Dublin where he studied drawing and draughtsmanship. He was later appointed (*c*.1759) as master of the Dublin Society's Schools of Architecture. Among his works were the Octagon Presbyterian Chapel, Norwich (1754), the King's Hospital (or Bluecoat School), Blackhall Square, Dublin (1773–80), an addition to Westport House, Co. Mayo (1778), the Lismore Bridge and Causeway, Co. Waterford (1779), and Newcomen's Bank, Dublin (*c*.1780). One of his pupils, James Hoban (1758–1831), was the architect of the American White House, Washington. He died in Dublin in December 1786. [Portrait in boardroom of King's Hospital]

J

JACK, Harry W. (1891–1977) Born Audley Place, Cork, the youngest of eleven children of Robert Jack, a Methodist who described himself as a saddler in the census of 1901. Harry was educated at CBC, Cork, and while still a schoolboy, represented Cork Constitution in the Munster Senior Cup. He then attended UCC with whom he won two Munster Senior Cup medals (1912–13). He played twice for Ireland (against Scotland and Wales) in 1914 but then World War I intervened. He took a doctorate in Agricultural Science and was later decorated with the OBE for his services in Malaya and Fiji. He played an essential part in the development of Fijian rugby, both as a player and coach. While on leave in Dublin, he played with Lansdowne RFC and won a third Irish cap in 1921 when he appeared at scrum-half against Wales. He eventually retired to Dublin and was president of Lansdowne for the 1960/61 season. He died at Bloomfield Nursing Home, Dublin, on 19 December 1977 and was buried in Dean's Grange Cemetery.

JACKSON, Joseph D. (1783–1857) Born Peterborough, Glasheen, Cork, the eldest son of Strettel Jackson. He was educated at TCD where he graduated BA (1806) and MA (1832). He studied at the King's Inns and was called to the Irish Bar in 1806. In 1831, he declined an offer to stand as a parliamentary candidate for Cork City. He was chairman of the County of Londonderry in 1834 when he was asked to stand as Conservative candidate for the Borough of Bandon. He resigned the chairmanship and was MP for Bandon from 1835 to 1842. He was appointed as solicitor-general for Ireland in 1842, and having resigned the Bandon seat, was elected as MP for Dublin University (TCD). He resigned this in turn in the following year on being appointed as judge of the Irish Court

of Common Pleas. He was styled 'Leather-lungs' by Daniel O'Connell (1775–1847) for 'the marvellous long-windedness of his forensic and parliamentary appeals'. He died on 19 December 1857.

JACOB, Brian (1938–2001) Born Cork, the son of Frank Jacob, provender miller. He was educated at Portora Royal School, Co. Fermanagh, and at TCD where he graduated B.Sc. (1960) and later M.Sc. in nuclear physics. In 1965, he became a scholar in the School of Cosmic Physics at the Dublin Institute for Advanced Studies (DIAS). Having developed an interest in seismology, he then worked at the Global Seismology Unit of the British Geological Survey at Edinburgh. He was co-leader of the international Lithospheric Seismic Profile in Britain (LISPB) study to determine the crustal structure from the north to the south of Britain. In 1976, he returned to DIAS on his appointment as professor of Geophysics. He was promoted to senior professor in 1990. He was deeply involved in the Rockall and Porcupine Irish Deep Seismic project which provided the essential framework needed for offshore hydrocarbon exploration. He also played a leading role in major international surveys of the East African Rift and of the Hawaiian Volcanic Chain. He was general secretary of the European Geophysical Society (1992–6) and was admitted as a member of the Royal Irish Academy in 1998. Previously, in 1989, he had been elected as an associate of the Royal Astronomical Society. He died at St Vincent's Private Hospital, Dublin, on 5 November 2001 and was buried in Shanganagh Cemetery.

JEFFERS, Wellington (1814–1896) Born Cork, the son of Robert Jeffers, a teacher. The family emigrated to Upper Canada (later

Ontario) when he was an infant. He was educated by his father and turned down a banking career to become an itinerant Methodist preacher. He was ordained in 1841. However, his health broke down and on his recovery, he was appointed as editor of the influential Toronto *Christian Guardian* – a position which he held from 1860 until 1869. In 1863, he was conferred with an honorary degree of DD by Victoria College and, in 1876, he was elected president of the Toronto Methodist Conference. He retired in 1884 to Belleville, Ontario, where he had spent the previous fifteen years in serving two congregations. He died there on 10 February 1896.

JENNINGS, Robert H. (1852–1918) Born Woodlawn, Cork, the eldest son of R. Jennings. He was educated at the Royal Military Academy, Woolwich, and travelled in Europe and the East. He joined the Royal Engineers in 1872 and served in Afghanistan and India, mainly as a political officer and British Consul. He undertook a major military exploration in the Persian area (1884/85) and served on the British army staff in India until 1890. He was promoted to the rank of colonel in 1903, having previously published many scientific and geographical articles on various countries in Mesopotamia. He was a fellow of the Royal Botanical Society and a member of the Royal Society of Arts. He died in London on 21 November 1918.

JEPHSON-NORREYS, Sir Charles Denham (1799–1888) He was the only surviving son of Lt.-Col. William Jephson of Mallow Castle, by his third marriage. Colonel Jephson died in 1816, having, in 1800, succeeded his first cousin, **Denham Jephson** in the Mallow Castle estate. He was educated at Brasenose College, Oxford, where he graduated BA (1827) and MA (1828). In March 1820, he unsuccessfully contested the Mallow parliamentary seat but was successful in 1826. He thereafter represented the

Whig/Liberal interest, with one notable exception, until his defeat in 1859. This exception was his loss of the seat for a few months after the election of December 1832 (for refusing 'to pledge himself to vote for the repeal of the Union'). However, he was re-instated on petition. In 1838, he was created a baronet and assumed the additional surname of Norreys to mark his descent and inheritance of the Mallow estate from Sir Thomas Norreys. He died at the Queen's Hotel, Queenstown (Cobh), on 10 July 1888 and was buried in Mallow.

JOHNSON, Philip F. (1835–1926) Born Mallow, Co. Cork. He received a good education locally and, as a young man, travelled in the South Seas and in India. On his return, he worked for a time for the Great Southern & Western Railway Company. In 1860, he took a tenancy on the Egmont Hotel, Kanturk, and later formed loose connections with the Fenians. In the wake of the Fenian uprising, he did some work for the Amnesty Association and soon became a popular speaker at the various rallies. He was also a supporter of Major Lawrence Knox, a Conservative Home Ruler (and owner of the *Irish Times*) and of **Isaac Butt**. In late 1869, a club to represent the rural labourers was founded in the hotel (The Kanturk Labourers' Club), of which he became secretary. This club made contact with similar bodies in England and soon expanded into the Irish Agricultural Labourers' Union (IALU) with Butt as president and Johnson as secretary. However, the decline of the Amnesty Movement had a huge effect on the IALU and it had disappeared by 1875. Johnson was a founder-member of the Irish National Land League in 1879 and was associated with the main leaders including **Michael Davitt**, **C.S. Parnell**, and **William O'Brien**. Unfortunately, the League's main interest rested with the tenants while the labourers were relatively ignored. Following incidents at Shanagarry, Co. Cork in October 1880 when demonstrating labourers forced the cancellation of two Land League meetings,

Parnell intervened and the Land League Labour Association was founded at Johnson's Hotel two months later. Eventually with the suppression of the Land League, the labourers' interest waned. Johnson left the national scene and concentrated on local politics. He moved to his daughter's home at Clifden, Co. Galway, where he died on 3 November 1926. He was buried in the nearby Ardbear Cemetery.

JOHNSON, Robert (1708–1767) Born Saintfield, Co. Down, the son of William Johnson, clergyman. He was educated at TCD where he graduated BA (1729), MA (1732) and DD (1756). He was consecrated as Church of Ireland bishop of Cloyne on 21 October 1759. He died at Cloyne on 16 January 1767 and was buried in his cathedral.

JOHNSON, Sir William M. (1826–1918) Born Anglesey, Wales, the only son of Rev. William Johnson, naval chaplain, whose subsequent clerical career was mostly spent in County Cork (rector of Clenor and chancellor of the diocese of Cloyne). He was educated at TCD where he graduated BA (1849) and MA (1856). He was called to the Bar in 1853, became law adviser to the Crown (1868–74), and was called to the Inner Bar in 1872. Having unsuccessfully contested the constituency of Mallow as a Liberal in 1874, he was elected MP there in 1880. He was then appointed as solicitor-general after the election. He successfully defended the seat in a by-election and sat for Mallow until 1883. He resigned this seat in 1883 on his appointment as a judge of the Irish High Court, having previously been appointed as attorney-general in November 1881. He led the prosecution in the Phoenix Park Murders trial. He was also a judge of the High Court of Admiralty from 1893. He retired from the Bench in 1909 and was created a baronet in that year. He died at his Leeson Street, Dublin, residence on 9 December 1918. Of Johnson, **A.M. Sullivan** remarked, '… he was a monument of kindness and stupidity; he was universally known as "Wooden-headed Billy"'.

JONES, Edward (1641–1703) Born Llwyn Ririd, Montgomeryshire, Wales, the son of Richard Jones, Esq. He was educated at Westminster School and at Trinity College, Cambridge, where he graduated BA (1664) and MA (1668). While at Cambridge, he was a fellow-student of the discoverer of gravity, Sir Isaac Newton (1642–1727). In 1670, he came to Ireland as chaplain to the lord lieutenant, the duke of Ormonde. He was consecrated as Church of Ireland bishop of Cloyne on 16 March 1683. In 1689, he fled with his family to England and was put on the List of Attainder by the Jacobite authorities. He never returned to Ireland and was appointed as bishop of St Asaph, Wales, on 13 December 1692. In 1701, he was suspended from office for six months on charges of simony and illegal promotions of clergy. He died on 10 May 1703, at College Court, Westminster, and was buried in St Mary's Church there.

JONES, Lloyd (1811–1886) Born Bandon, Co. Cork. In 1827, he settled in Manchester and was employed as a clothing cutter in the cotton industry there. He came under the influence of the social reformer, Robert Owen (1771–1858), who, on his return to London from Scotland in 1828, had begun to interest trades unions in his 'villages of co-operation'. He later edited periodicals in London and Leeds and wrote extensively on the theory and practice of co-operation. He also wrote *The Life, Times, and Labours of Robert Owen* (posthumously, 1889). He died in Stockwell, London, on 22 May 1886.

JONES, Mary H. (1837–1930) Born Cork, the daughter of Richard Harris, labourer, and sister of **W. Richard Harris**. Her father emigrated to America in 1835. His family followed and Mary was educated in Toronto, Canada, to where her father had temporarily moved. She worked as a teacher for a time in Memphis and Chicago and was married in 1861. However, her husband and four children died during a yellow fever epidemic in Memphis and another four years later she lost all her possessions in a Chicago fire. Shortly afterwards, she became interested in trades union affairs and featured prominently in most of the great American labour episodes, especially in the area of mining. In 1921, she addressed the Pan-American Federation of Labor in Mexico City and two years later she represented the striking West Virginia coal miners – at the age of 86 years! She died on 30 November 1930. 'Mother Jones' was buried in the United Mineworkers' Cemetery at Mount Olive, Illinois. [Autobiography (1925)]

JONES, William Bence (1812–1882) Born Beccles, Suffolk, the eldest son of William Jones, an officer of dragoon guards. He was educated at Harrow School and at Oxford where he graduated BA (1834) and MA (1836). In 1837, he was called to the Bar at the Inner Temple. A year later, he took over the management of the 4,000-acre Lisselan Estate near Clonakilty which had been bought by his grandfather, an absentee landlord. He lived permanently on the estate until 1880. Using his knowledge of farming methods, he made great improvements on the estate and farmed the 1,000-acre demesne himself. However, his attitude to leases after 1870 and his demand that tenants adhere to his prescribed farming methods, made him an unpopular figure in the area. He was also considered an unsympathetic JP. In 1880, as a result of his refusal to accept rent at Griffith's valuation (instead of his own stipulated rent), he was subjected to a boycott. This extended to the Cork shipping companies refusing to carry his livestock to Bristol – a dispute which excited attention in both the Irish and English press. His protagonist at local level was the parish priest of Clonakilty, **John O'Leary**. Jones' polemical *Life's work in Ireland of a landlord who tried to do his duty* (1880) was responded to by O'Leary in the *Contemporary Review*, eliciting a

defence from Jones in the same journal. He returned to England in January 1881 and died at his home at Elvaston Place, Queen's Gate, London on 22 June 1882.

JOYCE, John Stanislaus (1849–1931) Born Angelsea Street, Cork, the only child of James Augustine Joyce (1827–1866) and his wife Ellen O'Connell. A native of Fermoy, Joyce Sr. inherited a salt and lime works that went into liquidation in 1852–3 and was subsequently employed as an inspector of hackney coaches. John Stanislaus spent some time at St Colman's College, Fermoy, and was admitted to Queen's College, Cork in October 1867, where he studied medicine but left without graduating, though he had excelled in the College Dramatic Society. He worked as an accounts clerk in Cork before moving in 1873 to Dublin where he had obtained a position as Secretary of the Dublin Distilling Co., the principals of which had Cork connections. After this company was liquidated in 1878, he was secretary of the United Liberal Club. In May 1880 he married May Murray, daughter of a prosperous publican. In the following year, he obtained a civil service position in the Collector General's department. In February 1882 his second son James Augustine Joyce was born; the first child had only survived for a week. John Stanislaus' passions in life were singing, drinking and Parnell, and did not include attention to his employment. He contrived to lose his civil service job and his inheritance of property in Cork over ensuing years but his store of anecdotes gave his son valuable material for his future career and he appears in his son's books as Simon Dedalus. He died at the Drumcondra Hospital on 29 December 1931, survived by eight of his sixteen children and was buried at Glasnevin Cemetery. [Life by J. Wyse-Jackson and P. Costello (1997)]

JUMPER, Sir William (c.1660–1715) Born Bandon, Co. Cork, to a well-connected family. As a very young man, he entered the Royal

Navy. He was promoted to the rank of lieutenant in 1691 and to the rank of captain two years later. He took part in many sea battles and served under Admiral Sir George Rooke (1650–1709) against the French at the battles of Cadiz and Gibraltar. He was knighted in 1704 and later served under Sir Cloudesley Shovell (1620–1707). He died at Plymouth on 12 March 1715. [Sketch in Bennett's *History of Bandon* (1862, 1869)]

K

KANE, Paul (1810–1871) Born Mallow, Co. Cork, the son of Michael Kane, an English soldier. Around 1819 the family emigrated to Toronto, Canada, where the father became a wine and spirits merchant. Paul became interested in art and worked as a decorative painter of furniture and portraitist at Cobourg, Ontario. He then spent a period in Detroit before setting out for Europe in 1841. He studied and worked in Rome, Genoa, Florence and Paris. On his way back, he stopped over in London and met the American artist, George Catlin, whose great interest was in the recording of a vanishing North American Indian culture. This was to decide Kane's artistic future. He left Toronto with his portfolio and a gun in June 1845, and for the next three years, he made over 700 sketches of the various tribes and Indian personalities he encountered before returning to Toronto. He made one more short trip but spent the remainder of his life in Toronto executing the sketches. As well as tracing much of the social history of mid-nineteenth-century Canada, his work is of prime importance to ethnologists. His publication *Wanderings of an Artist among the Indians of North America* (1859) was reproduced in France (1861), Germany (1862) and Denmark (1863). The first major Canadian anthropological work, *Prehistoric Man: searches into the origin of civilisation in the old and the new world* by Kane's friend, Sir Daniel Wilson of Toronto University, was heavily influenced by the sketches and finished pictures. With failing sight, which he attributed to snow, Kane died on 20 February 1871 at his Toronto residence. [Catalogue edited by J.R. Harper (1971)]

KANE, Sir Robert J. (1809–1890) Born Dublin. He was educated at TCD where he graduated BA (1835). In 1831, he had been appointed as Professor of Chemistry at the Apothecaries' Hall and in the following year, he founded the *Dublin Journal of Medical Science*. In 1834, he was appointed as professor of Natural Philosophy at the Royal Dublin Society. He was appointed as first president of the newly founded Queen's College, Cork (now UCC) in 1845, and in the following year he became the director of the Museum of Irish Industry at St Stephen's Green, Dublin. In 1845, he was a member of a three-man commission formed to investigate measures to stop the spread of potato blight. He was knighted in 1846 and was elected as a fellow of the Royal Society in 1849. On resigning his Cork post in 1873, he was appointed as a Commissioner of National Education. He was elected as president of the Royal Irish Academy in 1877. On the establishment of the Royal University of Ireland in 1880, he was its first vice-chancellor. He died in Dublin on 16 February 1890. He published *Elements of Practical Pharmacy* (1831), *Elements of Chemistry* (1841) and *Industrial Resources of Ireland* (1844). [Portrait in the Aula Maxima, UCC]

KEANE, Augustus H. (1833–1912) Born Cork, the son of James Keane, city councillor. He was educated at the Catholic University, Dublin, and in Rome. Having spent a period teaching languages at Southampton, he was appointed as professor of Hindustani at the University of London. He established a firm reputation as an anthropologist. He was elected as a fellow of the Royal Geographical Society. His publications include *Ethnology* (1896), *Man: Past and Present* (1899) and *The World's Peoples* (1908). He also translated many works from French and German. He died in Hampstead, London, on 3 February 1912.

KEANE, Sir John (1757–1829) Born Belmont, Co. Waterford, the son of Richard Keane. He was MP in the Irish Parliament for Bangor (1791–7) and for Youghal (1797–1800). In 1799, he opposed the motion for the Union, but was induced to support it on its reintroduction and was created a baronet in August 1801. He sat in the Imperial parliament for Youghal (1801–6) and for Bangor (1807–18). He died on 18 April 1829. He was the ancestor of the present baronet and his second son was John, 1st Baron Keane (1781–1840), who was commander-in-chief of the British army in India and who conducted the Afghan Campaign of 1839. His great-great grandson, Sir John Keane, 5th Bart. (1873–1956), was a Free State Senator (1922–34) and a member of Seanad Éireann (1938–48).

KEANE, Seán (1899–1953) Born Mitchelstown, Co. Cork. In 1920, he joined the first active service unit of the IRA which had been formed in the Mitchelstown area. He was arrested and imprisoned in Wormwood Scrubs Gaol where he went on a hunger strike which lasted eighteen days. Following his release, he was again arrested and imprisoned at Spike Island. He joined the Free State army after the Treaty and served until 1924 having reached the rank of captain. He was elected as a Fine Gael member of Cork County Council in 1934 and served until his death although he had changed allegiance to the Labour Party in the meantime. He was unsuccessful as an independent candidate in the general election of 1943, but was elected as Labour TD for East Cork in 1948 and served until 1953. He died after a long illness at his residence in King Street, Mitchelstown, on 29 March 1953 and was buried in Kildorrery Cemetery.

KEANE, William (1805–1874) Born Castlemartyr, Co. Cork, the son of an employee of the Shannon Estate. He was educated locally and at the Irish College, Paris, where he was ordained in 1828 and worked on the staff until 1839. In that year, he returned to Ireland and served as a curate in Fermoy until 1841 when he was appointed as parish priest of Midleton. He became bishop of the restored diocese of Ross on 20 December 1850 and was translated to the see of Cloyne on 15 May 1857. He died on 15 January 1874 and was buried in a temporary vault in the Pro-Cathedral, Queenstown (Cobh). He was later re-interred in St Colman's Cathedral, Cobh. He was the uncle of Bishop **William Fitzgerald** of Ross.

KEARNEY, Denis (1847–1907) Born Oakmount, Kilbrittain, Co. Cork. He went to sea in 1858 and eventually became first officer on an American coastal steamer. Following his marriage in 1870, he settled in San Francisco, went into the draying business and was granted American citizenship in 1876. He became interested in trades union affairs and represented the Draymen and Teamsters' Union. He was later elected as president of the Workingmen's Party of California. Among other things, he opposed bank monopolies, unjust taxation, railroad domination and Chinese competition in the labour market. His diatribes against Chinese immigration led to the passing of the Expulsion Act of 1882. However, his influence and public profile began to wane in the late 1880s. He died at Alameda, California, on 24 April 1907.

KEEFE, Ernie (1919–1991) Born Beechmount, Carrigrohane, Cork, the son of C.G. Keefe. He played rugby for the Sunday's Well club and was a member of the side which took the club's first Munster Senior Cup title. He was a member of the first Munster side to play a touring side (Australia) on 9 December 1947, at the Mardyke. Munster lost by 6–5 in injury time. He gained six international caps and played against France in the Triple Crown year of 1948. He was also an international boxer, losing the 1945 national heavyweight title on a controversial points decision. He died at Cork University Hospital on 30 November 1991 and was buried in St Luke's Cemetery, Douglas.

KELLEHER, Daniel L. (1883–1958) Born Cork, the son of William Kelleher of King Street (now Mac Curtain Street), and younger brother of **Stephen B. Kelleher**. He was educated at CBC, Cork, and at UCC. He worked as a teacher in Liverpool and Dublin and developed an interest in prose, drama, and poetry. In 1910, his play, 'Stephen Grey', was produced at the Abbey Theatre. This was followed by *A Contrary Election* (1910) and *The Last Hostel* (1918) which he wrote with **T.C. Murray**. He also wrote travel and historical sketches which included *Paris, Its Glamour and Life* (1914), *Lake Geneva* (1914), *The Glamour of Dublin* (1918), *The Glamour of Cork* (1919), *Round Italy* (1923), *The Glamour of the West* (1928), *The Glamour of the South* (1929), *Great Days with O'Connell* (1929) and *It's Ireland* (1932). His poetry collections include *Cork's Own Town* (1920), *Poems Twelve a Penny* (1911) and *Twelve Poems* (1923). He died in Dublin on 6 March 1958.

KELLEHER, Jamesey (1878–1943) Born Clonmult, Co. Cork, the son of William Kelleher, farmer. A full-back, he was captain of the celebrated Dungourney hurling team which won the All-Ireland SHC on three occasions (1894, 1902–3) and being on the losing end on five other occasions (1901, 1904–5, 1907 and 1912). He was also an expert horseman and was successful in many point-to-point meetings all over Munster. He is generally regarded as the greatest Cork hurling icon after Christy Ring. He died on 10 January 1943 and was buried in Clonmult Cemetery. [Profiles by R. Henchion in *JCHAS*, 82 (1977); J.P. Power in *A Story of Champions* (1941) and T. Horgan in *Cork's Hurling Story* (1977)]

KELLEHER, Michael (1937–1998) Born Cork, the son of Denis P. Kelleher. He was educated at PBC, Cork, and at UCC where he graduated in medicine in 1964. He worked as a registrar at Bethlehem Royal Hospital and at the Maudsley Psychiatric Hospital, in London. He returned to Cork in 1970 and took up the appointment of clinical director of Our Lady's Hospital and St Anne's Hospital. He specialised in the study of suicide and tracked the trends on an inter-county basis. Through his influence, the Suicide Research Foundation was established in Cork in 1994 and was replaced two years later by the National Suicide Research Project with himself as director. However, he was forced to resign from the position through illness early in 1998. He died at his Kerry Pike, Blarney, residence on 9 August 1998 and was buried privately.

KELLEHER, Stephen B. (1875–1917) Born Cork, the son of William Kelleher of King Street (now Mac Curtain Street), and elder brother of **Daniel L. Kelleher**. He was educated at North Monastery CBS and at CBC, Cork. He obtained first place in Ireland in the matriculation examination of the Royal University. He entered Queen's College, Cork (now UCC), in 1892 and graduated MA in 1896. In 1898, he was appointed an examiner in mathematics by the Intermediate Board and in the same year, entered TCD where he graduated BA (1902). He became a fellow of TCD in 1904 and was appointed as Erasmus Smith Professor of Mathematics in 1914. He died in Dublin on 18 August 1917.

KELLER, Daniel (1839–1922) Born Inniscarra, Co. Cork. He was educated at St Vincent's Seminary at the former Mansion House, Cork (now the Mercy Hospital). He then attended the Irish College, Paris, where he was ordained in 1862. He served as a curate in Killeagh, Co. Cork, before teaching at St Colman's College, Fermoy, where he became dean under the presidency of the future archbishop of Cashel, **Thomas Croke**. After three years, he returned to Paris to take up an appointment as professor of Moral Philosophy at the Irish College. In 1870, he returned home once again and was made administrator of Queenstown (Cobh). He spent 16 years there and was intimately associated with the construction of St Colman's Cathedral. He was appointed parish priest of

Youghal in 1885 where he remained until his death. Arising from his support for the Plan of Campaign (1885–91), he was arrested on 18 March 1887 for contempt of court – refusing to disclose in a bankruptcy trial a conversation he had had with a tenant of the Ponsonby Estate. He was greeted by large crowds in every town on his way to Dublin, where the Lord Mayor and a procession of 20,000 people escorted him to his hotel. He was imprisoned until 21 May when the Court of Appeal gave judgement against the legality of the original arrest warrant. While in prison, he was made a canon of the Cloyne diocesan chapter on 7 April. He was made dean of Cloyne in 1894 and a monsignor in 1900 (while on a visit to Rome). He was heavily involved with the Home Rule movement as a supporter of the Irish Parliamentary Party. He took a keen interest in educational matters and was, for many years, the chairman of the Central Council of the Catholic Clerical Managers' Association. He died at his residence on 8 November 1922 and was buried in the grounds of Youghal Church.

KELLER, George (1842–1935) Born Cork, the son of Thomas Keller, a wallpaper manufacturer who emigrated to New York in 1850 where he operated as a building contractor. George and his brother joined the family two years later. He continued his education at the New York Free Academy and became an architect who specialised in the design of memorials. His most notable commissions were the design of the Gettysburg Memorial, the President Garfield National Memorial and the Hartford (Conn.) Memorial Arch. At his death, which occurred on 7 July 1935 at his Hartford residence, he was dean of the American Institute of Architects.

KELLY, Denis (1852–1924) Born Templederry, Killaneave, Co. Tipperary. He was educated at St Flannan's College, Ennis, and at the Irish College, Paris, where he was ordained in 1877. For the following twenty years, he worked on the staff of St Flannan's, having become president in 1890. He was consecrated as bishop

of Ross on 9 May 1897. An expert on educational matters, he sat on various royal and viceregal commissions. He was also prominent in the Home Rule movement and an outspoken supporter of the Irish Parliamentary Party. He died in Dublin on 18 April 1924 and was buried in St Patrick's Pro-Cathedral, Skibbereen.

KELLY, John Edward (1839–1884) Born Kinsale, Co. Cork. He emigrated to the United States where he worked as a compositor. He joined the Fenians and returned to Ireland to partake in the 1867 uprising, working in the meantime as a compositor at *The Cork Herald*. He was captured after the skirmish at Kilclooney Wood where **Peter O'Neill Crowley** was killed. He was sentenced to death but this was commuted to penal servitude for life. He was transported to Western Australia on the *Hougomont* and worked on the ship's newspaper, the *Wild Goose*. Having been pardoned in 1871 on condition of not returning to Britain, he worked as assistant editor of the Sydney *Irish Citizen*, a paper started by his fellow-Fenian, John Flood. Here he published his *Illustrious exiles, or military memoirs of the Irish Race* (1875). At the end of 1875, he left for San Francisco. 'The Protestant Fenian' died in Boston in January 1884 and was buried in Hope Cemetery where a monument, in the shape of a round tower, was unveiled at his grave by John Boyle O'Reilly in the following year.

KELLY, Timothy [Bro. Jerome] (1926–1999) Born Lehanemore, Beara, Co. Cork. He entered the Presentation Order at Cork in August 1944 and took his final vows in 1949. In the meantime, he had graduated from De la Salle Training College, Waterford, a year previously. He first taught at Greenmount NS, Cork, and attended courses at the Crawford Technical School and at UCC where he graduated BA. In August 1954, he was one of several Brothers sent to the West Indies to provide secondary education there at the request of Archbishop **Finbarr Ryan**. He taught chemistry at San Fernando, Trinidad, and was appointed principal at Presentation College there. His election as assistant to the superior general of the Order in 1969 necessitated a return to Cork where he combined his new post with that of principal of PBC (1969–81). Before his departure from Trinidad, he was made a freeman of San Fernando. In 1970, he established the Cork housing charity, SHARE, which proved a great success. In 1981, he was elected as superior general and in the following year, he was conferred with an honorary doctorate of the NUI. In March 1994, he received the freedom of Cork for his contribution to Irish education and for his innovative leadership of SHARE. He was diagnosed with leukaemia in 1995 but continued with his charitable work. He died in the Bon Secours Hospital on 19 January 1999 and was buried at Mount St Joseph's Cemetery, Cork.

KENEALY, Edward V. (1819–1880) Born Cork, the son of William Kenealy, merchant. He was educated at TCD where he graduated BA (1840) and LL.D (1851). He was called to the Irish Bar (1840), to the English Bar (1847), and to the English Inner Bar (1868). In 1873, he appeared as counsel in the Tichborne Trial which made national news. Following the trial, he founded *The Englishman* newspaper to plead his client's case. However, as a result of the tone and content of his paper, he was disbenched and disbarred. In 1875, he was elected as MP for Stoke and unsuccessfully moved in the House of Commons for an inquiry into the trial. He lost his seat in the election of 1880. As well as being a linguist of repute, he also wrote poetry, fiction and esoteric works. He died in London on 16 April 1880 and was buried at Hangleton, Sussex. [Memoirs by A. Kenealy (1908)]

KENEALY, William (1828–1876) Born Cloyne, Co. Cork, the son of a blacksmith. He qualified as a schoolmaster, but was dismissed in 1848 because of his association with the Young Ireland movement. He then took up a teaching appointment at the Diocesan College, Derry, but moved to Leeds and into journalism when he took over the editorship of *The Lamp*, a Roman Catholic organ. He returned to Ireland and became editor, in turn, of the *Tipperary Leader* and the *Kilkenny Journal*. He contributed poetry to the organ of the Young Irelanders, *The Nation,* under the pseudonym of 'William of Munster'. His ballad, 'The Moon Behind the Hill' (1856) became famous when it entered the repertoire of 'Christy's Minstrels' at St James's Theatre, London. He also wrote the introduction to Edward Hayes' *The Ballads of Ireland* (2 vols, 1855). He was twice elected as mayor of Kilkenny (1872, 1873) and was the recipient of a French Red Cross award for his help to the beleaguered Parisians during the Franco-Prussian War (1870/71). He died on 5 September 1876 and was buried in St Patrick's Cemetery, Kilkenny.

KENNEDY, Michael B. (c.1849–1912) Born Sraharla, Mitchelstown, Co. Cork. He was educated at Mount Melleray School, Co. Waterford, and at St Colman's College, Fermoy. He completed his clerical education at the Irish College in Paris and was ordained in Waterford in the late 1870s. He spent a few years on the Liverpool Mission before being appointed as a curate in Youghal from where he was transferred to Meelin. Taking a prominent role in the local branch of the National Land League, he and other leading members were prosecuted under the Coercion Acts in April 1888 at the Newmarket Petty Sessions. This occasion, and his subsequent arrest to serve a two-month prison sentence on 27 August, gave rise to the 'Meelin Cavalry' as 200 Meelin horsemen accompanied him on both journeys. His sojourn in Cork Prison was followed by a further three-month sentence later in the year. On his release in February 1889, he was triumphantly escorted back to Meelin by his loyal 'cavalry'. He spent subsequent periods as curate in Dungourney and Blarney, before his transfer to Fermoy in 1901. He died there after a long illness on 8 March 1912. A statue to his memory (by F.W. Doyle-Jones) was unveiled in Fermoy in October 1926.

KENNEY, Arthur H. (1776–1855) Born Cork, the son of John Kenney, vicar-general of the diocese of Cork. He was educated at TCD where he graduated BA (1795) and DD (1812). He was ordained in the Church of Ireland and after several preferments, he became rector of St Olave's, Southwark, London, in 1821. Here he engaged in theological controversy with representatives of the Roman Catholic Church. In 1845, his London living was sequestered on account of his unpaid debts. He retired to Boulogne-sur-Mer, France, where he died on 27 January 1855. His publications included *An Enquiry concerning some of the Doctrines maintained by the Church of Rome* (1818), *Principles and Practices of Pretended Reformers in Church and State* (1819), *Facts and Documents illustrative of the History of the Period immediately preceding the Accession of William III* (1827), and *The dangerous Nature of Popish Power in these Countries especially as illustrated from awful Records of the Time of James the Second* (1832).

KENNY, Joseph E. (1845–1900) Born Palmerston, Dublin, where his father was manager of a lead mine. He was educated in Dublin and Edinburgh where he received medical qualifications in 1868 and 1870. He then filled various medical posts in the North Dublin Union. Dismissed from his post in 1882 for his political activities, he contested the dismissal, was compensated and reinstated. In 1885, he was elected as a nationalist MP for the South Cork constituency, which he represented until 1892. A close confidante of **C.S. Parnell**, he sat as a Parnellite MP for College Green (Dublin) from 1892 to 1896, when he resigned his seat. He was crown coroner for the City of Dublin from July 1891 until his death, which occurred on 9 April 1900. He was buried in Glasnevin Cemetery.

KENT, David R. (1865–1930) Born Bawnard House, Castlelyons, Co. Cork, the son of David Kent, a prosperous farmer. He was the brother of **Thomas Kent** and **William Kent**. He was arrested in 1889 for his Land War activities and was imprisoned for six months. He joined the Irish Volunteers in 1914. He took part in the

defence of Bawnard House against police and military on the night of 1 May 1916. In the incident, he was wounded in the right side and lost three fingers of his right hand. When recovered from his wounds, he was transferred to Richmond Barracks, Dublin, tried by court-martial and sentenced to death. This was later commuted to five years penal servitude. He was subsequently released in June 1917 under a general amnesty but re-arrested in 1918 and sentenced to six months' imprisonment. He was elected to the First Dáil in 1918 for Cork East, in 1921 for Cork East/North East, and in the same constituency in 1922 as an anti-Treaty candidate. He was returned for East Cork in 1923 as a republican and in June 1927 for the Sinn Féin Party. He did not seek re-election in the following December but spent several months touring the United States as a Sinn Féin spokesman. He died at Bawnard House on 16 November 1930 and was buried in Castlelyons Graveyard.

KENT, Thomas (c.1867–1916) Born Bawnard House, Castlelyons, Co. Cork, the son of David Kent, a prosperous farmer. He was the brother of **David Kent** and **William Kent**. Having lived in Boston for some years, he returned home and became involved with Connradh na Gaeilge and with the Irish Volunteers. With his brothers, he was ready to participate in the Easter rising of 1916 but remained inactive when he received news that the plan had been cancelled. On the night of 1 May, Bawnard was surrounded by a force of RIC and a three-hour long gun battle ensued in which one of the brothers (Richard) and a head constable were killed. He was arrested, court-martialled at Victoria (now Collins) Barracks and executed on 9 May 1916. [Memorial by **Seamus Murphy** at Collins Barracks, Cork; Bust by James McCarthy at Kent Station, Cork]

KENT, William R. (1873–1956) Born Bawnard House, Castlelyons, Co. Cork, the son of David Kent, a prosperous farmer. He was the brother of **David Kent** and **Thomas Kent**. He was one of five brothers who were active in the Land

War period and served a period of imprisonment in the late 1880s. The brothers were also active in the Volunteers and on 1 May 1916, a party of armed police surrounded Bawnard House and called on the brothers to surrender. The Kents resisted and a three-hour gunfight ensued. A policemen was shot dead, David Kent was wounded, while Richard Kent was mortally wounded in attempting to escape. Thomas and William were court-martialled in Cork on 4 May. Thomas was sentenced to death and executed on 9 May while William was acquitted. He was co-opted to Cork County Council in 1917, elected as chairman (1918/19) and served as a county councillor (1917–25, 1928–34). He was elected to the Dáil as an East Cork Fianna Fáil TD in 1927, but lost his seat in 1932. He was re-elected in the following year as a Centre Party TD, but did not seek re-election in 1937. He died at Bawnard on 8 March 1956 and was buried in Castlelyons Graveyard.

KEOGH, John (1681–1754) Born Strokestown, Co. Roscommon, the eldest son of John Keogh, clergyman (also oriental scholar, mathematician, and metaphysician). He was educated at TCD where he graduated BA (1711). He was employed as chaplain to James King, 1st earl of Kingston. His *Botanologia Universalis Hibernica* (Cork, 1735) deals with the properties of herbs, while his *Zoologia Medicinalis* (Dublin, 1739) is medical in character. He also wrote *A Vindication of the Antiquities of Ireland* (1748).

KERRIGAN, Patrick F. (1928–1979) Born Old Youghal Road, Cork, the son of a taxi operator. He was educated at St Patrick's NS (Dillon's Cross) and at Cork School of Commerce. He joined the ITGWU (now SIPTU) in 1946 and later worked as a full-time trades union official. He served on Cork Corporation (1967–79) and was elected as Lord Mayor (1973/74). He contested Dáil elections in 1967, 1969 and 1973, before winning a seat for Labour in the 1977 general election. Previously he had been a member of Seanad Éireann (1973–7) as a Taoiseach's nominee. He died at

the North Infirmary Hospital, Cork, on 4 July 1979 and was buried in Rathcooney Graveyard, Glanmire.

KEYES, Raphael P. (1895–1977) Born Bantry, Co. Cork, the son of Michael Keyes. In 1917, he became captain of the Bantry Company of the Irish Volunteers. He took an active part in the War of Independence, including the raid on a naval sloop in Bantry Bay in November 1919. He was arrested on 31 January 1920 and jailed in Wormwood Scrubs Prison where he participated in a mass hunger strike. He was released in the following May but was arrested and interned with other Bantry officers in the following November. Having failed to win a West Cork seat for Fianna Fáil in the 1927 general election, he was elected in February 1932. However, he failed to retain his seat in the general election of January 1933 but served as a member of the Senate of the Irish Free State until 1936. He was also a member of Cork County Council from 1934 until 1942. A cinema proprietor in Bantry, he was a member of the town commissioners there for many years. He died in St Joseph's Hospital, Bantry, on 22 April 1977 and was buried in Abbey Cemetery.

KING, Edward (1795–1837) He was the son of **George King**, 3rd earl of Kingston, and brother of **Robert King** (1796–1867). On the death of the second earl in 1799, he was created Viscount Kingsborough. He was educated at Exeter College, Oxford and sat as MP for County Cork (1816–26). He decided to devote most of his time to the study of Mexican antiquities when he perused a Mexican manuscript in the Bodleian Library, Oxford. His *Antiquities of Mexico* in nine volumes were published between 1830 and 1848. However, at his death in 1837, seven volumes had been produced at a staggering cost of £32,000. He was imprisoned in the debtor's prison in Dublin where he died of typhus on 27 February 1837.

KING, George (1771–1839) He was the son of Robert King (1754–99), the 2nd earl of

Kingston, and the father of **Edward King**, and **Robert King** (1796–1867). On his father's death in 1799, he succeeded as 3rd Earl but was not allowed under the will to inherit the estate's revenues until the death of his mother in 1823. However, even then there were crippling debts on the estate. Nevertheless, 'Mad George', the 'King of the Galtees', had notions of becoming a feudal baron and employed **George Pain** and his brother, James, to design the neo-Gothic Mitchelstown Castle which was modelled on that of Windsor. The new edifice was estimated to have cost between £100,000 and £200,000 and took only two years to complete. Here, the most insignificant of guests were treated as royalty. By the early 1830s, the total Mitchelstown debt stood at £400,000. In 1833, he was publicly declared insane and his affairs were put into the hands of the Court of Chancery. He died in London on 18 October 1839.

KING, Robert (1796–1867) He was the second son of **George King**, 3rd earl of Kingston, and younger brother of **Edward King**, who resigned his County Cork parliamentary seat in favour of Robert in 1826. Robert represented the constituency until 1832 when he stood as a Liberal candidate and was heavily defeated. On his father's death in October 1839, he succeeded to the earldom as 4th earl as Edward had previously died in 1837. He died, unmarried, on 21 January 1867 and was succeeded by his younger brother, James.

KING, Robert (1815–1900) Born Cork, the son of Joseph King, merchant. He was educated at TCD where he graduated BA (1839). He entered the ministry of the Church of Ireland in 1841 and served as a tutor at St Columba's School, Dublin. He was subsequently headmaster of the diocesan school at Ballymena, Co. Antrim, from 1858 until his death. A fine Gaelic scholar and antiquary, he was the friend of **William Reeves** and John O'Donovan (1806–61). Among his Gaelic publications were *A Primer*, *A Catechism*, *A Life of Christ* and *The Book of Common Prayer*. His *History of the Church in Ireland* (3 vols) ran

to six editions. He also published *Memoir of the Primacy of Armagh* (1854). He died in Ballymena in 1900.

KINGSTON, Sir George S. (1807–1880) Born Bandon, Co. Cork, the son of George Kingston. Having trained as an architect and civil engineer, he moved to England. He was appointed as deputy surveyor-general of the new colony of South Australia and arrived there in September 1836. He eventually established himself in the Adelaide district and was instrumental in the establishment of the South Australian Mining Association in order to secure the colony's mineral riches from overseas speculators. He served as director (1848–56), deputy-chairman (1856–7), and chairman (1857–80) of the association and oversaw the development of the huge Burra copper mine, which, in its first five years of production, paid fifteen dividends of 200%. He entered the state Legislative Council as a republican in 1851 and was elected Speaker in the House of Assembly – a position which, excepting the years 1860–5, he held until his death. He was knighted in 1870. He died at sea on 26 November 1880 while voyaging to India for health reasons. [Life by D. Langmead (1994); Portrait by A. MacCormac at Parliament House, Adelaide; Cartoon by S.T. Gill at the South Australian Archives]

KIRCHHOFFER, John N. (1848–1914) Born Ballyvourney Glebe, Co. Cork, the son of Richard B. Kirchhoffer, clergyman, and brother of **Julia G.M. Kirchhoffer**. He was educated locally and at Marlborough College, England. He emigrated to Canada in 1864 and settled in Port Hope, Ontario. He became a lawyer and practised, in turn, at the Ontario and Manitoba Bars. During the Fenian Raid of 1866, he served in the 46th battalion of the Canadian Volunteers. He founded a successful settlement at Souris, Manitoba, and became its mayor in 1885. In the following year, he became a senator on the Manitoba Legislative Assembly. A keen sportsman, he captained the Canadian Cricket XI on several occasions. During a Canadian visit by the Prince of Wales in 1891, over 1,000 wild duck were shot in a single day at his shooting-lodge on Lake Manitoba. He died in Brandon, Manitoba, on 25 December 1914.

KIRCHHOFFER, Julia G.M. (1855–1876) Born Ballyvourney Glebe, Co. Cork, the daughter of Richard B. Kirchhoffer, clergyman, and sister of **John N. Kirchhoffer**. Her work, *Poems and Essays,* was published in Scotland and four pieces were included in 'Lyra Hibernica Sacra'. She died on 29 June 1876.

KIRK, Thomas (1781–1845) Born Cork. He trained as a sculptor in Dublin and was a founder-member of the Royal Hibernian Academy. He executed the statue of Admiral Horatio Nelson (1758–1805) which topped Nelson's Pillar in O'Connell Street, Dublin, and of Admiral Sir W. Sidney Smith (1764–1840) at Greenwich, London. He died in Dublin in 1845. His son, Joseph Robinson Kirk (1821–94), was also a noted sculptor and exhibitor.

KNAPP, Edmund (*fl.* 1720) He is associated with Knapp's Quay which he was allowed to build in 1707. He had been a freeman (1691), sheriff (1695), alderman and mayor of Cork (1703). He later represented Cork City as MP (1715–27). He was appointed, with Edward Hoare, to the weightmastership of Cork by parliament in 1723. However, this appointment did not sit well with most of the members of Cork Corporation and both he and Hoare were removed from the post in October 1724. Knapp later was awarded the contract for cleaning the streets of Cork in 1732. He was buried in the family vault at Shandon Graveyard.

KNOTT, Mary (1783–1859) Born Cork, the daughter of **Richard Abell (1750–1801)** and sister of **Abraham Abell**, **Joshua Abell**, **Richard Abell (1789–1840)** and **John Abell**. She married John Knott, a Dublin hosiery manufacturer and a Quaker trustee. Her skill in managing apprentices in her husband's firm is remembered in the pun, 'John was Knott, but Mary was Abell'. She published, *Two Months at Kilkee* (1836), a description of the West Clare holiday resort.

KNOWLES, James S. (1784–1862) Born Cork, the son of James Knowles (1759–1840), the lexicographer and publisher of *The Pronouncing Dictionary* (1835) and a first cousin of Richard Brinsley Sheridan (1751–1816), the playwright. He was also the father of the journalist, Richard Brinsley Knowles (1820–1882), who, despite his father's anti-Roman Catholic opinions, became editor of the *Catholic Standard.* In 1793, the family moved to London. Even though he graduated with a medical degree from the University of Aberdeen, he became interested in writing for the stage while at the same time he taught and lectured in Belfast and Glasgow. Among his plays were 'Leo, or The Gypsy' (1810), 'Brian Boroimhe' (1811), 'Caius Gracchus' (1815), 'Virginius' (1820), 'The Fatal Dowry' (1825), 'William Tell' (1825), 'The Hunchback' (1832) and 'The Love Chase' (1837). In 1844, he gave up the theatre and became a Baptist preacher. He wrote against the Roman Catholic Church with *The Rock of Rome, or the Arch-Heresy* (1849) and *The Idol demolished by its own Priest* (1851). He also wrote two novels, *Fortescue* (1846) and *George Lovell* (1847), during this period. In 1848, he was put on the Civil List at £200 a year. He died at Torquay on 30 November 1862. [Life by R.B. Knowles (1872); Plays edited by R.S. MacKenzie (1835, 1838), and by L.H. Meeks (1933)]

KYLE, Samuel (1770–1848) Born Co. Derry, the son of Samuel Kyle, gentleman. He was educated at Derry diocesan school and at TCD where he graduated BA (1793), MA (1799), and BD/DD (1808). He became a senior fellow of TCD and later served as Provost (1820–31). He was consecrated as Church of Ireland bishop of Cork and Ross on 27 March 1831 (the diocese of Cloyne was added on 14 September 1835). He died in Dublin on 18 May 1848.

L

LACY, Frederick St J. (1862–1935) Born Blackrock, Cork, the son of John F. Lacy, JP, army officer. He was educated at Castleknock College and at the Royal Academy of Music, London. He lived in London from 1886 to 1900 and held various appointments there, including that of director of music at St Augustine's, Ramsgate. He returned to Cork in 1900 and three years later, he founded the St John Lacy Chamber Music Concerts. In 1906, he was appointed as lecturer on Music at Queen's College, Cork (now UCC) and as professor of Music at the same institution four years later. He held this position until his resignation in 1934. He was instrumental in founding the Munster Association of Professional Musicians in 1909 and acted as its first chairman. He composed many songs (both sacred and secular), cantatas and concert overtures. He also published *Irish Tunes for Irish Regiments* in two volumes. He died on 31 August 1935.

LAMBKIN, Francis (1858–1912) Born 'Feltrim', Blackrock Road, Cork, the son of Robert Lambkin, JP. He was educated at Ratcliffe College, Nottinghamshire, and joined the British army as an administrative medical officer in 1881. He saw service in India, the West Indies and in South Africa (for the duration of the Boer War). He was subsequently employed in 1905 as a syphilologist at army headquarters in India. He then took up the post of lecturer in Syphilology at the Army Medical College, London, and was employed by the Colonial Office in 1907 to investigate the serious spread of syphilis in Uganda. In the previous year, he had been promoted to the rank of colonel. He published four major works, all of which dealt with syphilis. He died on 8 March 1912.

LANDES, Nicholas (d. *c.*1574) He was appointed as bishop of Cork and Cloyne on 27 February 1568, on the recommendation of Rev. David Wolfe (the papal commissary) and of the Munster bishops. However, with the Elizabethan Reformation in full swing, Landes never took possession of his united dioceses and the position went to **Richard Dixon**, the nominee of Sir Henry Sidney (1529–86), the Irish lord deputy.

LANE, David J. (1913–1955) Born Parnell Place, Cork. He was educated at CBC, Cork, where his rugby prowess was first noted. He played senior rugby with Cork Constitution before playing for UCC. He won four Irish international caps as wing-threequarter in 1934/35 (when Ireland took the International Championship) and was a member of three successive Munster Senior Cup-winning teams with UCC (1935–7). He died at Manchester Road, Crosspool, Sheffield, on 15 September 1955.

LANE, Denny (1818–1895) Born Cork, the son of Maurice Lane, the owner of Riverstown Distillery. He was educated at TCD where he graduated MA (1839) and in London where he took a law degree. He was called to the Bar (1842) and joined the Young Ireland movement in 1842. He became a regular contributor to *The Nation* newspaper mainly through his songs and poetry. One of his best-known ballads is 'Carrigdhoun'. He took part in the Young Ireland rebellion in 1848 and was subsequently imprisoned for four months. He took a keen interest in the commercial, cultural, and political life of Cork. He was a founder member of the Cork Historical and Archaeological Society and served as chairman of the Cork School of Science. He was for many years the secretary and resident engineer of Cork Gas Company and held directorships in the

Blackrock and Passage Railway Company, the Belvelly Brickworks, and the Springfields Starch Works. He also served as chairman of the Macroom Railway Company. He died at his South Mall, Cork, residence on 29 November 1895 and was buried in Matehy Cemetery. [Study by M. Cronin in *JCHAS* (1995, 1996); Commemorative plaque at 72, South Mall]

LANE, Sir Hugh (1875–1915) Born Ballybrack, Douglas, Cork, the son of James William Lane, rector of Redruth, Cornwall, who had inherited a small estate in Douglas. On his mother's side, he was the nephew of Lady Gregory (1852–1932), one of the principals of the Irish Literary Revival. Having made many continental tours with his mother, he set up as a London art dealer in 1898. His success was rapid and he was knighted in 1909 for his services to the British National Gallery. A year previously, he had lent a collection of thirty-nine mainly French Impressionist paintings to the Dublin Municipal Gallery at Harcourt Street, but these were removed in 1913 in a dispute with Dublin City Council. He perished as a passenger on the liner, *Lusitania*, which was sunk off the Old Head of Kinsale on 7 May 1915. An unwitnessed codicil to his will specified that the paintings should be returned to Dublin if a permanent home should be provided within five years. The dispute between the Dublin and London galleries went on until 1959 when an agreement was reached for alternate displays of the pictures. In the meantime, the former town residence of the earl of Charlemont at Parnell Square, Dublin, had been purchased to act as the permanent Municipal Gallery and the 'Lane Pictures' have been displayed there on and off since 1960. [Lives by Lady Gregory (1921, 1974) and T. Bodkin (1934); Portrait by J.S. Sargent]

LANE, Thomas [VC] (1836–1889) Born Cork. He joined the British army as a Private in the 67th Regiment. During the Chinese 'White Signal' Rebellion, Lane and Lieutenant Burslem swam the ditches of North Taku Fort on 21 August 1860, to enlarge a hole in the wall through which they then entered the fort during the assault by their own regiment. They were both severely wounded. For this act of bravery, they both were awarded the Victoria Cross. He died in Kimberley, South Africa, on 13 April 1889.

LANE, Walter P. (1817–1892) Born County Cork, the son of William Lane. In 1821, the family moved to the United States and settled in Ohio. While he was visiting his elder brother in Louisville, Kentucky, in 1835, he met the two Texas Commissioners, S.F. Austin and B.T. Archer, and took up the Texan cause against both the Mexicans and the Indians. On the outbreak of the Mexican War in 1846, he led a company of Texas Rangers and was subsequently involved in many dangerous assignments and adventures. He then got caught up in the Californian Gold Rush and in gold-mining activities in Nevada, Arizona and Peru. He had only returned to Texas when the American civil war broke out. He joined the Confederate army and was given the rank of lieutenant-colonel of the 3rd Texas Cavalry. At the end of this conflict, he had risen to the rank of brigadier-general. He then resumed his bachelor life as a merchant in Marshall, Texas, where he died on 28 January 1892. [*Adventures and Recollections* (1928)]

LANE, William J. (1849–1924) Born North Mall, Cork, the son of John Lane, merchant. He was educated at the Vincentian College, Cork, before starting on his career as a butter merchant. He was a member of Cork Corporation from 1881 and was closely involved in the commercial life of the city. As one of the originators of the Irish National Industrial Exhibition in Dublin in 1882, he took a prominent part in promoting the Cork Industrial Exhibition of the following year. From 1885 to 1892, he was nationalist MP for Cork East. He did not seek re-election in 1892, complaining previously in 1887 that his parliamentary duties had both exhausted his savings and damaged his livelihood. He later became an agent of the New York Life Insurance Company and on his appointment as their Irish manager, he moved to Dublin where he died in 1924.

LAWLESS, Clement Francis (1815–1877) Born Woodview, Cloyne, Co. Cork, the son of John Lawless, tithe proctor, and elder brother of **Paul Lawless**. The brothers emigrated to Queensland, Australia, in 1840, where, with other partners, they went into the cattle business. In 1847, they sold their holding licence and moved to the Burnett River area of Queensland where they took up extensive sheep farming. He returned to Ireland in 1859, married in 1860 and bought Kilcrone House near his native village. He visited Queensland in 1867 and again in 1873 when he sold his commercial interests to Paul's widow, Ellen. He died at Kilcrone on 22 May 1877 as a result of a hunting accident. He was buried in the graveyard of Cloyne Cathedral.

LAWLESS, Paul (1817–1865) Born Woodview, Cloyne, Co. Cork, the son of John Lawless, tithe proctor, and younger brother of **Clement F. Lawless**. The brothers emigrated to Queensland, Australia, in 1840, where, with other partners, they went into the cattle business. In 1847, they sold their holding licence and moved to the Burnett River area of Queensland where they took up extensive sheep farming. He returned to Ireland in 1855 and married in 1858. In the following year, he returned to Australia where he lived at Booubyjan – one of the brothers' sheep and cattle stations. His failing health forced the family to return to Ireland in 1865 and he died in Youghal on 7 August, soon after his arrival. His widow and family returned to Australia where their descendants still carry on the pastoral traditions of their pioneering predecessors.

LAWRENCE, Samuel H. [VC] (1831–1868) Born Cork. He joined the 32nd Regiment of the British army and rose to the rank of lieutenant. On 7 July 1857, during the Indian Revolt, he was the first to investigate a supposed mine in an occupied house at Lucknow. Even though his gun was knocked from his hand, he escaped with the relevant information. Ten weeks later, he advanced with two of his men and captured a 9-pounder cannon. For those actions, he was awarded the Victoria Cross. He was later promoted to the rank of major and died in Montevideo, Uruguay, on 17 June 1868.

LAWTON, Hugh T. (d. 1784) Born Castle Jane, Glanmire, Co. Cork, the son of Hugh Lawton, gentleman. He was largely responsible for the erection of the Cork House of Industry (Workhouse). He was high sheriff of Cork in 1767 and mayor in 1776. He was also a governor of St Stephen's Hospital in 1780. He was connected to the firm of Lawton, Carleton & Feray, merchants and bankers. He died in 1784. [Statue by John van Nost originally erected at the Cork Exchange, transferred to St Stephen's Hospital School and in 1916 to Cork Museum, but subsequently lost; Portrait at Cork Municipal Art Gallery]

LEADER, Nicholas P. (1773–1836) Born Mount Leader, Co. Cork, the eldest son of William Leader, gentleman, and father of **Nicholas P. Leader (1811–1880)**. He was educated at TCD where he graduated BA (1792) and was called to the Irish Bar in 1798. He succeeded to the estates of his Philpot grandfather. He unsuccessfully contested Cork County in the 1812 election, but was MP for Kilkenny City (1830–2). He died on 7 February 1836.

LEADER, Nicholas P. (1811–1880) Born Dromagh Castle, Co. Cork, the son of **Nicholas P. Leader (1773–1836)**. He was educated at TCD and was called to the Irish Bar in 1834. In 1832, he unsuccessfully contested the parliamentary borough of Harwich, Essex, as a Conservative. It was the same story for Cork County in the elections of 1841, and 1847. However, his luck changed in 1861 when he was elected for Cork County and he held this seat until his retirement in 1868. He inherited large estates in North Cork (in 1875, he owned 5,632 acres), of which he farmed over 2,000 acres on scientific principles. He also developed and worked the extensive coal mines at Dromagh, while he had mining interests in Bohemia. In his later years, he lived mostly in London, where he died at his residence following a long illness on 31 March 1880.

LEAHY, Con (1876–1921) Born Charleville, Co. Cork, the brother of **Pat Leahy**. A natural jumper, he competed in all three jumps; high, long, and triple. He won four British AAA titles (1905–8) and an American AAU title (1907) in the high jump. He was the winner of three Olympic medals. Representing Britain at the St Louis Olympics of 1904, he won the gold medal for the high jump and took the silver behind his fellow-Irishman, Peter O'Connor of Waterford, in the triple jump. Four years later, he won a joint silver medal at the London Olympics of 1908. Later that year he emigrated to the United States. He died in 1921.

LEAHY, John (1854–1909) Born Schull, Co. Cork, the eldest son of Patrick Leahy, farmer, and brother of **Patrick James Leahy**. He was educated locally and at the age of twenty-one, he emigrated to Queensland, Australia. He became a hotel proprietor and part-owner, with his younger brother, Patrick James, of a local newspaper. He entered the state Legislative Assembly as an independent in 1893 and was elected as Speaker in July 1907. He died at New Farm, Brisbane, on 20 January 1909 and, following a state funeral, was buried at Toowong Cemetery.

LEAHY, John P. (1802–1890) Born Cork. At the age of fifteen he set out for Lisbon where he joined the Dominican Order. He was ordained in 1826 and stayed on in Lisbon where he graduated DD and became rector of the Dominican College there. He returned to Ireland in 1847 where he was appointed as prior of St Mary's, Cork, and later as provincial of the Irish Dominicans. He was consecrated as coadjutor bishop of Dromore on 1 October 1854 and succeeded to that see in 1860. He was instrumental in the founding of St Colman's College, Newry and in the establishment of Mercy Convents at Newry, Rostrevor, and Lurgan. He opposed the doctrine of Papal Infallibility at the First Vatican Council but later accepted the dogma. He died in Newry, Co. Down, on 6 September 1890 and was buried in the Old Chapel Graveyard.

LEAHY, Pat (1877–1926) Born Charleville, Co. Cork, brother of **Con Leahy**. He excelled in all three jumping events (high, long, and triple), twice winning the British AAA title in the high jump (1898–9). He was also the winner of two Olympic medals when representing Great Britain. At the Paris Olympics of 1900 he took the silver medal in the high jump and the bronze in the long jump, but narrowly missed out in the triple jump when he finished in fourth place. He later competed with his brother, Con, in the high jump at the London Olympics of 1908. He died in 1926.

LEAHY, Patrick J. (1860–1927) Born Schull, Co. Cork, the eldest son of Patrick Leahy, farmer, and brother of **John Leahy**. He emigrated to Queensland, Australia, and founded the *Thargomindah Herald* newspaper in 1884. He also had grazing and mercantile interests. He sat in the Queensland Legislative Assembly (1902–8) and was also a member of the state's Legislative Council (1912–22). He died in 1927.

LEAMY, Edmund (1848–1904) Born Waterford, the son of J. Leamy. He was educated at the Jesuit College, Tullabeg, Co. Offaly and at University High School, Waterford. He was enrolled as a solicitor in 1878 and two years later was elected as MP for Waterford. In 1885, he was called to the Bar and also was elected as MP for Cork North East (1885–7). He further served as a member for Sligo South (1888–92) and for Kildare North (1900–4). He contested the constituencies of Waterford East (1892) and Galway (1895) as a Parnellite Home Ruler, but without success. He was editor of the Redmondite newspaper, *United Ireland,* in the 1890s. His publications included *Irish Fairy Tales*

(1899) and *By the Barrow River* (1907). He died at Pau, France on 10 December 1904 where he had lived for health reasons.

LECKY, Robert J. (1809–1897) Born Youghal, Co. Cork, the son of John Lecky (1764–1839). He was educated at the Quaker School at Ballitore, Co. Kildare. When he returned to Cork he went into partnership with his brother-in-law, **James Beale**, in ship-building and repair on Penrose Quay. He was responsible for the first Cork-built iron cutter, the *Charm*, and also for the first screw-driven ship, the *Rattler*. The company was eventually taken over by the shipbuilding concern of **Ebenezer Pike**. His gas fittings were approved for purchase by the United General Gas Company of London.

LEE, Grace Lawless (d. 1964) Born Cork, the daughter of Dr Philip G. Lee (d. 1934), a prominent Cork physician who was the hon. secretary of Cork Historical and Archaeological Society (1917–34) and also a founder-member. Grace was educated at the High School, Cork, and at TCD where she graduated BA (1928). An essay on the Huguenots in Ireland won her the Blake National History Scholarship and its publication in expanded form as *The Huguenot Settlements in Ireland* (1936) led to her appointment as a research assistant to the Huguenot Society of London. *The Huguenot Settlements* remains the standard work on the subject. Her scholarly history of a Huguenot family, *The Story of the Bosanquets* (1966), was published posthumously. In 1934, she married David Gwynn, brother of the historian, Professor **Denis Gwynn**, and resided in London where she died on 23 May 1964. She was cremated at Putney Vale Crematorium.

LEE, William (1876–1948) Born Mitchelstown, Co. Cork. He was educated at St Colman's College, Fermoy; at St John's College, Waterford, and at Oscott College, Birmingham. He was ordained in 1901 and appointed as secretary to the bishop of Clifton (Bristol) in the following year. Having become a canon, a domestic

prelate, and vicar-general of the diocese, he succeeded as bishop in 1932. During his episcopate, sixty new churches were built in the counties of Gloucester, Somerset and Wiltshire. He died in Bristol on 21 September 1948 and was buried in the Cemetery of All Souls Church there.

LEECH, Henry B. (1848–1921) Born Mitchelstown, Co. Cork, the second son of Rev. John Leech, chaplain of Kingston College. He was educated at TCD and at Gonville and Caius College, Cambridge, where he became a fellow. Having been called to the Irish Bar in 1872, he was professor of Jurisprudence and International Law (1878–88) and Regius professor of Laws (1888–1908) at TCD. He also acted as registrar of deeds (1891–1908) and registrar of titles (1893–1908) in Ireland. In 1902, he was elected a member of the American Academy of Political and Social Science. He died in London on 2 March 1921. His publications include, *Registration of Titles v. Registration of Assurances* (1891), *The South African Republics, their History and International Position* (1901), *The Irish University Question* (1905), *A Handbook for Unionist Speakers* (1910), and *The Continuity of the Irish Revolutionary Movement, 1847–1912* (1912).

LEHANE, Patrick Desmond (1907–1976) He was the son of Dónall Ó Liatháin, schools inspector and a native of Iveleary. He was the nephew of **Michael J. O'Lehane** and a first cousin of Con Lehane, TD (1912–83). He was educated at PBC, Cork; and at UCC. He farmed at Castletreasure, Douglas (which had been bought by his father following his retirement in 1921), and was county secretary of the Cork Farmers' Association. In 1930, he was a founding member of the Catholic Boy Scouts of Ireland in Cork. He contested the Dáil elections of 1943 and 1944 as a Clann na Talmhan candidate but lost narrowly on both occasions. He was elected for Cork South East in 1948 as a Clann na Talmhan member and again in 1951 – this time as an independent. He was defeated by

Fine Gael's **Tadhg Manley** in 1954 when standing as a Farmers' Party candidate. He was also a member of Cork County Council (1950–55). He died unexpectedly on 1 July 1976 at the North Infirmary Hospital and was buried in St Finbarr's Cemetery.

LENIHAN, Denis M. (1858–1930) Born Newmarket, Co. Cork. He was educated locally, but came to Cork at an early age and entered the drapery trade. He rose to a managerial position in 'The London House', Patrick Street and, following its take-over by **William Roche**, continued in the same capacity until his retirement. From the 1880s, he contributed short stories and verse to the periodical press, having begun as a contributor to the *Cork Herald*. His only full-length published work, set in the Land League period, was a novel, *The Red Spy* (*c*.1910), the central character being based on 'Red Jim' McDermott (a controversial Fenian). The novel was especially popular in the United States. He later produced a series of short stories on commission for the Catholic Truth Society. He died at his residence on Southern Road, Cork, on 9 November 1930.

LENIHAN, Thomas M. (1843–1901) Born at Rockhill, Mallow, Co. Cork, the son of Edmund Lenihan. He emigrated to the United States as a child and, following studies at seminaries in Kentucky, Missouri and Milwakee, was ordained in 1868. He served in the diocese of Dubuque, Iowa, until 1897 when he was consecrated as bishop of Cheyenne, Wyoming. He died, following a long illness, in Dubuque on 15 December 1901.

LEONARD, John P. (1812–1889) Born Spike Island, Co. Cork, the son of William Leonard, clerk of works. His two uncles, Brothers John P. Leonard and Joseph Leonard, were founder members of the Christian Brothers community in Cork. His father died in Paris in 1816 while on his way to the South of France to recuperate. John was enrolled at the College of Boulogne-sur-Mer in 1829, but was forced to return to

Ireland in the following year through ill health. However, he returned to France in 1834 and, aside from a few brief visits to Ireland, remained there for the rest of his life. He became a lecturer in English Language and Literature at the Municipal College Chapel of Paris University and acted as French correspondent for *The Nation* and *Cork Examiner* newspapers. He was a member of the Young Ireland movement and presented its leaders at a French Government reception and also at the United Irish Club of Paris in early 1848. He was instrumental in procuring French financial help for the relief of the famine-stricken inhabitants of Cape Clear Island in 1861. A member of the French Academy, he was conferred as Chevalier of the Legion of Honour for his distinguished service in the Franco-Prussian War of 1870. Though debarred on age grounds from military service, he served as a medical orderly. In the Paris Exhibitions of 1878 and 1889 (shortly before his death), he voluntarily promoted an 'Irish Pavilion' for Irish exhibitors. He died at his residence on Avenue de Villiers, Paris, on 6 August 1889 and was buried in the crypt of the parish church of St Francis de Sales. However, as he had previously wished, his remains were brought home to Ireland and buried in Templerobin Graveyard, Ballymore, Queenstown (now Cobh), on 27 October 1889. He published *Ireland under British Rule* (1864) and his translations from the French included Countess d'Hausonville's *Robert Emmet* (1858), Monseignor Dupanloup's *Sermon preached on behalf of the poor Catholics of Ireland* (1861), Cardinal Gaspard Mermillod's *Sermon ... on behalf of the distressed Irish ...* (1862) and General A.R. Dillon's *Historical notes on the services of the Irish officers in the French Army ...* (posthumously, 1905).

LEWIS, Bunnell (1824–1908) Born London. He was educated at Islington Proprietary School and at University College, London where he graduated BA (1843), MA (1849) and where he later was elected a fellow. He was professor of Latin at Queen's College, Cork (now UCC), from its establishment in 1849 to his retirement in 1905 at the age of 81 years. He died at his Cork residence on 2 July 1908.

LEWIS, Frank (*fl.* early 19th century) He worked in Cork and specialised in bookplate engraving, including a large one for the Cork antiquary, **John Windle**. He also cut seals from boxwood and produced artificial stones baked from clay for armorial seals. He exhibited seals at the Royal Hibernian Academy in 1842 from his address at 24, King Street (now Mac Curtain Street), Cork.

LEWIS, John T. (1825–1901) Born Garrycloyne Castle, Blarney, Co. Cork, the son of John Lewis, a curate at St Anne's, Shandon, who died young. He was educated at TCD where he graduated BA (1848), MA (1862) and DD (1862). Following his ordination in Lisburn in 1849, he followed his mother to Canada (she had settled there in 1848) as a missionary of the Society for the Propagation of the Gospel. In June 1861, following a bitter contest between Low- and High-Church interests, he was elected as first Anglican bishop of Ontario and chose Kingston as his see-city. However, he saw that Ottawa, as Canada's capital, was growing apace and he went to live there in 1870. But there was very little support for making an episcopal nucleus in the new capital and he returned to Kingston in the late 1880s. His diocese was enormous but his episcopate saw a large increase in the number of parishes (46 to 113). His health was ruined by travelling in extreme conditions, but for the financial support of the English missionary societies, his work would have been in vain. He had also lived in real poverty (his marriage produced eleven children, six of whom survived) and possibly his second marriage to a rich philanthropic lady in 1894 enabled his health to recover a little. He was made metropolitan of the Canadian ecclesiastical province in 1893 and in the following year he was elected as archbishop of Ontario. Following his resignation in 1900, he died at sea on 6 May 1901 while on his way to England. He was buried at Hawkhurst, Kent. [Life by D.M. Schurman (1991)]

LINDSAY, Thomas S. (1854–1933) Born Cork, the son of Joseph W. Lindsay, JP. He was educated at TCD where he graduated BD. Having been ordained in 1879, he served as curate in Enniscorthy and Bray, before becoming rector of Malahide in 1889 (where he ministered until his retirement in 1926). He had been archdeacon of Dublin from 1918. He died on 6 September 1933 and was buried in Malahide Graveyard. Among his publications were *Sunlit Hours* (1927), *Some Archbishops of Dublin* (1930), *What Think Ye of Christ?* (1931) and *From Gay to Grave* (1932).

LINEHAN, John (1865–1935) Born Cork, the eldest son of Matthew Linehan. He was educated at Farranferris College and at Tullabeg College, Co. Offaly. He worked as a journalist on the *Freeman's Journal* and as Dublin correspondent of the *Manchester Guardian*. He was called to the Bar (1891) and practised on the Munster Circuit. He was called to the Inner Bar in 1912 and in the same year was appointed as county judge of Tyrone and chairman of the Quarter Sessions. He died at the Tyrone County Club on 31 January 1935 and was buried at Leigh, Dorset, where he lived.

LINEHAN, Thomas (d. 1938) Born Whitechurch, Co. Cork, the son of Thomas Linehan. He was educated at Clongowes Wood College, Co. Kildare, and later became a full-time and extensive farmer on the family holding at Ballinvarrig, Whitechurch. In 1879, he became hon. secretary of the Cork branch of the Land League and was appointed a justice of the peace in 1893. He was a member of Cork County Council from its foundation in 1899 until his resignation in 1906 when he was appointed an assistant Land Commissioner. He resigned from the Land Commission in 1915 and was subsequently a trustee of the Irish Farmers' Union and chairman of its Cork branch. He was elected to Seanad Éireann in 1922 and was a prominent member of that House until its abolition in 1936. He died at his residence, Ballinvarrig House, on 15 October 1938 and was buried in St Joseph's Cemetery, Cork.

LINEHAN, Timothy (*fl.* 1937–1944) He was a solicitor of Coomlogane Street, Millstreet (admitted 1931) He was elected as a Fine Gael TD for North Cork in the 1937 general election and retained his seat in the elections of 1938 and 1943. However, he was defeated in the 1944 election.

LOMASNEY, William Francis ['Captain Mackey'] (1841–1884) Born either at Castlelyons, Co. Cork, the son of William Lomasney, or in Cincinnati, Ohio, of Co.Cork parents. He joined the Fenian movement in the US and travelled to Ireland in 1865 for the expected rising. He was arrested on arrival at Queenstown (now Cobh), charged with possession of a revolver and released on condition of leaving Ireland. However, he was re-arrested in Liverpool and released under the same conditions. He was one of the leaders of the Fenian rising in Cork and took part in the capture of Ballyknockane RIC barracks near Mourneabbey. After the rising, he became famous under his alias of 'Captain Mackey' for his successful arms raids on Cork gunshops and on Fota Martello Tower. He also used as aliases the names 'Francis Lomass' and 'Patrick Murphy'. He married Susan O'Connell of Paradise Place, Cork in July 1867. He was arrested in Cornmarket Street, Cork in February 1868. The death of a RIC constable in the course of the arrest caused him to be indicted for murder. He was tried at Cork in March 1868, acquitted on the murder charge but sentenced to twelve years penal servitude for treason felony. Released under the amnesty of 1871, he returned to the US and settled in Detroit as the proprietor of a book and stationery store. He remained active in Irish revolutionary circles and undertook missions to Ireland in disguise. Though he was critical of **O'Donovan Rossa**'s dynamite campaign, Lomasney's last mission was an attempt to blow up London Bridge on 12 December 1884, in which he, his brother Michael and John Fleming were killed. No bodies were recovered.

LONG, Sir James (1862–1928) Born Queenstown (now Cobh), Co. Cork, the son of James Long. He was educated at PBC, Cork. He entered the legal service and became the registrar of the County Court of Cork. In 1899, he was elected as a member of the first Cork County Council for the Queenstown division, and served as vice-chairman of the Council until 1902. In that year, he was re-elected but resigned without taking his seat. He was also chairman of Cork Harbour Commissioners for many years (1901–16). In 1916, he was appointed as secretary of the Cork Harbour Commissioners, and later, in 1925, as both secretary and general manager. He was knighted in 1910 on the occasion of the opening of an extension to Haulbowline Dockyard. He died at his residence, Spy Hill Villa, Cobh, on 17 September 1928 and was buried in Clonmel (Old Church) Graveyard, near Cobh.

LONGFIELD, Cynthia (1896–1991) Born Castlemary, Cloyne, Co. Cork or Belgravia, London. Her father was Mountiford Longfield, landlord and army officer. The family spent their winters in London and summers at Castlemary. On the outbreak of World War I, she served as a driver in the Royal Army Service Corps and later worked in an aircraft factory. With an abiding interest in natural science, she gained an international reputation as an entomologist specialising in the study of dragonflies. She later catalogued the Pacific Islands Collection of the British Museum. Her publications include *The Dragonflies of the British Isles* (1937) and (with P.S. Corbet and N.W. Moore) *The New Naturalist Dragonflies* (1960). She died at Castlemary on 27 June 1991 and was buried in the graveyard of Cloyne Cathedral. [Life by J. Hayter-Hames (1991); Bibliography by R.M. Gambles in *Odonatologica* 4 (1975); Book collection to Royal Irish Academy (1979)]

LONGFIELD, John (1741–1815) Born Longueville, Mallow, Co. Cork, the son of John Longfield, gent., and brother of **Mountiford Longfield** (1746–1819). In 1764, he married Elizabeth, the daughter of William Foster, MP. He was high sheriff of Cork in 1775. He sat as MP for Mallow in the Irish parliament (1790–1800) and in the British Parliament (1801–2). He died in 1815.

LONGFIELD, Mountiford (1746–1819) Born Longueville, Mallow, Co. Cork, the son of John Longfield, gent., and brother of **John Longfield**. He was MP in the Irish Parliament for Enniscorthy (1783–97) and for Cork City (1797–1800), while in the British Parliament he also represented Cork City (1801–18). He was a colonel in the Cork Militia and was appointed a commissioner of the Revenue in 1800. On the death of his cousin, **Richard Longfield** (Lord Longueville) in 1811, he inherited the Castlemary Estate, Cloyne, Co. Cork (comprising 10,800 acres in 1875). He died on 8 June 1819.

LONGFIELD, Mountiford (1802–1884) Born Desertserges, Enniskeane, Co. Cork, the son of Rev. Mountiford Longfield, and brother of **Robert Longfield**. He was educated at TCD where he graduated BA (1823) and LL.D (1831). He was appointed as professor of Political Economy at TCD in 1832, and two years later, he was appointed as professor of Feudal and English Law there. He was called to the Inner Bar in 1842 and served as a judge in the Land Courts (1858–67). He was also appointed as a commissioner of Irish National Education in 1853. In 1867, he became a member of the Irish Privy Council. He died in Dublin on 21 November 1884.

LONGFIELD, Richard (1734–1811) Born Castlemary, Cloyne, Co. Cork, the second son of Robert Longfield, landlord. He was MP for Charleville (1761–8), Clonakilty (1769–76), Cork City (1776–83 and 1791–5) and Baltimore (1783–90). He sat in the House of Lords on being created Baron Longueville in 1795. He became a viscount in 1800 and, following the Act of Union, was a representative peer at Westminster until his death in 1811. The titles became extinct on his death, *sine prole*, on 23 May 1811 and he was buried in the 'Longfield Chapel' of St Colman's Cathedral, Cloyne. In his youth, he was reputed to have been an avid patron of sport and cock-fighting.

LONGFIELD, Richard (1802–1889) Born Longueville, Mallow, Co. Cork, the eldest son of Lieutenant Colonel John Longfield. In 1832, he married a daughter of John McClintock, MP for County Louth. He was highsheriff of Cork in 1833. In January 1835, he contested the County Cork seat as a Conservative candidate. Though defeated at the polls, he was subsequently declared elected when **Fergus O'Connor** was unseated on petition. He sat until 1837 when he was defeated and was also unsuccessful for the Mallow seat in 1841. He was the owner of 9,400 acres in Co. Cork in 1875. He died on 18 June 1889.

LONGFIELD, Robert (1810–1868) Born Desertserges, Enniskeane, Co. Cork, the son of Rev. Mountiford Longfield, and younger brother of **Mountiford Longfield (1802–1884)**. He was educated at TCD where he graduated BA (1830) and MA (1832). He was called to the Irish Bar in 1834 and to the Inner Bar in 1852. He published several legal works, particularly on the law of landlord and tenant. He was elected as a Conservative MP for Mallow in 1859 and sat until 1865 when he did not contest the seat. He died on 28 April 1868.

LOONEY, Thomas D. (d. 1953) Born Blarney, Co. Cork. He was elected to Dáil Éireann in the June 1943 general election as a Labour Party TD for South East Cork. When the party split in January 1944, he was one of the five TDs who seceded to form the National Labour Party, under which banner he unsuccessfully sought re-election in the May 1944 general election. He was a member of Cork County Council from 1934 until 1950 (for the Labour Party [1934–45] and for the National Labour Party [1945–50]). In 1950, when he lost his council seat, he stood as an Irish Transport and General Workers' Union (ITGWU) candidate. He was branch secretary of the Blarney ITGWU for many years and was also deeply involved in local sports administration, being for a time president of the Cork County Cycling Board of the NACAI, and president of the National Cycling Association (NCA). He died at his residence, Waterloo Terrace, Blarney, on 11 February 1953 and was buried in Garrycloyne Cemetery.

LORD, David S.A. [VC] (1913–1944) Born Cork, the son of S.B. Lord. The family moved to Wrexham where he worked as an apprentice pharmacist. He joined the RAF in 1936 and served as a flight lieutenant with the 271 Squadron and with Transport Command. On 19 September 1944, at Arnhem, Holland, he flew a Dakota through intense German anti-aircraft fire in order to drop supplies to the 1st Airbourne Division. The aircraft was hit twice and the engine caught fire. He managed to make a drop but then found out that two containers still remained on board. He then turned back, made a second run, and, having dropped the containers, ordered his crew to bale out. However, a few seconds later, the Dakota crashed in flames and all the crew, with the exception of the navigator who was taken prisoner, were killed. He was posthumously awarded the Victoria Cross for his bravery. He had been previously awarded the Distinguished Flying Cross.

LORD, Percival B. (1807–1840) Born Mitchelstown, Co. Cork, the son of John Lord, the chaplain of Kingston College, Mitchelstown. He was educated at TCD where he graduated BA (1829) and MB (1832). Following a medical course in Edinburgh, he joined the East India Company as a surgeon in 1834 and saw service in Afghanistan. He became political assistant to Sir W.H. MacNaghten (1793–1841), but was killed in action at Purwan on 2 November 1840. He published *Popular Physiology* (1834, 1855) and *Algiers, with Notices of the neighbouring States of Barbary* (2 vols, 1835).

LOVELL, John (1810–1893) Born Bandon, Co. Cork, the son of Robert Lovell, farmer. In 1820, the family emigrated to Montreal, Canada, to take up farming there. However, John had no interest in this way of life and was apprenticed to a printer. In 1836, he and a partner published the region's first 'penny paper', the *Montreal Daily Transcript*. Three years later the partnership was dissolved and Lovell went into printing. In 1843, he imported the first steam-press into Montreal. In the following year, he went into partnership with his brother-in-law, John Gibson, and eventually the firm of Gibson & Lovell became a major publisher in British North America. Lovell had also a great interest in the promotion of French Canadian literature. To ensure financial solvency relative to the risks of publishing literature, the company also printed newspapers, magazines, directories, school textbooks and government publications in both languages. By 1866, the firm was employing 150 people and running twelve steam-presses. To escape some copyright laws, Lovell had also built a modern printing plant in the United States, at Rouses Point, New York. He was very prominent in the Anglican community of Montreal and was a large contributor to the building of Christ Church cathedral there. He was also prominent in the Irish Protestant Benevolent Society. He provided the Grey Nuns (Sisters of Charity) with a hand press and a font of type so that they could do their own printing. He died in Montreal on 1 July 1893.

LOWNEY, Denis M. (1863–1918) Born Castletownbere, Co. Cork, the son of Denis Lowney. He was educated in Montreal, New York, and was ordained in Montreal in December 1887. He engaged in pastoral work in Providence, Rhode Island, for twenty years and was chancellor and vicar-general of the diocese before being consecrated as auxiliary bishop of Providence in October 1917. He died at

Providence on 13 August 1918 and was buried there.

LUCEY, Cornelius (1902–1982) Born Windsor, near Ballincollig, Co. Cork. He was educated at St Finbarr's Seminary, Farranferris, and at St Patrick's College, Maynooth, where he was ordained in 1927. Following postgraduate studies at Innsbruck and at UCD, he held the chair of Philosophy and Political Theory at Maynooth (1929–50). Having an interest in social questions, he was one of the founders of the Christus Rex Society in 1941. He was consecrated as coadjutor bishop of Cork on 14 January 1951 and succeeded to the see on 24 August 1952. He initiated and oversaw an extensive building programme of churches and schools in Cork city and in other locations throughout his diocese. A controversial figure, both locally and nationally, he was later made a freeman of Cork. He retired on 23 August 1980 and, following a period of voluntary work in Turkana, Kenya, he died in Cork on 24 September 1982. He was buried in the grounds of the North Cathedral.

LUCEY, John (1945–2002) Born St Luke's, Cork, the son of Denis Lucey, city bus inspector. He was educated at St Patrick's NS and at Cork School of Commerce. In 1963, he joined the Air Corps and on completion of his training he joined the army and served with the 1st Battalion in Galway in the following year. Two years later, he joined the Irish Naval Service and worked as a telegraphist at Halbowline Naval Base where he attained the rank of chief petty officer in 1980 and warrant officer in 2001. In the late 1980s, he became a founder member and a chief spokesman for the Permanent Defence Forces Other Ranks Representative Association (PDFORRA) which campaigned for legal recognition to represent non-commissioned officers of the Defence Forces. In 1992, PDFORRA, along with the Representative Association for Commissioned Officers (RACO), was recognised under the Defence Forces Amendment Act. He became general secretary

of the association in 1994. A keen hill-walker, he was a founder member of the charity, Child Aid, which supports schools in Tanzania where he had previously had climbed Mount Kilimanjaro. He was killed in a mountain accident on the Magillicuddy Reeks, Co. Kerry, on 6 January 2002.

LUCY, John F. (1894–1962) Born Cork, the son of a cattle dealer and father of **Seán Lucy**. He was educated at North Monastery CBS. Following an altercation with their father, he enlisted with his younger brother, Denis, in the Royal Irish Rifles in January 1912. He served in France in World War I and was promoted to the rank of sergeant at the age of 20. However, he was wounded and invalided home in 1916. He rejoined his regiment in July 1917 as a commissioned officer and was badly wounded at Cambrai in December of that year. He served in the British army until his retirement in April 1935. He then took up journalism and worked for Radio Éireann where he devised and compered the first series of the programme, 'Question Time'. He published *Keep Fit and Cheerful* (1937) and followed this with his personal narrative, *There's a Devil in the Drum* (1938, new. ed. with biographical introduction, 1992). He rejoined the British army on the outbreak of World War II and was given the command of the leader training battalion, Royal Ulster Rifles, with the rank of lieutenant-colonel. He was awarded an OBE in 1945 and then returned to Cork where he was active in reorganising the British Legion. He played a prominent role in the Cork Civic Party and served on Cork Corporation (1955–62), latterly as an Independent councillor. He died at his son's residence on College Road, Cork, on 1 March 1962 and was buried in St Finbarr's Cemetery.

LUCY, Seán (1931–2001) Born Bombay, India, where his father, Lt. Col. **John F. Lucy**, was serving in the British army. The family returned to Cork in 1935 and Seán was educated at Glenstal Priory, Limerick, and at UCC where he graduated BA (1952) and MA (1957). He served as a lieutenant in the Royal Army Educational Corps (1954–7) and as senior English master at Prior Park College, Bath (1957–61). He was appointed as an assistant lecturer at UCC in 1962 and became professor of Modern English at the college in 1967. His publications include *T.S. Eliot and the Idea of Tradition* (1960) and *Unfinished Sequence and other poems* (1979). He was editor of *Love Poems of the Irish* (1967), *Five Irish Poets* (1970), *Irish Poets in English: Thomas Davis Lectures on Anglo-Irish Poetry* (1973) and *Goldsmith, the gentle master* (1984). Following his retirement, he lived in the United States. He died, following a short illness, at Evanston, Illinois, on 25 July 2001 and was cremated at Skokie, Illinois.

LYNCH, Charles (1906–1984) Born 'Parkgariff', Monkstown, Co. Cork, the son of an army officer. He was privately educated and studied piano at an early age. He won the Elizabeth Stokes Scholarship which enabled him to study at the Royal Academy of Music in London. While there, he took the Westlake Beethoven Prize before leaving the academy in 1924 to pursue further studies. He then embarked on a solo career and broadcast many times on the BBC before the outbreak of World War II. He returned to live in Ireland and performed regularly as a soloist with the RTÉ Symphony Orchestra, the RTÉ String Quartet and many others. He also made several foreign tours. He was in constant demand for piano recitals and for ballet accompaniment, being associated with the Cork Dance Company and with the Cork Ballet Company. In April 1981, he was conferred with an honorary D.Mus. degree by the National University of Ireland. He died at St Finbarr's Hospital, Cork, on 15 September 1984 and was buried in the 'musicians' corner' of St Finbarr's Cemetery. [Bronze bust at the Crawford Municipal Gallery, Cork]

LYNCH, Daniel (1842–1913) Born Baile Bhúirne, Co. Cork, the son of Donncha Ó Loingsigh. He was educated at Wall's School,

Macroom, at St Colman's College, Fermoy and at a school in England before enrolling at the Irish College, Paris, to study for the priesthood. He was there when the Franco-Prussian War broke out in 1870 and enrolled in the Zouave Corps to fight against the Prussians. Following the war, he abandoned his clerical studies and went to America to try his luck on the gold-fields. He returned to Ireland c.1887 and studied at Queen's College, Cork (now UCC) where he graduated in medicine. He was appointed as dispensary doctor at Baile Bhúirne where he spent the remainder of his life. He was determined to develop his native village as an independent entity and was directly responsible for opening both a shop and bakery there. He also established a monthly fair, cookery and dairy classes and a factory to produce knitted socks in the village. With an abiding interest in the Irish language, he was a prominent Connradh na Gaeilge figure at both national and local level. His enthusiasm for and the promotion of Irish at Baile Bhúirne were primarily responsible for the establishment of Coláiste Íosagáin there. He financed the construction of a meeting hall at Ballymakeera to promote the Irish language through concerts, meetings and feiseanna. He died at his residence, 'The Flatts', Baile Bhúirne, on 28 November 1913 and was buried in Reilig Ghobnatan.

LYNCH, Diarmaid C. (1878–1950) Born Granig, Tracton, Co. Cork, the son of Timothy Lynch, farmer. He was educated at Knocknamana NS and was orphaned at the age of 13 years. He became a sorting clerk in Cork GPO before obtaining a clerical post in the Post Office in London. Shortly afterwards, in March 1896, he emigrated to the US at the invitation of an uncle. He worked in a farm machinery business and became an American citizen in 1901. He was active in the Irish language movement in New York and was president of Connradh na Gaeilge in New York State in 1905. Returning to Ireland in July 1907, he became involved in the republican movement and joined the IRB in Dublin in the following year. He moved to

Cork in 1910 and was selected in the following year as divisional 'centre' for South Munster on the IRB Supreme Council. In 1914, he visited the US to raise funds, ostensibly for Connradh na Gaeilge, but also for the Volunteers. He served in the GPO as a staff-captain during the Easter rising. He was sentenced to death for his part in the rising, but this was commuted to ten years penal servitude on account of his US citizenship. On his release in June 1917, he became a member of the re-organised Supreme Council of the IRB. He was arrested and imprisoned in Dundalk Gaol in March 1918 and was served with a deportation order. While in jail, he secretly married Mary Quinn and she joined him later in the US. In the General Election of 1918, he was returned as Sinn Féin MP for Cork. From 1918 to 1932 he lived in the US and was national secretary of the Friends of Irish Freedom. On his return to Dublin in 1932, he undertook a thorough compilation of a record of the GPO garrison in 1916. In July 1938, he left Dublin and briefly resided near Mallow, before returning to his native Tracton in 1939 where he died on 9 November 1950. [His political career notes, edited by **F. O'Donoghue** and published as *The IRB and the 1916 Insurrection* (1957)]

LYNCH, Eamon (*fl.* **1925–1943**) Born Cuskinny, Cobh, Co. Cork. He was educated at Bellevue NS, at UCC and at the King's Inns. He became involved in the trades union movement as a full-time official. He represented the Labour Party on Cobh UDC and on Cork County Council (1925–34). He unsuccessfully contested a Dáil seat in Cork East in 1927 and 1932, and in Dublin South in 1938. In that year, he became a member of Seanad Éireann and served until 1943. He was also secretary of the Irish Trades Union Congress.

LYNCH, Eliza (1835–1886) Born Dundanion, Blackrock, Cork, the daughter of John Lynch, doctor. The family moved to Paris *c.*1845 and Eliza married a French army veterinary surgeon at the age of fourteen. Two years later, she returned to Paris alone and became the mistress of Don Francisco Solano Lopez (*c.*1826–70), the eldest son of the president of Paraguay. When Lopez returned to Paraguay in 1855, 'Madam Lynch' joined him. Following the death of the president in 1862, Don Francisco became president with Eliza as his consort. Two years later, however, Paraguay became involved in a war with the Triple Alliance (Brazil, Argentina and Uruguay). Eliza was made regent of the country while Don Francisco commanded the army. In 1870, he and his eldest son were killed by Brazilian forces and Eliza and her three other children were captured. She eventually returned to France and died, poverty-stricken, in Paris on 25 July 1886. Following the end of the Chaco War with Bolivia in 1932, Eliza's remains were re-interred in the Pantheon of the Heroes in Ascuncion, Paraguay. She was also the subject of two novels. [Life by H.L. Young (1966), and A. Brodsky (1975)]

LYNCH, George (1862–1928) Born Cork, the eldest son of George Lynch and brother of **Rose Lynch**. He travelled widely in the Antipodes in his 20s and contributed to many London newspapers and magazines. His reportage of the Spanish-American War for the *Daily Chronicle* established him as a leading correspondent. He reported on the Boer War for the *Illustrated London News*, was wounded at the Siege of Ladysmith and was captured and imprisoned by the Boers. He subsequently reported from every major theatre of conflict until 1920. His publications include *The War of the Civilisations* (1901) and *Impressions of a War Correspondent* (1903). He died in London on 29 December 1928.

LYNCH, Jack (1917–1999) Born Shandon, Cork, the son of Dan Lynch, tailor, who was a native of Bantry. He was educated at North Monastery CBS from where he entered the Civil Service. He studied at King's Inns and was called to the Bar in 1945. During this time he was making a legendary reputation for Cork (a senior player at the age of 18) on the hurling and football fields. He won five All-Ireland

SHC medals (1941–4 and 1946) and one All-Ireland SFC medal (1945). He also won three NHL medals (1940–1 and 1948) and three Railway Cup hurling medals (1942–4). At club level, he represented Glen Rovers, St Nicholas (the football section of the club) and Civil Service. He retired from the playing field in 1951. He was elected to the Dáil in 1948 as a Fianna Fáil TD for Cork City. Having served as a parliamentary secretary (1951–4), he subsequently held several Cabinet posts – Education (1957–9), Industry and Commerce (1959–65) and Finance (1965–6). In 1966, he succeeded Seán Lemass (1899–1971) both as Taoiseach and as leader of the Fianna Fáil Party. He was returned to office in the general election of 1969 but in the following year, as a result of the Northern Ireland 'Arms Crisis', he sacked two of his ministers (Charles Haughey and Neil Blaney) and accepted the resignations of two others (Kevin Boland and Micheál Ó Móráin). He headed the Irish negotiation team which was responsible for Ireland's admission into the European Economic Community in 1973. In that year, his party lost the general election and he was Leader of the Opposition until the landslide victory of 1977 put him back into power. However, there was growing opposition to him within his party, especially with regard to his policy of Unionist consent to ultimate Irish unity. This opposition was led by Charles Haughey who had been returned by Lynch to the Fianna Fáil front bench in 1975. He resigned as Taoiseach in 1979 following the defeat of his party in two by-elections in Cork and was succeeded by Haughey. He served on the boards of various companies during his retirement and always kept in contact with his native city and county. He died in Dublin on 20 October 1999 and was buried in St Finbarr's Cemetery, Cork. [Life by T.P. O'Mahony (1991), B. Arnold (2001), L. Ó Tuama (2000) and T. Ryle Dwyer (2001); Two bronze life-size busts by **Seamus Murphy** – one in private possession and the other at Fianna Fáil headquarters, Grand Parade; bronze, *in sede*, at Blackpool Shopping Centre]

LYNCH, Joe (1926–2001) Born Mallow, Co. Cork, the son of Jim Lynch, engine driver. He was educated at North Monastery CBS and at Blackrock College, Dublin. A keen sportsman, he turned down an offer to play professional football in England in order to embark on an acting career. He was a member of the Cork Shakespearean Company under the guidance of Rev. **James O'Flynn** and acted part-time at Cork Opera House. He became a member of the Radio Éireann Repertory Company on its foundation in 1947 and soon expanded his career with many radio and singing engagements. He particularly became identified with Radio Éireann's first comedy series, *Living with Lynch*, which ran from 1954 until 1958. He subsequently featured in many films and TV plays, and received highly favourable reviews for his parts as Blazes Boylan in Joyce's *Ulysses* and as Albert Einstein in Albrecht Duerrenmatt's *The Physicists*. However, he is chiefly remembered for his role as Dinny Byrne, initially in Wesley Burrowes' *Bracken* and then in the *Glenroe* series in which he starred from 1983 until 2000 when he left following a dispute over his contract. He died at his retirement home in Alicante, Spain, on 1 August 2001 and was cremated there.

LYNCH, Liam (1890–1923) Born Anglesboro, Co. Limerick. He was the commander of the Cork No. 2 Brigade of the IRA during the War of Independence. He took the anti-Treaty side during the Civil War and became chief-of-staff of the Irregular Forces. He died at St Joseph's Hospital, Clonmel, on 10 April 1923, following a shoot-out with Free State soldiers at Knocknafallen, Newcastle, nr. Clogheen, on the previous day. His request to be buried near his friend, **Michael Fitzgerald**, who had died on hunger strike, was honoured by General Prout of the Free State Army. He was buried in Kilcrumper Cemetery. His death signalled the virtual end of the Civil War when his successor as chief-of-staff, Frank Aiken (1898–1983), called a unilateral cease-fire on 30 April.

LYNCH, Patricia (1898–1972) Born Sunday's Well, Cork. On the death of her father, she was brought to London as a child. She was educated in London, Scotland, and Bruges. During the Easter Rising of 1916, she was sent to Dublin by the leader of the English suffragette movement, Mrs Emmeline Pankhurst (1858–1928), to report for the *Worker's Dreadnought*. This report was published in pamphlet form under the title, *Rebel Ireland.* She later settled in Dublin, having married the socialist writer, M.F. Fox, in London in 1922. She became a prolific writer of children's stories and the fifty or so books which she published included *The Cobbler's Apprentice* (1932), *The Turf Cutter's Donkey* (1935) and *Brogeen of the Stepping Stones* (1947). In 1967, she was elected as a member of the Irish Academy of Letters. She died on 1 September 1972. [Autobiographical early life (1947); Life by P. Young (2005)]

LYNCH, Rose (1872–1940) Born St Luke's, Cork, the second daughter of George Lynch and sister of **George Lynch**. A deeply religious woman with a devotion to Our Lady of Lourdes, she inaugurated juvenile pilgrimages to Lourdes and Rome in the late Twenties and early Thirties. She was commissioner of the Cork Girl Guides and her organisational talents were put at the disposal of many charitable causes. She also established the Saint Patrick's Lunch Room on Patrick's Quay where meals were provided for the poor. She was the author of two books on Lourdes and three novels *Mary Alannah* (1923), *The West a' Calling* (1925) and *The Call of the Orient* (n.d.). Her *Life in Many Lands* (1928) was a book of short stories. She died at the Bon Secours Hospital, Cork, on 2 January 1940 and was buried privately.

LYON, William (d. 1617) Born Chester, England. He was educated at Oxford and came to Ireland in 1570 as chaplain to the Lord Deputy, Lord Gray. He was consecrated as bishop of Ross (1582), while the dioceses of Cork (1583) and Cloyne (1586) were added to his temporalities. He built residences in Cork and at Rosscarbery. He improved the incomes of the dioceses of Cork and Ross but was unable to recover the see lands at Cloyne which had been alienated during the episcopate of his predecessor, **Mathew Sheyne**, to **Sir John Fitzedmund Fitzgerald** of Cloyne for £40. Lyon tried many times to recover the lands but failed each time as Fitzgerald had great influence (the lands were eventually restored in the 1660s). He died on 4 October 1617 and was buried in St FinBarre's Cathedral. [Portrait at episcopal residence, Cork]

LYONS, Francis (1795–1865) Born Cork, the son of Thomas Lyons, founder of the family wholesale drapery company. He was educated at the University of Paris and at Edinburgh University where he graduated MD (1822) but never practised. Having obtained his degree, he spent several years on the Continent. He subsequently joined his brother, Thomas, in the management of T. Lyons & Co. A Liberal in politics, he was elected as MP for Cork City in an 1859 by-election and sat until he resigned his seat in 1865. He had been in poor health for some years and died at his residence, 32, South Terrace, Cork, on 6 May 1865. He was buried in St Joseph's Cemetery.

LYONS, Peter (1735–1809) Born County Cork, the son of John Lyons. As a young man, he left Ireland to study law under his uncle, John Power of King William County, Virginia, and qualified as a lawyer in 1756. He eventually took over his uncle's practice and became one of the state's most noted lawyers. He was appointed as a judge of the general court of Virginia in 1779 and was advanced to the presidency of the Virginia Court of Appeal in 1803. He retired in 1807 and died in Hanover County, Virginia, on 30 July 1809.

LYONS, Robert S.D. (1826–1886) Born Cork, the son of Sir William Lyons, merchant, and mayor of Cork on two occasions (1848–9). He was educated at TCD where he graduated MB (1848). During the Crimean War, he became pathologist-in-chief to the British forces (1855–6). He returned to Dublin when he was appointed as professor of Medicine to the Catholic University and was elected as a member of the Royal Irish Academy. He also took a great interest in the reforestation of Ireland. He was elected as a Liberal MP for Dublin City (1880–5). He died in Dublin on 19 December 1886. His publications included *An Apology for the Microscope* (1851), *A Handbook of Hospital Practice* (1859), *A Treatise on Fever* (1861), *The Intellectual Resources of Ireland* (1873) and *Forest Areas in Europe and America, and probable future Timber Supplies* (1884).

LYSAGHT, Sidney R. (1856–1941) Born Hazlewood, near Mallow, Co. Cork, the eldest son of T.R. Lysaght, architect. He travelled widely before returning to Ireland in the early 1900s when he established a successful nursery business at Raheen, Co. Clare. He was the author of nine published works (including four novels) of which the better known were *Her Majesty's Rebels* (1907) and *My Tower in Desmond* (1925). He was the father of Dr Edward (Mac)Lysaght (1887–1986), the genealogist and historian. He died at Hazlewood on 20 August 1941.

LYSTER, Richard (1828–1863) Born Cork. He worked as a clerk and showing a talent for sketching and drawing, his employer, a Mr Murphy, helped him to travel to Rome to study. He remained there for five years and then returned to his native city. He exhibited at the Royal Hibernian Academy from 1858 to 1862. He died of consumption at his residence in Cove Street on 1 August 1863. [Commemorative plaque at his former residence, 43/44 Patrick's Street, Cork]

M

McADOO Henry R. (1916–1998) Born Ballintemple, Cork. He was educated at Cork Grammar School, Mountjoy School and TCD where he graduated in Irish and French (1938) and was conferred DD in 1939. He was ordained in the same year and served as dean of Cork from 1952 to 1962. In that year, he was elected as Church of Ireland bishop of Ossory, Ferns and Leighlin. He was advanced to the archbishopric of Dublin in 1977 and remained there until his retirement in 1985. He acted as co-chairman of the Anglican/Roman Catholic International Commission (ARCIC 1) and was instrumental in the production of the *Final Report* of 1982. He retired through ill health in 1985. He died at St Vincent's Hospital, Dublin, on 10 December 1998 and was buried at St Canice's Cathedral, Kilkenny. His publications include *The Structure of Caroline Moral Theology* (1949), *The Spirit of Anglicanism* (1965), *The Eucharistic Theology of Jeremy Taylor* (1988) and *The First of its Kind: Jeremy Taylor's Life of Christ* (1994).

McAULIFFE, Jack (1866–1937) Born Christ Church Lane, Cork, the son of Cornelius McAuliffe, cooper. The family emigrated to America when Jack was six years of age and settled in Brooklyn, New York, where he later took up boxing as a lightweight. In February 1886, he became to first Irish-born boxer to take a world title when he defeated the American, Jack Hooper, at lightweight. In the following six years, he successfully defended his title on six occasions. His most famous 'battle' was against Jem Carney of England at a secret venue (an old barn at Revere, Massachusetts) when the contest was declared a draw after seventy-four rounds and when a riot broke out at the decision. He came out of retirement in 1896 and fought on four occasions until he finally bowed out in the following year. Out of a total of seventy-seven bouts, he never had a decision against him. The 'Napoleon of the Ring' died at Forest Hills, New York, on 4 November 1937.

McAULIFFE, Patrick (1914–1989) Born Boherbue, Newmarket, Co. Cork, the son of Edmund McAuliffe. He was elected to Cork County Council for the Kanturk electoral area in 1942 and retained his seat at every local election up to 1979. He resigned in March 1985 on health grounds. He was unsuccessful as a Labour Dáil candidate in Cork North in 1943. However, he became a TD for that seat in the following year. He retained this seat at every election until his defeat in 1969 in the newly created North East Cork constituency. He was chairman of the now defunct Joint Cork Sanitoria Board for twenty years and also chairman of Cork Health Authority for nine years. He died on 13 October 1989 at St Colman's Hospital, Mallow, and was buried at Boherbue Cemetery.

MAC CARTAIN, Liam (1688–1724) Born Carrignavar, Co. Cork. Liam 'An Dúna' served with the forces of James II at the battles of the Boyne, Aughrim and Limerick. Following the war, he returned to his farm at Carrignavar. In 1705, he became head of the Blarney Court of Poetry (Cúirt Éigse na Blárnan) until his death in November 1724. He was buried at Whitechurch Graveyard, Blarney.

MacCARTHY, Aidan (1913–1995) Born Castletownbere, Co. Cork. He was educated at UCC and graduated as a medical doctor in 1938. Just before the outbreak of World War II, he joined the RAF and was stationed as medical officer at a base in East Anglia. While there, he rescued a pilot from a blazing plane which had hit an explosives dump – an action for which he was awarded the George Cross. He escaped from Dunkirk during the British retreat and was then posted to Java where he was interned by the Japanese. While being transported to a camp in Japan, the ship was torpedoed by an American submarine. He spent twelve hours in the water before being picked up by a Japanese destroyer, being beaten up, and being dumped back again into the sea. Eventually he was picked up by Japanese fishermen and was subsequently interned at a Nagasaki camp where only forty-two of the 1,000 prisoners there survived. After the war, he continued his service with the RAF and rose to the rank of air commodore. He died at his residence at Northwood, near London c.25 October 1995. He published an account of his experiences in *A Doctor's War* (1979).

McCARTHY, Alexander (1803–1868) Born Cork, the eldest son of Alexander McCarthy, a wealthy landowner who was descended from the McCarthys of Drishane. He was called to the Irish Bar in 1826 and entered parliamentary politics in 1832 when he unsuccessfully contested Limerick County as a Repealer. In 1846, he was elected unopposed as a Repeal MP for Cork City on the resignation of **Francis S. Murphy**, but lost his seat in the general election of the following year. He was again unsuccessful in a by-election for Cork City in 1849 when he stood as a Liberal. This was followed by a similar result in a Cork County by-election in 1855 before a successful return for that constituency in 1857. He did not seek re-election in 1859 but was persuaded to stand, albeit unsuccessfully, for Dublin City. He was elected as highsheriff for Cork City in 1856. He died on 2 January 1868 at his residence, 37 Upper Fitzwilliam Street, Dublin. McCarthy owned substantial property in Blackrock and Ballintemple, paying c.£14,000 for Lord Gort's Blackrock estate. His brother and heir, Daniel McCarthy, erected an elaborate memorial tower, designed by Cork arctitect, **William Atkins**, to Alexander's memory at Diamond Hill, Blackrock Road.

McCARTHY, Bartholomew (1843–1904) Born Ballynoe, Co. Cork. He was educated at St Colman's College, Fermoy, and in Rome where he graduated DD. He was ordained there in 1869 and returned to Ireland to teach for three years at St Colman's. He subsequently ministered at Mitchelstown, Macroom and Youghal, before being appointed as parish priest of Inniscarra in 1895. A German and Celtic scholar, he was Todd Professor of Celtic Languages at the Royal Irish Academy and Examiner in Celtic at the Royal University of Ireland. His annotated commentary on the Stowe Missal was published in the *Transactions* of the RIA in 1886. Later articles for the RIA included 'New textual Studies on the Tripartite Life of St Patrick' (1889) and the editing of volumes ii, iii and iv of *The Annals of Ulster* (1893–1901). His *The Codex Palatino-Vaticanus, No. 830; An 11th Century Irish MS. by Maranus Scotus* was also published by the RIA. He had almost completed an edition of the *Annals of Tighernach* when he died at Inniscarra on 5 March 1904. He was buried in the grounds of Macroom Church.

McCARTHY, Bridget G. (1904–1993) Born Cork. She graduated BA and MA at UCC and later took a PhD degree at Cambridge University. She was appointed as lecturer in Education at Craiglockhart Training College, Edinburgh, and in 1947, was appointed as professor of English Literature at UCC. She was the author of *Women Writers: their contribution to the English novel, 1621–1744* (1944) and *The Later Women Novelists, 1744–1818* (1947). These were volumes i and ii of *The Female Pen*, under which title they were reprinted in a single volume by Cork University Press (1994). She also wrote *Browning's Psychology of Genius* (1936). Her play, 'The Whip Hand: an Irish comedy', was produced at the Abbey Theatre in July 1942 and was staged by many amateur drama groups in later years. She edited *Some Problems of Child Welfare* (1945) and *Despite Fools' Laughter: poems of* **Terence MacSwiney** (1944). She also contributed essays to *Studies* and *The Dublin Magazine*. She died at Rosenalee Convalescant Home, Ballincollig, on 24 April 1993 and was buried in St Finbarr's Cemetery.

McCARTHY, Charles (1814–1896) Born Blarney, Co. Cork, the son of Denis McCarthy, farmer. He studied medicine in Glasgow, married in 1849, and emigrated to Melbourne, Australia, in 1853. He later took further medical degrees at the University of Melbourne. He took a great interest in the treatment of alcoholism and opposed the imprisonment of drunkards in the company of lunatics or criminals. In 1871, the government of Victoria established a centre to which alcoholics would have to go for treatment if ordered to do so by the courts. McCarthy was appointed as secretary and medical officer to the new establishment which opened in October 1873. The idea was ahead of its time and soon practical difficulties surfaced. The government subsidy was withdrawn and McCarthy was left unpaid for a year. Eventually, the centre was only open to paying patients. In 1877, McCarthy bought the property from the trustees. This was later challenged in court and eventually, in 1889, the government took over the whole project while McCarthy was employed to run it pending the appointment of a new superintendent. He died at Hawthorn, Victoria, on 29 February 1896.

McCARTHY, Charles (1924–1986) Born Cork, a member of a well-known family of Emmet Place plumbing contractors. He was educated at PBC, Cork; UCD and King's Inns where he was called to the Bar in 1958. Following a period as an actor with the Radio Éireann Players (whom he joined in 1948), he became a vocational schoolteacher and took an interest in trades union affairs. He served as general secretary of the Vocational Teachers' Association (VTA) for a period of eighteen years and was president of the Irish Congress of Trades Unions (ICTU) in 1963/64. He was appointed as lecturer (and later professor) in Industrial Relations at TCD in 1977. He subsequently headed the School of Business Studies there and was elected a fellow of that college. He acted as a consultant and mediator in many industrial disputes and was also as chairman of the board of the Abbey Theatre and

of the RTE Authority (1973–6). He died at his Dublin residence on 8 September 1986 and was buried in St Fintan's Cemetery, Sutton. His publications include *The Distasteful Challenge* (1968), *Industrial Democracy* (1971) and *Trades Unions in Ireland* (1977).

McCARTHY, Charles J.F. (1912–1999) Born Kenmare, Co. Kerry, the son of Thomas J. McCarthy, journalist and court stenographer. The family moved to Cork when he was two years old. He was educated at PBC, Cork; and at UCC where he graduated MComm. (1929). He then qualified as an accountant and, following some years with the firm Atkins, Chirnside & Co., he joined the Dwyer Group in 1941 where he remained until his retirement in 1972 as Group Secretary and Director. He was area operations officer in the Local Defence Force (LDF) during the Emergency and published a handbook (*Regional Defence*) for use by the local forces. He joined the Cork Historical & Archaeological Society in 1929 and made the first of many contributions to the *JCHAS* in 1932. In his latter years, he contributed a series of articles, *An Antiquary's Notebook*, comprising of notes on a varied range of historical topics. He also contributed articles to the *Evening Echo* and to other County Cork historical journals. He compiled and published privately monographs on topics such as *Early Medieval Cork* (1969) and *Cork Families* (1973). A member of the CHAS for seventy years and its president (1965–7), he was the last of the Cork antiquarian scholars and in his retirement enjoyed the role of the *eminence grise* of Cork local history. 'CJF' (as he was widely known) died at Cuskinny Nursing Home, Cobh, on 28 January 1999 and was buried in St Finbarr's Cemetery, Cork.

MAC CARTHY, Cormac ['Láidir'] (d. 1495) He was the son of Tadhg MacCarthy (d. 1448), Lord of Muskerry and father of **Cormac 'Láidir Óg' Mac Carthy**. He was the builder of Blarney Castle, Kilcrea Abbey and Ballymacadane Abbey. Blarney then became his principal residence. Following a skirmish at Dripsey between him and some of his relatives, he was wounded and died in Cork City. He was buried at Kilcrea Abbey.

MAC CARTHY, Cormac ['Láidir Óg'] (d. 1536) He was the son of **Cormac 'Láidir' Mac Carthy**. He carried on his father's policy of loyalty to the English Crown and this brought him into conflict with the powerful Desmond Geraldines whom he defeated at the battle of Mourneabbey in 1520. He died in 1536 and was buried at Kilcrea Abbey.

MAC CARTHY, Dermot (d. 1552) An Augustinian priest, he was appointed as bishop of Ross on June 6, 1526. He assisted at the consecration of **Dominic Tirry** as bishop of Cork and Cloyne in late September 1536.

MAC CARTHY, Donagh (c.1654–1726) He was of the Mac Carthy Reagh sept, the son of Seán Buí Mac Carthy and brother of the poet, Diarmaid Mac Sheáin Bhuí Mac Carthy. He studied on the Continent and was ordained in France in 1674. He graduated DD from the University of Paris in the same year. He returned to Ireland and ministered at Shandon, Cork. He was appointed by Bishop **John Baptist Sleyne** as vicar-general of the united dioceses of Cork and Cloyne in December 1707 and as coadjutor bishop on 16 August 1713 (eighteen months after Sleyne's death). He was arrested in late 1721 and died at North Gate Bridge Gaol, Cork, in March 1726. He was buried in Shandon Graveyard. [Sketch by **E. Bolster**, *A History of the Diocese of Cork* (1989), pp.34–44, 59–60]

MAC CARTHY, Donough (1594–1665) He succeeded his father as 2nd Viscount Muskerry in 1620 and was the grand-uncle of **Donough Mac Carthy (1668–1734)**. He fought on the Royalist side in the Confederate Wars and was a prominent member of the Confederation of Kilkenny. Blarney Castle was captured in 1649 and his other castles soon after. The campaign ended when he surrendered Ross Castle in 1652.

He lived in exile with King Charles II during the Cromwellian period and was created earl of Clancarty in 1658. At the Restoration in 1660, most of his former estates were restored under the Act of Settlement. He died in London in 1665.

MAC CARTHY, Donough (1668–1734) Born Blarney Castle, Co. Cork, a grand-nephew of **Donagh Mac Carthy (1594–1665)**, 1st earl of Clancarty. In 1676, he succeeded his uncle, Callaghan Mac Carthy, as 4th earl of Clancarty. In 1684, at the age of 16, he was married to the daughter of the earl of Sunderland, 11-year old Lady Elizabeth Spencer. He took the side of James II in the Williamite War, was attainted, and his estates were forfeited. Having escaped to France from the Tower of London in 1694, he returned four years later to strengthen his position by consummating his marriage. He was once again arrested but released on a pension of £300 a year subject to his residing abroad. His wife was granted £2,000 a year as compensation for the loss of the estates. He died in Hamburg on 19 September 1734.

MAC CARTHY, Florence (c.1562–1640) Florence 'Reagh' was born probably at Kilbrittain Castle, the son of Sir Donagh Mac Carthy Reagh, Lord Carbery. His marriage in 1588 to the daughter of Domhnall Mac Carthy Mór caused resentment to the English interest as primarily represented by Sir Valentine Browne who had hoped to have 'bagged' the Mac Carthy heiress for his own son. Florence was imprisoned in the Tower of London for this act and was also later accused of treason in the events surrounding the battle of Kinsale. He spent the remainder of his life in London – for the most part being imprisoned there. He was the author of 'Mac Cárthaigh's Book' which was copied for him in 1633 and which recounts much of Munster's history. He was buried at the Church of St Martin-in-the-Fields, London, on 18 December 1640. [Life and Letters by D. McCarthy (1867)]

McCARTHY, Florence (1761–1810) Born Macroom, Co. Cork. He was educated at the

Irish College in Rome where he took his DD degree. In 1803, he was appointed as vicar-general of Cork and (titular) bishop of Antinae. He caught a fever while attending a dying man and died in Cork in 1810.

McCARTHY, J. Bernard (1888–1979) Born Crosshaven, Co. Cork, where he worked as a postman. He was a prolific writer of plays, short stories, and novels. Four of his plays 'Kinship' (1914), 'The Supplanter' (1914), 'Crusaders' (1919) and 'Garranbraher' (1923), were produced at the Abbey Theatre, while many of his short stories were produced by the Catholic Truth Society. He also published three novels *Covert* (1925), *Possessions* (1926) and *Exile's Bread* (1927). He died on 18 January 1979 and was buried in Rathcooney Graveyard.

McCARTHY, Jeremiah (*c.*1758–1828) Born Co. Cork, the son of Calahan McCarthy. In 1777, he joined the Prince of Wales's American Regiment in New York State and two years later he was living in St Thomas, Quebec, running an army supply store and owning a farm. He developed an interest in land surveying and from 1783 to 1792 he had surveyed the entire landscape from the shores of the St Lawrence River to the Appalachian Mountains. He then spent a further four years (1792–5) on a survey of the St Lawrence River itself. He became involved in land-grant surveys, an area in which his career took a downward turn as his work was often successfully challenged in court suits by many complainants. While living in Quebec, he opened a mathematics school to 'teach a few young Gentlemen (not exceeding six at a time)… EUCLID'S ELEMENTS or GEOMETRY, TRIGONOMETRY both Plain and Spherical, ALGEBRA, ASTRONOMY, CONICK SECTIONS, GEOGRAPHY, or the use of the GLOBES and MAPS, MENSURATION, GUAGING, GUNNERY, FORTIFICATION, ARCHITECTURE, DIALLING MECHANICKS, and SURVEYING in all its branches both in Theory and Practice'. The courses, which were offered in French and English, produced many future surveyors. He died on 29 June 1828 in St Hyacinthe, Lower Canada.

McCARTHY, John (1815–1893) Born Fermoy, Co. Cork. He was educated locally and at St Patrick's College, Maynooth, where he was ordained in 1842. He served both as a curate and as parish priest of Mallow before his elevation to the see of Cloyne on 28 October 1874. He died on 9 December 1893 and was buried in the vault of St Colman's Cathedral, Queenstown (now Cobh). His *Relatio Status* of October 1880 provided an extensive profile of his diocese.

McCARTHY, John George (1829–1892) Born South Main Street, Cork. He worked as a solicitor and land agent. He was elected as a Home Rule MP for Mallow (1874–80) and was appointed, in 1885, as one of two commissioners to carry out the provisions of the Land Purchase Act of that year. He was president of Cork Catholic Young Men's Society and was made a Knight of St Gregory by Pope Leo XIII (1810–1903). He died in London on 7 September 1892 and was buried in Glasnevin Cemetery, Dublin. His publications included *A Small History of Cork* (1869), *Irish Land Questions, plainly stated and answered* (1870), *A Plea for Home Rule Government of Ireland* (1871), *The French Revolution of 1792* (1884) and *Henry Grattan, a Historical Study* (1886). [Sketch by T. Cadogan in *Mallow Field Journal* (1994); Commemorative plaque at CYMS premises, North Main Street, Cork]

McCARTHY, John W. (1854–1935) Born Kilworth, Co. Cork, the son of J. McCarthy. He was educated at Kilkenny College and at Queen's College, Cork (now UCC). In 1876, he was employed as a member of the British consular service in Japan and became the private secretary of the Japanese minister for Foreign Affairs in 1879 (to 1882). He studied law at Gray's Inn and was called to the English Bar in 1886. He served as counsel to the Chinese legation in London (1892–1902), before being appointed a judge of the county courts in Durham and Yorkshire. He was elected a Bencher of Gray's Inn in 1909. He retired from the Bench in 1929 and died in Harrogate, Yorkshire, on 19 July 1935.

Mac CARTHY, Justin (*c.*1643–1694) Born Co. Cork, the third son of **Donough Mac Carthy**, the 1st earl of Clancarty. He married a daughter of the earl of Strafford and served in Irish and English regiments in the pay of France. Following the accession to the English throne of King James II in 1685, he returned to Ireland and assisted the lord lieutenant, the earl of Tyrconnell, in removing Protestant officers from the army. He was created Viscount Mountcashel by James on his arrival in Ireland in 1689. Following the Jacobite defeat at Newtownbutler on 31 July 1689, he escaped from captivity and made his way to France where he later commanded the Irish Brigade in Savoy, Catalonia and in the Rhineland. He died at Bareges on 1 July 1694. [Life by J.A. Murphy (1959); Portrait by Sir P. Lely]

McCARTHY, Justin (1830–1912) Born Cork, the elder son of Michael F. McCarthy, a magistrates' clerk. In 1848, he began work as a journalist for the *Cork Examiner*. He left for Liverpool in 1852, settled in London in 1860 and became editor of the *Morning Star* (1864–8). In 1870, he moved to the *Daily News* as a leader writer. He entered politics and sat as a member of the Irish Parliamentary Party for Longford (1879) and for Derry City (1886–92). Following the 'Parnell Split' of 1890, he was chosen as chairman of the anti-Parnellite faction which he led until his resignation in 1896. He retired from active politics in 1900. In 1903, he was awarded a pension of £300 a year on the Civil List. He died at Folkestone, Kent, on 24 April 1912. His publications include *A Fair Saxon* (1873), *Dear Lady Disdain* (1875), *Miss Anthrope* (1878), *A History of Our Own Times* (5 vols, 1879), *Mononia* (1901) and *The Story of an Irishman* (1904). He co-edited *Irish Literature* (10 vols, 1904). [Life by E.J. Doyle (1996); Reminiscences (1899); Irish Recollections (1911)]

McCARTHY, M. Donal (1908–1980) Born Midleton, Co. Cork. He was educated at Rockwell College, UCC, and London University where he was awarded a doctorate in Statistics.

In 1931, he was appointed as a lecturer in Mathematics at UCC and later as professor of Mathematical Physics there in 1944 (to 1949). In 1949, he was appointed as deputy director of the Central Statistics Office and became director in 1957. He was director of the Economic and Social Research Institute on its foundation in 1966. He was elected as president of UCC in 1967 and served his term which ended in 1978. A member of the Carrigtohill club, he won an All-Ireland SHC medal with Cork in 1929. He died in 1980.

McCARTHY, Michael J.F. (1863–1928) Born Clonmult, Co. Cork, the son of a farmer. He was educated at Midleton CBS, Midleton College and TCD. He was called to the Bar in 1889. An anti-Home Ruler, he stood as a candidate for the St Stephen's Green Division, Dublin, in the general election of 1904 but eventually withdrew to avoid a split in the Unionist vote. However, his reputation rests with the many ponderous anti-Roman Catholic polemical works which he wrote. These include, *Five Years in Ireland, 1895–1900* (1901), *Priests and People in Ireland* (1902, 4th ed., 1914), *Galloglass, or, Life in the Land of the Priests* (1904), *Rome in Ireland* (1904) and *Irish Land and Irish Liberty: a study of the new lords of the soil* (1911). He had moved to England in 1904 and died at his Wimbledon residence in the last days of October 1928.

McCARTHY, Niall (1925–1992) Born Cork, the son of Joseph A. McCarthy, a judge of the Circuit Court. He was educated at Dun Laoghaire CBS, Clongowes Wood College and UCD where he graduated BA (1945). He was called to the Bar in 1946 and to the Inner Bar in 1959. He became a bencher of the King's Inns in 1975. Following a distinguished career in practice, in which he acted for the State in the McGee contraception case, defended Charles Haughey in the 1970 Arms Trial, and acted for Gulf Oil following the Whiddy Island disaster, he was appointed as a judge of the Supreme Court in 1982. He had served as chairman of the

Bar Council from 1980 until 1982. He was also appointed as chairman of the National Archives Advisory Council in 1986. While motoring with his wife in Spain, both were killed in a car accident on 1 October 1992. They were buried in Dean's Grange Cemetery, Dublin.

MAC CARTHY, Robert (1686–1770) Born Blarney Castle, Co. Cork, the son of **Donough Mac Carthy**, 4th earl of Clancarty. He succeeded as the 5th Earl on his father's death in 1734. As he was unable to obtain the return of his father's confiscated estates, he resigned his commission as a captain in the English Navy. He settled in France, and, on joining the army there, he received an annual pension of £1,000 and entertained regally in his chateau at Boulogne. He was heavily involved in the planning of the Jacobite rising in Scotland in 1745. He died in poor circumstances at Boulogne in 1770 – the last of his line. His illegitimate son, Robert, returned to Ireland at the outbreak of the French Revolution and was buried in the family vault at Kilcrea Abbey.

McCARTHY, Seán (1890–1974) Born Dunkereen, Upton, Co. Cork. He was educated at Knockavilla NS and at De la Salle Training College, Waterford, where he graduated in 1911. He later studied at UCC where he graduated BA and H.Dip. He worked as a teacher in Ringaskiddy, Brooklodge, Whitechurch, and at Blarney Street CBS. From 1919 to 1923, he was active as a justice in the Dáil and Sinn Féin Courts. He was chief liaison officer, Martial Law Area and liason officer (IRA) for County Cork in 1921. He took the Republican side in the Civil War and became Director of Publicity at the IRA headquarters at the Four Courts (1922–3). He later joined a West Cork active service unit, was sentenced to death and went on a thirty-eight-day hunger strike. He was subsequently imprisoned in Cork, Mountjoy Gaol and the Curragh Camp. He was elected as a Fianna Fáil TD for the Cork South East constituency in 1944, having been unsuccessful in the same constituency in the previous year.

He stood for Cork Borough in 1948, but was defeated. However, he won this seat in 1951 and remained a TD until his retirement in 1965. He was also a member of Cork Corporation (1945–67) and of Cork County Council (1945–67). He served as lord mayor of Cork on five occasions (1949/50, 1950/51, 1958/59, 1963/64, and for two months in 1967 following the death of **Seán Casey**). He was also intimately connected with the GAA. He became a member of the Cork County Board in 1913, representing his home club, Knockavilla. He served as chairman of the County Board (1917–37) and was elected as Life Honorary President in 1937. He was chairman of the Munster GAA Council for two periods (1929–32 and 1937–40) and president of the GAA (1932–5) which included the Golden Jubilee year of 1934. He wrote in the *Cork Weekly Examiner* under the pseudonym, 'Carbery'. He died in the Mercy Hospital, Cork, on 14 March 1974 and was buried in Innishannon Cemetery.

MAC CARTHY, Teige (c.1664–1747) Teige 'Rábach' was born (probably) at Timoleague, Co. Cork. He was educated at the Irish College, Paris, and was appointed as bishop of Cork and Cloyne on 7 April 1727 (consecrated in the following July or August). In 1730, he built a chapel on the present site of the North Cathedral and lived in Roebuck (a corruption of 'Rábach') Lane, off Shandon Street. He also acted as administrator of the diocese of Ross from 1733. In failing health, he petitioned for a coadjutor bishop in July 1746. No appointment was made before his death on 20 August 1747. He was buried in Shandon Graveyard. [Sketch by E. Bolster in *A History of the Diocese of Cork* (1989), pp. 44–58, 61–4]

McCARTHY, Timothy (c.1865–1928) Born Cloghroe, Inniscarra, Co. Cork, the eldest son of Denis McCarthy, farmer. Having been educated locally, he joined the staff of the *Cork Herald* and served his apprenticeship as a junior reporter in the days of the Land League. He moved to Dublin in 1893 and was associated for several years with the *Freeman's Journal* and the *Dublin Evening Telegraph*. He was also the acting editor of the *Irish People*, the organ of the United Irish League. In 1902, he served a three-month prison sentence for attacking Wyndham's Coercion Act. He spent two years in London, before returning to Ireland as the editor of the *Ulster Herald* group of newspapers. In November 1906, he was appointed as editor of the *Irish News*, the leading nationalist daily in Ulster. An associate of the nationalist leader, Joe Devlin, he pursued an official Home Rule Party approach in the *Irish News*, opposing the revolutionary and physical force movements. Having been in failing health for some months, he died at his Belfast residence on the Antrim Road on 30 December 1928.

McCARTHY, Welbore (1841–1925) Born Cork. He was descended from the Durrus branch of the MacCarthys. He was educated at TCD where he graduated. He entered the Church of England in 1867 and left to minister in India in 1874. He was appointed as archdeacon of Calcutta in 1892. He returned to England and was appointed as bishop of Grantham in 1905. He retired in 1918 and died at Ealing on 21 March 1925.

MACARTNEY, John A. (1834–1917) Born Creagh, Skibbereen, Co. Cork, the son of Hussey Burgh Macartney, clergyman. He was educated at Lucan School and by private tutors in Dublin. When the family moved to Melbourne, Australia, in 1848, he studied law and was appointed as judge-associate to **Sir Redmond Barry**. However, he gave up the law for the open spaces of Queensland and Northern Territory where he became a legend as a horseman and a horse-station owner. He also gained, through his many horse-rides, a reputation as an explorer and was elected as a fellow of the Royal Geographical Society in 1880. He died at Cleveland, Queensland, on 10 July 1917. [Autobiography (1909)]

McCAURA, Gerald (1871–1941) Born Skibbereen, Co. Cork, the son of Florence McCarthy, cooper. He emigrated to the United States c.1890 where he adopted the surname 'McCaura', probably a corruption of 'Mac Cárthaigh'. Having an inventive mind, he went to work in the laboratories of Thomas A. Edison (1847–1931). His best-known invention was the 'Pulsocon' or 'Oscilectron' – an apparatus for the electrical treatment of rheumatism, which he marketed widely. On his return to Ireland, he promoted the Pulsocon and also exhibited his skills in hypno-therapy, claiming to cure addictions such as smoking. He purchased a house at Lough Ine, Skibbereen, and was a benefactor of the National Volunteers. In 1915, he founded the Macaura Volunteer Band (now St Fachtna's Silver Band) and established the town's first cinema (The Kinemac) in 1917. He later purchased a large estate at Killymoon, Co. Tyrone. He died in May 1941.

Mac CURTAIN, Tomás (1884–1920) Born Ballyknockane, Burnfort, Co. Cork. He was educated at Burnfort NS and at North Monastery CBS. On leaving school, he took up the post of clerk at the City of Cork Steam Packet Company. He joined Connradh na Gaeilge and became the secretary of the Blackpool Craobh in 1902. In 1907, he joined the Cork Branch of Sinn Féin and became a member of the IRB. He was a contributor to Terence MacSwiney's short-lived 1914 newspaper, *Fianna Fáil*. At the time of the 1916 Rising, he obeyed Eoin MacNeill's orders to abort the planned insurrection and following a week's stand-off with the military, he surrendered the IRA weapons. Subsequently he spent the following two years in various English prisons. Having won a seat on Cork Corporation, he was elected on 30 January 1920 as the first Sinn Féin lord mayor of Cork. Seven weeks later, on 20 March, he was murdered by an RIC group operating from King Street (now MacCurtain Street) Station. A subsequent coroner's inquest found the RIC guilty of wilful murder. [Life by **Florence O'Donoghue** (1958); Larger than life-size bronze by **Seamus Murphy** at City Hall, Cork]

Mac DÓMHNAILL, Seán (1691–1754) Seán 'Clárach' was born in Charleville, Co. Cork. He was educated at the Charity School which had been founded by **Roger Boyle**, 1st earl of Orrery. He was a mill owner, a farmer, and a teacher, as well a being a firm Jacobite supporter – a trait which is always to the fore in his poetry. He often presided over the bardic school of poetry at Croom, Co. Limerick, and even more often he clashed with several of the major Munster poets of his time. He also made a copy of Geoffrey Keating's *Foras Feasa ar Éirinn* in 1720. In 1737, he was forced to leave his home as a result of a satirical poem ['Bás Dawson' ('The Death of Dawson')] on the death of a Tipperary landlord. He died on 7 January 1754. [Life and works by R. Ó Foghludha (1934); Headstone by **Seamus Murphy** at Holy Cross Cemetery, Charleville]

MacDONALD, Daniel (1821–1853) Born Cork, the son of **James MacDonald**. Like his father, he developed a talent for pen and ink portraits and caricatures, and exhibited at the Royal Hibernian Academy (1842–4). He also exhibited at the British Institution (1847, 1849–51) and at the Royal Academy (1853). His promising career was terminated by his sudden death in 1853.

MacDONALD, James (1789–p.1842) Born Cork as James McDaniel which he later changed to MacDonald. He was the father of **Daniel MacDonald**. He excelled in pen and ink drawings and in caricature. His pen sketches were exhibited at **Richard Milliken**'s Munster Exhibition of 1815. He later exhibited at the Royal Irish Academy in 1832. He lived in Patrick Street.

McDONALD, John B. (1844–1911) Born Fermoy, Co. Cork, the son of Bartholomew McDonald. The family emigrated to New York in 1847. Having worked as an inspector on railroad and dam projects, he established himself as a railroad contractor and became involved in railroad and tunnelling work in ten different states. One of his successes was the construction (1890–4) of a 3.2km (2 miles) tunnel under the city of Baltimore which connected two railway lines. However, his greatest challenge came when his company was awarded the $35,000,000 contract for the New York subway project. He took personal control of the whole operation from start to finish – a finish which was well within the time limit assigned to the operation. He also built the Jerome Park Water Reservoir in New York City – the biggest of its time. He was a bidder for the construction of the Panama Canal, but, much to his disappointment, the United States Government decided to directly undertake the work. He died in New York on 17 March 1911 with the funeral ceremonies being conducted at St Patrick's Cathedral. During the obsequies, the power on the New York Subway was switched off for two minutes as a mark of respect.

McDONALD, Sir John D. (1826–1908) Born Cork, the son of James McDonald, artist. He was educated at the Cork School of Medicine and at King's College Medical School, London. He joined the British Navy as an assistant surgeon in 1849. He was involved in a survey and exploration of microscopic life of the South West Pacific. In 1859, he was elected a fellow of the Royal Society. He was appointed as professor of Naval Hygiene at Netley in 1872. From 1883 until 1886, he was in charge of the Royal Naval Hospital, Plymouth, and was knighted in 1902. He published many scientific papers and had an interest in musical composition and oil painting. He died at Southall, Middlesex, on 7 February 1908. His publications included *The Analogy of Sound and Colour* (1869), *Outlines of Naval Hygiene* (1881) and *A Guide to the Microscopical Examination of Drinking Water* (1883).

Mac EGAN, Boetius (d. 1650) Born Duhallow Barony, Co. Cork. He joined the Franciscan Order and studied at various centres on the Continent, including Spain. He returned to Ireland in the late 1620s and was guardian of Buttevant Friary in 1641/42 on the outbreak of the Confederate War (1641–53). He attended the Franciscan Chapter meeting in Athlone in 1644 and was elected as a counsellor to the provincial. On 3 June of the following year, he attended the General Chapter of the Order at Toledo, Spain. He returned to Ireland around August 1645 and two months later accompanied the Papal Nuncio, Archbishop G.B. Rinuccini (1592–1663), to the confederation base at Kilkenny. He was appointed as chaplain to the Ulster army of Eoghan Rua O'Neill (c.1582–1649) and was present at O'Neill's famous victory at Benburb on 5 June 1646. He was consecrated as bishop of Ross in Waterford on 25 March 1648. However, with the split in the Confederation, the departure of Rinuccini, the arrival of Oliver Cromwell (15 August 1649) and the death of Eoghan Rua (6 November 1649), the Confederation War was nearing its end. While Cromwell was laying siege to Clonmel, an army from Kerry under Colonel David Roche set out to relieve the town. Cromwell ordered Lord Broghill (**Roger Boyle**, later 1st earl of Orrery) to intercept Roche. The two armies met at Macroom on 10 May 1650 and Roche's forces were routed, while MacEgan was captured. On the following day, he was brought before the beleaguered garrison at Carrigadrohid Castle and promised that his life would be spared if he should procure a surrender. He refused and was hanged from a nearby tree. He was most probably buried in Aghina Graveyard, nr. Macroom. [Life by C. Mooney (1950)]

Mac EGAN, Owen (c.1570–1603) Born probably in Co. Cork. He was educated in Spain where he graduated MA and BD. He returned to Ireland in 1600 as bishop designate of Ross, but shortly afterwards, he was sent to King Philip III of Spain (1578–1621) to request support. A force was eventually sent to Kinsale in September 1601, and the famous Battle of Kinsale took place in late December. Mac Egan arrived in Kenmare Bay in June of the following year with more Spanish troops and £12,000 in specie. He was killed in an encounter with an English force under the future Sir William Taffe

at Cladach, Timoleague, on 5 January 1603 and was buried in Timoleague Abbey.

Mac GEARAILT, Piaras (1702–1795) Born Ballymacoda, Co. Cork, the fourth son of Michael Fitzredmond Fitzgerald, landowner, of the Ballycrenane branch of the East Cork Geraldines. He was probably educated at Cadiz, Spain, where his uncle was a wine merchant. Though a strong supporter of the Stuart cause, he converted to Protestantism in order to retain his lands. A celebrated Munster poet, he is best known for his 'Rosc Catha na Mumhan' ('The Battle-hymn of Munster'). He spent the last years of his long life with his wife's people in Clashmore, Co. Waterford. He died in 1795 and was buried in Ballykinealy, his native townland. [Works edited by R. Ó Foghludha (1905)]

Mac GIOLLA PHÁDRAIG, Seosamh I. see **Fitzpatrick, Joseph J.**

McGRATH, Patrick (c.1895–1956) Born Cork. As a boy, he became an apprentice blacksmith and followed that trade until 1946 (General **Tom Barry** commissioned the iron cross at the site of the Kilmichael Ambush from 'Pa' – the first of many throughout the West Cork area). He had a smithy in Morgan Street, Cork. During the War of Independence, he was an officer of the 2nd battalion, Cork No.1 Brigade. He was a member of the jury which brought a verdict of wilful murder against the British Prime Minister following the murder of **Tomás MacCurtain**. An accomplished rugby player, he captained Cork Constitution to Munster Senior Cup wins in 1922 and 1923. He was elected to the Dáil as a Fianna Fáil TD in 1946 and held his seat until his death. He had been the Fianna Fáil director of elections in Cork in the 1943 and 1944 general elections. He was a member of both Cork Corporation and Cork County Council (1950–6) and served as lord mayor of Cork for four terms (1952–6). He died in Cork on 20 June 1956 and was buried in St Finbarr's Cemetery. [Headstone by **Seamus Murphy** at St Finbarr's Cemetery, Cork]

McHENRY, John J. (1898–1976) Born Dublin. He was educated at UCD (B.Sc., 1917 and M.Sc., 1918), Downing College and Cavendish Laboratory, Cambridge (MA, 1921) and UCG (D.Sc., 1931). In 1932, he was appointed as professor of Experimental Physics at UCC (to 1964). At various times, he served on the governing body of UCC, on the senate of the National University of Ireland, on the Atomic Energy commission and on the commission for Higher Education. He was elected as president of UCC in January 1964. He retired in June 1967 on reaching the statutory age. He died at the Bon Secours Home on 3 September 1976 and was buried in St Finbarr's Cemetery. [Headstone by **Seamus Murphy** at St Finbarr's Cemetery, Cork]

McKENNA, Sir Joseph N. (1819–1906) Born Artane, Dublin, the eldest son of Michael McKenna. He was educated at TCD and was called to the Irish Bar in 1848. However, he chose banking as a career and eventually became the chairman of the National Bank. Campaigning as a Liberal, he unsuccessfully contested parliamentary seats at New Ross (1859, 1863) and Tralee (by-election, 1865), but in the general election of 1865, he was elected MP for Youghal, heavily defeating **Isaac Butt**, apparently with the support of the clergy (McKenna was a Roman Catholic). However, he lost his seat in 1868 when he was defeated by another Liberal, Christopher Weguelin. Even though Weguelin was unseated on petition, McKenna did not claim the seat. In 1874, he regained Youghal when standing as a Home Rule candidate. He held it until 1885 when he failed to get sufficient support to contest the new constituency of Cork East. However, he was selected for and elected MP for South Monaghan which he represented until his retirement in 1892. He was knighted in 1867. He had extensive estates in Co. Waterford and resided at Ardrogena, Ardmore, which he had purchased in 1874. He was in financial difficulties in the 1880s and a Receiver was appointed over his estates in February 1887. In that year, he complained in the House of Commons that the Plan of Campaign (of the Land League) had been used against him despite his assertion that he was a good landlord. He died at Ardogena on 15 August 1906 and was buried in the local cemetery. His nephew, Reginald McKenna (1863–1943), was a banker, MP, and a leading Liberal politician who served as Home Secretary (1911–15) and Chancellor of the Exchequer (1915–16).

McKENNA, Matthew (1706–1791) Born Great Island, Co. Cork. He was educated at the Irish College, Paris (his gravestone describes him also as 'Doctor of the Sorbonne'). He appears to have been parish priest of Great Island prior to his succession to the bishopric of Cloyne and Ross on 7 August 1769. He continued to reside on Great Island during his episcopate. He died at Cove (now Cobh) on 4 June 1791 and was buried in Templerobin (Ballymore) Graveyard, near Cobh. [His Will is published in full among 'Catholic Episcopal Wills' in *Archivium Hibernicum*, vol. 3]

MACKESSY, Willie (1880–1956) Born Buttevant, Co. Cork. His family moved to Cork City and he came to prominence in Gaelic games as a hurler with Blackrock and as a footballer with Lees. He commenced his business career in Kinsale and later took up a clerical position at the Munster Arcade, Cork. In 1912, he opened a licensed premises ('The Vineyard') in Market Lane to which he added, in 1918, the Oliver Plunkett Street pub which bore the family name. These premises were among the most popular in Cork for over half a century. He was the first Cork dual All-Ireland medallist. In 1903, he won his All-Ireland SHC medal and followed this with a football one in 1911 (having played on the losing side in the finals of 1899, 1901, 1906–7). In 1911, he also played in the first hurling match on the Continent when he lined out for Cork against Tipperary in an exhibition match at Fontenoy. He won six Cork County Senior Football medals (1902–4, 1907–8 and 1911) and four Cork Senior Hurling medals (1903, 1910–12). He represented Cork on the

Munster Council for some years and was treasurer of that body in 1912. He died at the Bon Secours Hospital on 11 November 1956 and was buried in St Finbarr's Cemetery.

MACLISE, Daniel (1806–1870) Born Cork, the son of Alexander McLeish, a Scottish soldier who arrived in Cork with his regiment in 1797. On the departure of the regiment, Alexander stayed on and set up as a leather-cutter on the South Main Street. He was married on 24 December 1797 at the Presbyterian (Unitarian) Church, Prince's Street, by Rev. **Thomas Dix Hincks**. Daniel was educated locally and in 1820 he was employed at Newenham's Bank. However, he left soon after to study at the Cork Institute, which had been founded by Hincks. Through the patronage of **Richard Sainthill**, he was introduced to **T. Crofton Croker** and later illustrated the 2nd edition of Croker's *Fairy Legends* (1826). He then studied at the Cork School of Art and, in 1825, he sketched Sir Walter Scott who encouraged him to move to London – which he did in July 1827. He entered the schools of the Royal Academy in April 1828 and won the Gold Medal in 1831. In the meantime, he had built up a very successful practice in portraiture and continued to exhibit at the Royal Academy. In 1832, he visited Cork with Croker and was presented with an inscribed gold medal by the Cork Society of Arts. In 1830, he began to contribute character portraits to *Fraser's Magazine* – a series which was to continue until 1838 and which is preserved in the Foster Collection at the British Museum. Most successful are his huge frescoes, 'The Meeting of Wellington and Blucher' (1859) and 'The Death of Nelson' (1864) at Westminster Hall which were commissioned for the new parliament building following a competition in 1844. His 'The Marriage of Strongbow and Aoife' and 'Merry Christmas in the Baron's Hall' hang at the National Gallery of Ireland. He was elected as a member of the Royal Hibernian Academy in 1860. He declined, in 1866, both the presidency of the Royal Academy and a knighthood. He died of pneumonia at Chelsea on 25 April 1870 and was buried at Kensal Green. [Life by Justin O'Driscoll (1871) and by Nancy Weston (2001); Bust (1870) by E. Davis (1813–1878) at Burlington House, London; Bust by J. Thomas (1813–1862) at Birmingham Midland Institute; Exhibition catalogue at the National Gallery, Dublin, by R. Ormond and J. Turpin (1972); Self-portrait (1829) at the National Gallery, Dublin; Commemorative plaque at the site of the former Bolster's Bookshop, 70, Patrick's Street, Cork, where Maclise sketched the writer, Sir Walter Scott, in 1825]

McMULLEN, James Finbarre (1859–1933) Born Cork, the youngest son of Barry McMullen, builder and contractor. He was educated at Queen's College, Cork (now UCC) where he graduated BE and also studied architecture. He later established an architectural practice in Cork and his work include the Honan Chapel (UCC), the Lough Church, the Model Schools; the Eye, Ear and Throat Hospital, the Grand Hotel (Crosshaven) etc. In 1910, he was made a Knight Commander of St Gregory by Pope Pius X (1835–1914) in recognition of his contribution to church architecture. He was also elected as high sheriff of Cork (1907/8). He died at his Douglas Road residence on 31 March 1933 and was buried privately.

MacNAMARA, James A. (1777–1860) Born Cork. In 1813, he advertised the publication, in parts, of 'a new edition of the Catholic Bible', which would include the anti-Protestant 'Rhemish Notes'. However, before publication was complete, Mac Namara was declared bankrupt in December 1814 and a number of copies were completed by Richard Coyne of Dublin. The bible, which claimed the patronage of the Archbishop of Dublin, John Troy (1739–1823), became controversial. In 1818, MacNamara, now residing at Sunday's Well, Cork (having spent some years in Dublin), completed the publication in Cork of his own edition of the bible, which included the controversial notes and the apparent claim of hierarchical patronage. Its publication was criticised by many, including Daniel O'Connell (1775–1847), who described MacNamara as 'a very ignorant printer in Cork'. MacNamara, who seems to have left Cork shortly afterwards, died in London on 21 December 1860. His death notice described him as 'the publisher of the Douay Bible'.

MacNAMARA, Justin F. (1794–1845) Born Macroom, Co. Cork, a nephew of Bishop **Florence McCarthy** and a relation of Bishop **John Murphy**. He was educated at St Patrick's College, Maynooth and was ordained in Cork in 1817. He served as a curate in the city parish of SS. Peter and Paul until 1827 when he moved to Rome. There he renewed his friendship with sculptor **John Hogan** and accompanied him on visits to many art galleries and churches in Italy. He was appointed as parish priest of Kinsale and was responsible for the building, in 1834, of the parish church of St John the Baptist. Ten years later, he introduced the Sisters of Mercy to the town and was also responsible for introducing the Carmelites at a later date. In 1845, he set out once more on a visit to Rome but died at Gibraltar on 31 December of that year. His remains were disinterred in the following year and returned to Kinsale in April where they were laid to rest in a vault in his parish church. In 1849, Hogan's superb memorial, showing Mac Namara standing in the pose of a preacher, was erected in the church.

McNAUGHTON-JONES, Henry (1845–1918) Born Cork, the son of William Thomas Jones, physician. He was educated at Queen's College, Cork (now UCC), where he became a demonstrator in Anatomy at the age of nineteen and subsequently became professor of Midwifery there (1876–83). He was instrumental in the founding of several Cork medical institutions [including the Cork Ophthalmic Hospital (1868), the Cork Maternity Hospital (1872) and the Victoria Hospital (1883)], but moved to London in 1883. He was twice president of the British Gynaecological Society and, in 1912, represented

Britain and Ireland at the International Congress of Obstetrics and Gynaecology in Berlin. His *Manual of Diseases of Women* (2 vols, 1884) ran to nine editions, while his *Diseases of the Ear and Nasopharynx* reached a sixth edition in 1902. He died at Barnet on 16 April 1918.

McNEILL, Josephine (1895–1969) Born Patrick Street, Fermoy, Co. Cork, the youngest child of James Aherne, shopkeeper. She was educated at Loreto Convent, Fermoy, and at UCD where she graduated BA in Modern Languages. Her first teaching post was at the Ursuline Convent, Thurles, where she met and became engaged to Pierce McCann. However, McCann (who was elected a Sinn Féin MP for Tipperary East in the general election of 1918) was interned and died in Gloucester Gaol in March 1919. While in London in 1923, she met James McNeill (1869–1938), then the Irish Free State High Commissioner in London and a brother of Eoin McNeill (1867–1945), the political leader and historian. They married in that same year and in 1928, McNeill was appointed as Governor General of the Irish Free State in succession to **Tim Healy**. Mrs McNeill was an accomplished hostess at the Viceregal Lodge, but in October 1932, McNeill was dismissed from the post following a dispute with Eamon de Valera. Following her husband's death in December 1938, Mrs McNeill was for a time involved in the development of the Irish Countrywomen's Association (ICA) and, in the late 1940s, became a supporter of Clann na Poblachta. In February 1950, she was appointed as Irish Ambassador to The Hague, the first woman to be accorded ambassadorial status by the State. In 1955/56, she was Ambassador to Sweden and Norway and from 1956 to her retirement in June 1960, she was Ambassador to Switzerland. She retired to a residence in Leeson Park, Dublin, and died at St Vincent's Hospital, on 20 November 1969. She was buried beside her husband in Kilbarrack Cemetery.

Mac SUIBHNE, Pádraig (1871–1936) Born, Ring, Co. Waterford, the son of Tomás Mac

Suibhne, farm worker. When he was a boy, the family moved to Dungarvan where he was educated. He had a keen interest in Irish and was one of the founders of the Dungarvan branch of Connradh na Gaeilge in June 1895. He took up a clerical post in a solicitor's office in Fermoy, Co. Cork, and, again, was a co-founder of the Fermoy branch of the Connradh in 1900. On 5 October 1901, he chaired the Cork meeting in which the Cork Council of Connradh na Gaeilge was inaugurated. He was one of the main applicants in 1903 for the editorship of the Connradh's organ, *An Claidheamh Soluis* – a post which finally went to the 1916 leader, Patrick Pearse (1879–1916). In 1907, he was appointed as an inspector of Irish by the Irish National Board of Education, and later was a schools inspector of the department of Education until his retirement in 1936. He died at his residence at 54 Highfield Avenue, Cork, on 6 December 1936 and was buried in St Finbarr's Cemetery.

McSWEENEY, Fanahan (1948–1995) Born Castletownroche, Co. Cork. He was educated locally and at Doneraile CBS. He was awarded an athletics scholarship to McNeese State College, Louisiana, where he later graduated with an engineering degree. He held a number of Irish track records as well as a European Indoor 400m record. He represented Ireland in this event at the Munich Olympics of 1972. In 1986, he was diagnosed with cancer and shortly before his death, he published *Living and Loving with Cancer* (1994). He died at his Silver Heights, Cork, residence on 27 July 1995 and was buried in Ballyhooley Cemetery.

MacSWINEY, Mary (1872–1942) Born Surrey, the daughter of John MacSwiney, teacher, and sister of **Seán MacSwiney** and **Terence MacSwiney**. She was reared in Cork on her father's return there and was educated at the St Angela's Convent. She taught in England and briefly in France before acquiring a teaching diploma at Cambridge University. She taught at a Benedictine convent for some years before

returning to Cork on her mother's death in 1904. She took a great interest in the Suffragist movement until 1914 when she became a founder member and president of Cumann na mBan, the women's republican organisation. She worked as a schoolteacher at St Angela's until her dismissal for republican activities during the period of the 1916 Rising. She then founded her own school, St Ita's. Following the death of Terence, she was elected to the 2nd Dáil as a TD for Cork City in May 1921. She was elected to the 3rd Dáil as an anti-Treaty candidate and was subsequently elected as a republican abstentionist TD until 1927 when she refused to join Fianna Fáil and was defeated. She refused to recognise the legitimacy of the Irish Free State and continued to advocate militant opposition to it. She died at her residence at Belgrave Square, Wellington Road, on 8 March 1942 and was buried in St Joseph's Cemetery. [Life by C.H. Fallon (1986)]

MacSWINEY, Muriel Frances (1892–1982) Born Carrigmore, Cork, the daughter of Nicholas Murphy, of the distillery family. She married **Terence MacSwiney** at Bromyard in Herefordshire, where he was under detention for his political beliefs, on 9 June 1917, though the marriage did not win the approval of the Murphy family. In September 1917 they settled at Douglas Road, Cork, but their early married life was disrupted by his frequent arrests. Their daughter, Maire, was born in 1918. He succeeded **Tomás MacCurtain** as Lord Mayor in March 1920 but was arrested again in August and sentenced to two years' imprisonment and began the hunger strike that would end in 'his death on 25 October 1920. After his death, Muriel participated in nationalist activities, touring the US to speak on behalf of Sinn Féin. She left Ireland with her daughter in December 1923 and commenced a peripatetic existence that took her to Germany, France and England. She became involved in left wing politics and perhaps joined the Communist party. In 1932 **Mary MacSwiney**, her sister-in-law, took Maire back to Ireland, an act Muriel viewed as kidnapping. Her attempts to regain custody failed and thereafter she increasingly severed any links with either the MacSwiney or Murphy families. She suffered bouts of depression and other illnesses. She lived in Kent in her latter years and died at Oakwood Hospital, Maidstone on 26 October 1982.

MacSWINEY, Patrick (1790/91–1865) Born Ballyvolane House, Cork, the son of a miller. He was educated at St Patrick's College, Maynooth, where he was ordained a priest. He was professor of Theology at Carlow College (1819–25), but resigned his post in 1825 to engage in debate with evangelical controversialists (his bishop, James W. Doyle of Kildare and Leighlin [1786–1834], forbade retaliation). Dr MacSwiney emigrated to France where he became prefect of studies at the Irish College in Paris and superior in 1828. He was president of that college for 22 years (1828–50) and shepherded this institution through the revolutions of 1830 and 1848. In his early years at the college, he engaged, unsuccessfully, in trying to win compensation for the losses it suffered during the French Revolution of 1789. In 1847, he was awarded the rank of Chevalier of the Legion d'Honneur and an annual pension of 5,000 francs. He spent most of his retirement in Paris, but occasionally visited Ballyvolane, where he died on 14 August 1865. He was buried in Whitechurch Graveyard.

MacSWINEY, Seán (1889–1942) Born Cork, the son of John MacSwiney, teacher, and brother of **Mary MacSwiney** and **Terence MacSwiney**. He spent some time in Canada where he was involved in the anti-conscription campaign during World War I. He returned to Cork on the death of Terence. He was elected to the 2nd Dáil (1921) as a TD for the Rest of County Cork but was defeated in 1922 as an anti-Treaty candidate. He had been sentenced to fifteen years penal servitude in 1921 but had escaped from Spike Island. He served later terms of imprisonment for Republican activities and died at Belgrave Square, Wellington Road, Cork, on 22 January 1942.

MacSWINEY, Terence (1879–1920) Born North Main Street, Cork, the son of John MacSwiney, teacher, and brother of **Mary MacSwiney** and **Seán MacSwiney**. He was educated at North Monastery CBS. On leaving school in 1894, he took up an accounting position in the clothing firm of Dwyer & Company of Washington Street. In 1901, he was a founder member of the Cork Celtic Literary Society and later, in 1908, he founded with **Daniel Corkery**, the Cork Dramatic Society. Meanwhile, in 1907, he had taken the philosophy degree of the Royal University of Ireland. In 1911, he was employed by Cork County Council to organise commercial classes in all the county towns. He resigned from this position in 1915 to act as a full-time organiser for the Irish Volunteers which he had helped to form in Cork two years earlier. In the meantime, he had founded in 1914 a weekly newspaper, *Fianna Fáil*, which was suppressed by the authorities after only eleven issues. When the 1916 Easter Rising broke out, he obeyed the orders of Eoin MacNeill to call off operations and travelled to Tralee on a British permit in an attempt to persuade the Kerry volunteers to surrender their arms. He was subsequently imprisoned for short terms in 1916 and 1917. While in detention at Bromyard, Hertfordshire, he was married on 9 June 1917 to Muriel Murphy (see **Muriel MacSwiney**) with **Geraldine Neeson** as bridesmaid. He represented West Cork in the first Dáil Éireann and was involved in the setting up of the Sinn Féin arbitration courts. Following the murder of his friend, **Tomás MacCurtain**, lord mayor of Cork, in March 1920, MacSwiney was elected to succeed him. On 12 August of that year, he was arrested with others at City Hall on the charge of possessing an RIC cipher. All the accused decided to go on hunger strike and were, with the exception of MacSwiney, subsequently released. On 16 August, he was sentenced to two years imprisonment and removed to Brixton Prison, London. He died there on 24 October on the seventy-fourth day of his hunger strike – a phenomenon which had aroused media attention all over the world. His remains were returned to Cork and were buried in St Finbarr's Cemetery. He wrote the following plays for the Cork Dramatic Society, 'The Revolutionist', 'The Holocaust', 'The Warriors of Coole' and 'The Wooing of Emer'. His *Principles of Freedom*, which was published posthumously in 1921, is a collection of various articles he had written prior to 1916. [Life by D. O'Hegarty (1922), M. Chavasse (1961), D. Ó Briain (1979) and F.J. Costello (1995); Larger than life-size bust by **Seamus Murphy** at City Hall, Cork; Commemorative plaque at his birthplace, 23/24 North Main Street, Cork]

Mac WEENEY, Vera (1909–1981) Born St Helen's, Blarney, Co. Cork, the second daughter of Francis W. Mahony, woollen manufacturer by his second wife, May Ashlin. She was educated in Cork and Dublin. A noted sportswoman, she achieved interprovincial and international recognition in hockey, tennis and squash. As a member of Maids of the Mountain Hockey Club, she represented Leinster in 1927 and Ireland (at full-back) in 1932. She captained the Irish touring team to the United States in 1936. In 1940, she married Arthur Mac Weeney, the rugby correspondent of the *Irish Times*. Following her husband's death in 1958, she became a sports correspondent of the *Irish Times*, covering hockey, tennis and racket sports. She also served as president of the Irish Ladies Hockey Union (1951/2). She died at Sir Patrick Dun's Hospital, Dublin, on 9 January 1981 and was buried in Glasnevin Cemetery.

MacWHITE, Michael (1883–1958) Born at Reenogreena, Glandore, Co. Cork. He went to London at the age of seventeen and worked in a bank for several years. He then spent some years teaching in Scandinavia and travelling through Northern Europe. He returned to Ireland in 1910 but two years later he was in the Balkans when he enlisted as a volunteer in the Bulgarian forces during the war against the Turks. Having recuperated from his wounds in the south of France, he then joined the French Foreign Legion with whom he served with distinction during World War I. In 1918, he travelled to the United States as a member of the French military mission. A friend and correspondent of Arthur Griffith (1871–1922) and John Devoy (1842–1928), he joined the Dáil diplomatic service under Seán T. O'Kelly (1882–1966). He served, in turn, as secretary to the Dáil Éireann delegation to the Paris Peace Conference (1920–1), permanent delegate to the League of Nations (1923–9), vice-president of the International Labour Conference (Geneva), envoy extraordinary and minister plenipotentiary to the US (1929–38) and to Italy (1938–50). He retired in 1950. As well as being an explorer, soldier, and diplomat, he was also multilingual. He died in 1958.

MADDEN, Ambrose [VC] (1820–1863) Born Cork. He joined the British army and was promoted to the rank of sergeant in the 41st Regiment. On 26 October 1854, during the Crimean War, he headed a party of his regiment which captured a Russian officer and fourteen of his men, three of whom were personally captured by Madden. He was awarded the Victoria Cross for this action and was later promoted to the rank of lieutenant. He died in Jamaica on 1 January 1863.

MADDEN, Daniel O. (1815–1859) Born Mallow, Co. Cork, the son of Owen Madden, merchant. He moved to London in 1842 where he worked for *The Press* newspaper. He was the friend and correspondent of a leader of the Young Ireland movement, **Thomas O. Davis**. His publications include *The Age of Pitt and Fox* (first volume), *Ireland and her Rulers since 1829* (3 vols, 1843), *The Rt. Hon. J.P. Curran* (1846), *A Memoir of the Life of the Rt. Hon. Henry Grattan* (1846), The *Chiefs of Parties*, and *Revelations of Ireland in the Past Generation* (1848). He returned to Dublin in 1857 where he acted as correspondent for *The Athenaeum* and the *Daily News* of London. He died in Dublin on 6 August 1859 and was buried in Shandon Graveyard, Cork.

MADDEN, Sir Frank (1847–1921) Born Cork, the son of John Madden, solicitor, and brother of **Sir John Madden** and **Walter Madden**. He was educated in London, in Normandy and in Melbourne, Australia, to where the family had emigrated in 1857. He studied at Melbourne University and qualified as an attorney in 1869. He established a successful legal partnership and entered the Victorian Legislative Assembly in 1894. This was followed by a long term as speaker of the Assembly (1904–17) when, as a result of his anti-Irish outbursts and his criticism of Archbishop **Daniel Mannix**, he lost his seat. He had been knighted in 1911. He died at his residence at Kew, Victoria, on 17 February 1921 and was buried with Anglican rites in Boroondara Cemetery.

MADDEN, Sir John (1844–1918) Born Cork, the son of John Madden, solicitor, and brother of **Sir Frank Madden** and **Walter Madden**. He was educated in London, in Normandy, and in Melbourne, Australia, to where the family had emigrated in 1857. He continued his education at the University of Melbourne where he graduated BA (1864) and LL.B (1865). He was called to the Bar in 1865 and, with two solicitor brothers, he was successful as a barrister. He was elected to the Victorian Legislative Assembly in 1874 and served as minister for Justice for a short period. Following on the loss of his seat in 1883, he became Victoria's most celebrated barrister and was rewarded with the post of chief justice in January 1893 – the year in which he received a knighthood. In 1899, he was appointed both as Lieutenant Governor of Victoria and as vice-chancellor of Melbourne University. A keen sportsman, he was president of the Victorian Amateur Athletic Association and of the Olympic Sporting Federation. He died at South Yarra, Melbourne, on 10 March 1918 and was buried with Roman Catholic rites in Melbourne General Cemetery.

MADDEN, Patrick Joseph see **Ó MAIDÍN, Pádraig**

MADDEN, Walter (1848–1925) Born Cork, the son of John Madden, solicitor, and brother

of **Sir John Madden** and **Sir Frank Madden**. He was educated in London, in Normandy, and in Melbourne, Australia, to where the family had emigrated in 1857. Having served a period in the navy, he returned to Melbourne and set up as a surveyor, valuer and financial agent. He was elected to the Victorian Legislative Assembly in 1880 and represented the 'country' interest as a backbencher until his defeat in the election of 1894. He was a board member of the National Mutual Life Association of Australia from 1897 until his death. He died at his brother Henry's home at Flemington, on 3 August 1925 and was buried with Roman Catholic rites in Melbourne Cemetery.

MAGEE, William C. (1821–1891) Born at the library of St FinBarre's Cathedral, Cork, the eldest son of John Magee, the librarian and curate of St Finbarr's parish whose father, William Magee, had been dean of Cork and archbishop of Dublin. He was educated at Kilkenny College and at TCD where he graduated BA (1842), MA and BD (1854) and DD (1860). Following his ordination in 1844, he served as curate of St Thomas's, Dublin, but owing to ill-health, spent a short time in the south of Spain. In 1864, he was appointed both as dean of Cork and of the Chapel Royal, Dublin Castle. He was consecrated as bishop of Peterborough in 1868. He spoke strongly in the House of Lords against the disestablishment of the Church of Ireland. He was enthroned as archbishop of York on 17 March 1891 but died five weeks later, on 5 May, in London. He was buried in the grounds of Peterborough Cathedral. [Life by J.C. MacDonnell (2 vols, 1896); Portrait by Joseph Watkins (1870)]

MAGINN, William (1793–1842) Born Marlborough's Fort, Cork, the son of a schoolmaster. He was educated at TCD where he graduated BA (1811) and LL.D (1819). He returned to Cork to assist at his father's school and commenced a long association as a contributor to *Blackwood's Magazine*. He arrived in London in 1823 and wrote for various journals and, following a short stint in Paris, he became assistant editor of the London *Evening Standard*. In a temporary break with *Blackwood's* in 1828, he founded *Fraser's Magazine* two years later. However, his addiction to alcohol led to financial collapse and he found himself in the debtors' prison in 1837. He subsequently retired to Walton-on-Thames where he died on 21 August 1842. His publications included *Whitehall, or the Days of George IV* (1827) and *John Manesty, the Liverpool Merchant* which was finished by C. Ollier and published in 1844 to relieve the deceased's family. [Sketch by D. and M. Coakley (1975); Writings edited by R.S. MacKenzie (5 vols, 1855–7); Miscellanies edited by R.W. Montagu (2 vols, 1885); Portrait by **Samuel Skillen**, etched by J. Kirkwood]

MAGNER, Thomas J. (1850–1920) Born Ovens, Co. Cork, the son of John Magner. He was educated locally and at St Vincent's Seminary, Cork. He studied for the priesthood at the Irish College, Paris, where he was ordained in 1881. On his return to Cork, he taught at St Finbarr's Seminary for several years before his appointment to a succession of curacies at Kinsale, Bandon and Cathedral Parish. In 1907, he was appointed as parish priest of Dunmanway and later became a canon in the diocesan chapter. On the afternoon of 15 December 1920, while taking his daily walk, he was murdered by a deranged Auxiliary, Sgt. Vernon Hart, in one of the most pointless atrocities of the War of Independence period. A 22-year old parishioner of Canon Magner's, Tadhg Crowley, was also killed by Hart in the same incident. They were both buried in Dunmanway Cemetery, where a publicly subscribed memorial marks the canon's grave. A memorial to both victims was erected in 1924 at the site of the shooting.

MAGUIRE, John Francis (1815–1872) Born Cork, the eldest son of John Maguire, merchant. He founded the *Cork Examiner* in 1841 to support Daniel O'Connell and the Repeal movement. Two years later he was called to the Bar. He entered politics and sat as MP for Dungarvan (1852–65) and for Cork (1865–72). He took a keen interest in the affairs of his native city and was elected as lord mayor of the city on four occasions (1852, 1862–3 and 1864). He also took a great interest in the Papacy and was created a Knight Commander of St Gregory by Pope Pius IX (1792–1878) whom he had visited three times. He died in Dublin on 1 November 1872 and was buried in St Joseph's Cemetery, Cork. His publications include *The Life of Father Mathew* (1863), *Rome and its Rulers* (1856), *The Irish in America* (1866), *The Pontificate of Pius IX* (1870) and *The Next Generation* (3 vols, 1871). [Miniature by **Hugh Danckert**; Commemorative plaque at the offices of the *Irish Examiner*, Academy Street, Cork]

MAGUIRE, Margaret (d. 1905) Born Ringview, Passage West, Co. Cork, the daughter of Robert Baily, a wealthy landlord and property owner. She married **John Francis Maguire**, while her sister, Elizabeth Josephine, married **Edward Sullivan** of Mallow. She was author of several published works including *Beauty and the Beast: a play* (1878), *Two plays: Blue Beard – Cincerella* (1879), *Young Prince Marigold and other tales* (1873) and *Father Mathew and his times* (1903). Widowed in 1872, she survived her husband by over 30 years, dying at her residence, Weir View, Sunday's Well, on 19 November 1905.

MAGUIRE, Sam (1879–1927) Born Mallabracka, Dunmanway, Co. Cork. He moved to London and played on the losing London side in three All-Ireland Senior Football finals (1900–1 and 1903). A member of the Irish Republican Brotherhood (IRB), he was later elected as president of the London GAA Board. He died on 2 June 1927 and was buried in Dunmanway Cemetery. He has given his name to the All-Ireland Senior Football trophy which was first presented in 1928 – a year after his death.

MAHONEY, James (1810–1879) Born Cork, the son of Wm. Mahoney, carpenter. Showing an early interest in painting, he studied in Rome and travelled in Europe where he painted views in watercolour. He returned to his father's house in Nile Street, Cork, in 1842. He exhibited at the Royal Hibernian Academy until 1846 when he again left for Europe. Some of his Cork views featured in the Cork Exhibition of 1852. He also exhibited at the RHA between 1856 and 1859 (having become an associate member in 1856). Many of his works over this period are in the National Gallery, Dublin. He then settled in London where he exhibited at the Royal Academy and at the Watercolour Society. He changed direction and gained a firm reputation as an illustrator in newspapers, books, and magazines, most notably in the *Illustrated London News*. He was the illustrator of the *Household Edition* of the works of Charles Dickens (1812–70). This included 28 drawings for *Oliver Twist*, 58 for *Little Dorrit* and 58 for *Our Mutual Friend*. He died of apoplexy at Marylebone, London, on 29 May 1879.

MAHONY, Francis S. ['Father Prout'] (1804–1866) Born Cork, the son of the Blarney woollens manufacturer, **Martin Mahony,** and brother of **Ellen Woodlock**. He was educated at Clongowes Wood College, Co. Kildare. He joined the Jesuit Order and engaged in further studies in Paris and Rome. In 1830, he returned to Ireland and took up a teaching position at Clongowes. He left the Order shortly afterwards and returned to Rome to study at the Irish College there. It was here that he composed the celebrated Cork anthem, 'The Bells of Shandon'. Following his ordination in 1832, he returned to Cork to undertake parish work. However, following a disagreement with Bishop **John Murphy** of Cork in 1834, he moved to London and lived as a layman. Here he began to write for **William Maginn**'s *Fraser's Magazine* under the pseudonym of 'Father Prout' and a series in the magazine entitled, *Reliques of Father Prout*, established his reputation. He also wrote poems for *Bentley's Miscellany* which had been founded by the great novelist, Charles Dickens. In 1846, he settled in Rome to write for the London *Daily News* and two years later moved on to Paris. From 1858 until his death he was a correspondent for *The Globe* newspaper. He

died in Paris on 18 May 1866. His remains were brought back to Ireland and buried in the crypt of St Anne's, Shandon. [Lives by B. Jerrold (1876) and E. Mannin (1954); Portrait by **Richard Lyster**; Bust by **John Hogan**; Bust by **Richard Barter** at Cork School of Art; Drawing by **Daniel Maclise** at British Museum; Commemorative plaque at St Anne's, Shandon]

MAHONY, Martin (1764–1834) Born Cork, the third son of Timothy Mahony whose father, a native of Co. Kerry, had established a woollen industry near Cork in 1750. By the late eighteenth century, the business (principally in Blackpool) had expanded greatly under Martin and his elder brother, Timothy. In 1822, Martin transferred the business to Blarney where it was to prosper for 150 years. He died at his residence, Mayfield, Cork, on 15 February 1834 having 'during his fifty years in the business, conducted the woollen manufacture on a more extensive scale than any other employer in the South of Ireland'. He married twice, and by his second marriage was father of **Francis S. Mahony**, and **Ellen Woodlock**.

MAHONY, Pakey (1880–1968) Born Dublin Street, Blackpool, Cork, the son of James O'Mahony. Becoming a professional boxer in his mid-20s, he boxed some of the leading Irish and British heavyweights before winning the Championship of Ireland against Dan Voyles on 17 March 1913. Three months later, he boxed Bombardier Billy Wells, the champion, for the British heavyweight title. Despite suffering a broken jaw in Round Four, Mahony fought on before being knocked out in Round Thirteen. He retired from the sport soon afterwards. A resident of Blackrock from 1913, he trained the Rockies hurling team in the 1920s and was trainer of the Cork All-Ireland-winning hurling teams of 1928, 1929 and 1931. He died in September 1968.

MANDEVILLE, John (1849–1888) Born Ballydine House, Carrick-on-Suir, Co. Tipperary, the fourth son of James H. Mandeville, landowner, and nephew of the Fenian leader,

John O'Mahoney. Through the influence of his mother's family, the O'Mahoneys of Clonkilla, Mitchelstown, he became involved in the activities of the Irish National Land League in 1885. Early in 1886 the tenants of the earl of Kingston demanded an abatement of rents in view of the bad harvest of the previous year. A figure of 10% was offered by the Kingston estate but this was refused by the tenants who pressed for a 20% reduction. When this was refused, the 'Plan of Campaign' was adopted by the Kingston tenants in mid-December. Rents were withheld and lodged as a common fund in a bank by the local committee until a settlement would be agreed upon. With over fifty evictions pending, Mandeville and **William O'Brien**, MP, were prosecuted under the new Coercion Act and summoned to appear in Mitchelstown on 9 September 1887. They failed to turn up, but trouble broke out with the police who opened fire from their barracks and shot dead three men. Following the 'Mitchelstown Massacre', the two were convicted at Midleton, and Mandeville was sentenced to two months imprisonment. They were imprisoned at Tullamore, Co. Offaly, where they refused to wear prison clothes, to associate with criminals and to perform menial work. Mandeville's health began to decline as a result of exposure and ill treatment. He was released on Christmas Day 1887 and despite his condition, he continued to work for a settlement with the Kingston estate. This was achieved in February 1888 when the abatement of 20% was agreed upon. He died at his Clonkilla residence on 8 July 1888 and was buried in Kilbehenny Graveyard.

MANLEY, Tadhg (1893–1976) Born Ballinaglough, Carraig na bhFear, Co. Cork. He qualified as a primary teacher and was appointed in 1917 to a post at Midleton CBS. He was an active member of the 4th battalion, Cork No. 1 Brigade of the IRA and took part in many engagements in the East Cork area. He was arrested for his activities and imprisoned for periods in Pankhurst, Isle of Wight and Maidstone gaols. After the War of Independence, he resumed his teaching career at Ballinvriskig NS, White's Cross. He served as a Fine Gael TD for South Cork from 1954 to 1961 (when he did not stand for election). However, following the death of Deputy **John Galvin**, he returned to contest the Cork Borough by-election of 19 February 1964, but was unsuccessful. He died at St Patrick's Hospital, Cork, on 25 August 1976 and was buried in Dunbullogue Cemetery. He was the uncle of Fine Gael TD and former lord mayor of Cork, **Liam Burke**.

MANN, Isaac (1712–1788) Born Norwich, England. He was educated at TCD where he graduated BA (1732), MA (1735) and DD (1747). He was consecrated as Church of Ireland bishop of Cork on 15 March 1772. He rebuilt the present episcopal residence at Bishop Street. His famous *Familiar exposition of the Church Catechism in five Parts* ran to seventeen editions both in Ireland and England. He died at Bath on 10 December 1788 and was buried at Ballinaspig (Bishopstown) on 31 December. His remains were later re-interred in the foundations of the present St FinBarre's Cathedral during its construction.

MANNERS, Catherine R. (d. 1852) Born Lehena, Cork, the daughter of Francis Gray. She published *Review of Poetry* (1790) and *Poems with Portrait* (1793). In January 1790, she married William Manners, Lord Huntingtower. She died on 21 March 1852.

MANNING, Timothy (1909–1989) Born Ballingeary, Co. Cork, the son of Cornelius Manning, blacksmith. He was educated at St Patrick's Seminary, Menlo Park, California, and at the Gregorian University, Rome. In 1946, he was consecrated as titular bishop of Lesvi. He was transferred to Fresno, California, in 1967 and two years later he was appointed as titular bishop of Capri and coadjutor archbishop of Los Angeles. He succeeded as archbishop in 1970 and served until his retirement in 1985. He had previously been created a cardinal by Pope Paul VI (1897–1978) in 1973. He died in Los Angeles on 23 June 1989.

MANNIX, Daniel (1864–1963) Born Charleville, Co. Cork, the son of Timothy Mannix, farmer. He was educated at St Colman's College, Fermoy, and at St Patrick's College, Maynooth, where he graduated DD (1895). In 1895 also, he was appointed to the chair of Moral Theology at Maynooth. He was elected as president of Maynooth in 1903 and rose to the rank of monsignor in 1906. He was appointed as coadjutor bishop of Melbourne in October 1912, and, following a period of illness, he arrived in Australia at Easter 1913. He initially opposed the Rising of 1916, but with the execution of the leaders, he became firmly anti-British and opposed conscription during World War I. When he succeeded as archbishop of Melbourne on 6 May 1917, he was both one of the most revered and hated of Australian figures. On his way to Rome in May 1920, he spoke, along with Eamon de Valera (1882–1975), in support of Irish nationalism at mass meetings in the United States. With excitement at fever pitch awaiting him in Ireland, his ship was intercepted by the British Navy and he was landed in England where he was forbidden to make speeches. When he reached Rome he was successful in securing some Vatican support for the Irish cause. He arrived back in Melbourne in August 1921. He visited Ireland in 1925 shortly after his mother's death but was totally ignored by the Free State Government which he had severely criticised. He never visited Ireland again. His episcopate saw a huge increase in both the structure and importance of the Roman Catholic Church in Australia. He became a legend in his time but never obtained the cardinal's red hat. He died on 6 November 1963, following a collapse on the previous day and was buried with the minimum of ceremony. [Lives by F. Murphy (1972), W. Ebsworth (1977), M. Gilchrist (1982), C. Kiernan (1984) and B.A. Santamaria (1984)]

MARNANE, Edward J. (1933–1999) Born Cork, the son of William Marnane, shop assistant and later store manager. He entered the service of Cork County Council as a clerical officer in 1951 and became a fellow of the Chartered Institute of Secretaries. He graduated B.Comm. (1955) and M.Comm. (1975) at UCC. He advanced through the local government service and was appointed as County Secretary in 1976. For many years, he worked as a part-time lecturer in Public Administration at UCC, especially on the topic of Proportional Representation. He compiled *A Directory of Townlands and DEDs in County Cork* (1985) and *Cork County Council 1899–1885* (1986, rev. 1999). He died while on holiday at Owenahincha, Co. Cork, on 30 July 1999 and was buried in St Finbarr's Cemetery.

MARTIN, Henry (1763–1839) He was the second son of William Martin, a captain in the Royal Navy. His mother was a member of the Rowley family, who, with the de Cliffords, controlled the parliamentary borough of Kinsale. He was the nephew of the Kinsale MPs, **Sir Josias Rowley**, **William Rowley** and **Samuel Campbell Rowley**. He succeeded the latter as MP for Kinsale in 1806 and sat until 1818. He was appointed one of the masters-in-chancery and died on 19 July 1839.

MARTIN, Sir James (1820–1886) Born Midleton, Co. Cork, the eldest child of John Martin, castle steward. The family emigrated to Sydney, Australia, when he was a year old. He was educated at Sydney and became a solicitor and journalist. In 1849, he entered the Legislative Council of New South Wales and was called to the Bar. He was appointed as Attorney General in 1856 and served as premier of New South Wales in 1863, 1866 and 1870. He was knighted in 1869. He died of heart failure at his residence, Clarens, Sydney, on 4 November 1886. He published *The Australian Sketchbook* (1838). [Lives by E. Grainger (1970) and J.N. Molony (1973)]

MARTIN, Violet F. (1862–1915) Born Ross Castle, Oughterard, Co. Galway, the daughter of James Martin, a landed gentleman of an old Galway family. Owing to financial difficulties, she was brought to Dublin in 1872 and was educated at Alexandra College there. She developed an interest in writing and publishing and, with her second cousin, **Edith O. Somerville** of Drishane House, Castletownshend, Co. Cork, she formed in 1886 the world-famous writing partnership of 'Somerville and Ross' (Violet's pseudonym was 'Martin Ross'). She spent most of her time at Drishane House and died there on 21 December 1915. Publications of the writing partnership include *An Irish Cousin* (1889), *Naboth's Vineyard* (1891), *Through Connemara in a Governess's Cart* (1892), *In the Vine Country* (1893), *The Real Charlotte* (1894), *Beggars on Horseback* (1895), *The Silver Fox* (1898), *Some Experiences of an Irish RM* (1899), *Further Experiences of an Irish RM* (1908), *Dan Russel the Fox* (1911) and *In Mr Knox's Country* (1915). [Autobiographies 1906 and 1921; Studies by G. Cummins (1952), M. Collis (1968), J. Cronin (1972), and G. Lewis (1985); Letters edited by G. Lewis (1989); Archives edited by O. Rauchbauer (1993)]

MARTIN, William (1772–1853) Born Tookstown, Co. Tipperary, the son of a Quaker, William Martin. Following an apprenticeship in Cork, he eventually settled there. He started in business, but soon went bankrupt and earned his living as a baker. In 1829, he became interested in the emerging temperance movement and two years later he helped found an interdenominational temperance society in Cork. However, the society eventually ran into difficulties but in April 1838, Martin's friend Father **Theobald Mathew,** embarked on his famous temperance campaign at Cove Street. The 'Grandfather of the Temperance Cause', William Martin, died on 25 December 1853.

MATHEW, Sir James C. (1830–1908) Born Bordeaux, France, the son of Charles Mathew of Lehenagh House, Togher, and nephew of Father **Theobald Mathew**. He was educated at TCD where he graduated BA (1850). He was called to the English Bar and was knighted in 1881. Later, in 1892, he was appointed as chairman of a royal commission to examine the case of evicted tenants in Ireland. However, he was distrusted by the landlord and unionist interest as he was the father-in-law of the nationalist leader, John Dillon, MP (1851–1927). In 1901, he was appointed as a member of the Court of Appeal, but resigned four years later when he suffered a stroke. He died in London on 9 November 1908 and was buried in St Joseph's Cemetery, Cork.

MATHEW, Theobald (1790–1856) Born Thomastown Castle, Cashel, Co. Tipperary, the son of a land agent. Having initially studied for the priesthood at Maynooth (from where he was expelled), he joined the Capuchin Order and was ordained in 1814. For twenty-five years he worked among the poor of Cork and was the leader of the temperance movement which was founded in Cove Street in April 1838. It soon spread throughout the country and later to the Irish populations in both Britain and America. In 1847, he was granted £300 a year on the Civil List. In failing health, he went to live with his brother and died in Queenstown (now Cobh) on 8 December 1856. He was buried in St Joseph's Cemetery, Cork. [Lives by **J.F. Maguire** (1863), F. Mathew (1890), K. Tynan (1908), P. Rogers (1943), and Fr. Augustine (1947); Analysis by C. Kerrigan (1992); Portrait by **Daniel MacDonald**; Analysis of temperance movement by C. Kerrigan (1992); Statues by **John Hogan** at Patrick Street, Cork, and by Mary Redmond at O'Connell Street, Dublin; Portrait by **Samuel West**, engraved by W.O. Geller; Temperance medal by William Woodhouse (1805–1878); Limestone tablet by **Seamus Murphy** at the place of his death, 18 West Beach, Cobh; Commemorative plaque at his former residence, 10, Cove Street, Cork]

MAULE, Henry (1676–1758) Born Arklow, Co. Wicklow, the son of a revenue official. He was educated at TCD where he graduated BA (1696), MA (1699) and LL.D (1719). He was consecrated as Church of Ireland bishop of Cloyne on 11 September 1726. He was subsequently translated to the dioceses of Dromore (1732) and Meath (1744). He founded the Green

Coat School while rector of St Mary Shandon. He also played a central role in the foundation of the Incorporated Society, which administered the Irish Charter Schools. His *Pietas Corcagiensis* (1721) which he wrote while at Shandon, reflected his interest in the German Protestant pietistic reform movement. He died at the episcopal residence at Ardbraccan, Co. Meath, on 13 April 1758.

MEADE, Lizabeth T. (d. 1915) Born Bandon, Co. Cork, the daughter of Rev. R.T. Meade, clergyman. Having published her first book at the age of seventeen, she went to London in 1874 and married Toumlin Smith five years later. She wrote or collaborated in over forty novels (mainly for girls) and was, for a time, editor of *Atalanta*, a girls' magazine. She died in Oxford on 26 October 1915.

MEADE, William E. (1832–1912) Born Donoughmore, Co. Cork, the son of William Meade, clergyman. He was educated at Midleton College and at TCD where he graduated BA (1857), MA (1860) and DD (1873). He ministered for thirty years in the diocese of Armagh and also served as secretary of the general synod of the Church of Ireland. He was consecrated as Church of Ireland bishop of Cork, Cloyne and Ross on 6 January 1894. He died at his residence in Bishop Street, Cork, on 12 October 1912 and was buried in the ancestral plot at Ballymartle Cemetery.

MEAGHER, P.J. (1810–1880) Born Bantry, Co. Cork. With an interest in journalism, he was a contributor to *Bolster's Magazine* and other Cork periodicals. His *Zedechias, a Hebrew Tale and other poems* was published in Cork in 1827. **John Windele**, refers to Meagher's publication in his *Historical and Descriptive Notes of the City of Cork* and regrets that 'he (Meagher) did not persevere in the vocation of poesy; his strains breathe an unconquerable love of universal liberty and a strong ardour of patriotism, much feeling, and smooth and agreeable versification'. He subsequently worked as a special corre-

spondent for the London *Times* in France and Spain. In 1835, he volunteered to fight in the army of the Infanta of Spain, rising to the rank of captain and paymaster. Two years later he married a Frenchwoman, Adelaide de Brumont, of Bayonne. He returned to work in London but later resumed his job as *The Times* correspondent in Madrid and, in 1856, at Paris. He retired in 1869 and died at Bayonne in 1880.

MEANEY, Cornelius (1890–1970) Born Muniflugh, Clondrohid, Co. Cork. The family later moved to Millstreet. He served on Cork County Council as an ex-officio member (1920–3). He was elected to that body in 1928 and held his seat until his death. He won a seat in Dáil Éireann as a Fianna Fáil deputy for North Cork in 1937 but was defeated in 1943. He unsuccessfully contested his lost seat in 1944, 1948 and 1951, before he was returned for the Mid-Cork seat in the 1961 general election. He did not seek re-election in 1965 but was succeeded by his son, Tom (TD 1965–82 and minister of state 1971–81). He died at the Bon Secours Hospital, Cork, on 11 September 1970 and was buried in St Mary's Cemetery, Millstreet.

MECHAM, George F. (1828–1858) Born Queenstown (now Cobh), Co. Cork. He joined the Royal Navy in 1841 and rose to the rank of lieutenant in 1849. In March of the following year, he was third lieutenant of the barque, *Assistance* – one of four vessels ordered to Arctic waters in search of a previous expedition which had not been heard from since 1845. He commanded several sledge parties and mapped out many areas before the expedition returned to London in September 1851. In the following year, the same four vessels, along with a supply ship, set out once again on the same mission. This time, Mecham was first lieutenant on the *Resolute*. The expedition eventually ran into trouble on the ice and the total complement of the five vessels (263 men) crammed on board the *Northern Star*. To reach this ship, Mecham had covered a distance of 1,336 miles by sledge in seventy days. On their return to England, he was promoted to the rank of commander in October 1854. While commanding a steam vessel, the *Vixen*, in the Pacific, he was taken ill and died in Honolulu, Hawaii, on 17 February 1858. Two Arctic landmarks, Cape Mecham and Mecham Island, were named in his honour.

MEHIGAN, Patrick D. (1884–1965) Born Ardfield, Co. Cork, the son of Denis Mehigan, farmer. Having been educated at Mountain Common NS, he joined the Customs and Excise Service in 1899. He was transferred to London in 1902 and lined out with London against Cork in the 1902 All-Ireland Hurling final. On his return to Cork, he played for the county against Kilkenny in the 1905 All-Ireland Hurling final. He was also an accomplished athlete and took the Irish triple jump title in 1908. In 1922, he was transferred to the Irish Civil Service and helped in the organisation of the Tailteann Games. On 29 August 1926, he gave the first radio broadcast in Europe of an outdoor sports event when he commentated on the All-Ireland hurling semi-final. From then until 1932, he was a regular Radio Éireann broadcaster. On his retirement from the Civil Service and from radio work in 1934, he became a full-time journalist – as Gaelic games correspondent of the *Irish Times* and as 'Carbery' in the *Cork Examiner* and other publications. From 1939 until 1964, he published each Christmas a *Carbery's Annual* – selections from which were published in one volume in 1984 under the title, *Vintage Carbery*. He also published a collection of essays, *Mountain Heath* (1944). He died on 4 December 1965 at his residence, 35 Dartmouth Square, Dublin, and was buried in Dean's Grange Cemetery.

MEREDITH, Susanna (1823–1901) Born Cork as Susanna Lloyd, the daughter of the governor of the County Gaol. In 1840, she married a young doctor, but seven years later was a widow and childless. She then engaged in charitable work and ran a lace-making industrial school in Cork. On her father's death in 1860, she moved to London and became the editor of

The Alexandra, a journal which promoted women's rights and employment opportunities. She also became active in improving the plight of women convicts and provided sheltered accommodation and employment to many of them on their release. She testified before the Gladstone Committee on prisons and her evidence led to some reforms. In 1871, she opened her first village-home for the children of convicted criminals at Addlestone, Surrey, where she died in 1901. She published *A Book About Criminals* (1881) and *Saved Rahab!* (1881), both of which endeavoured to promote her aims.

MERRIMAN, Patrick J. (1877–1943) Born Dublin. He was educated at North Richmond Street CBS and at UCD where he graduated BA (1898) and MA (1899) in Modern Languages and Literature. He taught English at St Patrick's College, Maynooth, and later acted as registrar and bursar of UCD. In 1909, he was appointed as professor of History at UCC and later as registrar in 1915. In December 1919, he was elected as president of UCC in succession to **Sir Bertram Windle**. He held this position to his death, which occurred at the President's House, UCC, on 13 September 1943. He was buried in St Finbarr's Cemetery, Cork.

MILLIKEN, Richard A. (1767–1815) Born Castlemartyr, Co. Cork, the son of a Scottish Quaker, Robert Milliken, who was in the employ of the earl of Shannon. Richard worked for a short time as an attorney, but turned to literary pursuits and to publishing his poems in *The Cork Miscellany* and later in his and his sister Anna's *The Casket* which ran for only ten issues. He fought as a yeoman with the Cork Volunteers during the 1798 Rising and composed his famous burlesque, 'De Groves of de Pool' (based on his own 'The Groves of Blarney') on his company's return. He also published some long-forgotten plays including 'The Slave of Surinam' (1810), 'Darby in Arms' (1810) and 'Dungourney in Egypt'. He later returned to the law and practised for a time in Dublin. He died on 16 December 1815 and was buried in Douglas

Cemetery. He also had a strong interest in art and shortly before his death he founded the Cork Society for Promoting the Fine Arts and in that year (1815) the first Munster Exhibition was held at the new 'Deane's Buildings' (designed by **Sir Thomas Deane**) on the South Mall. The society continued to hold exhibitions until 1833. [Memoir by Anne Milliken (1823)]

MILLINGTON, James H. (1799–1872) Born Cork. He was reared in England but returned to Cork in 1821 and set up at 22, Patrick Street, as a painter of miniatures. However, he moved to Dublin in the same year and exhibited at the Society of Artists there. He then moved to London and entered the Royal Academy as a student in 1826. His 'Vulcan's Cave' was exhibited at the Academy in 1831. He continued to exhibit there until 1870 and was, for a while, curator of the School of Painting. He also exhibited at the British Institution and at the Society of British Artists. He died at Bayswater, London, on 11 August 1872.

MOCKLER-FERRYMAN, Augustus (1856–1930) Born Rockville, Co. Cork, the son of Edward Mockler and Julia Ferryman. He was educated at Cheltenham and at Sandhurst Royal Military College where he was commissioned in 1878. He served with the 43rd Light Infantry and the Oxfordshire Light Infantry before rising to the rank of lieutenant-colonel in 1900. With the exception of a five-year stint in Africa, he spent most of his career at Sandhurst where he rose to the position of professor of Military Topography. He was also employed as the compiler of the official history of the Boer War and as editor of the relevant maps. He was called to the English Bar in 1899. He was a prolific writer on military matters, travel and also wrote short stories. Among his many publications were, *The Oxfordshire Light Infantry* (28 vols, 1892–1920), *Up the Niger* (1892), *In the Northman's Land* (1896), *The Annals of Sandhurst* (1900), *British Nigeria* (1902), *Hemmed In, a Tale of the Western Soudan* (1902), *Military Sketching and Reconnaissance* (1903), *The Golden*

Girdle (1908), *Peeps at many Lands – Norway* (1909), *Confessions of a Robin* (1911), *Regimental War Tales* (1915), and *The Oxford and Bucks Light Infantry in the Great European War, 1914–18* (1920). He was also co-author of *The Military Geography of the Balkan Peninsula* (1905). He resided in Tavistock, South Devon, and died on 26 May 1930.

MOHER, John W. (1909–1985) Born Curraghmore, Mitchelstown, Co. Cork, the son of William Moher, farmer. He was educated at Ballygiblin NS, at Mitchelstown CBS and at PBC, Cork. He joined the British Civil Service and worked in a secretarial capacity at the Admiralty. He became a regular speaker on Irish issues at Hyde Park's Speaker's Corner and was an admirer of Éamon de Valera (1882–1975). He returned to work the family farm in 1945 and wrote for the *Irish Farmer's Journal*. He also contributed a weekly column on Irish matters to the *News Chronicle* of London. He was a member of Cork County Council (1950–74) and served as a Fianna Fáil TD for Cork East (1954–65), having failed to get elected in the general election of 1951 and in a by-election of 1953. He was a vigorous advocate for the setting up of the Agricultural Research Centre at Moorepark, Fermoy, and was also a leading figure in the provision of the Cork Regional (now University) Hospital at Wilton, Cork. He died at that hospital on 10 November 1985 and was buried in Mitchelstown Cemetery.

MOLONEY, T.F. [Barry] (1935–1992) Born Cork. Having qualified as an art teacher, he worked for a period as a graphic artist before obtaining a teaching position in Clonmel where he became head of the art department in the Central Technical Institute. In 1970, he returned to Cork as assistant principal of the Crawford Municipal School of Art. He became principal in June of the following year. A watercolourist, he regularly exhibited at the Munster Fine Art Exhibitions and, as a sculptor, was commissioned to execute the 'Echo Boy' sculpture at Cook Street which commemorates the anniversaries of the

Cork Examiner and *Evening Echo* newspapers. He was also commissioned to execute the bronze relief of Tim Severin's 'Brendan Boat' which topped the Tall Ships Trophy during the Tall Ships visit to Cork in 1991. He died at his Castletreasure residence in Douglas on 28 December 1992 and was buried in St Finbarr's Cemetery.

MONAHAN, Philip (1894–1983) Born Dublin. He was educated at Westland Row CBS and at North Richmond Street CBS before he began his working life as a teacher at Drogheda CBS. Having joined the Irish Volunteers, he was arrested and interned at Frongoch. On his release, he joined Sinn Féin and won a seat on Louth County Council. He became mayor of Drogheda in 1920. He supported the Treaty and was appointed as commissioner for Kerry (1922) and Cork City commissioner in 1924. When the Irish government introduced the American model of city management in 1929, he was appointed City Manager for life (to his retirement in 1958). His tenure was marked by the rebuilding of the City Hall, extensive slum clearance and house-building in the suburbs both north and south of the river. He died at his residence, Dundanion House, Church Road, Blackrock, on 18 April 1983 and was buried in the local St Michael's Cemetery. [Life by A. Quinlivan (2006)]

MOODY, John (alias COCHRANE) (c.1727–1812) Born Cork, the son of a hairdresser. He went to Jamaica in 1745 where he became noted as an actor. He returned to the London stage and played with the celebrated actor, David Garrick (1717–79), at Drury Lane. He was especially noted for his performances as a 'stage Irishman'. Due to his heavy weight, he was forced to retire from the stage c.1795, but returned to give his last performance for charity at Covent Garden on 26 June 1804. He subsequently lived in Barnes Common and grew vegetables for Covent Garden Market. He died on 26 December 1812 and was buried in Barnes Churchyard.

MOORE, Courtenay (1840 or 1842–1922) Born Rosnashane, Ballymoney, Co. Antrim, the sixth son of Alexander Moore, doctor. He was educated at TCD where he graduated BA (1862) and MA (1871). In 1866, he was ordained in the Church of Ireland ministry at Cork. His preferments were in the diocese of Cloyne and included the curacy of Brigown (1866–71), the rectorship of Faraghy (1871–5) and of Castletownroche (1875–82), before returning to Mitchelstown as rector of Brigown from 1883 until his retirement in 1915. A founder member of the CHAS, he was a frequent contributor to its *Journal*. He was editor of the *Irish Ecclesiastical Gazette* (1893–97) and was author (among other works) of two novels, *Con Hegarty: a story of Irish life* and *Jer Sheehy*. He also published *A Chapter of Irish Church History: being some personal recollections of life and service in the Church of Ireland* (1908). He died at his residence at Kingstown (now Dún Laoghaire) on 22 June 1922 and was buried there. His daughter, Jessie (**Mrs Victor Rickard**), who died in 1963, was a prolific and successful novelist with thirty novels to her credit.

MOORE, Henry Kingsmill (1853–1943) Born Liverpool, the son of a clergyman who later became headmaster of Midleton College, Co. Cork. He came to Ireland in 1863 and was educated at Midleton, at Bromsgrove School and at Balliol College, Oxford. He took a great interest in educational matters and was appointed as first principal of the Church of Ireland Training College in 1894 – a position which he held until 1927. He married a daughter of John Turpin, his father's predecessor at Midleton College. He also acted as chaplain to the lord lieutenant from 1906 until 1921. He was a member of the Royal Irish Academy and a fellow of the Royal Irish Society of Antiquarians. He died on 1 December 1943. He published *An Unwritten Chapter in the History of Education* (1904) and *Reminiscences and Reflections* (1930). He also published a didactic pamphlet, *The Teaching of Our Lord with Reference to Finance*.

MOORE, Terry (1945–2001) Born Cork. He was educated at North Monastery CBS where he played hurling, football and basketball. Though his older brother, Seán, was a prominent Cork footballer and sprinter, Terry opted for a rugby career, beginning with Highfield RFC's junior side in 1962. He was promoted to the senior side in the following year and helped the club to its first Munster Senior Cup title in 1966 and again in 1968. He toured Australia in 1967 with the Irish side and made his international debut against the Wallabies in what proved to be Ireland's first test victory there. However, he did not gain the second of his twelve international caps as a No. 8 until 1972. His international career lasted until 1974 when he was part of the team which won the Five Nations Championship. He died unexpectedly in Cork on 17 June 2001 and was buried in St Oliver's Cemetery.

MORGAN, Henry (fl. 1849) Born Cork. He was an amateur landscape painter and who is best known for his series of coloured lithographs on views of Cork Harbour. The twenty-eight views were published in Exeter in 1849. [republished as a bound volume (Cork, 1999)]

MORGAN, Jane (1832–1899) Born Prospect, Carrigrohane, Co. Cork, the daughter of James Morgan. She studied drawing, modelling, painting and sculpture in Cork and Dublin. With her sister, Maria, she moved to Rome and then to New York. They designed and built an unusual house at Staten Island which Jane, over a period of five years, decorated with carving and inlaid panels on the walls and ceilings. She died there of diphtheria on 4 April 1899. Her pictures and woodwork were later transferred to Hollybrook, Skibbereen, the residence of Colonel A. Hickman Morgan.

MORGAN, William J. (d. 1856) Born Cork. He worked as a landscape artist and exhibited at the Royal Hibernian Academy in 1847. Though possessed of much natural talent, he led an intemperate and irregular life. He died in Cork in August 1856.

MORIARTY, Abram Orpen (1830–1918) Born Cork, the son of **Merion M. Moriarty**, portmaster. The family moved to Sydney, Australia, in 1843. He worked as a clerk in various public departments of New South Wales and was elected to the Legislative Council in 1858. A year later, having resigned from the Council, he moved to Queensland and drafted the actual proclamation which established the colony on 10 December 1859. He returned to Sydney in the following year and held various public offices including that of chief commissioner of Crown Lands. He died at his residence at Goulburn, New South Wales, on 24 April 1856 and was buried in the local Anglican graveyard.

MORIARTY, Henry Augustus (1815–1906) Born Dursey Island, Co. Cork, the son of Commander James Moriarty, RN. He joined the British Navy in 1829 and rose to the rank of Captain in 1867. He is associated with the various attempts between 1857 to 1865 to lay the Atlantic telegraph cable and especially for the recovery of the broken cable in 1866. He published various pamphlets on seafaring and was a contributor to the *Encyclopaedia Britannica*. His four-volume work on sailing directions was privately published by the British Admiralty. He died at Lee, Kent, on 18 August 1906.

MORIARTY, Joan D. (1920–1992) Born Mallow, Co. Cork. She spent her childhood years in Liverpool, London and Paris, but eventually settled in Cork where she opened a ballet studio and founded the Cork Ballet Group (later the Cork Ballet Company). In 1959, she established a touring company, the Irish Ballet Theatre, which played all over Ireland but was wound up in 1964. She established the Irish Ballet Company in 1974 and continued as director until her resignation in 1988. Her dance version of Synge's 'Playboy of the Western World' was performed in London and New York to wide critical acclaim. She died on 24 January 1992 and was buried in St Finbarr's Cemetery, Cork. [Life by S. Mac Liammoir (1995); Essays, R. Fleischmann, ed.

(1998); Commemorative plaque at the former Cork Ballet School premises, 1 Emmet Place, Cork]

MORIARTY, John Francis (1854–1915) Born Mallow, Co. Cork, the son of John Moriarty, solicitor. He was educated at Stonyhurst School and at TCD where he graduated BA. Having studied law, he entered the Middle Temple (1875) and was called to the Bar (1877). He worked as a Crown prosecutor in Co. Cork before becoming a QC in 1905 and Law Sergeant (1908–13). He served as Solicitor General and as Attorney General during 1913 and 1914 prior to his appointment as Lord Chief Justice of Appeal later in the latter year. He became ill in April 1915 and went to England for treatment. Following a serious operation, he died at Edgebaston, Birmingham on 2 May 1915. He was buried in Glasnevin Cemetery.

MORIARTY, Merion M. (1794–1864) Born County Cork, the son of vice-admiral Sylverius Moriarty and father of **Abram Orpen Moriarty**. He joined the Royal Navy in 1807, was promoted to the rank of lieutenant but retired through ill health on half-pay in 1815. He married in 1816 and, having studied medicine at the University of Edinburgh, he graduated MD in 1821. He practised for a time in Dublin but was later employed by the St George's Channel Steam Navigation Company as a ship's captain on the Cork-Bristol route. In January 1843, he took up an appointment as the harbour-master of Sydney, Australia, and worked there until his retirement on pension in 1857. In August 1860, he was returned as a member of the New South Wales Legislative Assembly. He died on 10 January 1864 and was buried in the Anglican cemetery of St Leonard's, Sydney.

MORONEY, Tommy (1923–1981) Born Cork. He was educated at PBC, Cork, where he was an outstanding athlete and represented Munster schools in interprovincial rugby. On leaving school, he played rugby at out-half for Highfield, Cork Constitution and Munster. He won Munster Senior Cup medals with Constitution in 1943 and 1946. However, he opted to concentrate on soccer and won League of Ireland Championship medals (1945–6) and an FAI Cup medal (1947) with Cork United. In 1947, he signed for West Ham United and made 148 league appearances until 1952. In the meantime, he was capped twelve times for Ireland and was left-half on the team which had a famous victory over England at Goodison Park in 1949. On his return to Cork in 1953, he was manager, in turn, of Evergreen United, Cork Celtic and Cork Hibernians – all League of Ireland clubs. He died on 2 May 1981 and was buried in St Joseph's Cemetery.

MORRIS, Francis O. (1810–1893) Born Queenstown (now Cobh), the eldest son of Rear-Admiral Henry G. Morris. He was educated at Bromgrove School and at Worcester College, Oxford, where he graduated BA (1833). He was ordained in 1835 and spent the remainder of his ministry as rector of Nunburnholme, Yorkshire. He is best known for his works on birds, for his opinions on the theory of evolution and for his opposition to animal vivisection. He also wrote on religious and social subjects. He died on 10 February 1893. His publications include *A History of British Birds* (6 vols, 1851–1857), *Difficulties of Darwinism* (1869), *A Double Dilemma in Darwinism* (1870), *All the Articles of the Darwin Faith* (1877 and 1882), *The Demands of Darwinism on Credulity* (1890), *The Cowardly cruelty of the Experimenters on Living Animals* (1890) and *A Defence of our Dumb Companions* (1892). [Memoir by M.C.F. Morris (1897)]

MORRIS, William (d. 1680) He came to Ireland as a Baptist captain in the Cromwellian army. However, he was suspected of having Quaker tendencies and when these were confirmed, he was discharged from the army. He settled at Castlesalem or Benduff, near Rosscarbery, with his brother, Paul. As a Quaker, he objected to the payment of tithes and published the pamphlet *Tithes, No Gospel Ordinance*.

In 1670, **William Penn** visited him at Castlesalem and wrote his *Letter to the Young Convinced* from there.

MORRISON, Sir Richard (1767–1849) Born Midleton, Co. Cork, the son of John Morrison, architect, who is best remembered for his design of Kingston College, Mitchelstown. He was a pupil of James Gandon (1742–1823) and published a book entitled, *Designs* (1793). His patron was Bishop **Charles Agar** of Cloyne who went on to become archbishop of Cashel and Dublin. Morrison designed Sir Patrick Dun's Hospital, Dublin, and was elected as president of the Institute of Architects. He was knighted in 1841. He died in Bray on 31 October 1849 and was buried at Mount Jerome Cemetery, Dublin. His son, William Vitruvius Morrison (1794–1838), was also a noted architect. Father and son were responsible for the design of Fota House. [Biographical sketches and works of the Morrisons by the Irish Architectural Institute (1989)]

MORROGH, John (1849–1901) Born Cork, the son of Dominick Morrogh. He was educated at the Christian Brothers schools in Cork and emigrated to South Africa in the early 1870s. He was an early participator in the working of the Kimberley diamond mines and became one of the directors of the De Beers Diamond Company. He returned to Cork in the mid-1880s and turned his energy to local industry – reopening Douglas Woollen Mills after several years' closure. He was a director of the *Cork Herald* and *National Press* newspapers. He also embarked on a political career and was elected MP for Cork South East at a by-election in June 1889 as a Home Ruler. He retained his seat (as an anti-Parnellite) in the 1892 general election, but resigned in June 1893, pleading business commitments. He was a member of Cork Corporation for three years and was elected to the first Cork County Council in 1899. He died at his residence, Mount Grange, Douglas, on 4 October 1901 and was buried in Douglas Cemetery. He was the grand-uncle of

Sheelagh Murnaghan (1924–93), Liberal MP for Queen's University in the Stormont Parliament (1961–9).

MOUNTAINE, James (c.1819–1868) Born Cork. Throughout his adult life, he was prominent in revolutionary nationalism in Cork. A supporter of Repeal in his early years, he became a member of the Young Ireland movement and was active in Cork during the rising of 1848. When James Stephens (1824–1901) founded the Irish Republican Brotherhood in 1858, Mountaine was his contact-man in Cork where the latter organised Fenian meetings at his 73 North Main Street shoemaking premises. He was also prominent in Cork nationalist organisations such as the Davis Institute, the Cork National Reading Rooms and the Brotherhood of St Patrick. He was arrested in 1863 on suspicion of inciting the 'Prince of Wales Riots' in the city but was acquitted. During a series of Fenian arrests in 1865, he was arrested in late October and, following a period on remand, was tried in Cork on 27 December where he was defended by **Isaac Butt** and found not guilty. He was arrested again in 1867 and spent several months in Cork Gaol. However, his health was impaired by his periods in prison and he died on 6 November 1868. His funeral to St Joseph's Cemetery was attended by an estimated 6,000 people but his grave remains unmarked.

MOYLAN, Jack (d. 1949) Born Churchtown, Mallow, Co. Cork. Though he was to become noted as a flat race jockey, he finished second in the Aintree Grand National in 1924 riding Fly Mask. He rode seven Irish Classic winners in his career (1,000 Guineas, 1926; 2,000 Guineas, 1944; Irish Derby, 1944 and 1945; Irish Oaks, 1944; and Irish St Leger, 1939 and 1946). He was father-in-law of Jimmy Eddery, Irish champion jockey, and grandfather of Pat Eddery, one of the great modern flat race jockeys. He died at Churchtown in 1949.

MOYLAN, Francis (1735–1815) Born Cork, the son of a valuator to Cork Corporation and brother of **Stephen Moylan**. He was educated at the Irish College, Toulouse. He was ordained on 11 June 1761 and spent his first years as a priest at Chatou, near Paris. He returned to Cork in 1764 and ministered in the North Parish at St Mary's and at SS. Peter and Paul's for ten years before moving to St Finbarr's, South Parish, in 1774. In the following year, he was appointed as bishop of Ardfert and Aghadoe. On 17 June 1787, he was translated to the diocese of Cork and Ross on the resignation of Bishop **John Butler**, Lord Dunboyne. He favoured the Act of Union but reacted strongly against the English Government's proposal of a veto on Roman Catholic episcopal appointments in return for a state endowment of Roman Catholic clergy and the recommendation to implement Catholic Emancipation. He also supported **Nano Nagle** in the founding of the Order of Presentation nuns. He died at Chapel Lane, Cork, on 10 February 1815 and was buried in his cathedral. [Monument by Peter Turnerelli at North Cathedral; Portrait by **William Willes** (head by **John Corbett**)]

MOYLAN, Seán (1887–1957) Born Kilmallock, Co. Limerick, the son of Richard Moylan of Newmarket, Co. Cork, where Seán was reared. He was educated at Newmarket NS. At the age of sixteen he was apprenticed to a carpenter and, following a spell in Dublin, he set up as a building contractor in the Newmarket area in 1914. He joined the Irish Volunteers and became the commandant of the Newmarket battalion of the IRA in 1917. However, he was arrested and imprisoned in the following year. In 1920, he played a prominent role in the capture of Mallow military barracks, in the capture of General Lucas and in the ambushes of Tureengarriffe and Clonbanin. He was captured in May 1921, tried, and sentenced to fifteen years imprisonment. While he was imprisoned on Spike Island, he was elected to the 2nd Dáil and was released in July following the Truce. He subsequently opposed the Anglo-Irish Treaty and spent some time in the United States before returning in 1924. He served as Fianna Fáil TD for Cork North (1932–57) and was minister for Lands (1943–8) and minister for

Education (1951–4). He was defeated in the general election of 1957 but was appointed by Taoiseach Éamon de Valera as a member of the Seanad. He was then appointed as minister for Agriculture – only the second Senator to hold ministerial status. He died at his residence at Clontarf, Dublin, on 16 November 1957 and was buried in Kiskeam Cemetery. [Headstone by **Seamus Murphy** at Kiskeam]

MOYLAN, Stephen (1734–1811) Born Cork, the son of a valuator to Cork Corporation and brother of Bishop **Francis Moylan**. He was educated locally and in Paris. He spent three years in the shipping business in Lisbon before emigrating to America in 1768 and setting up as a merchant in Philadelphia. He was elected as president of the Friendly Sons of St Patrick in 1771 (and also later, in 1796). At the outbreak of the American War of Independence, he sided with the colonists and in August 1775 he was appointed as muster-master general of the army. In March 1776, he became secretary to General George Washington (1732–99), the future first US President, and was promoted to the post of quartermaster general in the following June. Following a disagreement with a congressional committee, he resigned his commission and rejoined the army as a volunteer. However, in December of that year, he was requested by Washington to form a cavalry regiment. The regiment (nicknamed 'Moylan's Dragoons') was ready by April 1777 and Moylan commanded until the end of the war, when, through ill health, he retired to Philadelphia. By then, he had married Mary R. van Horn of Phil's Hill, New Jersey in 1778. On 3 November 1783, he was honoured with the rank of brigadier-general by the American Congress. He died in Philadelphia on 13 April 1811 and was buried in Old St Mary's Graveyard there. Moylan Park in Philadelphia was dedicated to his memory in 1922. [Life by M.J. Griffin (1909); Assessment by F. Monaghan in *Studies* (1930)]

MOYNIHAN, Denis (1885–1975) Born Rathmore, Co. Kerry. He was educated at St

Brendan's College, Killarney and at the Irish College, Paris, where he was ordained in 1909. He ministered in Liverpool until 1918 when he returned to the diocese of Kerry and worked in Caherdaniel, Tralee and Killarney. He was consecrated as bishop of Ross at St Patrick's Pro-Cathedral, Skibbereen, on 21 September 1941. He was translated to the diocese of Kerry on 10 February 1953 and to the titular see of Suacia on 17 July 1969. He died on 5 December 1975 and was buried in the grounds of St Mary's Cathedral, Killarney.

MOYNIHAN, James (1893–1970) Born Cúil Aodha, Co. Cork, the son of Con Moynihan, farmer. During the War of Independence, he was captain of 'A' company, 8th batt., Cork No.1 Brigade of the IRA and was interned several times. He took the Republican side during the civil war and later served as a Fianna Fáil county councillor for a period of forty-two years (1928–70). He died while attending a Vocational Education Committee meeting on 1 October 1970 and was buried in Reilig Ghobnatan, Baile Bhúirne. His son, Donal, is a Fianna Fáil TD for the constituency of Cork North West. [Memorial at Cúil Aodha]

MULDOON, John (1865–1938) Born Dromore, Co. Tyrone, the third son of James Muldoon. He was educated locally and at Queen's College, Galway (now UCG). He was called to the Bar in 1894 and practised on the North Western Circuit. Having been assistant secretary to the Irish National Federation, he was elected as a nationalist MP for Donegal North in a 1905 by-election, but did not seek re-election in the following year. In 1907, he was returned as MP for Wicklow East in a by-election. He resigned this seat in 1911 to provide Capt. **Anthony J.C. Donelan** with a safe seat and was elected for Cork East in Donelan's stead (Donelan had been deprived of his seat following an election petition). He retained the Cork East seat until 1918. He was appointed as registrar in Lunacy (1921) and as registrar to the Chief Justice (1926). He retired in 1935. An authority on land

law and local government, he collaborated in the compilation of several texts on legal topics. He was also well versed in electoral law and had charge of many election campaigns. He died at his Dún Laoghaire, Co. Dublin, residence on 20 November 1938 and was buried in Dean's Grange Cemetery, Dublin.

MULHARE, Edward (1923–1997) Born Cork. He was educated at St Nessan's NS and at North Monastery CBS. He briefly studied medicine. He took an interest in acting and made his stage debut at Cork Opera House at the age of nineteen. He first appeared on the London stage in the 1951 production of '*Othello*' under the direction of Sir Laurence Olivier and replaced Rex Harrison in the Broadway production of '*My Fair Lady*'. His earliest film role was in *Hill 24 Doesn't Answer* (1954) and in the 1960s he had prominent roles in several films including *Von Ryan's Express* (1965) and *Caprice* (1967). He reached a wide audience through his leading roles in the popular TV series, *The Ghost and Mrs Muir* (1968–9) and *Knight Rider* (1982–7). He died in Los Angeles, USA, on 25 May 1997.

MULLANE, Anthony John [Tony] (1859–1944) Born Cork, the son of Denis Mullane. The family emigrated to the United States c.1864 and settled near Erie, Pennsylvania. He became a professional baseball player and made his debut in 1881 with the Detroit Wolverines. He played thirteen seasons with eight different teams and ended his major league career in 1894. He is claimed to have been the best pitcher in baseball of his day and was one of the game's high earners during his career. He was also distinguished by being ambidextrous to a unique level. Nicknamed, 'The Apollo of the Box' or 'The Count', he had a colourful career and life. On retirement, he worked for a time as a professional umpire and later as a policeman. He died in Chicago on 25 April 1944.

MULLIGAN, William A. (d. 1919) He became headmaster of the Crawford Municipal School of Art on the resignation of **James Brenan** in

1889. His watercolours were exhibited at the Royal Hibernian Academy until 1916.

MULLINS, Thomas Lincoln (1903–1978) Born New Rochelle, New York, the only child of Martin (of Galway) and Catherine Mullins (of Cork). He returned to Ireland as a child and was educated at Presentation Brothers School, Kinsale, and at St Enda's, Rathfarnham, Dublin. As a member of the IRA, he participated in the War of Independence and was imprisoned in Wormwood Scrubs, where he took part in a hunger strike. On his release, he returned to active service, but was again captured and interned at Spike Island, Co. Cork, and later at Ballykinlar Camp, Co. Down. He was released in July 1921 following the Truce. He took the Republican side in the civil war and was again interned, this time in Mountjoy Gaol and took part in a long hunger strike. A founder member of Fianna Fáil in 1926, he accompanied Eamon de Valera (1882–1975) on a tour of West Cork establishing cumainn and a West Cork constituency executive. He was elected to Dáil Éireann as a Fianna Fáil TD for West Cork in June 1927 but did not seek re-election in 1932. He was involved in the publicity section of Fianna Fáil (1933–40), was sub-editor of the *Irish Press* (1941–4) and was general secretary of Fianna Fáil from 1945. He was a Senator and Leader of the House from 1957 to 1973. He had stood for the Dublin County Dáil by-election in 1947 and, despite topping the poll, he was defeated by Seán McBride (1904–88), the leader of Clann na Poblachta. He died at Ashford nursing home, Dublin, on 2 November 1978 and was buried in Dean's Grange Cemetery.

MUNSTER, Henry (*fl.* 1870–90) Henry Munster was English, Roman Catholic, a graduate of Cambridge and a barrister, though he never practised. He had valuable interests in collieries and iron works in the Sheffield area. His English home was at Tunbridge Wells, but in 1868 he moved residence to Cashel to contest the parliamentary seat there. Despite spending over £6,000, he failed to win the seat, though the election was declared void and the borough was disenfranchised for persistent corruption. He then turned his attention to Mallow and won a nomination to contest the seat in the Liberal interest in May 1870. He was successful at the polls, but on petition was unseated and a new writ was issued. He supported the candidacy of his son **William Felix Munster** at Mallow in 1872 and was successful in getting the Munster surname into the House of Commons. He made his final foray in Irish parliamentary politics in 1887 when he contested Donegal South as a Liberal Unionist, but was outpolled by five to one by the nationalist candidate, J.G.S. McNeill.

MUNSTER, William Felix (1849–1877) Born at Mortier near Tours, France, the eldest son of **Henry Munster**, barrister and industrialist. He was educated at Stonyhurst and at London University, where he graduated BA. In 1872, aged only 23, he won a nomination as a Liberal to contest the Mallow parliamentary seat left vacant by the retirement of **George Waters**. His opponent was the Liberal Home Ruler, **John George McCarthy**. Munster was victor by a margin of thirteen votes (91–78) and was elected to the House of Commons. His tenure was a short one. Rumours of his resignation had circulated in early 1874, but he retained the seat until a general election was called later that month. He did not contest the seat. He spent some time in the US after 1874 and in January 1877 he married Blanche Lynch, daughter of a prominent citizen of St Louis. Following a society wedding, the couple toured the southern States on honeymoon, before returning in April to St Louis, where they took rooms in the Southern Hotel. During their stay a disastrous fire engulfed the hotel on 11 April 1877 and eleven people lost their lives. The Munsters escaped the blaze, having initially despaired of rescue. The next morning Munster visited the scene and was described as being in a state of 'shock and excitement'. On returning to his room, he committed suicide by shooting himself with his revolver.

MURPHY, Bartholomew (1789–1872) Born Cork. An ordinary working man, he founded the Sick Poor Society movement in Cork city around 1830, at a time when the poverty of the Cork lower classes was compounded by outbreaks of disease. Murphy began the movement by collecting a few pennies from people in his neighbourhood to aid a poor family laid low by sickness. This grew into more formally organised fundraising and distribution to the sick poor in the North, Middle and South Parishes. The society played a prominent role in alleviating distress in the city during economic crises and epidemics over the following century. He died on 4 August 1872 and was buried in St Joseph's Cemetery. A headstone was unveiled over his grave in 1937 by the North Parish branch.

MURPHY, Charles K. (1890–1956) Born Cork. He was educated at PBC (Cork), in Munich and at UCC where he graduated MA (1913) and LL.D (1917). He qualified as a solicitor in 1917 and subsequently became professor of Jurisprudence and dean of the Law Faculty at UCC. He also acted as agent for the Labour Party candidates in the 1922 general election. He had been appointed as hon. secretary of the St Vincent de Paul Society of Cork in 1918 and remained thereafter its most prominent member in the city, being President from 1941 until his death. He was instrumental in the building of the hostel for homeless men on Merchants' Quay and was also the initiator of the annual Eucharistic procession in Cork City. He wrote several books and pamphlets on the St Vincent de Paul Society and on Roman Catholic social action, notably *The Spirit of the Society of St Vincent de Paul* (1940), *The Spirit of Catholic Action* (1943) and *The Lay Apostolate of Charity* (posthumously, 1959). He died, following a brief illness at the Mercy Hospital, Cork, on 9 September 1956 and was buried privately.

MURPHY, Daniel (1815–1907) Born Belmont, Moviddy, Co. Cork, the son of Michael Murphy. He was educated at a local seminary and at St Patrick's College, Maynooth, where he was ordained in June 1838. In the following year, he commenced his missionary service at Hyderabad, India, and was consecrated as coadjutor bishop in October 1846. He resigned in 1864 through ill health and returned to Ireland. Two years later, he was appointed as bishop of Hobart, Tasmania and immediately became involved in the controversy surrounding the granting of state aid to denominational schools. He attended the First Vatican Council and voted for the dogma of papal infallibility. He became a metropolitan in May 1889 as a consequence of the diocese of Hobart being made into an archbishopric. Having four nephews and a sister among the religious of his see, he was often accused of being 'nephew-ridden'. Among his interests was the study of astronomy and he read a paper to the 1895 Congress of the Australasian Science Association at Brisbane. He died at Low Head, Tasmania, on 29 December 1907 and was buried in Hobart. [Memoir by M. Beechinor (1916)]

MURPHY, Denis (1833–1896) Born Scarteen, Newmarket, Co. Cork, the son of Timothy Murphy. He studied at Jesuit seminaries in England, Germany and Spain before being ordained to the Order in 1849. He taught at Clongowes Wood College, Co. Kildare, and at Crescent College, Limerick, before his appointment as professor of Moral Theology at the Jesuit Institute, Milltown, Dublin. When the Jesuits took over the running of the old Catholic University in Stephen's Green under Rev. William Delany (1835–1924) in 1883, Murphy declared, 'I am his librarian and his bursar, yet I have not a penny in my burse nor a book in my library.' A keen historian, his *Cromwell in Ireland* was published in 1883. He also compiled a history of Holycross Abbey, Co. Tipperary, and researched in continental archives on Irish Roman Catholic martyrs since the time of King Henry VIII (1491–1547). He was a very keen antiquarian and was, for a time, the editor of the *Kildare Archaeological Journal*. He played the cello in a string quartet which frequently performed at the Royal Irish Academy of Music in Dublin. He died at University College, Dublin, on 18 May 1896 and was buried in Glasnevin Cemetery.

MURPHY, Sir Francis (1809–1891) Born Cork, the son of Francis D. Murphy, 'Superintendent of the Transportation of Convicts from Ireland'. He attended TCD and later studied medicine taking the Diploma of the Royal College of Surgeons of which he later became a member. In June 1836, he emigrated to Sydney as a colonial surgeon. Four years later, he resigned his position and engaged in farming a holding of 50,000 acres. In 1852, he sold out and moved to Melbourne where he entered politics. He became speaker of the Victorian Assembly in 1856 and served five terms over a fourteen-year period. He was knighted in 1860 and was a founder member of the University of Melbourne. He died in Melbourne on 30 March 1891 and, following an Anglican service, was buried in Boroondara Cemetery.

MURPHY, Francis S. (1807–1860) Born Hyde Park, Cork, the son of Jeremiah Murphy, merchant and distiller. He was the nephew of Bishop **John Murphy** and of **James Murphy**. He was educated at Clongowes Wood College, Co. Kildare and at TCD where he graduated BA (1829), and MA (1832). He was called to the English Bar in 1833. A year later, he wrote for **William Maginn's** *Fraser's Magazine* and helped **Francis S. Mahony**, his former teacher at Clongowes, with his *Reliques of Father Prout*. In 1837, he was elected as MP for County Cork and served for a total of sixteen years. He was appointed a sergeant-at-law in 1842 and in 1853 he resigned his parliamentary seat when he was appointed a commissioner in Bankruptcy. He died on 17 June 1860. [Portrait in the *Maclise Picture Gallery* (1883)]

MURPHY, James (1769–1855) Born South Main Street, Cork, the eldest son of Jeremiah Murphy (1746–1802), tanner and leather merchant. He was the brother of Bishop **John Murphy** and uncle of **Francis S. Murphy**. He

took over his father's business in the first decade of the nineteenth century, and with his younger brothers, Nicholas, Daniel and Jeremiah, they became one of the city's wealthiest merchant families, operating their shipping base from Morrison's Island. In 1825, James and his brothers bought a disused woollen mill and former army barracks from Viscount Midleton and established a distillery in Midleton town. The distillery, trading under the name of 'James Murphy & Co.', proved to be very successful. The firm later amalgamated with other Cork distilleries to form the Cork Distilling Company, which became one of the founding companies of Irish Distillers plc. [Bust by **John Hogan** at the Old Distillery, Midleton]

MURPHY, James C. (1760–1814) Born Blackrock, Cork, the son of a bricklayer. He worked as a bricklayer, studied architecture in Dublin and later Gothic architecture on the Continent. He supervised some additions to the Irish House of Commons to the design of the famous architect, James Gandon (1742–1823). He studied Moorish architecture in Cadiz and Batalha (Spain) and left a large number of drawings. He died in London on 12 September 1814. His publications include *Discourse on the Principles of Gothic Architecture* (1795, Ger. trans., 1828), *Travels in Portugal* (1795, Ger. trans., 1796; French trans. in 2 vols, 1797), *A General View of Portugal* (1798) and *Arabian Antiquities in Spain* (1813–16).

MURPHY, James J. (1825–1897) Born Morrison's Island, Cork, the son of Jeremiah James Murphy (1795–1851), merchant and distiller. His grandfather, **James Murphy**, was a co-founder of Midleton Distillery. In 1856, he sold his shares in the distillery, and, with his brothers William, Jerome, Francis and Nicholas, he established the Lady's Well Brewery at the site of the former Cork Foundling Hospital under the title of 'James J. Murphy & Co.' The brewery was a great success and made him one of Cork's most eminent businessmen. He also took an interest in banking and, as one of the directors of the Munster Bank, he took the principal role in rescuing the bank when it sensationally collapsed in 1885. A new bank, the Munster & Leinster Bank (now AIB), was then formed with Murphy as chairman and all outstanding debts of the failed Munster Bank were honoured. Many commercial bodies made presentations and congratulatory addresses to the man who had saved them from financial ruin. As well as being a notable contributor to many Cork charities, he also took a lively interest in the newly founded GAA. He died at his home near Passage West on 26 October 1897 and was buried in the family vault at Carrigrohane.

MURPHY, James V. (1880–1946) Born Knocknacool, Bandon, Co. Cork, the son of Timothy Murphy, farmer, horse-dealer and Poor Law Guardian. He was educated at Farranferris College and at Maynooth Seminary and was ordained to the priesthood in 1904. In 1906, he was sent to minister at Rochester, New York, but soon lost his priestly vocation. He returned to Europe and became chief of the Italian Information Bureau in London (1916–19). After some freelance periods in Italy and Germany, he married an upper class Englishwoman, Mary Crowley, who was twenty years his junior. He moved back to Germany where he became interested in the rise of National Socialism. He published *Adolf Hitler: the drama of his career* (1932) and worked for the Nazi Propaganda Ministry until 1938. In the following year, he published the first unabridged English edition of Hitler's *Mein Kampf.* He then moved to England where he spent World War II in poor health. Never a Fascist, he died at Bishop's Stortford on 4 July 1946 and was buried in Broxbourne graveyard. [Life by J. and P. Burns (1987)]

MURPHY, Jeremiah (1840–1915) Born Inniscarra, Co. Cork. He was educated at St Colman's, Fermoy and at St Patrick's College, Maynooth, where he was ordained in 1871. He was appointed as parish priest of Macroom in 1897. He was well known as a contributor to many of the leading journals, as a fluent Irish

speaker and as an accomplished traveller. He had a large library which was later sold in Cork.

MURPHY, Jeremiah D. (1806–1824) Born Cork, a cousin of **Francis S. Murphy**. A gifted linguist, he had mastered seven languages before his early death at the age of eighteen years. He was also a contributor to *Blackwood's Magazine*.

MURPHY, Jeremiah (1895–1966) Born Ballincollig, Co. Cork, whose father was a builder and whose mother was a teacher. He was educated at North Monastery CBS and at UCC where he graduated MA (1926). Later, in 1932, he graduated PhD for his translation into Irish of the Anglo-Saxon Chronicles. He worked as a secondary schoolteacher at Carlow CBS and at CBC, Cork, and was an assistant to the professor of English at UCC, **Daniel Corkery**. In 1934, he was appointed as professor of English Language and Literature at UCG – a post which he held until his retirement in 1965. He was the author of two novellas, entitled, *Hewn of the Rock* (1933) and also of a number of short stories. In his later years, he was a regular essayist in the *Capuchin Annual*. Having a deep interest in theatre and drama, he was associated with St Aidan's drama group of Ballincollig and also with the Cork Shakespearean Society ('The Loft'). He was producer with the Ballincollig group of the first stage production of Padraig Pearse's 'The Singer' at the Peacock Theatre, Dublin. In Galway, he was closely involved with An Taibhdhearc as actor, writer, director, and, for over a decade, chairman. At UCG, he founded the dramatic society, the arts society and the boat club. He died in 1966.

MURPHY, John (1772–1847) Born South Main Street, Cork, the second son of Jeremiah Murphy (1746–1802), tanner and leather merchant. He was the younger brother of **James Murphy** and uncle of **Francis S. Murphy**. He studied for the priesthood at Paris and Lisbon and was ordained in 1794. He returned to Cork in 1797 where he served, in turn, as curate and parish priest of the Middle Parish. He was consecrated as bishop of Cork and Ross in 1815. He was a promoter of the arts and a student of Gaelic, which he learned at the age of forty. He was the first patron of the sculptor, **John Hogan**, who executed many of the wooden carvings in the sanctuary and reredos of the North Cathedral. He built up a massive library of 70,000 volumes, which unfortunately was divided up and sold by Sotheby's of London after his death. In his will, he bequeathed 120 volumes of Irish manuscripts to St Patrick's College, Maynooth. He was also associated with the establishment of Cork Savings Bank in 1817. He died on 1 April 1847 and was buried in his cathedral.

MURPHY, John (1796–1883) Born Ringmahon, Cork, the son of **James Murphy**, merchant and distiller. Following his education in England, he was employed by the East India Company and in 1816, at the age of twenty, he started work with the Hudson Bay Trading Company at New Brunswick, Canada. On his return to Ireland two years later, he went into business with his brothers. However, the venture was not successful and he returned to Canada where he took up trapping. He travelled with a tribe of Indians who nicknamed him 'The Black Eagle of the North'. He eventually returned home and decided to enter the priesthood. He studied in Rome and, following his ordination in 1823, ministered in Liverpool. He was recalled to Cork in 1847 after the death of his uncle, Bishop **John Murphy**. He ministered in Bandon and Schull before his appointment as administrator of Cork's Middle Parish in 1848. He was the main force behind the building of the Church of SS. Peter and Paul (1866) and also with the foundation of the Mercy Hospital at the old Mansion House. He was made archdeacon of Cork in 1874 when he retired to St Vincent's, Sunday's Well. He died on 10 March 1883 and was buried in the family vault at Carrigrohane.

MURPHY, John Nicholas (1816–1889) Born at Clifton, Cork, the eldest son of Nicholas Murphy, one of the co-founders of James Murphy & Co., distillers. He was educated at Clongowes Wood College, Co. Kildare. He took a part in the family businesses in later life, but also devoted himself to charitable projects and, in his prime, to municipal affairs. He was mayor of Cork in 1854 and high sheriff of the city in 1857. He was the founding president of the St Vincent de Paul Society in Cork and was responsible for the establishment of the Sisters of Charity Children's Hospital on Wellington Road in 1877. He also wrote extensively on religious matters and his works include *Ireland: industrial, political and social* (1870), *Terra incognita; or the convents of the United Kingdom* (1873) and *The Chair of Peter* (2 vols), a study of the Papacy. In recognition of his literary services, he was created a Count of the Holy Roman Empire by Pope Leo XIII (1810–1903). He died at Clifton on 11 September 1889 and was buried at the family burial place in Carrigrohane Graveyard.

MURPHY, Michael (1826–1868) Born Cork. He came to Toronto, Ontario, as a young boy where he worked as a cooper and eventually opened a tavern. As a result of a Hibernian/Orange confrontation in Toronto on St Patrick's Day, 1858, the Hibernian Benevolent Society of Canada was formed and Murphy was elected as its first president. The society spread and in 1863, its organ, the *Irish Canadian* was founded. Soon afterwards, the society was accused by the *Toronto Globe* of having strong Fenian links – an accusation strenuously denied by Murphy, although he himself had attended the first national convention of the Fenians in November 1863. In March 1866, Murphy and six companions were arrested at Cornwall, Ontario, while on their way to Portland, Maine, to help in a Fenian attack. They were charged with treason but on the night of 1 September, Murphy and five others escaped and crossed into the United States. He settled in Buffalo, New York, where he was the owner of the Irish Arms Hotel. He died of tuberculosis in Buffalo on 11 April 1868 and the funeral service took place at St Michael's Cathedral, Toronto. [Biographical article by C.P. Stacey in the *Canadian Historical Review*, 15 (1934)]

MURPHY, Michael (1924–1996) Born Kilmichael, Co. Cork. He was orphaned at the age of 7 years, and, having attended Toames NS, went to live with relatives in Macroom. He was educated at St Finbarr's College, Farranferris, where he excelled at hurling – winning an All-Ireland MHC medal in 1941. He then studied at St Patrick's College, Maynooth, where he was ordained in June 1949. He ministered in Washington until 1955 and, on his return to the diocese of Cork, he worked as a curate in Ballingeary and at the North Cathedral. He then served on the Peru Mission from 1961 to 1969 when he was recalled to act as president of Farranferris College. He was consecrated as coadjutor bishop of Cork on 23 May 1976 and succeeded to the see on 23 August 1980. He died at his home on 7 October 1996 and was buried in the grounds of his cathedral.

MURPHY, Michael Pat (1919–2000) Born Coarliss, Drimoleague, Co. Cork. He moved to Schull where he ran a bar with his wife, Hettie, the daughter of Ned Roycroft, a member of the first Cork County Council in 1899. He was co-opted to Cork County Council in 1948 and sat for the Skibbereen electoral area until his retirement in 1985. He was elected as Council chairman on four occasions (1958/59, 1965/66, 1968/69 and 1969/70). He was Labour TD for Cork South-West from 1951 until his retirement in 1981. He was parliamentary secretary to the minister for Agriculture and Fisheries from 1973 until early 1977, and when in opposition, he was Labour spokesman on agriculture. He died at the Victoria/South Infirmary Hospital, Cork, on 28 October 2000 and was buried in Schull Cemetery. His son, Michael Pat Jr., was an independent member of Cork County Council, and his daughter, Kate Ann, is the wife of the Fianna Fáil minister for Sport and Cultural Affairs, John O'Donoghue, TD.

MURPHY, Nicholas D. (1811–1889) Born Cork, the fourth son of Daniel Murphy, tanner, of the brewing and distilling family. He was educated at Clongowes Wood College, Co. Kildare, and at the King's Inns, Dublin. He was admitted a solicitor in 1834 and built up a large practice which, however, he abandoned on the death of his father to take over the management of his tanning business. He entered parliamentary politics on February 1865 when he was returned unopposed as Liberal MP for Cork City in place of **William Trant Fagan**. He retained his seat until 1880 when his defeat in the famous election of that year marked the end of the Liberal Party as a force in Cork and of Murphy involvement in parliamentary politics. His defeat was attributed to being a lukewarm Home Ruler and too zealous a supporter of the liquor interest. He died at his residence in Roseneath Villas, Military Road, Cork, on 6 January 1889.

MURPHY, P.A. ['Weeshie'] (1919–1973) Born Bere Island, Co. Cork. He was educated at St Brendan's Seminary, Killarney, and at UCD where he qualified as a veterinary surgeon, setting up practice in Cork City. The pinnacle of his football-playing career was as full-back on the Cork team which won the 1945 All-Ireland title. He also won three Railway Cup medals (1946, 1948–9) and a National League medal. He won a County senior football medal with Beara in 1940 and, having helped to reorganise Lees football club in 1950, he won his second county medal with that club in 1955. In that year, he was elected as chairman of Cork County GAA Board and held this position until 1965. In 1970, he was elected as chairman of the Munster GAA Council, a post he still held when he died suddenly in Dublin on 2 September 1973 (All-Ireland hurling final day). [Headstone by **Seamus Murphy** at St Finbarr's Cemetery, Cork]

MURPHY, Patrick Stephen (1889–1968) Born Mitchelstown Co. Cork, and a solicitor by profession. He represented the Mallow area in the Cork County Council as a Fianna Fáil member (1928–42). In 1932, he was elected to Dáil Éireann for the East Cork constituency and was re-elected in 1933. Two years later, his family home was burned down by the Blueshirts. **John**

L. O'Sullivan, the prominent Blueshirt, was jailed for five years by the Military Tribunal for his part in the burning, though it was widely believed that in fact he had tried to prevent it, but that his loyalty to his comrades prevented him from telling the full story at his trial. Murphy unsuccessfully contested the newly created constituency of North Cork in 1937 and also did not seek re-election to the county council in 1942. He died on 1 May 1968 and was buried in Kilgullane Cemetery.

MURPHY, Robert (1806–1843) Born Mallow, Co. Cork, the son of a clergyman. At the age of eleven, while laid up with a broken thighbone, he developed an interest in mathematics and seven years later published, in Mallow, a pamphlet on the subject. He was sent to Cambridge by public subscription. In 1831, he became a fellow and dean of Gonville and Caius College, Cambridge. Owing largely to his drinking habits, he was forced to leave Cambridge. He later became examiner in mathematics at the University of London in 1838. He died on 12 March 1843.

MURPHY, Seamus (1907–1975) Born Mallow, Co. Cork, the son of a train driver. He received his early education at St Patrick's NS, Dillon's Cross, where he came under the influence of **Daniel Corkery**, who encouraged him to study sculpture. He attended the Cork School of Art where he won the Gibson Travelling Scholarship in 1931. Following further studies in Paris, he returned to Cork in 1933 and opened his own studio. As his reputation grew, he received commissions to carve many national figures. He was a frequent exhibitor at the Royal Hibernian Academy and was for a time Professor of Sculpture there. He was elected as a member of the Royal Hibernian Academy in 1966. In 1969, he received an honorary LL.D degree from the National University of Ireland. He died at his residence at Wellington Road, Cork, on 2 October 1975 and was buried in Rathcooney Graveyard. [Autobiography (1950); Commemorative plaque at Wellesley Terrace, Wellington Road, Cork]

MURPHY, Seán Óg (c.1892–1956) Born Windmill Road, Cork. He was educated at South Monastery CBS and at North Monastery CBS. A famous hurling full-back of the Blackrock club, he also captained the Nils to a County senior football title in 1919. He won four All-Ireland SHC medals (1919, 1926, 1928–9), captaining the team in three successive finals (1926–8). He also captained the winning Cork team in the inaugural National Hurling League final of 1926. He won two Railway Cup hurling medals with Munster (1928–1929). He retired from hurling in 1929 as a result of a shoulder injury. He later became secretary of the Cork County GAA Board (1929–56) and also served on the Munster Council (1924–56). He died at the Bon Secours Hospital, Cork, on 13 June 1956 and was buried in St Finbarr's Cemetery.

MURPHY, Thomas J. (b. 1881) Born Cork, the son of M.J. Murphy, sculptor. He was educated at the Oratory and at King's College, London. He studied sculpture at Lambeth and Royal Academy Schools. He was a frequent exhibitor at the Royal Academy. Among his works were the Bodley Memorial Portrait, the earl of Devon Monument at Hickleton and the Portraits of Lord and Lady Halifax.

MURPHY, Timothy (1789–1856) Born Dromatimore, Aghabullogue, Co. Cork. He was educated at St Patrick's College, Maynooth, and was ordained in 1815. Having served as a curate in Doneraile, he was transferred to Fermoy where he spent the rest of his life, serving, in turn, as curate, administrator and parish priest. He was consecrated as bishop of Cloyne and Ross on 16 September 1849 and continued to live in Fermoy where he had founded St Colman's College and had introduced the Presentation and Loreto orders of nuns to the town. He retained the diocese of Cloyne when it was separated from Ross on 17 December 1850 – the latter diocese being given to his eventual successor in Cloyne, **William Keane**. He died on 4 December 1856 and was buried in the grounds of Presentation Convent, Fermoy.

MURPHY, Timothy J. (1893–1949) Born Clondrohid, Co. Cork. He was educated at Clondrohid and Macroom National Schools. He was influenced in his teens by the Irish Land and Labour Association and by O'Brienite politics. Moving to Dunmanway around 1920, he became involved in trade union and Labour Party activities. He was elected as a Labour Party TD for West Cork in the 1923 General Election and represented this constituency until his death (being successful in 10 Dáil elections). As a member of the first Inter-Party Government, he was appointed as minister for Local Government in February 1948. He sat on Cork County Council from 1925 (and as acting chairman in 1947) but resigned on his being appointed to the Cabinet. He collapsed and died while speaking at an Inter-Party public meeting at Pearse Square, Fermoy, on 29 April 1949. Following a state funeral, he was buried in Dunmanway Cemetery.

MURPHY, William A. (1930–1982) Born Ballyvolane, Cork, the son of Daniel Murphy, farmer. 'Tony' later became a prosperous builder and businessman in Cork. A flamboyant figure (whose silver Rolls Royce was his hallmark), he masterminded the *Gay Future* betting coup in 1974. This attempt to 'catch' the big British bookmakers involved the horse, *Gay Future*, who romped home a 10/1 winner of a novice hurdle at Cartmel, on the August Bank Holiday of 1974. Unfortunately, the matter ended up in court and most of the £300,000 winnings were withheld. A television production (*Murphy's Stroke*), featuring Niall Toibín as Murphy, was made of the story and a book, *The Gay Future Affair*, by Larry Lyons, was published in 1983. Tony Murphy died in at his South Douglas Road residence on 31 October 1982 and was buried in Rathcooney Cemetery.

MURPHY, William Martin (1844–1919) Born Bantry, Co. Cork, the son of a building contractor. Following his education at Belvedere College, Dublin, he took over the family business at the age of 19 on the death of his father. In 1870, he married the only daughter of

James Lombard of Dublin, who had made a fortune in the construction of tramways and in the drapery business. He eventually owned Clery's of Dublin and founded the Dublin United Tramways Company. He served as Nationalist MP for St Patrick's Division, Dublin (1885–92). In 1905, he founded the *Irish Catholic* and the *Irish Independent* and this was followed a year later by the *Sunday Independent*. He was the main mover behind the Irish National Exhibition of 1907 and refused a knighthood on King Edward VII's visit to Ireland in that year. In 1912, he founded the Dublin Employers' Federation as a reaction to the growing power of organised labour. When workers refused to withdraw from trades unions he led the employers in the Dublin Lockout, which lasted from August 1913 until the end of January 1915. With the outbreak of World War I, he supported Irish enlistment in the British army, but later opposed the idea of partition, publishing in 1917 *The Home Rule Act of 1914 Exposed*. He died in Dublin on 26 June 1919 and was buried in Glasnevin Cemetery. [Life by T. Morrissey (1997)]

MURPHY, Willie ['Long Puck'] (1915–1977) Born Ballincollig, Co. Cork. A Ballincollig and Cork hurling corner-back, he was renowned for his huge clearances and puckouts (hence 'Long Puck'). He won five All-Ireland SHC medals (1941–4 and 1946). He also won three NHL medals (1940, 1941, and 1948) and seven Railway Cup medals (1940–3, 1945–6 and 1948). He died at his Bishopstown, Cork, home on 24 August 1977 and was buried in St John's Cemetery, Ballincollig.

MURRAY, James [VC] (1859–1942) Born Cork. He joined the British Army and was promoted to the rank of lance-corporal in the 2nd battalion, Connaught Rangers. During the First Anglo-Boer War (1880–1), he was awarded the Victoria Cross for his bravery near Pretoria on 16 January 1881. Under heavy fire from about sixty Boers, he advanced with Limerick-born trooper John Danagher and rescued a soldier who had been severely wounded 500m beyond the British lines. Murray was shot through the body and was taken prisoner by the Boers. He was subsequently released. Danagher was also awarded with a similar decoration. Murray died in Our Lady's Hospice, Harold's Cross, Dublin, on 19 July 1942 and was buried in Glasnevin Cemetery.

MURRAY, Thomas C. (1873–1959) Born New Street, Macroom, Co. Cork, the son of a shop-keeper. He was educated at St Patrick's College of Education, Dublin, and later worked as a teacher in Cork (where he was a co-founder of the Cork Little Theatre) and Dublin. A prolific playwright, he also wrote poetry and was a contributor to *The Bell*, the *New Ireland Review* and the *Dublin Magazine*. He served as the president of the Irish Playwrights' Association, and as vice-president of the Irish Academy of Letters. He received an honorary D.Litt degree from the National University of Ireland in 1949. He died in Ballsbridge, Dublin, on 7 March 1959 and was buried in Glasnevin Cemetery. His plays included 'Wheel of Fortune' (1909), 'Birthright' (1910), 'Maurice Harte' (1912), 'Sovereign Love' (1913), 'The Briery Gap' (1917), 'Spring' (1918), 'Aftermath' (1922), 'Autumn Fire' (1925) and 'Michaelmas Eve' (1932). His *Spring Horizon* (1937) is a short autobiographical novel. [Sketch by M. Ó hAodha (1961)]

N

NAGLE, David Augustine (1823–1884) Born Annakissa, Mallow, Co. Cork, the son of Pierce Nagle by his second marriage. He was also the nephew of **Edmund Bailey O'Callaghan**. He qualified as a solicitor and took a prominent role in Cork City politics as well as acting for many of the public utility companies in both the city and county. In the early 1860s, he purchased a controlling interest in the *Cork Herald* and established it as Cork's first daily newspaper. He was a member of Cork Corporation for a number of years and twice served as mayor of Cork (1874/5 and 1875/6). A resident of Queenstown (now Cobh), he also served for several years as chairman of Queenstown town commissioners. In 1874, he contested for the Mallow parliamentary seat as an alternative Home Ruler but polled disappointingly. He died, after a long illness, at his residence, 2, South Mall, Cork, on 16 July 1884 and was buried in Mallow.

NAGLE, Sir Edmund (1757–1830) Born Cork, the son of Edmund Nagle and grandson of Garrett Nagle of Ballinamona Castle, Shanbally-more. In 1770, he joined the British Navy and was promoted to the rank of lieutenant in 1777. Following an engagement with a French frigate, he was knighted in 1794. In 1803, he settled in Brighton to command the Sussex Sea Fencibles. He was promoted to the rank of rear admiral in 1805 and two years later was made a vice-admiral. In 1813, he was appointed as governor of Newfoundland, Canada. He was promoted to the rank of admiral in 1819. He died in East Molesey, Sussex, on 14 March 1830.

NAGLE, John C. (1910–1996) Born Cork, the son of Michael Nagle. He was educated at CBC, Cork; UCC, TCD and Cambridge University. He served in the department of Finance but was transferred to the department of Agriculture where he was secretary from 1958 until his retirement in 1971. He also served as chairman of the EC Committee on the control of foot and mouth disease. He was appointed chairman of the National Council of Educational Awards (NCEA) and later was awarded an honorary degree of LL.D by that body. He died in 1996. He published *Agriculture Trade Policies* (1976).

NAGLE, Nano (1728–1784) Born Ballygriffin, Mallow, Co. Cork, the daughter of Garret Nagle, a prosperous North Cork landowner. Honoria (Nano) was educated locally and in Paris and returned to Cork in 1750. In the following few years she founded nine Cork schools to cater for the needs of the poor and in 1771, she invited the French Ursuline nuns to run one of these. However, she later decided to found her own congregation, the Sisters of the Charitable Instruction of the Sacred Heart of Jesus (later constituted as the Presentation Sisters in 1802). The first convent (the South Presentation, Cork), which she built at her own expense, was set up in 1777. She died and was buried there on 20 April 1784. [Lives by T.J. Walsh (1959) and M.P. O'Farrell (1996); Portrait at Ursuline Convent, Blackrock, Cork; Commemorative plaque at entrance to South Presentation Convent, Douglas Street, Cork]

NAGLE, Sir Richard (1636–1699) Born Clogher, Doneraile, Co. Cork, the son of James Nagle. He was appointed as attorney-general of the Jacobite administration and helped to pass the Bill of Attainder against prominent Irish Protestants. He was chosen as speaker of James II's 'Patriot Parliament' of 1689, as well as being the king's private secretary. He left for France with Patrick Sarsfield (*c.*1655–93) following the Treaty of Limerick. He died at the Jacobite court in St Germain, Paris, on 4 April 1699.

NAGLE, Thomas (d. 1944) He was elected to the 3rd Dáil in June 1922 as a Labour Party member for the 'Rest of County Cork' constituency. He subsequently represented North Cork from 1923 until 1927 when he did not seek re-election. He resided in Ranelagh, Dublin, but died while cycling at Enniscorthy, Co. Wexford, on 5 November 1944. He was described as 'a Dublin official of the ITGWU and an old and esteemed member of the Ancient Guild of the Brick- and Stone-layers' Union'.

NALDER, Hubert H. (d. 1961) A native of Newcastle-on-Tyne, he came to Cork in 1898 as assistant engineer to Charles Merz, who was then undertaking the task of laying Cork's tramways and developing electricity as a medium of public lighting and power supply. Merz's stay was brief and, by 1900, Nalder was manager of the Cork Electric Tramways & Lighting Company, which he directed for the whole of its existence up to 1931. He played a significant role in the Cork Exhibition of 1902–03, being responsible for the electrical engineering element and for the colourful illuminations. On the winding up of the tramways, he continued in the employment of the ESB for some years. He died at his residence, Ashton Park, Cork, on 17 September 1961 at an advanced age and was buried in St Lappan's cemetery, Little Island.

NAUGHTON, Bonaventure (d. 1587?) see **Ó NEACHTAIN, Bonaventura**

NEALE, Samuel (1729–1792) Born Dublin, the son of a Quaker, Thomas Neale. On his mother's death, his father emigrated to America while the children were left in care. At the age of eighteen he inherited a large estate from his grandfather at Christianstown, Co. Kildare. However, he took to high living but was converted back to Quaker principles largely as a result of a 1751 encounter in Cork with two Quaker women preachers. One of those was Mary Peisley whom he married in 1757 but who died only two days after their wedding! Three years later he married Sarah Beale, a grand-daughter of **Joseph Pike** (1657–1729), and they lived at Springmount, Glanmire, where Neale had leased some lands. He later entered into a business partnership with his brother-in-law, Caleb Beale (1730–96) and Thomas Bond of Riverstown, a paper manufacturer. The new partnership employed fifty hands at Ballinglanna, Glanmire. However, Neale got tired of business and opted for America and the Quaker ministry. He returned to Glanmire in 1772 and died there twenty years later.

NEESON, Geraldine (1895–1980) Born Geraldine Sullivan at Sunday's Well, Cork, and wife of **Seán Neeson**. She was educated at St Angela's College, Patrick's Hill, and studied music under Frau Tilly Fleischmann. She later became both a concert pianist and teacher at her old school. She was a close friend of **Muriel Murphy** and was bridesmaid at her marriage to **Terence MacSwiney** on 9 June 1917 while the latter was in detention at Bromyard, Hertfordshire. In 1925, she married Seán Neeson, a native of Belfast who was then teaching at Mount Melleray Abbey, Co. Waterford. They later returned to Cork and settled at Mount Verdon Villa on the Wellington Road. A close friend of the actors, Micheál Mac Liammoir and Hilton Edwards, she founded the Cork Drama League which later saw the involvement of the writer, **Frank O'Connor**. She also featured in many productions under the auspices of the Little Theatre Society. In addition to her many cultural activities, she later became a distinguished music and theatre critic of the *Cork Examiner*. She died at Mount Verdon Villa on 10 November 1980 and was buried in St Finbarr's Cemetery. [Life-size plaster bust by **Seamus Murphy** in private possession]

NEESON, Seán (1891–1964) Born Fall's Road, Belfast, Co. Antrim, the son of Owen Neeson, shipyard worker, and husband of **Geraldine Neeson**. Seán was reared by his mother and her brothers who were both musicians (his father had gone to the goldfields of South Africa and was never heard of again). He was educated at St

Patrick's College of Education, Dublin, and at Queen's University, Belfast, where he graduated BA (1913). He was a co-founder of the Sinn Féin Party in Belfast and was interned following the 1916 Rising. On his release, he worked as a teacher in Drogheda, Kilorglin and Cork. He served as an intelligence officer for the southern division during the War of Independence. He took the Republican side during the Civil War and was interned at Gormanstown. He then worked as a teacher at Mount Melleray Abbey School, Co. Waterford, and following his marriage, he returned to Cork where he acted as director of the Cork radio station (1927–31). Following the closure of the station, he worked for the Cork office of Irish Hospital Sweepstakes. He was also on the staff of the music department of UCC where he lectured on Irish traditional music. The Neeson home at Mount Verdon Villa, Wellington Road, became a mecca for many Cork music and theatre enthusiasts. He died at Mount Verdon Villa on 21 May 1964 and was buried in St Finbarr's Cemetery.

NELSON, Havelock (1917–1996) Born Cork. He was educated at TCD (where he graduated MA, M.Sc. and PhD) and at the Royal Irish Academy of Music. He was a founder member of the Dublin Orchestral Players in 1939. He served in the RAF during World War II. He joined BBC Northern Ireland in 1947 and founded both the Studio Symphony Orchestra and the Studio Opera Group. He worked as both a conductor and broadcaster. He was a guest conductor of international renown and conducted with the Sadler's Wells Opera Company. In 1976, he was appointed as artistic director of the Trinidad and Tobago Opera Company. In 1966, he was awarded the OBE for his services to music. He was awarded the honorary degree of D.Mus. from Queen's University, Belfast, and the honorary fellowship of the Royal Irish Academy of Music in 1985. He died in Belfast on 5 August 1996 and was buried privately.

NEVILLE, Henry (1822–1889) Born St Finbarr's Parish, Cork, a nephew of **J.J. Callanan**. He was educated at O'Regan and Moynihan's School, Cork, and at St Patrick's College, Maynooth, where he was ordained in 1847 for the Cork diocese. He was appointed as professor of Philosophy at Maynooth in 1852 but resigned on health grounds five years later. He was then appointed as parish priest of Passage and Monkstown and also to a canonry of the Cork diocesan chapter. He was prominent at the various synods and attended the First Vatican Council as theological consultor to Bishop Moriarty of Kerry. In 1875, he became parish priest of St Finbarr's as well as dean and vicar general of Cork. In the same year, he published *Comments* – a reply to William Gladstone's (1809–98) *Expostulation*. From 1879 until 1883 he was rector of the Catholic University while retaining his diocesan offices, having been created a domestic prelate with the title of 'Monsignor' in 1880. During his pastorates, he was responsible for building churches at Monkstown (1871) and The Lough (1881). Despite his successful career, Neville was not popular with his contemporaries and was unsuccessful in the campaign for the co-adjutorship of Cork in 1884. He died on 15 December 1889 and was buried in a vault adjoining the old St Michael's Church, Blackrock.

NEWENHAM, Sir Edward (1732–1814) Born Coolmore, Carrigaline, Co. Cork, the son of William Newenham, Esq., and the uncle of **Thomas Newenham**. He was educated at TCD, but did not graduate. He was elected as MP for Enniscorthy (1769–76) and for County Dublin (1776–97). He was an active supporter of the Irish Volunteers but disagreed with Henry Grattan (1746–1820) in supporting the Act of Union. He was knighted in 1764. In 1778, he unsuccessfully attempted to add a clause to the Catholic Relief Bill which would also remove the disabilities of Dissenters under the Test Act. Even though the move failed, the Test Act was finally repealed two years later. He died in Blackrock, Dublin, on 2 October 1814. His son, Robert O'Callaghan Newenham (1770–1849), was a prominent landscape and topographical draughtsman [he edited *Sketches in Ireland*

(1826)], while his grand-daughter, Eliza, married the Cork architect, **Sir Thomas Deane**.

NEWENHAM, Frederick (1807–1859) Born County Cork. He settled in London where he established a reputation as a fashionable painter of ladies' portraits. He exhibited at the Royal Academy (1838–55) and at the British Institution (1841–52). His commissioned portrait of Queen Victoria was exhibited at the Royal Academy in 1844. He died on 21 March 1859.

NEWENHAM, Thomas (1762–1831) Born Coolmore, Carrigaline, Co. Cork, the son of Thomas Newenham by his second wife, and nephew of **Sir Edward Newenham**. He was educated at TCD but did not graduate. He was admitted to the Middle Temple, London, in 1782 but was not called to the Bar. He was elected as MP for Clonmel and opposed the Act of Union. He lived in England after the Union and wrote extensively on the state of Ireland and the need for reform. An advocate of Catholic Emancipation, he unsuccessfully corresponded with Bishop J.W. Doyle of Kildare and Leighlin (1786–1834) in an attempt to unite the Roman Catholic and Protestant churches in Ireland. He died at Cheltenham, Gloucestershire, on 16 October 1831. His publications included *A Statistical and Historical Inquiry into … the Population of Ireland* (1803), *The Natural, Political, and Commercial Circumstances of Ireland* (1809) and *A Series of Suggestions and Observations relative to the State of Ireland* (1825) [Sketch by H.D. Gribbon in *Irish Population, Economy, and Society* (1981)]

NEWMAN, Sir John R.P. (1871–1947) Born Dromore (Newberry Manor), Kilshannig, Co. Cork, the son of J.A.R. Newman, JP, DL, and extensive landowner. He was educated at Charterhouse and Cambridge where he graduated BA (1893). In the same year, he succeeded to his father's estates. He was highsheriff of County Cork in 1898 and was involved in local Unionism in County Cork to 1909. He was Unionist MP for the Enfield Division of Middlesex (1910–18) and for Finchley (1918–23). He served in World War I as a Major in the 17th Battalion, Middlesex Regiment. He died at his residence in Farnham, Surrey, on 12 March 1947.

NEWSOM, Samuel Henry (1847–1927) Born Tellingana, Cork, the son of a Quaker, Samuel Newsom. His grandfather, John Newsom (1779–1846), was a wholesale and retail tea and coffee merchant. Samuel held directorships in the Cork Improved Dwellings Company, the Cash Bakery and Cork Commercial Buildings Company. He was a trustee and treasurer of the South Infirmary Hospital, a trustee of Cork Savings Bank, the secretary of the Cork Hospital Saturday Collection Movement, the president of Cork Chamber of Commerce and a Cork Harbour commissioner. He was also deeply involved in the administration of the Cork Quaker community. He died in 1927.

NÍ CHÉILEACHAIR, Síle (1924–1985) Born Coolea, Co. Cork, the son of Domhnall Bán Ó Céileachair, whose autobiography, *Sgéal mo Bheatha* was published in 1940. She was educated at Coláiste Bhríde, Falcarragh and at Mary Immaculate College, Limerick, where she qualified as a primary teacher. Moving to Dublin, she taught in Harold's Cross and later in Crumlin. She retired from teaching on her marriage in 1953. She collaborated with her brother, **Donncha Ó Céileachair**, in the publication, *Bullaí Mháirtín* (1955), a book of short stories which was very well received. She died at St Vincent's Hospital, Dublin, on 26 August 1985 and was buried in Boharnabreena Cemetery, Dublin.

NÍ CHONAILL, Eibhlín (c.1748–1800) Eibhlín 'Dubh' was born in Derrynane, Co. Kerry, the daughter of Dónal Mór Ó Conaill. She was the aunt of Daniel O'Connell (1775–1847), the Liberator. Following the death of her husband around 1763 (six months after her marriage at the age of fifteen) she married **Art Ó Laoghaire** (Arthur O'Leary) of Macroom in December 1767. Following a long and bitter dispute with the highsheriff of Cork, Abraham

Morris, Ó Laoghaire was shot dead by a soldier at Carraig an Ime on 4 May 1773. He was buried at Kilcrea Abbey, Co. Cork. Eibhlín is said to have immediately composed the famous *Caoineadh Airt Uí Laoghaire*, one of the greatest Gaelic laments. The poem was written down many years later from oral tradition. It has been edited by Seán Ó Tuama (1961) and translated by **Frank O'Connor** (1962).

NÍ CHRÓINÍN, Eibhlín (1879–1964) Born Céim Chorrbhuaile, Ballingeary, Co. Cork, the daughter of Concubhair Ó Cróinín, farmer. She was educated locally and spent some time as a monitor at Kilnamartra NS and then at her old school. In 1901, she was appointed as a peripatetic teacher under the auspices of the Kilkenny Branch of Connradh na Gaeilge. She spent over sixty years working there, although when she arrived she could only speak Irish and had to take English lessons at a local convent. During each summer break, she taught at Coláiste na Mumhan, Ballingeary, for over forty years. To mark her fiftieth anniversary as a teacher, a special concert which included the Radió Éireann Light Orchestra and Cór Cois Laoi, was given at Kilkenny. Yet she carried on for another decade! She died at St Anthony's Hospital, Dunmanway, on 9 October 1964 and was buried in Inchigeela Cemetery. [Memorial plaque at Rothe House, Kilkenny]

NÍ CHRÓINÍN, Eibhlís (1879–1956) see **CRONIN, Elizabeth**

NÍ LAOGHAIRE, Máire Bhuí (1774–c.1849) Born Toureennanean, Inchigeelagh, Co. Cork, the eldest of eight children of Diarmaid Buí Ó Laoghaire, farmer. At the age of eighteen she eloped with a Skibbereen horse trader named James Burke and the couple settled near Ballingeary where Burke became a very successful tenant farmer and father of nine children. However, times became very difficult for the Burkes from the 1820s and they were finally evicted from their main holding in 1847. Máire died at her son's farm at Inchimore, Ballingeary,

c.1849 and was buried at Inchigeelagh Graveyard. Though illiterate, her poems and songs were passed on by oral tradition, including her famous 'Cath Céim an Fhia' ('The Battle of Keimaneigh') which describes an engagement at the Pass of Keimaneigh between the Whiteboys and a detachment of the Muskerry Blue Light Dragoons in January 1822 during the Tithe War. her brother, Barra, was one of the four who lost their lives in that incident. [Life and works by B. Brennan (2000); Works edited by D. Ó Donnchú (1917 and 1931)]

NOBLETT, Henry J. (1812–p.1844) Born Grand Parade, Cork, the son of George Noblett, hosier. He trained as a landscape painter in oils and watercolour. He moved to London in 1831 where he exhibited at The Royal Academy, the Society of British Artists and the New Society of Painters in Watercolours. He returned to Cork in 1835 where he lived with his two sisters at their hosiery business at 29, Grand Parade. He contributed illustrations to Mr and Mrs Hall's *Ireland* (3 vols, 1841–3) and also exhibited at the Royal Hibernian Academy in 1844.

NOLAN, Seán (d. 1939) Born Cork. He became a member of the Irish Republican Brotherhood c.1908 and was subsequently prominent in the Volunteer movement in Cork. In February 1917, he was one of several Republican leaders in Cork who were arrested and served with banishment orders. He spent several months in Bromyard Prison with **Terence McSwiney**. On his return, he became adjutant of the Cork brigade of the IRA. In May 1921, he was one of the Sinn Féin candidates elected to the 2nd Dáil Éireann and took the anti-Treaty side in the January 1922 debates. He was elected for the North-, Mid-, South-, South East-, and West-Cork combined constituency. When he sought re-election as an anti-Treaty candidate in June 1922, he was defeated. He was a member of Cork Corporation in the early 1920s up to its dissolution in 1924 when he retired from politics. An auctioneer by profession, he latterly resided in Magazine Road but was in poor health for several years. He died at St Joseph's Hospital, Cork, on 29 October 1939 and was buried in St Joseph's Cemetery.

NOTTER, J. Lane (1843–1923) Born Carrigduve, Blackrock, Cork, the son of Richard Notter, merchant and landowner. He was educated at TCD and took first place on entering the army medical service in 1866. He served as an assistant surgeon with the Royal Artillery in Canada and Malta before becoming professor of Military Hygiene at the army medical school at Netley, Hampshire. He subsequently was appointed as examiner in Public Health at many universities including those of Cambridge, Liverpool and Wales. He was a fellow of the Royal Society of Medicine and president of the Epidemiological Society of London. He was the co-author of *The Theory and Practice of Hygiene* which ran to nine editions. He was editor of the 8th Edition of *Parke's Manual of Practical Hygiene* and wrote numerous articles on both hygiene and preventative medicine. He had residences at Rock Island, Crookhaven (which he inherited as part of his family's lands in the Mizen Peninsula), and at Earl's Court, London. He died at a Southampton nursing home on 24 October 1923.

NYHAN, John ['Flyer'] (1892–1934) Born Clonakilty, Co. Cork, the son of Daniel Nyhan. At an early age, he went to live with his Barrett grandparents near Ballineen. Until 1914, he was an outstanding footballer and hurler with Clonakilty and worked in the local electric light station in Clonakilty and in Deasy's Brewery. He joined the Irish Volunteers in 1915 and became active in organisational and training matters. By 1917, he was quartermaster of his battalion and a staff captain of the Cork No.1 Brigade. Arrested in March 1920, he was jailed in Wormwood Scrubs where he went on hunger strike. He was released two months later but was captured at Shannonvale on the following St Stephen's Day and was interned for a year at Ballykinlar Camp, Co. Down. He took the anti-Treaty side during the civil war and was severely wounded by a Free State patrol near Ring on St Stephen's Day 1922. However, he managed to escape and found refuge in Bandon Nursing Home. Following the civil war, he emigrated to Scotland where he worked with an engineering firm (1924–1933). As he was returning by ferry to Clonakilty for Christmas 1933, he caught a chill which quickly turned to pneumonia. He died at the Bon Secours Nursing Hospital, Cork, on 6 January 1934 and was buried in Ballymoney Cemetery, near Ballineen.

O

Ó BRIAIN, Micheál (1866–1942) Born Ballinora, Ballincollig, Co. Cork, the son of Denis O'Brien. He worked as a teacher in Ballingeary pre-1897 and later at Ballyvourney where he collected Irish words and folklore. He wrote songs, poetry and some sketches for the stage. He was very active in assisting the lexicographer and editor, Rev. Pádraig Ó Duinnín, with his famous *Foclóir Gaedhilge agus Béarla* (1904, 1927, 1934). He died at Ballymakeera on 27 December 1942. His *Cnósach Focal ó Bhaile Bhuirne i gConndae Chorcaí. Micheál Ó Briain (1866–1942) a bhailigh* (ed. B. Ó Cuív) was published in 1947.

Ó BRIAIN, Pádraig (c.1848–1913) Born Ballydehob, Co. Cork, the son of Cornelius Ó Briain, farmer. A native Irish speaker, he emigrated to America where he worked for a German printing company, becoming a fluent German speaker in the process. Having married, he returned to Ireland and eventually lived in Cuffe Street, Dublin, where his wife ran a small provisions shop and where he established a printing press (with a fount of Irish type) at the rear. He was one of the ten founder members of Connradh na Gaeilge which was founded in Dublin on 31 July 1893. As well as delving into the book-selling business, he also published (at his own expense) editions of many works (by himself and others) in Irish. These included, *Bláith-fhleasg de mhilseáinibh na Gaedhilge: a garland of Irish selections* (1893), *Bruighean Eochaidh Bhig Dheirg* (1894), *Sgeulaidheacht Chúige Mumhan, Eochair-Sgiath an Aifrinn* (1898), *Cnuasacht Chomhagail* (1901), *Cúirt an Mheadhon Oidhche* (1908), *Sgéalta gearra an Iarthair* (1910) and *Eachtra Mhacaoimh an Iolair Mhic Ríogh na Sorcha* (1912). His 'The Dentist / An Fiaclóir' (1898), was one of the first plays ever published in Irish. Following an accident,

he sold the printing press and went to live in West Lombard Street, Dublin, around the year 1912. He died on 17 November 1913.

O'BRIEN, Con (1883–1946) Born Ballinagrath, Ballyhea, Co. Cork, the son of Patrick O'Brien. He spent several years in the US and on his return, settled down in his native area. In the 1920s and 1930s, he earned the name of 'The Bard of Ballyhea' for his regular contributions to the 'Humour and Poetry' columns of the *Cork Weekly Examiner*. He vied each week for the 10s. prize with rivals such as Ned Buckley of Knocknagree. He died on 14 February 1946 and was buried in the Abbey Churchyard, Buttevant. In 1981, *The Poems of Con O'Brien, the Bard of Ballyhea* (ed. J. Meagher) was published and contained a hundred of his best-known poems. It was reprinted in the following year.

O'BRIEN, Cornelius M. (1868–1916) Born Girrlough, Balineen, Co. Cork. He was educated at Ballinacarriga NS, Farranferris College, Cork and at the Irish College, Paris, where he was ordained in 1892. For several years, he worked as a teacher at Farranferris and held curacies in city parishes before being appointed as curate at Douglas around 1904. His *Life of St Finbarr*, a forty-page pamphlet, was published in Cork in 1902. He was principal editor of the *Journal of the Ivernian Society* (1908–15). A competent organist, he was also an amateur artist of some repute and studied locally at the Cork School of Art and in London and Munich. He specialised in portraiture. He died at the Mercy Hospital, Cork, on 4 March 1916 and was buried in St Joseph's Cemetery.

O'BRIEN, Dennis (1792–1865) Born Fermoy, Co. Cork. He emigrated to the United States in 1811 and lived in Maine where he operated as a foot pedlar in hardware and tinware. He moved to Canada in 1820 and set up in London, Ontario, as a general merchant. He soon branched out into other activities, including a gristmill, a distillery and a chain of general stores. He was also one of the incorporators of the London and Gore Railroad. He later built London's largest hotel, 'The Western'. He was a prominent supporter of the Irish Benevolent Society and of Roman Catholic charities. He died at Westminster Township, near London, on 16 May 1865.

O'BRIEN, Fitzjames (1828–1862) He was the son of James O'Brien, solicitor. He was reared in Castleconnell, Co. Limerick. Having written some verse to the *Dublin University Magazine* and *The Nation*, he settled in London where he worked as a journalist and at the same time, went through a large inheritance. He later emigrated to the United States where he wrote short stories on horror and occult themes including *The Diamond Lens*, *What Was It?* and *The Wondersmith*. On the outbreak of the American civil war, he joined the Union army and died from his wounds in 1862. His stories were collected and published in 1881. He is best known in Ireland for his poem 'Lough Ine'. [Surveys by F. Wolle (1944) and M. Hayes (1977)]

O'BRIEN, Sir Ignatius J. (1857–1930) Born Cork, the son of Mark J. O'Brien, chandler and brewer's agent of King Street (now Mac Curtain Street) and freeman of Cork. He entered the Royal University of Ireland where he studied for two years. He then worked as a journalist on *Saunder's Newsletter* and on *The Freeman's Journal* in Dublin. He was called to the Bar in 1881. In 1887, he established his reputation through his defence of Canon **Daniel Keller** of Youghal in a famous Land War case. He then retired from the Munster Circuit to devote his career to chancery and bankruptcy. Following his call to the Inner Bar in 1907, he was appointed, in succession, a serjeant-at-law (1910), solicitor-general for Ireland (1911), attorney-general and member of the Irish Privy Council (1912), and Lord Chancellor of Ireland (1913). However, he

was forced to resign from the chancellorship by the British Conservative Government in 1918. He accepted a British peerage and chose the title of Baron Shandon. He went to live in the Isle of Wight and was called to the English Bar in 1923. He died in London on 10 September 1930.

O'BRIEN, James F.X. (1828–1905) Born Dungarvan, Co. Waterford, the son of Timothy O'Brien, merchant and ship owner. As a young man, he took part in the attack on Cappoquin police barracks in the abortive Young Ireland rising of 1848 and escaped to Wales in one of his father's vessels. He later returned home. On his father's death in 1853, he sold the business and studied for a while at Queen's College, Galway (now UCG), continued with his medical studies in Paris and sailed for New York in 1856. Two years later, he joined the Fenian movement and served in 1861 as an assistant surgeon for a militia regiment in the American civil war. He returned to Ireland in 1862 and organised the Fenians in Cork while at the same time engaging in the tea and wine business. During the Fenian Rising of March 1867, his men captured the Ballyknockane (Mourneabbey) police barracks and took the arms. They then marched towards Bottle Hill but scattered at the approach of the British infantry. He was captured, convicted of high treason and sentenced to death. However, the sentence was commuted to life imprisonment. He was released two years later and returned to his Cork business. He later joined the Home Rule movement, served as MP for South Mayo (1885–95) and for Cork City (1895–1905). He also worked as British secretary of the United Irish League. He died at Clapham, London, on 28 May 1905 and was buried at Glasnevin Cemetery, Dublin.

O'BRIEN, John (1701–1769) Born Ballyvaddy, Glanworth, Co. Cork. With the intention of studying for the priesthood, he attended the University of Toulouse and the Sorbonne, Paris, where he graduated STL and DCL. Following his ordination around 1727, he worked as a tutor in Spain. However, he returned to Ireland in 1738 and was appointed as parish priest of Castlelyons and lived at Ballinterry, Rathcormac. On 10 January 1748, he was appointed as bishop of Cloyne and Ross. A noted linguist, he made several trips to the Continent during his episcopate and died at Lyons on 30 March 1769. He published in Paris the *Focalóir Gaoidhilge/Sax-Bhéarla or An Irish-English Dictionary* (1768) [Life by **J. Coombes** (1981)]

O'BRIEN, John (*c.*1848–1893) Born Ballymartin, Dungourney, Co. Cork, of 'respectable' farming stock. At the age of fourteen, he was sent to Cork to be apprenticed to the drapery trade at the establishment of John Daly of George's Street (now Oliver Plunkett Street). Having reached a management position in the company, he left in 1878 to open his own woollen and drapery business in Patrick Street. He was also instrumental in establishing a 'home-made boot factory' in Blackpool. A supporter of the Fenians, he later became a supporter of Parnell and was a popular speaker at meetings around the county. He was elected to Cork Corporation in 1882 and subsequently became an alderman. In 1883, he was jailed for two months arising from a public meeting in the Bantry area at which he spoke. He was twice elected as mayor of Cork (1887 and 1888). During his tenure as mayor, he was involved in several wrangles with the authorities and in February 1888, was sentenced to fourteen days imprisonment. He became ill with pneumonia while on business in Co. Kerry and died at Killarney on 15 April 1893. He was buried in Dungourney.

O'BRIEN, Michael J. (1870–1960) Born Fermoy, Co. Cork. He was educated at Fermoy CBS and at St Colman's College, Fermoy. Following a period of employment in Ireland, he emigrated to the United States in 1889. Arriving in New York, he obtained a position with the Western Union Telegraph Company. He worked for this company for forty-five years until his retirement in 1935. By 1900, he had begun researching the contribution of the Irish to early American colonial history. His early researches, published in *The Gaelic American* and *The American-Irish Historical Society Journal,* were consolidated in his book, *A Hidden Phase of American History* (1919). A further seven books appeared up to 1941, including *In Old New York* (1928) and for many years up to 1933, he was historiographer to the AIHS. In 1930, he was awarded an honorary degree of LL.D by UCD, 'in recognition of his works, involving prolonged researches on the history of the Irish in America'. His research and writings provided a valuable corrective to previous academic neglect of the Irish contribution, though he occasionally exaggerated his case. A further four volumes of his work was published posthumously, including his *The Irish at Bunker Hill* (1968). He died at Yonkers, New York, on 4 November 1960.

O'BRIEN, Murrough (1614–1674) Born Co. Clare, the son of Dermot O'Brien, 5th Baron of Inchiquin. He was a royal ward between 1628 and 1635, and converted to Protestantism. He joined the Spanish service and campaigned in Italy before returning to Ireland in 1639. He fought against the Irish forces at the outbreak of the Rising of 1641. In the following year, he succeeded his father-in-law, **Sir William St Leger**, as governor of Munster and won battles at Liscarroll and Bandon. With the cessation of hostilities in September 1643, he travelled to Oxford in the following February to obtain Charles I's commission as president of Munster, but this was not granted. Later in that year, he inclined towards the parliamentary side in the English civil war and expelled Roman Catholics from many Munster towns (earning the title, 'Murchadh na dTóiteán' or 'Morrough of the Burnings'). Having massacred the garrisons of Adare and Cashel, and having won a great victory over Lord Taaffe's confederate forces in 1647, he went over to the royalist side for the remainder of the conflict. With the execution of King Charles I (1600–49) and the parliamentary victory under Oliver Cromwell (1599–1658), he followed King Charles II (1630–85) into exile in 1650. He was created 1st earl of Inchiquin in

1654 and re-converted to Roman Catholicism. He returned to Ireland in 1662, having received extensive estates in Munster and financial compensation for his losses during the Confederate War. He retired to his Rostellan estate on the banks of Cork Harbour and made a double marriage settlement with his old enemy, **Roger Boyle**, 1st earl of Orrery. He died at Rostellan on 9 September 1674 and was buried in the Thomond Tomb in St Mary's Cathedral, Limerick.

O'BRIEN, Paddy (*c.*1896–1984) Born Liscarroll, Co. Cork. He joined the Irish Volunteers in 1917 and led a 'Flying Column' which was formed in 1920. However, he was wounded in the attack on Milford police barracks in November of that year. In the following year, on the arrest of **Seán Moylan**, he took command of the Cork 4th Brigade of the IRA and afterwards became second-in-command to **Liam Lynch** in the 1st Southern Division. He took the republican side in the civil war. During the 'Emergency', he was area commander of the LDF in North Cork. In later life, he became prominent in the ICMSA and was acting president prior to the election of **James O'Keeffe**. He died at Mallow Hospital on 6 September 1984 and was buried in Buttevant cemetery.

O'BRIEN, Patrick (*c.*1761–1806) See **COTTER, Patrick**.

O'BRIEN, Patrick ['Rocky Mountain'] (1851–1919) Born Dromore, Caheragh, Co. Cork, the son of John O'Brien. He joined the local Fenian group, but was forced to flee to New York in 1868. He was one of the Fenian 'army' which attempted an 'invasion' of British Canada in May 1870 under the command of General John O'Neill who had fought in the American civil war. Following this fiasco, he fled to the 'Wild West' and gained contracts from mining companies to supply their workers with meat. It was his skill as a big game hunter that he acquired the sobriquet, 'Rocky Mountain'. He eventually settled in New York and raised a

family there. He later paid many holiday visits to Ireland which he usually spent in Bantry. His *Birth & Adoption* (1904) is mostly a collection of recitation-type verse which is still popular in West Cork. He died at St Mary's Hospital, Long Island, on 8 February 1919 and was buried in Calvary Cemetery, New York.

O'BRIEN, William (1832–1899) Born Broomfield, Midleton, Co. Cork, the eldest son of John O'Brien, grocer. He was educated at Midleton College and at the King's Inns, Dublin. He was editor of the *Cork Examiner* before he was called to the Bar in 1855. He practised on the Munster Circuit and was called to the Inner Bar in 1872. He stood as a Home Rule candidate for the Ennis constituency on two occasions (1879 and 1880) but was defeated each time. He was appointed as a judge of Common Pleas, but transferred to the Queen's Bench division in 1882. In that year, he was the presiding judge at the trial of the Invincibles who had carried out the Phoenix Park murders on 6 May 1882. He died at his Dublin residence at 79, Merrion Square, on 5 December 1899 and was buried in the vaults of St Andrew's Church, Westland Row.

O'BRIEN, William (1852–1928) Born Mallow, Co. Cork. He was educated at the Cloyne Diocesan College of the Church of Ireland and at Queen's College, Cork (now UCC). During the Land League period, he was a staunch supporter of **C.S. Parnell** and was reputed to be the author of the 'No Rent Manifesto' of 1881. A journalist by profession, he was editor of the Land League's organ *United Ireland*. He was arrested for incitement but on his release, he was elected as MP for Mallow. He was the driving force behind the 1886 'Plan of Campaign' for rent reduction. Following the 'Mitchelstown Massacre' of 8 September 1887, he was again imprisoned. In 1891, he took the anti-Parnellite side in the 'Parnell Split', but took little interest in nationalist politics during the 1890s when he married a wealthy Frenchwoman, Sophie Raffalovich. In 1898, he founded the United

Irish League which, in 1900, united with the Irish Parliamentary Party under John Redmond (1856–1918) and John Dillon (1851–1927). This lasted until 1903 when he resigned from the party. By the time he founded his All for Ireland League in opposition to the UIL in 1910, his political influence was in terminal decline. He supported Sinn Féin following the election victory of 1918. He died in London on 25 February 1928 and was buried in Mallow. He wrote several novels including *'Neath Silver Masks* (1871), *Kilsheehan* (1872), *When We Were Boys* (1890) and *A Queen of Men* (1898). His political works included *Recollections* (1908) and *The Irish Revolution* (1928). [Lives by McDonagh (1928) and by P. Bull in the *History Association of Ireland* series (forthcoming); Studies by J.V. O'Brien (1976) and by S. Warwick-Haller (1990)]

O'BRIEN, William (1881–1968) Born Ballygurteen, Clonakilty, Co. Cork, the son of a police constable. He moved to Dublin and commenced work as an apprentice tailor in 1898. He also joined the Irish Socialist Republican Party in that year. In 1908, he worked with Jim Larkin (1876–1947) to found the Irish Transport and General Workers Union (ITGWU) and was the secretary of the workers' committee during the Dublin Lockout of 1913. Following the 1916 Rising, he was interned in England and again in 1920 when he was released following a hunger strike. On Larkin's return in 1923 from detention in America, a bitter struggle took place with O'Brien for leadership of the ITGWU. This led to Larkin forming the Workers' Union of Ireland (WUI) in the following year. O'Brien served as general secretary of the ITGWU until his retirement and was president of the Irish Trades Union Congress on four occasions. He was also elected as a TD for Dublin South City (1922–3), and for Tipperary (1927 and 1937–8). He died in Bray on 30 October 1968 and was buried in Glasnevin Cemetery. [Edited autobiography by E. MacLysaght (1969); Life-size plaster by **Seamus Murphy** in private possession]

Ó BRÚDAIR, Dáibhidh (*c.*1625–1698) Born Carrigtohill, Co. Cork, of a fairly prosperous family. He received his linguistic and poetic education at a bardic school and came under the influence of the great Gaelic historiographer, Geoffrey Keating (*c.*1580–*c.*1644). From around 1660, he lived in West Limerick in fine style but by the mid-70s, he had lapsed into relative poverty. His poetry reflects the sentiments of those who, depending on the patronage of the Gaelic nobility, were losing their status and livelihoods to the advancing settler culture. A firm Jacobite, he celebrated the advent of the lord deputyship of Richard Talbot, earl of Tyreconnell (1630–91), when the Protestant ruling elite was replaced. However, the defeat of James II (1633–1701) and the Williamite triumph plunged him once more into despair and hopelessness – feelings which are brilliantly reflected in his later poems. He died in January 1698. [Works edited by J.C. Mac Erlean (3 vols, 1910–17), and M. Hartnett (1985); Limestone tablet by **Seamus Murphy** at Springfield Castle, Drumcollogher, Co. Limerick]

Ó BUACHALLA, Tadhg (1863–1945) Born Kilgarvan, Co. Kerry, the son of Pádraig Ó Buachalla, farmer. At the age of nine, he contracted infantile paralysis and, like many other sufferers, this decided the nature of his future career. At the age of thirteen, he became an apprentice tailor in Kenmare and, when 'out of his time', he worked in Killarney, Mallow, Cork City, Youghal and Dublin. He also spent some time in Scotland. Returning to Cork, 'Tim Buckley' married Anastasia Nic Cárthaigh ('Anstey') in June 1906 and settled down in Gougane Barra where he gained a fine reputation as a storyteller. The couple came to national notice when their conversations formed the basis of **Eric Cross**'s book, *The Tailor and Anstey*, which was published in 1942 and was banned by the Irish Censorship Board shortly afterwards. He died on 21 April 1945 and was buried in Gougane Barra. [His transcriptions (by **Seán Ó Crónín**) were edited by **Andrias Ó Muimhneacháin** under the title, *Seanchas an*

Táilliúra (1978); Account of Senate debate in M. Adams, *Censorship: the Irish Experience* (1968); Five life-size bronzes – three in private possession, AIB and Board of Works / headstone at Gougane Barra, Co. Cork by **Seamus Murphy**]

Ó CADHLAIGH, Cormac (1884–1960) Born Kinsale, Co. Cork, the son of Jeremiah Kiely, cobbler. He was educated at St Colman's College, Fermoy and at Rockwell College. He became interested in the study of Irish and having qualified as a teacher of the subject, worked as a peripatetic teacher with Connradh na Gaeilge in various parts of the country. In 1909, he was teaching at his old school in Fermoy, and, while there, he was one of the three founder members of the Association of Secondary Teachers of Ireland (ASTI). He graduated BA (1912) and MA (1913) from the Royal University of Ireland. In 1923, he was appointed as an assistant in the Irish Department and in the library at UCC, becoming a lecturer in 1930. Two years later, he was appointed as professor of Modern Irish at UCD. He was a contestant for the presidency of UCC in 1943, but Professor **Alfred O'Rahilly** was appointed. On his retirement in 1954, he moved to Killorglin, Co. Kerry, his wife's birthplace. He died on 1 December 1960 and was buried in Drom a'Bhaile Cemetery. He will always be associated with his school textbook, *Slighe an Eolais* (1923) which served thousands of Irish students for well over forty years. His book of proverbs, *Eagna an Ghaedhil*, was published in 1924. He also translated many school texts from French and Latin and even a papal encyclical, Leo XIII's *Rerum Novarum* (1891). His other publications include *Ceart na Gaedhilge* (1922), *Cormac Mac Airt* (1927), *An Fhiannaíocht* (1936), *Guaire an Oinigh* (1939), *Gnás na Gaedhilge* (1940), *Diarmaid Mac Cearbhaill* (1950) and *An Rúraíocht* (1956). [Biographical article by Rev. **Tadhg Ó Murchú** in *Feasta* (Feb., 1961)]

Ó CAITHNIA, Liam P. (1925–2001) Born Cork, the third child of Leo Canny, fitter/turner. He was educated at the Model Schools and at Sullivan's Quay CBS before joining the Order of Christian Brothers at the age of thirteen. He entered the Order's novitiate in 1941 and qualified as a primary teacher at the Marino College of Education, Dublin. He had a great interest in the Irish language, sport and culture which he promoted in the many schools in which he served. His extensive research into the early history of hurling resulted in the publication of his *magnum opus*, *Scéal na hIománá* (1980). In the previous year, he had been co-editor of a poetry collection (*Art Mac Bionaid – Dánta*) with the future Irish cardinal, Tomás Ó Fiaich (1923–90). A companion volume to *Scéal na hIománá* and which dealt with the early history of Gaelic football was published under the title, *Báirí Cos in Éirinn* in 1984. In the same year, his study on narrative motifs in bardic poetry, *Apalóga na bhFilí*, was published. His biography of the founder of the GAA, Michael Cusack, under the title *Micheál Ciosóg*, had been published in 1982. He held the appointment as Visiting Loftus Professor at Iona College, New York, for the academic year of 1982/83. He died at St Patrick's Home, Baldoyle, Co. Dublin, on 25 September 2001 and was buried in the community graveyard there.

O'CALLAGHAN, Edmund Bailey (1797–1880) Born Mallow, Co. Cork. He was educated in Dublin, Paris and Quebec, and qualified as a Canadian doctor in 1823. Taking more of an interest in literary matters, he became editor of the *Montreal Vindicator* in 1834 and was elected to the parliament of Lower Canada Parliament two years later. However, he fled the country in November 1837 on the outbreak of the revolt of Louis J. Papineau (1786–1871), whom he had supported. He settled in Albany, New York, where he resumed his medical practice. He still took an interest in literature, poetry and history. He accidentally came across extensive deposits of early Dutch settler manuscripts and records in the office of the New York State Secretary. He learnt Dutch and subsequently published *The History of New Netherland* (2 vols, 1846–8). The New York authorities then persuaded him to edit the records – a task which took him all of twenty-two years. He published *The Documentary History of the State of New York* (4 vols, 1849–51) and the first series of *Documents Relative to the Colonial History of the State of New York* (vols I-XI, 1853–61). In 1870, following the request of the mayor of New York, he commenced work on editing the minutes of the Common Council of New York. The eight volumes were partially published in 1872 before printing was halted for financial reasons (the volumes were eventually published in 1905). He was twice married but a child from each marriage died in infancy. He died on 29 May 1880.

O'CALLAGHAN, Sir Francis L. (1839–1909) Born Dunmanus, Co. Cork, the son of James O'Callaghan, JP. He was educated at Queen's College, Cork (now UCC), but his engineering talents were formed during terms of railway construction in Cork and Wales between 1859 and 1862. He entered the Indian Department of Public Works and qualified as a civil engineer. He supervised the construction of a bridge over the Indus River and of the railway through the Bolan Pass. He eventually became consultant engineer to the Government of India for State Railways. He retired in 1894 and was knighted in 1902. He was a member of the Institute of Civil Engineers and a fellow of the Royal Geographical Society. He died in Guildford, Surrey, on 14 November 1909 and was buried there.

O'CALLAGHAN, Jeremiah (1780–1861) Born Aghinagh, Co. Cork, the son of Jeremiah O'Callaghan, farmer. He was ordained priest for the diocese of Cloyne and Ross in 1805 and served as a curate on Cape Clear Island and in Aghnakishey. He became involved in the question of the taking of usury (high interest) in financial transactions and was transferred to the parish of Rosscarbery in 1818. However, in the following year, he refused absolution to a dying usurer (pending compensation to the debtors) and was suspended from office. In 1823 he emigrated to New York but was not accepted there. It was the same in Baltimore and Quebec. While staying in Montreal he published *Usury,*

or Interest, Proved to be Repugnant to the Divine and Ecclesiastical Laws, and Destructive to Civil Society (1824). The book sold very well. The English social reformer, William Cobbett (1763–1835), republished the book in 1825 and in 1828 he forwarded the profits to O'Callaghan. In 1830, O'Callaghan was accepted for the diocese of Boston and was posted to the state of Vermont – he being the only priest there! For twenty-four years he traversed Vermont, ministering to the frontier settlements of French Canadians and Irish immigrants. His mission was so successful that he earned the title of 'The Apostle of Vermont'. In 1854, he moved to Holyoke, Massachusetts, where he died on 23 February 1861. He was buried in St Jerome's Church, which he had built shortly after his arrival at Holyoke. His other publications included *A Critical Review of Mr J.K. Converse's Calvinistic Sermon* (1834), *The Creation and Offspring of the Protestant Church* (1837), *The Hedge around the Vineyard* (1844), *Banks and Paper Money* (1852) and *Exposure of the Vermont Banking Companies* (1854).

O'CALLAGHAN, John (d. 1913) Born Killavullen, Co. Cork. He acted as a district correspondent of the *Cork Examiner* before emigrating to the US where he became involved in Irish nationalist organisations and proved himself an effective organiser. He acted as American correspondent of the *Irish Daily Independent* (1893–6). From its foundation, he was national secretary of the United Irish League of America and represented that organisation at political conventions in Dublin. He died in Boston on 27 July 1913.

O'CALLAGHAN, Kathleen (1888–1961) Born Crossmahon, Lissarda, Co. Cork, she was a member of a farming family with strong nationalistic traditions. She was educated at the Dominican Convent, Eccles Street, Dublin; at the Royal University, Dublin; and at Cambridge University where she graduated MA in Languages. She took up a teaching post at Mary Immaculate Training College, Limerick, and later married Councillor Michael O'Callaghan who was elected mayor of Limerick in 1920. On 7 March 1921, Mayor O'Callaghan was murdered in her presence by British forces. She was elected to the 2nd Dáil as a Sinn Féin TD for Limerick City-Limerick East in May 1921 and re-elected in 1922 as an anti-Treaty TD. However, she failed to be re-elected in 1923. She played a prominent part in Limerick's cultural life and was a founder member of Féile Luimní. She died at St John's Hospital, Limerick, on 16 March 1961 and was buried at Mount St Lawrence Cemetery. Her sister, Marie O'Donovan (d. 20 January 1961), was also a member of the staff of Mary Immaculate College. She was Deputy mayor of Limerick from May 1921 to January 1922 – the first woman to hold that position.

O'CALLAGHAN, Kevin (1921–1974) Born at Skarragh, Lombardstown, Co. Cork, the son of **William O'Callaghan,** farmer and senator. He was educated at the Dominican College, Newbridge, Co. Kildare. He became a member of the Fianna Fáil party in 1945 and enhanced his political connections in 1954 when he married Stephanie, daughter of the Fianna Fáil stalwart **Seán Moylan.** He was elected to Cork County Council in 1950 (Mallow Area) and unsuccessfully contested a Dáil seat in the following year's general election. He did not seek re-election to the Council in 1955, but was elected to Seanad Éireann in a 1970 by-election and was re-elected on the agricultural panel in 1971. He was Fianna Fáil director of elections in North East Cork for the 1973 general and presidential elections. An extensive farmer, he was a director of Erin Foods Ltd (1963–70). He died at his residence, Eden Hill, Mallow on 24 January 1974 and was buried in St Joseph's Cemetery, Mallow.

O'CALLAGHAN, Pat (1905–1991) Born Derrygallon, Kanturk, Co. Cork. He qualified as a doctor at the Royal College of Surgeons at the age of 20 years. Having been refused permission to practise on age grounds, he joined the medical corps of the RAF. He became an all-round athlete in field events but specialised in hammer throwing. He won his first gold medal at the Amsterdam Olympics in 1928 with a throw of 51.39m and repeated the performance four years later at the Los Angeles Olympics with 53.92m. With a third Olympic title at his mercy, he was unable to compete in the Berlin Olympics of 1936 as the Irish athletics body, the National Athletics and Cycling Association (NACA), was banned from international competition. Following his retirement from athletics, he took up professional wrestling for a while in the USA before resuming his medical career in Clonmel. He died at Ardkeen Hospital, Waterford, on 1 December 1991 and was buried in Powerstown Cemetery, Clonmel.

O'CALLAGHAN, Sir Robert W. (1777–1840) Born Cork. He joined British Army in 1764 and served in the Peninsular War. He rose to the rank of general in 1814 and was knighted in the following year. He later served in Scotland and India. He was awarded the Grand Cross of the Bath in 1838. He died in London in 1840.

O'CALLAGHAN, Seán (1918–2000) Born Killavullen, Co. Cork, the son of Con O'Callaghan, small farmer and county council ganger. He was educated at Wallstown NS, at Doneraile CBS and at the Military College, Co. Kildare. For a time, he was a member of the IRA (1934–6), but was commissioned as an officer of the Irish Army in 1936 and served until after the Emergency. He left the army and worked as a journalist in Fleet Street with *The Dispatch, The Chronicle* and *John o' London's Weekly.* He moved to Africa in 1952 where he worked for the *East African Standard* in Nairobi as a roving reporter. Following the publication of his *The Easter Lily* (1956), he devoted his time to writing. Other subsequent publications included *The Slave Trade, The Jackboot in Ireland, Execution* and *To Hell or Barbados* (2000). He resided in Malta in his latter years and died in August 2000. [Autobiography (1992); Film of his *Slave Trade* by Malenotti of Rome]

O'CALLAGHAN, Thomas A. (1839–1916) Born Cork. He was educated at North Monastery

CBS and at St Vincent's, Sunday's Well. He entered the Dominican Novitiate at Tallaght, Co. Dublin, in 1857 and, following further studies at Minerva College, Rome, he was ordained in July 1863. He was consecrated as coadjutor bishop of Cork in Rome on 29 June 1884. He succeeded to the see of Cork on 14 November 1886. He died on 4 June 1916 and was buried in St Joseph's Cemetery.

O'CALLAGHAN, William (1881–1967) Born Scarragh, Lombardstown, Co. Cork. He was educated at Dromore NS, at Buckley's Academy, Cork and at Albert College, Dublin. He was co-opted to Cork County Council in March 1914, but was unsuccessful in retaining his seat three months later when he contested the Kanturk division as an O'Brienite candidate. In 1942, he was elected to the same council for the Mallow area as a member of Fianna Fáil and retained his seat until 1950 when he declined to go forward. He was elected to Seanad Éireann in 1938 on the agricultural panel and retained this seat until 1961, with the exception of 1943–44. In 1938, he purchased Longueville, Mallow, the 18th-century mansion of the Longfield family (opened as a restaurant and guest house in later years by his son and daughter-in-law). He was a founding member and first treasurer of the Irish Dairy Shorthorn Breeders' Association and also chairman of the Irish Sugar Beet Growers' Association. Mixing farming with business, he was, at various times, a saw-mill operator, ice-cream manufacturer and a director of Clover Meats, Waterford. He died on 28 January 1967 at Longueville and was buried in Gould's Hill Cemetery. His son, **Kevin O'Callaghan**, was a senator from 1970 to his death in 1974.

Ó CATHÁIN, Seán (1873–1937) Born Anglesboro, nr. Mitchelstown, Co. Cork, the son of Patrick O'Keane, farmer. He was educated at Kilbehenny NS and at Gleann na gCreabhar NS where he worked for a time as a monitor. In 1892, he was appointed as a customs officer in London. Having learnt Irish, he was secretary of the London branch of Connradh na

Gaeilge for seven years. He was transferred to Belfast in 1905 and was active in the training of teachers of Irish under the aegis of the Connradh. In 1909, he published his *Ceachta Cainte Gramadaighe* which ran to eight editions. He also taught at both Coláiste na Mumhan, Ballingeary and at Coláiste an Daingin. In 1922, he was transferred to Cork as a tax inspector, but was again transferred to Dublin in the following year as assistant collector at Dublin Harbour. He died on 4 February 1937.

Ó CAOIMH, Eoghan (1656–1726) Born Glenville, Co. Cork, the son of a prosperous farmer. He received a classical education and, in his twenties, was transcribing manuscripts at various places in Munster. Following his marriage to Eleanor Nagle of Brosna, Co. Kerry, in 1681, he settled in Kerry but returned to Cork when he was evicted in 1692. While in prison between 1698 and 1703, he was supported by the bishop of Cork, **John Baptist Sleyne**. Following the deaths of his wife (October 1707) and son, he was ordained in the priesthood in 1717 and was appointed as parish priest of Doneraile where he corresponded with the noted Gaelic poet, **Seán Clárach Mac Domhnaill**. He died on 5 April 1726 and was buried in Oldcourt Cemetery. His tombstone was encased in a more eleborate memorial in 1911 by a successor at Doneraile, Canon **Patrick A. Sheehan**. [Sketches in *Gadelica 1* (1912–1913), and by B. Ó Conchúir (1982)]

Ó CAOIMH, Pádraig (1897–1964) Born Co. Roscommon. He was educated at CBC and PBC, Cork, and at UCC. When he was 17 years old, he, along with two others, founded the Nemo Rangers Football Club. In 1916, he joined the Volunteers and later that year he went to London to undertake a teacher-training course. In 1920, while serving as a captain in the 1st Cork Brigade of the IRA, he was arrested and sentenced to fifteen years' imprisonment (later commuted to ten years). He was imprisoned in England but was released in 1922. He took the anti-Treaty side during the Civil War, but after this he returned to his teaching career. In July 1920, he was elected as secretary of the Cork county board of the GAA, a position he held until his appointment as general secretary of the GAA and manager of Croke Park in 1929. During his tenure at the helm of the GAA, he was responsible for the expansion of Croke Park, the establishment of the National League and Railway Cup competitions, and the management of a greatly enlarged organisation. He died at the Mater Hospital, Dublin, on 15 May 1964 and was buried in Glasnevin Cemetery. County Cork's GAA stadium, Páirc Uí Chaoimh, is named in his honour.

Ó CEALLACHÁIN, Dónal (1892–1962) Born Great William O'Brien Street, Cork, the son of William O'Callaghan who worked as a labourer at the nearby North Presentation convent. He was educated at Eason's Hill NS and at North Monastery CBS. He learnt Irish and won many prizes in conversation and recitation at various feiseanna. He competed as a member of the North Parish branch of Connradh na Gaeilge at the Oireachtas in Dublin in 1903. He was chairman of Cork County Council (1920–4), but did not seek re-election in 1925. He was also a Sinn Féin member of Cork Corporation and, following the death of Lord Mayor **Terence Mac Swiney**, he was elected in his place on 4 November 1920. He fled to the US and was re-elected for 1921, *in absentia*. In the following year, he took the Republican side in the civil war but was once more elected as Lord Mayor and was so again in 1923. He resigned the mayoralty in January 1924. He left Cork and spent some years in Europe before taking up work with the ESB as an accountant. He was elected to the 1st Dáil in May 1921 as TD for Cork City. He died on 12 September 1962 and was buried in Dean's Grange Cemetery, Dublin.

Ó CÉILEACHAIR, Aindrias (1883–1954) Born Na Milíní, Baile Bhúirne, Co. Cork, the son of Domhnall Ó Céileachair, farmer. He was educated locally, at St Colman's College, Fermoy and at St Patrick's College, Maynooth, where he was ordained in 1908. Possessing a rare ability in the study of Old Irish, he lectured in Celtic Studies at the Dunboyne Institute, Maynooth, and later at Liverpool University. In November 1916, he was awarded a research scholarship at Illinois University, and while there, he worked with the German scholar, Gertrude Schoepperle, to produce an edition of *Betha Colaim Cille* (1918). He returned to Ireland shortly afterwards and resumed his spiritual duties. From 1920 to 1940, he worked as chaplain at the Preparatory College, Mallow. When the college was transferred to Baile Bhúirne in 1940, he retired to Coachford on grounds of ill-health. He later moved to Carrigrohane, Cork, and died at Mount Desert on 28 July 1954. He was buried in Coolea Cemetery. His Irish translation of H. Sienkiewicz's *Quo vadis?* (1895) was published in 1936.

Ó CÉILEACHAIR, Donncha (1918–1960) Born Coolea, Co. Cork, the son of Domhnall Bán Ó Céileachair, whose autobiography, *Sgéal mo Bheatha* was published in 1940. He was educated locally, at the Preparatory College, Mallow and at De la Salle Training College, Waterford, where he qualified as a primary teacher. He graduated MA at UCD with a thesis on the Irish of Muskerry. He held various posts in Clare, Leitrim and Dublin before being seconded by the Department of Education to be part of the editorial team of Tomás de Bhaldraithe's *English-Irish Dictionary*. He later returned to teaching and worked at Belgrove NS, Clontarf. He collaborated with his sister, **Síle Ní Chéileachair**, in the publication, *Bullaí Mháirtín* (1955), a book of short stories which was very well received. He produced, with Proinsias Ó Conluain, *An Duinníneach* (1958), a biography of the Gaelic lexicographer, Pádraig Ó Duinnín (1860–1934). The diary of his pilgrimages, *Dialann Oilithrigh*, was published in 1953. His other publications included, *An Ungáir* (with Joseph Szoverffy, 1958), *Leabhar Lourdes* (1958) and *Iognáid Loyola* (posthumously, 1962). He died of polio on 21 July 1960 and was buried in Glasnevin Cemetery. [Analysis of style by P. Riggs (1978)]

Ó CÉILLEACHAIR, Séamas (1916–1988) Born Doirín Álainn, Baile Bhúirne. He worked as a primary school teacher at Skeheenarincky, Ballyporeen, Co. Tipperary. He is especially noted for his school text, *An Graiméar Nua* (1962), which ran to eight editions and for the editorship of his poetry anthologies *Nua-Fhilí, 1942–52* (1956, 1962, 1965); *Nua-Fhilí, 1953–63* (1968); and *Nua-Fhilí 3* (1979). His own poetry collections *Bláth an Bhaile* (1952) and *Coillte an Cheoil* (1955) were well received. He also wrote a children's nursery rhyme collection, *Hup Hup* (1952). He died at St Joseph's Hospital, Clonmel, on 27 September 1988 and was buried in Reilig Ghobnatan, Baile Bhúirne.

Ó CIOSÁIN, Seán (c.1896–1982) Born Blackpool, Cork, the son of John Cashman, storekeeper. He was educated at North Monastery CBS and at De la Salle Training College, Waterford, where he qualified as a primary teacher in 1915. However, he developed an interest in Irish and was employed as a peripatetic teacher by Connradh na Gaeilge (1917–20), working mainly in West Cork. He held various positions within the Connradh before his appointment as a primary schools inspector in 1925. He worked in many parts of the country before he retired from the inspectorate following a disagreement with a bishop. He worked as a lecturer in Irish at De la Salle College (1930–9). On the outbreak of World War II, he moved to England where he taught in Dorset and Derby. He returned to Ireland in 1956 and worked as an official translator in the Translation Section, Leinster House. He was a frequent contributor to many Gaelic journals and published three collections of short stories, *Scéalta cois Laoi* (1935), *Idir Chéin agus Chomhgar* (1952) and *Príomhthairgí an Domhain* (1957). His translations include those of *The Vicar of Wakefield* (*Viocáire Wakefield*, 1931) and *Wuthering Heights* (*Árda Wuthering*, 1934). He died at his residence in Clontarf, Dublin, on 26 January 1982 and was buried in St Fintan's Cemetery, Sutton. [Autobiographies, *Cois Laoi na sreath* (1970) and *Is ait an mac an saol* (1973)]

Ó COILEÁIN, Conchubhair (1911–1965) Born Ballymah, Waterfall, near Cork, the son of William Collins, railroad worker. He was educated at Ballinora NS and at North Monastery CBS. He taught for a time (1929–32) as a Christian Brother, then as a promoter of An Fáinne for Connradh na Gaeilge, before moving to Dublin in 1937 as a peripatetic Irish teacher for Dublin VEC. He became principal officer of the Dún Laoghaire school attendance committee in 1940 and was associated with the revived Oireachtas na Gaeilge in the previous year. He became full-time secretary of Connradh na Gaeilge in December 1943. He then worked as assistant librarian at the *Irish Press* newspaper and from 1954 until his death, he was head of Irish news at Radio Éireann and later at Radió Teilifís Éireann. He was the instigator of the noted Irish news programme, *Nuacht Anall, Nuacht Abhus*. He died at his residence in Dean's Grange, Dublin, on 18 June 1965 and was buried in St Finbarr's Cemetery, Cork.

Ó COILEÁIN, Seán (1754–1817) Born Dunmanway/Drimoleague, Co. Cork, the son of a small farmer who died while Seán was young. In 1773, he spent four months at a seminary at Coimbra in Portugal. On his return, he settled at Myross, Union Hall, where he ran a school at Stookeen until a few years before his death. He married a local girl by the name of Coughlan and the couple had three or four children. However, the marriage failed and he took up with his wife's sister who gave birth to a daughter. He left Myross in 1814 and lived with his daughter's family on Main Street, Skibbereen, where he continued to teach. He died on 18 April 1817 and was buried in Cill Míne Cemetery. Even though very little of his poetic output remains in manuscript form, his reputation largely rests with his poems 'An Buachaill Bán' (1782), 'Machnamh an Duine Dhoilíosaigh' (1813), his translation of 'The Exile of Erin' ['An Díbirteach ó Éirinn'] (1816) and his English translation of 'Agallamh an Othair leis an mBás'.

Ó CONAILL, Daithí (1938–1991) Born Lough Road, Cork. He joined the Morrison's Island branch of Sinn Féin in 1955 and, as an IRA member, took part in the raid on Brookeborough Barracks on New Year's Day, 1957, in which Seán South and Fergal O'Hanlon were killed. He was subsequently arrested and served prison sentences in Mountjoy Jail and at the Curragh Camp, Co. Kildare. He escaped from the Curragh in 1958, and in November 1959, was critically wounded by the RUC and B-Specials at Ardboe, Co. Tyrone. He was later sentenced to eight years' imprisonment but was released from Crumlin Road Jail, Belfast, in 1963. He unsuccessfully stood as a Sinn Féin candidate for Cork borough in the general election of 1961 and polled just under 2,000 first preference votes. He was appointed as a vocational teacher in building construction and worked for a time in Glencolumcille, Co. Donegal, later at Ballyshannon Technical School, Co. Donegal, and at Old Bawn Community School, Tallaght, Co. Dublin. He became vice-president of Provisional Sinn Féin in 1971 following the split with Official Sinn Féin. In the early 1970s, he was the chief Republican negotiator in the 'Feakle Talks' which sought a basis for a permanent peace in Ireland. He was arrested in Dublin in July 1975 and staged a forty-seven-day hunger strike at Portlaoise Prison. He left Provisional Sinn Féin when it was decided at its Ard Fheis in November 1986 that its elected TDs would sit in Leinster House. He became vice-president of Republican Sinn Féin in 1987. He died at his Rathgar, Dublin, home on 1 January 1991 and was buried in the Republican Plot in Glasnevin Cemetery.

O'CONNELL, Denis J. (1849–1927) Born Donoughmore, Co. Cork, the son of Michael O'Connell. He was educated in Maryland, USA, and at Urban College of Propaganda, Rome, where he was ordained in 1877. He was engaged in pastoral work in Richmond, Virginia, and acted as secretary to Bishop Conroy of Ardagh and Clonmacnoise on a papal mission to Canada. He then served as rector of the North American College, Rome (1885–95), vicar of Santa Maria Church, Rome (1895–1903) and rector of the Catholic University of America, Washington (1903–8). He was consecrated as titular bishop of Sebaste in May 1908. He was appointed as auxiliary bishop of San Francisco in the following December and as bishop of Richmond in January 1912. Following his resignation, he was named as titular archbishop of Marianne in January 1926. He died in Richmond on 1 January 1927 and was buried locally.

O'CONNELL, John (1810–1858) Born Dublin, the third (and favourite) son of Daniel O'Connell (1775–1847), the Liberator. He was educated at Clongowes Wood, Co. Kildare, and at TCD. He was called to the Irish Bar in 1837 but never practised. He was a Repeal MP for Youghal (1832–7), Athlone (1837–41), Kilkenny City (1841–7), Limerick City (1847–51) and Clonmel (1853–7). He resigned his Clonmel seat in February 1857 on being appointed Clerk of the Hanaper in Ireland. Even though he was his father's chief lieutenant, he was adjudged to have been 'an inept leader' of the Repeal Association after his father's death. Among his publications were, *The Repeal Dictionary* (1845), *The Life and Speeches of Daniel O'Connell* (1846) and *Recollections* (1846). He died at his Kingstown (now Dún Laoghaire) residence on 24 May 1858 and was buried in Glasnevin Cemetery.

O'CONNELL, Timothy (1882–1970) Born Aghabullogue, Co. Cork. He was educated at the Royal College of Science, Dublin. He worked in the technical division of the Department of Agriculture and was in charge of agricultural policy during World War II. He was then involved in the implementation of the American-sponsored Marshall Plan which tackled the problem of German reconstruction after that war. His specialisation was in the growing and production of wheat. He died in 1970.

O'CONNOR, Arthur (1763–1852) Born Mitchelstown, Co. Cork, the brother of **Roger**

O'Connor, Esq., and uncle of **Fergus O'Connor**. He was educated at TCD where he graduated BA (1782). He was called to the Bar in 1788 and sat as an MP for Philipstown. He joined the Society of United Irishmen and edited its organ, *The Press*. He was arrested in England in 1798, tried for high treason and acquitted. However, he was re-arrested an imprisoned at Fort George in Scotland. On his release in 1803, he went to France and was recognised as the representative of the United Irishmen by Napoleon. In 1807, he married Eliza, the daughter of the Marquis de Condorcet (1743–94), the French philosopher and mathematician [whose works O'Connor helped to edit in twelve volumes (Paris, 1847–9)]. In 1834, he had been permitted by the British government to return to Ireland for two months to dispose of his properties. He died at his chateau in Bignon on 25 April 1852. [Bust (1833) by P.J. David (1788–1856)]

O'CONNOR, Dominic (d. 1935) Born Cork, the nephew of Rev. Luke Sheehan, a Capuchin missionary priest of Oregon, USA. Dominic also joined the Capuchin Order and served as a chaplain to the Allied Forces in Greece during World War I. He returned to Ireland in 1917 and was appointed as brigade chaplain to the Cork Volunteers by **Tomás MacCurtain**. He was the first to arrive at the Mac Curtain home on the morning of his murder. He later acted as chaplain to **Terence Mac Swiney** and remained with him during the long days of his hunger strike at Brixton Prison. In January 1921, he was arrested at Church Street Friary (Dublin), taken to Dublin Castle and was sentenced to five years' imprisonment. He was released from Pankhurst Prison in January 1922 under the general amnesty following the Anglo-Irish Truce. Himself and Rev. Albert (Bibby) acted as chaplains to the Republican garrison at the Four Courts. Both men were subsequently ordered to serve on the Capuchin mission in America. Dominic was allocated to Bend (Oregon) where his uncle, Luke Sheehan, had pioneered Irish Capuchin missionary work. He served in various capacities there and undertook research into the Roman Catholic history of Oregon, publishing *A Brief History of the Diocese of Baker* in 1930. In 1934, he was involved in a motor accident in Portland, Oregon, which led to his death in October 1935. He was buried at Bend. On 13 June 1958 the remains of Rev. Dominic and Rev. Albert (who had died in 1925) were repatriated to Ireland and were re-interred on the following day at the Capuchin Cemetery, Rochestown, Cork.

O'CONNOR, Fergus (1794–1855) Born Connorville, Fermoy, Co. Cork, the son of **Roger O'Connor** and nephew of **Arthur O'Connor**. He was educated at Portarlington Grammar School and possibly at TCD. He was called to the Bar in 1830. He campaigned in England for the Reform Bill of 1832. He was elected as a Repeal MP for Mallow in 1832, but was unseated in 1835 for failing to meet the property qualification for MPs. In 1837, he became editor of the Leeds *Northern Star*, a radical newspaper, which became in the following year the leading Chartist organ. In 1841, he broke away and founded the National Charter Association. He was elected as MP for Nottingham in 1847. Following the failure of parliamentary petitions in 1842 and 1848, the movement declined. His mind became unbalanced and he was admitted into care in 1852. He died in London on 30 August 1855. [Life by D. Read and E. Glasgow (1961)]

O'CONNOR, Frank (1903–1966) Born Douglas Street, Cork, as Michael O'Donovan, the son of a soldier. The father being an alcoholic, the family was raised in poor circumstances. Having moved to Blarney Street and then to Dillon's Cross, he received his early education at St Patrick's NS, where he came under the influence of **Daniel Corkery** who encouraged his literary interests. He was active in the War of Independence and took the Republican side in the civil war, for which he was interned in 1923. He was appointed as Cork County librarian in December 1925, but threw up the post and left

Cork for Dublin where he was appointed as librarian at Pembroke Library. He served as director of the Abbey Theatre from 1935 until 1939 and in that year he married a Welsh actress, Evelyn Bowen, and devoted himself to literature. He settled in Co. Wicklow and as well as his literary endeavours, he also was a regular broadcaster with Radio Éireann (now RTÉ). However, through the 1940s, he became disillusioned with the prevailing atmosphere in Ireland as, among other things, many of his books were banned by the Censorship Board. In the war years, he acted as the poetry editor of **Seán O'Faolain's** publication, *The Bell*. In 1951, with his marriage broken up, he left for America where he attained celebrity status on the campus circuit. Here he met and married Harriet Rich in 1953. He returned to Ireland in 1960 and was appointed as lecturer in English at TCD in 1963. He died in Dublin on 10 March 1966 and was buried in Dean's Grange Cemetery. His publications include *Guests of the Nation* (1931), *The Saint and Mary Kate* (1932), *Bones of Contention* (1936), *Dutch Interior* (1940), *Lords, Kings, and Commons* (1959), *The Lonely Voice* (1963) and *The Backward Look* (posthumously, 1967). [Autobiographies (1961 and 1968); Four life-size bronzes by **Seamus Murphy** at The National Gallery, RTÉ, Cork City Library, and UCC; Commemorative plaque at 31, Douglas Street, Cork]

O'CONNOR, George B. (1851–1921) Born Ballineen, Co. Cork, the son of Roger O'Connor of Fort Robert, and grand-nephew of the Chartist leader, **Fergus O'Connor**. He joined the British Army and served abroad with the 19th Hussars and the Queen's Bays regiment where he rose to the rank of major. He wrote two well-received histories, *Elizabethan Ireland* (1906) and *Stuart Ireland* (1910). He also wrote *Irish and other Fragments* (1910). In the general election of December 1910, he stood as a Unionist candidate for the College Green (Dublin) constituency but was unsuccessful. He was nominated to contest the Cork City constituency in the general election of 1918 but withdrew before the poll. He was a supporter of Horace Plunkett's (1854–1932) short-lived Irish Dominion League in 1919. He was shot dead outside his residence, Illane Roe, Rochestown, on 11 July 1921.

O'CONNOR, James (1823–1890) Born Cobh, Co. Cork, the son of Charles O'Connor and younger brother of Bishop **Michael O'Connor**. He left Ireland around 1839 with his brother who had been appointed as rector to a seminary in Philadelphia. He studied at the seminary and later in Rome where he was ordained in March 1848. He returned to America and worked in his brother's diocese (who was now the bishop of Pittsburgh). In 1862, he accepted the rectorship of his old seminary in Philadelphia and worked there until 1872. Following a further four years of pastoral work in Philadelphia, he was appointed titular bishop over the states of Nebraska, Wyoming, Montana and the Dakotas in August 1876. In 1885, due to an expanding church, he was appointed as first bishop of Omaha with jurisdiction over Nebraska and Wyoming. Through his encouragement of various religious orders to work in his diocese, he built up a full religious, social and educational structure. At the time of his death on 27 May 1890, his original diocese had been subdivided into five independent bishoprics.

O'CONNOR, John (1850–1928) Born Mallow, Co. Cork, the son of W. O'Connor. He was educated at North Monastery CBS and worked as a commercial traveller. His erect stature of 1.90m (6'4") earned him the nickname of 'Long John'. Elected MP for Tipperary County in a January 1885 by-election, he retained his seat to 1892 sitting for Tipperary South. In July of that year, as an anti-Parnellite nationalist, he unsuccessfully contested both Tipperary South and Kilkenny City. He was called to the English Bar in 1893, but continued his association with nationalist politics. He was elected MP for Kildare North in a 1905 by-election and sat for that constituency until 1918, when he was defeated by Sinn Féin's Domhnall Ó Buachalla, later governor-general of the Irish Free State. He was called to the Inner Bar in 1919, but did not practise. He died at his residence at Hampstead, Camden Town, on 28 October 1928 and was buried in Kensal Green Cemetery.

O'CONNOR, Michael (1810–1872) Born Cobh, Co. Cork, the elder brother of Bishop **James O'Connor**. He left Ireland in 1824 to study for the priesthood in France. Following further studies in Rome, he was ordained in June 1833 and graduated DD in the following year. He spent a time teaching languages before returning to Ireland to take up a curacy at Fermoy. He moved to Philadelphia around 1839 to take up the rectorship of a seminary there. He was transferred to Pittsburgh, Pennsylvania, in 1841 and two years later was consecrated as first bishop of Pittsburgh. He made huge strides in the development of the new diocese and before his cathedral was completed in 1855 the diocese had been split in two and he had accepted the poorer diocese of Erie. However, on foot of public demand, a straight swap took place and he returned to Pittsburgh. In 1859 he travelled to Rome and obtained permission to join the Jesuit Order following his resignation as bishop. He was received into the Order in December 1862. He carried on his missionary work in the US, Cuba and Canada before his death at Woodstock, Maryland, on 18 October 1872. He was buried in the Jesuit Cemetery there.

O'CONNOR, Pat (1921–1986) Born Tureenavauscane, Kiskeam, Co. Cork, the son of J.J. O'Connor, farmer. He was educated at Boherbue NS. He emigrated to London at the age of sixteen and, having an interest in boxing, joined a club in Hammersmith. Following a string of victories, he turned professional in 1939 and boxed as a middleweight. He took the Irish middleweight title from John Roche over fifteen rounds in Clonmel in 1942 and defeated the British and Empire middleweight champion, Ernie Roderick, in a London tournament in the following year. He also took and successfully defended the Irish cruiserweight title. With 200 victories behind him, he left for the United States in 1947 where he gained eighteen victories and was a serious contender for the legendary Sugar Ray Robinson's middleweight crown. However, a series of injuries finished the promising career of 'The Clouting Celt from County Cork', and he went to live in San Francisco. He returned home to Ireland in spring 1986 and was hospitalised soon after at St Patrick's Hospital, Kanturk, where he died on 18 June. He was buried in Keady, Co. Armagh – his wife's homeplace.

O'CONNOR, Richard (1810–1876) Born Mangan Castle, Bandon, Co. Cork, the eldest son of Arthur O'Connor. He emigrated to Sydney, Australia, in 1835 and held various clerical positions in the New South Wales legislative assembly and legislative council. In 1864, he was appointment as clerk of both houses and he produced the first edition of the *Parliamentary Handbook* in 1868. In the meantime, he was a fellow of St John's College at the University of Sydney, a trustee of the Savings Bank of New South Wales and a member of the board of management of the Government Asylums for the Infirm and Destitute. In failing health, he retired in March 1871, leaving a lasting legacy to the orderly administration of the state's parliamentary system. He died at his home at Glebe Point, Sydney, on 27 June 1876.

O'CONNOR, Richard F. (d. 1940) Born Cork to a family of prominent timber merchants. He was educated at Queen's College, Cork (now UCC) where he graduated BA and BE. Following some years in private practice, he was appointed as county surveyor (North) to Cork County Council in 1907 and from 1929 acted in this capacity for the whole county. He played a major role in the modernisation of the county's roads and was mainly responsible for the laying-out of the Carrigrohane Straight. Subsequently, he was in charge of developing the famous Cork Motor Race circuit on the Carrigrohane and Model Farm Roads and was chief engineer of the organising committee for each race. He was a tireless promoter of the need for an airbase in

Cork and presented comprehensive plans in the late 1930s for airports at Belvelly and (later) Midleton. He died at his resdience, 'Clydaville', Mallow, on 3 March 1940 and was buried privately.

O'CONNOR, Roger (1762–1834) Born Connerville, Fermoy, Co. Cork, the brother of **Arthur O'Connor** and father of **Fergus O'Connor**. He was educated at TCD, but did not graduate. He was called to the Irish Bar in 1783 and to the English one in the following year. Having joined the Society of United Irishmen, he was arrested in 1797 at the insistence of his brother, Robert, but acquitted. He was arrested again during the 1798 Rebellion and imprisoned for a while in Scotland. He was suspected of being involved in an arson attack on his residence, Dangan Castle (Trim, Co. Meath), shortly after the building had been insured. He eloped with a married woman and was acquitted on the charge of robbing the Galway mail coach. In 1822, he published *The Chronicles of Eri* – a work purporting to have been translated from the Phoenician. He died at Kilcrea, Cork, on 27 January 1834.

O'CONOR, William A. (1820–1887) Born Cork, of a Roscommon family which had moved there. He was educated at TCD where he graduated BA (1853). Following his ordination in the Church of England in 1853, he ministered in Liverpool before finally settling in Manchester in 1858 where he ministered to the poor parishioners of St Jude's. He developed an interest in literary and social pursuits and contributed articles to the Manchester Statistical Society and to the Manchester Literary Club. He was a strong advocate of Irish Home Rule and his anti-English *History of the Irish People* (2 vols, 1882), ran to three editions. His *Essays in Literature and Ethics* was published posthumously (1889). He died in Torquay on 22 March 1887 and was buried there.

O'CONROY, Timothy (1883–1935) Born Castleinch, Ovens, Co. Cork, the son of Jeremiah Conroy, labourer. He joined the Royal Navy in June 1898 and served in South America, Africa and Arabia. He left the navy in 1905 and for the next five years travelled on the Continent where he developed his capacity for linguistics – eventually becoming fluent in nine languages. From 1910 until 1913, he was employed as a tutor at the Russian Imperial Household where he became acquainted with the notorious Rasputin (1871–1916). He returned to London in 1913 and took up a position with the Lunn Travel Agency as its Geneva representative. He took part in the dramatic negotiations on the outbreak of World War I to evacuate 500 British travellers back to England. He spent the war as an interpreter in Russia, and, as a result of a brief visit to Japan, he went to live there from 1918 until 1933. He married a Japanese girl and was appointed as professor of English at Keio University, Tokyo. While travelling around the country in his study of Japanese culture and life, he also had access to many state functions and banquets. However, with growing militarism in Japan and with the annexation of Manchuria by Japan in 1931, he became disillusioned and returned to England in September 1933, having to leave his wife behind. This concern led to a final illness which bordered on paranoia. A month later, his *The Menace of Japan* was published. He died in Hampstead General Hospital on 5 November 1935. [Biographical article by T. de Bhaldraithe in *Comhar*, 11 (Samhain, 1985)]

Ó CRÓINÍN, Seán (1915–1965) Born Ballymakeera, Co. Cork, the son of Seán Ó Cróinín and **Elizabeth Cronin**. He was educated locally and at a Cork City commercial school, but owing to poor health, did not complete the course. He was employed for a time by the Cork Committee of Agriculture as a cow-tester. He then worked in Dublin with the folklorists, Séamus Ó Duilearga and Seán Ó Súilleabháin. In 1938, he became a full-time folklore collector for County Cork and worked in that capacity until 1944. When he married in 1943, he settled in Macroom, where he eventually found suitable work as a rate collector. A second manuscript collection period lasted from 1959 until his early death. During those periods, he amassed a huge total of almost 31,000 pages of manuscript from Mid-Cork, South Cork and East Cork – nearly 50% of the entire Cork Folklore Collection. Some of his material has been subsequently edited by **Andrias Ó Muimhneacháin** (1978) (this included his transcriptions from **Tim Buckley** of *The Tailor and Anstey* fame). He died suddenly at his residence at Casement Street, Macroom, on 14 March 1965 and was buried in the local St Colman's Cemetery. [Cork Folklore Collection and Cork Schools Collection in microfilm at Special Collections, Boole Library, UCC]

Ó CRUADHLAOICH, Diarmuid (1875–1947) Born Kilbrittain, Co. Cork, the son of John Crowley. He became a customs officer and worked in Donegal and Trim before being transferred to London in 1902. Having previously become a member of the Gaelic League in Donegal, he represented London at the General Convention in Dublin later in 1902. He resigned his post in 1916 and qualified as a barrister. He was a district judge of the Republican Courts which were (unofficially) instituted in 1920. He was arrested in Dublin and served a period of two years imprisonment. He returned to the Bench after the War of Independence but, as a result of his anti-Treaty opinions and judicial actions, was imprisoned for a time by the Provisional Government. He resigned from the judiciary in 1924 to pursue a pay claim. Afterwards, he was active in the Sinn Féin Party and published a pamphlet, *The Oath of Allegiance* (1925). He was strongly opposed to Eamon de Valera (1882–1975) and the Fianna Fáil Party and later published an anti-de Valera pamphlet, *Step by Step from the Republic back into the Empire*. He died at his residence in Charleville Road, Dublin, on 4 November 1947 and was buried in Clogagh Graveyard, Co. Cork. [Account of judicial career in M. Kotsonouris, *Retreat from Revolution: the Dáil Courts 1920–1940* (1993)]

Ó CRUADHLAOICH, Pádraig (*c.*1861–1949) Born Ballyvourney, Co. Cork, the son of

Diarmaid Ó Cruadhlaoich, tailor. He, in turn, became a tailor and settled in Macroom in 1885 where he married two years later. He learned to read and write Irish and became a friend of An t-Ath. **Peadar Ó Laoghaire**. He was the author of the Oireachtas na Gaeilge Ode in 1908 and later was president the Muskerry Court of Poetry which was founded in 1926. Under his pseudonyn, 'Gaedheal na nGaedheal', 170 of his poems were published in two books (1936, 1942). In his later years, much of his folklore was transcribed by his Macroom neighbour, **Seán Ó Cróinín**. He died at his residence in Castle Street, Macroom, on 15 March 1949 and was buried in Reilig Ghobnatan, Baile Bhúirne. [Autobiography, *Cuimhne Sean-leinbh* (1946); Works edited by Donncadh Ó Cróinín as *Seanchas Phádraig Í Chrualaoi* (1982)]

Ó CUILEANÁIN, Concubhar (1917–1960) Born Oldcourt, Skibbereen, Co. Cork, the son of Micheál Ó Cuileanáin, teacher. He was educated at De la Salle College, Skibbereen, and at UCC where he graduated BA in Celtic Studies (1940). While at UCC, he held positions in various societies and was editor of the student magazine, *The Quarryman*. He pursued his vocational school teaching career in counties Cork, Kildare, Longford and Dublin while at the same time, was heavily involved in the affairs of Connradh na Gaeilge. He was editor of the Connradh's journal, *Feasta* (which was first published in April 1948) and was the author of the Connradh's promotional pamphlet, *What you can do*. Later, he was appointed as the first editor of the GAA's *Our Games Annual*. He contested the presidency of Connradh na Gaeilge in 1950 but was unsuccessful. He died (as a result of an accident) at Sir Patrick Dun's Hospital, Dublin, on 11 March 1960 and was buried in Skibbereen Cemetery.

Ó CUILL, Micheál (1888–1955) Born Clondrohid, Co. Cork, the son of Micheál Ó Cuill, farmer. As a teenager, he taught Irish in the locality, but when he was 17 years old, the family moved to Cork. He became a member of the Irish Republican Brotherhood (IRB), acted as an organiser for Fianna Éireann and was pivotal in the formation of Cumann na mBan in the city. He was also deeply involved in the Irish Volunteers and, on the outbreak of the Easter Rebellion, set off for Dublin by train only to travel as far as Sallins, Co. Kildare. He walked the rest of the way, but was arrested in the outskirts of the city and was interned in Frongoch Camp. Thus he was later affectionately known as 'The Man who walked to Dublin'. In 1920, he was elected a member of Cork Corporation and it was he who proposed **Tomás Mac Curtain** for the office of Lord Mayor. He was a lifelong member of Connradh na Gaeilge and worked as an inspector of Irish under the aegis of Cork Vocational Education Committee. He collapsed in Marlborough Street, Cork, on 17 September 1955 and died shortly afterwards. He was buried in St Finbarr's Cemetery. [His collection of short stories, *A Cheart Chuige*, was published in 1956]

Ó CUILL, Seán (1882–1958) Born Na Doirí, Cúil Aodha, Co. Cork, the youngest child of Micheál Ó Cuill, carpenter. On the death of his mother, he was reared in County Kerry by his maternal grandmother. Having won two Oireachtas first prizes for his poetry and proverbs (1902, 1903), he spent a year studying at UCC before he departed to the Netherlands (Aappeldoorn) and Belgium (Bruges) to teach English at the Berlitz schools there. He returned to Cork and a collection of his essays, *Céad Flós an Earraigh*, was published in 1908. He held various teaching positions in Leinster and in Cork before he went into the retail newspaper business through his outlet at 95, Patrick Street. However, by selling Republican and Irish magazines, he invoked the wrath of the authorities and was eventually forced to close his business. He was deeply involved with the Irish Volunteers, and after the War of Independence, he was provided with a position in the civil service. He then worked as a proof-reader for An Gúm (the Government Publications Office) from 1929 to 1947. His series of didactic wall charts (with the handbook entitled, *An Módh Ceart*) was published by Browne and Nolan and were to be seen in hundreds of Irish schools. He also studied at UCD and graduated BA in 1931. He later took up the study of the etymology of words and his *Europe's First Language: prehistoric man as fruitgrower* was published in 1953. At about the same time, he launched a monthly magazine entitled, *An Litríocht*, but it only survived for a few editions. He died at Our Lady's Hospice, Harold's Cross, Dublin, on 19 May 1958 and was buried in Reilig Ghobnatan, Baile Bhúirne.

Ó CUILLEANÁIN, Cormac (1902–1970) Born Glanmire Road, Cork, the son of John Cullinane, railway clerk. He was educated at North Monastery CBS and at UCC where he graduated BA. He was a member of the 1st Cork Brigade of the IRA, was interned in the Curragh Camp during the civil war, and later joined the Fianna Fáil Party. He was appointed lecturer in Irish at UCC in 1932 and was made professor of the History of Modern Irish Literature in 1950. With his wife, Eilís (née Dillon), he administered the Honan Hostel at UCC (1949–63). He retired in 1965 and moved the Rome for health reasons. He returned to Cork four years later and died in St Vincent's Hospital, Dublin, on 26 October 1970. He was buried in St Joseph's Cemetery, Cork.

Ó CÚIV, Shán (1875–1940) Born Macroom, Co. Cork, the son of John O'Keeffe, tanner. He was educated at the Model School Dunmanway, and at other schools before taking up employment in 1898 as a reporter on the *Cork Herald*. He joined Connradh na Gaeilge and moved to Dublin in November 1900 where he worked for the *Evening Telegraph* and the *Freeman's Journal* until 1924. He also acted as editor of the journal, *Glór na Ly* (1911–12), and of the *Irish Opinion* (1916). He later worked for *The Irish Independent* and was appointed as Irish editor of the paper in 1931. He was the first to hold the position of Director of the Government Information Bureau (1934). He had a great interest in the teaching of Irish and was associated with **Osborn Bergin**

and others in the development of 'An Leitriú Shímplí' – a phonetical method to simplify the writing of Irish. He died at his residence at Harcourt Street, Dublin, on 13 August 1940 and was buried in Glasnevin Cemetery. His publications include *The Sounds of Irish* (1921), *Fuaimeanna agus Blas na Gaedhilge* (1922), *The Short Cut to Irish* (1927–9), *An Eochair chun Labhartha na Gaedhilge* (1932), and *Prós na hAoise* (1933)

Ó DÁLAIGH, Tadhg (*fl.* 1618) A descendant of the bardic Ó Dálaigh family whose members were in the retinue of the Norman Carew family of Bantry. Around 1618, Tadhg, in search of patronage, addressed his poem, 'Gabh mo gheráin, a Sheoirse' ('Pardon my complaint, George'), to the Lord president of Munster, Sir George Carew (1555–1629), in the mistaken belief that he was a descendant of the Bantry line, when in fact he was an English adventurer who had come to Ireland in 1574 and was a skilful exponent of the art of brute force.

Ó DONNCHADHA, Éamonn (1876–1953) Born Carraig na bhFear, Co. Cork, the son of Donnchadh Ó Donnchadha, farmer, and brother of **Tadhg Ó Donnchadha**. He was educated locally and at St Patrick's College of Education, Dublin, where he qualified as a primary teacher. He later worked as principal teacher at Clogheen NS, Cork. He was very active in the affairs of Connradh na Gaeilge and published such schoolbooks as *Mionchaint Scoile* (1906) and *Bunús na hEolaíochta, Uimhríocht* (1928). He also published an Irish grammar, *Graiméar Gaedhilge* (1923). He worked as a full-time lecturer at UCC from 1909. He was a member of Sinn Féin and acted as a judge of the Republican courts. He died at his residence on Glasheen Road, Cork, on 11 March 1953 and was buried in Whitechurch Graveyard.

Ó DONNCHADHA, Tadhg (1874–1949) Born Carraig na bhFear, Co. Cork, the son of Donnchadh Ó Donnchadha, farmer, and brother of **Éamonn Ó Donnchadha**. He was educated at North Monastery CBS and at St Patrick's College of Education, Dublin. He taught in Dublin and joined Connradh na Gaeilge where he wrote under the pseudonym, 'Tórna'. He was the editor of *Irisleabhar na Gaedhilge* (1902–9), while his first collection of poems, *Leoithne Andeas,* was published in 1905. In addition to editing the works of many of the eighteenth-century Munster poets, he also produced an instruction book for poets, *Bhéarsaidheacht Gaeilge* in 1936. He was also professor of Irish at UCC (1916–44). He died on 21 October 1949 and was buried in St Finbarr's Cemetery. [Festschrift by **S. Pender**, ed. (1947); Life-size bronze by **Seamus Murphy** at UCC]

O'DONOGHUE, Bruno (1905–1990) Born Curraclogh, Bandon, Co. Cork. He was educated at Laragh NS and at PBC, Cork. He worked as a clerk at Irish Steel, as a milk tester at Bandon Co-op and in later years as a clerk at Collins' Barracks, Cork. He saw service with the Irish Brigade during the Spanish civil war. A keen local historian, he edited and prepared for publication Jeremiah O'Mahony's *West Cork and its story* (1961). His *magnum opus* in local history was *his Parish histories and placenames of West Cork* (1986). He died on 5 June 1990 at Millbrook Nursing Home, Bandon and was buried in Kilbrogan Cemetery.

O'DONOGHUE, Gregory (1951–2005) Born Ballinlough, Cork, the son of Robert O'Donoghue, literary editor of the *Cork Examiner*. He was educated at CBC, Cork, and at UCC where he graduated MA. He moved to Ontario, Canada, where he married, took his doctorate, and lectured at Queen's College there. Previous to this, he had contributed to the *Faber Book of Irish Verse* and had published his own collection in his *Kicking* (1975). He moved to Britain in the early 1980s and worked on the freight railways before returning to Cork ten years later. He became associated with the Munster Literature Association and became the poetry editor of the magazine, *Southward*. He later published two collections, *The Permanent*

Way (1996) and *Making Tracks* (2001). He also contributed to the Cork 2005 *Translations* series. He died at the South Infirmary on 27 August 2005 and was buried in St Michael's Cemetery, Blackrock.

O'DONOGHUE, Florence (1894–1967) Born Rathmore, Co. Kerry. He was educated locally and at the Cork School of Commerce. He joined the Irish Volunteers in Cork in 1917 and served as adjutant and intelligence Officer of Cork No.1 Brigade from March 1918 to March 1921. He held similar positions in the first southern division of the IRA from its formation in April 1921 until March 1922. In that month he became a member of the army executive and adjutant general of the IRA until the following June. He was the agreed choice for the post of adjutant general in the army unification proposals of 1922. In peacetime, he worked as a rate collector for Cork County Council. He joined the Defence Forces in 1940 and retired in November 1945 with the rank of Major. During the Emergency, he had served as editor of *An Cosantóir*, the journal of the Defence Forces, and was a member of the advisory council of the Bureau of Military History from its foundation. In December 1946, he was seconded for eighteen months to the Department of Defence for the purpose of collecting records for the Bureau. He was the leading authority on the history of the War of Independence in Munster and contributed articles to many journals. He published a study of the military role of General **Liam Lynch** in *No Other Law* (1954) and also edited Diarmaid Lynch's papers in *The IRB and the Rising* (1957). His *Tomás Mac Curtain* was published in 1958. He died at the Mercy Home, Cork, on 16 December 1967 and was buried in St Finbarr's Cemetery.

O'DONOVAN, Denis (1836–1911) Born Kinsale, Co. Cork, the son of William O'Donovan. He was educated in Ireland and France, and on completion of his studies, he toured Europe. He then returned to France as professor of Modern Languages and Literature at the College des Hautes Etudes. His *Memories of Rome* (1859) earned him a medal from Pope Pius IX (1792–1878). Having spent some time in London, he moved to Melbourne, Australia, in 1866 and later ran a school there. In August 1874, he was appointed as librarian to the parliament of Queensland and moved to Brisbane. In 1883, he produced an innovative library catalogue which won him acclamations by many European learned societies. He retired from the library in 1902 and moved to France. He died, while visiting a son, at Claremont, Western Australia, on 30 April 1911.

O'DONOVAN, John (1858–1927) Born Lissard, Rosscarbery, Co. Cork, the son of Florence O'Donovan. He was educated at Mount Fachnanus NS and was employed there as a monitor (1872–5). He emigrated to New Zealand in 1878 and a year later he joined the police force as a constable. He rose through the ranks until he was appointed commissioner of the New Zealand police force in 1916. He retired in 1921. He previously studied law under the aegis of the University of New Zealand and qualified as a solicitor in 1893. He died in Wellington in late April 1927.

O'DONOVAN, John (1908–1982) Born Macroom, Co. Cork, the son of Cornelius O'Donovan, ARCScI. He was educated at UCD and Oxford. He won a Rockefeller Scholarship to Harvard University in 1932. In the following year, he joined the Irish civil service. He was an administrative officer in the department of Finance (1933–51) and served as private secretary to the minister for Finance (1941–2). From 1951, he was also lecturer in Economic Theory at UCD. In 1954 he was elected as a Fine Gael TD for Dublin South East and was chosen as Parliamentary Secretary to the Government (1954–7). He lost his Dáil seat in 1957 and failed to regain it at the next general election in 1961. He was chosen as a member of Seanad Éireann (1957–61). He brought the action in the High Court which resulted in the Electoral Act (1959) being declared unconstitutional. He joined the Labour Party in 1965, but unsuccessfully contested the Dublin South West seat in that year. However, he was elected for Dublin South Central in 1969 – a seat which he lost in 1973. He died in Dublin on 17 May 1982 and was buried in Dean's Grange Cemetery. He was the author of *The Economic History of Livestock in Ireland* (1940).

O'DONOVAN, Paddy (d. 1990) Born Douglas, Cork. A hurling half-back, he played for the Glen Rovers club and winning ten county championship medals. He won five All-Ireland SHC medals (1941–4 and 1946) as well as three Railway Cup hurling medals (1945, 1948–9). His last Munster final appearance was in the defeat by Tipperary at Killarney in 1950. He died in June 1990.

O'DONOVAN, Seán S. (1893–1975) Born Cashelisky, near Clonakilty. He was educated locally and at UCD where he graduated in Veterinary Medicine in December 1918. A fine exponent of hurling and football, he played junior football for Cork in 1912. He won a county intermediate football medal for Clonakilty in 1913 and as a student in Dublin, was a founder-member of the Collegians team. He represented Dublin, winning an All-Ireland junior football medal in 1916 and an All-Ireland senior hurling medal in the following year. Following the Easter Rising, he was arrested and interned at Wakefield Gaol. He later served as an officer of the Cork No. 3 Brigade of the IRA and took the anti-Treaty side in the Civil War. In 1920/21, he was chairman of Clonakilty Rural District Council and an *ex-officio* member of Cork County Council. In the 1920s, he entered the service of the veterinary department of Dublin Corporation and subsequently became chief veterinary officer. He was a founder member of Fianna Fáil and served for a time as joint honorary treasurer of that organisation. He was married to Kathleen Boland, a sister of Harry and Gerald Boland. In March 1938, he was elected to Seanad Éireann and served for three periods (1938–48, 1951–4 and 1957–69). He

died at his Clontarf Road residence on 22 February 1975 and was buried in St Fintan's Cemetery, Sutton.

O'DONOVAN, Timothy J. (1881–1957) Born Killeagh, Rosscarbery, Co. Cork. He was educated at Bealad NS and in his early years he served some time as a flax instructor under the department of Agriculture in Ulster. He later operated a flax mill of his own in Rosscarbery. Farming extensively at Inchidoney, near Clonakilty, he took a prominent role in agricultural societies and was president of Clonakilty Agricultural Society from 1929 and a past-president of Cork Farmers' Union. He served as a TD for West Cork (1923–44), as a farmers' representative up to 1933 and subsequently as a member of Fine Gael. He was defeated in the 1944 general election, but was later in that year elected to Seanad Éireann. He was subsequently Leas-Chathaoirleach (1943–8) and Cathaoirleach (1948–54) of that House. He died at his residence, Island House, Inchidoney, on 28 July 1957 and was buried in Rossmore Cemetery.

O'DONOVAN ROSSA, Jeremiah (1831–1915) Born Rosscarbery, Co. Cork, the son of a farmer and linen weaver. He founded the Phoenix Literary and Debating Society in Skibbereen in 1856 and joined the Fenians two years later. Between 1863 and 1865, he managed and contributed to the Fenian organ, the *Irish People*. In 1865, he was arrested with other Fenian leaders and sentenced to twenty years' penal servitude. In 1871, he and four other Fenians ('The Cuba Five') were released on condition that they would leave Ireland. He settled in America but visited Ireland in 1894. Among his publications were *O'Donovan Rossa's Prison Life* (1874, reprinted 1882) and *Rossa's Recollections* (1898). He died in New York on 30 June 1915. His remains were buried in Glasnevin Cemetery on 1 August, with Patrick Pearse delivering the famed funeral oration. [Circular bronze plaque by **Seamus Murphy** at St Stephen's Green, Dublin]

O'DRISCOLL, Patrick (*c.*1875–1940) Born Drinagh, Co. Cork. He pursued a journalistic career and was associated in a managerial capacity with *The Southern Star* for some time. He was secretary of the *Cork Sun* weekly newspaper (1903–05) before establishing his own weekly newspaper, *The West Cork People*, in Clonakilty in 1905. He married in 1901 Margaret Collins, a national schoolteacher and sister of **Michael Collins**. She later became a TD (see **Margaret Collins-O'Driscoll**). The *West Cork People* had both high ambitions and a torrid existence. Its slogan was 'All wide-awake West Cork men read the *West Cork People*' and it claimed an hyperbolic readership of 200,000. In January 1907, Edward Gillman sued the newspaper's printers, News & Sons, for a libel published in the paper. Gillman was ultimately vindicated and subsequently, O'Driscoll was convicted on a charge of assaulting **John F. Moriarty**, Gillman's solicitor. The *West Cork People* did not long survive this episode and O'Driscoll was next associated with the O'Brienite newspaper, *The Cork Accent* in 1910 and its successor, the *Cork Free Press* (1910–16). Following a period as Irish correspondent of the *Catholic Herald*, he obtained a position as a member of the reporting staff of the Dáil. He died at the Richmond Hospital, Dublin, on 29 August 1940 and was buried in Glasnevin Cemetery.

O'DRISCOLL, Patrick F. (1878–1949) Born Coolbawn, Caheragh, Co. Cork. He was educated at Gurrane NS and Bauravila NS. He was elected as a member of Skibbereen Rural District Council in 1911 and served until its abolition in 1925. He was elected to Cork County Council in 1934 as a Farmers' candidate and retained his seat until his death. In 1943, he was elected to Dáil Éireann as a Clann na Talún member for West Cork. He did not seek re-election in 1948. He died at his residence, Coolbawn, Caheragh, on 8 August 1949 and was buried in the Abbey Burial Ground, Skibbereen.

O'DRISCOLL, Stephen (1825–1895) Born Cork. His premises were in Pembroke Street

where he worked as a lithographer, caricaturist and silhouettist. He designed and lithographed the address which was presented to Queen Victoria (1819–1901) on her visit to Cork. His 'Assembly of Citizens in front of the Commercial Buildings, South Mall' (a composition of hundreds of silhouettes pasted onto a colour background) also included the help of his sister, Mary. He is also known for his silhouette group of '**Father Mathew**, **Dan Callaghan**, MP; and the King of the Cork Beggars' (1843) which is in Cork Museum. He died on 20 February 1895.

O'DRISCOLL, T.J. (1908–1998) Born Cork, the eldest child of Michael O'Driscoll, leather merchant. He was educated at PBC, Cork, and at TCD where he graduated BA (1934). He was later awarded an honorary LL.D. He entered the civil service in 1928 and served as assistant secretary at the Department of Foreign Affairs (1950–1). In 1951, he was appointed as first chairman and chief executive of the Irish Export Board (An Córas Tráchtála) – a position he held until 1955 when he was appointed as Irish Ambassador to The Netherlands. In the following year, he was appointed as director general of the Irish Tourist Board and was central to the expansion and success of Bórd Fáilte where he promoted overseas marketing and encouraged the development of large hotels. On his retirement in 1971, he took up various consultancies in the private sector, including executive director of the European Travel Commission (1971–86) and chairman and president of An Taisce, the Irish Heritage Trust. He was also a noted sportsman in both squash and rugby. He won the Irish Open Squash Championship in 1942, having won his first international cap in 1939. In rugby, he played for both TCD and Lansdowne and gained an interprovincial cap in 1932. He died at a Co. Dublin nursing home on 23 October 1998 and was buried at Kilmashogue Cemetery, Rathfarnham. He was the father of Liz Mac Manus, the Wicklow TD.

Ó DROIGHNEÁIN, Muiris (1901–1979) Born Clohonora House, Newtownshandrum,

Co. Cork, the eldest child of James Drinan, farmer, and a cousin of Archbishop **Daniel Mannix**. He was educated locally, at Charleville CBS, and at UCC where he graduated BA (1927) and MA (1929). His thesis on the history of modern Irish literature, *Taighde i gcomhair Stair Litridheacha na Nua-Ghaedhilge ó 1882 anuas*, was published in 1936. Following a teaching spell at Mullingar CBS and at Synge Street CBS, Dublin, he took up a teaching position at St Malachy's College, Belfast, where he spent the remainder of his career. His best known work is *An Sloinnteoir Gaeilge agus an tAinmneoir* was published in 1966 and later ran to two further editions. As an 'addendum' to De Bhaldraithe's *English-Irish Dictionary*, he published *Nua gach Bia: a dictionary of culinary terms* (1973). He died on 28 June 1979. [Papers in the Franciscan Archive, Dublin]

O'DWYER, Andrew C. (1801–1877) Born Cork, the second son of Joseph O'Dwyer, merchant. He was prominent in the Catholic Association in the late 1820s and was called to the Irish Bar in 1830. Having exerted himself in the registration under the Reform Act of 1832 in Drogheda, he was chosen as a Repeal candidate there and was elected MP in that year. Even though he was re-elected as a Liberal Repealer in January 1835, he was unseated as unqualified. In the following April, he was again elected in a by-election, but was once again unseated on petition. In 1837, he was appointed (through the influence of Daniel O'Connell) as Filacer of the Exchequer. This office was abolished shortly afterwards, leaving O'Dwyer with an annual pension of £3,000. He subsequently resided in London, but unsuccessfully contested Waterford City as a Liberal candidate in 1857. He died in London on 15 November 1877.

O'FAOLAIN, Eileen (1900–1988) Born Sunday's Well, Cork, the daughter of Joseph Gould. She was educated at UCC. She married the novelist and writer, **Seán O'Faolain**, in 1928 (they had met ten years before in the West Cork Gaeltacht) and was a noted writer of children's

fiction, and of Irish myths and legends. Her publications included *The Little Black Hen* (1940), *The King of the Cats* (1941), *The Children of Crooked Castle* (1945), *May Eve in Fairyland* (1945), *Miss Pennyfeather and the Pooka* (1949), *The Shadowy Man* (1949), *The White Rabbit's Road* (1950), *Irish Sagas and Folktales* (1954), *High Sang the Sword* (1959) and *Children of the Salmon and Other Irish Folktales* (1965). She died at St Vincent's Hospital, Dublin, on 21 September 1988 and her body was donated for medical research. There was a memorial service at the Chapel of TCD.

O'FAOLAIN, Seán (1900–1991) Born Cork, the son of Denis Whelan, a police constable and a native of Stradbally, Co. Laois. He was educated at PBC, Cork, at UCC and at Harvard University where he graduated MA in English Literature in 1929. Previous to this, however, he interrupted his studies at UCC when he became involved in the War of Independence. He opposed the Anglo-Irish Treaty and was involved with the first southern division of the IRA in the civil war. Disillusioned with political developments, he returned to his studies. Following his marriage in America to Eileen Gould (**Eileen O'Faolain**) and a teaching stint in England, he returned to Ireland as a writer in 1933. During the war years, he founded and edited the periodical, *The Bell*, which, through encouraging young writers and liberal views, fell foul of the Irish censorship board. In later years, he was employed as visiting professor in many American universities. In 1986, he was elected to the title of 'Saoi' in the institution of Aosdána and a year later he was conferred with the freedom of his native city. He died on 20 April 1991. His publications include *Midsummer Night Madness and Other Stories* (1932), *Eamon de Valera* (1933), *Constance Markievicz* (1934), *A Nest of Simple Folk* (1934), *Bird Alone* (1936), *A Purse of Coppers* (1937), *The King of Beggars* (1938), *Come Back to Erin* (1940), *The Great O'Neill* (1942), *Teresa and Other Stories* (1947), *The Irish* (1948), *The Short Story* (1948), *I Remember, I Remember* (1948), *A Summer in Italy* (1949), *The Man Who Invented*

Sin (1949), *Newman's Way* (1952), *South to Sicily* (1953), *The Heat of the Sun* (1956), *The Talking Trees* (1971), *Foreign Affairs* (1976), *And Again* (1979) and *Collected Stories* (3 vols, 1980–2). [Autobiography (1963, 1964, 1993); Life by M. Harmon (1994); Critical Introduction by M. Harmon (1966); Two life-size bronzes by **Seamus Murphy** at UCC and Cork City Library]

O'FIHELY, Maurice (d. 1513) Born Co. Cork. He was educated at Oxford but spent most of his life as a professor at the universities of Milan, Venice and Padua. He edited the works of the Irish medieval philosopher, John Duns Scotus (d. 1308). He was appointed as archbishop of Tuam in 1506. He died in Galway in 1513.

O'FLANAGAN, James R. (1814–1900) Born Fermoy, Co. Cork, the son of a barrack-master. He was educated at TCD and was called to the Bar in 1838. He subsequently practised on the Munster Circuit before taking up a post in Dublin at the Insolvency Court in 1847. Retiring on pension, he moved to London in 1870 where he continued with his literary work. However, he returned to Fermoy a few years after, having built a new residence there. In 1885, he established and edited the short-lived *Fermoy Journal*. He died in Fermoy on 25 March 1900 and was buried in Castlehyde Graveyard. Among his publications were *The Blackwater in Munster* (1844), *Gentle Blood* (1861), *The Life and Adventures of Bryan O'Regan* (1866), *The Bar Life of O'Connell* (1869), *The Lives of the Lord Chancellors of Ireland* (2 vols, 1870) and *Captain Shaugnessy's Sporting Career* (1873). With J. D'Alton, he wrote *A History of Dundalk* (1861). [Autobiography (1898)]

Ó FLOINN, Donnchadh (1760–1830) Born Carraig na bhFear, Co. Cork, but lived from 1782 in Shandon Street, Cork, where he kept a grocery shop. He studied for a time in France, probably as a seminarian. He copied over fifty Gaelic manuscripts and his surviving correspondence of twenty-two letters provides a survey of the mentalities and activities of many of Cork's Gaelic scholars in the first quarter of the nineteenth century. He died on 7 October 1830 and was buried in Dunbullogue Cemetery.

Ó FLOINN, Donnchadh (1902–1968) Born Kilbrin, Kanturk, Co. Cork, the son of Jeffrey O'Flynn, leather merchant. He was educated locally, at North Monastery CBS, St Colman's College, Fermoy, and at St Patrick's College, Maynooth, where he graduated BA and was ordained in 1927. He was professor of English and Logic at All Hallows College, Dublin, before his appointment as professor of Irish at Maynooth. From 1945, he was a pivotal member of the *ad hoc* commission which undertook to translate into Irish, firstly the New Testament and then the whole Bible, directly from the Greek. In 1964, he was appointed as parish priest of Our Lady of Peace Parish, Bray, Co. Wicklow. He died on 2 April 1968 and was buried in Mount Jerome Cemetery, Dublin. His publications include *The Integral Irish Tradition* (1954).

O'FLYNN, James C. (1881–1962) Born Mallow Lane, Cork. He was educated at North Monastery CBS, Farranferris College, and St Patrick's College, Maynooth, where he was ordained in 1909. He took a great interest in all facets of Irish culture and served as president of the Cork City Branch of Connradh na Gaeilge and of Feis na Mumhan. In 1926, he rented a room over the sweet factory at Mulgrave Street, Shandon, which subsequently gained fame as 'The Loft' – the headquarters of the Cork Shakespearean Company which produced many plays at Cork Opera House. Having served at various posts in the diocese of Cork, he was appointed as parish priest of Passage West in 1946 and remained there for the rest of his ministry. He died in Cork on 18 January 1962. [Life by R. Smith and R. O'Donoghue; A BBC broadcast by H. Davis, *It Happened to Me*, (1961)]

Ó FOGHLUDHA, Risteárd (1873–1957) Born Knockmonalea, Youghal, Co. Cork, the eldest of twelve children of Richard Foley (1830–1910), farmer. He was educated at Youghal CBS and moved to Dublin in 1888 where he worked as a journalist for the *Freeman's Journal*. He was a founder member of Connradh na Gaeilge's Craobh an Chéitinnigh (Keating Branch) in 1901 (and acted as secretary until his marriage in 1909). He then worked in a number of English cities, latterly as a salesman for the Underwood Typewriter Company. In 1905, he was transferred to the company's offices in Belfast and Dublin. He had a great interest in shorthand and typing and was one of the clerks of the First Dáil Éireann in January 1919. He was later associated with the foundation of the Dublin Institute of Shorthand Writers. He worked for Underwoods until 1936 when he moved to the book-publishing section of the Government Publications Office (An Gúm). In 1946, he was appointed by Eamon de Valera (1882–1975) as a member of the Placenames Commission (Coimisiúin na Logainmneacha). His main contribution to Irish literature was his editions of the lives and works of fifteen of Munster's major poets and his 1952 collection of the poets of the Maigue (*Filí na Máighe*). He also published, *Cúirt an Mhéan Oíche* (1912), *Logainmneacha i.e. Dictionary of Irish Place-names (7,000), English-Gaelic* (1935), *Carn Tighearnaigh* (1938) and a translation, *Tiarnaí deireanacha Urmhumhan* ('The Last Lords of Ormond') (1956). He was conferred with an honorary D.Litt by the National University of Ireland in 1939. He died at his residence at Eaton Square, Terenure, Dublin, on 20 August 1957 and was buried in Mount Jerome Cemetery.

Ó GALLCHOBHAIR, Tomás (1894–1982) Born Conna, Co. Cork, the son of Patrick Gallagher, farmer and tavern owner. He was educated at Conna NS and at St Patrick's College, Maynooth. Following his ordination, he graduated MA at UCG. He ministered as a curate in various parishes until his appointment, in succession, as parish priest of Kilnamartra and Ballymacoda. He had a great interest in the activities of Ring College (Coláiste na Rinne), Co. Waterford, of which he was a shareholder since 1916. He is chiefly known for his

translations which included *Críost an Uile* (*Christ Is All* by J. Carr), *Teacht Chúchulainn* (*The Coming of Cuchulainn* by S. O'Grady), *Scéal an Bhíobla le Pictiúirí – An Tiomna Nua* (Schuster's Bible), *Amhránaithe Breathnach* (*A Welsh Singer* by A. Raine) and *Muiris Ó hAirt* (*Maurice Harte* by **T.C. Murray.** He retired from the ministry in 1980. He died at Ladysbridge on 17 May 1982 and was buried in Mogeely Cemetery.

O'GORMAN, David L. (*c.*1860–1945) Born Fermoy, Co. Cork, the son of David O'Gorman. He was educated at Belvedere College, Mount Melleray School and at Tullabeg College. In his early years, he travelled and worked extensively in Australia and in the South Seas. On his return to Fermoy, he took an interest in local politics and won a seat for the Fermoy electoral area in the first Cork County Council in 1899, serving until 1920. He returned to the County Council in 1925, and represented the Mallow area to 1934 as a Farmers' candidate. From then until his death, he represented Fine Gael on the council. He contested a Dáil seat for East Cork in 1923, but was unsuccessful. He became a TD in June 1927 but lost the seat again three months later. He was again unsuccessful in 1932. He represented the County Council on the Governing Body of UCC (1926–45). He lost a leg as a result of being shot during the civil war and wore a prosthesis for the remainder of his life. He died on 27 January 1945 at his Fermoy residence and was buried in Kilcrumper Cemetery.

O'GRADY, Standish J. (1846–1928) Born Castletownbere, Co. Cork, the son of Rev. Thomas O'Grady, the local rector. He was educated at Midleton College and at TCD where he graduated BA (1868). He was called to the Bar in 1872 but instead pursued a literary career. As well as having a keen interest in Irish history, he is chiefly remembered for his fine novels which are based on Irish legend and myth and which were hugely influential at the time. In his later years, he edited *The All-Ireland Review* and *The Kilkenny Moderator,* and contributed many articles to prestigious journals. Being in bad health, he retired to the Isle of Wight in 1918 and died there on 18 May 1928. His publications include *History of Ireland: the Heroic Period* (1878), *Early Bardic Literature, Ireland* (1879), *History of Ireland: Cuchulain and his Contemporaries* (1880), *History of Ireland: Critical and Philosophical* (1881), *Cuchulain: An Epic* (1882), *The Crisis in Ireland* (1882), *Toryism and Tory Democracy* (1886), *Finn and his Companions* (1892), *The Coming of Cuchulain* (1894), *Pacata Hibernia* (1896), *The Flight of the Eagle* (1897), *In the Gates of the North* (1891), *The Queen of the World* (1906) and *The Triumph and Passing of Cuchulain* (1920) [Lives by H.A. O'Grady (1929), P. Marcus (1970) and J. Cahalan (1982)]

O'GRADY, William J. (*c.*1790–1840) Born Co. Cork. He was educated for the priesthood and was ordained *c.*1816 at St Mary's College, the diocesan seminary of Cork. He was a curate at the Cathedral parish in 1820 when the cathedral was gutted by fire, reputedly set by local Protestants incensed by a sermon on the Blessed Sacrament preached by O'Grady. In 1827, he embarked as a chaplain on an ill-fated Irish emigration scheme to Brazil. However, he seems to have persuaded a large contingent of the emigrants to settle in Upper Canada, and in June 1828, he arrived at York, Toronto. Here he presented testimonials from the bishop of Cork and was given faculties by Bishop McDonnell of Kingston. In a politically charged environment where lower class Irish emigrants were becoming the majority of Roman Catholics, he became embroiled in controversy with his bishop on account of his support for the Irish element. This culminated in his suspension in 1832. In the following year, he set out for Rome to put his case to the Pope and Curia but, however, his suspension was only confirmed. He returned to Upper Canada where he became involved in reform politics. In 1834, he became the sole owner of the reform newspaper, *The Correspondent*, but sold it in 1837 when he retired from active politics. He took up farming

in Vaughan township where he died suddenly on 18 August 1840.

Ó hAIMHIRGÍN, Osborn (1873–1950) see **BERGIN, Osborn**

Ó hANNRACHÁIN, Peadar (1873–1965) Born Skibbereen, Co. Cork, the son of Seán Ó hAnnracháin, farmer. He was educated locally and joined Connradh na Gaeilge, of which he became an organiser in 1901. He turned to journalism and was editor of *The Southern Star* for two years (1917–18). He took part in the War of Independence and spent some time in jail. He later bought a farm and worked as a registrar for Cork County Council. He published an extensive account of his Connradh activities in *Fé Bhrat an Chonnartha* (1944). He also published two books of poetry, *An Chaise Gharbh* ['The Coarse Affection'] (1918) and *An Chaise Riabhach* ['The Fallow Affection'] (1937). His play, 'Stiana' (1944) was produced at the Abbey Theatre. In 1938, he sold his farm and moved to Dublin where he got a post in the Pigs and Bacon Commission. He died at his residence, 'Cuan Dor', Baldoyle, Co. Dublin, on 29 March 1965 and was buried in St Fintan's Cemetery, Sutton, Co. Dublin. He was the father of the noted actor, Kieron Moore.

Ó hANNRACHÁIN, Tadhg (1855–1949) Born Mitchelstown, Co. Cork, the son of Timothy Hanrahan. He was educated at Mitchelstown CBS and at St Colman's College, Fermoy, before moving to Kilkenny in 1872 where he attended St Ciaran's College. He later became a successful bacon merchant and businessman there. With a great interest in Irish (he was one of the founders of Connradh na Gaeilge in Kilkenny) and antiquities, he purchased and restored the Tudor Rothe House and established it as a cultural venue. He also served as a prominent member of Kilkenny Corporation for many years. He died on 24 February 1949. [Memorial plaque at Rothe House]

Ó hAODHA, Seámas (1886–1967) Born Cork, the son of Christopher Hayes, carpenter. He was educated at CBC, Cork, and at UCC where he graduated BA (1909) and MA (1917). He qualified as a teacher and later became a primary schools' inspector in 1939. He had become a devoted Gaelic scholar and poet following a visit to Ballingeary in 1908, when, for the first time, he heard Irish being spoken. He died at his residence, 23, Green Road, Blackrock, Co. Dublin, on 20 March 1967 and was buried in St Joseph's Cemetery, Cork. His poetic publications include *Uaigneas* (1928), *Caoineadh na Mná* (1939), *Dánta Eile* (1939) and *Ceann an Bhóthair* (1966). One of his five plays (on the life of the poet, Donncha Rua Mac Conmara) was produced at the Abbey Theatre (1939).

O'HARA, Henry Michael (1853–1921) Born Cork, the son of Henry O'Hara, merchant. He was educated at Stonyhurst College, Lancashire, but, being orphaned in 1866, was sent to Melbourne, Australia, to be looked after by his aunt, Margaret Madden, the mother of **Sir Frank Madden**, **Sir John Madden** and **Walter Madden**. He studied law for a period at the University of Melbourne, but returned to Ireland in 1874 to study at the Royal College of Surgeons, Dublin. Having qualified as a surgeon, he returned to Melbourne in 1878 and quickly established himself as an outstanding surgeon and medical witness. He was elected a fellow of the Royal College of Surgeons in 1888 and was president of the surgical section of the Fourth Intercolonial Medical Congress of Australasia in 1896. As well as having a great interest in horses and horse racing, he was also an accomplished baritone and was encouraged by the celebrated Australian soprano, Dame Nellie Melba (*c.*1861–1931), to pursue a professional career. He was also the doctor and friend of the composer and concert pianist, Percy Grainger. He died at his residence at Portsea on 7 April 1921.

O'HEA, John F. (*c.*1838–1922) Born Clonakilty, Co. Cork, the son of James O'Hea, lawyer. He trained in the Cork School of Design, the Dublin School of Art and exhibited at the Royal Hibernian Academy. He is best known as an illustrator and cartoonist of many journals and newspapers. As 'Spex', he was the colour cartoonist of *The Weekly Freeman*. He also painted 'The Prince of Wales at Punchestown'. He spent periods both in London and Dublin, but settled in London following the Parnell split. He died in West Kensington on 2 September 1922.

O'HEA, Michael (1808–1876) Born Woodfield, Rosscarbery, Co. Cork. He was educated locally and at the Irish College, Paris, where he was ordained in 1843. He initially ministered in the diocese of Cloyne (which was united to Ross at that time) before being appointed as parish priest of Ross in 1850. On the separation of the dioceses in 1851, he was named as vicar general of Ross. He was consecrated as bishop of Ross on 7 February 1858 at the Pro-Cathedral, Skibbereen. He died on 18 December 1876 and was buried in his cathedral.

O'HEA, Patrick (1852–1925) Born Clonakilty, Co. Cork, the son of Dr Patrick O'Hea and nephew of **John McCarthy**, bishop of Cloyne. He was educated at Gayfield, Dublin, a college affiliated to the Catholic University. He was admitted a solicitor in 1875 and practised in Cork. A member of Cork Corporation, he became an eloquent speaker at Irish Parliamentary Party meetings in the 1880s and was elected as an MP for Donegal West in 1885. He resigned his seat in 1890 and emigrated to South Africa where he practised law. He died at Dundee, Natal Province, on 7 August 1925.

O'HEA, Timothy [VC] (1846–1874) Born Bantry, Co. Cork. He enlisted in the 1st Battalion of the Rifle Brigade and was posted to Canada. On the night of 16 June 1866, a railway truck, loaded with gunpowder and attached to a train with 800 German migrants aboard, caught fire. O'Hea was a member of the military escort on board. He single-handedly put out the fire, having mounted the carriage nineteen times with buckets of water. For this action, he was awarded the Victoria Cross (the first to be awarded in peacetime) 'for conspicuous courage under circumstances of great danger'. He subsequently left the army, and having served for a period in the New Zealand Mounted Constabulary, he settled in Sydney, Australia, in June 1874. A few days later, he joined an expedition to North West Australia. The project ended in tragedy when the party ran out of water in the Graham's Creek area of Queensland and split up to look for water. O'Hea had collapsed on 6 November and his body was later found by a party of Aborigines. [Life by A.H. Chisholm (1955)]

O'HEGARTY, Patrick S. (1879–1955) Born Evergreen Road, Cork, the son of John Hegarty, plasterer and worker in stucco. He was educated at North Monastery CBS where he was a fellow-pupil and friend of **Terence Mac Swiney**. He joined the postal service in 1897 and represented Cork GPO at the Connradh na Gaeilge Árdfheis of 1906. He was transferred to London where he joined the Irish Republican Brotherhood and became editor of the movement's organ, *Irish Freedom*. In 1913, he was appointed as postmaster at Queenstown (now Cobh), but on account of his Republican activities, was transferred to Shrewsbury in the following year. Following a further spell at Welshpool, Montgomeryshire (now Powys), he returned to Ireland in 1918 and opened, with a colleague, an Irish bookshop in Dawson Street, Dublin – the shop subsequently becoming a 'safe house' during the War of Independence. On the foundation of the Irish Free State, he was appointed as director of the GPO, Dublin, and later as secretary of the Department of Posts and Telegraphs where he remained until his retirement in 1945. Both a writer and historian, his publications included *John Mitchel, an appreciation* (1917), *The Indestructible Nation* (1918), *Sinn Féin, an illumination* (1918), *Ulster, a brief statement of fact* (1919), *A Short Memoir of Terence Mac Swiney* (1922), *The Victory of Sinn Féin* (1924) and *A History of Ireland under the Union, 1801–1922* (1952). Writing in *The Separatist* (of which he was editor) in September 1922, he praised the recently published *Ulysses* of James

Joyce – Ireland's first favourable critique. He died at his Rathgar residence on 17 December 1955 and was buried in Templeogue Cemetery. His son, Seán Sáirséal Ó hEigeartaigh (1917–1967), was the noted Irish publisher and founder of the publishing house, Sáirséal & Dill (1945).

Ó hEIGEARTAIGH, Diarmuid (1856–1934) Born Letter, Caheragh, Co. Cork, the son of Jeremiah Hegarty, farmer, and father of **Diarmuid Ó hÉigeartaigh (1892–1958)**. He was educated locally, and took up the post of monitor in the local national school in 1874. By 1882, he was the principal teacher of Kilcomane NS on the Mizen Peninsula. He moved to Lowerstown NS in 1887 and taught there until his retirement in 1921. Self-taught in Irish, he was the author of *Tadhg Ciallmhar* (1934) and of *Is Uasal Ceird* (posthumously, 1968), an autobiographical memoir. He died at Lowertown on 18 March 1934 and was buried in Caheragh.

Ó hEIGEARTAIGH, Diarmuid (1892–1958) Born Lowerstown, Schull, Co. Cork, the eldest son of **Diarmuid Ó hÉigeartaigh (1856–1934)**, teacher. He was educated locally and in Skibbereen. He entered the civil service and worked in the department of Agriculture and Technical Instruction. He was sworn into the Irish Republican Brotherhood by Seán Mac Diarmada (1884–1916) and took part in the Easter Rising in Dublin. He was then interned for a short period in Knutsford Detention Barracks, Cheshire. A close confidante of **Michael Collins**, he was elected to the executive of the IRB in November 1917. He was, in turn, chief clerk of the First Dáil, one of three assistant secretaries to Erskine Childers in the Treaty delegation, secretary of the Executive Council of the Irish Free State and principal private secretary (1923–32) to **W.T. Cosgrave**. He was described by Frank Pakenham in his *Peace by Ordeal* as 'the civil servant of the revolution'. In 1932, he was appointed as a commissioner of Public Works and seventeen years later, as chairman of the Commission. He held this post until his retirement in 1957. He died at his Donnybrook, Dublin, residence on 14 March 1958 and was buried in Dean's Grange Cemetery.

Ó hÉIGEARTAIGH, Pádraig S. (1879–1955) see **O'HEGARTY, Patrick S.**

O'HERLIHY, Thomas (d. 1580) Born in the barony of Carbery. He was nominated as bishop of Ross on 17 December 1561 and was consecrated in Rome. He was one of the Irish bishops in attendance at the Council of Trent in May 1562. He returned to Ireland and, in 1569, he travelled to Spain with Archbishop Maurice Mac Gibbon of Cashel to offer the kingship of Ireland to King Philip II (1527–98) or to his nominee. He was subsequently arrested, lodged in the Tower of London and brought before the English Privy Council. Having been imprisoned for three years, he returned to Muskerry and rented a farm in 'Densus Saltus' (probably near Macroom). Here he lived in solitude until his death on 11 March 1580. He was buried in Kilcrea Abbey.

O'HEYNE, John (d. p.1556) He was nominated as bishop of Cloyne and Cork on 5 November 1540, in succession to Louis MacNamara who had died in the previous September but who had never been consecrated. Due to the effects of the Henrician Reformation, he was unable to take possession of his united dioceses and was translated as administrator of the diocese of Elphin on 20 February 1545, where he served until 1553/54.

O'HIGGINS, Thomas F. (1890–1953) Born Stradbally, Co. Laois, the son of Dr T.F. O'Higgins. His maternal grandfather was **Timothy D. Sullivan**. Both his father and brother, Kevin (d. 1927), were shot dead by Republicans in the aftermath of the civil war. He qualified as a medical doctor and, following imprisonment in the period 1919–1921, joined the medical corps of the Free State army in May 1922. In February 1929, he resigned his commission as director of Medical Services. He was

subsequently elected as a TD for North Dublin (1929–31) and for Leix-Offaly (1931–48). In 1948, he was elected as TD for Cork City and was a sitting TD at the time of his sudden death on 1 November 1953. He was minister for Defence in the first Inter-Party Government (1948–51) and of Industry and Commerce for the last three months of that administration. His son and namesake was a government minister (1954–7) and an unsuccessful presidential candidate (1966).

O'KEEFE, Eugene (1827–1913) Born Bandon, Co. Cork, the son of John Keeffe. When he was five years old, the family left for Canada and settled in Toronto. Following his education at Roman Catholic schools in the city, he helped his widowed sister to run a hotel. In 1856, he joined the Toronto Savings Bank as a clerk and worked there until 1861 (however, he maintained his connection with this institution as a director, vice-president, and president when the bank had become the Home Bank of Canada). In that year he, along with two partners, purchased the Victoria Brewery which, following massive expansion and innovation, eventually was incorporated as the O'Keefe Brewery Company of Toronto Ltd. In 1879, the company manufactured Canada's first large-scale production of lager beer and was eventually taken over by the Carling Company. He also served as president of the Ontario Brewers' and Maltsters' Association. He was a noted philanthropist and spent huge sums of money on church building projects, hospitals and charitable organausations – especially on the Society of St Vincent de Paul. He died at his Toronto home on 1 October 1913 with a huge crowd attending the obsequies.

O'KEEFFE, Bartholomew (1856–1927) Born Charleville, Co. Cork, the youngest son of Bartholomew O'Keeffe. He was educated at St Colman's College, Fermoy, and at the Irish College, Rome. He graduated DD and was ordained in 1879. He held several curacies in the Cloyne diocese and also spent some time ministering at the St John of God Hospital, Dublin. He returned to Youghal in 1906 and spent eighteen years there, partly as chaplain to St Raphael's Hospital. While he had been in Dublin, he did some research at the Public Record Office and transcribed a number of Cloyne documents from the surviving originals. He presented a transcription of the 1766 Cloyne religious census and presented them in 1904 to his bishop, **Robert Browne**. Subsequently, the originals perished in the attack on the Four Courts during the civil war. He returned to St John of God's on his retirement in 1925. He died there on 21 November 1927 and was buried in Dean's Grange Cemetery.

O'KEEFFE, Constance (1671–1745) Born Pobul-O'Keeffe, Duhallow, Co. Cork, the fourth son of Art O'Keeffe, landowner. Having lost their lands after the Williamite war, Constance and his three brothers joined the French Army. The three brothers were killed, while Constance, now a captain in Clare's Irish Regiment, was badly wounded in the battle of Ramillies in 1706. Three years later, he took part in the minor Jacobite invasion of Scotland, was arrested and imprisoned for over a year in London. He returned to France where he campaigned until his retirement from the French Army after nearly forty years' service. He died at St Germain, near Paris, on 5 February 1745.

O'KEEFFE, Dan ['Danno'] (1907–1967) Born Fermoy, Co. Cork. His parents came from Kerry and he lived in Tralee from an early age where he was educated as the local CBS. He worked as a clerical officer with Kerry County Council. His great career as a Kerry Gaelic football goalkeeper commenced with capturing Munster and All-Ireland JFC medals in 1930. He made his senior debut in All-Ireland final of the following year when he was on the winning side. He followed this with a tally of six more (1932, 1937, 1939–41 and 1946). On his retirement following the 1948 All-Ireland semi-final, he had won fifteen Munster SFC medals, three Railway Cup medals, and one NFL medal. As well, he had played in ten All-Ireland SFC finals. In the 1984 *Sunday Independent* 'Team of the Century',

he was named in the goalkeeping slot. He died unexpectedly at his Tralee residence on 2 June 1967 and was buried in Rath Cemetery, Tralee.

O'KEEFFE, Denis (1810– p.1851) Born Cork. He worked in Dublin as a wood engraver in the 1840s and 1850s. His woodcuts appeared in the *Irish Penny Magazine* in 1841.

O'KEEFFE, Eoghan (1656–1726) See **Ó CAOIMH, Eoghan**.

O'KEEFFE, James (1865–1937) Born Kanturk, Co. Cork, the son of Patrick O'Keeffe, farmer. He was educated locally and at Blackrock College, Co. Dublin, and subsequently obtained a clerical post at the War Office, London. While there, he became a prominent member of the Irish Literary Society and of the London branch of Connradh na Gaeilge where he gained a fine reputation as a teacher of Irish dancing. He was co-editor of *Rince Gaodhalach – A Handbook of Irish Dances with an Essay on their Origin and History* (1902). On his transfer to Dublin in 1902, he continued with his Connradh activities and acted as treasurer of the School of Irish Learning and of the Irish Texts Society. In 1912, he was transferred from Dublin and worked as a British Government financial representative in the United States and Canada during World War I. On his retirement in 1926, he was awarded the CBE. He died in Richmond, Surrey, on 6 December 1937. His publications include *Táin Bó Cuailgne from the Yellow Book of Lecan* (1912) [as co-editor] and *Buile Suibhne* (1913, repr. 1931).

O'KEEFFE, James (1920–1981) Born Newmarket, Co. Cork, the eldest child of Murt O'Keefe, farmer and county engineer. He was the elder brother of **Patrick O'Keefe**. He was educated at Newmarket NS and became a progressive dairy farmer with a herd of eighty cattle on a 120-acre farm. Having become a member of the National Council of the Irish Creamery Milk Suppliers Association (ICMSA) in 1962, he was elected as president of that organisation in 1968. He held this position until

1978 – during a period of intense campaigning by farmers for better prices. He was a member of the Study Group which published the two-tier milk study report in 1968 and was appointed to the Economic and Social Committee formed on Ireland's entry into the EEC in 1973. In the following year, he was appointed to the board of An Bórd Bainne of which he was made chairman in 1975. He died at his home in Scarteen, Newmarket, on 5 November 1981 and was buried in Clonfert Cemetery.

O'KEEFFE, John (c.1797–1838) Born Fermoy, Co. Cork, an apprentice to a coach painter. Having served his time, he worked as an heraldic painter but later switched to portraiture. He then moved to Cork where he married and found work in painting religious pictures and altarpieces for many of the newly built Roman Catholic churches in the city and county. He moved to Dublin in 1834 and exhibited at the Royal Hibernian Academy. His reputation was growing when he died suddenly on a visit to Limerick in 1838. His best work, 'Sibyl', was raffled for the support of his wife and family and is now in the Cork Museum.

O'KEEFFE, Manus M. (1834–1868) Born Cork. He initially worked as a saddler and as an attorney's clerk but later became particularly noted for his illuminations of ancient Ireland. He died in poor circumstances at the Mercy Hospital, Cork, on 3 May 1868.

O'KEEFFE, Mary C. (1902–2000) Born Schull, Co. Cork, the daughter of Maurice O'Keefe, farmer and businessman. She was educated locally and at the Ursuline Convent, Waterford. As a member of the Sisters of Charity, she pursued a nursing career in London and Dublin. She served as matron of St Vincent's Hospital (St Stephen's Green), before moving to Temple Street Hospital. She returned to St Vincent's in 1968 to supervise the moving of the hospital to Elm Park, Donnybrook. On her retirement in 1974, she was appointed as superior of the Sisters of Charity Nursing Home

at Donnybrook. She became a fellow of the Nursing Faculty of the Royal College of Physicians in 1983, and in the following year was conferred with an honorary LL.D by the National University of Ireland. She died on 4 January 2000. She was the aunt of the Fine Gael TD for West Cork, Jim O'Keefe.

O'KEEFFE, Patrick (1881–1973) Born Cullen, Co. Cork, the son of Daniel J. Keeffe, farmer. He obtained a post in the civil service in Dublin and was a prominent member of Connradh na Gaeilge and a close friend of the political leader, Arthur Griffith (1871–1922). He became a co-treasurer of Sinn Féin and partook in the Easter Rising of 1916. He was subsequently imprisoned in England and Wales. On his release from prison, he was dismissed from his post, but was appointed (with salary) as Árd-Rúnaí of Sinn Féin. He was returned unopposed as Sinn Féin MP for Cork North in the 1918 general election, while he was imprisoned in England. He supported the Anglo-Irish Treaty and was appointed as Deputy Governor of Mountjoy Prison at Griffith's request. This position disturbed him greatly, especially as many of the inmates were his former colleagues during the War of Independence. He was subsequently appointed as assistant clerk of Seanad Éireann and held this position until his retirement in 1946. He died on 20 October 1973.

O'KEEFFE, Patrick (1897–1980) Born Schull, Co. Cork, the son of Maurice O'Keeffe, merchant. He was educated at Schull NS and at Clongowes Wood College. At the age of seventeen, he joined his mother's family firm, James Lyons of Bantry, and subsequently became managing director of G.W. Biggs & Co., the leading merchants in that area. He established a fishing company, expanded the Biggs firm (absorbing the timber exporters, Murphy & O'Connor) and was a director of Bantry Bay Towing Company. His abiding interest was in local history, and though he published only one article, he amassed a huge collection of notes, transcripts and diaries, which are deposited in the Cork Archives Institute. He was also a keen yachtsman and was a founder member of the Irish Cruising Club. He died at St Joseph's Hospital, Bantry, on 31 January 1980 and was buried in Abbey Cemetery.

O'KEEFFE, Patrick (1921–1999) Born Newmarket, Co. Cork, the son of Murt O'Keefe, farmer and county engineer. He was the younger brother of **James O'Keefe (1920–1981)**. In 1940, he joined the Munster and Leinster Bank as a clerk and soon advanced to various executive positions. On the formation of Allied Irish Banks in 1970, he was appointed as manager of the Munster Region. In 1975, he was transferred to the head office in Dublin and in 1981, was appointed as the bank's first Group Chief Executive. He retired in 1984 having played a leading role in his bank's take-over of the First National Bank of Maryland – the first American acquisition by an Irish bank. He played a pivotal part in the development of modern Irish banking. He died in Dublin on 5 June 1999 and was buried in Shanganagh Cemetery.

O'KEEFFE, Timothy J. (1910–1943) Born Cork. Playing as a left-winger, he started his soccer career with Cork FC with whom he won a FAI Cup medal in 1934. On leaving the Cork club for Waterford United, he had scored a total of 105 goals – the first League of Ireland winger to reach the 'century'. He also won another Cup medal with Waterford in 1937. He was then transferred to Hibernian of Scotland for a League of Ireland record fee of £400. He won three caps for Ireland – one in 1934 and two in 1938. He died of cancer at the early age of thirty-three years in 1943.

O'KELLY, G. Cornelius (1886–1947) Born Dunmanway, Co. Cork. He left for England in 1903 and two years later he won the British heavyweight wrestling championship. He represented Great Britain at the London Olympics in 1908 where he took the gold medal in the heavyweight division. He later turned to professional boxing and boxed in America, Ireland and England. He died in England in 1947.

O'KELLY, Michael J. (1915–1982) Born Abbeyfeale, Co. Limerick. He was educated at Rockwell College and at UCC. In 1944, he was appointed as curator of Cork Public Museum which he set up before being appointed as professor of Archaeology at UCC in 1946 (he retained the curatorship in a part-time capacity until 1963). His distinguished archaeological career was highlighted by his excavations at Newgrange (1962–76) – the results of which were published as *New Grange: Archaeology, Art, and Legend* (1982). His book, *Early Ireland: an introduction to Irish pre-history*, was edited by his widow, Claire, and was published in 1984. He was editor of the *JCHAS* (1947–64) and was also president of the CHAS (1962, 1977/78). He died on 14 October 1982, having oficially retired from his university position a month earlier.

Ó LAOGHAIRE, Art (d. 1773) Born Raleigh, near Macroom, Co. Cork. He served as a captain in the Hungarian Hussars in the service of Austria. On his return to Ireland in 1767, he married, at short notice, the 'Widow Connor of Iveragh', i.e. **Eibhlín Dhubh Ní Chonaill** of Derrynane, Co. Kerry – an aunt of Daniel O'Connell, the Liberator. Following a long and bitter dispute with the high sheriff of Cork, Abraham Morris, and his followers, Ó Laoghaire was shot dead by a soldier at Carraig an Ime on 4 May 1773. He was buried at Kilcrea Abbey, Co. Cork. The famous Gaelic lament 'Caoineadh Airt Uí Laoghaire' is attributed to Eibhlín Dhubh, although she seems not to have written any other poetic work. Others attribute the work to Eoghan Rua Ó Suilleabháin (1748–84) who included some names from the Ó Laoghaire incident in one of his poems.

Ó LAOGHAIRE, Diarmaid (1871–1942) Born Lios Carragáin, Clondrohid, Co. Cork, the son of Jeremiah O'Leary, farmer, and related on both sides to the writer, An tAth. **Peadar Ó Laoghaire**. As a result of his kinsman's writings, he became interested in Irish and later became a peripatetic teacher of Irish before taking up a post at Coláiste na Mumhan, Ballingeary – a post which he held before he inherited the family farm. He wrote regular newspaper articles and his publications included a novel, *An Bhruinneall Bhán* ['The White Maiden'] (1934) and a collection of essays, *Saothar Bliana: aistí ar chuireadóirescht agua ar ghnóthaibh na feirmeach* (1934, repr. 1945). He died on 3 April 1942 and was buried in Reilig Ghobnatan, Baile Bhúirne.

Ó LAOGHAIRE, Donnchadh (1877–1944) Born Derreenaculling, Baile Bhúirne, Co. Cork, the son of Donnchadh Ó Laoghaire, farmer, and father of **Liam O'Leary**. He was educated locally and worked on the family holding until he moved to Cork City in 1898 where he worked at O'Dwyer's and at Beamish & Crawford. He took up the playing of the uilleann pipes and performed at the 1907 St Patrick's Day concert at the Queen's Hall, London (and later gave many recitals on the newly-formed Radio Éireann). He was then employed as a 'timire' (promoter) by Connradh na Gaeilge, but shortly afterwards, set out for the Continent where he studied French and German at the universities of Paris, Dijon and Cologne. On his return, he taught these languages at Mt. Melleray School, Co. Waterford, at Wexford CBS and at St Peter's College, Wexford. He retired in 1942 and moved to Youghal (his wife's birthplace) where he opened an antique shop. He died in Youghal on 3 April 1944 and was buried in North Abbey Cemetery there. He contributed poems and essays to many Gaelic publications including *Fáinne an Lae*, *Irisleabhar na Gaeilge* and *An Claidheamh Solais*. His translations into Irish included *Eachtraí an Ghiolla Mhóir* (1936), *Eachtra an Impire agus a chuid Éadaigh* (1939), *Feoil agus Ceoil* (1939) and *An Péarla Dubh* (posthumously, 1952).

Ó LAOGHAIRE, Pádraig (1853–1932) Born Kilbrittain, Bandon, Co. Cork, the son of Timothy O'Leary. He was educated in Cork City, at the Irish College, Paris, and was ordained in June 1879. He ministered as chaplain at St Patrick's Hospital, Wellington Road, and at St Marie of the Isle Convent. From 1890 to 1915, he served as curate in the Lough Parish and took a leading part in the temperance movement. The Fr. O'Leary Temperance Hall on the Bandon Road is named in his honour. He later ministered as parish priest in Glounthaune and in Cork's Middle Parish. He was a passenger on a train which was ambushed and six civilians killed at Upton Viaduct on 15 February 1921 – an incident from which he never recovered. He died on 24 January 1932 and was buried in St Finbarr's Cemetery. He also had a great interest in and affection for the Irish language. His *Caint na nDaoine* was published in 1920.

Ó LAOGHAIRE, Pádraig (1870–1896) Born Inches, Eyeries, Co. Cork, the son of Patrick Lynch, farmer. He was appointed as a monitor at the local primary school and, having spent some time in London and Belfast, worked as a teacher in Terenure, Dublin. He published the important *Sgéalaidheacht Chúige Mumhan* (1895) – a pioneering collection of stories from the mouths of many Munster storytellers. Suffering from TB, he returned to Béara and died in Eyeries on 29 October 1896.

Ó LAOGHAIRE, Peadar (1839–1920) Born Lios Carragáin, Clondrohid, Co. Cork. He was educated at St Colman's College, Fermoy and at St Patrick's College, Maynooth, where he was ordained in 1867. Following various postings in the diocese of Cloyne, he was appointed as parish priest of Castlelyons in 1891. He became very active in promoting the aims of both the Land League and Connradh na Gaeilge. He then decided to turn to writing and produced a style which was attractive to members of the new language movement. He was a great favourite at the huge feiseanna which were held all over the county in the early years of the new century. With the noted Celtic philologist, Professor Kuno Meyer (1858–1919), he was given, in 1912, the freedom of both Cork and Dublin. He died on 20 March 1920 and was buried at Castlelyons Cemetery. His publications included *Aesop a Tháinig go hÉirinn* (1900–1902, 1903), *Séadna*

(1904), *Eisirt* (1909), *An Cleasaí* (1913), *Caitilína* (1913), *Aithris ar Chríost* (1914), *Lughaidh Mac Con* (1914), *Na Ceithre Soiscéil as an dTiomna Nua* (1915), *Bricriu* (1915), *Guaire* (1915), *Don Cíochóté* (posthumously, 1921), *Gníomhartha na nAspal* (posthumously, 1922) and *Lúcián* (posthumously, 1924). [Autobiography (1915)]

Ó LAOGHAIRE, Pilib (1909–1976) Born Roman Street, Cork, the youngest son of Cornelius O'Leary, cooper. He was educated at Eason's Hill NS, and at North Monastery CBS. He showed an interest in music at an early age and became a chorister at the North Cathedral under Aloys Fleischmann, senior. He was appointed as a peripatetic teacher of Irish and then as county music director by the Cork Vocational Education Committee. For a time, he studied choral conducting under Sir Hugh Robertson and sang in the latter's famous Glasgow Orpheus Choir. He later became conductor of Cork's Cór Chois Laoi which had been founded in 1949. He performed with this choir all over Ireland and at many festivals abroad. Having read for a B.Mus. degree at UCC, he did part-time work in the music department there. He died at the Mercy Hospital, Cork, on 30 May 1976 and was buried in St Finbarr's Cemetery.

Ó LAOIRE, Donncha (1912–1965) Born Inchigeelagh, Co. Cork, the son of Con O'Leary, farmer. He was educated at St Kevin's Preparatory College and at De la Salle Training College, Waterford, before qualifying as a primary schoolteacher. He subsequently taught in Wexford and Inchigeelagh before graduating BA at UCC. He then moved to Dublin where he was appointed as full-time secretary of Comhdháil Náisiúnta na Gaeilge in 1947 – a post which he held until his death. He was associated with An Club Leabhar and An Cumann Drámaíochta and presented many Irish programmes on RTÉ. He died at his Baldoyle, Co. Dublin, residence on 25 May 1965 and was buried in Ballygriffin Cemetery.

O'LEARY, Arthur (1729–1802) Born Acres, near Dunmanway, Co. Cork. He was educated

at St Malo, France, where he had entered the Capuchin Order and was ordained there. He was appointed by the French government as chaplain to the prison camp and hospital at St Malo. He returned to Cork in 1771 and preached to huge congregations where he denounced the agrarian activities of the Whiteboys, the threatened French invasion of 1779 and supported the establishment of the Irish Volunteers. In receipt of a secret English government pension for his loyalist efforts in the newspapers and among the public, he also reported on the deliberations of the Catholic Committee which had been founded in 1760 and of which he was a member. In 1789, he took up a position as chaplain to the Spanish Embassy in London. He died there on 1 January 1802. [Bust by Peter Turnerelli (1802)]

O'LEARY, Con (1887–1958) Born Cork, the son of James O'Leary, a nationalist member of Cork Corporation. He was educated at Rochestown College and at UCC where he graduated BA (1913). He was involved with the Cork Dramatic Society under the guidance of **Daniel Corkery** and **Terence MacSwiney**. He then worked as a journalist on the *Freeman's Journal* and on the *Manchester Guardian*. He was brought to London by the Irish journalist and politician, T.P. ['Tay Pay'] O'Connor (1848–1929), where he was employed as assistant editor of *T.P.'s Weekly*. He continued with his busy journalistic career and worked at the London office of the *Irish Press* for the last ten years of his life. He died at Whittington Hospital, London, on 11 November 1958 and was buried in Surbiton Cemetery. He was also a writer of note and his publications include the novels *Break o'Day* (1926), *This Delicate Creature* (1928), *A Hillside Man* (1933) and *Passage West* (1945); his travel book, *A Wayfarer in Ireland* (1935); and his historical study, *Grand National* (1945, 1947). He was the author of two plays, 'The Crossing' (1914) and 'Queer Ones' (1919).

O'LEARY, D.F. (1801–1854) Born Cork, the son of Jeremiah O'Leary, merchant, and grandnephew of Rev. **Arthur O'Leary**. In 1817, he enlisted in Britain as a mercenary in the forces of Simón Bolívar (1783–1830), the future liberator of Venezuela and of the eponymous Bolivia. In March 1820, he was appointed as aide-de-camp to Bolívar and was later raised to the rank of lieutenant-colonel. He took part in many campaigns which involved various factions (and even countries) and was at Bolívar's side when the latter died on 17 December 1830. He then moved, in turn, to Jamaica and Venezuela, and represented the Venezuelan Foreign Service in various European cities. In January 1841, he changed services and worked for the British Foreign Office, subsequently holding various consular positions. He died at Bogotá on 24 February 1854. [Recollections edited by R.A. Humphreys (1969)]

O'LEARY, Daniel (*c.*1846–1933) Born Clonakilty, Co. Cork. He emigrated to America in 1866 and worked in Chicago as a book pedlar. The walking experiences of his job led to his interest in the long-distance walking exploits of Edward P. Weston (1839–1929), then at the height of his career. He consequently left the book trade and became a professional walker. From 1875 to 1877, he held nearly all the American long-distance records. Probably the most noted of those was his reduction of the 500-mile record to a time of 139 hours, 32 minutes. In 1896, he competed against Weston over a distance of 2,500 miles. Weston covered the distance in nine weeks, leaving O'Leary some 200 miles behind! However, O'Leary recorded probably his greatest feat in 1907 at Cincinnati, when, at the age of 61 years, he walked a mile at the beginning of each hour for 1,000 hours with only naps in between! Even in his eighties, he used to walk 100 miles on each birthday. He died in Los Angeles on 29 May 1933. [Life by J. Jackson (1881)]

O'LEARY, Daniel A. (1877–1951) Born Ballymakeera, Co. Cork. A member of Cork County Council, he was elected to Dáil Éireann in September 1927 as a Cumann na nGaedheal TD for North Cork. He was re-elected in 1932 and 1933. In 1937, he was returned for the West Cork constituency. However, he was defeated in the 1938 election. He also failed in 1943 and in 1944 when he stood as a Clann na Talún candidate. A farmer and a publican, he died at his residence, the Hibernian Hotel, Ballymakeera, on 30 March 1951 and was buried in Reilig Ghobnatan, Baile Bhúirne.

O'LEARY, Daniel H. (1875–1954) Born Glendart House, Drimoleague, Co. Cork, the fifth son of Florence O'Leary. He was educated privately, at Queen's College, Cork (now UCC), and at the King's Inns, Dublin. He was called to the Bar in 1902 and practised on the Munster Circuit. He unsuccessfully contested the two 1910 parliamentary elections as a Redmondite candidate in West Cork and suffered a similar fate in the 1911 County Council election, his nemesis on each occasion being an O'Brienite. On the death of **James Gilhooly** in 1916, he was elected as MP for West Cork, but did not seek re-election in 1918. He subsequently practised law (being admitted as a solicitor in 1921) in Arklow, Co. Wicklow. He died in a nursing home at Edgeworthstown, Co. Longford, on 23 December 1954 and was buried in Dean's Grange Cemetery, Dublin.

O'LEARY, Goodwin Purcell (1817–1876) Born Mourneabbey, Co. Cork, the son of Cornelius O'Leary, barrister, and grandson of **Art Ó Laoghaire**. He was educated in Paris from the age of five but returned to Ireland *c.*1830. He graduated from TCD in 1833 and later graduated in medicine at Edinburgh University. Following another period of residence on the Continent, he graduated Bachelor of Letters from the University of Paris. In 1857, he was appointed to the chair of Materia Medica at Queen's College, Cork (now UCC). When Denmark was threatened with invasion in 1864, he offered to raise a force of a hundred Irishmen to come to its aid. For this, he was awarded the Order of Danneborg by the Danish Court. He died at his cousin's residence at Chatsworth, Manchester, on 9 June 1876 and was buried at Kilcrea Abbey. The Purcell's Range in the American Rockies was named after him by his friend, John Palliser, mountaineer and explorer.

O'LEARY, Henry (1832–1897) Born Co. Cork, the son of Theophilus O'Leary. He arrived in Canada in 1852 and two years later, settled in Richibucto, New Brunswick, where he bought a store and wharf. He went into the canning of salmon and lobster for export to England and the United States. Shortly before his death, he owned over thirty canneries in New Brunswick alone. He went into lumber and shipbuilding as ancillary industries for his canning business. In December 1873, he won a seat in the New Brunswick House of Assembly and held it until the dissolution of the House in 1878. In that year, he contested for a seat in the Canadian House of Commons, but was defeated. He died in Dorchester, New Brunswick, on 7 November 1897. Two of his sons, Henry Joseph and Louis James, became Roman Catholic bishops of Edmonton and Charlottetown respectively.

O'LEARY, John (1850–1921) Born Barryroe, Co. Cork. He was educated at Castleknock College and at St Patrick's College, Maynooth. In 1874, he was ordained to the priesthood to serve in his native diocese of Ross. As a curate in Clonakilty in the early 1880s, he had a celebrated dispute with **William Bence Jones**, the local landlord. He was a prominent supporter of **C.S. Parnell** and, unlike most of his clerical colleagues, remained steadfastly so after the 'Split'. He became parish priest of Clonakilty in 1889 and supervised the completion of the town's Church of the Immaculate Conception. He was also responsible for the building of the church at Darrara. When the *Southern Star* newspaper was purchased from its founder in 1891 and incorporated, Monsignor O'Leary was appointed chairman of the new company and retained that position for many years, becoming the main shareholder in 1909. In 1897, he was one of the three candidates for the vacant see of Ross, but Rev. **Denis Kelly** was eventually

chosen. He died in Clonakilty on 31 October 1921 and was buried in the churchyard there.

O'LEARY, John (1929–1999) Born Cork, the eldest son of Frank O'Leary. He studied at the Cork School of Art and having graduated in 1958, studied in Paris for a further two years under the Gibson Bequest travel scholarship. His first solo exhibition was staged at the Dublin Painters' Gallery in 1961. He returned to Cork where he taught at Cork County vocational schools and at the Crawford Gallery. He was a founder member of the Cork Arts Society. In 1974, he moved with his family to Sligo where he was appointed as head of the arts department of Sligo Regional Technical College. He was involved in the establishment of the Sligo Art Gallery and later served as its artistic director (1994–9). He is represented in the collections of the Crawford Gallery and at the Niland Gallery of Sligo. He died in Sligo General Hospital on 17 November 1999 and was buried in Sligo Cemetery.

O'LEARY, Joseph (1792–1864) Born Cork, the eldest son of Jeremiah O'Leary, woollen manufacturer. He was educated at TCD where he graduated BA (1818). He attended at King's Inns and was called to the Bar in 1825. He became an expert on the laws of tithe and though he published *The Law of Statuable Composition for Tithes in Ireland* (1834), *Rent Charges in Lieu of Tithe* (1840) and *Dispositions for Religious and Charitable Uses in Ireland* (1847), his detractors described him as a failed barrister when he was appointed professor of History and English Literature at Queen's College, Galway (now UCG) in 1852. Though he was a Roman Catholic, his appointment was seen as 'political jobbery' and was controversial. However, he remained in his position and was active in teaching until his death in 1864.

O'LEARY, Joseph (c.1795–1855) Born Cork. As a songwriter, he contributed to such local periodicals as *The Freeholder*, *The Bagatelle* and the *Cork Merchantile Chronicle*. He also contributed to *Bolster's Cork Quarterly* and to two London periodicals. He moved to London in 1834 to become a parliamentary and police reporter for the *Morning Herald*. Being unsuccessful there, he drowned himself at the Limestone Cut of the River Lea (i.e. Regent's Canal), near London, in 1855.

O'LEARY, Liam (1910–1992) Born Youghal, Co. Cork, the son of **Donnchadh Ó Laoghaire**, teacher. When he was three years old, the family moved to Wexford. He was educated at UCD. He entered the civil service and also worked part-time as film critic for *Ireland Today* magazine. He was also interested in theatre and was a co-founder of Dublin Theatre Guild in 1934. He founded the Irish Film Society in 1936. He was seconded from the civil service to work as a producer for the Abbey Theatre, but left to become a freelance. He was appointed by the then Foreign Minister, Seán Mac Bride (1904–88), as a member of the Cultural Relations Committee, having already made a publicity film, *Our Country* (1948) for Mac Bride's Party, Clann na Poblachta. However, with the return of Fianna Fáil to government, the committee's future film plans were scrapped. He moved to London in 1953 and was appointed as acquisitions officer of the British National Film Archive. He returned to Dublin in 1967 and worked with the RTÉ film department until his retirement in 1987. As an actor, he had parts in the films, *Men against the Sun* and *Stranger at My Door*. He published *Invitation to the Film* (1945) and *The Silent Cinema* (1965). In 1980, he published *Rex Ingram*, the biography of the Dublin-born silent film director. He founded the National Film Archive in 1986, and the Irish Film Centre opened a few months before his death which occurred at St Vincent's Hospital, Dublin, on 14 December 1992. [Film documentary, *At the Cinema Palace: Liam O'Leary* by D.T. Black]

O'LEARY, Michael [VC] (1888–1961) Born Inchigeela, Co. Cork. He joined the 1st Battalion of the Irish Guards, rose to the rank of lance-corporal, and fought on the Western Front in World War I. On 1 February 1915, at Cuinchy in the Pas-de-Calais, he single-handedly took two German positions, killing eight and taking two soldiers prisoner. For this action, he was awarded the Victoria Cross. He later served during World War II with the Middlesex Regiment (1940–4) and with the Pioneer Corps (1944–5). He died in London on 2 August 1961.

O'LEARY, Patrick ['Pagan'] (*c.*1825–1895) Born Macroom, Co. Cork. He emigrated to the United States and studied for the priesthood. However, he defected from his seminary to take part in the Mexican War of 1846. During this campaign, he received a head wound, as a result of which he became eccentric (he renounced his baptismal vows on the grounds that St Patrick had demoralised the Irish people by teaching them to forgive their enemies!). He returned to Ireland and became a highly effective Fenian organiser in the British army. He was arrested in 1864 and was sentenced to seven years penal servitude. On his release in 1871, he returned to the US and settled for a short time in New York. He entered the National Military Home in Norfolk, Virginia, under the name 'Charles Smith', his *nom-de-guerre* in Mexico. He died there on 4 March 1895 and was buried in the National Cemetery with full military honours.

O'LEARY, Paddy (1918–1992) Born Evergreen Street, Cork. A free-scoring soccer centre-forward, he found the net 118 times in the League of Ireland with Limerick, St James' Gate, Cork United and Cork Athletic. He won three League of Ireland medals – one with Cork United (1946) and the other two with Cork Athletic (1949 and 1951). He also won two FAI Cup medals – one with Cork United (1947) and the other with Cork Athletic (1951). He died on 18 June 1992.

O'LEHANE, Michael J. (1873–1920) Born Kilbarry, Inchigeela, Co. Cork, the son of Cornelius O'Lehane, farmer and uncle of **Patrick Desmond Lehane**. He was educated at

North Monastery CBS and worked as a drapery assistant at Cash & Co., London House and Queen's Old Castle before moving to Cannock's of Limerick in 1898 and to Arnott's of Dublin in 1900. He was actively involved in both Connradh na Gaeilge and the GAA. He was involved in the foundation of the Irish Drapers' Assistants Benefit and Protective Association (later the Irish Distributive and Clerical Workers' Union) in 1902 and was the first full-time secretary and later the editor of the union's organ, the *Distributive Worker*. He led his members in many strikes for better pay and conditions and was elected as the first president of the Dublin Council of Trade Unions. He was a Sinn Féin member of Dublin Corporation (Kilmainham Ward) and was one of the founders of the Irish Labour Party in 1912. He died in March 1920, and was buried in Glasnevin Cemetery. [Account in D. Keogh, *The Rise of the Irish Working Class* and (do.) the *Capuchin Annual* (1976)]

OLLIFFE, Sir Joseph F. (1808–1869) Born Cork, the son of Joseph Olliffe, merchant. He was educated in Paris where he graduated MA (1829) and MD (1840). He soon established a successful medical practice and, in 1852, was appointed as physician to the British Embassy in Paris. He was knighted in the following year and was created an officer of the Legion of Honour by Napoleon III (1808–73) in 1855. It was he who established Deauville as a premier French resort through his influence on the duke of Morny, the brother of Napoleon III. He died on 14 March 1869.

Ó LOINGSIGH, Amhlaoibh (1872–1947) Born Cúil Aodha, Co. Cork, the son of Conchúir Ó Loingsigh, farmer. A born storyteller, he was the first winner of the Oireachtas Storytelling Competition in 1902 and took many prizes at various feiseanna up to 1910. He died at his Cúil Aodha residence on 24 January 1947 and was buried in Reilig Ghobnatan, Baile Bhúirne. His stories and conversations were collected by **Seán Ó Cróinín** and edited by his son, Donncha, under the titles, *Scéalaíocht*

Amhlaoibh Í Lúinse (1971) and *Seanchas Amhlaoibh Í Lúinse* (1980).

Ó LOINGSIGH, Micheál (1883–1942) Born Baile Bhúirne, Co. Cork, the son of Con Ó Loingsigh, farmer. In 1900, he joined the civil service as a boy-copyist in London before his transfer to the Irish Land Commission in Dublin. He joined Connradh na Gaeilge and Sinn Féin, and was elected a member of Dublin Corporation. He took part in the Easter Rising of 1916 and was later interned in Frongoch (Wales) and Ballykinlar Camp, Co. Down. He was appointed as official translator to the First Dáil in June 1919 and later as principal translator from 1925 until his death. He was a member of An Comhar Drámaíochta and was, for a period, a member of the executive committee of Connradh na Gaeilge. He was also connected with the founding, in June 1932, of the magazine, *An Camán* – sponsored jointly by Connradh na Gaeilge and the GAA. He died on 14 March 1942.

Ó LONGÁIN, Micheál Óg (1766–1837) Born Tobairín Maighir, Carraig na bhFear, Co. Cork, the son of Micheál Mac Peadair Ó Longáin, scribe and poet. He was orphaned as a young boy, and, having spent some years working on a farm as a 'milk boy', returned to school where he learned arithmetic, Latin and mensuration. He was a prolific poet who composed in the region of 300 poems and was also a professional scribe and teacher who, for a time, worked in transcribing manuscripts for the bishop of Cork, **John Murphy**, and for the banker, **James Roche**. Prior to the Rebellion of 1798, he was an organiser for the United Irishmen in the Carraig na bhFear area and, on the failure of the rebellion, went into hiding for a some time afterwards. In 1815, Bishop Murphy founded a group called Comhthionól Gaedheal Chorcaighe (Cork Irish Society) to preserve and promote Irish literature, and Ó Longáin, living at the time at Blair's Hill, was a member. He died at Knockbuidhe, Carraig na bhFear, on 17 May 1837 and was buried in Whitechurch Graveyard.

His three sons, Peadar Ó Longáin (1801–*p.*1853), Pól Ó Longáin (1801–66) and Seosamh Ó Longáin (1817–80), were notable poets and scribes. [Survey by B. Ó Conchúir in *Scríobhaithe Chorcaí 1700–1850*, pp.91–158]

O'MAHONEY, John (1816–1877) Born, Clonkilla, Mitchelstown, Co. Cork, the son of Daniel O'Mahoney, gentleman. He was educated at Hamblin's School, Cork, and at TCD but did not graduate. He joined the Young Ireland movement and following the abortive rising of 1848, he fled to France and then to New York. Here, in 1857, he published a translation of Geoffrey Keating's *Foras Feasa ar Éirinn*. In 1858, he was a founder member of the Fenian Brotherhood (later called the Irish Republican Brotherhood or IRB). In 1864, he raised the 99th Regiment of the New York National Guard to fight for the Yankees in the American civil war and became its colonel. In the following year, a split developed in the American Fenian movement when James Stephens (1824–1901), who had been planning an Irish rising, escaped to America and took over the leadership. This led to the abortive 'invasion' of Canada in 1866 which O'Mahony opposed. However, O'Mahony resumed the leadership again in 1872 and held the position until his death in New York on 6 February 1877. His remains were brought back to Ireland and, following a huge funeral, were interred at Glasnevin Cemetery on 4 March. [Portrait by an unknown artist at the Dublin Municipal Gallery]

O'MAHONY, Danno (1912–1950) Born Ballydehob, Co. Cork. He emigrated to America in 1934 where he took up professional wrestling. He took the World Heavyweight title on 30 July 1935 when he defeated the reigning champion, Ed Don George, in Boston. He successfully defended his title at Dalymount Park, Dublin, on 9 August 1936. He was renowned for his speciality, the 'Irish Whip', a throw which he had developed. He served in the US army for the duration of World War II. He died on 2 November 1950, following injuries which he received in a car crash near Portlaoise on the previous day. He was buried in Schull Cemetery. [Life by J.W. Pollard *et al.* (n.d.)]

O'MAHONY, Edward J. (d. 1918) Born Mardyke Street, Cork. He worked in the composing department of the *Cork Examiner* for many years, but being possessed of a remarkable singing voice, left Cork for Italy in 1878 to perfect his musical education under maestro Sangiovanni. In the following year, he took leading parts in three operas at the Pavia Opera House. Known as 'The Irish Basso', he spent some years in the United States where he had several successful concert tours and popularised Irish songs. He returned to Cork and resided at Albert Lodge, Glenbrook. In failing health for some time, he died at the South Infirmary Hospital, Cork, on 3 July 1918 and was buried privately.

O'MAHONY, Eoin (1904–1970) Born Monkstown, Co. Cork, the eldest son of Daniel John O'Mahony, city analyst. Nicknamed 'The Pope', he was educated at PBC, Cork, at Clongowes Wood, Co. Kildare, at UCC and TCD. He was called to the Irish Bar in 1930 and practised on the Munster Circuit. He was also called to the English Bar in 1933. He joined the Fianna Fáil Party in 1931 but was unsuccessful in his pursuit of a Dáil or Seanad seat. He was an active member of the Irish Georgian Society, the Military History Society and the Knights of Malta. He also had an abiding interest in genealogy and his 'Meet the Clans' radio programme ran for seven years and was highly popular. He unsuccessfully contested the Presidential Election of 1966. From 1966 to 1968, he was Visiting Professor at the University of South Illinois. He died at Monkstown, Co. Dublin on 15 February 1970 and was buried in St Joseph's Cemetery, Cork. [Life-size bronze by **Seamus Murphy** at the Royal Irish Academy, Dublin]

O'MAHONY, James Edward (1897–1962) Born Mitchelstown, Co. Cork, the son of James

O'Mahony. He was educated at Rochestown College and entered the Capuchin Order in 1913. He engaged in further studies at UCC (BA and MA), at the Gregorian University, Rome (BD), and at the University of Louvain (Lic. Phil. and PhD). In 1928, he was granted the title 'Professor Agrégé' – the first Irishman and the first Capuchin to receive the honour. He was appointed as deputy professor of Philosophy at UCC in 1933 and succeeded to the professorship four years later when he succeeded Rev. **Edwin Fitzgibbon**. He was elected as provincial of the Irish Capuchin Order in 1943. He was the author of several book and pamphlets on philosophy and religion. His books included, *Christian Philosophy: essays* (1939) and *The Music of Life* (1944). He died at the Bon Secours Hospital, Cork, on 31 July 1962 and was buried in the community cemetery at Rochestown College.

O'MAHONY, John (1844–1912) Born Bally-velone, Enniskeane, Co. Cork, the eldest son of James O'Mahony, farmer, and cousin of **Thaddeus O'Mahony**. He was educated at Lordan's School, Bandon, at Sullivan's Classical School, Cork, and at St Patrick's College, Maynooth, which he entered in September 1861. Following an outstanding period of study, he was ordained in May 1871 and took up the position of curate in St Finbarr's Parish, Cork, until 1881. In the previous year, he was instru-mental in having **C.S. Parnell** nominated for Cork City in the general election, principally in opposition to the nominal Home Ruler, **Nicholas Dan Murphy**. As a censure for his behaviour, he was transferred to a curacy in Kinsale where he ministered until 1886. In that year, he was appointed as administrator of St Mary's Cathedral and later as parish priest of Kilmurry in August 1893. He published articles in the *Irish Theological Quarterly* and read several papers at the Maynooth Union, of which he became President in 1910. His *magnum opus* was his 'History of the O'Mahony Septs of Kinelmeky and Ivagh' which was published in *JCHAS* (1906–10) and later in book form. He died at his residence in Crookstown on 11

January 1912 and was buried in the grounds of Cloghdubh Church where a marble statue to his memory was unveiled in 1917.

O'MAHONY, John Eager (1849–1900) Born Skibbereen, Co. Cork, a relative of **Jeremiah O'Donovan Rossa**. A journalist, he was chief reporter/assistant editor of *The West Cork Eagle* in Skibbereen from the early 1870s to 1887. In September 1887, he left Skibbereen to take up a post as editor/manager of the *Tipperary Nationalist*. Becoming embroiled in the land agitation in Tipperary, he served two periods of imprisonment for his espousal of the cause and during this period, he established a short-lived newspaper called *New Tipperary*. In 1892, he became founding proprietor and editor of the *Waterford Star* and five years later he established a sister newspaper, the *Tipperary Champion*. He died of pneumonia following a short illness at his residence, The Quay, Waterford, on 13 January 1900. After his death, his widow, Annie (née O'Callaghan) and a native of Skibbereen, took over the newspaper until her death in 1913 when it passed to his son, Con.

O'MAHONY, Thaddeus (1821–1903) Born Enniskeane, Co. Cork, the son of Cornelius O'Mahony, farmer, and cousin of Canon **John O'Mahony**. Having converted to the Church of Ireland, he attended TCD and graduated BA in 1856. He had been ordained deacon in the previous year and then ministered as a curate and as a rector from 1857 to 1872. He was also professor of Irish at TCD from 1861 until 1879. A member of the Royal Irish Academy, he edited the 'Senchas Mór' under the title, *The Ancient Laws of Ireland* (4 vols, 1865–79). He also published a translation of C. Wordsworth's *St Patrick, the Apostle of Ireland, his Life and Times* under the title, *Naomh Pádraig: a Bheatha agus a Aimsir* (1854). He died on 27 July 1903 and was buried in Mount Jerome Cemetery.

O'MAHONY, Thomas (1862–1924) Born Fermoy, Co. Cork. He was educated at Fermoy CBS. He was apprenticed to the building trade and established himself later in life as a substantial building contractor. From 1911 until 1914, he was a member of Cork County Council as the ex-officio representative of Fermoy Rural District Council. He was also a member of Fermoy Urban District Council and, for several years, its chairman. In 1923, he was elected to Dáil Éireann as Cumann na nGaedheal TD for East Cork but died less than a year later on 20 July 1924 at his residence, 'Sunmount', Fermoy. He was buried in Kilcrumper Cemetery.

O'MAHONY, Timothy (1825–1892) Born Aherla, Co. Cork. He studied for the priesthood at the Irish College, Rome, and was ordained in 1849. He returned to Cork and ministered there until November 1869 when he was consecrated as bishop of the huge diocese of Armidale, New South Wales, Australia. However, O'Mahony's drinking habits and a false claim that he had fathered a child led to considerable friction between Irish and non-Irish bishops in Australia. Following a Vatican-sponsored inquiry, O'Mahony was cleared of the main charges but was forced to resign and travel to Rome. He was then appointed as auxiliary bishop of Toronto, Canada, in 1878. He died in Toronto on 8 September 1892 and was buried in St Paul's Church.

O'MAHONY, Timothy J. (1839–1917) Born Cathedral Parish, Cork, the nephew of Rev. **Francis S. Mahony** ('Fr. Prout'). He was educated locally, studied for the priesthood in Paris and Rome, and graduated DCL and DD. He was ordained in 1852 and was professor of Theology at All Hallows College, Dublin. He wrote poetry for many Roman Catholic periodicals and his published collections include *A Wreath of Song: Souvenir of a Course of Philosophy* (1881), *Wreaths of Song from Fields of Philosophy* (1890), *Thought Echoes* (1891), *Wreaths of Song from a Course of Divinity* (1903) and *Allelulia's Sequence* (1913). He died on 19 March 1917 and was buried in All Hallows Cemetery.

O'MAHONY, Timothy J. (1864–1914) Born Rosscarbery, Co. Cork. As a young man, he showed huge prowess as an athlete and specialised in the 440 yards race in which he broke many local records. His maintainence of pace in this difficult event earned him the nickname 'The Rosscarbery Steam Engine'. In the early days of the GAA (founded 1884), the promotion of athletics was an important part of the association's activities and O'Mahony took full advantage of this by winning at many meetings. He was also a strong nationalist and, in June 1888, was jailed for a fortnight in Cork Gaol following an incident involving the RIC. Later that year, he left for Boston and New York where he won three international races in the 440 yards. After retirement, he took a great interest in GAA affairs, both as a football referee and as a prominent member of Carbery Rangers. He was also associated with athletics and acted both as starter and handicapper at many meetings. He moved to Dublin in the mid-1890s as a journalist. He died there on 10 September 1914.

Ó MAIDÍN, Pádraig (1919–1981) Born Limerick, the son of Patrick Madden. Having been educated at Limerick CBS, he joined the Limerick County library service in 1937 and was appointed as Monaghan County Librarian nine years later in 1946. In the following year, he was appointed as Cork County Librarian – a position he held until his death in 1981. During his tenure in Cork, he greatly expanded the library service and especially highlighted awareness of the public library as a popular resource. His most notable contribution to the cultural life of his adopted county was the development of interest in local historical research. He instigated the publication of the *Cork Historical Guides* series of town history booklets and was a prime mover in the foundation of the Cork Archives Institute. From 1968 to the year of his death, he wrote an historical column entitled, 'Today', for the *Cork Examiner* which was enormously popular. He contributed many articles to the *JCHAS*, most notably editing *Pococke's Tour of the South of Ireland* for publication. In his earlier years, he contributed poetry to *Irish Writing*. He died at Cork Regional

Hospital on 13 December 1981 and was buried in St Finbarr's Cemetery.

Ó MATHGHAMHNA, Finghín (*c.*1430–1496) Born Rosbrin Castle, nr. Ballydehob, Co. Cork, the third son of Diarmaid 'Rúntach' Ó Mathghamhna, 7th Lord of Ivagh. He later succeeded (by tanist law) to the chieftainship as 10th Lord. He was the translator of *Mandeville's Travels* from the Anglo-French into Irish. The book, by Sir John Mandeville (*fl.* 1356) of St Albans, dealt with a journey to the Holy Land, the Near East and India. Some parts of the stories were probably original but were heavily embellished with Mandeville's imaginary additions. Finghín's translation was discovered at Rennes public library in 1869. He died in December 1496.

O'MEARA, Barry E. (1786–1836) Born Churchtown, Mallow, Co. Cork, the son of Jeremiah O'Meara, a lawyer. In 1804, he was appointed as an assistant surgeon to the 62nd Regiment and saw service in Sicily, Calabria and Egypt. Through his involvement in a duel, he was dismissed from the army but he continued his career as surgeon in the Royal Navy. In 1815, he was aboard the ship which was bringing the Emperor Napoleon (1769–1821) from Rochefort to Plymouth. Napoleon was impressed by O'Meara's command of Italian and requested that the surgeon would accompany him as his personal physician for his impending exile on the island of St Helena in the South Atlantic. However, tensions soon developed between O'Meara and the governor of the island, Sir Hudson Lowe. O'Meara was dismissed from his post and returned to England in late 1818 where the controversy with Lowe dragged on – this time in print. He published *Napoleon in Exile, or a Voice from St Helena* (2 vols, 1822), which was an extended version of the earlier *Exposition* of 1819. The 1822 publication reached three editions and was also published in three volumes in France (1822 and 1825). He died in London on 16 June 1836 and was buried in St Mary's Church, Paddington.

Ó MUIMHNEACHÁIN, Andrias (1905–1989) Born Ballingeary, Co. Cork. He worked as a teacher of Irish at Coláiste Chaoimhín, Dublin, and later at Cathal Brugha Street College, Dublin. He was intimately connected with Connradh na Gaeilge and served for forty years on its governing body. He was involved in the re-establishment of Oireachtas na Gaeilge in 1939 and served for twenty-five years as its chairman. He was a member of the Irish Folklore Commission for many years and also served as a member of the Commission on the Restoration of the Irish Language (1959–64). He presented his Irish language course, 'Listen and Learn' on Radio Éireann in the 1940s and 1950s. He published *An Claidheamh Solais* (1955), *Na Múinteoirí Taistil* (1962) and *Dóchas agus Duainéis* (1975). A personal friend of **Tadhg Ó Buachalla**, he edited the latter's transcriptions by **Seán Ó Crónín** under the title, *Seanchas an Táilliúra* (1978), as a possible corrective to **Eric Cross**'s, *The Tailor and Anstey*. He died at Lansdowne House Nursing Home, Dublin, on 14 November 1989 and was buried in Glasnevin Cemetery.

Ó MUIMHNEACHÁIN, Conchubhar (1870–1945) Born Ballingeary, Co. Cork, the son of Conchubhar Ó Muimhneacháin, farmer. Having been educated locally, he joined Connradh na Gaeilge and became secretary of the Ballingeary Branch. He won many prizes at the Oireachtas for his stories and poetry. He worked as a peripatetic teacher of Irish in counties Clare, Carlow and Kilkenny. He later qualified as a secondary teacher and worked at St Kieran's College, Kilkenny, while he spent his summers working at Coláiste na Mumhan in his native village. He returned there in his retirement and died on 24 December 1945. He was buried in Reilig Ghobnatan, Baile Bhúirne. His publications include *Fionn agus Lorcán* (1901), *Amhráin Shéamuis Mhóir Uí Mhuimhneacháin* (1924) and *Béaloideas Bhéal Átha an Ghaorthaigh* (1934). He translated J. Murphy's *The Priest Hunters* [*Sealgairí Sagart* (1952)], and C. Kickham's *The Homes of Tipperary* [*Scéalta ó Thiobraid Árann* (1953)]. He also translated plays and collections of short stories as well as contributing many articles to the various magazines.

Ó MUIRTHILE, Seán (1881–1941) Born Leap, Co. Cork, the son of Páid Hurley, boatman. Following a spell as a postman, he was appointed by Connradh na Gaeilge in November 1907 as a peripatetic teacher of Irish for the Kenmare district. He later taught in counties Clare, Limerick and Tipperary. He joined the Irish Republican Brotherhood (IRB) in 1915 and became secretary of the Supreme Council of that body in August 1916. Following a period of exile in Yorkshire in 1917, he returned to Dublin in the following year and continued with his teaching duties. He served as general secretary of Connradh na Gaeilge from November 1920 to July 1922 when he was appoointed governor of Kilmainham Jail. He took the pro-Treaty side during the civil war and served as a lieutenant-general in the Free State Army. However, he, and **Gearóid O'Sullivan**, were forced to resign their commissions on account of the 'Army Mutiny' of 1924. He stood for election to Seanad Éireann in the following year, but was unsuccessful. In 1930, he was appointed as the manager of the Cork City office of Irish Hospital Sweepstakes. He died while undergoing minor surgery on 28 June 1941 and was buried in Leap Cemetery. His two plays, 'Pósadh an Iascaire' ['The Fisherman's Wedding'] and 'An Cníopaire' ['The Miser'] were produced in 1913 and 1915 respectively.

Ó MULLÁIN, Dónall (1880–1965) Born Cúil Aodha, Co. Cork, the son of Seán Ó Mulláin, stonemason and builder. He was the uncle of the noted writer of Irish, **Donncha Ó Chéileachair**. He spent his life as a farmer and took a keen interest in Irish music, poetry, dancing, and, above all, song-writing. His song, 'An Poc ar Buile', as well as winning an Oireachtas prize, was probably the most popular Irish song ever recorded. He died at his Cúil Aodha residence on 12 January 1965 and was buried in Reilig Ghobnatan, Baile Bhúirne. His son, Seán, is a noted novelist and writer of adventure stories in Irish.

Ó MURCHADHA, Seán (1700–1762) Born Rathanny, Carraig na bhFear, Co. Cork, the son of Diarmuid Ó Murchadha, land tenant. 'Seán na Raithíneach' took over the land holding on the death of his brother, Dónall, in 1719. A major Munster Gaelic poet, he transcribed many valuable historical tracts into Irish. He was also the president of An Cúirt Filíochta at Carraig na bhFear and other locations. He died in September 1762 and was buried in Whitechurch Graveyard.

Ó MURCHADHA, Tadhg (1843–1919) Born Macroom, Co. Cork. He attended Wall's School, Macroom, for a time but became a tailor and moved to Cork in 1864 where he worked at the Munster Arcade (now Penny's). He was a founder member of the Cork branch of Connradh na Gaeilge in 1894. Under the pseudonym 'Seandún', he wrote a column in Irish for the *Cork Weekly Examiner*. His special interest was in translation work – his main effort being *Eachtra Robinson Crúsó* (1915) which **Osborn Bergin** helped to produce. He died on 13 April 1919. [Works edited by **Terence Mac Swiney** in *Sgéal Sheandúin* (1920)]

Ó MURCHÚ, Tadhg (1908–1971) Born Killaminoge, Ballinhassig, Co. Cork, the only child of Bartholomew Murphy, farmer. He was educated at Innishannon NS, Farranferris College and at St Patrick's College, Maynooth, where he graduated BA in Celtic Studies. He was ordained in 1935 and later graduated MA at UCC. He worked at Farranferris for twenty-five years and was appointed as curate at Carraig na bhFear in 1960. Aside from his clerical duties, he spent his life in the promotion of Irish as a spoken language and helped to produce *Faiche na bhFilí* (1962) in bilingual form. He was appointed as parish priest of Murragh in 1970. He died at the Bon Secours Hospital, Cork, on 11 December 1971 and was buried in the grounds of Murragh Church. [Life by P. Tyers (2000) and by D. Breathnach and M. Ní Mhurchú (1986); Life-size bronze bust by **Seamus Murphy**]

Ó NEACHTAIN, Bonaventura (d. 1587) Possibly born in Limerick, the son of a smith. It is generally accepted that it was he who was appointed bishop of Ross on 2 August 1580. In 1621, he was named by Don Philip O'Sullivan in his *Historiae Catholicae Iberniae Compendium* as the re-builder of the monastery of Dursey Island, Beara. However, it seems that he spent most of his time in exile in Spain. 'Bonaventura Nectarius' died at Evora, Portugal, on 14 February 1587.

O'NEILL, Billy (c.1876–1963) Born Sarsfield's Court, Glanmire, Co. Cork, the son of John O'Neill, farmer. He was one of Cork's greatest all-round sportsmen. A founder member of the Sarsfield's GAA Club, he won two All-Ireland SHC medals – one with Dungourney (1902) and the other with Blackrock (1903). In 1910, he played with the Cork touring hurling side in Flanders. He was also a prominent rugby player with Cork Constitution, with whom he won two Munster Senior Cup medals. His chance of an international rugby cap was dashed by the introduction of the GAA ban in 1905. He also excelled at athletics and ran all distances from the sprints to the marathon. He died in 1963 and was buried in Ballylucra Cemetery.

O'NEILL, Eamon (1882–1954) Born Kinsale, Co. Cork, the son of James O'Neill, merchant, businessman, and a member of the first Cork County Council. He was the brother of **Philip O'Neill**. He was educated at Youghal CBS, Kinsale PBS, Mungret College, and at the Royal University of Ireland where he graduated BA (1901). Inheriting the family business, he was one of the founders of the Irish Master Bakers' Association and played a prominent role in local commercial development. Through his efforts, electric lighting was introduced to Kinsale in 1920. He served on Cork County Council (1925–8) and unsuccessfully contested the 1927 general election for the Cumann na nGaedhal Party in the constituency of West Cork. However, he was elected to the Dáil in 1932 and held his seat until 1943. He regained it in the following year, but was again unseated in 1948 when he contested the new Cork South constituency. He held the post of leas Ceann Comhairle of the Dáil (1939–43 and 1944–8). A prominent all-round sportsman, he was the donor of the O'Neill Cup for junior rugby clubs in County Cork, and was also an accomplished singer and musician. He died at his residence, Knockduff House, Kinsale, on 3 November 1954 and was buried in Clontead Graveyard.

O'NEILL, Eliza (1791–1872) Born Drogheda, Co. Louth, the daughter of a local theatre manager. Having appeared on both the Belfast and Dublin stages, she made her Covent Garden debut in October 1814, in *Romeo and Juliet*. She enjoyed great success over the following five years, but in December 1819, she announced her retirement from the stage as she was to marry **William W. Becher**, MP for Mallow. He was created a baronet in 1831. Lady Becher died in Mallow on 29 October 1872. [Portrait by Thomas C. Thompson]

O'NEILL, Francis (1849–1936) Born Bantry, Co. Cork. He emigrated to America at the age of 16 years and eventually became chief of the Chicago police department in 1905. In his young days he had been a noted performer on the flute and a collector of Irish folk music. With his namesake from Co. Down, James O'Neill, he published thousands of songs and airs which had been collected from Irish musicians in America. He died in 1936. His library and manuscripts were bequeathed to Notre Dame University. He published *The Music of Ireland* (1903), *The Dance Music of Ireland* (1907), *O'Neill's Irish Music for Piano and Violin* (1908), *Irish Folk Music, a fascinating Study* (1910), *Irish Minstrels and Musicians* (1913) and *Waifs and Strays of Irish Melody* (1916, 1922).

O'NEILL, Pádraig (1928–1995) Born Aughadown, Co. Cork, the son of Harry O'Neill. He was educated at St Fachtna's High School, Skibbereen, at PBC, Cork and at St Patrick's College of Education where, succeeding to his mother's calling, he qualified as a primary teacher. In his early teaching career, he trained as an actor before joining the Radio Éireann Players in 1951. He then moved to production at the station and was associated with such popular radio programmes as 'Take the Floor', 'Question Time' and 'The School around the Corner'. In the 1960s, he scripted and produced 'Murphy agus a Cháirde', one of the first homemade TV programmes for children. Under the name of 'Paddy O'Brien' he established a reputation as a commentator on greyhound racing. His intimate knowledge and expertise in the greyhound industry led to his appointment as chairman of Bórd na gCon. He was also executive producer of Community Radio at RTÉ, from which organisation he retired in 1990. He died in Dublin in June 1995.

O'NEILL, Peter (1757–1846) Born Conna, Co. Cork. He was educated at a classical school at Kilworth and at the College of the Lombards, Paris, where he was ordained. He returned to minister in Ireland in 1781. He held a curacy at Skibbereen before being appointed in 1786 by Bishop **Matthew McKenna** of Cloyne and Ross as parish priest of Ballymacoda. During the Rebellion of 1798, he was accused of being a member of the Society of United Irishmen and of being involved in the murder of a suspected government spy. He was arrested in Ballymacoda by a detachment of the Wexford Militia on 1 June. Imprisoned in Youghal, he underwent a savage flogging three days later to extract information and to force a confession. He was subsequently imprisoned in Cork and was transported to Australia at the end of June 1800. An order from the lord lieutenant to stop this arrived too late. He was sent to Norfolk Island in the Pacific Ocean. He was finally released on 19 November 1802 and returned to Ireland where he resumed his pastoral duties in Ballymacoda. He died there on 30 June 1846 and was buried in the church grounds. [Life by P. O'Neill (1998)]

O'NEILL, Philip (1885–1937) Born Kinsale, Co. Cork, the son of James O'Neill, merchant,

businessman, and a member of the first Cork County Council. He was the brother of **Eamon O'Neill**. He settled in Co. Kilkenny and became a leading newspaper columnist under the pseudonym, 'Sliabh Ruadh' and wrote especially on GAA affairs. His *Twenty Years of the GAA, 1910–1930* was published at Kilkenny in 1931. He had earlier published a pamphlet, *St Elton of Kinsale*. He also wrote an unpublished history of the Kinsale barony as well as a large body of ballads and verse. He died in Kilkenny on 17 September 1937 and was buried in Foulkstown Cemetery.

O'RAHILLY, Alfred (1884–1969) Born Listowel, Co. Kerry, the son of T.F. Rahilly, clerk of the Petty Sessions. He was educated at Blackrock College, Dublin, and at the Royal University, Dublin. In 1908, he entered the Jesuit Order at Stonyhurst College but left having taken a D.Phil. In 1914, he joined the staff of University College, Cork, and was appointed as professor of Mathematical Physics there in 1917 (to 1943). In the same year, he joined Sinn Féin and later, in 1921, he was imprisoned for six months at Spike Island in Cork Harbour. In the meantime, he had been appointed as registrar at UCC and held this post until 1943 when he became president. He sat as a TD for Cork City from 1923 to 1924, having previously contributed to and supported the Treaty. At UCC, he founded the chair of sociology, the Cork University Press, provided extra-mural courses for workers and farmers and expanded the college library tenfold. He was appointed as president of UCC in 1943 and held the post until his retirement in October 1954. Following the death of his wife, he took up residence on the grounds of his old school, Blackrock College, and was ordained a priest in December 1955. He was promoted to the dignity of monsignor soon after and was made a Knight of St Gregory. He died in Dublin on 2 August 1969. [Life by J. Gaughan (4 vols, 1986–93); Limestone tablet by **Seamus Murphy** at the Boole Library, UCC]

O'REGAN, Jim (1901–1982) Born Castle Park, Kinsale, Co. Cork. He was educated at

Ringrone NS, at Presentation School, Kinsale and at De la Salle Training College, Waterford, where he qualified as a primary school teacher. In 1924, while teaching in Birr, he was a member of the Offaly team which won the Leinster junior hurling championship. In the following year, he played on the Dublin team which won the Leinster SHC, but the title was later awarded to Offaly on an objection. He later won four All-Ireland SHC medals with Cork (1926, 1928–9 and 1931), playing at centre-back. He was also a dual interprovincial player with Munster. At the time of his death, he was president of Cork County GAA board. He died at the North Infirmary Hospital on 31 October 1982 and was buried in St Finbarr's Cemetery.

O'REILY, Jeremiah J.P. (1798–1880) Born Cork, he entered the novitiate of the Capuchin Order in September 1826 at Frascati, Italy, where he completed his studies and where he was ordained. In 1833, he was appointed guardian of the Church Street (Dublin) Capuchin community and six years later was appointed to a similar post at Kilkenny Friary. He left Ireland for New Zealand in 1842 and was the first pastor of a small Roman Catholic community at Port Nicholson (now Wellington). Having built a church (1843) and a school (1847), he was the only permanent priest in the area until 1850. In 1868, he undertook a three-year visit to Europe. He was the author of a catechism (1844) which was published for his community, and of a tract, *Ex Horto Ecclesiae* (1850). In 1865, he translated *Meditations and Prayers in Honour of St Joseph* from the French. He died in Wellington on 21 July 1880 and was buried in Mount Street Roman Catholic Cemetery where his grave is marked by a Celtic cross.

O'REILLY, Maurice J. (1866–1933) Born Cobh, Co. Cork, the son of Thomas O'Reilly, shopkeeper and stevedore. He was educated at St Colman's College, Fermoy, and at St Patrick's College, Maynooth. In 1887, he entered the Vincentian Order and was ordained three years later. He volunteered for the Australian mission

and arrived in Melbourne in November 1892. He served as president of St Stanislaus' College, Bathurst, New South Wales, from 1903 until 1914 when he returned to Ireland to take up the position of president of Castleknock College, Co. Dublin. However, his stay at Castleknock was a short one as he was appointed in June 1915 as rector of St John's College at the University of Melbourne. Here he campaigned against conscription and supported Archbishop **Daniel Mannix** against his many critics. He also engaged in theological controversy and defended the doctrine of transubstantiation before the beginning of the International Eucharistic Congress in Sydney in 1928. Previously, in 1926, he had become provincial of his Order. He died at St John's College on 25 September 1933 and, following a massive funeral, was buried at Rookwood Cemetery. He had a keen interest in poetry and published *Poems* in 1919. [Memories by F.D. King (1953); Analysis by J.P. Wilkinson in *Australian Catholic Historical Society Journal*, 7, iii (1983); Portraits at St Stanislaus' and St John's Colleges]

Ó RIADA, Seán (1931–1971) Born Erinville Hospital, Cork, the son of an Adare (Co. Limerick) policeman. He was educated at Adare and later studied music at UCC under Professor **Aloys Fleischmann**. Following further studies in France and Italy, he was appointed as musical director of the Abbey Theatre in 1951. He came into both national and international prominence with his musical scores for Louis Marcus's films *Mise Éire* (1959) and *Saoirse* (1961). He also wrote the musical scores for *The Playboy of the Western World* (1962), *Young Cassidy* (1964) and *An Tine Bheo* (1966). He founded the group, Ceoltóirí Chualann, which specialised in presenting Irish traditional music both on radio and television. He was also a composer of note, especially for his series *Nomos 1–4* for choir and orchestra. On being appointed to a lectureship at the department of Music, UCC, he settled in Cúil Aodha in 1963. However, in failing health, he was removed to King's College Hospital, London, for special treatment. He died there on

3 October 1971 and was buried in Cúil Aodha Graveyard. [Life by T. Ó Canainn and G. Mac a' Bhua (1993); Assessment by B. Harris and G. Freyer (1981); Headstone at Cúil Aodha Graveyard, Co. Cork, life-size bronze at RTÉ, Dublin, and death mask, all by **Seamus Murphy**]

Ó RÍORDÁIN, Seán (1916–1977) Born Baile Bhúirne, Co. Cork. Following the death of his father, the family moved to Inniscarra in 1932 and he attended North Monastery CBS, Cork. In 1937, he took a job as a clerk with Cork Corporation, but a year later, tuberculosis was diagnosed and eventually he was hospitalised at Doneraile where he wrote his first poem in 1944. His mother died in the following year – an event which profoundly affected him and which produced his noted poem 'Adhlacadh mo Mháthar' ('My Mother's Burial'). In 1965, he resigned from the Corporation through ill health. He worked as a part-time lecturer at UCC from 1969. He was conferred with an honorary degree of D.Litt. by the National University of Ireland in 1976. He died in Cork on 21 February 1977 and was buried in Reilig Ghobnatan, Baile Bhúirne. His poetic collections include *Eireaball Spideóige* (1952), *Brosna* (1964), *Línte Liombó* (1971), and *Tar éis mo Bháis* (posth. 1979). With Séamus Ó Chonghaile, he published *Rí na hUile* (1967) – a compilation of modern translations of medieval Irish religious poetry. [Life and Works by S. Ó Coileáin (1982)]

Ó RÍORDÁIN, Seán P. (1905–1957) Born Monkstown, Co. Cork. He qualified and worked as a primary school teacher before he was awarded a travelling scholarship by the National University of Ireland in 1931 to study archaeology in Great Britain and on the Continent. He worked in the National Museum before being appointed as professor of Archaeology at UCC (1936–43). He moved to UCD in 1943 and took up the position of professor of Celtic Archaeology which he held until his death. He is associated with the excavations at Lough Gur, Tara, and Newgrange. He was also a former editor of the *JCHAS*. He died in Dublin on 11 April 1957. His publications include *The Antiquities of the Irish Countryside* (1942) and *Tara: the Monuments on the Hill* (1954). He was also the co-author of *Newgrange and the Bend of the Boyne* (posthumously, 1964). [Four life-size bronzes by **Seamus Murphy** – three in private possession and one at UCC]

ORPEN, Charles H. (1791–1856) Born Cork. He studied for medicine and was the founder of the Claremont Institution (1816) for the deaf and dumb. He emigrated to South Africa and was ordained there in 1848. He was appointed as rector of Colesberg and wrote many religious works. He died in Port Elizabeth in 1856. [Life by Alicia le Fanu]

O'RYAN, Edmund (1825–1903) Born Cork, the son of John J. O'Ryan, doctor, and brother of **Julia M. O'Ryan**. In his early years, he wrote newspaper articles and poetry for *The Nation* (the organ of the Young Ireland movement), for *The Tablet* of London and for *The Lamp* – a London periodical. He graduated MD at St Andrew's University, Edinburgh, practised as a doctor in Clonakilty and then at Clashmore Dispensary, Co. Waterford, where he remained for forty years until his retirement. He died at his residence in Shanacoole, Co. Waterford, on 31 December 1903 and was buried in the Mass Yard, Youghal.

O'RYAN, Julia M. (1823–1887) Born Cork, the daughter of John J. O'Ryan, doctor, and sister of **Edmund O'Ryan**. She wrote stories and poems for the *Irish Monthly*, *Chamber's Journal* and the New York *Catholic World*. She died on 14 May 1887.

Ó SCANAILL, Tadhg (1883–1967) Born Baile Bhúirne, Co. Cork, the son of Peadar Ó Scanaill, saddler. He was educated locally and at PBC, Cork. He joined the Post Office and having spent some time as a sorter on the railway between London and Bristol, was appointed to a position in the GPO, Dublin, in 1910. He was an active member of Connradh na Gaeilge and was one of a group which founded 'An Fáinne Gaelach' in the spring of 1916. He was also a member of the Volunteers but was in Co. Tipperary when the Easter Rising broke out in 1916. He was later employed as a translator in the office of Dáil Éireann – a position which led to his appointment as secretary of the Gaeltacht Commission. He was also interested in acting and was a founder member of An Comhar Drámaíochta. His novel, *Thall is Abhus,* was published in 1953. He died in Jervis Street Hospital (as a result of a motor accident) on 8 January 1967 and was buried in Swords Cemetery, Co. Dublin.

Ó SEAGHDHA, Mortimer (1897–1981) Born Glengarriff, Co. Cork, the son of **Pádraig Ó Seaghdha,** teacher. He was educated in Cork and Rome and was subsequently ordained as a member of the Capuchins taking the name of An tAth. Casáin. He published some short stories in *Éarna* and in *The Capuchin Annual.* He also published *Gleann an Uaignis* (1922) and *An Londubh agus Scéalta Eile* (1937). He died in California on 16 February 1981.

Ó SÉAGHDHA, Pádraig (1864–1955) Born Glengarriff, Co. Cork, the son of Séamus Ó Séaghdha, farmer, and father of **Mortimer Ó Séaghdha.** He became a monitor at Glengarriff NS and, on completion of his course, attended Marlborough Street Training College, Dublin, where he qualified as a primary schoolteacher. He worked at Glengarriff for the rest of his career. A member of Connradh na Gaeilge, he had close connections with Coláiste na Mumhan at Ballingeary. He was a frequent contributor to the various Gaelic journals and also published his *Annála na Tuaithe* (1905–7). He wrote three plays, 'An Sgoraíocht' (n.d.), 'Déanamh an Chleamhnais' (1926) and 'Fastuím' (1926). He died on 9 February 1955.

Ó SÉAGHDHA, Seán P. (1887–1971) Born George's Street (now Oliver Plunkett Street), Cork, the eldest child of James O'Shea, printer. On the death of the father, the family moved to London. Seán later got a job with a railway

company in Birmingham and joined Connradh na Gaeilge where he was active on the branch committee. He moved to Dublin in 1912 and, following his marriage, took up a clerical post with the Great Northern Railway Company. He then worked, in turn, as a representative and manager of the Irish Cutlery Manufacturing Company – a concern which he later purchased. He was interned in England following the Easter Rising of 1916 on the grounds that his cutlery facility had been illegally used by the Volunteers. He was president of the Dublin Industrial Development Association (1920–3) and was nominated by the Free State government as a representative on the National Agricultural Industrial Development Association (NAIDA). Following the failure of his clothing company (The Moore Clothing Co.) in the early 1930s, he was appointed as full-time secretary of NAIDA and was responsible for the initial 'Buy Irish' campaign. He also inaugurated the Dublin St Patrick's Day parade and was its organiser until the early 1960s. Following his wife's death, he married for a second time in 1948 and died at his Dundrum, Co. Dublin residence on 8 April 1971. He was buried in Dean's Grange Cemetery.

O'SHAUGHNESSY, Andrew (1866–1956) Born Coolbane Mills, Freemount, Co. Cork. He spent several years of his late teens in the United States where he absorbed some American business and manufacturing ideas. On his return, he opened a creamery at Newmarket in 1895 and added other branches to it, thereby creating a chain under the name, The Newmarket Dairy Company. In 1903, he purchased Dripsey Mills and reorganised it with specialisation in quality woollen goods. In the next few years, he added Bridgetown Flour Mills and Sallybrook Woollen Mills to his operation, while, in 1929, he bought Kilkenny Woollen Mills. In 1923, he was elected as a TD for Cork Borough, winning the fifth and last seat for the Progressive Association. He did not seek re-election in 1927. He resided in several locations in Cork and its hinterland during his long life, but latterly made his home at Dripsey Castle. He died at Nazareth Home,

Mallow, on 1 January 1956 and was buried in Ballyhea Cemetery.

O'SHEA, James (1870–1959) Born Ardgroom, Co. Cork, the son of Bartholomew O'Shea, farmer. Following some family disagreement, he converted to Protestantism and left for New York in 1889 where he found employment as an accountant. While considering entering the ministry through Columbia University, he contracted typhus and returned to Ireland in October 1893. He subsequently matriculated at TCD as a sizar and graduated BA (1897). Following a three-year period as a peripatetic preacher (in Irish and English), he was ordained in 1900 and ministered in the diocese of Ferns. He moved to the diocese of Tuam in 1902 when he became rector of Letterfrack. On 15 June 1919, he was one of the first persons to reach the landing place of the flyers, Alcock and Brown, who had flown across the Atlantic Ocean in their converted bomber. He subsequently ministered in Burrisholme and Newport. He died at his residence in Phibsboro, Dublin, on 7 August 1959. He was a member of Connradh na Gaeilge in its early days and wrote many articles in the various journals and newspapers. He had his own column in the *Church of Ireland Gazette* for almost fifty years. His publications include *Kerry Pie and Other Indigestibles* (1902), *Scríbhinní Naoimh Phádraig* (1932) and a play, 'Fé'n Sceich Sídhe' (1936). He also translated many prayers into Irish. [Diary extracts in the *Church of Ireland Gazette* (January-July, 1952); Selection of poems in C. Ó Coigligh (ed.), *Cuisle na hÉigse* (1986)]

O'SHEA, Timothy P. (1902–1979) Born Carrigaphooka, Clondrohid, Co. Cork, the second youngest of eleven children of Timothy O'Shea, farmer. He was educated at Carrigadrohid NS and at Rochestown College. He entered the Capuchin novitiate at Kilkenny in 1920 and later studied at UCC where he graduated BA. He was ordained priest at Holy Trinity Church, Cork, in June 1928. In 1931, he commenced his missionary work in southern Africa and in the following year, he and two other Capuchin priests established a mission in Western Province, Rhodesia (now Zambia) – the first Roman Catholic missionaries in the region. He established schools and helped to promote secondary education for girls in Zambia. On his return to Ireland in September 1950, he was consecrated bishop in Dublin and appointed vicar apostolic of Livingstone when he returned to Africa. In 1959, he became the first bishop of Livingstone when a diocese was established there. He retired in 1974 and spent his final years in Lukulu where he had established his first mission station. He died on 26 May 1979 and was buried there.

Ó SÍOCHÁIN, Pádraig Augustine (1905–1995) Born Cork, the son of **Daniel D. Sheehan**, MP and barrister. He was educated at Rochestown College, Farranferris College, University of London and at UCD. He began work as a journalist with the *Irish Times* (1925–31), the *Irish Press* (1931–2) and as editor of the *Garda Review*. In 1936, he was called to the Bar and later was promoted to SC. He was the author of *Criminal Law of Ireland* (1940, 5th ed. 1966) and of *Law of Evidence in Ireland* (1953), both of which were translated into Gaelic. He also published *Aran: islands of legend* (1962). He was the founder of the National Language Revival Movement. He died at his Dublin residence on 19 December 1995 and was buried in Cruagh Cemetery, Rathfarnham.

Ó SÍOCHÁIN, Seán F. (1914–1997) Born Kilnamartra, Macroom, Co. Cork, the son of Daniel Sheehan, shopkeeper. He was educated at St Patrick's College of Education where he qualified as a primary teacher in 1935. A fine Gaelic footballer, he played for both Cork and Munster. He became assistant to the general secretary of the GAA, **Pádraig Ó Caoimh**, in 1946 and worked at this post until his appointment as general secretary in 1964. He retired in 1979, but was active in the fund-raising effort for the 'new' Croke Park until 1982. He was a prominent member of the Dublin Grand Opera

Society and sang the bass part of Mozart's *Magic Flute* in Dublin with the great New Zealand mezzo-soprano, Joan Hammond, in 1943. He was also regularly featured on Radio Éireann and toured America. He died at his Clontarf, Dublin, residence on 2 February 1997 and was buried in Fingal Cemetery.

Ó SUILLEABHÁIN, Diarmaid (1932–1985) Born Eyeries, Co. Cork, the son of John O'Sullivan. Having qualified as a primary teacher, he spent his teaching career in Co. Wexford where he wrote the novels which established his reputation. In these novels, the themes of historical nationalism, existentialism, and social economics are deeply explored. His publications included *Súil le Muir* (1959), *Dianmhuilte Dé* (1964), *Caoin Tú Féin* (1967), *Maeldún* (1972), *Ciontach* (1983), *Aistear* (1983), *Saighdúir gan Claoimh* (1985), *An Uain Bheo* (posthumously, 1988) and *Bealach Bó Finne* (posthumously, 1988). He died on 5 June 1985.

Ó SÚILLEABHÁIN, Proinsias (1889–1956) Born Adrigole, Co. Cork, the son of Eugene O'Sullivan. He qualified as a primary school-teacher *c.*1910 and worked in Dublin and Glin (Co. Limerick) before leaving for Germany in 1920. He studied at Freiburg University where he graduated PhD. He returned to Ireland in 1925 and was appointed as a primary schools inspector. A member of Connradh na Gaeilge since his early student days, he wrote many books for schoolchildren including *Scéal na hÉireann i gcomhair Páistí Scoile* (1922), *Beidh Rinnce Againn* (1923), *Seanchaíocht, Prós, agus Filíocht* (1924), *An Circín Rua* (1924), *Scéilíní I gcomhair na bPáistí* (n.d.), *150 de Dhánta Gaeilge* (1936), and *Stair na hÉireann ó Aimsir N. Pádraig go dtí an Lá Inniu* (1938). In 1934, he founded the Schools Drama Association (Cumann Drámaíochta na Scol) and later published *An Lámhleabhar Drámaíochta* (1936). He was appointed as chief inspector of Vocational Schools in 1943 and was called to the Bar in 1949. He was also president of the Irish-German Society and after World War II, was active in the welfare of orphaned and displaced German children. He died at his Rathgar, Dublin, residence on 27 February 1956 and was buried in Glasnevin Cemetery.

Ó SÚILLEABHÁIN, Tadhg (*c.*1715–1795) Born Tournafulla, Kileedy, Co. Limerick. Around 1740, 'Tadhg Gaelach' travelled to County Cork where he spent the following thirty years mainly in the east of the county, but especially in the 'Barony' area south of the Midleton–Youghal road. He was renowned for the high quality of his Gaelic poetry, but his religious compositions were best remembered and were posthumously published as *Timothy O'Sullivan's Pious Miscellany* in 1802. While in Cork, he was acquainted with Bishop **Richard Walsh** of Cork and Bishop **John O'Brien** of Cloyne. Around 1769 he moved, firstly to Dungarvan and then on to Waterford City. It is held that he died at the 'Big Chapel' Waterford, on 22 April 1795. He was buried in Ballylaneen Graveyard, near Bunmahon, Co. Waterford. [Life by **R. Ó Foghludha** (1929)]

O'SULLIVAN, Cornelius (1841–1907) Born Bandon, Co. Cork, the son of James O'Sullivan, a merchant. In 1862, he won a scholarship to the Royal School of Mines, London, where he developed an interest in chemistry which resulted, in 1865, in a teaching position at the Royal College of Chemistry, London. However, he left the college in the following year to take up the position of assistant brewer and chemist at Bass & Co. of Burton-on-Trent. He later became head of the scientific and analytic staff at the brewery. His researches into the nature of maltose led to his lucrative patenting of dextrin-maltose relative to the brewing process. His series of papers on brewing technology was published by the Chemical Society between 1872 and 1896. He was elected a fellow of the Chemical Society in 1876 and of the Royal Society in 1885. He died at Burton-on-Trent on 8 January 1907 and was buried in Ballymodan Cemetery, Bandon. His brother, James O'Sullivan (1856–1939), succeeded him as chief chemist and head brewer at Bass & Co. [Life by H.D. O'Sullivan (1910)]

O'SULLIVAN, Daniel J. (b. 1906) Born Castletownbere, Co. Cork, the son and grandson of lighthouse keepers. His father was killed in an accident on the Bull Rock when Daniel was only a boy. He and his brothers, Eugene and Hugh, followed their father's vocation. Throughout his career, he had a great interest in naturalist pursuits and in writing. For twenty years, he wrote the 'Land and Water' column in the *Irish Press* and also published a poetry collection, entitled, *Lighthouse Keeper's Lyrics* (1947). He later became Principal Keeper at Inishtrahull Island, Co. Donegal.

O'SULLIVAN, Denis John (1918–1987) Born Millstreet, Co. Cork. He was active in the Fine Gael Party from an early age. In 1948, he was a candidate for a Dáil seat in North Cork, but lost by only 300 votes. However, he was successful in the same constituency in 1951 and served for ten years before being returned in 1961 for the Mid-Cork constituency. He was defeated in 1965 and served in the Senate until 1969. Previously, he had been parliamentary secretary to the Taoiseach and Minister for Defence (1954–7). In 1972, he unsuccessfully contested the Mid-Cork by-election which had been caused by the death of **Patrick Forde**. He was a member of Cork County Council for the Bandon Electoral Area (1960–85) and was elected as chairman of that body in 1970. 'Dinny Owen' died at the Bon Secours Hospital, Cork, on 21 July 1987 and was buried in Bandon.

O'SULLIVAN, Gerald R. [VC] (1888–1915) Born Frankfield, Douglas, Cork, the son of Lt. Col. George L. O'Sullivan of the 91st Argyll & Sutherland Highlanders. He was gazetted to a commission in the 1st Battalion, Inniskilling Fusiliers, in May 1909. He served in China and India and was promoted to the rank of lieutenant in March 1913 and captain in February 1915. He was awarded the Victoria Cross for conspicious bravery on two occasions at

Gallipoli in June/July 1915. He was killed while leading his men in the attack on Hill 70 at Suvla Bay on 21 August 1915. His body was not recovered.

O'SULLIVAN, Gearóid (1891–1948) Born Coolnagarrane, Skibbereen, Co. Cork, the son of Michael O'Sullivan, farmer. He graduated in Celtic Studies (1913) and also took an MA degree (1915) at UCD. He joined the Irish National Volunteers and fought in the GPO during the Easter Rising of 1916, following which he was interned in England. He later became adjutant–general of the IRA during the War of Independence. He was appointed as adjutant general on the Free State army but was forced to resign in 1924 as a result of the 'Army Mutiny'. However, his character was later vindicated. He served as a Cumann na nGael TD for Carlow/Kilkenny (1921–3) and Dublin County (1927–37). He was called to the Bar in 1926 and was appointed as Judge Advocate General in 1927. He died at his Dartry, Dublin, residence on 26 March 1948 and was buried in Glasnevin Cemetery. [Memorial plaque in Town Hall, Skibbereen]

O'SULLIVAN, Gerry (1936–1994) Born Cork. He was educated at Sullivan's Quay CBS. He was employed as a security officer at Dunlop's and was a section representative of the ITGWU (now SIPTU). He was elected as a Labour Party member of Cork Corporation in 1979 and served until his ministerial appointment in 1993. He also served as lord mayor of Cork (1986/1987). Having unsuccessfully stood in the general election of 1987, he was returned as a Labour TD for Cork North Central in 1989 and 1992. In January 1993, he was appointed minister of state at the Department of the Marine. Following a long illness, he died at his Gurranebraher residence on 5 August 1994 and was buried in St Finbarr's Cemetery.

O'SULLIVAN, Jeremiah (1842–1896) Born Kanturk, Co. Cork, the son of John O'Sullivan. He went to the US in 1863 and studied at seminaries in Maryland. He was ordained at Baltimore in 1868 and worked there until 1885 when he was consecrated as fourth bishop of Mobile, Alabama, in September of that year. He died in Mobile on 10 August 1896, and was buried there.

O'SULLIVAN, John (1878–1948) Born Cork. On the death of his father, he was brought as a boy to Rouen by his mother and was sent to be educated at the Lycée Corneille there. He sang as a leading boy treble in the choir of Rouen Cathedral. He made his operatic debut in Toulouse in 1911 as Romeo in Gounod's opera, *Roméo et Juliette*. Following a success as Raoul in Meyerbeer's *Les Huguenots* in July 1914, he was contracted to the Paris Opera until 1933. He subsequently performed major operatic roles at La Scala, Milan; at the Arena de Verona, at Covent Garden and at the Theatre Royal, Dublin. He found an enthusiastic but controversial patron and promoter in the writer, James Joyce (1882–1941), when the latter lived in Paris. In a 1954 interview, the writer and playwright, Samuel Beckett (1906–89), recalled that, while a teacher in Paris in 1929, he was one of a party which accompanied Joyce to hear O'Sullivan sing. During the performance, Joyce called out in a loud voice, 'Up Cork!' O'Sullivan retired from the stage in 1938 and died in Paris on 9 February 1948.

O'SULLIVAN, John L. (1901–1990) Born Carrigroe, Clonakilty, Co. Cork, the son of John O'Sullivan, farmer. He was educated at Lisavaird NS. He joined the Volunteers in 1919 and was Captain of 'L' company, 2nd batt., 3rd Cork Brigade. He was arrested in 1920 and spent the last ten months of the War of Independence in Portlaoise and Spike Island prisons. During the civil war, he took the pro-Treaty side and served as a captain in the Free State army to 1925. In 1932, he became actively involved in the Army Comrades Association and continued his association with the its members during the Blueshirt period. He was imprisoned at Arbour Hill in 1933 for cattle

seizing and was detained until 1937. An unsuccessful Dáil candidate for Cumann na nGaedheal in West Cork in 1937, he was again unsuccessful in 1951, 1954, 1961 and 1965 before winning a Fine Gael seat in the general election of 1969. He lost this seat in the 1977 general election. He was a member of Seanad Éireann (1954–61) and of Cork County Council (1950–90). He served as Chairman of Cork County Council (1972–3) and in 1969, was the first Munsterman to be elected as chairman of the Fine Gael Parliamentary Party. He died at the Mercy Hospital, Cork, on 28 February 1990 and was buried in Rathbarry Cemetery.

O'SULLIVAN, Michael J. (1794–1845) Born Cork, the son of Daniel O'Sullivan, draper. He was educated at Maginn's Academy where a fellow-pupil was **William Maginn**, the son of the propreitor. He was called to the Bar in 1817 and in the following year was editor of the *Freeman's Journal* and the *Theatrical Observer*. At this time, he was also a contributor to *Frasier's Literary Chronicle* and was poet laureate to the Grand Lodge of Freemasons of Ireland. His poetic collections include *The Prince of the Lake* (1815) and *A Fasciculus of Lyric Verses* (1846). A collection of his songs was published in Cork under the title of *Harmonica* in 1818. He also wrote several plays and operas including, 'The Corsair' (1814), 'Lalla Rookh' (1815) and 'The Maid of Milan'. He had an interest in the theory of education and published *The Art of Learning* which was based on the work of the Swiss educationalist, J.H. Pestalozzi (1746–1827). He died of consumption in 1845.

O'SULLIVAN, Richard (c.1840–1880) Born Bantry, Co. Cork, the son of Daniel Sullivan, and brother of **A.M. Sullivan**. He was educated at St Xavier's College, Dublin, and at the Catholic University where he graduated BA (1862). He worked as a journalist in Dublin but ill health forced him to emigrate to Sydney, Australia, in 1865. He quickly became editor and part-proprietor of the *Freeman's Journal*, the organ of Irish Roman Catholic nationalism in

New South Wales. His anti-English and pro-Fenian editorials made him many enemies. With the attempted assassination of the duke of Edinburgh in March 1868, the premier of New South Wales, Sir **James Martin**, immediately added clauses to the British Treason Felony Act – many of which were directly aimed at O'Sullivan, but ultimately of no avail. In the following year, he was fired from the newspaper by his co-proprietors because of his support for the Fenian prisoners in Western Australia. He moved to San Francisco where he worked as editor of the Irish *Catholic Monitor* and was admitted to the Bar there. He died of pneumonia on 15/16 January 1880.

O'SULLIVAN, Richard (1888–1963) Born Maryville, Friar's Walk, Cork, the son of Richard O'Sullivan, ship's engineer. He was educated at North Monastery CBS and, in 1906, he passed the examination for the executive grade of the civil service. He was posted to the revenue and audit Department of the Treasury in London. Supplementing his income as the London Correspondent of the *Cork Examiner*, he studied at London University and was called to the English Bar in 1914. On the outbreak of World War I, he was commissioned in the Royal Artillery and served throughout the war. Retaining his Cork links, he stood in the 1918 general election as a nationalist candidate for Cork City and polled respectably. He then resumed his legal career in London and was called to the Inner Bar in 1934. He was appointed as Recorder of Derby in 1938 and, in the following year, was prosecuting counsel in the IRA Coventry bombing trial. He was appointed as lecturer in Common Law at London University from 1946. In 1928, he had founded the Thomas More Society (an association of Roman Catholic lawyers) and played a significant role in More's canonisation. He was the author of several books on common law and translator of two volumes by French author, Jacques Maritain. His collection of essays, *The Spirit of the Common Law*, was published posthumously. He died on his 75th birthday, 18 February 1963.

O'SULLIVAN, Timothy T. (1899–1971) Born Bantry, Co. Cork, the son of Daniel O'Sullivan. He joined the Irish Volunteers in 1914 and was an active participant in the IRA following the 1916 Rising. By 1922, he was the O/C of Cork No.5 Brigade, and had participated in the major engagements in West Cork. He was a member of Cork County Council (1928–55), and sat as a Fianna Fáil TD for West Cork (1937–54). He was subsequently a member of Seanad Éireann (1954–69). He lived in Ardgroom until 1928, before moving to Cork City. He died at the Mercy Hospital, Cork, on 3 March 1971 and was buried in Douglas Cemetery. He was the father of Donal O'Sullivan, a prominent Cork GAA administrator.

O'SULLIVAN, William (1907–c.2000) Born Tracton, Co. Cork, the son of John O'Sullivan. He was educated at Farranferris College (1920–4), De la Salle, Mallow and Waterford (1924–7) and at UCC (1928–31). He worked as a teacher from 1928 until 1939 before being appointed to a position in the Art and Industrial Division of the National Museum where he stayed until 1952. Following a period as secretary to the Arts Council, he returned as keeper to his old job at the National Museum in 1957 until his appointment by the Royal Irish Academy as secretary to the New History of Ireland Project in 1968. He was the author of *The Economic History of Cork City from the Earliest Times* (1937), and *The Earliest Irish Coinage* (reprin. 1969). He died c.2000.

O'SULLIVAN, William (1921–2000) Born Main Street, Bantry, Co. Cork, the son of W.H. O'Sullivan, JP, coal and general merchant. He was educated at Mungret College, at University College, London and at TCD where he graduated during World War II. He was appointed as keeper of the manuscripts at TCD where he gained a great reputation through his reorganisation of his department and through his assistance to countless students and researchers. He was also a member of the Royal Irish Academy. He died at the Blackrock Clinic on 21 December 2000 and was buried in Dean's Grange Cemetery, Dublin. [Festschrift by T. Barnard, K. Simms and D. Ó Cróinín (eds) (1998)]

O'SULLIVAN BEARE, Dónal (1560–1618)
Born Dunboy Castle, Co. Cork, the only son of Dónal O'Sullivan (1537–63), Lord of Beare and Bantry. He was educated in Waterford where he learnt English and Latin. On his father's death, the titles of Lord of Beare and Bantry went (under Irish law) to his uncle, Owen O'Sullivan (d. 1594). In 1587, he challenged his uncle's succession rights and following a court case which lasted for two years, was granted the larger portion of his late father's lands. He took no part in the Desmond Rebellion, but entered the Nine Years War in September 1601 when a Spanish force landed in Kinsale. A large Ulster force under Hugh O'Neill (c.1550–1616), earl of Tyrone, marched southwards to join them. On Christmas Eve, the surrounded English force broke through the Irish lines and inflicted heavy casualties. O'Sullivan Beare retreated westwards to Dunboy Castle. This castle eventually fell on 18 June 1602 but he had previously left to meet an expected Spanish force at Ardrea on Kenmare Bay. On New Year's Eve, he set off from Glengarriff with a thousand followers to avoid an oncoming English force. Fifteen days later, he obtained refuge from Brian O'Rourke

at Leitrim Castle. Only thirty-five of his followers remained due to the severity of the weather and the march itself. He fled to Spain where he was well received by King Philip III (1578–1621) and granted a pension. In 1617, Philip granted him the title of Count of Berehaven. He was stabbed in the throat in Madrid on 16 July 1618 by John Bathe, an Anglo-Irish refugee. He had been attempting to stop a duel between his cousin, **Philip O'Sullivan Beare** and Bathe. Bathe eventually settled in London where he was granted a pension of £500 a year by King James I (1566–1625).

O'SULLIVAN BEARE, Philip (c.1590–c.1634)
Born Beara, Co. Cork. Following the destruction of Dunboy Castle and a retreating march to County Leitrim in 1602, he left for Spain with his cousin, **Dónal O'Sullivan Beare**, who was later assassinated in Madrid by an English agent. He was educated at St James' College, Compostella, and served for a time in the Spanish Navy. He later became a staunch Counter-Reformation propagandist for the Irish/Catholic cause against English historians and Anglo-Irish ecclesiastics. He was last heard of in Portugal in the 1630s. His publications included *Historiae Catholicae Iberniae Compendium* (1621), *Vindiciae Hiberniae Contra Giraldum Cambrensem et alios …* (1626), and *Patritiana Decas* (1629).

P

PAIN, George R. (1792/3–1838) Born Isleworth, Middlesex, the son of James Pain, builder and surveyor, and grandson of William Pain, architect. He and his brother, James (1779/80–1877), were apprenticed to the celebrated architect and town planner, John Nash (1752–1835). Around 1817, the brothers came to Ireland to work on Viscount Gort's Lough Cutra Castle in Co. Galway, which had been designed by Nash. George subsequently settled in Cork, while James opted for Limerick. James was appointed as Munster architect to the Board of First Fruits and was responsible for designing numerous churches, mainly in the Gothic revival style. Cork buildings with which one or both brothers were involved include The County Club, St Patrick's Church, Cork Courthouse, Holy Trinity Church and Monastery, Blackrock Castle, Cork County Gaol, St Luke's Church, the Mathew Tower, Castlehyde Church, Mitchelstown Castle, and churches at Frankfield, Carrigaline, Blackrock and Fermoy. Further afield, James re-designed Dromoland Castle, Adare Manor, Strancally Castle and Castle Bernard. He also designed the tower and spire of St Carthage's Cathedral, Lismore. George died on 26 December 1838 and was buried in Shandon Graveyard, while James died in Limerick on 13 December 1877 and was buried in St Mary's Cathedral there.

PALLISER, William (1646–1727) Born in Kirkby-Wiske, Yorkshire, the son of John Palliser. He was educated at TCD where he graduated BD (1674) and DD (1679). He was consecrated as Church of Ireland bishop of Cloyne on 5 March 1693 and was subsequently raised to the archbishopric of Cashel on 26 June 1694. He died at his residence in Rathfarnham, Dublin, on 1 January 1727 and was buried in St Andrew's Church, Dublin.

PARKER, Richard D. (c.1805–1881) Born Carrigrohane House, Cork, the son of Robert Parker. An amateur who specialised in the painting of birds, he resided at Landscape House, Shanakiel, Cork. In 1843, he exhibited some of his 'birds' when the British Association for the Advancement of Science met in Cork. He also exhibited at the National Arts Exhibition which was held in Cork in 1852. His collection of 170 pictures, including c.260 birds, is now in the Ulster Museum. He died at his residence on 15 April 1881.

PARKS, Edward (c.1773–d. p.1828) A Cork artist and a member of the Dublin Society of Artists, he exhibited in Dublin (1812 and 1813) and Cork (1815). He specialised in portraiture and especially in Shakespearean subjects. He was living in Cork in 1828.

PARNELL, Charles Stewart (1846–1891) Born Avondale, Co. Wicklow, the son of a landlord of nationalist sympathies. He was educated in England and at Magdalen College, Cambridge, but did not take a degree. He was elected as MP for Meath in 1875 and joined the Home Rule League which had been founded by **Isaac Butt** in 1873. In 1879, he took over the party on the death of Butt and in the same year he joined forces with Michael Davitt's Land League to agitate for landlord/tenant reform. He was elected as MP for Cork in 1880 and served until his death in 1891. In the meantime, he led the Irish Party at Westminster to unprecedented heights in gaining the Land Act of 1881 and in bringing the Irish Home Rule issue to the forefront of British politics. However, the 1899 divorce petition of Captain William O'Shea, by whose wife, Katherine, Parnell had three children, led to a split in the Irish Party and the effective end of his political career. He died in

Brighton on 6 October 1891, only five months after his marriage to Mrs O'Shea. He was buried in Glasnevin Cemetery, Dublin. [Life by R.B. O'Brien (2 vols, 1898), K. O'Shea [Parnell] (2 vols, 1914), W. O'Brien (1926), C.C. O'Brien (1957), R.F. Foster (1976), P. Bew (1980); Memoirs by **T.P. O'Connor** (1891), J.H. Parnell (1916), and by E. Byrne (ed. by F. Callanan, 1981)]

PARR, Richard (1617–1691) Born Fermoy, Co. Cork, the son of Richard Parr, a clergyman. He was educated at Exeter College, Oxford, where he graduated BA (1639), MA (1642) and DD (1660). Following his ordination, he met with the archbishop of Armagh, James Ussher (1581–1656), at Exeter College in 1643 and was appointed as chaplain to the archbishop. During the Commonwealth, he took up the post of vicar of Camberwell, Surrey, in 1653. He later declined both the deanery of Armagh and an Irish bishopric. A very able preacher, he also wrote *The Life of Ussher* (1686) and *Christian Reformation* (1660). The latter work was addressed to his 'dear kindred and countrymen of County Cork'. He died at Camberwell on 2 November 1691 and was buried there.

PAYNE, James Warren (1883–1954) Born Monkstown, Co. Cork, the son of Somers Payne, company director. He entered the service of the Munster & Leinster Bank in 1901, from which he retired in 1937. He served in World War I with the Connaught Rangers and reached the rank of captain. A member of the Royal Munster Yacht Club, he was an outstanding dinghy yachtsman. He won the international 12ft. dinghy race on the Brussels ship canal in 1924, an event then designated as a world championship. He subsequently retained his title in Cork Harbour in August 1925. For his achievements, he was made an hon. life member of the RMYC. He died at his Passage West home on 18 March 1954.

PAYNE, Robert (*fl.* 1589) Born Nottinghamshire, but lived for a while at Poyne's End, Co.

Cork. He had an interest in agriculture and published in 1583 his *Hillman's Table* ('which sheweth how to make Ponds to continue Water in high and drie Grounde, of what Nature soeuer') and his *Vale-man's Table* ('shewing how to drain Moores and all other wett Groundes, and to lay them drie for euer. Also how to measure any roufe Grounde, Wood, or Water, that you cannot come into'). He was sent to Munster by his neighbours at the time of the Munster Plantation to ascertain the risks involved in settling there. As a result of his observations, he published in 1589 *A Brief Description of Ireland, unto XXV (i.e. 25) of his Partners, for whom he is Undertaker there.* His report was favourable, but it seems that the syndicate did not act on his recommendations. [His *Description* – edited by A. Smith (1841)]

PAYNE-TOWNSHEND, Charlotte Frances ['Mrs G.B.S.'] (1857–1943) Born at Derry, Rosscarbery, Co. Cork, the eldest child of Horace Townshend (he changed his surname by royal licence in 1863), a substantial landowner. She was educated privately and accompanied her mother on trips to London and the Continent. The death of her mother in 1891, six years after her father's death, left her a wealthy woman. She was independent-minded and had attitudes and sympathies at variance with her social background. Establishing a residence in London, she became friendly with Sidney (1859–1947)and Beatrice Webb (1858–1943) and joined the Fabian Society, through which she met the playwright, George Bernard Shaw (1856–1950), in 1896. In June 1898, she and GBS were married in Henrietta St Registry Office, London. Theirs was a marriage of companionship rather than compatibility, either sexual or intellectual and it is believed that the marriage was unconsummated. She translated plays by the French dramatist, Eugene Brieux (1858–1932), acted as Shaw's secretary, had her *Selected Passages* from Shaw's works published and had a close friendship with T.E. Lawrence (1885–1930). In her final years, she suffered from bone disease and was tenderly cared for by Shaw. She died on

12 September 1943. She was cremated and following Shaw's death and cremation in 1950, their ashes were mixed and the joint remains scattered on the flower beds at Ayot St Lawrence, their country home since 1906. [Life by J. Dunbar (1963)]

PEARSON, Charles Yelverton (1857–1947) Born Kilworth, Co. Cork, the son of William W. Pearson, medical doctor. He spent his youth at Carrigaline, where his father was the dispensary doctor. He was educated at the Model Schools, Cork and at Perrott's School, Cork. In 1874, he entered Queen's College, Cork (now UCC) and graduated MD, M.Ch (1878) after a distinguished student career. On graduation, he became a senior demonstrator in Anatomy (1878–1884). He was appointed as professor of Materia Medica and lecturer in Medical Jurisprudence in 1884 and retained this position until 1898 when he was appointed as professor of Surgery. He retired in 1928. In the meantime, he had also been surgeon to the North Infirmary and Victoria Hospitals. In the 1880s, he was medico-legal advisor to the Crown in criminal cases and conducted both the post-mortem and analysis in the 'Coachford Poisoning Case' which resulted in the conviction and execution of Dr **Philip Cross**. He published an account of this case in the medical press. He died at his residence, Knockrea Park, Douglas Road, on 13 May 1947 and was buried privately.

PENDER, Seamus (1906–1990) Born Waterford, the eldest child of William Pender. He was educated at Mount Sion, Waterford and at UCC where he graduated BA (1927). He undertook further studies in Berlin. From 1932 to 1937, he was an assistant librarian at the Royal Irish Academy until his appointment as lecturer in history through Irish at UCC in the same year. He occupied the (newly-created) professorship of Irish History at UCC from 1955 to his retirement in June 1971. He was also dean of the Faculty of Arts (1958–70). A member of the Irish Manuscripts Commission, he edited for publication, *A 'Census' of Ireland c.1659* (1939),

The Council Books of the Corporation of Waterford 1662–1700 (1964) and three significant contributions to *Analecta Hibernica*. He was long connected with the Cork Historical & Archaeological Society of which he was president (1953–5) and to whose journal he contributed a seventeen-part study of the municipal documents of Waterford City, and also a preliminary report on Fenian documents in the Catholic University of America. He edited the festschrift in honour of **Tadhg Ó Donnchadha**, *Féilscríbhinn Thórna* (1947). He died at the Bon Secours Hospital, Cork, on 14 November 1990 and was buried in St Finbarr's Cemetery.

PENN, William (1644–1718) Born London, the son of Sir William Penn (1621–1670), the naval commander who was granted the castle and manor of Macroom in 1654 but who had to exchange these for lands at Shanagarry in East Cork. He entered Christ Church, Oxford, in 1660 but was sent down in the following year owing to his non-conformist views. Following periods in Paris and Turin, he travelled to Dublin in 1665 where he found favour with the lord lieutenant, James Butler, Duke of Ormonde (1610–88). He was appointed as victualler to the naval squad at Kinsale and resided at his father's seat at Shanagarry. In 1667, he attended a Quaker meeting in Cork to hear his friend, Thomas Loe, preach and was converted. A subsequent meeting on 3 September was broken up by soldiers and, as a result, he spent a month in prison – the first of many subsequent incarcerations. He paid further visits to County Cork in 1669 and 1690. In March 1681, he received the royal charter to establish the Quaker colony of Pennsylvania. He died on 30 July 1718 and was buried in the Quaker burial ground near Chalfont St Giles, Buckinghamshire.

PENROSE, Cooper (1736–1815) Born Waterford, the son of a Quaker, John Penrose. He married Elizabeth Dennis, whose father was a partner in a Cork timber business. He became very wealthy through his property investments and built a fine residence at Woodhill, which was designed by his architect cousin, Michael Penrose. As a patron of the arts, he helped many artists and painters, including **Daniel Maclise**, with their careers. Following the execution of Robert Emmet in 1803, Penrose's house provided a refuge for **Sarah Curran**. He was disowned by Cork Quakers in 1786 for having been at a horse race, for owning a billiard table and for keeping a musical instrument. He died in 1815.

PENROSE, Mary E. (d. 1942) Born Kinsale, Co. Cork, the daughter of Henry Lewis. She was educated at Rochelle School, Cork, and at TCD where she graduated BA in German and English Literature. In 1889, she married Harry Hugh Penrose (of the Penrose-Welsted family of Ballywalter and Shandangan) and it was under the name Mrs H.H. Penrose that she later became a prolific novelist while residing in Surrey. She was the author of twelve novels published between 1905 and 1915, with three of them having an Irish setting – *Denis Trench* (1911), *A Faery Land Forlorn* (1912) and *Burnt Flax* (1914). She also contributed stories to various periodicals such as *Temple Bar* and *The Windsor*. She died on 23 August 1942.

PERCEVAL, Sir John (1683–1748) Born at Burton, Churchtown, Co. Cork, the son of Sir John Perceval who owned large estates in North Cork. Both parents died while he was still a child and he was sent in 1698 by his guardian, Sir Robert Southwell, to Westminster School. He entered Magdalen College, Oxford, in late 1699, but left in 1701 without taking a degree though he was elected as a fellow of the Royal Society in the following year. He was MP for County Cork (1703 and 1713) and for Harwich (1727). He was also was a member of the Irish Privy Council (1704 and 1714). He was created Baron Perceval of Burton (1715), Viscount Perceval of Kanturk (1723) and 1st earl of Egmont (1733). He took a great interest in the colonisation of Georgia and was a friend and patron of the philosopher/bishop, **George Berkeley**. He died in London on 1 May 1748

and was buried at Erwarton, Suffolk. [Portrait by G. Kneller; Diaries in the *7th Report of the Historical Manuscripts Commission*]

PERDUE, Richard G. (b. 1910) He was the son of Richard Perdue. He was educated at TCD where he graduated BA (1931), MA (1938) and DD (1938). Following his ordination in 1934, he served in various posts in the dioceses of Dublin, Kildare and Killaloe. He was consecrated bishop of Killaloe on 19 February 1957. He was translated to the united diocese of Cork, Cloyne and Ross on 19 February 1957. He resigned from the episcopacy on 20 May 1978 and later settled in Timaru, New Zealand.

PERRIER, Sir Anthony (c.1770–1845) Born Dublin, the son of Anthony Perrier (1712–1772), merchant, and younger brother of **Sir David Perrier**. He became a freeman of Cork in 1792 and was the operator of the Spring Lane Distillery from 1806 – a plant which was owned by David. In 1822, he patented one of Europe's first continuous whiskey stills, but it was not a success. He served as a county magistrate for thirty-seven years and was the treasurer of the Pipe Water Company. He served as mayor of Cork in 1820/21. In 1823, he was appointed as Cork agent to the Atlas Assurance Company of London and operated from 68, South Mall. The business was continued until 1925 by his son and grandson, in turn. He was knighted by the lord lieutenant, the duke of Richmond, on his visit to Cork in 1829, when Perrier was high sheriff. He died at his South Mall residence on 24 April 1845 and was buried in St Peter's Graveyard, North Main Street. His remains were later re-interred at St Luke's, Douglas.

PERRIER, Sir David (1765–1826) Born Dublin, the son of Anthony Perrier (1712–72), merchant, and elder brother of **Sir Anthony Perrier**. With the death of his father, his mother and her eight children moved to Cork to be near her relatives. He worked as an apprentice at Burnett's Glass House Company at Hanover Street, and having been become a freeman of

Cork in 1787, he acquired, with his younger brother, George (1767–1850), the Red Abbey Sugar House and resided at Douglas House. However, the sugar plant was totally destroyed by fire on 7 December 1799. He later owned the Spring Lane Distillery, which was managed by his brother, Anthony. He served as high sheriff of Cork in 1794 and was knighted in September of the following year on the visit of the lord lieutenant. He later served as mayor of Cork (1813/14). On his death on 1 December 1826, he was buried in St Nicholas Churchyard, Cork.

PHAYRE, Robert (c.1619–1682) Born Kilshannig, Co. Cork, the son of Emanuel Phayre, the local vicar. During the Confederate Wars, he fought on the side of the English parliament and rose to the rank of lieutenant-colonel. He was taken to London as part of a prisoner exchange and there he became friendly with Oliver Cromwell (1599–1658). He was one of the three officers to whom the warrant for the execution of King Charles I (1600–49) was addressed, and was present at the execution. He returned to Ireland with Cromwell and commanding a Kentish regiment, he captured Youghal and defeated the Royalist forces under Bishop **Boetius Mac Egan** of Ross. He served as governor of Cork from 1651 until 1654 and resided both at Rostellan and at Ovens. In 1658, he married Elizabeth Herbert, the daughter of Sir Thomas Herbert (who had attended the late king at his execution), as his second wife. At the Restoration of King Charles II in 1660, he was arrested in Cork and confined in the Tower of London. He was saved from execution through the Herbert connection and through the efforts of **Donough Mac Carthy**, 1st Earl Clancarty, whose life Phayre had spared during the Confederate Wars. He returned to Ireland and became interested in a sect called the Muggletonians (founded c.1651). He died at Grange, Ovens, in September 1682, and was buried in the Baptist Cemetery, Cork.

PHILLIPS, Robert A. (1886–1945) Born Courtmacsherry, Co. Cork. Though not a professional naturalist, he became an expert on land and fresh-water molluscs and also investigated many of Ireland's fauna and flora. He combined his investigations with his job as a commercial traveller for Guys of Cork, having been with the firm since the age of fourteen years.

PIGOT, David R. (1797–1873) Born Kilworth, Co. Cork, the son of Dr John Pigot, physician, and father of **John Edward Pigot**. He was educated at TCD where he graduated BA (1819) and MA (1832). He studied medicine for a while but soon abandoned it in favour of the law. His rise was a rapid one. He was called to the Bar in 1826 and to the Inner Bar in 1835. In 1839, he was appointed as solicitor-general for Ireland and as attorney-general in the following year. He became chief baron of the Irish Exchequer in 1846. He served as a Liberal MP for Clonmel from 1839 until 1841. He died in Dublin on 22 December 1873.

PIGOT, John E. (1822–1871) Born Kilworth, Co. Cork, the eldest son of **David R. Pigot**. He was educated at TCD where he graduated BA (1843). He was called to the Bar in 1844. He was involved with the Young Ireland movement and contributed songs, articles and poems to the movement's organ, *The Nation,* under the pseudonym of 'Fermoy'. With the failure of the 1848 Rising, he acted for the leaders, John Mitchel (1815–75) and William Smith O'Brien (1803–64), in their state trials. He became a member of the Repeal Association and, in 1851, he became joint secretary of the Society for the Preservation and Publication of the Melodies of Ireland. He toured the country and amassed a collection of 2,000 tunes, which was deposited at the Royal Hibernian Academy. He emigrated to India in 1865 and established a successful legal pracrice in Bombay. He was on holiday when he died at his father's Dublin residence on 1 July 1871.

PIKE, Ebenezer (1806–1883) Born Cork, the son of a Quaker, Joseph Pike (1768–1826), banker. He was largely instrumental in the setting up of the Cork Steamship Company in

1843/44 (when the St George Company was wound up) and was involved in a ship-repair and shipbuilding yard at Hargreaves Quay where he built many iron steamers. He was also a partner in Sir Joseph Pease's shipyard at Jarrow-on-Tyne. For many years, he served on the board of Cork Harbour Commissioners and helped in Quaker relief work during the Famine. He resided at Bessborough House, Blackrock, where he died on 29 March 1883. His estate was valued at £168,000.

PIKE, Joseph (1657–1729) Born Kilcrea, Co. Cork, the son of a Quaker, Richard Pike (1627–1668), who had been in the army of Cromwell. At the age of 18 years, he entered the wool-buying business and with his brother Richard, he opened the first linen-draper's shop in Cork. He later expanded this business with the help of his wife's marriage dowry. He also went into banking, and through his friend, **William Penn**, he owned large amounts of land in Pennsylvania. He wrote a private account of the siege of Cork in 1690 and published *A Treatise concerning Baptism and the Supper* (1710).

PIKE, Mary (1776–1832) Born Cork, the daughter of Samuel Pike, banker, and niece of **Cooper Penrose**. On her father's death in 1796, the 20-year old heiress stood to inherit £20,000. However, Sir Henry Brown Hayes of Vernon Mount, Cork, who was relatively 'hard up', decided that a marriage to Miss Pike would be a very desirable arrangement. On 2 February 1797, Sir Henry dined with Cooper Penrose at Woodhill – an engagement which he used to glean information concerning Mary Pike. Shortly afterwards, Mary was kidnapped when her coach was stopped by five armed men. She was taken to Vernon Mount, where, in the presence of a priest, she was forced to go through a marriage ceremony. She eventually escaped and fled to England. Cooper Penrose offered a large reward for her abductor and on 13 April 1801, Sir Henry was brought to trial and sentenced to transportation to Botany Bay, Australia. This famous abduction incident is recalled in the song, 'Merrily kiss the Quaker'. However, Mary fell foul of the Cork Quaker community as she had testified on oath during the trial. She died in 1832, of unsound mind and with her estate of £55,000 being administered by her guardians.

PILON, Frederick (1750–1788) Born Cork. He initially studied medicine but later he opted for the theatre and also wrote for the London *Morning Post*. His first play, 'Invasion', was successfully staged at Covent Garden and was followed by many others including a farce, 'The Deaf Lover' and a comedy, 'He would be a Soldier'. He also wrote for the Drury Lane stage. He died at Lambeth on 19 January 1788 and was buried there.

PIPER, Oliver J.S. (1886–1933) Born Aberavon, Wales, the son of Oliver J.S. Piper, the owner of Passage Docks. While studying engineering at Glasgow, he showed promise as a rugby player and, on his return to Cork, he played with Cork Constitution, gaining eight Irish caps (1909–10). He was a member of the first truly representative team to tour South Africa in 1910. He was also a prominent member of Cork Harbour Rowing Club. He later resided in London where his death occurred on 22 April 1933.

POLLAND, Madeleine (1918–2005) Born Madeleine Cahill at Kinsale, Co. Cork, the daughter of a police sergeant. She was reared in Hertfordshire, England, and served in the intelligence section of the Women's Auxiliary Air Force during World War II. She married and returned to Hertfordshire where she began to write children's fiction and short stories. She later settled with her husband in Spain. Her children's stories include *Children of the Red King* (1960), *The Town Across the Water* (1961), *Beorn the Proud* (1961), *Fingal's Quest* (1961), *The White Twilight* (1962), *Chuiraquimba and the Black Robes* (1962), *City of the Golden House* (1963), *The Queen's Blessing* (1963), *Flame Over Tara* (1964), *Mission to Cathay* (1965), *Queen*

Without Crown (1965), *Deirdre* (1967), *To Tell My People* (1968), *Stranger in the Hills* (1968), *To Kill a King* (1970), *Alhambra* (1970), *A Family Affair* (1971), *Daughter to Poseidon* (1972) and *Prince of the Double Axe* (1976). She also turned to the novel and included many Irish and Spanish themes as well as topographical descriptions. Included in this genre are *Thicker then Water* (1967), *The Little Spot of Bother* (1967), *Random Army* (1969), *Package to Spain* (1971), *Double Shadow* (1977), *All Their Kingdoms* (1981), *Their Heart Speaks in Many Ways* (1982), *No Price Too High* (1984) and *As It Was in the Beginning* (1987). She died in 2005.

POLLOCK, James A. (1865–1922) Born Douglas, Cork, the son of James Wheeler Pollock, cloth manufacturer. He was educated at Manchester Grammar School and at Queen's College, Cork (now UCC) where he graduated BE in 1884. In the following year, he emigrated to Sydney, Australia. He studied mathematics and physics at the University of Sydney and graduated B.Sc. in 1890. He was appointed as professor of Physics there in 1899 and was awarded a D.Sc. in 1909 for his work on Hertzian Waves. He was elected a fellow of the Royal Society in 1916. In that year, he enlisted in the Australian Imperial Force and was attached to the 177th Tunnelling Company of the Royal Engineers with responsibility for the Mining School at Poperinghe, Belgium. He directed the mining operation which, undetected, was responsible for the destruction of the German fortifications at the Messines and Wytschaete Ridges on 7 June 1917. Ten days before the end of the war, he was promoted to the rank of major and returned to Sydney in April 1919. He resumed his university duties and died, unmarried, in Sydney on 24 May 1922.

PONCE, John (1603–1670) Born Cork, by the name of John Punch. In his publications, he used the Latin name of 'Pontius' which was re-translated as 'Ponce'. He entered the Franciscan Order at Louvain and studied there and at Cologne. He became a professor at St Isidore's, Rome, and rector of the Irish College there. He collaborated with Rev. Luke Wadding in preparing an edition of the works of the Irish medieval philosopher, John Duns Scotus (d. 1308). He wrote both on theological topics and on Irish social problems. His publications include *Philosophiae cursus integer* (1656 and 1672), *Deplorabilis populi Hibernici ... status* (1651), *Cursus theologicus* (1652), *Judicum doctrinae Augustini et Thomae* (1657), *Scotus Hiberniae restitutus* (1660) and *Commentarii theologici* (1661). [Portrait at St Isidore's College, Rome]

PONSONBY, George (1773–1863) Born Bishop's Court, Co. Kildare, the son of William Brabazon Ponsonby, 1st Baron Ponsonby. He was educated at TCD where he graduated BA (1794). He served as MP for Lismore (1797–1806), Cork County (1806–12). Defeated for Cork County in 1812, he was subsequently elected as MP for Youghal (1826–32). He was also a lord of the Irish Treasury. He died in Midhurst, Sussex, on 5 June 1863.

POOLEY, John (1645–1712) Born Ipswich, England. He was educated at TCD where he graduated DD (1692). He was consecrated as Church of Ireland bishop of Cloyne on 5 December 1697. He was subsequently translated to the diocese of Raphoe (1702). While in Cloyne, he tried unsuccessfully to regain the demesne lands which had been alienated since the end of the sixteenth century. Of High-Church leanings, his claim to fame was his imprisonment by the Irish House of Lords for protesting against an 'adjournment of the House to a Church Holyday'. He died in Dublin on 16 October 1712.

POPE, Alexander (1763–1835) Born Cork, the son of a miniature-painter. He received his artistic education at the Dublin Society's drawing school in which he was enrolled in 1776. He exhibited crayon drawings and portraits at the Irish Society of Artists (1777–80). He returned to Cork in 1781 where he established a firm reputation as a portraitist. However, he opted for the theatre as his main occupation and appeared at Covent Garden in 1785. From 1801 until 1828, he appeared in hundreds of performances at Covent Garden, Drury Lane, The Haymarket and many provincial centres. Throughout his stage career, he held an unrivalled reputation as a Shakespearean actor. He also continued to paint miniatures and exhibited at the Royal Academy. In 1828, he was granted a pension of £100 a year from the Covent Garden Fund as he had fallen into financial difficulties on account of his overspending. He died at Bedford Square, London, on 22 March 1835.

POPE, Richard T.P. (1799–1859) Born Cork, the eldest son of Thomas Pope, solicitor, alderman, and mayor of Cork (1829). He was educated at Winchester School and at TCD where he graduated BA (1821) and MA (1839). He was ordained as a minister of the Church of Ireland in 1821, and six years later, he engaged with Fr. Tom Maguire in one of the most celebrated religious debates of the day. It was held in Dublin and lasted six days, the proceedings being published in several versions. He died at Kingstown (now Dún Laoghaire), Co. Dublin, on 7 February 1859.

POWER, John (1792–1849) Born Tullineaskey, Rosscarbery, Co. Cork, the son of Andrew Power, brother of **Maurice Power** (1764–1831), and first cousin of Rev. **Maurice Power** (1791–1877). He was educated in Cork and at St Patrick's College, Maynooth. Following his ordination, he served as a curate in Youghal before emigrating to New York as pastor of St Peter's Church where he remained for the rest of his life. With his brother, Dr William Power, he was active in the Irish Emigrant Society and kept in contact with his brother, Maurice, the MP. He developed into an eloquent preacher and theologian and twice served as vicar general of the New York diocese. However, despite the efforts of his friend, Bishop **John England** and others, he was unsuccessful on two occasions in achieving episcopal status. A noted controversialist, he wrote for the periodicals, *The Truth Teller* and *The United States Catholic Miscellany*. He was also editor of the *Laity's Directory* (1822) and compiler of *The New Testament by Way of Question and Answer* (1824). He produced a manual of prayers, *True Piety,* in 1832. He died in New York on 14 April 1849.

POWER, John (1820–1872) Born Belle-Vue, Youghal, Co. Cork. He qualified as a civil engineer having trained in the offices of Sir John Rennie, but he devoted more of his time to the world of letters than to engineering. He spent some years in Central America where he established and edited the *Panama Star and Herald* newspaper, but ill health obliged him to return to London in the early 1860s where he engaged in bibliographic projects. In 1865, he issued the first number of the *Irish Literary Inquirer*, but only four issues appeared. His *List of Irish Periodical Publications*, dedicated to his townsman, **Samuel Hayman**, appeared in 1866, and in 1870, he published his *Handy Book about Books*. During this period, he was working on a major project, namely, *Bibliotheca Hibernica*, but poor health hindered his progress on it. His manuscript notes became scattered after his death which occurred at St Leonard's-on-Sea, East Sussex, on 13 May 1872.

POWER, Maurice (1791–1877) Born Tullineaskey, Rosscarbery, Co. Cork, the son of Andrew Power, first cousin of **John Power** (1792–1849) and of **Maurice Power** (1811–1870). He was ordained in Paris in 1827. He acted as Administrator in Skibbereen for a year before moving to Ladysbridge as curate to Rev. **Peter O'Neill** of Ballymacoda. He was appointed as parish priest of Killeagh in 1839 and remained there until his retirement in 1876. As well as having a great interest in Gaelic literature, he translated many French sermons and composed many of his own in beautiful Irish. He died in Youghal on 26 July 1877 and was buried in Killeagh Graveyard. [Sermons by B. Ó Madagáin (1974)]

POWER, Maurice (1811–1870) Born Deelish, Skibbereen, Co. Cork, the fourth son of Andrew Power, first cousin of Rev. **John Power** (1792–1849) and of Rev. **Maurice Power** (1791–1877). Educated at Stonyhurst College, he later qualified as a medical doctor, but never practised. He married Catherine Livingston, the daughter of a Supreme Court judge, in New York in 1832. By 1839, they were living near Clonakilty where he became the first chairman of Clonakilty Town Commissioners. In 1844, they moved to Cove (now Cobh) where Power also filled the post of chairman of Cove Town Commissioners. He was chosen as a Repeal candidate for Cork County in 1847 to succeed Daniel O'Connell, the Liberator, on the latter's death. He won the by-election and was re-elected in a general election a month later. In 1852, he resigned his parliamentary seat on being appointed as Governor of St Lucia. He lived there until 1855 when he retired to Freiburg, Germany, on health grounds. The Powers returned to Cove in 1862 and purchased Ringacoltig House and estate where he died on 28 December 1870. Early in the following year, his remains were exhumed and re-interred in the family burial ground at Rosscarbery.

POWER, Michael (1911–1989) Born Douglas, Cork, the son of Joseph Power, steward of Douglas Golf Club. 'Mick' was educated at the local Douglas school and at North Monastery CBS. Though he played golf from an early age, he did not take it up seriously until he was almost thirty. His first championship success was in the South of Ireland event in 1950. He won the same tournament in 1952 when he defeated Norman Drew, later a Walker Cup and Ryder Cup player. He was runner-up in the South of Ireland on three occasions (1953, 1956 and 1957). In 1951, he took both the Irish Close Championship (by defeating the legendary Joe Carr) and the East of Ireland titles. He played most of his golf at the Muskerry club where he was captain in 1950 and whom he assisted to Irish Senior Cup victories in 1946–7 and 1953. In 1949, he reached the last eight of the Open

Amateur Championship. He played in seven series of Home Internationals for Ireland (1947–54) and had a 50% success rate. He died at Cork Regional (now University) Hospital on 14 October 1989 and was buried in St Finbarr's Cemetery.

PRIOR, Michael (1942–2004) Born Cork. On leaving school, he joined the Vincentian Order and graduated in Physics at UCD. Following his ordination, he studied Semitic Languages in Rome and gained a Licentiate in Sacred Scripture in 1972. He moved to England and, following a teaching period in Coventry, he was appointed as Lecturer in Theology and Religious Studies at Strawberry Hill, later a college of Surrey University. He gained a doctorate at King's College, University of London, in 1987 and spent a year as visiting professor at the University of Bethlehem. A fervent supporter of Palestinian rights, he constantly emphasised the fundamental difference between religious Judaism and secular Zionism – especially the latter's attitude towards the Palestinians. His writings include *Paul the Letter-writer and the Second Letter to Timothy* (1989), *Jesus the Liberator: Nazareth Liberation Theology* (1995), *The Bible and Colonialism: a moral critique* (1997) and *Zionism and the State of Israel: a moral enquiry* (1999). He died at Osterley, Middlesex on 21 July 2004.

PULLEIN, Tobias (1648–1713) Born Middleham, Yorkshire, the son of Joshua Pullein. His family was of Flemish descent. He was educated at TCD where he graduated DD (1688). He was consecrated as Church of Ireland bishop of Cloyne in November 1694. He was subsequently translated to the diocese of Dromore on 7 May 1695. He died on 22 January 1713 and was buried in the churchyard of St Peter's Church, Drogheda.

PULVERTAFT, Robert J.F. (1897–1990) Born Cork, the son of a clergyman. He was educated at Westminster School and won a scholarship to Trinity College, Cambridge. With the outbreak of World War I, he joined the Royal Flying Corps (later RAF) and saw action as a pilot in the Middle East and in France. After the war, he returned to Cambridge where he graduated in clinical medicine and took MD in Microbiology. He then worked as head of Clinical Pathology at Westminster Medical School before spending World War II as a lieutenant-colonel in the Royal Army Medical Corps in the Middle East. Here he was assistant director of Pathology, and for this work, he was awarded the OBE in 1944. On his return to Westminster Medical School, his main area of research was into melanoma. He was professor of Clinical Pathology at London University (1950–62) and was extern examiner in Pathology to many universities. He published *Studies on Malignant Disease in Nigeria by Tissue Culture* and also many other articles in medical journals. He died at Macclesfield, England, on 30 March 1990.

PUNCH, John (1603–1670) See **PONCE, John**

PURCELL, John B. (1800–1883) Born Quartertown, Mallow, Co. Cork, the son of Edmond Purcell. He emigrated to America, arriving at Baltimore in 1818 where he worked as a private tutor. With the intention of entering the priesthood, he studied in Emmitsburg, Maryland, and later at the Seminary of St Sulpice, Paris. He was ordained at Notre Dame Cathedral in May 1826 and returned to Emmitsburg Seminary where he eventually became president. In October 1833, he was consecrated as bishop of Cincinnati. He was promoted to the rank of archbishop in 1850 when Cincinnati became an archbishopric. He encouraged many orders of priests and nuns (including the Sisters of Mercy, Kinsale) to minister in his diocese and further afield during the American civil war. He was an ardent supporter of the temperance movement following a visit by Father **Theobald Mathew**. He attended the First Vatican Council where he voted against the definition of papal infallibility, but later conformed. However, in 1879 came the collapse of the 'Purcell Bank' with a deficit of four million dollars. This was a trust which had been administered by his brother, the Rev. Edward Purcell, and involved millions of dollars which had been invested in church properties on behalf of private investors before and during the civil war. Following the appointment of a coadjutor, he retired to a convent and died on 4 July 1883. [Life by M.A. McCann (1918); Biographical article by R. Forde in *The Mallow Field Journal*, 6 (1988)]

Q

QUAIN, Sir John Richard (1816–1876) Born Rathealy, Fermoy, Co. Cork, the youngest son of Richard Quain, brother of **Richard Quain** and half-brother of **Jones Quain** and cousin of **Sir Richard Quain**. He was educated at the universities of Goettingen and London [where he graduated LL.B (1839)]. He was called to the English Bar in 1851 and to the Inner Bar in 1866. He was later appointed as Attorney General of County Durham. He was knighted in 1872 and in the same year he was appointed as a judge. He died on 12 September 1876 and was buried at Finchley. [Bust (1878) by J. Woolner (1825–1892) at the Middle Temple]

QUAIN, Jones (1796–1865) Born Rathealy, Fermoy, Co. Cork, the son of Richard Quain, half-brother of **John Richard Quain** and of **Richard Quain** and cousin of **Sir Richard Quain**. He was educated at TCD where he graduated BA (1816) and MB (1820). He was appointed as professor of Anatomy (1831) and as a senator (1836) of University College, London. He published *Elements of Anatomy* (1828). He died on 31 January 1865.

QUAIN, Richard (1800–1887) Born Rathealy, Fermoy, Co. Cork, the son of Richard Quain, the brother of **John Richard Quain,** half-brother of **Jones Quain** and cousin of **Sir Richard Quain**. He was educated at Paris and London. He was elected as a member of the Royal College of Surgeons in 1828, as a fellow in 1843 and as a fellow of the Royal Society in 1844. He became president of the Royal College of Surgeons in 1834. He was also surgeon at University Hospital, London, and surgeon extraordinary to Queen Victoria. In 1844, he published *The Anatomy of the Arteries* which was illustrated by the Cork artist, Joseph Maclise – a younger brother of **Daniel Maclise**. He died on

15 September 1887 and was buried at Finchley. He had married in 1859, Ellen Brodrick, the widow of the 5th Viscount Midleton, but the marriage was childless. He left his fortune of £75,000 towards studentships in English literature and natural science at London University. [Portrait by G. Richmond; Bust (n.d.) by T. Woolner (1825–1892) at the Royal College of Surgeons, London]

QUAIN, Sir Richard (1816–1898) Born Mallow, Co. Cork, the son of John Quain and cousin of **Jones Quain, Sir John Richard Quain** and **Richard Quain**. In 1837, he entered University College, London, where he graduated MB (1840). He was elected as a fellow of the Royal Society in 1871. He became president of the General Medical Council in 1891 and was knighted in that year. He was also physician to Queen Victoria (1819–1901). He edited *A Dictionary of Medicine* (1882). He died at Harley Street, London, on 13 March 1898 and was buried at Hampstead Court. [Portrait by J. Millais at the College of Physicians, London]

QUILL, Timothy (d. 1960) Born Clondrohid, Co. Cork. He was active in the trades union movement and joined the Labour Party. He became a TD in June 1927 when he was elected for the North Cork constituency. However, he was unseated three months later and unsuccessfully contested a seat in the elections of 1937 and 1938. He served on Cork County Council for two periods (1925–34 and 1942–5) and was also a member of Cork Corporation. He had moved to the city in the 1930s to take up a post as manager and secretary of the Cork Co-operative Bakery Society. While there, he purchased a farm near Blackrock, the result of which he devoted himself full-time to farming. He became prominent in the Irish Friesian Society and served as its hon. secretary for some years. He later purchased a farm near Blarney ('Example Farm') and where he achieved distinction as a Friesian breeder. He died at 'Example Farm' on 10 June 1960 and was buried in St Finbarr's Cemetery.

QUIN, Edward (*p.*1839) Born Cork, the brother of **Simon Quin**. He became a popular local songwriter and two of his songs, 'Bobety Dawly' and 'Shandrum Boggoon', were published in **Thomas Crofton Croker**'s *Popular Songs of Ireland* (1939). He later set up as a coachbuilder in London.

QUIN, Simon (*p.*1839) Born Cork, the brother of **Edward Quin**. He was a popular local songwriter and his 'The Town of Passage is neat and spacious' was included in **Thomas Crofton Croker**'s *Popular Songs of Ireland* (1839). He later worked at his brother's coachbuilding establishment in London.

QUINLAN, John (1826–1883) Born Cloyne, Co. Cork, the son of John Quinlan. In 1844, he emigrated to the USA and was later ordained by Archbishop **John B. Purcell** for the Cincinnati diocese in August 1852. He held the position of rector of Mount St Mary of the West Seminary from 1854 until 1859. He was consecrated as second bishop of Mobile, Alabama, in December 1859. He was engaged in the infrastructural reconstruction to his diocese in the aftermath of the American civil war. He died in New Orleans on 9 March 1883 and was buried in Mobile.

QUINN, Edel (1907–1944) Born Kanturk, Co. Cork, the daughter of a bank manager. Having been unable, through illness, to join the order of Poor Clares, she took up a secretarial post in the Legion of Mary, which she had previously joined. In 1936, she volunteered for Legion work in Africa and founded many praesidia from her base in Nairobi, Kenya. She subsequently worked in Mauritius, Nyasaland and Tanganyika. In failing health, she returned to Nairobi and died on 12 May 1944. [Lives by L-J Suenens (1954) and D. Forristal (1994)]

QUIRKE, John (1911–1983) Born Milltown, Co. Kerry, but reared in Blackrock, Cork, to where the family had moved when he was only a year old. His hurling career began with Blackrock in 1928 with which he won three county senior hurling medals (1929–31). He made his inter-county debut in 1932 but had to wait until 1939 for his first All-Ireland final which was a defeat by Kilkenny (the 'thunder and lightning' final). However, he won four consecutive All-Ireland medals (1941–4) and retired in 1945 after winning a total of seven Railway Cup medals with Munster (as captain in 1945). He also won two NHL medals with Cork. He died on 24 August 1983 and was buried in St Michael's Cemetery, Blackrock.

R

RALEIGH, Sir Walter (*c.*1552–1618) Born Hayes Barton, Devonshire, of a local family. He was educated at Oxford University but did not graduate. In 1580, he came to Ireland as an army captain with Lord Deputy Grey. He fought to suppress the Desmond Rebellion and was granted large estates on the defeat of the Fitzgeralds. He was elected as mayor of Youghal in 1588. In the following year, he left for England to supervise the publication of **Edmund Spenser's**, *The Faerie Queen*. In 1602, he sold most of his Munster estates to **Richard Boyle**, 1st earl of Cork. His Youghal residence, Myrtle Grove, was that of the former warden of St Mary's Collegiate Church and, on Raleigh's departure, it was repaired and remodelled (largely as it stands today) by Sir George Carew (1555–1629), lord president of Munster. He was beheaded at the Tower of London on 29 October 1618 and was buried in St Margaret's Church, Westminster. [Portrait by A. Verrio (*c.*1590) at the National Gallery, Dublin]

RAY, R.J. (*c.*1865–*c.*1958) see **BROPHY, Robert J.**

REEVES, William (1815–1892) Born Charleville, Co. Cork, the son of Boles D'Arcy Reeves, attorney. He was educated at TCD where he graduated BA (1835) and MB (1837). Following his ordination in 1838, he served as curate of Kilconriola, Co. Antrim, from 1841 until his appointment as headmaster of the Diocesan School, Ballymena, in 1849. He was vicar of Lusk, Co. Dublin, from 1857 until his appointment as librarian at Armagh Public Library in 1861. He worked at the library until 1875 when he was appointed as dean of Armagh. He became Church of Ireland bishop of Down, Connor and Dromore in 1886. A foremost authority on antiquities and manuscript collections, he was elected as president of the Royal Irish Academy in 1891. He wrote an edition of Adamnan's *Life of Columba* (1857); *Ecclesiastical Antiquities of Down, Conor and Dromore* (1847); and *The Acts of Archbishop Colton* (1850). He died in Dublin on 12 January 1892 and was buried in Armagh. [Life by Mary C. Lady Ferguson (1893); Memorial discourse by J.E.L. Oulton (1937)]

REIDY, John W. (1918–1965) Born Macroney, Kilworth, Co. Cork, and was educated at St Colman's College, Fermoy. During World War II, he served with the American naval forces and later returned to Cork where he established a successful haulage business. He also became involved in the entertainment industry via two very popular dance halls, the 'Palm Grove' in Cork and the 'Crystal Ballroom' in Carrigaline. In 1954, he unsuccessfully contested the general election in Cork Borough as an Independent candidate and also contested the 1956 by-election caused by the death of **Pa(trick) McGrath**. However, in 1955, he was elected to Cork Corporation as an Independent and retained a seat to his death, being latterly the senior alderman on the Corporation. A witty and colourful character, he campaigned under the slogan 'The needy need Reidy and Reidy needs your votes'. His principal issue was 'housing for the people' and he was well known to city centre shop staff, whose political support he canvassed by advising them on the best housing opportunities. He died at his residence, Temple Villa, Beaumont Park, Ballintemple on 21 February 1965 at the early age of 47. He had not been in the best of health prior to his death. He was buried at St Finbarr's Cemetery.

REILLY, Joseph (1889–1965) Born Dublin, the son of J. Reilly of Granard, Co. Longford. He was educated at St Mary's College, Dublin, at

UCD and at the universities of Cambridge, Geneva and Berlin. He worked as chemist-in-charge at the Royal Navy cordite factory, Dorset (1915–21) and as head of branch of the research department at Woolwich Arsenal, London (1921–4). In 1925, he was appointed as assistant state chemist, Dublin, but later in the same year, he was appointed as professor of Chemistry at UCC and held this position until his retirement in 1960. He was a member of most of the prestigious chemistry societies and was a Boyle Medallist of the Royal Dublin Society. He was also a keen student of local history and was editor and publisher of the *Blarney Magazine* (1948–64) under the imprint of the Woodland Press (he resided for many years at 'Woodlands', St Ann's Hill, Blarney). He died at his Bishopstown Avenue residence on 18 September 1965.

RENOUF, Louis P.W. (b. 1887) Born Lewisham, England, the son of Sir Peter le Page Renouf. He was educated in Birmingham and at Trinity College, Cambridge, where he graduated BA and Dip. in Agriculture. He worked as a demonstrator at Cambridge and as a lecturer at Glasgow University. From 1915 to 1920, he was director of the Bute Laboratory and Museum at Rothesay, Scotland. He lectured in biology at Bradford before being appointed as professor of Zoology at UCC in 1922 (to 1954). He was awarded the D.Sc. of the National University of Ireland and was the founder of the Biological Station at Lough Ine, near Skibbereen (1925). He founded and edited the *Mendel and Pasteur Review*.

RICE, Richard (1846–1925) Born Ballynacarriga, Kilworth, the son of Edmund Rice. He was educated at St Colman's College, Fermoy, and was admitted a solicitor in 1871. He worked as a local solicitor and was elected as coroner of Cork East Riding in 1872. Among his famous inquests were those on the victims of the Mitchelstown shootings of 1887 and of the sinking of the *Lusitania* in 1915. He was also prominent in the Land League agitation and in Redmondite Home Rule politics. He died at his Kilworth residence, Killaly House, on 20 November 1925 and was buried in Macrony Graveyard, Kilworth.

RICH, Mary (1625–1678) Born Youghal, Co. Cork, the seventh daughter of **Richard Boyle**, 1st earl of Cork. When her mother died in 1628, she was brought up by the wife of Randal Clayton of Mallow. Having refused to marry the earl of Clanbrassil at the age of thirteen, she married Charles Rich, the second son of the 3rd earl of Warwick, three years later. Her husband eventually succeeded to the earldom in 1659. Of Calvinist leanings, she wrote many devotional books. She died at Leighs Priory, Felsted, Essex, on 12 April 1678 and was buried in the local church. [Lives by C.F. Smith (1901) and M.E. Palgrave (1901)]

RICKARD, Jessie Louisa [Mrs Victor Rickard] (1876–1963) Born Dublin, the younger daughter of Canon Courtenay Moore, then rector of Castletownroche and later of Brigown (Mitchelstown), a noted antiquarian and a Protestant Home Ruler. She spent her youth in Mitchelstown and married Robert Ackland, whom she later divorced and caused a rift with her father. She then married Victor Rickard, an officer of the Royal Munster Fusiliers. Lt. Col. Rickard features prominently in the painting 'The Last Absolution of the Munsters' by the war artist Matania, which depicts the second battalion of the Munsters on the eve of the second Battle of Ypres in April-May 1915, in which Rickard and many of his colleagues were to die. Having previously published two novels and now widowed with a son to support, she reverted to writing as a source of income. From *The Story of the Munsters* (1915) to *Shandon Hall* (1950), she wrote over forty novels ranging in genre from light comedy to detective novels. These were not of great literary merit, but earned her a living as a popular novelist. Almost all of her works were published under the name, 'Mrs Victor Rickard'. She was a close friend of Lady Hazel Lavery (1880–1935) who was the subject of her novel *A Bird of Strange Plumage*

(1927). She became a convert to Roman Catholicism in 1925 and lived in Cork from 1946. She suffered a debilitating stroke c.1950 and, in her latter years, lived in the Montenotte home of **Denis Gwynn** whose wife was a daughter of Lady Lavery by her first marriage. She died on 28 January 1963.

RING, Christy (1920–1979) Born Cloyne, Co. Cork, the son of Nicholas Ring. Having won two All-Ireland MHC medals (1937 and 1938), he went on to win another eight in the senior ranks (1941–4, 1946, and 1952–4). He created records in the Railway Cup championships, appearing in twenty-two finals and winning eighteen of them between 1942 and 1963. He won four NHL medals (1940–1, 1948, and 1953), while he won an unprecedented eleven Cork County Senior Hurling Championship medals with his club, Glen Rovers. In 1954, he was on the St Nicholas team which took the Cork senior football championship title. He was also a noted squash player at local level. He died on 2 March 1979 and was buried in Cloyne Cemetery. [Life by V. Dorgan (1981, 1999); Biopic by L. Marcus (1964)]

RIORDAN, M. Augustine (1783–1848) Born Doneraile, Co. Cork. He worked as an architect and builder before joining the teaching community of Edmund Ignatius Rice (1762–1844) in 1814. He taught at the Brothers' first Cork school at Chapel Lane. In 1826, he left the North Monastery with a minority group, which had decided to remain as Presentation Brothers. He opened a large school in Tower Street where he acted as superior. He subsequently designed and built numerous chapels, churches and schools in the dioceses of Cork, Cloyne and Kerry. Austin Riordan died at the Presentation Monastery, Douglas Street, on 20 January 1848 and was buried in the monastery grounds. [Profile in D.H. Allen, *The Presentation Brothers* (1993)]

ROACH, John (1813–1887) Born Mitchelstown, Co. Cork. He emigrated to America at the age of sixteen and settled in New Jersey as an iron moulder. Having failed as a farmer in Illinois, he moved to New York and bought a small iron works. After many disappointments, his break came in 1860 when he was awarded the contract for the construction of an iron drawbridge over the Harlem River. By the end of the civil war, he owned one of the best foundries and engine plants in America. He now concentrated on the iron shipbuilding industry and moved his headquarters to Pennsylvania. Between 1872 and 1886, the 'father of iron shipbuilding in America' launched 126 vessels (most of them for the US Navy) from his shipyard. He died in New York on 10 January 1887. [Life by H.B. Grose (n.d.)]

ROBERTS, Michael (1817–1882) Born Peter Street, Cork. He was educated at Midleton College and TCD where he graduated BA (1838) and was elected as a fellow in 1843. He was appointed as professor of Mathematics, TCD, in 1862. He enjoyed an international reputation through his many contributions to mathematical journals. He died on 4 October 1882.

ROBERTS, Richard (1803–1841) Born Passage West, Co. Cork, the son of Richard Roberts. He joined the Royal Navy and took part in various hunts for slave ships off the West Coast of Africa. From 1830, he was captain of the steamer *Victory* which belonged to the St George Steam Packet Company of Cork and was engaged in the trade between Cork and Bristol. In late 1837, he was appointed as captain of the British & American Steam Navigation Company's *British Queen* which was in competition for an Atlantic crossing with I.K. Brunel's (1806–1859) *Great Western*. As the *British Queen* was unfinished, the company hired the St George Company's *Sirius* to compete, with Roberts as captain. The *Sirius* won this historic race to New York. He later sailed the *British Queen* on the London–New York run (1839–40). Early in 1841, he was transferred to the sister ship, *President*. However, the craft was lost, with all hands, in a storm in March 1841 on the return trip to London.

ROBERTS, William Randal (1830–1897)
Born Mitchelstown, Co. Cork, the son of Randal Roberts, baker and publican. He emigrated to New York city in 1849 and worked as a dry goods clerk for eight years before establishing his own business, which collapsed in the economic slump of 1857. In 1858, he opened another store which so prospered that, by 1869, he could retire as a millionaire. He was described by the Fenian, John Devoy (1842–1928), as 'a successful dry goods merchant who was vain and shallow but showy'. During the Civil War years he became involved in Irish societies in New York. In 1865, he became president of the Knights of St Patrick and president of the Fenian Brotherhood's newly created senate, which curbed the power of Head Centre, **John O'Mahony.** A dispute soon arose between O'Mahony and the senate, resulting in O'Mahony losing his position to Roberts. This allowed the Roberts faction to proceed with their ill-conceived invasion of Canada in June 1866. After the failure of the Canadian venture, Roberts was briefly imprisoned in the US for breach of neutrality laws. At the end of 1867, he resigned his Fenian presidency. He then embarked on a political career in New York and in 1870 was elected to the House of Representatives as a Democrat; during his period of service which lasted until 1874, he pursued a Fenian agenda, attacking British policy at every opportunity. Later in the decade he was president of the board of aldermen in New York. He supported Grover Cleveland (1837–1908) in state and national campaigns and on Cleveland's election as president of the US, Roberts was appointed US Minister to Chile in 1885. In 1889 he suffered a paralytic stroke, from which he never recovered, though he lived for eight more years. Roberts returned to the US and having separated from his wife, died at Bellevue Hospital in New York on 9 August 1897.

ROBINSON, E.S. Lennox (1886–1958) Born Douglas, Cork, the son of a Church of Ireland rector and former stockbroker. He was educated at Bandon Grammar School. Following an early interest in the theatre, his first play, *The Clancy Name* (1908), was produced at the Abbey Theatre, Appointed as Abbey Theatre manager for short periods in 1910 and 1919, he became a director in 1923. He also served as the director of the Abbey School of Acting and as a librarian for the Irish Carnegie Trust. In 1938, he was awarded the honorary degree of D.Litt. from TCD. His plays include 'Patriots' (1912), 'The Dreamers' (1915), 'The Whiteheaded Boy' (1916), 'The Lost Leader' (1918), 'Crabbed Youth and Age' (1922), 'The Round Table' (1922), 'Never the Time and the Place' (1924), 'Portrait' (1925), 'The White Blackbird' (1925), 'The Big House' (1926), 'The Far-off Hills' (1928), 'Ever the Twain' (1929), 'Drama at Inish' (1933), 'Church Street' (1934), 'Killycreggs in Twilight' (1937) and 'Bird's Nest' (1938). He also published: *Further Letters of J.B. Yeats* (1920), *Lady Gregory's Journals* (1946), *Ireland's Abbey Theatre* (1951) and *I Sometimes Think* (1956). He died at Monkstown, Co. Dublin on 14 October 1958. [Autobiography (2 vols) *In Three Homes* (1938) and *Curtain Up* (1941); Portrait by J. Sleator at the Abbey Theatre]

ROBINSON, George (1819–1902) Born Moate, Co. Westmeath, the son of a Quaker, George Robinson (d. 1776). The family emigrated to New York but he returned to Ireland and settled in Cork where he established a shipbuilding and ship-repair company at Water Street which, as Cork's premier shipyard, employed some 500 workers by 1859. He was responsible for building Ireland's first iron three-master, the *Mulgrave*, and also built the *Ilen* for the Skibbereen Steamship Company in 1872 – the last ship to be built by a city dockyard. A slump in the trade caused the yards to close. The plant was later acquired by Cork Harbour Commissioners in 1877. He died in 1902.

ROCH, Sampson T. (1759–1847) Born Youghal, Co. Cork, the son of Luke Roch. A deaf mute, he showed early artistic promise and was sent by his father to study in Dublin. He eventually set up as a painter of miniatures in Capel Street and later in Grafton Street. He left

Dublin in 1792 and settled in Bath where he was very successful and painted several members of the British royal family. He retired to Ireland and lived with his relations at Woodbine Hill, Co. Waterford. He died in February 1847 and was buried in Ardmore Graveyard.

ROCHE, Augustine (1849–1915) Born Douglas Street, Cork, the son of Michael Roche, a prominent businessman. Having been privately educated, he entered the family business and became one of the leading wine and spirits merchants in the city and county. He was elected to Cork Corporation in 1883 and twice served as mayor (1893 and 1894), highsheriff (1902 and 1903) and lord mayor (1904). As a Parnellite candidate, he unsuccessfully contested Cork City in the general elections of 1894 and 1895. However, he was returned, unopposed, in 1905, in place of **James F.X. O'Brien** on the latter's death. He retained his seat until the general election of December 1910 when two O'Brienite nationalist candidates were returned for Cork City. In March 1911, he was returned, unopposed, to the vacant North Louth seat which he represented until his death. During his term as mayor in 1893/94, he initiated excursions to the seaside at Youghal for poor children, which later became an annual event. With Lord Chief Justice O'Brien, he organised the international regatta on the River Lee in 1903. A lifelong collector of antiques and curios, he amassed a valuable collection which he gave on loan to the Cork School of Art. After his death, it was sold over a period of five days at Marsh's auction rooms in July 1916, being comprised of 6,000 ounces (17kg) of old Irish and English silver as well as artworks, furniture etc. He died at his residence, 73 Douglas Street, on 7 December 1915 and was buried in St Finbarr's Cemetery.

ROCHE, Eamon (d. 1952) Born Bansha, Co. Tipperary. During the War of Independence, he was an officer in the West Limerick IRA and was elected a TD for Kerry–West Limerick (1921–23). He took no part in the civil war. In 1925, he was appointed as manager of Mitchelstown Co-operative Creamery and over the next quarter century, established the company as a progressive element in the dairy industry, thus laying the foundations of one of the most successful agribusinesses in the country. By 1950, the Mitchelstown plant employed some 500 workers. He died suddenly in Dublin while visiting a niece on 7 September 1952 and was buried in St Michael's Cemetery, Tipperary. He was the father of Kevin Roche, the internationally acclaimed architect.

ROCHE, Edmund Burke (1815–1874) He was the son of Edward Roche of Trabolgan and Kildinan. Through his mother, Margaret Curtain, he was related to the orator and statesman, Edmund Burke (1729–1797). In 1837, he was elected as a Repealer MP for Cork County. He retained his seat until his resignation in 1855 when he was created Baron Fermoy in the Irish peerage. He later represented the English constituency of Marylebone (1859–65). He was one of the magistrates dismissed because of their activities on behalf of Repeal in 1843. He was lord lieutenant and custos rotulorum (commissioner of customs) for Cork city and county from c.1860. The owner of large estates in County Cork, he took a great interest in agricultural development and improvement. He promoted the growing of flax in the county after the Famine and became Ireland's largest grower in 1853, having established a flax mill at Trabolgan in the previous year. He died from a chill caught following his daily sea-bath, at Trabolgan on 17 September 1874 and was buried in Corkbeg Graveyard, Whitegate.

ROCHE, James (1770–1853) Born Limerick, the son of Stephen Roche, merchant. At the age of 15 years, he enrolled in a school at Saintes on the Charente River and later joined his brother, George, as a partner in a Bordeaux wine business. He was a supporter of the French Revolution and among his acquaintances was the eponymous Dr Guillotine. He left France in 1797 and settled in Cork where he founded a bank. When this failed in 1819, he was forced to sell his library in London to pay off the debts. He returned to France and settled in Paris for two years before returning to Cork in 1832 where he spent the remainder of his life. In 1851 he published his *Essays of an Octogenarian* and wrote many articles in local journals. He died on 1 August 1853.

ROCHE, James J. (1872–1956) Born Midleton, Co. Cork, the son of a Midleton poor law union clerk. He was educated at St Colman's College, Fermoy, and at St Patrick's College, Maynooth, where he was ordained for the diocese of Cloyne in 1893. Having worked on the staffs of St Patrick's College, Carlow, and of Fermoy, he held various ministries in the diocese. He was consecrated as bishop of Ross on 31 March 1926. He was translated as coadjutor bishop of Cloyne on 26 June 1931 and succeeded Bishop **Robert Browne** on 23 March 1935. He died on 31 August 1956 and was buried in the grounds of St Colman's Cathedral, Cobh.

ROCHE, Kennedy F. (1911–1999) Born Mullingar, Co. Westmeath, the eldest child of Maurice Roche. He was educated at the Patrician Academy, Mallow, and at UCC where he graduated BA (1938) and MA (1943). He joined the staff of the history department at UCC in 1948 as a part-time demonstrator while he was clerk of the district courts at Mallow and Buttevant. He resigned the clerical positions on being appointed an assistant in the UCC History Department in 1952. He was subsequently appointed as a statutory lecturer in History in 1962 and as professor of the History of Political Ideas in 1976. He retired in 1981. He died at St Joseph's Hospital on 20 April 1999 and was cremated at Glasnevin Crematorium, Dublin. His *Rousseau: Stoic and Romantic* (1974) was well received. He also contributed important essays to *Daniel O'Connell: centenary essays* (1949) and to *Historical Studies III and IX* (1961, 1974).

ROCHE, William (1874–1939) Born Kilcanway, Killavullen, Co. Cork, the son of David Roche, farmer. He was educated locally and was apprenticed to the drapery trade with Cash's of Cork for five years. Having made several attempts to establish himself in business, he spent some years in England before returning to Cork in 1901. Here he established the Cork Furniture Stores in Merchant Street. In 1919, he purchased 'The London House', Patrick Street, and in September of that year, the firm was renamed Roche's Stores Ltd. Even though most of the premises were destroyed in the burning of Cork in December 1920, he was back in temporary business within days. The new premises, built with the help of compensation (£24,500), were completed in January 1927, the year in which he acquired the Henry Street Warehouse in Dublin. In 1937, the Limerick firm, McBirney & Co., was added to the chain. He had moved to Dublin in 1927 and died at his residence on Breffni Road there on 23 February 1939. He was buried in Dean's Grange Cemetery.

ROE, William (d. *c*.1850) He was trained at the Royal Dublin Society's schools and specialised in landscapes. Having begun to exhibit at the Royal Hibernian Academy in 1826, he left Dublin in 1835 to settle in Cork. He was responsible for a number of pencil sketches, entitled, 'Views of Cork and Its Environs' (reproduced in *JCHAS*, vols VIII and IX). Some of his works were exhibited at the Cork Exhibition of 1852.

RONAN, Stephen (1848–1925) Born Cork, the son of Walter Ronan, solicitor. He was educated at Queen's College, Cork (now UCC) where he graduated MA. He was called to the Irish Bar in 1870 and to the Irish Inner Bar in 1889. He was called to the English Bar in 1888 and to the English Inner Bar in 1909. He was appointed Queen's Advocate for Ireland in 1892. He died in Dublin on 3 October 1925.

RONAYNE, Charles O'Lomasney (1845– 1929) Born Youghal, Co. Cork, the son of Richard C. Ronayne. He was educated at the Royal University of Ireland and at TCD. He served as a doctor in the Franco-Prussian war of 1870 and was awarded the Croix Rouge Française and the Medaille Militaire for his services [his memoir of the period, 'Reminiscences of an Ambulance Surgeon in the Franco-Prussian War', was published in the *JCHAS* (1918)]. On his return to Youghal, he was prominent in local and national affairs and was for a time chairman of Youghal town commissioners. He was deprived of his position of justice of the peace for authorising **William O'Brien**, in defiance of the Crimes Act, to hold a public meeting in Youghal in March 1888 for distressed tenants of the Ponsonby Estate. Besides his work as a doctor, he also contributed many articles on local history to the *Dungarvan Observer*. He was the author of *The History of the Earls of Desmond... and a history and guide to the ecclesiastical and collegiate foundations in Youghal*, which was published in London in 1929. He died at his residence at South Abbey, Youghal, on 6 May 1929.

RONAYNE, Joseph P. (1822–1876) Born Cork, the son of Edmund Ronayne, proprietor of the Terrace Glassworks, South Terrace, and the nephew of **Francis S. Mahony** ('Fr. Prout'). Having served his apprenticeship as a surveyor, he joined the firm of Sir John MacNeill (road, bridge and railway builder) where he worked on the construction of the Cork-Dublin railway. He then worked as assistant engineer for the Cork and Bandon Railway Company whose line was opened in December 1851. With the rejection of his pamphlet, *The Supply of Water to Cork* (1854), he left for California where he worked on the project to divert the waters of the Sierra Nevada for use on the goldfields there. He returned to Cork in 1859 and set up his own business as a contractor. He designed and constructed both the Queenstown (now Cobh) Junction-Queenstown and Cork-Macroom railway lines. He became a member of Cork Corporation and supported the Fenian movement but did not take part in the uprising of 1867. He also took part in the Home Government movement which was founded by **Isaac Butt**. In 1873, he succeeded **John Francis Maguire** as Home Rule MP for Cork City. However, he died at his residence, 'Rinn Ronain', Rushbrooke (now a hotel), from haemorrhage following a leg amputation, on 7 May 1876 and was buried at St Joseph's Cemetery, Cork.

RONAYNE, Philip (1683–1755) Born at Hodnet's Wood, Great Island, where the family were landowners. 'Widely esteemed for his knowledge of mathematics', he is said to have been a personal friend and correspondent of Sir Isaac Newton (1642–1727). His learning contributed to him being accorded magical powers and he figures in **Crofton Croker**'s *Fairy Legends and Traditions of the South of Ireland* (1825). He lived for some time on a small island in the Upper Lake, Killarney (still known as Ronayne's Island), where he is reputed to have had a Negro servant (illustrated in Carr's *Stranger in Ireland*, 1806). Here he enjoyed seclusion and fishing, until one morning he discovered that the earl of Shannon was also fishing nearby. Whereupon, he remarked to his servant that 'this place is getting far too crowded' and returned to his Great Island home. He published *A Treatise of Algebra* (1717) of which a second edition also appeared. He also invented 'Ronayne's Cubes', a mathematical puzzle. He died at Hodnet's Wood on 23 April 1755.

RONAYNE, Thomas (1848–1925) Born Youghal, Co. Cork. He was educated at Corsham (Wiltshire) and Wakefield. He was employed at the Inchicore Works (Dublin) of the Great Southern & Western Railway and then with the firm of Sharpe, Stewart, & Co. (Manchester). He emigrated to New Zealand in 1875 where he worked as locomotive engineer and/or general manager of various railways. He was appointed as a railway commissioner in 1904 and as general manager of New Zealand Railways (1905–14). He lived in Wellington and died on 7 September 1925.

ROSS, John (1827–1897) An accomplished Cork engraver on silver and other plate, he was responsible for many of the monumental brasses of St Fin Barre's Cathedral. He was also noted for his heraldic designs on plate and on bookplates. He died in Cork on 1 December 1897.

ROSS, Sir Thomas (1797–c.1875) Born Rossford, Skibbereen, Co. Cork, the second son of Thomas Ross. He entered the Royal Navy in July 1812 as a First Class volunteer and served as a midshipman for the remainder of the Napoleonic War. From 1815, he served on several ships on anti-smuggling patrol, on coast blockade and on coast guard duty. He was advanced to the rank of Commander in 1833 and then as Inspecting Commander in the coast guard (1834–43). For his leading role in rescuing men from a wreck near Malahide, Co. Dublin, in November 1838, he was awarded a Lifeboat Gold Medal and received a knighthood from the Viceroy. In later years, he lived at Dardistown Castle, Co. Meath, and died c.1875.

ROWE, Charles H. (c.1893–1943) Born Cork, the son of James Charles Rowe, a Unionist member of Cork Corporation. He was educated at UCC and TCD where he had a brilliant undergraduate career. He was elected as a fellow of TCD in 1920. He was given a year's leave of absence to study at the Sorbonne, Paris, and on his return to TCD, was appointed Erasmus Smith professor of Mathematics there. Specialising in geometry, he made contributions on Riemannian Geometry in various international mathematics journals. He also edited an edition of **George Salmon**'s *Geometry of Three Dimensions*. He was the founder of the College Mathematical Society and edited the TCD Calendar from 1933. As well a being a fluent Irish speaker, he also 'wrote in impeccable English and French'. He was appointed as junior dean in 1943. However, he was found dead in his rooms at TCD on 4 December 1943 and subsequently a verdict of death 'from coal gas poisoning while of unsound mind' was returned at the inquest into his death. He was buried in Mount Jerome Cemetery, Dublin.

ROWLEY, Sir Josias (1765–1842) He was the second son of Clotworthy Rowley, barrister (and MP for Downpatrick, 1801), the brother of **Samuel C. Rowley** and **William Rowley**. His mother was Letitia Campbell of Mount Campbell, Co. Leitrim. He was also the uncle of **Henry Martin**. His maternal aunt was the wife of Edward Southwell, 20th Baron de Clifford, who was the patron of the parliamentary boroughs of Downpatrick and Kinsale, hence the Rowley connection with both boroughs. In 1778, he entered the naval service under his uncle, Sir Joshua Rowley, and had a successful career. He was created a baronet (1813), promoted to the rank of rear admiral (1814), and was commander-in-chief on the Irish coast (1818–21). In 1825, he was elevated to the rank of vice-admiral and was commander-in-chief in the Mediterranean (1835–7). He was MP for Kinsale (1821–6) and died, unmarried, at Mount Campbell on 10 January 1842.

ROWLEY, Samuel C. (1774–1846) He was the third son of Clotworthy Rowley, barrister (and MP for Downpatrick, 1801), and brother of **Sir Josias Rowley** and **William Rowley**. His mother was Letitia Campbell of Mount Campbell, Co. Leitrim. He was also the uncle of **Henry Martin**. His maternal aunt was the wife of Edward Southwell, 20th Baron de Clifford, who was the patron of the parliamentary boroughs of Downpatrick and Kinsale, hence the Rowley connection with both boroughs. He entered the Royal Navy and rose to the rank of rear-admiral to command the *Terror* (burnt at the battle of Copenhagen, 1801) and the *Laurel* (wrecked in January 1812). He was MP for Downpatrick (1801–2) when the seat was vacated by his father on his appointment as a commissioner of the Irish Revenue. He sat as MP for Kinsale (1802–6), was twice married and died in January 1846.

ROWLEY, William (d. 1811) He was the eldest son of Clotworthy Rowley, barrister (and MP for Downpatrick, 1801), and brother of **Samuel C. Rowley** and **Sir Josias Rowley**. His mother was Letitia Campbell of Mount Campbell, Co. Leitrim. He was also the uncle of **Henry Martin**. His maternal aunt was the wife of Edward Southwell, 20th Baron de Clifford, who was the patron of the parliamentary boroughs of

Downpatrick and Kinsale, hence the Rowley connection with both boroughs. He was educated at TCD where he graduated BA (1783) and LL.B (1787). He was called to the Irish Bar in 1787. He was recorder and custos rotulorum (commissioner of customs) at Kinsale before being returned as MP for that borough in 1801. He was succeeded by his brother, Samuel, in the following year. He died, unmarried, in 1811.

RUISÉAL, Liam (1891–1978) Born White Street, Cork, the son of William Russell, general worker. He was educated by the Presentation Brothers at the South Monastery and at the age of fifteen, was employed in the new bookshop of Cornelius O'Keeffe in George's Street (now Oliver Plunkett Street). He was an enthusiastic member of Connradh na Gaeilge and attended the Cork School of Commerce where one of his teachers was **Terence Mac Swiney**. From 1916 to 1927, he had his own bookshop (An Siopa Gaelach / The Fountain Bookshop) on the Grand Parade. In the latter year, he took up a position as manager of Browne and Nolan's bookshop on Cook Street (now 'Specsavers') before opening his own outlet on Oliver Plunkett Street in 1929 – a shop which was to become a Cork 'institution'. He was a member of the Irish Republican Brotherhood (IRB) and of the Cork Volunteers before serving on Cork Corporation (1920–4). He was also a prominent member of the Cork praesidium of the Legion of Mary. He died at his Western Road residence on 26 October 1978 and was buried in St Joseph's Cemetery. [Autobiography (1978)]

RUSSELL, Bartholomew T. (1799–1890) Born Cork. He entered the Dominican Order in 1817 and finished his studies in Corpo Santo, Lisbon. He returned to Cork in 1823 and was based in Dominick Street. The 'silver-tongued preacher' was responsible for the building of St Mary's Church and Priory, Pope's Quay. He died on 10 July 1890, in the Dominican Priory and was buried in St Mary's Cemetery. His younger brother, Patrick B. Russell (1809–1901), was also a distinguished member of the Dominican Order who spent all his adult life at Corpo Santo. He was a significant benefactor of the Dominican foundation at Tallaght, Co. Dublin, and also the founder of Dominican convents in Portugal. He died at Corpo Santo on 16 November 1901.

RUSSELL, Lord John (1792–1878) Born Westminster, the third son of John Russell, 6th Duke of Bedford and Viceroy of Ireland (1806–7). He was educated at Westminster School and at the University of Edinburgh. He was MP for Tavistock (1814–20) and for Huntingdonshire (1820–6). On his electoral defeat in the latter constituency in 1826, he was returned for Bandon on the nomination of the duke of Devonshire and sat for this constituency until the general election of 1830 when he was eventually returned for Tavistock. He later held various ministerial appointments and served as Prime Minister (1846–52). His reputation rests with his successful running of the 1832 Reform Bill for Earl Grey's government. He died on 28 May 1878 at Richmond Park, Surrey, and was buried in the family vault at Chenies, Buckinghamshire.

RUSSELL, John ['Jack'] (1909–1977) Born Queenstown (now Cobh), Co. Cork. He was educated at St Colman's College, Fermoy and at UCC where he graduated MB. He played club rugby with UCC and won three successive Munster senior cup medals (1935–7). A second-row forward, he was capped nineteen times for Ireland (1931–7) and played in three of the four matches in the 1935 championship-winning team. He died at his Blarney residence on 13 May 1977 and was buried in St Colman's Cemetery, Cobh.

RUSSELL, Thomas (1767–1803) Born Kilshannig, Co. Cork, the son of John Russell, and army commander. He joined the British army in 1782 and saw service with his brother, Captain Ambrose Russell, in the 52nd Regiment in India. While stationed in Belfast in 1791, he became friendly with some of the northern leaders of the Society of United Irishmen including Samuel Neilson (1761–1803) and Henry Joy McCracken (1767–98). Previous to this, however, he had met Theobald Wolfe Tone (1763–98) at an Irish House of Commons debate. In 1794, he became librarian of the Linen Hall Library, Belfast. Two years later, he was arrested and imprisoned at Fort George, Scotland, until his release in 1802. He was landed at Cuxhaven, Holland, and travelled to Paris where he met with Robert Emmet (1778–1803) who was planning to stage an Irish rising in the following year. He returned to Ireland in April 1803, and was arrested in Dublin following the failure of the rising. He was tried for high treason in Downpatrick and hanged there on 21 October 1803 – the day sentence was passed. [Life by MacGiolla Easpaig [as Gaeilge] (1957), Carroll (1995), Quinn (2002) and Gallagher (2003); Journals and remains by C.J. Woods, ed. (1991); Biographical poem, 'The Man from God Knows Where' by F.M. Wilson]

RYAN, Sir Andrew (1876–1949) Born Ronayne's Court, Douglas, Cork, the son of Edward Ryan, soap manufacturer, and brother of Archbishop **Finbarr Ryan**, **Sir Thomas Ryan**, and Professor **Mary Ryan**. He was educated at CBC, Cork, and at Queen's College, Cork (now UCC) where he graduated BA (1896). He later studied at Cambridge University. Entering the diplomatic service in 1897, he was stationed at Constantinople (1903–23) and was a member of the British delegation at the Near East Peace Conference at Lausanne (1922–3). He was consul general at Rabat, Morocco (1924–30), and minister plenipotentiary at Jedda, Saudi Arabia (1930–6). In 1936, he was appointed envoy extraordinary and minister plenipotentiary in Albania. He was knighted in 1925. He died on 31 December 1949.

RYAN, Finbarr (1882–1975) Born Ronayne's Court, Douglas, Cork, the son of Edward Ryan, soap manufacturer and brother of **Sir Andrew Ryan**, **Sir Thomas Ryan** and Professor **Mary Ryan**. He was educated at CBC, Cork, and at

Clongowes Wood College. He entered the Dominican Order in 1899, studied at Tallaght Priory and UCD before completing his studies in Rome where he was ordained in 1905. He returned to Ireland and acted as prior in Dublin and Cork before twice being selected as provincial of the Order (1921–6 and 1930–4). In April 1937, he was consecrated as coadjutor to Archbishop Dowling of Port of Spain, Trinidad. Before leaving, he was made freeman of Cork. He succeeded to the archbishopric in 1940. On his retirement in 1966, the government of Trinidad awarded him with the country's highest honour, the Trinity Cross, in recognition for his services to education in the West Indies. He returned to Cork in 1966 and lived in the Dominican retreat house, Ennismore, Mayfield. He died at the Bon Secours Home, Cork, on 10 January 1975 and was buried in the Dominican plot at St Joseph's Cemetery. He published a book on Fatima (1939) and was the editor of the *Irish Rosary* (1908–20).

RYAN, Frank (1900–1965) Born Fermoy, Co. Cork, but moved at an early age to Tallow, Co. Waterford, where the family were victuallers. He joined the Irish Volunteers and became commandant of the 2nd battalion, West Waterford IRA. He was in his mid-twenties when it was discovered that he possessed a magnificent tenor voice. His singing career began with Fermoy Choral Society. He won the award for solo tenor at the Dublin Feis Cheoil in 1931 and took the honours in many other feiseanna. He turned professional in 1939 when he joined the Dublin Operatic Society and took leading roles in many of its performances. He toured extensively and appeared at the Royal Albert Hall, London. He toured America on five occasions and appeared at Carnegie Hall, New York, in 1948. He died at his home, 'The Grange', Curraglass, Co. Cork, on 17 July 1965 and was buried in Tallow Cemetery.

RYAN, Mary (1873–1961) Born Ronayne's Court, Douglas, Cork, only daughter of Edward Ryan, soap manufacturer, and sister of **Sir**

Andrew Ryan, Sir Thomas Ryan and Archbishop **Finbarr Ryan**. She was educated at Ursuline colleges in Cork and Berlin; in France and at UCC where she was appointed lecturer in German in 1909. In the following year, she was made professor of Romance Languages at UCC, becoming the first woman in Britain to hold a professorial chair. She was made a chevalier of the French Legion of Honour in 1935 and retired in 1938. In 1952, she was awarded the degree of D.Litt (Hon.) for her published works, *Alfred Noyes on Voltaire* (1938); *Introduction to Claudel* (1950); and for her essays published in *Studies*. She died at her residence, 'Gortalough', Rochestown Road, Cork, on 16 June 1961 and was buried in St Joseph's Cemetery.

RYAN, Sir Thomas (1879–1934) Born Ronayne's Court, Douglas, Cork, the son of Edward Ryan, soap manufacturer, and sister of **Sir Andrew Ryan**, Professor **Mary Ryan** and Archbishop **Finbarr Ryan**. He was educated at CBC, Cork, and at the Royal Indian Engineering College.

He entered the Indian Colonial service in 1898. He held prominent posts in various departments of the Indian civil service before his appointment as joint secretary of the Industries and Labour department in 1928. In 1931, he became director general of Posts and Telegraphs in India – a position he held at the time of his death in New Delhi on 12 March 1934, some weeks before he was due to retire. He had been knighted in the previous year.

RYAN, Vincent W. (1816–1888) Born Cork, the son of John Ryan, a captain of the 82nd Regiment of Foot. He was educated at Magdalen Hall, Oxford, where he graduated MA (1848). He served as a curate on the island of Alderney and later as headmaster of the Liverpool Institution. In 1850, he was appointed as principal of Highbury Training College at Islington, London. Four years later, he was consecrated as bishop of Mauritius and was responsible for many improvements until his retirement in 1867. He died in 1888.

S

SADLEIR, George F. (1789–1859) Born Cork, the second son of John Sadleir (originally of Co. Tipperary and later of Shannonvale, Clonakilty, Co. Cork), a cotton manufacturer and high sheriff of Cork in 1791. In April 1805, he joined the 47th Regiment of Foot as an ensign. He was promoted to the rank of lieutenant in 1806 and to that of captain in 1813. Almost all of his military service was passed in the Persian Gulf and in India. In 1819, in the course of a diplomatic mission, Sadleir crossed the Arabian Desert from the Persian Gulf to the Red Sea – becoming the first European to make a recorded crossing of the peninsula (his *Diary of a Journey* … was published posthumously in 1866). He returned to England in 1828 and retired from the army with the rank of major in 1837. That same year he was elected as high sheriff of Cork. He emigrated to New Zealand around 1855 and died at Upper Queen Street, Auckland, on 2 December 1859.

SADLEIR, Richard (1794–1889) Born Cork, the son of James Sadleir, landowner and merchant. He was educated at Bandon Classical School and joined the British Navy in 1808. He returned to Ireland in 1821, but in 1824, he was commissioned to study the condition of the Australian Aborigines. He travelled to New South Wales and, three years later, he placed his report before the state's Legislative Council. In the meantime, he had been granted a large tract of land in the Hunter Valley area and was appointed as master of the male orphan school at Liverpool, New South Wales – a position which he held until 1851. He then entered politics and succeeded in being returned as a Radical member of the state's Legislative Council. His parliamentary career ended in 1864, but he continued to play an active part in local politics and served as mayor of Liverpool.

He took a great interest in theological matters and served as joint secretary of the Church of England Constitution Defence Association. He published *The Aborigines of Australia* (1883). He also produced a range of pamphlets on such diverse subjects as railway expansion, city water supply, homeopathic medicine and non-combustible light! He died at Liverpool on 6 March 1889.

SADLIER, William C. (1867–1935) Born Bandon, Co. Cork, the son of Christopher Sadlier, journalist, who later settled with his family in Melbourne, Australia. He was educated at Trinity College, Melbourne, where he graduated MA. He was also a BD graduate of London University and held a Lambeth DD degree. Following his ordination as priest in 1892, he served in various positions in Melbourne before his consecration as bishop of Nelson, New Zealand, in 1912. Following his retirement in 1934, he settled in Sussex, England, where he died on 1 February 1935.

SAIDLÉAR, Annraoi (1896–1976) Born Buttevant, Co. Cork, the third child of James Sadlier, policeman. He was educated at Mallow and Doneraile CBS, before entering UCC on a scholarship in 1914. He left in the following year to attend a London training college for primary teachers. However, he worked as a secondary school teacher in Galway, Gorey, Waterford, Glasnevin and at Coláiste Mhuire, Dublin. He became a prominent member of Connradh na Gaeilge in those various places. A playwright, three of his dramas, 'Misneach', 'Oíche sa Tabhairne' and ''Bhfuil Gealt Anseo' were published in 1929, 1945 and 1945 respectively. Further plays were published in *Ceithre Drámaí don Aos Óg* (1936) and *An Púca* (1936). His novel for children, *An Smuigléir*, was written anonymously. His later plays were subsequently published as *An Charraig Bhán agus Connla* (1936), *Aisling cois Mara* (1956), *An Bóthar ó Thuaidh, 1798* (1962), *Gleann an Áir* (1962) and *An Draoi Dríochta* (1966). He died on 13 June 1976.

SAINTHILL, Richard (1787–1869) Born Topsham, Devon, the son of Captain Richard Sainthill, Royal Navy, who had come to reside in Cork *c.*1800. Sent to London by his father to learn the wine trade, the young Richard developed a strong interest in antiquities, literature and numismatics. While researching in the British Library in late 1828 or early 1829, he came across a manuscript in the Harleian Collection, which, he thought, was a copy of the charter of Cork granted by King John of England (1167–1216). It was, in fact, a body of statutes from the time of King John's great-grandson, King Edward III (1312–77), but with an earlier preamble. The 'discovery' was announced in the *Cork Constitution* of 7 May 1829 and generated much local interest. Sainthill published the results of his researches in *Olla Podrida* in two volumes (1844 and 1853). He also published *The Old Countess of Desmond* in 1861. He carried on his wine business at Nelson (now Emmet) Place. He died at Nelson Place on 13 November 1869 and was buried in the family plot in Rathcooney Graveyard. [Portrait by **Daniel Maclise**; Commemorative plaque and window in the south aisle, St Fin Barre's Cathedral.]

ST LAWRENCE, Thomas (1755–1831) He was the son of Thomas St Lawrence, 1st earl of Howth. He was educated at TCD where he graduated BA, LL.B and LL.D (1796). He was appointed as dean of Cork on January 7, 1796, before being consecrated as Church of Ireland bishop of Cork and Ross on 27 September 1807. He died at the episcopal residence, Cork, on 10 February 1831 and was buried in St Fin Barre's Cathedral.

ST LEGER, Francis B.B. (1790–1829) Born Co. Cork, the second son of Colonel Richard St Leger, and grandson of 1st Viscount Doneraile. He was educated at Rugby School and worked with the East India Company from 1816 until 1822. He edited *The Album* and other magazines. Among other novels, he wrote *Gilbert Earle*, which was very popular in its day. He died on 20 November 1829.

ST LEGER, Sir William (d. 1642) He was the son of Sir Warham St Leger (d. 1600), military officer and colonist. He served in Holland for eight years and was knighted for his services in April 1618. He also received large grants of crown lands in Laois and Limerick. Following a period in London, he returned to Ireland in July 1627, having been appointed as president of Munster and as a member of the Irish Privy Council. He was made a freeman of Cork on 27 June 1628. The minutes of the Council Book of Cork Corporation record that St Leger ordered the discontinuance of the playing of hurling and football on the streets of Cork! He was a firm supporter of Lord Deputy Wentworth (1593–1641). He attended the parliaments of 1634 and 1639 as a member for County Cork and helped in the raising of a large Irish army in support of King Charles I of England. Also, in 1639, the manor of Doneraile was established by statute. St Leger built a church there (replaced in 1726) and was in residence when the Irish Rebellion of 1641 broke out on 23 October. Surrounded by hostile rebels, he made his headquarters in Cork, but was in Dungarvan when the city was threatened by the forces of **Donough Mac Carthy**, 1st Earl Clancarty. His forces made it back to Cork on time and the city was beseiged until its relief in late April by his son-in-law **Murrough O'Brien**, later 1st earl of Inchiquin. He died in Cork on 2 July 1642. His Doneraile seat was later burned by the Irish rebels in 1645.

SALMON, George (1819–1904) Born Cork, the son of Michael Salmon, linen merchant. He was educated at TCD where he graduated BA (1839), MA (1844) and DD (1859). He was ordained in 1844. He was elected as a fellow of the Royal Society in 1858. He was appointed as professor of Divinity at TCD in 1866 and held this position until 1888 when he was appointed as provost of the college. He established a firm reputation both as a mathematician and theologian. He received the freedom of Dublin in 1892. He died at TCD on 22 January 1904 and was buried in Mount Jerome Cemetery. His mathematical publications included *Conic Sections* (6 eds, 1847–1876), *Higher Plane Curves* (3 eds, 1852–1879), *Lessons Introductory to the modern Higher Algebra* (4 eds, 1859–1885) and *Geometry in Three Dimensions* (5 eds, 1862–1912). His theological works included *The Eternity of Future Punishment* (1864), *The Reign of Law* (1873), *Non-miraculous Christianity* (1881 and 1887), *Introduction to the New Testament* (7 eds, 1885–94), *Gnostic and Agnostic* (1887), *Thoughts on the Textual Criticism of the New Testament* (1897) and *The Infallibility of the Church* (1889). His *The Human Element in the Gospels* was edited by N.J.D. White (1907). [Portraits by B. Constant in Provost's House, TCD, and by S. Purser in the Common Room, TCD; Bronze by A. Bruce-Joy in St Patrick's Cathedral, Dublin; Statue (*in sede*) by J. Hughes at TCD]

SAMPSON, John (1862–1931) Born Schull, Co. Cork, the son of James Sampson, chemist and mining engineer, and brother of **Ralph Allen Sampson**. His father died in Liverpool in 1871, and, in 1876, he was apprenticed to a Liverpool lithographer. He read widely and gave up the printing business to become the first librarian of University College, Liverpool, in 1892 – a post which he held until his retirement in 1928. He became interested in the study of Romany (gypsy) dialects and lived among gypsies for long periods. He contributed numerous articles to the *Journal of the Gypsy Lore Society*. In 1926, he published *The Dialect of the Gypsies of Wales* which was considered to be a masterpiece. He later published *The Wind on the Heath* (1926), *Romane Gilia* ('Romani Poems', posth., 1934) and *In Lighter Moments* (posthumously, 1934). Those works dealt with gypsy themes in verse and prose. In his *Poetical Works* (1905), he restored the text and added a

commentary on the lyrics of William Blake (1757–1827). He died on 9 November 1931 at West Kirby, Cheshire, and his ashes were scattered above the village of Llangwm, Conway, Wales. In a *Sunday Times* review of 11 May 1997, it was observed that as 'An intellectual hobo, a raffish pedant, Sampson was also for thirty years the fastidious librarian of Liverpool University, but he was known to all as "The Rai" ("gentleman" in Romany)'. [Life by A. Sampson (1997)]

SAMPSON, Ralph A. (1866–1939) Born Schull, Co. Cork, the son of James Sampson, chemist and mining engineer and brother of **John Sampson**. The family, with little means, moved to Liverpool in 1871 but James died in 1873. Ralph was educated at the Liverpool Institute and at St John's College, Cambridge, where he became a fellow in 1890. In the meantime, he was a mathematics lecturer at King's College, London, and returned to Cambridge in 1891 to take up the first Isaac Newton Studentship in Astronomy and Physical Optics. He was elected as a fellow of the Royal Society in 1903. He subsequently held professorships of mathematics at Newcastle and Durham before moving to Edinburgh University in 1910 to take up the post of professor of Astronomy and also Astronomer Royal of Scotland. He was awarded the Gold Medal of the Royal Astronomical Society in 1928 for his work on the satellites of Jupiter. He resigned in 1937 through ill health. He died at Bath on 7 November 1939. He published the *Tables of the Four Great Satellites of Jupiter* in 1910 – the culmination of 10 years work on the subject.

SANDES, John (1863–1938) Born Cork, the son of Samuel Dickson Sandes, clergyman. He was educated at King's College School, London, at Trinity College, Stratford-on-Avon and at Magdalen College, Oxford, where he graduated BA (1885). He emigrated to Melbourne, Australia, in 1887 and joined the staff of the Melbourne *Argus*. Following his marriage in 1897, he moved to Sydney in 1903 and joined the *Daily Telegraph* where he wrote leaders, articles and columns on a variety of subjects. His first novel, *Love and the Aeroplane* was published in 1910 and this was followed by nine adventure romances under the pseudonym, 'Don Delaney'. He wrote many articles and poems concerning happenings in World War I and attended the Versailles peace conference as London correspondent of the *Daily Telegraph*. He subsequently wrote for the *Sydney Morning Herald* and from 1925 until his death, he was editor of the Sydney shipping magazine, *Harbour*. He died on 29 November 1938 at Wauchope, New South Wales, and was cremated in Sydney.

SANDFORD, Arthur W. (1858–1939) Born Co. Tipperary, the son of Canon Sandford, rector of Clonmel. He was the second husband of **Lady Mary Carbery** whom he married in February 1902. He was educated at Queen's College, Cork (now UCC) and graduated MD in 1882. He later lectured on ophthalmics and otology at that college. He lived at Frankfield House, Douglas, (*c.*1890–1920) and was one of the founders of the Eye, Ear and Throat Hospital (known colloquially as the 'Iron Throat') Western Road, in 1897. He died at his residence near the Welsh border, Eye Manor, on 12 May 1939 and was buried in Eye Graveyard. His son, Christopher (b. 1902), was a noted printer and was the founder of the Boar's Head Press. Later he became the owner of the Golden Cockerel Press which had been previously owned by **Robert Gibbings**.

SANDHAM, Robert (1620–1675) Born Petworth, Sussex, of Baptist parents. He came to Ireland with the army of Cromwell and settled in Youghal. Having heard the Quakeress, Elizabeth Fletcher, preach in Youghal, he converted and was a founder of the Youghal Connexion. In 1662, the Quakers were forbidden to meet in Youghal and Sandham was arrested. He was forced to walk to Charleville to appear before the Lord president of Munster, **Roger Boyle**, 1st earl of Orrery. To the disappointment of the Youghal magistrates, he was released.

SARSFIELD, Edmund (1736–*p.*1791) Born Doughcloyne, Cork, of the Cork branch of the Sarsfield family. He went to France and joined Rothe's Irish regiment as a cadet in 1752. He later rose to the rank of lieutenant-colonel in Walsh's Regiment and for his bravery he was made a Chevalier of St Louis. When the Irish Brigade was dissolved in 1791, he remained on in the 92nd Regiment (which had replaced Walsh's) and fought for the Revolutionary army in which he rose to the rank of general.

SAUL, John (1819–1897) Born Deerpark, Castlemartyr, Co. Cork, the son of James Saul, head gardener at Carewswood, the dowerhouse of the Shannon estate. As he grew up, he was trained in the science of landscape gardening and in his early 20s he went to England where he managed extensive nurseries. Following his arrival in Washington DC in May 1851, he was engaged by the American government to lay out the Smithsonian Grounds, Lafayette Square and other public parks. In 1852, he purchased a property, 120 acres of which he set out in nursery stock. He imported new plants from Europe as soon as they had come on the market and orchids from Africa, Mexico and South America. He shipped plants to all parts of the United States and also some native American plants to Europe. He was for many years a member of the Parking Commission in Washington and ultimately its chairman. He died in Washington on 11 May 1897.

SAUNDERS, George (1823–1913) Born Cork, the son of Lieutenant-Colonel R. Saunders. He was educated at St Bartholomew's Hospital, London, and, having qualified as a doctor, he entered the British army as a surgeon in the 47th Regiment. He saw service throughout the Crimean War and then served in China, Hong Kong, Japan and Cape Province. During his stay in China, he was decorated in 1869 for his services during an epidemic. Before his retirement in 1871, he had become Deputy inspector-general of the army. He returned to his native city and was appointed as a consultant surgeon at the Eye, Ear and Throat Hospital. He also served as president of the Medical Missionary Association and as deputy inspector of hospitals. He died on 6 March 1913. He published several works including *The Healer-Preacher, Stories of Medical Mission Work* and *Reminiscences*.

SAVAGE, Robert (1818–1888) Born Cork, the son of Francis Savage, gentleman. He was educated at Rutland Square, Dublin, and entered TCD in October 1834 with a church career in mind. He never graduated, however, but emigrated to Australia where he lived as a sheep farmer and local magistrate at Nangeela, Victoria. Subsequently, he moved around Victoria as a farmer and land reformer and published the *International Exhibition Essays* (1872–3) which dealt with state agricultural matters. However, his great interest was in the field of inventions. He invented items as diverse as reaping machines, stone-breakers, cement, paint, sewing machines, elevators, steam vacuum lift pumps, electric shearing machines and even a torpedo which he hoped to sell to the Italian Government! He died in Melbourne on 12 July 1888 and was buried in St Kilda Cemetery there.

SAWARD, Pat (1928–2002) Born Cobh, Co. Cork, but was raised in South London. Displaying football talent as a teenager, he played for Crystal Palace as an amateur, before signing professionally for Millwall in July 1951. A tall well-built left-half or inside-left, he played 120 League games and scored fourteen goals for Millwall, before transferring to Aston Villa for a fee of £16,000 in August 1955. He made 162 League appearances for Villa, won an FA Cup medal with them in 1957 and captained the team to the Second Division Championship in 1959/60. In March 1961, he transferred to Huddersfield Town and made fifty-nine League appearances for them before retiring in October 1963 to become coach at Coventry City. He was manager of Brighton from 1970 to 1973, taking them into the Second Division in 1971–72. He later coached the Saudi Arabian club AL-NASR and ran a holiday business in Minorca. He

made eighteen international appearances for the Republic of Ireland between 1953 and 1962. He captained the team which defeated West Germany 1–0 in May 1960. He died at Newmarket in Cambridgeshire on 20 September 2002.

SCANNELL, Richard (1845–1916) Born Sheanliss, Cloyne, Co. Cork, the son of Patrick Scannell. A fluent Irish speaker, he was educated at All Hallows College, Dublin, and was ordained there in 1871. He immediately departed for the United States and undertook pastoral work in the diocese of Nashville until 1887, being administrator of the diocese from 1880. He was consecrated as bishop of the newly created diocese of Concordia, Kansas, in November 1887. He was translated to the diocese of Omaha, Nebraska, in January 1891. He died in Ohama on 8 January 1916 and was buried there.

SCULLY, Harry (c.1863–1935) Born Cork. He initially worked as a bookkeeper, but having an interest in painting, he enrolled in the Cork School of Art and later studied at Heatherley's Academy, London, where he specialised in watercolours. Following a further period of study on the Continent, he returned to Cork and set up a studio at Nelson's Place (now Emmet Place). His exhibitions at the Royal Hibernian Academy began in 1893 and he was made a full member of this institution in 1906. Some of his works were also shown at the Royal Academy, London (1896, 1900–1). His portrait of UCC president, **Sir Bertram Windle,** hangs in the Aula Maxima there. Among his pupils in Cork were **Lady Katherine Dobbin** and **Robert Gibbings**. He left Cork in the late 1920s and went to live Orpington, Kent. After being involved in a street accident, he died at a London hospital on 21 July 1935.

SCULLY, Vincent (1810–1871) Born Dublin, the son of Denis Scully, advocate, political writer and a native of Co. Tipperary. He was educated at Oscott College, at TCD and at Trinity College, Cambridge. He was called to the Bar in 1833 and to the Inner Bar in 1849. He was the author of several notable pamphlets on the Irish Land Question such as *Free Trade in Land* (1853). He was elected as Liberal MP for Cork County in a March 1852 by-election, but lost his seat in 1857. He regained it two years later, but was defeated again in 1865. He died on 4 June 1871.

SEYMOUR, Henry J. (1876–1954) Born Co. Cork, the eldest son of M.S. Seymour, schools inspector, who resided in Dunmanway and who later held the position of senior secretary of the National Board of Education. Henry was educated at the Royal College of Science, at Queen's University, Belfast, and at UCD. In 1898, he was appointed as temporary assistant geologist to the Geological Survey of Ireland and was promoted to geologist to the survey three years later. He retired from the service in November 1909 when he was appointed as professor of Geology at UCD – a post which he held until his retirement in 1947. He died at his residence on the Stillorgan Road, Dublin, on 28 January 1954 and was buried in Dean's Grange Cemetery.

SHANAHAN, Michael (1731–1811) Born Co. Cork, where he owned a marble works. He came to the notice of the bishop of Cloyne, **Frederick A. Hervey**, who, when translated to Derry in 1768, took Shanahan along to plan and supervise his many huge building projects in that diocese. He travelled to Italy with Hervey in the early 1770s where he was employed to measure and draw several Swiss, Italian and French bridges which had been designed by the Grubermann brothers. While in Vicenza he began work on an architectural book which, however, was never published. Among many others, he designed the Mussenden Temple and St Rémy Monument at Downhill, Co. Derry, and Hervey's residence at Ballyscullion, Co. Derry. He was also responsible for designing and building (1788–91), at a cost of £13,000, the old St Patrick's Bridge, Cork, which was swept away by floodwaters in 1853 and replaced by the present structure. He was also the architect of the Spike Island fortifications in Cork Harbour. He died at White Street, Cork, on 22 May 1811.

SHARKEY, Patrick (*c.*1772–1840) Born Co. Roscommon. He was educated at TCD where he graduated BA (1799), MA (1801) and MB (1802). While at college, he won several prizes for Greek and Latin verse. He worked as senior physician at Cork General Dispensary and died at Castletownbere in 1840. He published *Poema Heroicum Graecum* (1804) and wrote several poems for various Cork journals.

SHAW, Sir Eyre M. (1828–1908) Born Ballymore, Cobh, Co. Cork, the son of Bernard R. Shaw, merchant. He was educated at Dr Coghlan's School, Queenstown (now Cobh) and at TCD where he graduated BA (1848) and MA (1854). He spent some time at sea on the Cork-Quebec timber route and served in the British army from 1854 to 1859. In 1859, he was appointed as chief constable of police and fire services of Belfast and was promoted to head the London Fire Engine Establishment in 1861. An expert in fire protection, he was knighted on his retirement in 1891 and received the freedom of the City of London in the following year. Among his publications were *A Complete Manual of the organisation, machinery, discipline and general working of the fire brigade of London* (1876, rev. ed. 1890) and *Fires in Theatres* (1876, 2nd ed. 1889). He died at Folkestone, Kent, on 25 August 1908 and was buried in Highgate Cemetery, London. Shaw was lampooned in the Fairy Queen's air in Gilbert & Sullivan's *Iolanthe* of 1882:

'On fire that glows with heat intense
I turn the hose of commonsense,
And out it goes at small expense!
We must maintain our fairy law
That is the main on which to draw –
In that we gain a Captain Shaw!

Oh, Captain Shaw!
Type of true love kept under!
Could thy brigade with cold cascade
Quench my great love, I wonder?'
[Life by R. Cox (1998)]

SHAW, William (1823–1895) Born Moy, Co. Tyrone, the son of Samuel Shaw, clergyman. Following a period at TCD, he trained for the Congregational ministry at Highbury College, Middlesex, and took up a position at the Congregational Church, George's Street (now Oliver Plunkett Street), Cork, in 1846. He married into a wealthy Cork family in 1850 and left the ministry to pursue a business career. Going into politics, he became MP for Bandon in 1868 as an independent Liberal candidate and served until 1874 when the constituency was dissolved. Previously, in 1870, he had become associated with the Home Government Association of **Isaac Butt** and presided at the founding of the Home Rule League at the Rotunda, Dublin, in November 1873. He was returned as a Home Rule MP for Cork County in 1874 and was elected as party chairman at Westminster after the death of Butt in 1879. He topped the poll for the County in the general election of 1880 but broke with **C.S. Parnell** after the latter was chosen by ballot as party chairman. He continued in Parliament as an independent Liberal before his retirement from politics in 1885. While an MP, he played a leading role in the development of industry and commerce in Cork and was particularly associated with the Cork Flax Spinning Company. He was also a director of the Munster Bank which collapsed in 1885 (it was subsequently saved as the 'Munster and Leinster Bank' [now AIB] through the efforts of the Cork brewer, **James J. Murphy**). Shaw went bankrupt shortly afterwards and went to live in London. He died at Enniskerry, Co. Wicklow, on 19 September 1895.

SHEA, John A. (1802–1845) Born Cork, and worked as a clerk at the Beamish & Crawford Brewery. He wrote poetry for both the *Cork Merchantile Reporter* and *Bolster's Cork Quarterly* before emigrating to the United States in 1827. His publications include, *The Lament of Hellas* (1826), *Adolph* (1831), *Parnassian Wild Flowers* (1836), *Clontarf* (1843) and *Poems* (posthumously, 1846). He died in New York on 15 August 1845.

SHEAHAN, Denis B. (1843–1924) Born Buttevant, Co. Cork, he emigrated to the United States where he studied art and astronomy at Yale University. A sculptor, astronomer and inventor, he perfected instruments and charts later used by the US Navy and other government departments. As a sculptor, his bust of Thomas Moore (1779–1852) graces The Mall in Central Park, New York. Other works include statues of Daniel O'Connell (1775–1847) and General George Custer (1839–76). He also produced equestrian statues of General Robert E. Lee (1807–70) and General Guzmán Blanco (1829–99). He died on 11 October 1924.

SHEAHAN, Thomas (1797–1836) Born Dominick Street, Cork, the son of Thomas Sheahan, self-employed carpenter. He received a good education locally and studied for the priesthood for a period. In 1823, he took up employment as tutor to the Deasy family of Clonakilty, one of his pupils being the future MP, **Rickard Deasy**. Sheahan became politicised during this period by his observation of the magistracy in action at the local courts and through his involvement with the Catholic Association. He spent most of 1825 in London where his political tract, *Excursions from Bandon* (1825), was published. In January 1826, he became editor of the *Cork Mercantile Chronicle*, a Liberal and pro-Catholic newspaper. He became a leading figure in Cork radical politics, was a propagandist for Catholic Emancipation, municipal reform and for measures to alleviate the plight of the poor. He played a key role in establishing the Cork Trades Association in 1832. Resigning as editor of the *Chronicle* in 1833, he published his best-known work, *Articles of Cork Manufacture*, later that year. He died of a fever at Dominick Street on 29 March 1836 and was buried in St Joseph's Cemetery, where a substantial monument was erected over his grave by the Cork Trades Association later that year. [Life by Fintan Lane (2001)]

SHEARES, Henry (*fl.* 1761–1774) A banker, he was a partner in the firm of Rogers, Travers

& Sheares. He was the father of **Henry Sheares** and **John Sheares** of the Society of United Irishmen who were executed in July 1798 while planning for the insurrection of that year. He sat as MP for Clonakilty (1761–8) and founded, in 1774, a Cork society for the relief and discharge from the Debtors' Prison of inmates owing only small amounts. He was also a noted figure in the Cork literary world of his day.

SHEARES, Henry (1753–1798) Born Cork, the son of **Henry Sheares**, banker and MP. He was educated at TCD and later joined the British Army. On leaving this, he was called to the Bar in 1789. When his first wife died in 1791, his four children were reared by her parents in Paris. While visiting them with his younger brother, **John Sheares**, in 1792, he embraced Republicanism and on their return to Ireland, they joined the Society of United Irishmen. As plans were being drawn up for the 1798 Rising, the brothers were arrested on 21 May and hanged for high treason at Newgate Prison, Dublin, on 14 July 1798.

SHEARES, John (1766–1798) Born Cork, the son of **Henry Sheares**, banker and MP. He was the younger brother of **Henry Sheares (1753–1798)**. He was educated at TCD and called to the Bar in 1788. Following a visit to Paris in 1792, he and his brother joined the Society of United Irishmen on their return. He became a regular contributor to the society's paper, *The Press*. With his brother, he was arrested on 21 May 1798 having been betrayed by an informer. The brothers were executed at Newgate Prison, Dublin, on 14 July 1798.

SHEEHAN, Daniel D. (1874–1948) Born Knockardrahan, Dromtariff, Co. Cork, the second son of Daniel Sheehan, tenant farmer, who, following his eviction in 1880, became a licensed vintner in Kanturk. While still in his teens, 'D.D.' was secretary of the Kanturk Land and Labour Association, a farm labourers' organisation. He pursued a successful career in journalism for several years and was managing

editor of the Preston *Catholic News* for two years before becoming editor of the Skibbereen *Southern Star* (1898–1901). He played a prominent role in the Irish Land and Labour Association and, espousing the cause of small tenant farmers and agricultural labourers, unsuccessfully sought nomination in 1900 as a Labour candidate in South Cork. In 1901, he won selection as the nationalist candidate in a Mid-Cork by-election. He was returned unopposed and successfully defended his seat five times until 1918. An ally of **William O'Brien**, he resigned from the Irish Parliamentary Party in 1906, was an Independent Nationalist (1907–10) and, on the formation of O'Brien's All-for-Ireland League in 1910, became its secretary. Having obtained a law degree at UCC in 1909, he was called to the Bar in 1911. He volunteered for service on the outbreak of World War I, was commissioned captain in the Royal Munster Fusiliers and served in the British Expeditionary Force in France. He was later invalided home because of deafness caused by shellfire. His two eldest sons, Daniel and Martin, were killed in 1918 while serving in the Royal Flying Corps (now RAF). Another son, Michael, left Farranferris College to join the British army and eventually became the youngest officer to be wounded in action. His daughter, Eileen, who was serving as a nurse at the front, also lost her fiancé who was an officer. Daniel resigned his parliamentary seat in 1918 and lived in England for several years. He returned to Dublin following the ending of the civil war and was appointed as Editor of the *Dublin Chronicle*. His book, *Ireland since Parnell* (1921), is an account of Irish politics from the death of Parnell to 1918. He died at Queen Anne Street, London, on a visit to his daughter on 26 November 1948. He was buried in Glasnevin Cemetery.

SHEEHAN, Patrick A. (1852–1913) Born Mallow, Co. Cork, the son of a small businessman. He was educated at St Colman's College, Fermoy and at St Patrick's College, Maynooth. Following his ordination in 1875, he served on the English mission and, on his return, he served in various curacies in the diocese of Cloyne. He was appointed as parish priest of Doneraile in 1895 and was elevated to the cathedral chapter in 1903. He established a firm reputation as a novelist through his books which included *Geoffrey Austin, Student* (1895), *The Triumph of Failure* (1898), *My New Curate* (1898), *Glenanaar* (1905), *Luke Delmege* (1905), *Lisheen* (1907) and *The Graves at Kilmorna* (1916). He also published a collection of poems, *Cithara Mea* (1900). He died on 5 October 1913. His brother, D.B. Sheehan, who worked as a bank clerk in Cork, was a local poet. [Red marble tablet by **Seamus Murphy** at the Technical School, Mallow]

SHEEHAN, Richard A. (1845–1915) Born Bantry, Co. Cork. He was educated at St Vincent's, Cork and at St Patrick's College, Maynooth, where he was ordained in 1868. Having served as a curate and canon in the diocese of Cork, he was consecrated as bishop of Waterford and Lismore on 31 January 1892. He was a founder member and first president of the Cork Historical and Archaeological Society (1891). He was also a founder member and first president of the Waterford and South East of Ireland Archaeological Society. Before his episcopal appointment, he had been president of Cork Catholic Young Men's Society. He died in Waterford on 14 October 1915 and was buried in Holy Trinity Cathedral.

SHEEHAN, Thomas (*c.*1796–1880) Born Friar's Walk, Cork, the eldest son of Thomas Sheehan, nurseryman and seed merchant. Thomas and his younger brother Remigius (Remmy) purchased the staunchly Conservative *Dublin Evening Mail* newspaper from Timothy Haydn in 1833. With Thomas as proprietor and Remmy as editor, they pursued an anti-Roman Catholic line and poured scorn on Daniel O'Connell. Both brothers were noted for their satiric wit. On one occasion Remmy assaulted O'Connell with an umbrella and was sentenced to three months imprisonment for his valour.

After Remmy's early demise, Thomas carried on the paper on his own until 1858 when he sold it to Maunsell & Co. Thomas lived to a good age, was reputedly reconciled to the Roman Catholic church and died at his residence, Mespil House, Dublin on 25 March 1880. He was buried in Glasnevin Cemetery. Their younger brother, George (1810–87), was ironically a priest of the Diocese of Cork, who died as parish priest of St Patrick's parish and vicar general of the diocese.

SHEEHY, Samuel J.A. (1827–1910) Born Cork, the son of John Sheehy, carpenter and builder. The family emigrated to Sydney, Australia, in 1838. He was educated at St Mary's Seminary and entered the Benedictine Order in August 1849. Following his ordination in March 1852, he taught at St Mary's Day School and held various chaplaincies. He was elected as a fellow of St John's College, University of Sydney and in 1866 he was appointed as auxiliary bishop to the archbishop of Sydney. However, the consecration did not take place as he was charged of 'having connived at the apostasies of certain monks' and of having left his room in a drunken state. He resigned the appointment but remained as vicar general of the archdiocese until 1873. He held various parochial appointments and presided over the secularisation of the Australian Benedictines before his death at Randwick, New South Wales, on 14 September 1910.

SHEEHY, Timothy (1855–1938) Born Skibbereen, Co. Cork, the second son of Timothy Sheehy. He was educated locally and at Castleknock College, Co. Dublin. He was a member of Skibbereen Town Commissioners from 1885 and of its successor, Skibbereen Urban District Council, from its establishment in 1900, being chairman in its first year. In all, he was prominent in public affairs in Skibbereen for nearly sixty years. He was a member of Cork County Council (1902–20 and 1925–38) and a Redmondite in the 1910–14 period. He was elected as a Fine Gael TD for West Cork in 1927, but lost his seat in the general election of

1932 while he was 'Father of the Dáil'. He died on 5 November 1938 and was buried in Castlehaven Graveyard.

SHEEHY-SKEFFINGTON, Hanna (1877–1946) Born Mill House, Kanturk, Co. Cork, the daughter of David Sheehy, mill owner and MP. She was educated at the Dominican Convent, Eccles Street, Dublin and at the Royal University of Ireland where she graduated BA (1902). She worked as a teacher at the Rathmines School of Commerce and, in 1903, married the socialist and pacifist, Francis Skeffington, a university registrar. The pair were co-founders of the Irish Women's Franchise League and founded the influential paper, the *Irish Citizen*, in 1912. She was imprisoned for her suffragette activities and was sacked from her teaching post. The Skeffingtons were involved with James Connolly (1868–1916) in the Dublin Lockout of 1913. Hanna was subsequently arrested, as was her husband for his anti-recruitment activities at the outbreak of World War I. During the Rising of 1916, Francis was arrested and murdered by British soldiers at Portobello (now Cathal Brugha) Barracks – an event which led to an enquiry by a royal commission at the insistence of Hanna. She toured America on behalf of Sinn Féin and Cumann na mBan, and, on her way home, was again arrested but subsequently released after going on hunger strike. She then served on the executive of Sinn Féin and was appointed as a judge in the republican courts. She took the anti-Treaty side during the civil war and was appointed as a member of the first executive of Fianna Fáil in 1926. However, she soon left and became the assistant editor of *An Phoblacht* (the organ of the IRA) in 1932. Despite campaigning intensively as an independent candidate on a feminist 'ticket' in the general elections of 1938 and 1943, she failed to take a seat. She died in Dublin on 20 April 1946. [Life by L. Levenson/J.H. Natterstad (1986) and M. Luddy (1995).]

SHEIL, Edward (1834–1869) Born Coleraine, Co. Derry. He was a pupil at the Cork School of Art and was eventually appointed as headmaster in 1859. However, due to the state of his health, he was forced to resign in the following year, having been presented with a testimonial by the committee of management. Following a spell in Italy, he returned to Cork where he worked as an artist, specialising in subject painting. He exhibited at the Royal Hibernian Academy (1855–60) and at the Royal Academy, London, in 1866. He was elected as a member of the Royal Hibernian Academy in 1864. He died at the South Mall residence of **Denny Lane** on 11 March 1869.

SHERIDAN, Patrick (*c.*1638–1682) Born Kilmore, Co. Cavan, the son of Denis Sheridan, vicar of Killasher and a former Roman Catholic priest. He was the brother of William Sheridan (1635–1711), non-juror bishop of Kilmore (i.e. who refused to swear allegiance to Queen Mary (1622–94) and King William III (1650–1702) and was deprived of his temporalities but not of his title) and of Sir Thomas Sheridan (1642–1712), author, and secretary of King James II (1633–1701). He was educated at TCD where he graduated BD (1665) and DD (1681). He was elected as vice-provost of TCD in 1666. He was consecrated as Church of Ireland bishop of Cloyne on 27 April 1679. He died in Dublin on 22 November 1682 and was buried in the Chapel of TCD.

SHEYN, Matthew (d. 1582/83) He was born in County Tipperary. He was educated at Peterhouse, Cambridge, but probably did not graduate. The letters patent for his consecration as Church of Ireland bishop of Cork and Ross were issued on 29 May 1572. He alienated episcopal land in both the dioceses of Cork and Cloyne. He was responsible for the first recorded iconoclasm in Cork when, in October 1578, he publicly burned a statue of St Dominic at the 'High Cross of Cork' on the North Main Street. As a contemporary witness noted, 'he was very active in correcting the gross superstitions of the lower orders, especially with regard to the worship of images'. He died either on 13 June 1582, or in August 1583.

SIGERSON, Hester (d. 1898) Born Cork, the sister of **Ralph Varian**. She married the historian and translator, George Sigerson (1836–1925), and subsequently moved to Dublin. Her poems were published in many newspapers and periodicals including, the *Irish Fireside*, the *Cork Examiner*, the *Boston Pilot*, the *Irish Monthly* and *Young Ireland*. She died at her Clare Street, Dublin, residence on 15 April 1898 and was buried in Glasnevin Cemetery.

SIMMONS, Bartholomew (1804–1850) Born Kilworth, Co. Cork. He worked as a clerk in the Cork Excise Office. He took to writing poetry and contributed to *Bolster's Quarterly Magazine* and *Blackwood's Magazine* as well as other periodicals. He published *Legends* in 1843. He died, unmarried, in London on 21 July 1850 and was buried in Highgate Cemetery.

SIMMS, George O. (1910–1991) Born Dublin, the son of John F.A. Simms, Crown Solicitor. He was reared at Lifford, Co. Donegal, and educated at Lifford, Hindhead (Cheltenham) and at TCD where he graduated BA (1932), MA (1935), BD (1936) and DD (1936). He was ordained in 1936 and returned to TCD in 1939 as both a lecturer and dean of residence. He remained until 1952 when he was appointed as dean of Cork. Five months after taking up this position, he succeeded Bishop **Thomas Hearn** as bishop of Cork, Cloyne and Ross on 28 October. He was translated to the archbishopric of Dublin on 11 December 1956. He was elected as Church of Ireland Primate on 17 July 1969. He retired on 11 February 1980 and moved to Templeogue, Dublin, where he died on 15 November 1991. He was buried privately. An expert on the Book of Kells and a fluent Irish speaker, he was elected as a member of the Royal Irish Academy in 1957. [Life by L. Whiteside (1990)]

SIMPSON, Maxwell (1815–1902) Born Co. Armagh. He was educated at TCD where he graduated BA (1837) and MB (1847). Having studied chemistry in London and Germany, he was elected as a fellow of the Royal Society in 1862. He was professor of Chemistry at Queen's College, Cork (now UCC), from 1872 until 1891 and enjoyed the highest reputation in his field, being the first chemist to synthesise succinic acid. He died in London on 26 February 1902. [Commemorative plaque at his former residence, 11, Dyke Parade, Cork]

SISK, John G. (1911–2001) Born Cork, the son of John V. Sisk whose father, John Sisk, had founded the family building firm (specialising in the growing business of church-building) in 1859. He was educated at Clongowes Wood College, Co. Kildare and at UCC where he graduated BE (1932). Following his marriage, he moved to Dublin in the mid-1930s where he built up a steady business resulting in the construction of the US army camps in Derry and Fermanagh during World War II. During the post-war reconstruction period in Europe, he established Ascon Construction in a joint venture with the Dutch group, Hollandsche Beton. He also established another company, Beaver Distribution. His greatest satisfaction came in the field of church building, being responsible for the construction of Galway and Cavan Cathedrals as well as Mutare Cathedral, Zimbabwe. He retired in 1974 and served as a non-executive director of Allied Irish Banks for the following five years. By that time, his firm had become the largest construction company in Ireland. He died at his residence on Cowper Road, Rathmines, Dublin on 11 March 2001 and was buried in Bohernabreena Cemetery, Co. Dublin.

SKIDDY, Roger (d. c.1588) Born Cork, of a prominent and wealthy local family. He was appointed as Dean of Limerick in 1552. Following the death of Bishop **Dominic Tirrey**, he was granted the temporalities of the dioceses of Cork and Cloyne by Queen Mary (1516–58) on 18 September 1557. He was not consecrated until 30 October 1562 (letters patent of Queen Elizabeth I (1533–1603) on July 31, though **A. Bolster** argues in *The History of the Diocese of*

Cork [vol. 1] that the consecration date was not correct). The consecration was not recognised by the Papacy. He resigned on 18 March 1567 for some unspecified reason. He was pardoned for his resignation on 7 May following and was appointed as warden of St Mary's Collegiate Church, Youghal. He died *c.*1588.

SKILLEN, Samuel (*c.*1819–1847) Born Cork. Showing considerable talent as an artist, he was helped by **Richard Sainthill** who was also a patron of **Daniel Maclise**. He received his artistic education at the Royal Hibernian Academy School and in London. His two-year visit to countries of southern Europe was described in a series of letters to the *Literary Gazette*. He subsequently exhibited at the Royal Hibernian Academy (1842–3) and returned to Cork shortly before his death at his sisters' haberdashery premises in Patrick Street on 27 January 1847. [Portrait by **William Fisher** at Cork Municipal Museum]

SKINNER, Leo B. (d. 1970) Born Mitchelstown, Co. Cork, the son of James G. Skinner, solicitor. He was educated at Clongowes Wood College and at UCD. During the War of Independence, he was a member of the Mitchelstown unit of the IRA and subsequently took the Republican side in the civil war. He qualified as a solicitor in 1930. He was later elected as a Fianna Fáil TD for North Cork in the general election of 1943 and held his seat in the following year. In 1948, he stood for the new Cork East constituency but was unsuccessful. He was appointed a district justice for the Ballinasloe area in 1954 and was transferred to the Tipperary area later in the same year. He died at the Bon Secours Hospital, Cork, on 27 January 1970 and was buried in Mitchelstown Cemetery.

SKOTTOWE, Charles (*fl.* 1829–1842) He was born in 1793 and practised in Cork where he earned a reputation as a portrait painter. In 1829, he exhibited at the Royal Hibernian Academy and then settled in London. His works were regularly exhibited at the British Institution and at the Royal Academy between 1834 and 1842.

SLEIGH, Joseph F. (1733–1770) Born Cork, the son of William Sleigh and Anne Fenn (the family which has given its name to Fenn's Quay). He was educated at the Quaker school at Ballitore, Co. Kildare, where one of his fellow-pupils was the orator, Edmund Burke (1729–97). He attended Cambridge University and became friendly with the poet, Oliver Goldsmith (*c.*1728–74), who wrote an elegy on Sleigh's death. He later qualified as a doctor. He was on the medical staff of the North Infirmary Hospital from 1759 until his death on 10 May 1770.

SLEVIN, Gerard (1919–1997) Born Cork. He entered the civil service in 1944 and worked in the Genealogical Office. He was appointed as chief herald of Ireland in 1954 and held this position until his retirement in 1981. He died on 18 January 1997 and was buried privately.

SLEYNE, John Baptist (1639–1712) Born Cloyne or Midleton, Co. Cork, the son of John Sleyne. He was educated at the University of Paris where he graduated MA (1661) and DD (1670). In 1672, he was appointed as vicar apostolic and dean of Cloyne. He went to Rome in 1676 where he acted as the agent of Bishop **Peter Creagh** and also taught as a professor at the College of Propaganda. He was consecrated as bishop of Cork and Cloyne on 3 November 1692, having been nominated by the exiled King James II (1633–1701). He arrived in Ireland in late January or early February 1694 and lived under the patronage of **Sir James Cotter** of Carrigtohill. He was arrested in 1697 under the Banishment Act. A trial followed in July 1702 and he was sentenced to be banished to Portugal. He was deported in March 1703 and was accommodated in Lisbon by the Irish Dominicans. He resigned on 22 January 1712 and died three weeks later on 16 February. He was buried in the convent of Buom Successo, Lisbon. [Profile and portrait in **A. Bolster** *A History of the Diocese of Cork* (vol. 2, 1989)]

SMIDDY, Richard (1811–1878) Born Bally-makea, Killeagh, Co. Cork. He held several curacies in the diocese of Cloyne before his appointment as parish priest of Aghada in 1854. Though best known for his archaeological writings, his earliest publication was *The Holy Bible and the manner in which it is used by Catholics* (1850) and in 1857, he was responsible for a revision of an Irish catechism for diocesan use, *An Teagasc Chríostaidhe, de réir ceist is freagra ...* In 1866, he published anonymously, *Tobar Mhuire, or Lady's Well in Aghada* – a work which was reprinted in 1897. His best known work, *Essay on the Druids, Ancient Churches, and Round Towers of Ireland* (1871) was later published in abbreviated form (1976), but like most of his contemporaries on the subject, his theories would not pass muster with modern scholarship. Canon Smiddy died on 11 June 1878 and was buried in Aghada Graveyard. A Celtic memorial cross was erected over his grave around 1879.

SMIDDY, Timothy A. (1876–1962) Born Cork, the son of William Smiddy of Kilbarry House. He was educated at St Finbarr's College, Farranferris and at UCC where he graduated MA (1907). He later studied in Paris and at the Handelshöchschüle of Cologne. He was professor of Economics and dean of the faculty of Commerce at UCC (1909–24). In 1921, he was the economic advisor to the Irish plenipotentiaries at the Anglo-Irish Treaty talks in London and from 1922 to 1924 was envoy of Dáil Éireann to the United States. From then until 1929, he was envoy extraordinary and minister plenipotentiary of the Irish Free State to Washington. During the 1930s, he chaired several government committees (Trade Loans Committee, 1933–7; Commission on Agriculture, 1939; Summer Time Committee, 1940). He was also a director of the Central Bank of Ireland (1943–55). In retirement, he became Chairman and Managing Director of Arklow Pottery (1946–59) and placed this firm on a firm foundation before he left in 1959. He died in Dublin on 9 February 1962 and was buried in Dean's Grange Cemetery.

SMITH, Charles (c.1715–1762) Born Co. Waterford. He practised as an apothecary in Dungarvan. He published *The Antient and Present State of the County and City of Cork* in 1750 under the auspices of the Physico-Historical Society of Ireland in Dublin. He also published histories of counties Kerry, Waterford and (with Walter Harris) Down. In 1756, he was a founder member and first secretary of the Medico-Philosophical Society which lasted in Dublin until 1784. He died in Bristol in July 1762.

SMITH, Lucy E. (d. 1929) She was the daughter of J.A. Smith, a Presbyterian minister who resided in Cork City and who served his community at Aghada, Co. Cork. In 1896, she and Dora A. Allman became the first women medical graduates at Queen's College, Cork (now UCC). She is always referred to as 'the first lady doctor in Cork' and was the first female doctor to set up a practice there. She was a past-president of the Munster branch of the British Medical Association, and an examiner of the Central Board for Midwives in Ireland. She was closely associated with the Erinville Hospital and The Home for Protestant Incurables. She died at her residence, 2 Verdon Place, Cork, on 23 March 1929 and was buried in St Luke's Cemetery, Douglas. Her brother, Major General J.B. Smith (1865–1928), was a distinguished medic in the Indian Service.

SMITH-BARRY, Arthur H. (1843–1925) He was the eldest son of James Hugh Smith-Barry of Fota Island and of Marbury Hall, Cheshire. He was educated at Eton College and Christ Church, Oxford. In February 1867, he was selected (with the support of the Roman Catholic clergy) as a Liberal candidate for Cork County to succeed the late **George R. Barry**. He was returned unopposed. He was MP until 1874 when he did not seek re-election. The owner of 12,000 acres in Co. Cork, and with estates in Co. Tipperary, Cheshire and Huntingdon, he was high sheriff for Cheshire in 1883 and for Cork in 1886. He was a

Conservative Unionist MP for South Huntingdon from July 1886 until he retired in 1900. He came to national prominence during the Plan of Campaign (1886–91). He was co-founder of the Cork Defence Union in 1885 and a leader of landlord opposition to tenant demands. In 1889, his eviction of 152 tenants in Tipperary led to the foundation of the Tenants' Defence League and the establishment of 'New Tipperary' to house the evicted tenants. He was a vice-president of the Irish Unionist Alliance and its chairman (1911–13). He was also vice-president of the Irish Landowners Convention. He was a keen sportsman, having a great interest in cricket and hunting. He was also admiral of the Royal Cork Yacht Club. He was created 1st Baron Barrymore in 1902. He died at his London residence on 22 February 1925 and was cremated at Golders Green Crematorium.

SNOW, Joseph (*fl.* 1840) A Cork poet, he wrote for local journals under the pseudonym, 'Oberon'. He moved to London in the early 1830s and was called to the English Bar in the 1840s. However, he eventually settled for a career in journalism. He also published travel books in 1835 and 1838 under the pseudonym, 'George St George'.

SOMERVILLE, H. Boyle T. (1863–1936) Born Castletownshend, Co. Cork, the third son of Lt. Col. Thomas H. Somerville, army officer, landowner, high sheriff of Cork (1888) and brother of **Edith O. Somerville**. Having been educated at various naval academies, he entered the Royal Navy, where he had a distinguished career. He retired in 1919 with the rank of vice-admiral and was subsequently employed by the Admiralty Hydrographic Department. His publications following his retirement included, *The Chartmakers* (1928), *Commodore Anson's Voyage* (1934) and *Will Mariner* (1936). He was co-author with Edith of the family history, *Records of the Somerville Family* (1940). A keen amateur archaeologist, he contributed several articles to the *JCHAS*. Having retired to Castletownshend, he was in the habit of

providing references to local young men wishing to join the Royal Navy. This was interpreted by the IRA as recruiting for the British Forces and he was shot dead at Castletownshend on 24 March 1936.

SOMERVILLE, Edith O. (1858–1949) Born Corfu, Greece, the daughter of Thomas H. Somerville, army officer, landowner, high sheriff of Cork (1888) and sister of **H. Boyle T. Somerville**. The father retired in 1859 and returned to his home, Drishane House, Castletownshend. Edith was privately educated there and at Alexandra College, Dublin. Having studied painting in London and on the Continent, she returned home and began a literary partnership with her Galway cousin, Violet Martin ('Martin Ross'). The pair ('Somerville and Ross') published: *An Irish Cousin* (1889), *Naboth's Vineyard* (1891), *Through Connemara in a Governess's Cart* (1892), *In the Vine Country* (1893), *The Real Charlotte* (1894), *Beggars on Horseback* (1895), *The Silver Fox* (1898), *Some Experiences of an Irish RM* (1899), *Further Experiences of an Irish RM* (1908), *Dan Russel the Fox* (1911) and *In Mr Knox's Country* (1915). Further publications subsequent to Violet Martin's death in 1915 (still under the title of 'Somerville and Ross') included *Irish Memories* (1917), *Mount Music* (1919), *The Big House of Inver* (1925) and *The States through Irish Eyes* (1931). A founder member of the Irish Academy of Letters and the Munster Women's Franchise League (which she founded with **Geraldine Cummins** and **Suzanne Day**), she died at Drishane on 8 October 1949. [Life by **G. Cummins** (1952) and G. Lewis (2004); Bibliography (New York, 1942)]

SOUTHWELL, Edward (1671–1730) Born St Martin-in-the-Fields, London, the son of **Sir Robert Southwell**. He was educated at Merton College, Oxford, and worked as a clerk of the English Privy Council. He was appointed as vice-admiral of Munster in 1699 and succeeded his father as Irish chief secretary on the latter's death in 1702 which position, in 1720, was granted to him and his son, Edward, for life at

£300 a year. He married Elizabeth Cromwell, the daughter of the earl of Ardglass, and thus obtained extensive properties in Co. Down. Following the union of England and Scotland in 1707, he was appointed as clerk to the Privy Council of Great Britain. He became a member of the Irish Privy Council in 1714 and was MP for Kinsale until his death. He died on 4 December 1730 and was buried at his residence, King's Weston, Gloucestershire. [Portrait (1708) by J. Kneller]

SOUTHWELL, Robert (1607–1677) Born Kinsale, Co. Cork, the son of Anthony Southwell, a landowner who came to Ireland in the wake of the Munster Plantation and father of **Sir Robert Southwell**. He was appointed as collector of the Port of Kinsale in 1631. He lived there during the Confederate Wars and took the side of the Royalists. Under the Cromwellian administration he lost a fifth of his estates, but following the Restoration, he was granted the forfeited estate of Philip Barry Óg in 1666. This included the liberty of Kinsale and the lands of Ringcurran. In 1670, he was appointed as vice-admiral of Munster and a member of the provincial council. He died on 3 April 1677 and was buried at St Multose's Church, Kinsale.

SOUTHWELL, Sir Robert (1635–1702) Born Battin Warwick, Kinsale, Co. Cork, the son of **Robert Southwell**. He was educated at Queen's College, Oxford, where he graduated BA (1655). He subsequently studied law at Lincoln's Inn, London. In 1665, he was knighted and appointed as envoy to the Court of Portugal (1665–9) and to Brussels (1671–2). In the meantime, he was appointed in 1680 as chief commissioner of the excise at Kinsale with a salary of £500 a year. In 1679, he purchased the manor of King's Weston, Gloucestershire, and in 1682 he founded and endowed an almshouse 'for eight helpless men and women' in Kinsale. He lived at King's Weston until the English revolution of 1689 and accompanied King William (1650–1702) to Ireland in the following year. Following his victory in Ireland, William appointed him as

Irish chief secretary – a post which he held for the rest of his life. In 1690, he was elected as president of the Royal Society and held this position until 1695. He died at King's Weston on 11 September 1702 and was buried in Henbury Church, Gloucestershire. [Portrait by J. Kneller at the Royal Society]

SPENCE, Robert W. (1860–1934) Born Cork, the son of Robert Spence. He was educated locally and entered the Dominican Novitiate at Tallaght, Dublin, in 1878. Following his studies at Corpo Santo College, Lisbon, he was ordained there in December 1882. He then returned to Ireland where he ministered at St Mary's, Cork and at St Catherine's, Newry. In 1892, he was appointed as prior of Black Abbey, Kilkenny, where he restored the old church and built a new abbey. He was appointed as prior of the Dominican Order's first Australian house in 1898 and took up residence in Adelaide, South Australia. Following a period as advisor to Archbishop John O'Reily of Adelaide, he was appointed as the latter's coadjutor bishop in July 1914 and succeeded to the archdiocese in August of the following year. He subsequently carried out major church and school building projects and proved himself to be an outstanding prelate. He was made a freeman of Cork on August 27, 1920, while on a visit to his native city. Before he returned to Australia, he severely criticised the British Government over its handling of the Irish situation. This led to much controversy in Australia. He died on 5 November 1934 and was buried in West Terrace Cemetery, Adelaide.

SPENSER, Edmund (c.1552–1599) Born Smithfield, London, the son of John Spenser, 'a gentleman by birth'. He was educated at Merchant Taylors' School and at Pembroke College, Cambridge, where he graduated BA (1573) and MA (1576). He became secretary to the bishop of Rochester, John Young, and then entered the service of the earl of Leicester. In July 1580, he was appointed as secretary to the lord deputy of Ireland, Lord Arthur Grey, and landed in Dublin on 12 August of that year.

Having been appointed as clerk of the Irish Court of Chancery in 1581, he secured much landed property in counties Wexford and Kildare. He resigned his Dublin position in 1588 and took up a new post as clerk of the Council of Munster. Following the defeat of the earl of Desmond, he was granted in 1589 over 3,000 acres at Kilcolman, near Doneraile, where he wrote his celebrated allegory, *The Faerie Queene*. However, there was continual acrimony between him and Viscount Maurice Roche of Fermoy and in 1594 he lost a land case to Roche which resulted in his resignation from the Munster Council. That same year he married Elizabeth Boyle, a relative of the earl of Cork, **Sir Richard Boyle**. Following his London visit of 1598, he wrote his *View of the Present State of Ireland* in which he recognised no native Irish rights and claims, but he also criticised many aspects of English administration in Ireland. In September 1598, he was appointed as sheriff of Cork – just before the outbreak of the Nine Years War in Munster. Kilcolman Castle was burnt and he fled to Cork with his wife and four children. On 9 December, he was sent to London by the president of Munster, Sir Thomas Norreys, to report on the situation to Queen Elizabeth. However, he died at King Street, Westminster four weeks later, on 13 January 1599 and was buried in Westminster Abbey. [Portrait by B. Wilson at Pembroke College, Cambridge]

SPERRIN-JOHNSON, John C. (1885–1948) Born Grenville House, Cork, the eldest son of A. Johnson (he adopted 'Sperrin' as an additional surname). He entered Queen's College, Cork (now UCC), in 1903 and studied medicine for three years. He graduated BA (1908) in Animal and Vegetable Physiology and Chemistry and MA (1910) in Biological Sciences. Having graduated MB, B.Ch, and BAO in 1913, he entered St John's College, Cambridge, as an advanced student. In that year, he was appointed as professor of Biology at the University of Auckland, New Zealand. He resigned from this position in 1931 through ill health. He then spent a year as naturalist to the British School of

Archaeology in Egypt under Sir Flinders Petrie (1853–1942). He was appointed as professor of Botany at UCC in 1932 (to 1948) and took up residence at Blackrock Castle. He published numerous articles in learned journals on science, travel and folk music. In his will, he bequeathed his collection of music scores and books on music to UCC. He died at the Mercy Hospital, Cork, on 19 May 1948 and was buried in St Joseph's Cemetery.

SPILLAN, Daniel (1797–1854) Born Bantry, Co. Cork, the son of Daniel Spillan, woollen draper. Though a Roman Catholic, he entered TCD in 1817 and graduated BA (1822), and MA and MB (1826). In 1826, he was admitted a licentiate of the College of Physicians in Ireland and was elected a fellow in 1830. A prolific scholar and medical writer, his earliest publications (in Dublin) were critical translations of the classics such as, *The Oration of Aeschines against Ctesiphon* (1823) and *The Orestes and Phoenissae of Euripides* (1826). He moved to London in the early 1830s, where he practised medicine (apparently without great success) and continued his scholarly work. He published translations of medical texts on various topics, as well as original works, such as *A Manual of Chemistry* (1837), manuals on general therapeutics, clinical medicine and a homeopathic Pharmacopoeia. Even though his works were well received, his industry was not rewarded with financial success. He was reduced to destitution and died in St Pancras Workhouse on 20 June 1854.

STAWELL, Sampson (1785–1849) Born Kilbrittain, Co. Cork, the son of Sampson Stawell and nephew of Francis Bernard, 1st earl of Bandon. He joined the British army and served in the Peninsular War with the 12th Lancers. He also fought at the battle of Waterloo and eventually rose to command the regiment in 1827 – a position which he held until 1847. In 1832, on the death of his brother, James Ludlow Stawell (b. 1783), who was a candidate for the borough of Kinsale, Sampson was put forward as a Whig (Liberal) candidate and was elected. He retired in 1835 and died on 21 August 1849.

STAWELL, Sir William F. (1815–1889) Born Oldcourt, Mallow, Co. Cork, the son of Jonas Stawell, barrister and classical scholar. His mother was Anna, the daughter of Bishop **William Foster** of Cork. He was educated at TCD where he graduated BA (1837). He was called to both the Irish and English Bars in 1839. He practised on the Munster Circuit, but emigrated to Melbourne, Australia, three years later when he saw 'forty hats on the Circuit and not enough work for twenty'. He became one of the most prominent barristers in Melbourne and took a leading part in the campaign for the foundation of the state of Victoria which was separated from New South Wales in 1851. It was he who decided on the names of the two houses of the new parliament – the Legislative Assembly and the Legislative Council. He became chief justice of Victoria in February 1857 and was knighted in the following July. He played a leading part in the development of the Victorian Supreme Court and presided over many notable cases. He visited Ireland in 1873 and was conferred with the honorary degrees of MA and LL.D by TCD. He resigned as chief justice in September 1886 and was then appointed as lieutenant-governor of the state. He left Australia in February 1889, but died at Naples on 12 March. He was buried in the English Cemetery there. The town of Stawell, Victoria, is named after him. He took a great interest in many aspects of Victorian life. He was the superintendent of the ill-fated Burke-Wills Expedition of 1861 and headed the mourners at the explorers' funeral. He was also a member of the council of Melbourne University and succeeded his friend, **Redmond Barry** as chancellor for a short period. He was an active member of the Church Synod of Victoria and was one of the framers of its constitution. [Portrait at the Victorian Supreme Court]

STEWART, Isabella (d. 1867) Born Cork, the daughter of Robert Travers, solr., and niece of

Admiral **Sir Eaton Stannard Travers**. She wrote various novels and poems and, in 1827, married Thomas Stewart of Yarmouth. She died on 23 April 1867 and was buried at Gunton Churchyard, Suffolk.

STOCKLEY, William F.P. (1859–1943) Born Templeogue, Co. Dublin, the son of John S. Stockley, RHA. He was educated at Rathmines School and at TCD where he had a brilliant academic career. After graduation, he emigrated to Canada to take up the post of professor of English at the University of New Brunswick (1886–1902) and subsequently at the University of Ottawa (1902–3). He then took up the post of headmaster of St Mary's College, Nova Scotia (1903–5). On his return to Ireland, he was appointed as professor of English at UCC in 1905 and held this position until his retirement in 1930. He joined Sinn Féin in 1916 and was an alderman of Cork Corporation (1920–25). He was also TD for the National University constituency (1921–23). He published *Essays in Irish Biography* (1933) and several other books on aspects of English literature. He died at his residence, 'Arundel', Ballintemple, on 23 July 1943 and was buried in St Finbarr's Cemetery. [Portrait bust by **Joseph Higgins** at UCC]

STOKES, George J. (1859–1935) Born Sligo, the only son of Robert Stokes. He was educated at the Diocesan School, Sligo, at TCD (where he graduated MA), and at the Universities of Heidelberg and Berlin. He studied at Lincoln's Inn, London, and was called to the Bar. He held the chairs of Mental and Social Science (1884–1909) and of Philosophy and Jurisprudence (1909–24) at UCC. He died in London on 6 March 1935. His publications include *The Objectivity of Truth* and many articles on philosophy, mathematical logic and jurisprudence.

STOPFORD, James (1697–1759) Born Dublin, the son of Joseph Stopford, an English army captain. He was educated at TCD where he graduated BA (1715) and MA (1718). He was consecrated as Church of Ireland bishop of

Cloyne on 11 March 1753 in succession to Bishop **George Berkeley**. It was he who was Dean Swift's 'Jim Stopford' and was an executor of the dean's will. He died in Cloyne on 23 August 1759 and was buried in St Ann's Church, Dawson Street, Dublin.

STOPFORD, Robert L. (1813–1898) Born Dublin, but settled in Cork as a young man where he worked as a teacher, and as a cor-respondent of the *Illustrated London News* and other newspapers and magazines. His reputation stands as a landscape and marine watercolour painter. Many of his lithographs describe local Cork scenes. He exhibited at the Royal Hibernian Academy in 1858 and 1884. His son, **William H. Stopford** was also a noted artist. He died at his Monkstown, Co. Cork, residence on 2 February 1898.

STOPFORD, Thomas (1739–1805) Born England, the third son of 1st earl of Courtown (Wexford). He was educated at TCD where he graduated BA (1762), MA (1769) and DD (1794). He was consecrated as Church of Ireland bishop of Cork on 29 June 1794. While in Cork, he made substantial additions to St FinBarre's Diocesan Library (now at UCC). He died in Dublin on 24 January 1805.

STOPFORD, William H. (1842–1890) Born Cork, the son of **Robert L. Stopford**. He received his artistic training from his father, at the Cork School of Art and at South Kensington, London. In 1868, he became headmaster of the Halifax School of Art and settled there until his death. He exhibited in London and in the north of England from 1867 to 1880. His lithograph, 'Blarney Castle', sold 140,000 copies in America alone. He died at Halifax on 15 February 1890.

SULLIVAN, Alexander M. (1830–1884) Born Bantry, Co. Cork, brother of **Timothy D. Sullivan** and **Donal Sullivan** and father of Alexander M. Sullivan (law sergeant). He was educated locally and during the Famine years, was employed as a clerk in local relief schemes.

He supported the Young Ireland movement in 1848 and moved to Dublin in 1853 to work as an artist. Following a spell in Liverpool, he returned to Dublin in 1855 to become assistant editor of *The Nation*, and, in 1858, its editor and owner. Even though he did not agree with the policies of the Fenians, he was imprisoned for an article which he wrote in his *Weekly News* on the events which surrounded the execution of the 'Manchester Martyrs' in 1867. During his impris-onment, a sum of £400 was collected for his support. However, he donated this towards the erection of the statue of Henry Grattan which now stands in College Green, Dublin. Originally, Dublin Corporation had earmarked the site for a statue of Prince Albert, the Prince Consort, but this had been defeated, largely through the efforts of Sullivan, who was a member at the time. He was a founder member of the Home Rule movement in 1870 and was returned as a Home Rule MP for Louth (1874–80). Even though he had topped the poll in 1880, as a supporter of the temperance movement, he refused to take his seat for Louth as his fellow-MP for the constituency was a representative of the licensed vintners. He was presented with a seat for Meath in the same year by **C.S. Parnell**. However, through ill health, he resigned the Meath seat in 1881. In the meantime, he had been called to the Irish Bar in 1876 and to the English Bar in the following year. He died at his Dublin residence in Rathmines on 17 October 1884 and was buried in Glasnevin Cemetery. His publications include, *The Story of Ireland* (1870), *New Ireland* (1877) and *A Nutshell History of Ireland* (1883).

SULLIVAN, Dave (1877–1929) Born Cork. He emigrated to America as a young boy and later took up a career in professional boxing. He won the World Featherweight Championship in New York in 1898, but lost it again within two months. His attempt to regain the title in 1904 failed and he retired in the following year. He died in 1929.

SULLIVAN, Donal (1838–1907) Born Bantry, Co. Cork, the son of John Sullivan of Dublin.

He was the brother of **Alexander M. Sullivan (1830–1884)** and **T.D. Sullivan**. A suspected Fenian in the early 1860s, he followed his brothers to Dublin and became manager of the publishing division of *The Nation* newspaper until he entered politics. He was elected MP for Westmeath South in 1885 and represented this constituency until his death. He was described by his nephew, Alexander M. Sullivan, as 'the man who never made a speech and never missed a division'. He was secretary of the Irish Parliamentary Party (1893–8). An anti-Parnellite, his account of the crucial party meetings in Committee Room 15 at the time of the Parnell 'Split', was published as a pamphlet. He died in London on 3 March 1907.

SULLIVAN, Sir Edward (1822–1885) Born Mallow, Co. Cork, the son of Edward Sullivan, merchant. He was educated at Midleton College and at TCD where he graduated BA (1845). He was called to the Bar in 1848 and to the Inner Bar in 1858. He was returned as MP for Mallow and served until 1870. He was appointed as solicitor general in 1865 and prosecuted many Fenians after the Rising of 1867. As attorney general, he worked with the English Prime Minister, William Gladstone (1809–98), in effecting the disestablishment of the Church of Ireland. He became master of the rolls in 1870, was knighted in 1881 and was appointed as Irish Lord Chancellor in 1883. He died at his Dublin residence on 13 April 1885.

SULLIVAN, John (1749–1839) Born Cork, the second son of Benjamin Sullivan, barrister, land and house-property owner. He was the elder brother of **Sir Richard J. Sullivan** and younger brother of Sir Benjamin Sullivan (1747–1810). In 1765, he joined the Madras section of the East India Company through the influence of his relation, **Laurence Sullivan**. His rise and prosperity in the company was rapid and on his return to work in England in 1785, he bought an estate in Buckinghamshire. In 1789, he married the daughter of the future 3rd earl of Buckinghamshire and sat in the Commons for the constituency of Old Sarum (1790–7). Through the Buckinghamshire connection, he served as under secretary for war and the colonies (1801–4), but still remained as a director of the East India Company until 1828. He died at his Buckinghamshire seat on 1 November 1839.

SULLIVAN, John [VC] (1831–1884) Born Abbey, Bantry, Co. Cork, the son of a coastguard. He was educated at the local national school, before joining the naval brigade of the Royal Navy in 1846. He rose to the rank of boatswain's mate on HMS *Rodney* and saw action in the Crimean War. On 10 April 1855, while under continuous rifle fire, he volunteered to place a flag on a mound to act as an aiming point for his battery. For this act, he was awarded the Victoria Cross (gazetted 24 February 1857). He was later awarded the Royal Humane Society's silver medal for the rescue of a drowning colleague in September 1858. He ended his naval career as chief boatswain of Portsmouth Dockyard and retired early in 1884 after 37 years' service with a pension of £150 a year. Although he had been unwell prior to his discharge, he purchased a farm at Ballindeasig near Tracton. He committed suicide at Ballindeasig on 28 June 1884 and was buried in Nohoval Cemetery.

SULLIVAN, Laurence (c.1713–1786) Born Co. Cork, the son of Philip O'Sullivan. In 1739, he worked as a private merchant at the settlement of the East India Company in Bombay of which he became a member of the council. He returned to England in 1755 and served as an east India Company director for almost his entire remaining career, residing mainly in London. He acted as chairman and deputy chairman on three occasions each. He also had a political career, being MP for Taunton (1762–8) and Ashburton (1768–74). He died on 21 February 1786 and was buried at the church of St George the Martyr, London.

SULLIVAN, Sir Richard J. (1752–1806) Born Dromina, Co. Cork, the third son of Benjamin Sullivan, barrister, land and house-property owner. His eldest brother, Sir Benjamin Sullivan (1747–1810), was a judge of the Supreme Court of Madras, while his second brother, **John Sullivan**, was under-secretary at the War Office. Through his relation, **Laurence Sullivan**, he was sent to India as a young man where he developed an interest in writing. On his return to England, he was elected as a fellow of the Society of Antiquaries in 1785 and as a fellow of the Royal Society in the same year. He was twice elected as MP for the English constituencies of New Romney (1787–96) and Seaford (1802–4) and was created a baronet in 1804. He died at his residence at Thames Ditton, Surrey, on 17 July 1806. His publications include *An Analysis of the Political History of India* (1779, 1784; Ger. trans., 1787), *Thoughts on Martial Law* (1779, 1784), *Philosophical Rhapsodies* (3 vols, 1785), *Thoughts on the Early Ages of the Irish Nation and History* (1789) and *A View of Nature, in Letters to a Traveller among the Alps* (6 vols, 1794; Ger. trans., 8 vols, 1795–1800).

SULLIVAN, Robert B. (1802–1853) Born Bandon, Co. Cork, the son of Daniel Sullivan, merchant. He was also the nephew of **William W. Baldwin**. In 1819, he emigrated to Toronto, Ontario, but with his father's death in 1822, his uncle William took him in hand and having studied law, was called to the Bar in 1828. Within the space of three years, however, he had married, and his wife and only child had both died. Things took a turn for the better in 1833 when he married a lady of a prestigious family and two years later he was elected as mayor of Toronto. He caused a sensation in 1836 when he changed from the Whigs to the Tories for a seat on the Upper Canadian Executive Council which came his way in 1839. He also received the plum job as commissioner of Crown Lands. He quietly served as president of the Council from 1841 to the following year. He then began to drink heavily, but nevertheless held his Council seat until May 1851. In early 1848, he had been appointed as provincial secretary and later in the year had been appointed as a judge in the Court of Queen's Bench. He was promoted to the Court of Common Pleas in January 1850 and held this position until his death in Toronto on 14 April 1853.

SULLIVAN, Timothy D. (1827–1914) Born Bantry, Co. Cork, the son of Daniel Sullivan of Dublin. He was the elder brother of **A.M. Sullivan (1830–1884)** and **Donal Sullivan**. He worked as a poet and journalist for the Young Ireland organ, *The Nation*, and among his compositions was the famous anthem, 'God Save Ireland'. From 1880 to 1900, he sat at various times as MP for Westmeath, Dublin and Donegal. He took part in the Land League agitation and opposed **C.S. Parnell** following the split in the Irish Parliamentary Party. His works include *Greenleaves* (1875), *Dunboy and other Poems* (1861), *The death of King Conor Mac Neasa: lays of the Land League* (1887), *Poems* (1888), *Lays of Tullamore Prison* (1888), *Blanaid and other Poems* (1891) and *A Selection of the Songs and Poems of T.D. Sullivan* (1899). He died at his residence in Belvedere Place, Dublin, on 31 March 1914 and was buried in Glasnevin Cemetery. [Memoirs (1905)]

SUPPLE, Gerald H. (1823–1898) Born Cork, the eldest son of Thomas Supple. He was educated in Dublin and became a member of the Young Ireland movement. He wrote for *The Nation* newspaper and following the failure of the 1848 Rising, he moved to London where he wrote articles for various journals and newspapers. He emigrated to Melbourne, Australia, in 1857 and continued with his journalistic work. He also studied law and was called to the Bar in December 1862. However, due to the bad state of his eyesight, he was forced to return to journalism and became a popular leader and article writer. In 1862, following a disagreement with George P. Smith, the editor of *The Age*, he left, but eight years later on 17 May 1870, he shot Smith in the arm on a Melbourne street and killed a bystander. He was found guilty and sentenced to death but following two unsuccessful appeals, the sentence was commuted to one of life imprisonment in September 1871.

Following the death of Smith, he was released on compassionate grounds in October 1878. He then moved to Auckland, New Zealand, to live with his two unmarried sisters. He subsequently wrote for the *New Zealand Herald* and died in poor circumstances in Auckland on 16 August 1898. His long poem, 'The Dream of Dampier', was published by his Melbourne friends in 1892. He also published *The History of the Invasion of Ireland by the Anglo-Normans* (1856).

SWAIN, Isaac (1874–1963) Born Co. Down, the son of James Swain. A member of a Quaker family, he was educated at the Friends' School, Lisburn, and was a teacher in Friends' secondary schools until 1902. He subsequently held a scholarship at the Royal College of Science for Ireland (1902–5) and then worked as a demonstrator in Geology there (1906–10). On the foundation of the National University of Ireland, he was appointed as professor of Geology and Geography at UCC in November 1909. He occupied this Chair until his retirement in 1944. From 1911, he also acted as supervisor of examinations in the college. More noted as a lecturer and field-geologist than as a writer, his most notable contribution (apart from articles in journals) was the section on Munster geology in Fletcher's *Provinces of Ireland* handbook. Following his retirement, he lived in Co. Kildare. He died after a short illness on 9 December 1963, at Bangor, Co. Down, and was buried in the Friends' Burial Ground, Blackrock, Co. Dublin.

SWANSTON, Alexander (1809–1882) He was the son of Peter John Swanston, a Scot, who was resident local agent of the Devonshire estates in Bandon from 1819, having previously worked at the other Devonshire estates in Lismore, Co. Waterford. He succeeded his father as Bandon agent around 1838 and managed the estates until 1858 when he resigned to follow a business career in London. He maintained his links with Bandon, however, and, in 1874, was prevailed upon to stand as a Liberal candidate for Bandon in the parliamentary election. He became an MP by the slender margin of five votes. Re-

nominated in the 1880 general election, he retired from the contest at the eleventh hour in the face of strong Tory support, leaving **Richard Lane Allman** to contest it (unsuccessfully) as a last-minute substitute. Swanston returned to England and died in London on 24 June 1882.

SWANTON, James (c.1760–1828) Born Cork. He was sent to France as a young boy and joined Berwick's Regiment of the Irish Brigade in 1780. He had reached the rank of captain by the outbreak of the French Revolution in 1789 and was imprisoned at Perpignan in 1792. He was eventually released and later served in both the Revolutionary wars and in the various Napoleonic campaigns. He died in Paris at the home of his daughter, Madame Swanton Belloc (the grandmother of the poet and writer, Hilaire Belloc [1870–1953]).

SWANZY, Henry (1915–2004) Born Cork, the son of S. Leonard Swanzy, rector of Rathcooney Union, Glanmire. When he was five, the family moved to London on the death of the father. He worked as a literary editor at the start of his career and then became a producer with the BBC at the end of World War II. He was appointed as producer of the BBC's *Caribbean Voices* which was broadcast from London and covered all the countries of the region. This provided a special cultural link with the thousands of immigrants who were domiciled in Great Britain. Among those who made broadcasts were the writers Derek Walcott and V.S. Naipaul, both future Nobel prizewinners. He retired from the programme in 1976 and died on 19 March 2004.

SWAYNE, Hugh (c.1762–1836) Born Cork, the son of John Swayne, collector of excise. In April 1782, he was appointed a second lieutenant in the Royal Irish Artillery. He rose to the rank of lieutenant colonel and retired on full pay in September 1800 when his regiment was amalgamated with the Royal Artillery. He took a great interest in the Napoleonic wars and, in 1810, published in London *A sketch of the état major: or general staff of an army in the field, as* *applicable to the British service; illustrated by the practice in other countries.* This publication was chiefly instrumental in his appointment as administrator of Cape Breton Island, Nova Scotia, in August 1812. He immediately began to build up the island's defences by founding a militia, largely against American privateers. He also took a strong stance against threats to the island's coalmines. However, his health began to fail and he left on leave of absence to England in July 1815. He was promoted to the rank of lieutenant general in May 1825. He died in Paris on 31 October 1836.

SWEENY, Thomas W. (1820–1892) Born Dunmanway, Co. Cork, the son of William Sweeney. Having emigrated to America as a boy, he took part in the Mexican War in the 1840s, fought against the Yuma and Sioux Indians, and had a distinguished record in the Union army during the American civil war. Having become interested in the Fenian movement, he organised and led the ill-fated raid on Canada in 1866. He was arrested by the American authorities for absence without leave but was soon released. He rejoined the army and retired in 1870 with the rank of brigadier-general. He died at his home in Long Island on 10 April 1892. [Life by J. Morgan (2005); Sketch by W.M. Sweeny (1899)]

SWINEY, J.M. (d. *p.*1781) Born Cork, the son of Eugene Swiney, printer. He also went into the printing trade and published a collection of poems, entitled, *The Juvenile Muse* (1781) which included a dramatic piece, 'The Alarm'.

SYNG, Philip (1703–1789) Born Cork, the son of a local 'Goldsmith and Gentleman'. In 1714, the family emigrated to America and around 1723 Philip took over the running of his father's shop in Philadelphia. His silver inkstand, which he sold to the Philadelphia Assembly for £52 16s. in 1752, was used at the signing of the Declaration of Independence and of the American Constitution. As well as being an excellent craftsman, he was also associated with Benjamin Franklin (1706–90) in the latter's experiments on electricity. He was a member and officer of the American Philosophical Society and one of the founders of the University of Pennsylvania. He was also a member of the first Masonic Lodge in America of which he was junior warden. He died on 8 May 1789. [Life by P.S.P. Conner (1891)]

SYNGE, Edward (d. 1678) Born Bridgnorth, Shropshire. He was educated in Ireland under the direction of his brother, Bishop **George Synge** of Cloyne. He attended Drogheda School and TCD where he graduated BA. He was awarded the degree of DD in 1661. He was consecrated as Church of Ireland bishop of Limerick on 27 January 1661. He was translated to the united diocese of Cork, Cloyne and Ross on 21 December 1663. He also held the wardenship of Youghal from 1664 until his death on 22 December 1678. He was buried in St FinBarre's Cathedral, Cork.

SYNGE, Edward (1659–1741) Born Innishannon, Co. Cork, the son of Bishop **Edward Synge (d. 1678)**. He was educated at Christ Church, Oxford, where he graduated BA, and at TCD where he graduated MA. He became Church of Ireland bishop of Raphoe in 1714 and archbishop of Tuam in 1716. He was appointed as a member of the Irish Privy Council in 1714. One of the most prolific theological writers of the eighteenth century, his *An Essay towards making the Knowledge of Religion easy to the meanest Capacity* ran to 26 editions. He died at Tuam on 23 July 1741.

SYNGE, Edward (1691–1762) Born Cork, the son of Archbishop **Edward Synge (1659–1741)**, brother of Bishop **Nicholas Synge (1693–1771)** and grandson of Bishop **Edward Synge (d. 1678)**. He was educated at TCD where he graduated BA (1709), MA (1712) and DD (1728). He became Church of Ireland bishop of Clonfert (1730), Cloyne (1732), Ferns (1734) and Elphin (1740). He died in Dublin on 27 January 1762 and was buried in the churchyard of St Patrick's Cathedral. [Life by R.R. Hartford (1947); Letters by Marie-Louise Legg (1996)]

SYNGE, George (1594–1653) Born Bridgnorth, Shropshire, the elder brother of Bishop **Edward Synge (d. 1678)**. He was educated at Balliol College, Oxford, where he graduated BA (1613) and MA (1616). He came to Ireland as chaplain to the Archbishop of Armagh, Christopher Hampton (1552–1625). He was consecrated as Church of Ireland bishop of Cloyne on 11 November 1638. On the outbreak of the 1641 Rebellion, he fled to Dublin and became a member of the Irish Privy Council. Having been nominated as archbishop of Tuam in 1647, he was unable to take possession of his see and he returned to England. He died in his native Bridgnorth and was buried there on 31 August 1653 at the Church of St Mary Magdalene.

SYNGE, Nicholas (1693–1771) Born Cork, the son of Archbishop **Edward Synge**, brother of Bishop **Edward Synge (1691–1762)** and grandson of Bishop **Edward Synge (d. 1678)**. He was educated at TCD where he graduated BA (1712), MA (1715) and DD (1734). He became Church of Ireland bishop of Killaloe in 1746. He was the ancestor of the playwright, J.M. Synge (1871–1909). He died on 19 January 1771.

T

TALBOT, John R. (1835–1905) Born Cork, the son of Richard Talbot, naval lieutenant. He worked as an apprentice ironmoulder in London before marrying and emigrating to Sydney, Australia, in 1860. He became very interested in labour affairs and in October 1872, he founded the Friendly Trade Society of Ironmoulders of New South Wales. Although a member of a craft union, he supported the Trades and Labour Council in its efforts to promote the acceptance of unskilled workers into the labour movement. In 1888, he was elected as president of the Labour Council, but, in 1892, did not support plans for political action by means of a parliamentary party. In 1893, he became president of both the Ironmoulders' Society and the Iron Trades Conference of New South Wales. He died at Surry Hills, Sydney, on 5 October 1905.

TANNER, Charles K.D. (1849–1901) Born Cork, the son of Dr W.K. Tanner, a prominent Cork physician who was professor of Surgery at Queen's College, Cork (now UCC) from 1864 to 1880. He was educated at Winchester School, at Queen's College, Cork, and on the Continent. He qualified as a medical doctor and established a successful practice in Cork. Conservative in politics by family background, he severed his connection with this party in 1884 and declared himself as a Home Ruler. In the following year, he was selected as a nationalist candidate for Mid-Cork and won an overwhelming victory over Patton, a token Loyalist candidate. He represented this constituency until his death and was an anti-Parnellite following the 'Split'. He was imprisoned on two occasions under the Coercion Act in 1888, the same year in which he became of member of Cork Corporation. In the House of Commons, he espoused the labourers' cause and his introduction of the measure by which labourers'

cottages were allocated one acre of land led to the term, 'Tanner's Acre'. Having become a convert to Roman Catholicism in 1897, he died in Reading, Berkshire, on 20 April 1901 following a long illness.

TANNER, Edmund (1524–1579) Born Leinster. He joined the Jesuit Order in Rome (1565) and studied there and at the University of Dillingen. Through ill health, he left the Jesuits in 1570 and travelled to Louvain to offer his services for the Irish mission. The archbishop of Milan, Charles Borromeo (1538–1584), provided him with a canonry in Milan before his consecration as bishop of Cork and Cloyne on 6 February 1575. Following extended stays in Madrid and Lisbon, he arrived in Galway on 21 June 1576. He was apprehended two months later and sent to Clonmel where, with the help of the Church of Ireland bishop of Waterford, Patrick Walsh, and Lord Barrymore, he escaped. For nearly three years afterwards, he secretly administered his dioceses but never regained their temporalities. A sick man, he fled Munster on the outbreak of the Desmond Rebellion and died at Cullahill, Co. Laois, on 4 June 1579.

TAYLOR, William C. (1800–1849) Born Youghal, Co. Cork, the son of Richard Taylor, manufacturer. He was educated at Robert Bell's School, Youghal, and at TCD where he graduated BA (1825). He returned to Youghal shortly afterwards as a teacher in his old school and wrote his first book, *A Classical Geography for the use of Youghal School*. He took an interest in writing and translating and wrote extensively on a huge number of topics. As a tribute to the high standard in such a number of works, he was awarded the degree of LL.D by TCD in 1835 with all fees remitted. He took a lively interest in the system of Irish National Education, in the

French educational system and in the issues of Free Trade and the Corn Laws. He was earmarked for the presidency of the new Queen's College, Cork (now UCC), but the position was given to **Sir Robert Kane**. He died of cholera at Herbert Street, Dublin, on 12 September 1849 and was buried in Mount Jerome Cemetery.

THADDEUS, Henry Jones (1860–1929) Born Cork. He was originally named Henry Thaddeus Jones but changed the surname in his adult life. He studied at the Cork School of Art before moving to London and Paris where he enrolled in the Academie Julian. Despite his early works as a landscape painter, his reputation stands as a portraitist. In 1884, he exhibited portraits of the duke and duchess of Teck at the Royal Academy, London, and one of Pope Leo XIII (1810–1903) in the following year. He later painted in Egypt, Australia and the United States. In July 1892, he personally presented his half-length portrait of the Khedive of Egypt to Queen Victoria (1819–1901). He commenced exhibiting at the Royal Hibernian Academy in 1886 and was elected a member in 1901. He died in the Isle of Wight in 1929. [Autobiography (1912)]

THERRY, John J. (1790–1864) Born Cork, the son of John Therry. He was educated locally and at St Patrick's College, Carlow. He was ordained in 1815 and served for a time as the secretary of Bishop **John Murphy** of Cork. He became interested in the plight of prisoners facing transportation to Australia, and, with the encouragement of Murphy, he arrived in Sydney in May 1820 with a hundred prisoners. The pastoral tasks which he faced over the remaining forty-four years of his life were enormous – especially that of obtaining funds to support his schools, churches and various charities. He also took a great interest in the affairs of the Aborigines and was very popular with them. He held many posts as parish priest and spent some time on pastoral duties in Van Diemen's Land. In 1859, he was elected on the founding council of St John's College – a college within the University of Sydney. He also went into the

property market in an effort to provide more churches and schools for the growing Roman Catholic community. He died on 25 May 1864 and, following an enormous funeral, was buried in the crypt of St Mary's Cathedral, Sydney. Later, a Lady Chapel in the cathedral was built in his memory. [Life and letters by E.M. O'Brien (1922)]

THERRY, Sir Roger (1800–1874) Born Cork, the son of John Therry, a revenue official. He was educated at Clongowes Wood College, Co. Kildare and at TCD, but did not graduate. He was later called to the Irish Bar. In 1822, he was appointed as secretary of the National Society for the Education of the Poor in Ireland and worked with Daniel O'Connell (1775–1847) in the Catholic Emancipation movement. He was called to the English Bar in 1827 and two years later was appointed as commissioner of the Court of Requests in New South Wales, Australia. He served as Attorney General from 1841 until 1843 when he was elected to the Legislative Council. He vacated his seat in 1845 having been appointed a judge in the previous year. In February 1846, he was appointed to the Supreme Court of New South Wales and held this position until his retirement to England in 1859. Apart from his legal career, he had taken a great interest in the affairs of the Roman Catholic Church in Australia and had sat on the senate of the University of Sydney. He was knighted in 1869 and died at Bath in May 1874. He published *The Speeches of George Canning* (1828), and *Reminiscences of Thirty Years' Residence in New South Wales and Victoria* (1863).

THOMAS, Henry (p.1835) He was an officer in the British army who served in the Peninsular Wars, in Canada, and in India, rising to the rank of lieutenant-colonel. In 1835, he was elected as a Conservative MP for Kinsale which he represented until his retirement in 1841. In the 1837 election, he was defeated by Pierce Mahony, but regained his seat on foot of an election petition. At the time of his marriage in 1836, he was described 'of Old Derrig, Queen's County' (Co. Laois).

THOMPSON, John V. (1779–1847) He grew up in Berwick-on-Tweed, Scotland. At the age of twenty he joined the British army as an assistant surgeon and saw service in the West Indies where he became interested in zoology. On his return to England in 1810, he was elected a fellow of the Linnaean Society. In 1816, he was appointed as district medical inspector of Cork and became deputy inspector-general there in 1830. While in Cork, he made some fundamental discoveries in the field of marine biology. In 1835, he emigrated to Sydney, Australia, where he became acting officer of health. He died there on 21 January 1847. He published *A Memoir on Pentacrinus Europaeus, a recent Species discovered in the Cove of Cork* (1823) and *Zoological Researches* (6 numbers, 1828–1834).

THOMPSON, Richard R. (1877–1908) Born Cork, the youngest son of Samuel Malenoir Thompson, merchant baker. He was educated locally and studied medicine at Queen's College, Cork (now UCC), from 1895 to 1897 but did not graduate. Shortly afterwards, he emigrated to Canada and lived in Ottawa. On the outbreak of the Boer War (1899), he volunteered for service as a medical assistant in the 2nd battalion of the Royal Canadian Regiment of Infantry and arrived at the front in November 1899. His regiment took part in battle at Paardeberg in the following February. On the 18th, Thompson remained for seven hours in an exposed position while maintaining pressure on the jugular vein of a private. On the 27th, he ventured across bullet-strewn ground to attend a wounded soldier. On finding that the soldier had died, Thompson returned while still under enemy fire. Though he did not receive the Victoria Cross, he was awarded the Queen's Scarf – one of four which Queen Victoria (1819–1901) had designed and crocheted for the bravest colonial soldiers. In the following October, Thompson was forced to return to Canada because of sunstroke. However, he returned to South Africa, and following a few months' service as a lieutenant in the South African Constabulary, he became an employee of De Beers Consolidated Mines at Kimberley. He did not remain in South Africa for long and died of appendicitis on 6 April 1908, at Buffalo, New York. He was accorded full military honours at his funeral in Ottawa and was buried at Chelsea, Quebec. At a special ceremony on Parliament Hill, Ottawa, on 24 May 1965, Thompson's 'Queen's Scarf' was presented by his nephew, Samuel F. Thompson of Cork, to the Canadian people. The Scarf was deposited in the Canadian War Museum.

THOMPSON, William (1775–1833) Born Cork, the son of John Thompson, a prosperous merchant and mayor of Cork (1794/5). A 'scientific' socialist (*avant la lettre*) and promoter of the co-operative movement, he was a totally atypical landlord in his dealings with his tenants – his will being successfully reversed by his relatives on his leaving his wealth to the co-operative movement. He was also a feminist and with his partner, Anna Wheeler (1785–1848), he wrote *An Appeal of One Half of the Human Race, Women, against the Pretensions of the Other Half, Men, to Restrain them in Political and thence in Civil and Domestic Slavery* (1825). In the previous year he had published *An Inquiry into the Principles of the Distribution of Wealth most conductive to human Happiness.* He also published *Labour Rewarded* (1827) and *Practical Directions for the speedy and economical Establishment of Communities* (1830). He died at Middle Farm, Rosscarbery, on 28 March 1833. Following problems as to burial, his body was donated to medical research. [Life by R.K.P. Pankhurst (1954)]

THORPE, John H. (1887–1944) Born Cork, the son of Rev. J.H. Thorpe, rector of St Peter's, Cork (1887–92) and later Archdeacon of Macclesfield, Cheshire. His mother was Martha Aylmer Hall of Rockcliffe, Cork. He was educated at Leatherhead and at Oxford University. He served in World War I and was awarded the OBE in 1919. He was Unionist MP for the Rusholme Division of Manchester (1919–23). A barrister, he was recorder of Blackburn from 1925 and was called to the Inner bar in 1935. His son, Jeremy Thorpe, MP, was the leader of the Liberal Party (1967–76).

THROSSELL, George (1840–1910) Born Fermoy, Co. Cork, the son of Michael Throssell, mail clerk. When he was ten years old, the family moved to Perth, Western Australia. He worked in a store and following his marriage in 1861 he opened his own business in Northam, Western Australia, and became very successful. He was involved in the Church of England and was a founder member of the Northam Mechanics Institute. From 1890 until 1904, he represented a growing Northam in the state Legislative Assembly and earned the nickname, 'The Lion of Northam'. He became Premier of Western Australia on 15 February 1901 but his ministry lasted only three months when he lost his majority and returned to the backbenches. However, he was elected to the state's Legislative Council in 1909. Following a domestic accident, he died on 30 August 1910 and was buried in Northam Cemetery. His son, Hugo V.H. Trossell (1884–1933), was awarded the Victoria Cross for bravery at Gallipoli during World War I – the first to be awarded to a Western Australian soldier.

THURSTON, Katherine C. (1875–1911) Born Wood's Gift, Cork, the only child of Paul Madden, banker and twice mayor of Cork (1885–7). She was privately educated and following her marriage to the English novelist, Ernest T. Thurston (1879–1933) in 1901 (dissolved in 1910), she developed an interest in writing novels. She died of asphyxia at Moore's Hotel, Cork, on 5 September 1911 and was buried privately in the family plot. Her publications include, *The Circle* (1903), *John Chilcote, MP* (1904), *The Gambler* (1906), *The Mystics* (1907), *The Fly on the Wheel* (1908) and *Max* (1910).

TIERNEY, George (1761–1830) Born Gibraltar, the third son of Thomas Tierney, merchant, and native of Limerick. He was educated at Eton College and at Peterhouse, Cambridge. He was called to the Bar in 1784 but never practised. A Whig with republican sympathies, he held several parliamentary seats including that of Bandon Bridge (1807–12) which was provided by his fellow-Whig, the duke of Devonshire. In 1827, he became master of the Royal Mint and enjoyed a seat in the British cabinet. However, he was dismissed a year later by the duke of Wellington when the latter was forming his new administration. He voted for the Catholic Emancipation Act in April 1829. He died at Savile Row, London on 25 January 1830. [Life by H.K. Olphin (1934)]

TIRREY, Dominick (d. 1557) A Cork City chaplain and Rector of Shandon. His patent of appointment (of 25 September 1536) by King Henry VIII (1491–1547) as bishop of Cork and Ross was opposed by the Farnese Pope, Paul III (1468–1549), who, two years later, excommunicated Henry. Tirrey was consecrated later in that month. He was probably a supporter of the Protestant Reformation and survived as a bishop on the accession of Queen Mary (1516–58) largely because he was unmarried. However, his episcopate was never recognised by the Papacy even though he was absolved from 'heresy' by Cardinal Pole (27 November 1556). Having made no effort to impose the new religion in Cork, he died in August 1557.

TIVY, Henry L. (1848–1929) Born Cork, the son of Henry Laurence Tivy. Educated privately, he became the proprietor of the *Cork Constitution* newspaper in 1882, purchasing the newspaper for £5,310. In 1883, a weekly edition, the *Cork Weekly News*, was established. He extended his newspaper interests in 1915 when he purchased the *Dublin Evening Mail* and allied journals from the executors of Arthur Guinness, Lord Ardilaun (1840–1915). A Unionist in politics, his publications reflected his political views. The destruction of the plant and machinery of the *Constitution* by Republican forces in 1922 dealt him and the paper a blow from which neither recovered. He was active in the promotion of both Cork Exhibitions (1883 and 1902/03) and acted as hon. treasurer of the latter exhibition.

He was also instrumental in raising a fund for the erection of the South African War memorial in Cork. He died at his residence, 'Barnstead', Blackrock, Cork, on 29 June 1929 and was privately buried.

TOBIN, Sir Thomas (1807–1881) Born Liverpool, the eldest child of Thomas Tobin, merchant in the African trade, including, at one time, the slave trade. In 1834, a Tobin syndicate purchased the disused gunpowder mills from the Board of Ordnance and Thomas Jr. was dispatched to be its overseer. He married in 1835 and, taking up his position as managing director of the Ballincollig Royal Gunpowder Mills Co., he settled at Oriel House, Ballincollig. He became very active in the civic and cultural life of Cork. A member of the executive of the 1852 Cork Exhibition, he was chairman of the board of directors of the Athenaeum (later the Opera House) which was built with surplus funds and materials from the exhibition. On the opening of the Athenaeum in 1855, he was knighted by the Viceroy. He also served on charitable committees and played a key role in the establishment of the Victoria Hospital, of which he was the hon. treasurer and secretary from 1878. He was an active member of several antiquarian societies and visited the Middle East to further his interest in the subject. He died on 9 January 1881 and was buried in Inniscarra graveyard. His wife, Catherine (d. 1903), who was a native of Northumberland, shared his interest in the antiquities. She was also an author of two books, *Shadows of the East* (1855) and *The Land of Inheritance* (1863). She translated P.E. Botta's (1802–1870) five-volume *Monument de Ninive* as *Illustrations of Discoveries at Nineveh* in 1850.

TÓIBÍN, Seán (1882–1971) Born Passage West, Co. Cork, the son of Thomas Tobin, gardener. He initially worked as a school monitor for a few years and then, under the auspices of Connradh na Gaeilge, as a peripatetic teacher of Irish in County Clare. He was the organiser of the 1914 Oireachtas at Killarney and opened his own summer school in Kerry. He was editor of *An Lóchrann* while it was being printed in Cork (1916–21). His office was burned by the Black and Tans while he himself was beaten as he was under suspicion of being an intelligence officer of **Tomás Mac Curtain**. From 1920, he worked as a teacher at Cork School of Commerce and did not take any side in the civil war. He died at the Mercy Hospital, Cork, on 11 November 1971 and was buried in Douglas Cemetery. Apart from his many translations of books from the English, his publications include, *Luibh-eolas* (1918), *Irish for All* (1922), *Ursa an Anama* (1923), *Tíreolaí Tosaigh* (1930), *Tíreolaí na hÉireann* (1934), *Blátha an Bhóithrín* (1955), *Oileán an Anró* (1958), *Trasna na mBánta* (2nd ed., 1973) and *Cúig Cúigí Éireann: tíreolas dúchais na Gaeilge* (1963). He was the father of the noted actor and comedian, Niall Tóibín.

TOLEKEN, John (1803–1887) Born Grand Parade, Cork, the son of John Toleken, goldsmith. He was educated at TCD where he graduated BA (1825), MA (1837) and MB/MD (1841). He is associated with the song, 'St Patrick was a Gentleman' which he and **Henry Bennett**, posing as ballad mongers, sang at a masquerade ball in Cork in 1814 or 1815. He later moved to Dublin and died there on 13 December 1887.

TONSON, Richard (1695–1773) He was the eldest son of Henry Tonson whose father had fought in the Confederate Wars. He was MP for the borough of Baltimore (1727–73), a total of forty-six years. He established Tonson's Bank of Paul Street, Cork, in May 1768. He lived in Dunkettle and died on 24 June 1773. His large estate went to his natural son, Colonel William Hull, who took the name of Tonson on the death of his father and continued as a partner in the bank while being raised to the peerage as Baron Riversdale in 1783.

TORPY, James (1832–1903) Born Fermoy, Co. Cork, the son of James Torpy, miller. He emigrated to Australia in 1853 and worked a mine in the goldfields of New South Wales. He was working as a hotel keeper and was one of the Miners' Protection League when the anti-Chinese riots broke out in 1861. Following his marriage in 1862, he moved to Orange, New South Wales, where he ran a hotel. In 1876, he visited Ireland and on his return to Orange he opened as a wine and spirit merchant. He was elected as mayor of Orange in 1879 and 1880, and became the owner of the *Western Daily Advocate* newspaper in 1886. He was elected to the New South Wales Legislative Assembly in 1889 and served until 1894. In that year, he was nominated to a seat on the Legislative Council but was rejected by the state governor. He was president of the Central Western Rugby Football Union and a member of many organisations in Orange. He died there on 22 June 1903 and was buried in the Church of England Cemetery.

TORRENS, Sir Richard R. (1814–1884) Born Cork, the son of lieutenant-colonel Robert Torrens, soldier and political economist. He was educated at TCD where he graduated BA (1835). He went to South Australia in 1840 where he worked as a collector of customs. He entered politics and, in 1855, he was elected as a member of the South Australian Legislative Council. He became the first Premier of South Australia two years later in 1857. In 1858, he saw the Torrens Act into law. This act established title to land through a process of public registration – a practice which was adopted throughout the whole of Australia by 1862. In 1859, he had published *The South Australian System of Conveyancing by Registration of Title* – a book which explained the system's operation. He had previously resigned his parliamentary seat in 1858 to take up the post of registrar-general, which position would be responsible for the implementation of the Act. In 1862, he left (without pay) for the British Isles to promote his system and never returned to Australia. He sat as MP for Cambridge from 1868 until 1874 – the year in which he retired from public life. He had been knighted in 1872. He died at Falmouth on 31 August 1884 and was buried at Leusdon Churchyard, Devon.

TOWNSEND, Richard (c.1618–1692) He was probably descended from the Townsends of Rainham, Norfolk. He fought on the side of Parliament in the English civil war and was sent to Ireland with his regiment in June 1647 to help the forces of **Murrough O'Brien**, 1st earl of Inchiquin. With Inchiquin, he took part in the defeat of the Royalist forces near Mallow on 13 November. Soon after, he defected to the Royalists with Inchiquin, but fell under suspicion as a spy and was forced to return to England. He returned to Ireland in the wake of the execution of King Charles I (1600–49) and was soon implicated in a plot to seize Inchiquin and take over Youghal. He retired from service soon afterwards and settled in Castletownshend. At the restoration of King Charles II (1630–85) in 1660, he was allowed to hold his lands and sat in the Irish Parliament as the member for Baltimore. He held his ground during the Williamite Wars for which he later received a parliamentary grant of £40,000 for services rendered. He died in the latter part of 1692 and was buried in Castlehaven Graveyard. [Life by R. and D. Townsend (1892)]

TOWNSEND, Richard (1821–1884) Born Baltimore, Co. Cork, the son of Commodore Thomas Townsend. He was educated at TCD where he graduated BA (1842) and MA (1852). An eminent mathematician, he lectured at TCD before being appointed as professor of Natural Philosophy in 1870. He was elected as a fellow of the Royal Society in 1866. Between 1863 and 1865, he published *Chapters on the Modern Geometry of the Point, Line, and Circle*. Following the disestablishment of the Church of Ireland in 1869, he collected some £2,500 from his former pupils to endow his native parish of Tullagh. He died in Dublin on 16 October 1884 and was buried in Mount Jerome Cemetery.

TOWNSHEND, Horatio (1750–1837) Born Rosscarbery, Co. Cork, the son of Captain Philip Townshend. He was educated at TCD where he graduated BA (1770) and MA (1776). He also attended Magdalen College, Oxford.

He entered the Church of Ireland ministry in 1770 and held various livings in the three County Cork dioceses until his death on 19 December 1837. He was buried in Douglas Churchyard. His publications included *A Statistical Survey of the County of Cork* (1810), *Observations on Dr Coppinger's Letter to the Royal Dublin Society* (1811), *Observations on the Criminal and Civil Judicature in County Cork* (1817) and *A Tour through Ireland and the Northern Parts of Great Britain* (1821). He was also a regular contributor to *Blackwood's Magazine* and *Bolster's Cork Magazine*. [Monument at Ross Cathedral]

TRAVERS, Aloysius (1870–1957) Born Cork. In 1887, he joined the Capuchin Order and was ordained priest seven years later. He was elected as definitor of the Irish Province for the first time in 1904 and held that position on six other occasions. He also served as provincial of the Irish Province (1913–16). During his term as president of Fr. Mathew Hall, Dublin, he founded (with Arthur Darley) the Feis Maitiú. In 1908, he founded the *Father Mathew Record* and was its editor until 1913. He attended many of the leaders of the 1916 Rising and played a prominent role in conveying messages between the leaders in the final phases of that episode. His 'Personal Recollections' of Easter Week were published posthumously in the *Capuchin Annual* of 1966. He was the author of a series of prayer books and other publications including *The Catholic Home* (1945). He died at the Capuchin Friary, Church Street, Dublin, on 2 May 1957.

TRAVERS, Sir Eaton Stannard (1782–1852) Born Douglas, Cork, the son of John Travers. He joined the Royal Navy in 1798 and served in many campaigns in the West Indies, in Canada, and in Europe during the Napoleonic Wars. He was promoted to the rank of commander in 1814, having fought in over a hundred engagements against the French. He was knighted in 1834 and was promoted to the rank of rear admiral on the retired list in 1855. He died at Great Yarmouth on 4 March 1858.

TRAVERS, James [VC] (1820–1884) Born Cork. During the Indian War, he was Colonel of the 2nd Bengal Native Infantry. In July 1857, the residency at Indore came under rebel gunfire. Travers and five other ranks charged and cleared the rebels' gun position, thus enabling those in the building to escape a certain slaughter. Having later risen to the rank of general, he died in India on 1 April 1884.

TRAYNOR, Anthony H. (*fl.* 1821–1848) He worked as a copperplate engraver in George's Street (now Oliver Plunkett Street), Cork. He moved to Dublin and worked as a portrait painter from 1827 until his death. He exhibited portraits and miniatures at the Royal Hibernian Academy, Dublin.

TRENCH, Frederick Herbert (1865–1923) Born Midleton, Co. Cork, the son of W.W. Trench of Bournemouth. He was educated at Keble College, Oxford, where he graduated BA (1888) and later became a fellow of All Souls College, Oxford. He worked as an examiner in the English Board of Education from 1891 until his early retirement in 1909. He was associated with the Haymarket Theatre, London, from 1911. Even though his four-act play *Napoleon* was produced in 1919, it is as a poet that he is chiefly remembered. His poetic publications include *Deirdre Wed and other Poems* (1900), *The Death of the Gods, translated from Merejkowski* (1901), *New Poems* (1907), *Lyrics and narrative Poems* (1911), *Ode from Italy in Time of War* (1915) and *Poems, with Fables in Prose* (1918). He died at Boulogne-sur-Mer on 11 June 1923 while on a visit to France. [Collected works with memoir by H. Williams (1924)]

TRESTON, Hubert J. (1888–1959) Born Ballyhaunis, Co. Mayo. He was educated at St Jarlath's College, Tuam, and at St Patrick's College, Maynooth, where, for a time, he studied for the priesthood. He graduated BA (1909) and MA (1911) from the Royal University of Ireland. He undertook further studies in London and later received a D.Litt degree from the National University of Ireland (1925). He worked for some years as a lay teacher at Maynooth before his appointment as professor of Ancient Classics at UCC in 1915. In 1920, he became dean of the faculty of Arts. He retired from these posts on reaching his 70th birthday in December 1958. He was the author of *Poine, a study in ancient Greek Blood-vengeance* (1923). He died at the Bon Secours Home on 5 February 1959 and was buried in St Finbarr's Cemetery.

TUCKEY, James K. (1776–1816) Born Mallow, Co. Cork, the son of Thomas Tuckey. His parents died in his infancy and he was reared by his maternal grandmother. He joined the Royal Navy in 1793. He served in the East Indies and took part in many engagements before being invalided to India at the end of 1800 while suffering from liver disease. In 1802, he saw service in Australia and made a survey of Port Phillip Harbour and environs. He published an account of this in his *Account of a Voyage to establish a Colony at Port Phillip …* (1805). On a voyage to the island of St Helena in 1805, he was captured by the French and spent nine years in a French prison, during which time he married a fellow-inmate, Margaret Stuart. On his return to England in 1814, he published his *Maritime Geography and Statistics* (1815). Having been promoted to the rank of commander, he was sent on an expedition to the Congo on a specially built ship, the *Congo*, which was capable of penetrating far up the River Congo. He died there on 4 October 1816. His diary was published in 1818 under the title, *A Narrative of an Expedition to explain the River Zaire, usually called the Congo, in South Africa in 1816, under the Direction of Captain J.K. Tuckey, RN.*

TUIGG, John (1820–1889) Born Donoughmore, Co. Cork, the son of Patrick Tuigg (Twohig). He was educated at All Hallows College, Dublin, and at St Michael's Seminary, Pittsburgh where he was ordained in May 1850 by Bishop **Michael O'Connor**. He became O'Connor's secretary and engaged in pastoral

work in the diocese until 1876. When the diocese of Pittsburgh was divided in 1876, he was consecrated as bishop of Pittsburgh in March of that year. There followed great bitterness over the division of the see and, in 1877, he was appointed as administrator of the diocese of Allegheny City (the other part of the old diocese) on the resignation of its bishop. However, his see was suppressed in 1889 and reunited to Pittsburgh. He died on 7 December 1889 at Altoona, Pennsylvania, and was buried there.

TUOMEY, Michael (1807–1857) Born Cork, the son of Thomas Tuomey, a skilled mechanic. In 1824, he took up a teaching post in Yorkshire before arriving in New York in November 1830. He held a teaching post in Maryland before opening a school in Patersburg, Virginia. He later studied at the Van Rensselear Polytechnical Institute in Troy, New York. Having made valuable mineral discoveries in Virginia, he was appointed as State Geologist of South Carolina in 1844. He issued two reports on the geology of South Carolina and, as a result, was appointed to the chair of geology, mineralogy and palaeontology at the University of Alabama in 1847. In the following year, he was appointed as State Geologist of Alabama and issued his report in 1856. He died at work at Tuscaloosa, Alabama, on 30 March 1857 and was buried in New Cemetery there.

TWOMEY, Edward (1951–2005) Born Farrenbrien, Minane Bridge. One of six children, he left home to work in his uncle's butcher shop in Midleton and, in 1976, bought a butcher shop from another uncle in Clonakilty. Using an old recipe, he produced the famous Clonakilty Black Pudding which was a great success on the European market and beyond. Previous to this, in the early 1990s, he had won the Irish Food Writers' Guild Food Award. He was a founder member of the Clonakilty Business Association and was closely associated with the West Cork Drama Festival. He died at Marymount Hospital, Cork, on 17 October 2005 and was buried in St Mary's Cemetery, Clonakilty.

TWOMEY, Maurice ['Moss'] (1896–1978)
Born Clondulane, Fermoy, Co. Cork, the son of
a mill worker. He was educated at Fermoy CBS
and later worked in a managerial post at the
Clondulane Flour Mills. He joined the Volunteer
Movement in 1917 and became staff-commandant
of the 1st Southern Division of the IRA. He
played a major part in the abduction of General
Lucas and two aides in Cork. He took the anti-
Treaty side during the civil war and was arrested
in 1923. He later became chief-of-staff of the
IRA two years after his release in 1924. When
the movement was outlawed in 1936, he was
imprisoned at the Curragh Camp, but resumed
his IRA activities on his release in 1938. However,
in 1939, he split with the IRA leadership over
the bombing campaign in England and opened
a shop in O'Connell Street, Dublin, which
became a future Republican venue. He died at
St Vincent's Hospital, Dublin on 6 October
1978 and was buried privately. He was
predeceased by his wife of 48 years, Kathleen
(née MacLaughlin), by six months.

TWOMEY, Michael (1930–1997) Born Fermoy,
Co. Cork. He and his widowed mother emigrated to England after World War II and, in
1946, he found work as the luggage lift operator
at London's Ritz Hotel. Two years later, he was
promoted to the Palm Court where he eventually rose to the position of headwaiter. His
function was to meet guests on arrival and
manage the team of the restaurant's waiting
staff. In his fifty years of service at the Palm
Court, he became acquainted with the world's
rich and famous. He never retired but only
worked shorter hours. He died of a stroke on 22
July 1997.

U

UNIACKE, Richard J. (1753–1830) Born Castletownroche, Co. Cork, the fourth son of Norman Uniacke, gentleman. He was educated in Lismore and then articled to a Dublin attorney. However, he emigrated to the West Indies, but arrived in Philadelphia in 1774 where he formed a partnership with a trader from Nova Scotia, Canada. He then moved to New Brunswick where he married his partner's 12-year-old daughter, Martha Maria Delesdernier (d. 1803), in 1775 (they had six sons and six daughters). He became involved in the American War of Independence and was tried by the British for treason. However, he was released and returned to Dublin in 1777 to finish his legal studies. He was called to the Irish Bar in 1779 and to the Bar of Nova Scotia in 1781. In the same year, he was appointed as solicitor-general of Nova Scotia and two years later was elected to the House of Assembly. He served as Speaker of the Assembly for two periods (1789–93 and 1799–1805). In 1805, he published a compilation of Nova Scotian statutes which became known as 'Uniacke's Laws'. A conservative both in politics and religion, he strongly supported Canadian unification and sent his 'Observations on the British Colonies in North America with a Proposal for the Confederation of the Whole under one Government' to the British Colonial Office. He also supported the *status quo* of the Church of England as the established church of Canada, but at the same time, he supported the emancipation of Roman Catholicism from all penal legislation. He amassed considerable wealth from his legal work and built his country residence, Mount Uniacke, on 11,000 acres north of Halifax, Nova Scotia. He died there on 11 October 1830. [Life by B. Cuthbertson (1980)]

UPINGTON, Sir Thomas (1844–1898) Born Lisleigh House, Ballyclough, Co. Cork. He was educated at TCD where he graduated MA (1868). He was called to the Bar in 1867 and was appointed as private secretary to the Lord Chancellor, Lord O'Hagan. In 1874, he emigrated to Cape Province, South Africa, where he became, in turn, attorney-general (1878–81) and Premier (1884–6). In 1892, he became a judge of the Supreme Court. He died at Wyberg, near Cape Town, on 10 December 1898.

USBORNE, Cecil V. (1880–1951) Born Queenstown (now Cobh), Co. Cork, the second son of George Usborne (d. 1925), a naval captain who served as deputy harbour master (1883–1922) and harbour master (1922–5). He was educated at The Philberds, Maidenhead, and at naval college, gaining five firsts in passing out as a naval lieutenant in 1911. At the outbreak of World War I, he was in command of HMS *Colossus*, at which time he invented the apparatus which led to the introduction of paravane mine-protection for ships. On promotion to the rank of captain, he served as senior British Naval Officer at Salonica (1917) and Corfu (1918), and commanded the naval Brigade at the Danube (1918–19). Following the war, he was director of both the naval Tactical School and naval Intelligence Division. He was promoted to the rank of rear admiral in 1928 and retired in 1933. On the outbreak of World War II in 1939, he was appointed Director of Censorship under the Home Office but resigned in the following year when he was recalled to the Admiralty for special service (1942–5). He was the author of several memoirs and naval histories including, *Smoke on the Horizon: Mediterranean Fighting 1914–1918* (1933), *The Conquest of Morocco* (1936) and *Blast and Counterblast* (1935), as well as novels such as *Malta Fever* (1936) and *Blue Tally-ho* (1947). He died at his residence, 97 Cadogan Gardens, London, on 31 January 1951.

V

VARIAN, Isaac S. (1812–1868) Born Cork, the cousin of **Ralph Varian** and **Hester Sigerson**. He worked as a brush manufacturer in London and then in Dublin. He was a member of the Young Ireland movement and was imprisoned following the uprising of 1848. While in London, he wrote poetry for the *Douglas Jerrold's Magazine*. He died in Dublin on 26 November 1868.

VARIAN, Ralph (c.1820–c.1886) Born Cork, the husband of **Elizabeth W. Varian**, brother of **Hester Sigerson**, and cousin of **Isaac Varian**. He wrote some poetry for *The Nation*, the organ of the Young Ireland movement and for *The Irishman*. He published *Street Ballads, Popular Songs* (1865) and *The Harp of Erin* (1869). He died c.1886.

VARIAN, Elizabeth W. (1821–1896) Born Brigadier House, Co. Antrim, the daughter of John Treacy and wife of **Ralph Varian**. She wrote a large number of poems for *The Nation* under the pseudonym, 'Finola'. She married Ralph Varian in 1871 and lived in Blackrock, Cork. She published *Poems* (1851), *Never Forsake the Ship and other Poems* (1874) and *The Political and National Poems of Finola* (1877).

VAUGHAN, Daniel (1897–1975) Born Ballyhoulihan East, Boherbue, Co. Cork, the son of John Vaughan, farmer. He was a member of Kanturk Rural District Council and was a prominent IRA member in North Cork during the War of Independence. He took part in many engagements, including the Clonbanin Ambush. At the 1922 general election, Captain Vaughan was nominated by the Farmers' Union Party for the 'Rest of the County' constituency and elected. In 1923 and 1927, he was returned for North Cork, again as a farmers' candidate. In

1932, he was again elected, but this time as a Centre Party candidate. In the following year, he was defeated by less than 500 votes. He retired from politics and later farmed at Gurteragh, Boherbue. He died at the Mercy Hospital, Cork, on 23 September 1975 and was buried in Clonfert Cemetery, Newmarket.

VERLING, James Roche (1787–1858) Born Cove (now Cobh), Co. Cork, the second son of John Verling, whose family had for generations been settled in the area. Pursuing a medical career, he was apprenticed to Sir Arthur Clarke, a Dublin physician, and studied at Edinburgh University where he graduated MD in December 1809. In the following month, he entered the Ordnance Medical Department as second assistant surgeon and served in the field for the duration of the Peninsular War. In July 1815, having been promoted to assistant surgeon, he was ordered to join a Royal Artillery company on the journey to St Helena with the exiled Napoleon Bonaparte (1769–1821). From 1815 to 1818, he was stationed at Jamestown, St Helena, with the Royal Artillery. In July 1818, on the dismissal of Dr **Barry O'Meara**, as Napoleon's medical attendant, Verling was appointed in his place. In fact, he was never allowed to attend on Napoleon at his house 'Longwood', as the latter was determined not to accept a nominee of the Governor, Sir Hudson Lowe. Finally, in September 1819, Dr Verling was allowed to resign his medical 'non-role' at 'Longwood', but did not leave St Helena until April 1820. Subsequently, he was promoted to the rank of surgeon in 1827, and in 1843 senior surgeon to the Ordnance Medical Department. Seven years later, he was appointed deputy inspector-general and was stationed at Woolwich, London, until his retirement in 1854. He spent his last days in Cove, where he died at his residence, 'Bellavista', on 1 January 1858. He was buried in the family vault at Clonmel (Old Church) Graveyard, Cobh. His 'St Helena Diary' is published in J.D. Markham, ed., *Napoleon and Dr Verling in St Helena* (2005).

VESEY, Sir Thomas (1673–1730) Born Cork, the eldest son of John Vesey (1638–1716), archbishop of Tuam (then dean of Cork), by his first marriage. He was educated at Christ Church and Oriel College, Oxford. He was consecrated as Church of Ireland bishop of Killaloe on 12 July 1713 and was subsequently translated to the diocese of Ossory on 28 April 1714. He died on 6 August 1730. He was the lineal ancestor of the Viscounts de Vesci of Abbeyleix, Co. Laois.

VOYNICH, Ethel L. (1864–1960) Born Cork, the daughter of **George Boole**, Professor of Mathematics at Queen's College, Cork (now UCC). She was educated locally and following further studies in Germany and Russia, she married an exiled Polish nobleman, Count Wilfrid Voynich. The couple moved to New York in 1916. Prior to this, she had developed an interest in writing and published her first book, *Stories from Garshin* in 1893. Her reputation rests primarily with the first volume of her trilogy, *The Gadfly* (1897) [set to music in 1955 by Russian composer Dmitry Shostakovich (1906–75)], which was a huge success. This was followed by *An Interrupted Friendship* (1910) and by the third volume, *Put Off Thy Shoes* (1945). She died in New York 27 August 1960. [Letters edited by P.J. Kavanagh (1982)]

W

WALKER, Robert (1834–1910) Born Cork, the son of Robert Walker (d. 1881) who succeeded Sir John Benson as City and Harbour Engineer in 1873. He trained in the offices of Henry Clutton, the London architect and engineer, before establishing an architectural practice in Cork. As an architect, he was responsible for some of the city's most attractive Victorian facades (Thompson's Bakery, Mac Curtain Street; SS. Peter and Paul's School, Paul Street; No. 5, South Mall; Methodist Church, Military Road), and was the architect of Frankfield Terrace (1885), one of Cork's first middle-class housing developments. He was also architect to the Cork Exhibition of 1883. A leading figure in the foundation of the Society of Architects, London, he was elected president of that body for four years. His health declined in his latter years and his son, Robert (d. 1937), took over the practice. He died at his South Mall residence on 30 January 1910.

WALLACE, Richard (d. 1951) Born Cork, the son of Captain Richard Wallace, master of one of the Cork, Blackrock & Passage Railway Company's 'greenboat' steamers. He started as a booking clerk at the CB&PRC but soon launched out on his own as a carrier and furniture remover. He later joined with Captain Palmer of Ringaskiddy to form Messrs. Palmer & Wallace operating both pleasure steamers and tender services for transatlantic liners. In public life, he was elected to the first Cork Board of Guardians under the 1899 Act, and in 1923, he was elected to the Cork Harbour Board to represent the mercantile body. He served as chairman of that Board (1928–33 and 1945) and was a member up to his death. He had the unique distinction of having a tugboat (the *Richard Wallace*) and a Cork street (Wallace's Avenue) named in his honour during his

lifetime. He was also very influential in the sporting arena. He served as president of Blackrock Hurling Club, as chairman of the Cork County GAA Board, and was instrumental in reviving the famous Cork City Regatta. He died at the South Infirmary Hospital on 28 February 1951 and was buried in St Joseph's Cemetery.

WALLER, John (d. 1743) Born Kinsale, Co. Cork, the son of James Waller, MP, and grandson of Sir Hardress Waller, a Congregationalist and one of the judges who condemned King Charles I (1600–49) to death. He sat as MP for Doneraile (1727–43) and, in 1736, he was referred to in Jonathan Swift's (1667–1745) 'Legion Club' (i.e. the Devil's club) which satirised the Irish Parliament –

'Who is that hell-featured brawler?
Is it Satan? No! 'tis Waller.
In what figure can a bard dress
Jack, the grandson of Sir Hardress?
Honest keeper, drive him further,
In his looks are hell and murther.'

He was living at Castletown, Co. Limerick, when he died in 1743.

WALSH, David (1796–1849) Born Cork, the nephew of Dr David Walsh, parish priest of Barryroe (1794–1815) and of Clonakilty (1815–28). Following his ordination, he served as curate to his uncle and succeeded him as parish priest of Clonakilty in 1828. On the death of the bishop of Cloyne and Ross, **Michael Collins**, in 1831, Walsh was one of three candidates selected by the diocesan clergy to succeed him. However, the president of St Patrick's College, Maynooth, **Bartholomew Crotty**, was chosen. When Crotty convoked his clergy in 1846 to select a co-adjutor, Walsh was the unanimous choice. Following Crotty's death, he was consecrated as bishop on 2 May 1847. During his episcopate, his *Statutes for the Regulation of the Diocese* were published. He died at his residence, Youghals House, Clonakilty, on 19 January 1849 and was buried beside his uncle in the old chapel yard in Clonakilty. In 1936, their remains were transferred to their present resting-place in the grounds of the Church of the Immaculate Conception, Clonakilty.

WALSH, Edward (1805–1850) Born Derragh, Kiskeam, Co. Cork. He spent thirty years in Millstreet where he worked as a hedge-school teacher. He was appointed to Toureen NS, Co. Waterford in 1837 and ten years later he took up a teaching post in Spike Island. Within a year, he had been dismissed on account of an unofficial interview with the Young Ireland patriot, John Mitchel (1815–75), who was awaiting transportation to Tasmania. In 1848, he was appointed as a teacher at the Cork Workhouse. He died on 6 August 1850 and was buried in St Joseph's Cemetery. His *Reliques of Irish Jacobite Poetry* and *Irish Popular Songs* were published in 1844 and 1847 respectively. [Memoir by J. Maher (ed.) in *The Valley near Slievenamon* (1942); Life by John J. Ó Ríordáin (2005); Commemorative plaque at his place of death, 13 Prince's Street, Cork]

WALSH, Francis A. (1807–1851) Born Cork, the son of Dr Francis Walsh. He was educated at Farrell's School, Cork, at the King's Inns, Dublin, and was called to the Bar in 1836. He was a supporter of Father **Theobald Mathew** and was a powerful speaker at temperance meetings. In 1845, he was appointed as the first professor of Law at the new Queen's College, Cork (now UCC). He died of fever at his residence, Rafeen, near Monkstown, Co. Cork, on 21 August 1851.

WALSH, Henry N. (c.1892–1958) Born Cork. He was educated at North Monastery CBS and at UCC where he graduated BE. In 1921, he succeeded **Conel W.L. Alexander** as professor of Engineering and was dean of the faculty until

his death. During his long career, he was both vice-president and president of the Institute of Civil Engineers of Ireland. He died on 27 November 1958 while giving a lecture at his old school. He was buried in St Finbarr's Cemetery.

WALSH, James J. (1880–1948) Born Raharoon, Bandon, Co. Cork, the son of James J. Walsh, farmer. He was educated locally and at King's College, London. He obtained a position as a sorting clerk in the Cork GPO and became involved in GAA administration. He was elected as chairman of the Cork County Board in 1910 and contested the presidency of the GAA in 1912. In 1914, he was transferred to Bradford (Lancashire) Post Office because of his political activities. He returned to Ireland two years later but was not allowed to reside in Cork. He took part in the Easter Rising of 1916, was arrested, convicted, and sentenced to death but this was later commuted to ten years penal servitude. Having been released in the 1917 amnesty, he was banned from visiting Cork, but was elected as a Sinn Féin MP for Cork City in the following year. He was a member of the First Dáil (1919–20), Second Dáil (1921–2), and Third Dáil (1922–3). He served as a Cumann na nGaedhal TD (1923–7) and during that time he was Postmaster General (1922–3) and then Minister for Posts and Telegraphs (1923–7). He retired from politics in September 1927 when he did not seek re-election. He had also been a member of Cork Corporation (1912–18) and an alderman (1918–22). He was both the director and chief organiser of the revived Tailteann Games in 1924. He lived in Dublin from the late 1920s and became a leading industrialist there. He revived the long-idle Kileen and Clondalkin Paper Mills and established Solas Teoranta as well as serving on the boards of several other companies. He died at his Ailesbury Road residence on 3 February 1948. [Autobiography (1944)]

WALSH, Jeremiah C. (1938–1992) Born Shandon Street, Cork, the son of a pharmacist. 'Jerry' was educated at PBC, Cork, and at UCC where he qualified as a doctor. A gifted rugby centre, he was capped twenty-six times for Ireland while playing for both UCC and Sunday's Well. He toured Australia and New Zealand with the British and Irish Lions in 1966, but was forced to return prematurely for family reasons. He also played representative rugby for the Combined Irish Universities and for the Barbarians. He won a Munster Senior Cup medal with UCC in 1963. He was widely recognised as one of the hardest tacklers of his time. He died suddenly in Cork on 28 September 1992 and was buried in Innishannon Cemetery.

WALSH, John (1856–1925) Born Bandon, Co. Cork. He was a prominent businessman who was chairman of the Beamish & Crawford Bottling Company in Bandon, and an extensive farmer. He was elected to the first Cork County Council in 1899, but was unseated on petition some months later. He was subsequently a member of the County Council (1910–20) in his capacity as chairman of Bandon Rural District Council. In December 1910, he was elected MP for South Cork as an O'Brienite candidate and sat until 1918. He died at Harbour View, Kilbrittain, on 26 August 1925 and was buried privately.

WALSH, Michael (1810–1859) Born near Cork, the son of Michael Walsh. He was brought to America as a child where his father became the owner of a New York mahogany yard. 'Young Mike' worked as a printer and newspaper correspondent and became interested in social matters – especially in the plight of the young labourers of New York City. These were known as the 'Subterraneans' on account of their being ignored by the various elected political leaders. He organised those labourers into the Spartan Association – one of America's first 'political gangs'. In 1843, he established his own newspaper, *The Subterranean*. A year later, this organ was merged with the *Working Man's Advocate*, but the new partnership was soon dissolved. He was elected to the New York State Assembly in 1846 and served three terms until 1852. In that year, he was elected to the US

Congress but was defeated by the Irish-American, John Kelly, in 1854. He then made two trade trips to Russia and Mexico but was soon back again in New York and in very poor means. Following another unsuccessful foray into journalism, his alcoholism was becoming an ever-increasing problem. He was found dead on the street on 17 March 1859 and foul play was suspected.

WALSH, Richard (*c.*1697–1763) Born Gortroe, Mallow, Co. Cork. He was educated on the Continent, and on Bishop **Teige Mac Carthy Rabach's** death in 1747, was appointed as vicar general of the diocese of Cork. He was appointed as bishop of Cork on 10 January 1748, while the dioceses of Cloyne and Ross were united under Bishop **John O'Brien**. It was during his episcopate that **Nano Nagle** began to establish her network of six city schools for the poor. He died at his Mallow Lane residence on 7 January 1763 and was buried in Shandon Graveyard.

WALSH, T. John (1906–1984) Born Marble Hall, South Parish, Cork. 'Jack' was educated at Farranferris College and at St Patrick's College, Maynooth, where he was ordained to the priesthood in 1930. Having served as a curate in various Cork City parishes, he was appointed as parish priest of Munitir Bháire (1965) and of Blackrock (1970). In 1979, he was appointed as a canon of the Cork Chapter. The most notable clerical local historian of his generation in Cork, he was a frequent contributor to the *JCHAS* and to the *Capuchin Annual* from the late 1940s. He also published short histories of the South Parish (1951) and of Blackrock (1955). His principal publications were *Nano Nagle and the Presentation Sisters* (1959) and *The Irish Continental College Movement* (1973). He died at the Bon Secours Hospital, Cork, on 27 June 1984 and was buried in St Michael's Cemetery, Blackrock.

WALSH, Thomas (1871–1943) Born Youghal, Co. Cork, the son of Patrick Walsh, cobbler. He went to sea and settled in Brisbane, Australia, where he worked on coastal steamers. Following his marriage in 1899, he moved to Newcastle, New South Wales, where he became agent for the Federated Seamen's Union of Australasia. He became the New South Wales branch secretary in 1912. When his wife died in 1914, he moved to Melbourne for the duration of World War I. While there, he met the feminist, Adela Pankhurst, daughter of the famous English sufragette, Emmeline Pankhurst (1858–1928), and the couple were married in September 1917. They then moved to Sydney where Tom was appointed as general secretary of the Seamen's Union. He organised the 1919 strike and was imprisoned in Melbourne for three months. Tom and Adela were both founder members of the Communist Party of Australia but soon withdrew. In 1922 Tom became federal president of the Seamen's Union and the following years were spent in a vicious struggle to prevent shipowners having the union deregistered. Tom had to supplement his meagre income by writing, while Adela earned money from her speaking engagements. They visited Japan in the winter of 1939/40 and on their return they held and propagated the view that the Japanese had no warlike intentions. Following the Japanese attack on Pearl Harbour, Adela was interned in March 1942. She was released in the following October after going on hunger strike. Tom was terminally ill at this stage and he died in North Sydney on 5 April 1943. Adela survived until 23 May 1961. [Account in M. Pugh, *The Pankhursts* (2001)]

WARBURTON, C. Mongan (1754–1826) Born Co. Monaghan as Charles Mongan, but changed the surname to Warburton after the English bishop and theologian, William Warburton (1698–1779), bishop of Gloucester. He also changed his denominational allegiance as he had been born into a Roman Catholic family. In 1800, he became precentor of St Patrick's Cathedral, Dublin and chaplain to the lord lieutenant, the duke of Bedford. He was consecrated as Church of Ireland bishop of Limerick on 13 July 1806. He was translated to

the diocese of Cloyne on 20 September 1820. He died on 9 August 1826 and was buried in St Colman's Cathedral, Cloyne.

WARD, John ['Zion'] (1781–1837) Born Cove (now Cobh), Co. Cork. In 1790, he was taken to Bristol where he worked as a shipwright. He took part in the battle of Copenhagen in 1801. On his return to England in 1803, he worked as a shoemaker and became, in turn, a member of many religious sects before founding his own 'gathered' community and bestowing the title of 'Zion' on himself. He was later imprisoned for eighteen months at Derby in 1832 on a charge of blasphemy. On his release, he founded another sect at Bristol. He subsequently settled in Leeds where he died on 12 March 1837. [Memoir by C.B. Holinsworth (1881)]

WARD, Joseph [VC] (1832–1872) Born Kinsale, Co. Cork. He served as a Sergeant with the 8th Hussars of the King's Royal Irish Regiment during the Indian War. On 17 June 1858, he, with three other ranks, attacked a rebel gun battery at Gwalior following a covered charge by the Hussars. They succeeded in bringing back two captured guns to the British camp. All three were awarded the Victoria Cross for their bravery. He died in Longford on 23 November 1872.

WARREN, Robert (1828–1915) Born Castlewarren, Barnahely, Cork, the son of Robert Warren, gentleman, who subsequently disposed of his Cork residence and lands in 1851 and went to live with his family at Mayview, Co. Sligo. Robert Jr. showed an early interest in natural history, often accompanying his father on boating expeditions to ornithological sites near Cork Harbour. He corresponded with the Belfast naturalist, William Thompson, who referred to Warren in his *Natural History of Ireland*. Following the family's move to Sligo, his attention focused on the bird life of Killala Bay and the surrounding country, of which he was to be a devoted observer for fifty-eight years. He was a frequent contributor to the *Proceedings of* *the Dublin Naturalists' Society* and to many other natural history magazines. He became, through his personal observation of birds, the leading Irish authority on the subject. In 1900, he was joint author with R.J. Usher of *The Birds of Ireland.* Around 1910, he returned to his native locality and died in Monkstown on 26 November 1915.

WARREN, Robert R. (1817–1897) Born Wellington Place, Cork, the only son of Henry Warren, army officer, whose father was Robert Warren of Warrenscourt, Co. Cork. He was educated at TCD where he graduated BA (1838), MA (1864), LL.B and LL.D (1868). He was called to the Irish Bar in 1839 and to the Inner Bar in 1858. He was elected as a Bencher of King's Inns in 1865. In 1867, he was appointed solicitor-general for Ireland in March, was elected as Conservative MP for Dublin University (in a by-election) in August and was appointed as attorney-general for Ireland in October. He did not contest the Dublin University seat in 1868, but was appointed a judge of the Court of Probate in October of that year. He was a member of both the General Synod and the Representative Body of the Church of Ireland from 1870 until his death, which occurred on 24 September 1897.

WATERS, George (1827–1905) Born Cork, the son of George Waters, brewer and distiller. He was educated at Hamblin's School, Cork, and at TCD where he graduated BA (1849) and MA (1864). He was called to the Bar in 1849 and to the Inner Bar in 1859. In 1852, he married the younger daughter of Charles Hamilton Teeling, the Belfast United Irishman. In a by-election of 1870, he was elected as Liberal MP for Mallow, but resigned his seat in 1872 on his appointment as chairman of the Quarter Sessions of Waterford County. He was subsequently appointed as county court judge for Cavan and Leitrim. From 1889 to 1896, he was president of the Dublin St Vincent de Paul Society. He died on 21 April 1905 at his Simmonscourt, Dublin, residence and was buried in Glasnevin Cemetery.

WATERS, George J. (1705–*p*.1789) Born Macroom, Co. Cork, the son of George Waters, a Parisian banker and formerly of Newcastle West, Co. Limerick (the original home of the Waters family was in Macroom and Mrs Waters had come from Paris to her father-in-law's house for the birth). On the death of his father in 1752, he became the owner of the Paris bank. He was the family banker of the exiled Stuarts and advanced a loan of 180,000 livres to Prince Charles Edward Stuart ['Bonnie Prince Charlie'] (1720–88) before the latter's departure on his ill-fated expedition to Scotland in 1745. A similar loan was advanced in 1749. His son, who continued as banker to the Stuarts, was later created Count Waters by King Louis XVI (1754–93) and was involved in the failed plan to rescue Queen Marie Antoinette of France (1755–93) during the Revolution of 1789.

WATSON, Henry (1822–1911) Born Cork, the son of Henry Watson, and younger brother of **Samuel Watson**. He worked as a coach-painter and also painted some local views. Following the death of his father in 1836, he and Samuel moved to Dublin. Henry then studied at the Royal Hibernian Academy School. He earned a good living through his painting of portraits, still life and animal subjects. Later in his career, he returned to coach painting and invented a type of 'transfer' which was painted in oils on special paper and transferred to wood and other materials. He died on 27 July 1911.

WATSON, Samuel (b. 1818) Born Cork, the son of Henry Watson and elder brother of **Henry Watson**. On the death of his father in 1836, he and Henry settled in Dublin. Samuel established an extensive practice as a lithographer, specialising in maps and plans of towns, railway projects etc. He also painted in oils and watercolours, mainly on rural themes. He was one of the first artists to produce works of chromo-lithography. As well as drawing many of the Young Ireland leaders, he also produced three book illustrations for the writer, **Gerald Griffin**. He produced *Historic Furniture of*

Ireland (1853), on which his reputation mainly rests. He exhibited at the Royal Hibernian Academy between 1845 and 1848.

WATSON, Sir William H. (1796–1860) Born Bamburgh, Northumberland, the eldest son of Captain John Watson of the 76th Foot. He entered the army as a cornet in 1811, was promoted to the rank of lieutenant, and served in the Peninsular War. He was subsequently present at the battle of Waterloo. He was placed on half-pay in 1816 and then studied at Lincoln's Inn, London. He practised as a special pleader until he was called to the Bar in 1832 and to the Inner Bar in 1843. As a Liberal MP, he represented Kinsale from 1841 until 1847 when he lost his seat though his opponent was unseated on petition. He unsuccessfully contested Newcastle-on-Tyne in 1852, but was MP for Hull from 1854 until 1856 when he was appointed as Baron of the Exchequer and knighted in November of that year. His career on the bench was cut short by his death (of apoplexy) at Welshpool on 13 March 1860.

WEBSTER, Charles A. (c.1866–1946) Born Bandon, Co. Cork, the eldest son of George Webster and brother of **Hedley Webster**. He was educated locally and at TCD where he graduated BA (1890) and BD (1900). He was ordained as a minister of the Church of Ireland in 1891. He served as curate of Nohoval (1890–2) and Marmullane (1892–1901), before becoming rector of the latter parish in 1901. He later served as incumbent of St Michael's, Blackrock, and was appointed as dean of Ross in 1926 – a position he held for over ten years until his retirement. He was elected as a member of the Royal Irish Academy in 1929. His publications include *The Church Plate of the Diocese of Cork, Cloyne, and Ross* (1909), *The Diocese of Cork* (1920) and *The Diocese of Ross and its Ancient Parishes* (1936). He died in Bandon on 8 April 1946 and was buried in St Michael's cemetery, Blackrock, Cork.

WEBSTER, Hedley (1880–1954) Born Bandon, Co. Cork, the son of George Webster and brother of **Charles A. Webster**. He was ordained as a Church of Ireland minister in 1903 and became rector of Kinneigh (1913–16), Holy Trinity, Cork (1916–26) and St Michael's, Blackrock (1926–45). He became a member of the Cork Chapter (1936) and archdeacon of Cork (1938). He was consecrated as bishop of Killaloe on 25 July 1945. He retired in 1953 and died at Blackrock, Cork, on 28 June 1954. He was buried in St Michael's Cemetery, Blackrock.

WELLAND, Joseph (1798–1860) Born Killeagh House, Midleton, Co. Cork, the son of William Welland, land agent. Through the influence of his patron, Archbishop **Charles Brodrick**, he served his architectural apprenticeship under John Bowden of Dublin and later became Bowden's assistant. For seven years, he was architect to the Board of First Fruits and when the Board of Ecclesiastical Commissioners was set up in 1833, he was appointed as a member. In 1843, he was appointed as sole architect to the commissioners and was responsible for the design of a hundred churches countrywide. His designs included the church of St Nicholas (Cork), St Peter's (Bandon), and those at Kanturk, Rushbrooke, Ballymoney, Carrigrohane and Innishannon. He was elected as vice-president of the Royal Institute of Architects (1849/50). He died at Upper Rutland Street, Dublin, on 6 March 1860 and was buried in St George's Graveyard.

WESLEY, Sir Samuel R. (c.1790–1877) Born Mount Crozier, Cove (now Cobh), Co. Cork, the son of Robert Wesley. He joined the Royal Marines and saw service in Guadeloupe and in the Peninsular War. He was raised to the rank of major general and deputy adjutant general of the Royal Marines in 1857 and was knighted five years later. He married Mary, the sister of **Isaac Butt**. He died in London in 1877.

WEST, Samuel (c.1810–p.1867) Born Cork, the son of William West, a native of Croydon, Surrey, who operated as a bookseller in Cork (1808–30) and who wrote *A Guide to Cork*.

Samuel studied painting in Rome and became a frequent exhibitor at the Royal Academy until his death. In 1847, he exhibited at the Royal Hibernian Academy. A woodcut of his drawing 'The New Court-house, Cork' was published in the *Irish Penny Journal* in May 1833.

WESTROPP, Hodder M. (1820–1885) Born Waterpark, Carrigaline, Co. Cork, the son of Henry Bruen Westropp, sheriff of Cork, and the brother of **Sir Michael R. Westropp**. He was educated at TCD where he graduated BA (1844). He became interested in archaeology and carried out investigations in Rome. He lectured there and in London and also translated several works from the Italian. Among his publications were *Fanaux de Cimetieres and Irish Round Towers* (1865), *A Handbook of Archaeology* (1867), *A Manual of Precious Stones and Antique Gems* (1874), *A Handbook of Pottery and Porcelain* (1880), *Early and Imperial Rome* (1884) and *Primitive Symbolism* (1895). He died in Ventnor, Isle of Wight, on 10 February 1885.

WESTROPP, Sir Michael R. (1817–1890) Born Waterpark, Carrigaline, Co. Cork, the son of Henry Bruen Westropp, sheriff of Cork, and the brother of **Hodder M. Westropp**. He was educated at TCD where he graduated BA (1838) and was called to the Irish Bar in 1840. He settled in Bombay where he was admitted to the Indian Bar in 1844. He subsequently became a member of the Legislative Council and was appointed as chief justice of Bombay. He was knighted in 1870. He died on 14 January 1890.

WETENHALL, Edward (1636–1713) Born Litchfield, England. He was educated at Trinity College, Cambridge, where he graduated BA (1659). He subsequently entered Lincoln College, Oxford, where he graduated BA (1660) and MA (1661). He was consecrated as Church of Ireland bishop of Cork on 23 March 1679. He was translated to the diocese of Kilmore on 18 April 1699. He died in London on 12 November 1713 and was buried in Westminster Abbey. He was incarcerated in Cork during the Jacobite occupation (1689–90) and released when John Churchill, Duke of Marlborough (1650–1722) recaptured the city. Previously, he had engaged in a pamphlet controversy with **William Penn** and the Quakers. While bishop of Cork, some of his publications included *The Protestant Peacemaker* (1682), *Judgement of the Comet* (1682), *Hexapla Jacobaea* (1686), *A plain Discourse proving the Authority of the Scriptures* (1688), *Pastoral Admonitions directed by the bishop of Cork… and a Sermon on the late Sufferings and Deliverance of the Protestants of the said City and County* (1691), *The Case of the Protestants in relation to recognising or swearing Allegiance to, or praying for King William and Queen Mary, stated and resolved* (1691) and '*Be ye also ready*' – a *Method and Order of Practice to be always prepared for Death and Judgement* (1694).

WHITCOMBE, John (1694–1753) Born Cork, the son of Edmund Whitcombe (Whetcombe), merchant. He was educated at TCD where he graduated BA (1716), MA (1719), BD (1728) and DD (1731). He was consecrated as Church of Ireland bishop of Clonfert on 4 January 1736. He was translated to the diocese of Down and Connor on 20 May 1752. Later in that year (August 12), he was raised to the archbishopric of Cashel. He died at Cashel on 23 September 1753 and was buried in the Cathedral on the Rock. His wife was the widow of Ambrose Congreve of Mount Congreve, Co. Waterford. He was nicknamed 'Cíorbhán' (i.e. 'white comb') by the native Irish.

WHITE, George B. (1802–1876) Born Bantry, Co. Cork, the son of Boyle White, Royal Navy. Following a period at sea, he arrived in Sydney, Australia, in January 1826 and was appointed as a clerk in the Colonial Secretary's Office. He soon left and in the following year he was appointed as an assistant surveyor in the surveyor-general's department. He worked in the Hunter Valley district of New South Wales where he also farmed (without success). From 1831 until 1853 he surveyed both the valley and the Barwon River. He retired on pension in

1853. He was elected to the New South Wales Legislative Assembly in 1858 but lost his seat in the following year. In declining health, he was declared bankrupt in 1867. He died at his son's Sydney home on 25 May 1876.

WHITE, William J. [Jack] (1920–1980) Born Cork, the son of William Luke White, accountant. He was educated at Midleton College and at TCD where he graduated BA (1940) and LL.B (1942). He joined the *Irish Times* in 1942 and was with the paper until 1961 – including a period as London editor (1946–52). He joined RTÉ in 1961 and held various managerial positions until his death, when he was head of broadcasting resources. He was attending a broadcasting conference in Stuttgart, Germany, when he died on 13 April 1980. He wrote three popular novels – *One for the Road* (1956), *The Hard Man* (1958) and *The Devil You Know* (1962). His play, 'The Last Eleven' (1967), was performed at the Abbey Theatre and won the Irish Life Drama Award. His play, 'Today the Bullfinch', was also performed at the Abbey, in 1969. His *Minority Report* (1975) examined the experiences of Protestants in a new Ireland. He resided at Booterstown Avenue, Dublin, but died on 13 April 1980 at a hotel in Stuttgart where he was attending a European Broadcasting Union conference.

WILLES, Sir James S. (1814–1872) Born Brown Street, Cork, the son of a chemist and brother of **William Willes**. He was educated at TCD where he graduated BA (1836). He was called to the English Bar and while still a junior barrister, was appointed a judge. He was knighted in 1855. His main work as a judge was in the area of election petitions. Under strain of work, he shot himself at his Watford home on 2 October 1872, and was buried in Brompton Cemetery.

WILLES, William (d. 1851) Born Brown Street, Cork, the son of a chemist and brother of **Sir James S. Willes**. He studied medicine at Edinburgh University before turning to art and becoming a pupil of **Nathaniel Grogan**. He

later studied at the Royal Academy in London where he exhibited in 1820/21. He also exhibited both in Cork (the Munster Exhibition of 1815) and at the Royal Hibernian Academy. He returned to Cork in 1823, and, in 1849, became the first headmaster of the Cork School of Art where he was a great but short-lived success. He contributed to Mr and Mrs Hall's *Ireland* (3 vols, 1841–3). He died in January 1851.

WILLIAMS, Barney (1823–1876) Born Cork as Bernard Flaherty, the son of Michael Flaherty who emigrated to New York in the early 1800s. Young Bernard became interested in acting, took the name of Williams, and made his stage debut in New York's Franklin Theatre in 1836. He later found his niche as 'Irish Barney', the quintessential stage-Irishman. In 1849, he married Maria Prey, a popular actress and singer. The pair toured England (1855–9) and then returned to America. Barney then tried unsuccessfully to try theatre management and returned again to the stage in 1869. His last appearance was on Christmas Night, 1875, at the Booth Theatre, New York. He died at his residence on Murray's Hill, New York, on 25 April 1876 and left a large fortune.

WILLIAMSON, Benjamin (1827–1916) Born Cork. He was educated at Kilkenny College and at TCD where he graduated BA (1824) and MD (1845). A noted mathematician, he was appointed as professor of Natural Philosophy at TCD in 1884 and was elected as vice-provost in 1908. He was also a fellow of both TCD and of the Royal Society. He was awarded the DCL of Oxford University in 1892. He died on 3 January 1916. His publications included *Treatise on the Differential Calculus* (1872) and *The Mathematical Theory of Stress and Strain* (1893).

WILMOT, Catherine (1773–1824) Born Drogheda, Co. Louth, but reared in Cork City. On her 'Grand Tour' with Lord Mountcashell's party, she dined with Napoleon (1769–1821), met with Bishop **Frederick Augustus Hervey**, Angelica Kaufmann (1741–1807) and Pope Pius

VII (1742–1823). She later travelled to Russia with instructions to bring home her sister, **Martha Wilmot**, who was the guest of the elderly Princess Daschkaw. In the event, Catherine returned home without her sister. She later settled in Paris and died on 28 March 1824. [Diary by T. Sadlier, *An Irish Peer on the Continent* (1920]

WILMOT, Edward (*c.*1800–1874) Born Cork, the son of Robert Wilmot (1772–1815), barrister and deputy recorder of Cork. He was the nephew of **Catherine Wilmot** and **Martha Wilmot**. He was educated at TCD where he graduated BA (1824). He published *Ugoline and other Poems* in 1828. In 1841, he assumed the additional surname of Chetwood. He lived at Woodstock, Co. Laois, and married Lady Janet Erskine, daughter of the 31st earl of Mar.

WILMOT, Martha (1775–1873) Born Cork, the daughter of the port surveyor. She left for Russia in 1803 to stay with a family friend, Princess Daschkaw, the director of the Academy of Arts and Sciences at St Petersburg. In 1808, she was forced to leave the country as Russia and England were at war. Her sister, **Catherine Wilmot**, had failed to persuade her to return home in 1807. The elderly princess died shortly afterwards. Martha later married an English rector and embassy chaplain and when he died in 1857, she returned to Ireland and lived with her daughter in Dublin. She died on 18 December 1873. She published *Memoirs of Princess Daschkaw* (1840). She was also a watercolour and portrait painter whose works are more of an historical than an artistic record. One of her watercolours portrays Peter the Great's (1672–1725) watch! [The Marchioness of Londonderry and M. Hyde (eds), *The Russian Journals of Martha and Catherine Wilmot, 1803–1808* (1934); and *More Letters from Martha Wilmot: Vienna, 1819–1829* (1935)]

WILSON, Bartholomew S. (1884–1938) Born Queenstown (now Cobh), Co. Cork, the son of James Wilson. He was educated locally and at

Rockwell College, Co. Tipperary. He worked for four years in a Fermoy jewellery shop, but returned to Rockwell in 1904 to enter the Holy Ghost Order and subsequently studied in France. He was ordained in 1913. He served as a chaplain with the 15th Division in World War I, was wounded, and was awarded the Military Cross, having been recommended for the Victoria Cross. He was invalided home, was then appointed as dean of discipline at Rockwell, and later as director of studies at Blackrock College, Dublin. He subsequently engaged in missionary work in Africa and was made vicar apostolic of Bagamoyo, Tanganyika, in 1924. He was consecrated as bishop of Bagamoyo and vicar apostolic of Sierra Leone in St Colman's Cathedral, Cobh, on 9 June 1933. Two years later, he was ordered home on health grounds and died at Woodfort, Mallow, on 28 October 1938. He was buried in the community cemetery, Rockwell College.

WILSON, Edward D.J. (1844–1913) Born Ballycurrany, nr. Midleton, Co. Cork. He was educated at TCD and at Queen's College, Cork, where he graduated BA (1865). He emigrated to London where he worked as a journalist for the *Morning Star* under **Justin Mac Carthy**. He later joined *The Times* and worked as a leader writer for 33 years. Under the pseudonym, 'Pactum Serva', he published *The Separatist Conspiracy in Ireland* (1907). He died at Camberwell, London, on 28 June 1913.

WILSON, James (1779–1857) Born Newry, Co. Down, the son of James Wilson, merchant. He was educated at TCD where he graduated BA (1802), MA (1809) and DD (1830). He was consecrated as Church of Ireland bishop of Cork, Cloyne and Ross on 30 July 1848. He died, unmarried, on 5 January 1857 and was buried in St FinBarre's Cathedral. [Memorial window at St Nicholas Church, Cork]

WILSON, John C. (1825–*c.*1890) Born Mallow, Co. Cork. He contributed poems to many English periodicals and to the *Dublin*

University Magazine. He was a member of the Savage Club – a literary club founded in 1857 and named after the poet, Richard Savage (c.1697–1743). His collections include *The Village Pearl* (1852), *Elsie: Flights of Fancy* (1864) and *Lost and Found* (1865). He also wrote a novel, *Jonathan Oldaker.* He died c.1890.

WINDELE, John (1801–1865) Born Cork. He worked in the sheriff's office there and showed an early interest in folklore and in antiquarian studies. He collected ogham stones and kept them at his residence in Blair's Hill (they were subsequently taken to UCC where they are now to be seen in the Stone Corridor). With **Jeremiah J. Callanan** and **Thomas Crofton Croker**, he formed a study group called the 'Anchorites' which frequently contributed to *Bolster's Quarterly Magazine* of which Windele was editor (1826–30). His chief publication was his *Historical and Descriptive Notes of the City of Cork* (1839). His manuscript collection (130 volumes) was purchased by the Royal Irish Academy. He died at his residence in Blair's Hill, Cork, on 28 August 1865.

WINDLE, Sir Bertram C.A. (1858–1929) Born Mayfield, Staffordshire, England, the son of Rev. S.A. Windle, clergyman. His mother was Katherine, the daughter of Admiral Sir Josiah Coghill, Baronet. The family moved to Kingstown (now Dún Laoghaire) when he was four years of age. He was educated at Repton College and at TCD where he graduated in medicine. While practising in Birmingham, he converted to Roman Catholicism, married, and became involved in Liberal politics. He became professor of Anatomy at Queen's College, Birmingham, which became the University of Birmingham in 1900, and married for a second time in the following year. He was appointed as president of Queen's College, Cork (now UCC), in 1904 (to 1919). He was professor of Anatomy (1907–9) and later professor of Archaeology (1910–15) at the college. He also lectured on English, Anthropology and other general subjects. Due to political pressure exerted by members of Sinn Féin both from within the college and without, he resigned from his position in mid-1919 to take up an appointment as a philosophy professor at the University of Toronto. He died there on 14 February 1929. His diverse publications while at UCC included, *The Prehistoric Age* (1904), *A School History of Warwickshire* (1906), *What is Life?: a study of Vitalism and Neo-Vitalism* (1906), *A Century of Scientific Thought* (1915), *The Church and Science* (1917) and *Science and Morals* (1919). [Analysis of UCC career in J.A. Murphy, *The College* (1995), 164–213]

WOLFE, Jasper T. (1872–1952) Born Skibbereen, Co. Cork, the son of William J. Wolfe. He was educated at Bishop's School, Skibbereen, and was admitted a solicitor in 1893. Having obtained first place in his final examination and having been awarded the Findlater Scholarship, he set up practice in Skibbereen. He served on Skibbereen UDC for some years and was a director of the *Skibbereen Eagle* newspaper. He also served as crown solicitor for Cork City and for the West Riding (1916–23). He was an Independent TD for West Cork (1927–33), but did not seek re-election in the latter year. In 1941, he became the first Corkman to hold the office of president of the Incorporated Law Society of Ireland. He died at his residence, 'Norton', Skibbereen, on 28 August 1952 and was buried in Aughadown Cemetery.

WOOD, James J. (1856–1928) Born Kinsale, Co. Cork, the son of Paul Wood. In 1864, the family moved to Connecticut where James started work in a lock company at the age of 14 years. When the family moved to Brooklyn, New York, he attended night school and worked for an engineering company (Brady Manufacturing) by day. He graduated in engineering from the Collegiate and Polytechnic Institute, Brooklyn, and began to take a keen interest in electric lighting, as Brady's were involved in the manufacture of dynamo castings for various concerns. He built and patented his arc-light dynamo in October 1880, with the result that the Fuller Electric Company abandoned the manufacture of its own product and formed a new concern, the Fuller-Wood Company. In all, Wood patented some 240 products (mainly electrical) in his lifetime. He then went into consultancy and one of his clients, the Thompson-Houston Company, became involved in a huge merger from which the General Electric Company (GEC) was formed. He eventually became consultant engineer of the new conglomerate and was based in Fort Wayne, Indiana. He was a pioneer in the development of floodlighting and invented the system which was first used to illuminate the Statue of Liberty in 1885. He also designed and manufactured the first internal combustion engine which was used by the inventor, Clare-born John Holland, in his 1898 submarine, later named the USS *Holland*. He was honoured with a fellowship of the American Institute of Electrical Engineers. He died in Asheville, North Carolina, on 19 April 1928.

WOOD, John (d. 1874) Born 'Wood's Gift', Diamond Hill, Blackrock, Cork. He became an army officer and lived for many years on the South Mall. He wrote poetry for *The Cork Southern Reporter* under the pseudonym of 'Lanner de Waltram'. Some of his poems appeared in **Thomas Crofton Croker**'s *Popular Songs of Ireland* (1852). He and his brother, Atteywell W.A. Wood, were well-known dandies, both in Cork and Dublin, and were nicknamed 'Noodle and Doodle'. Their costume, as appeared in a contemporary Dublin print, is described as 'chimney-pot hats, not tall, the leaf turned up sharply, white cravat, and collar up to the ears; black dress coats, with extra long swallow tails; tightly-laced vests; long trousers showing the boots, with long brass spurs and rowels (i.e. small wheels at the end of a spur) as large a halfcrowns; yellow gloves and a huge bunch of gold seals'. He died at 'Wood's Gift' on 22 February 1874.

WOODLOCK, Ellen (1811–1884) Born Cork, the daughter of **Martin Mahony** and sister of

Francis Sylvester Mahony ('Father Prout'). In November 1836, she married Thomas Woodlock of Dublin (whose brother was Roman Catholic bishop of Ardagh [1879–94]). Though she lived most of her married life in Dublin, she was distinguished for her philanthropic work in Cork, especially in the training and industrial education of girls and young women. For the realisation of this ideal, she founded the Elizabeth Society. Following her husband's death, she returned to live in Cork and died at 8, Sidney Place on 13 July 1884. She was buried in St Joseph's Cemetery in the family vault of her nephew, Edward Ronayne Mahony.

WOODWARD, Richard (1726–1794) Born Grimsbury, near Bristol. He was educated at Wadham College, Oxford, where he graduated BCL (1749) and DCL (1759). He was later awarded TCD degrees of B.Mus (1768), D.Mus (1771) and DD (1781). He was consecrated as Church of Ireland bishop of Cloyne on 4 February 1781. His apologetic *Present State of the Church of Ireland* (Dublin and London, 1787) ran to several editions and caused a sensation in the 'Established Church' controversy. Among his other publications was *Considerations on the Immorality and pernicious Effects of dealing in smuggled Goods. Addressed to the Inhabitants of the Diocese of Cloyne* (1783). He died at Cloyne on 12 May 1794 and was buried in his cathedral. His daughter, Mary, married the future Archbishop of Cashel, **Charles Brodrick**.

WRENNE, Joseph F. (1888–1966) Born Mallow, Co. Cork. He was educated at the local Patrician College and joined Cork County Council in 1906 as one of the first three clerical staff appointed by competitive examination. He studied at UCC where he graduated BA (1915) and MA (1916). He was deputy professor of History at UCC from 1920 to 1924. In 1932, he was appointed Secretary to Cork County Council, having been in charge of the Roads Department since 1925. In August 1942, he was appointed as the first Cork County Manager – a post which he held until his retirement in 1954.

Twice a prizewinner and medallist at An t-Oireachtas, his literary achievements in later life were as a playwright, his 'Sable and Gold' having a three-week run at the Abbey Theatre, Dublin, in 1918. He wrote under the pseudonym, 'Maurice Dalton'. He was president for several years of the Munster Dramatic Society. He died at the Bon Secours Home, Cork, on 13 June 1966 and was buried in St Finbarr's Cemetery.

WRIGHT, George (1847–1913) Born Fernhill House, Clonakilty, Co. Cork, the son of Thomas H. Wright, solicitor. He was educated at Portora Royal School, Co. Fermanagh, and at TCD where he graduated BA (1867). At TCD, he became a keen oarsman and rowed for the senior crew. He was called to the Bar in 1871 and joined the Munster Circuit where he earned a reputation as a formidable barrister. He was called to the Inner Bar in 1884. Among the notable cases in which he appeared was the famous Cork Card Case (*Beamish v. Pike*). In 1895, he unsuccessfully contested the Dublin University (TCD) parliamentary seat. He was appointed solicitor-general for Ireland in 1900 and a year later was elected to the judicial bench of the High Court. He presided over several celebrated murder trials during his judgeship, many of them on the North-East Circuit. He died suddenly of heart disease at his residence, 'Aircroft', Bray, Co. Wicklow, on 15 May 1913 and was buried in Mount Jerome Cemetery, Dublin.

WRIGHT, John W. (1769–1805) Born Cork. He entered the British Navy at the age of 12 years. He spent five years in Russia where he proved to be an excellent linguist. He later sailed with the famous British admiral, Sir W. Sidney Smith (1764–1840). During the Napoleonic Wars, he was in command of a brig, but in 1804 he surrendered to a squadron of French gunboats and was taken prisoner. In the following year, he was found with his throat cut in mysterious circumstances while still in captivity.

WRIGHT, Joseph (1834–1923) Born Cork, the son of Thomas Wright, a druggist of Patrick's Street. He was educated at Newtown School, Waterford, and developed an interest in geology. He was a member and later a president of the Cork Cuvierian Society. He was also a fellow of the Royal Geological Society of Ireland (1864). In 1868, he moved to Belfast, married, and entered the grocery trade. He became an expert on Irish fossils and his collection from the carboniferous rocks near Little Island was lodged in the British Museum. He spent the academic year of 1859/1860 at TCD as assistant to the professor of Geology. He died in 1923.

WRIXON, Sir Henry J. (1839–1913) Born Cork. He was educated at TCD where he graduated BA (1860). In the following year, he was called to the Bar. He emigrated to Australia and was elected as a member of the Legislative Assembly of Victoria. He later became attorney-general of Australia and vice-chancellor of Melbourne University. He was knighted in 1892. In 1901, he became the president of the Australian Legislative Council. He died on 9 April 1913.

WYCHERLEY, Florence (1908–1969) Born Rosscarbery, Co. Cork, the son of Geoffrey Wycherley, farmer, journalist and a member of Cork County Council (1909–20). He was educated locally and at technical and agricultural colleges. A progressive farmer, he was well known as a breeder of bloodstock and of greyhounds and was active in organisations such as Macra na Feirme and the Cork Farmers Association, which he served as county chairman. In 1950 he was an unsuccessful candidate for the Farmers' party in the County Council elections and three years later was unsuccessful in the 1954 general election standing as a Farmers' candidate in West Cork. In 1955 he was elected to Cork County Council and was a member from that date to 1967. In 1957 he was elected to Dáil Eireann, winning the last seat in West Cork by 50 votes from sitting TD **Seán Collins**, but failed to retain it at the next general election in 1961. When he lost his Council seat in 1967 he retired from active politics. He died unexpectedly at his residence, Gortnaclohy, Skibbereen on 23 April 1969 and was buried in the New Cemetery, Skibbereen.

WYCHERLY, Sir George (d. 1892) He was a member of Cork Corporation and was City highsheriff in 1883 and 1885. He was knighted in 1883. He held considerable property in the counties of Cork and Tipperary. He was a prominent medical practitioner in Cork for many years and died at his South Mall residence on 23 May 1892. He was buried privately.

Y

YELVERTON, Barry (1736–1805) Born Blackwater, Newmarket, Co. Cork, the son of Frank Yelverton. He was educated at Midleton College and at TCD where he graduated BA (1757). He was called to the Bar in 1764 and to the Inner Bar in 1772. He sat as MP for Donegal (1774) and for Carrickfergus (1776). He was appointed as attorney-general in 1782 and as chief baron of the Irish Exchequer in the following year. Even though he supported the Irish Volunteers, he was in favour of the Act of Union. He was created 1st Baron Avonmore in 1795 and 1st Viscount Avonmore in 1800. He was nicknamed the 'Goldsmith of the Irish Bar' and was both patron and friend of **John Philpot Curran**. He died at his Dublin residence, Fortfield, Rathfarnham, on 18 August 1805. [Portrait by H. Hamilton at King's Inns, Dublin]

YOUNG, Jim (1915–1992) Born Ballabuy, Dunmanway, Co. Cork, the eldest son of Jack Young, teacher, who won an All-Ireland SFC medal with Cork in 1911. His brother, Eamon, was also a holder of an All-Ireland SFC medal which he won with Cork in 1945. He was educated at Farranferris College, Cork and at St Patrick's College, Maynooth, where he graduated BA (1936). Following a year in the civil service, he studied medicine at UCC where he graduated in 1943. Jim won five All-Ireland SHC medals (1941–4 and 1946), three NHL medals (1940–41 and 1948), and four Railway Cup hurling medals (1943–46). While a student at UCC, he won two Fitzgibbon Cup (hurling) medals and two Sigerson Cup (football) medals. He later won eight Cork county senior hurling championship medals with his club, Glen Rovers. He was also both a squash player and golfer of repute and acted as non-playing captain of the Irish Davis Cup tennis team in 1967. An outdoor sportsman, he was a founder of the Cork Federation of Gun Clubs. He died at his residence 'Foxfield', Boreenmanna Road, on 23 August 1992 and was buried in St Catherine's Cemetery, Kilcully.

Z

ZAJDLIEROWA, Zoe Girling (b. 1905) Born Drinagh, Co. Cork, the daughter of Frederick Girling, clergyman. The family moved to England in 1921 because of the 'Troubles' and Zoe received her education in Dublin, England and France. However, her first published fiction, under her own name, appeared in the Irish literary magazine, *Banba*, in 1921 and 1922. Her first novel, *Butler's Gift*, written under the name 'Martin Hare', was published in 1932. She married a Polish officer, Alexander Piotr Zajdlier, and moved to Warsaw. She became as patriotic a Pole as any native and following the Nazi invasion in 1939, she identified with the suffering of the Poles. She and her husband fled Warsaw in early September 1939 and reached Estonia, but the ship they boarded for Sweden was intercepted and taken to Germany. She was separated from her husband who later joined the Polish Resistance, but disappeared during the war. She was allowed to go to Sweden and thence to England where she began to write about her experiences. Her *My Name Is Million*, though published anonymously, appeared in 1940. In 1943, she began *The Dark Side of the Moon*, which drew on first-hand accounts of the Polish deportees and on access to the records of the Polish government-in-exile. It was again published anonymously in 1946 (2nd ed., 1990) with a preface by T.S. Eliot (1885–1965). It is on this book that her reputation rests.

INDEX OF PLACES

This index indicates places in Cork city and county with which individual
entries in the Dictionary are associated. For example, those associated
with Mallow will be found under the entry 'Mallow'.